# GODS IN DWELLINGS

# Society of Biblical Literature

Writings from the Ancient World Supplement Series

Amélie Kuhrt, Editor

Number 3

Gods in Dwellings:
Temples and Divine Presence in the Ancient Near East

# GODS IN DWELLINGS

## Temples and Divine Presence in the Ancient Near East

Michael B. Hundley

# GODS IN DWELLINGS

Copyright © 2013 by the Society of Biblical Literature

**Library of Congress Cataloging-in-Publication Data**

Hundley, Michael B., 1978-
  Gods in dwellings : temples and divine presence in the ancient Near East / Michael B. Hundley.
      pages cm. — (Writings from the ancient world supplements / Society of Biblical Literature ; no. 3)
  Includes bibliographical references and index.
  ISBN 978-1-58983-920-5 (hardcover binding : alk. paper) — ISBN 978-1-58983-918-2 (paper binding : alk. paper) — ISBN 978-1-58983-919-9 (electronic format)
  1. Temples—Middle East—History—To 1500. 2. Middle East—Religion. I. Title.
  BL1060.H86 2013
  203'.509394—dc23
                    2013035222

Printed in the United States of America on acid-free, recycled paper conforming to ANSI/NISO Z39.48-1992 (R1997) and ISO 9706:1994 standards for paper permanence.

# CONTENTS

## PART 2: DIVINE PRESENCE IN ANCIENT NEAR EASTERN TEMPLES

# PREFACE

TEMPLES AND CULT IMAGES were seemingly ubiquitous in the ancient Near Eastern world, and are scarcely less so in modern scholarly writing. Temples and the cultic care within them served as the primary and official way of interacting with and influencing the otherwise distant deities who controlled the cosmos, thereby affording humans some security in an otherwise insecure world. In the temple, heaven met earth, allowing regular and regulated interaction with the deity to the benefit of all parties involved.

The following study is an attempt to understand how the people from the various ancient Near Eastern regions (Egypt, Mesopotamia, Hittite Anatolia, and Syria-Palestine) built, used, and understood their temples, and how they installed, served, and understood the divine presence within them. Given the vast amount of ground covered, it makes no attempt to be encyclopedic in its presentation of data. Likewise, given the proliferation of literature available on temples and divine presence in and across cultures and the advances in complementary fields like architectural and spatial theory, ritual theory, theories of language, art history, archaeology, and comparative studies, this book makes no attempt to master every discipline and sub-discipline. In fact, the book's primary aim is not to amass data, methodologies, or interpretations. Rather, it attempts to identify the common ancient Near Eastern temple systems, more particularly, the temple structures and practices and the thought worlds that informed them. In other words, it is a study in religious norms, exploring normative ways of conceptualizing and constructing temples and envisioning, enabling, and maintaining divine presence within them. In turn, rather than attempt to be exhaustive, it presents a wide range of data that help to illumine the common religious systems, giving the reader some access to the normative worlds of the temple, at least as far as the data will allow.

This book also recognizes the importance of understanding systems of thought and practice in their own rights and for comparative purposes. It attempts to situate the individual data in the larger systems of thought and practice, contending that such integration allows for a more robust analysis of the systems and their parts. The individual data are best interpreted in light of the larger system, its cultural context, to see how and if they fit and, if they diverge, why and in what ways. As the context informs the individual data, the analysis of their parts likewise illumines the system as a whole. A better understanding of the system and its parts consequently allows for richer comparisons of the systems themselves and their various constituent parts.

This project began during my Ph.D. at the University of Cambridge, where I sought to understand the biblical Priestly system designed to safeguard the divine presence in the Priestly tabernacle. Rather than comparing select elements in the Priestly system with isolated ancient Near Eastern rites, I attempted to compare the various systems of thought and practice. Since most existing comparative work was either too general or too specific, I attempted to gather and synthesize the vast ancient Near Eastern material and construct an interpretive lens through which to view it. This book, since significantly expanded and updated, is the result of that endeavor.

In short, *Gods in Dwellings* examines temples and the gods who inhabit them in ancient Egypt, Mesopotamia, Hittite Anatolia, and Syria-Palestine. It is thus concerned with official religion, with exploring the interface between human and divine in the major temples of the ancient Near Eastern. As far as possible, each region's system(s) is allowed to emerge in their own terms, contexts, and complexities. While the focus is on identifying commonalities, various differences are also noted. Where data are lacking, I fill in the blanks tentatively with comparative data. In the course of investigating each region, comparisons are also made across regions. At the end of each major section, syntheses are offered with a view toward finding common ground, despite the different ways temples and divine presence are presented in the different contexts.

Given that the data are remarkably diverse and only partially preserved, the generalizations posited do not hold for every place and every time, either within or across regions.[1] This study paints in broad strokes and invites specialists in each field and subfield to test the validity of the portrait painted and to add the detailed time- and place-specific brushstrokes.

This study has been written with several audiences in mind. Its fundamental aim is to familiarize the reader with the various ancient Near Eastern systems of thought and practice regarding temples and divine presence, thereby granting greater access to those cultures and even to the Hebrew Bible that emerged from them. Since the present work analyzes each region in its own right before offering a synthesis, it also may be used as a reference for each particular region as well as for comparative analysis (both with biblical and other ancient and modern religions). The principal audience is biblical scholars, who generally do not have sufficient access to all of the ancient Near Eastern discussions or to the systems of thought that inform them. This study attempts to provide access and ample material for comparison with various biblical texts relating to temples, divine presence, and, more broadly, conceptions of the divine. However, it explicitly does not make the comparisons itself, contending that each cultural system must be understood in its own right before such comparisons are undertaken, so as not to compromise

---

1. While I recognize that the generalizations posited by necessity do not do full justice to all of the data, the search for common elements remains helpful in granting greater access to the common ancient Near Eastern systems of thought and practice. For an assessment of the limited data and the limitations of making generalizations, see the individual chapters.

the integrity of the primary investigation or the secondary comparison with biblical texts.[2] I also hope to engage ancient Near Eastern specialists by contributing a macroanalysis of the most common systems of thought and practice in addition to the multiple excellent microanalyses already in print. I invite the specialists to test my methodology and interpretations and continue to extend the investigation to specific times and specific places. By minimizing technical language and writing as accessibly as possible without unnecessarily sacrificing the complexity of the subject matter, I also hope that nonspecialists can benefit from it.

I realize that in attempting to address specialists and nonspecialists alike I am in some way working at crosspurposes. In turn, I hope that specialists will forgive me for excluding some of the data and some of its diversity and that nonspecialists will forgive me for including too much data and diversity. Nonetheless, I believe that nonspecialists can benefit from the added detail and complexity and hope that specialists can benefit from a broader and more synthetic analysis that seeks to identify commonalities despite the diversity.

At this point, a few clarifications are in order. First, given the sheer volume of material, many worthy contributions have been omitted from direct consideration. Instead of collecting every relevant piece of primary and secondary literature, the references mentioned serve as a representative sample, representing the works used and some of the best resources available for further inquiry both in general and with regard to specific issues. Again, my goal was not to be encyclopedic but to use the data to paint a picture of the common ancient Near Eastern temples and temple cults. I have also showed a preference for English books since my primary audience is English. The reference list represents my selective presentation as it lists only the works cited.

Second, I have generally attempted to present the various primary languages in a way accessible to the general readership. Person and place names as well as the names of various (especially mythological) texts have been written in transcribed form without diacritic markers (except in citations). In other words, I write non-English words with English letters and vocalizations. For example, instead of identifying the Hittite capital as Ḫattuša, I have written it Hattusa. The goddess Ištar instead appears as Ishtar, while Nabû appears as Nabu. In addition, the myth describing the exaltation of Marduk, transliterated as the *Enūma eliš*,[3] has been written *Enuma Elish*. I have also generally rendered "š" as "s," except where "sh" is more common in English (e.g., Ishtar and Enuma Elish). However, foreign words that do not fall into these categories (i.e., words that are not proper nouns) are written in full transliterated form, with diacritics and in italics (e.g., the Hittite standing

---

2. If readers are interested in how I make such comparisons, they may refer to my previous (and upcoming) publications.

3. Transliteration refers to the conversion of a text from one writing system to another.

stone has been written *ḫuwaši*).[4] My rendering of Egyptian words requires further clarification. Although I follow the above rules for the most part, certain major concepts, such as *ba* (instead of *b3*), *ka, maat, sekhem,* and *ankh,* have been transcribed instead of transliterated for the convenience of nonspecialists. In addition, some words that would otherwise appear in transliterated form are transcribed because they appear in a citation or are transcribed in accord with a nearby citation. When referring to a deity, the neuter pronoun "it" will be used to avoid the cumbersome "she or he" or the incomplete "he" or "she."

Third, regarding references to specific texts and verses, I have tried to be as consistent as possible across cultures. I insert a period (.) between the numbers identifying a text, and spaces between the text numbers and the numbers (and letters) identifying a line. For example, in *KUB* 7.5 iv 11–16, *KUB* indicates the publication, "7" the volume, and "5" the text number within that specific volume, while "iv" indicates column 4 and "11–16" lines 11–16.[5] I use lowercase roman numerals to indicate columns (as in the previous example) and upper case roman numerals to identify the tablet numbers of the large Akkadian texts with individuals titles (e.g., for *Enuma Elish* tablet 5 verse 1, I write *Enuma Elish* V 1 instead of *Enuma Elish*.V 1, *Enuma Elish* 5 1, or *Enuma Elish*.5 1).[6] A single quotation mark (e.g., 1') after a line number indicates the line number as preserved on the tablet when the tablet is broken.

Finally, I must pause to express my thanks to those who have made this book possible. Graham Davies once again deserves pride of place. I am grateful for the patience he showed in allowing me to fumble my way around the ancient Near East as an early Ph.D. student and for encouraging me to turn my fumblings into a second book. Without his support, this book would not have been written. So, it is only fitting that I dedicate *Gods in Dwellings* to the one who shares its initials, Graham I. Davies.

---

4. Sumerian texts form the primary exception. Logograms are written in small caps, while Sumerian texts are written without italics and with extended spaces between the letters.

5. This is but one example. Different publications follow different rules in identifying their texts. For example, the RIMA series uses a different combination of letters and numbers. In A.0.77.1.13, e.g., "A" stands for Assyrian period, "0" indicates that the dynasty is inapplicable, "77" refers to the ruler number (in this case Shalmaneser I), "1" to the text, and "13" to the specific exemplar of that text. For an explanation, see A. Kirk Grayson, *Assyrian Rulers of the Early First Millennium BC I (1114–859 BC)* (RIMA 2; Toronto: University of Toronto, 1991), *xiii–xiv.*

6. To be consistent, I notate columns in Ugaritic texts with a lower case roman numeral instead of the normal practice (see, e.g., Mark S. Smith, *The Ugaritic Baal Cycle,* Vol. 1: *Introduction with Text, Translation & Commentary of KTU I.1–I.2* [VTSupp 53; Leiden: Brill, 1994]) of writing the column in upper case (*KTU* 1.3 vi 17–19 instead of *KTU* 1.3 VI 17–19).

I would like to thank Baruch Schwartz who read an early version of Part 2, which little resembles the one presented here, and offered his encouragement. The Alexander von Humboldt Foundation deserves high praise for allowing me the time and resources to finish this book (and the ability to do it in such a great location as Munich). I thank Ludwig-Maximilians-Universität München for giving me access to their facilities and scholarly discussions during my time as a Humboldt scholar. I am also in Christoph Levin's debt for giving me some leeway to diverge from my primary Humboldt project and for his genuine concern for my well-being. Thanks are also due to Princeton Theological Seminary for letting me use their extensive library during my time there.

I am grateful to Jared Miller for his interest and insights into all things Hittite, and Friedhelm Hoffmann for his invaluable guidance in matters Egyptian. They each offered helpful feedback, prevented several missteps, and are in no way responsible for any of my errors. Billie Jean Collins also deserves significant credit, for initially accepting the manuscript for publication, for supporting the project as it neared completion, and for offering her expert advice on the Hittite elements. I would also like to thank Amélie Kuhrt for taking on editorship of the series.

As always, I am indebted to my family, to my parents, Timothy and Virginia Hundley, for their unfailing support and to my wife's parents (Charles David and Virginia Susann Jones) for their loyalty and invaluable financial support. I would like to thank my three young children, Kaya Elana, Evangeline Grace, and Matthew Johannes, for making my life richer and more exciting, if not always easier. Finally, I would like to thank my wonderful wife, Susan, who has always supported me through thick and thin, believed in the project from the beginning, and enabled me to finish it in various ways, including by acting as its primary editor. Once again, she has been my inspiration and encouragement. In lieu of the expensive jewelry she deserves, I can only offer her my love and gratitude.

*Michael B. Hundley*
Munich, December 13, 2012

# LIST OF FIGURES

*Chapter 2*

## Chapter 3

## Chapter 4

## Chapter 5

## Chapter 8

## Chapter 9

## Chapter 10

## Chapter 11

# ABBREVIATIONS

| | |
|---|---|
| A | tablets in the collections of the Oriental Institute, Univ. of Chicago |
| ÄA | Ägyptologische Abhandlungen |
| ÄAT | Ägypten und Altes Testament |
| AB | The Anchor Bible |
| ADFU | Ausgrabungen der Deutschen Forschungsgemeinschaft in Uruk-Warka |
| AEL | Miriam Lichtheim, *Ancient Egyptian Literature*. 3 vols. Berkeley: University of California Press, 1973-1980 |
| AfO | *Archiv für Orientforschung* |
| AHw | W. von Soden, *Akkadisches Handwörterbuch*. 3 vols. Wiesbaden: Harrasowitz, 1959 – 1981 |
| ANEP | J. Pritchard, ed., *The Ancient Near East in Pictures Related to the Old Testament*. 2nd ed. Princeton: Princeton University Press, 1969. |
| ANET | J. Pritchard, ed., *Ancient Near Eastern Texts Relating to the Old Testament*. 3rd ed. Princeton: Princeton University Press, 1969 |
| AO | museum siglum Louvre (Antiquités orientales) |
| AOAT | Alter Orient und Altes Testament |
| AoF | *Altorientalische Forschungen* |
| ArOr | *Archiv Orientalni* |
| ASJ | *Acta Sumerologica* |
| ASOR | American Schools of Oriental Research |
| AT | The Alalakh Tablets |
| AuOr | *Aula Orientalis* |
| AuOrS | Aula Orientalis Supplement |
| BA | *Biblical Archaeologist* |
| BaF | *Baghdader Forschungen* |
| BaM | *Baghdader Mitteilungen* |
| BAR | *Biblical Archaeology Review* |
| BASOR | *Bulletin of the American Schools of Oriental Research* |
| BBB | *Bonner Biblische Beiträge* |
| BBVO | *Berliner Beiträge zum Vorderer Orient* |
| Bib | *Biblica* |
| BibB | *Biblische Beiträge* |
| BICS | Bulletin of the Institute of Classical Studies |

| | |
|---|---|
| *BiOr* | *Bibliotheca Orientalis* |
| *BJS* | *Brown Judaic Studies* |
| BM | museum siglum of the British Museum, London, or Baal miniature art |
| *BMCR* | *Bryn Mawr Classical Review* |
| BMECCJ | Bulletin of the Middle Eastern Culture Center in Japan |
| BMSAES | British Museum Studies in Ancient Egypt and Sudan |
| *Boreas* | *Boreas: Uppsala Studies in Ancient Mediterranean and Near Eastern Civilizations* |
| BR | Babylonian recension of the mouth-washing ritual |
| BS | Baal statue |
| *BzÄ* | *Beiträge zur Ägyptologie* |
| *BZAW* | *Beihefte zur Zeitschrift für die alttestamentliche Wissenschaft* |
| *CAD* | Ignace Gelb et al., eds., *The Assyrian Dictionary of the Oriental Institute of the University of Chicago.* 21 vols. Chicago: University of Chicago, 1956-2010 |
| *CANE* | J. M. Sasson, ed., *Civilizations of the Ancient Near East.* 2 vols. Peabody, MA: Hendrickson, 2000 |
| *CAT* | W. Dietrich, O. Loretz and J. Sanmartín, eds., *The Cuneiform Alphabetic Texts: from Ugarit, Ras Ibn Hani and other places (KTU).* 2nd. ed. Münster: Ugarit-Verlag, 1995. |
| CBET | Contributions to Biblical Exegesis and Theology |
| CBOT | Coniectanea biblica. Old Testament series |
| *CBQ* | *Catholic Biblical Quarterly* |
| CDOG | Colloquien der Deutschen Orient-Gesellschaft |
| CEPOA | Centre d'Étude du Proche-Orient Ancien, Université de Genève |
| CG | Catalogue General du Musee du Caire |
| ChS | Corpus der Hurritischen Sprachdenkmäler |
| *CHD* | H. G. Güterbock and H. A. Hoffner, Jr., eds., *The Hittite Dictionary of the Oriental Institute of the University of Chicago.* Chicago: University of Chicago, 1991– |
| *CLL* | H. C. Melchert. *Cuneiform Luvian Lexicon.* Chapel Hill, NC, 1993 |
| CM | Cuneiform Monographs |
| *COS* | W. W. Hallo and K. L. Younger, eds., *The Context of Scripture.* 3 vols. Leiden: Brill, 1997–2002 |
| *CRB* | *Cahiers de la Revue biblique* |
| *CTH* | E. Laroche, *Catalogue des textes hittites.* Paris: Klincksieck, 1971. |

| | |
|---|---|
| CUSAS | Cornell University Studies in Assyriology and Sumerology |
| *DBH* | *Dresdner Beiträge zur Hethitologie* |
| *DDD* | K. van der Toorn et al., eds., *Dictionary of Deities and Demons in the Bible*. 2nd ed. Leiden: Brill, 1999 |
| EA | El Amarna Tablets |
| *Ee* | *Enuma Elish* |
| Emar | Emar texts |
| *FAT* | *Forschungen zum Alten Testament* |
| *GGIG* | O. Keel and C. Uehlinger. *Gods, Goddesses, and Images of God in Ancient Israel*. Minneapolis: Fortress, 1998 |
| *HÄB* | *Hildesheimer Ägyptologische Beiträge* |
| *HAT* | *Handbuch zum Alten Testament* |
| HdO | Handbuch der Orientalistik |
| *HED* | J. Puhvel. *Hittite Etymological Dictionary*. Berlin: de Gruyter. 1984– |
| *HEG* | J. Tischler. *Hethitisches etymologisches Glossar*. Innsbruck: Institut für Sprachwissenschaft der Universität Innsbruck, 1977- |
| HEO | Hautes études orientales |
| *HrwG* | H. Cancik et al. *Handbuch religionswissenschaftlicher Grundbegriffe*. 5 vols. Stuttgart: Kohlhammer, 1988–2001 |
| HS | Tablet siglum of the Hilprecht Collection in Jena (Hilprecht-Sammlung) |
| HSS | Harvard Semitic Studies |
| *HW²* | J. Friedrich et al., eds. *Hethitisches Wörterbuch*. 2nd ed. Heidelberg: Winter, 1975– |
| *HUCA* | *Hebrew Union College Annual* |
| HUCASup | Hebrew Union College Annual Supplements |
| *IEJ* | *Israel Exploration Journal* |
| IT | Incantation Tablet(s) in Walker and Dick 2001 |
| *JANER* | *Journal of Ancient Near Eastern Religions* |
| *JAOS* | *Journal of the American Oriental Society* |
| *JBTh* | *Jahrbuch für biblische Theologie* |
| *JCS* | *Journal of Cuneiform Studies* |
| *JEA* | *Journal of Egyptian Archaeology* |
| *JEOL* | *Jaarbericht van het Vooraziatisch-Egyptisch Genootschap (Gezelschap) „Ex Oriente Lux"* |
| *JESHO* | *Journal of the Social and Economic History of the Orient* |
| *JNES* | *Journal of Near Eastern Studies* |
| *JNSL* | *Journal of Northwest Semitic Languages* |

| | |
|---|---|
| K | museum siglum of the British Museum in London (Kuyunjik) |
| KAI | H. Donner and W. Röllig, *Kanaanäische und aramäische Inschriften*. 3 vols. Wiesbaden: Harrasowitz, 1962–1964 |
| *KBo* | H. Otten and C. Rüster, eds., *Keilschrifttexte aus Boghazköi*. Leipzig-Berlin: Hinrichs-Gebr. Mann, 1916– |
| *KlF* | *Kleinasiatische Forschungen* |
| *KTU* | M. Dietrich, O. Loretz, and J. Sanmartín, eds., *Die keilalphabetischen Texte aus Ugarit*. Neukirchen: Neukirchen-Vluyn, 1976 |
| *KUB* | *Keilschrifturkunden aus Boghazköi*. Berlin: Akademie, 1921– |
| *LÄ* | W. Helck et al., eds., *Lexikon der Ägyptologie*. 7 vols. Harrasowitz: Wiesbaden: 1975–1992 |
| LACMA | Los Angeles County Museum of Art |
| *LKU* | A. Falkenstein, *Literarische Keilschrifttexte aus Uruk*, Berlin: Staatlichen Museen, 1931 |
| *MARG* | *Mitteilungen für Anthropologie und Religionsgeschichte* |
| *MARI* | *Mari, Annales de Recherches Interdisciplinaires* |
| *MÄS* | *Münchner Ägyptologische Studien* |
| *MDOG* | *Mitteilungen der Deutschen Orientgesellschaft* |
| *MIO* | *Mitteilungen des Instituts für Orientforschung* |
| *MKNAW* | *Mededeelingen der Koninklijke Nederlandsche Akademie van Wetenschappen* |
| *NEAEHL* | E. Stern, ed. *The New Encyclopedia of Archaeological Excavation in the Holy Land*. New York: Simon & Schuster, 1993. |
| *NEA* | *Near Eastern Archaeology* |
| NR | Nineveh recension of the mouth-washing ritual |
| OBO | Orbis Biblicus et Orientalis |
| *OEAE* | D. Redford, ed., *The Oxford Encyclopedia of Ancient Egypt*, 3 vols. Oxford: Oxford University Press, 2001. |
| *OEANE* | *The Oxford Encyclopedia of Archaeology in the Near East*. 5 vols. Oxford: Oxford University Press, 1997 |
| OIC | Oriental Institute Communications |
| OLA | Orientalia Lovaniensia analecta |
| OIP | Oriental Institute Publications |
| OIS | Oriental Institute Seminars |
| ORA | Orientalische Religionen in der Antike |
| *Or* | *Orientalia Nova Series* |
| *OrAnt* | *Oriens Antiquus* |

| | |
|---|---|
| RAI | Rencontre Assyriologique Internationale |
| *RÄRG* | H. Bonnet, *Reallexikon der Ägyptische Religions-geschichte*. 3rd. ed. Berlin: de Gruyter, 2000 |
| *RB* | *Revue biblique* |
| *RDE* | *Revue d'égyptologie* |
| *RHA* | *Revue hittite et asianique* |
| *RHR* | *Revue de l'histoire de religions* |
| RIMA | The Royal Inscriptions of Mesopotamia, Assyrian Periods |
| *RIMA 2* | A. Kirk Grayson, *Assyrian Rulers of the Early First Millennium BC I (1114–859 BC)*. Toronto: University of Toronto, 1991 |
| *RlA* | E. Ebeling et al. eds., *Reallexikon der Assyriologie und vorderasiatischen Archäologie*. Berlin: de Gruyter, 1928– |
| RS | Ras Shamra |
| *SAA* | *State Archives of Assyria 2, 3, 12* |
| *SAA 2* | S. Parpola and K. Watanabe. *Neo-Assyrian Treaties and Loyalty Oaths*. Helsinki: Helsinki University Press, 1988. |
| *SAA 12* | L. Kataja and R. Whiting, *Grants, Decrees, and Gifts of the Neo-Assyrian Period*. Helsinki: Helsinki University Press, 1995 |
| *SAAB* | *State Archives of Assyria Bulletin* |
| SAALT | State Archives of Assyria Literary Texts |
| SAGA | Studien zur Archäologie und Geschichte Altägyptens |
| SAK | Studien zur altägyptischen Kultur |
| SANER | Studies in Ancient Near Eastern Records |
| SANTAG | Arbeiten und Untersuchungen zur Keilschriftkunde |
| SAOC | Studies in Ancient Oriental Civilization |
| SBLWAW | SBL Writings from the Ancient World |
| SBLWAWSup | SBL Writings from the Ancient World Supplement Series |
| SCCNH | Studies on the Civilization and Culture of Nuzi and the Hurrians |
| *SEL* | *Studi epigrafici e linguistici* |
| *SMSR* | *Studi e materiali di storia delle religioni* |
| StBoT | Studien zu den Boğazköy-Texten |
| STT | The Sultantepe Tablets |
| Studia Pohl | Studia Pohl: Dissertationes scientificae de rebus orientis antiqui |
| T. | Tello |
| *TDOT* | G. J. Botterweck et al., eds. *Theological Dictionary of* |

|  |  |
|---|---|
|  | *the Old Testament.* 15 vols. Grand Rapids, MI: Eerdmans, 1974–2006 |
| *TU* | F. Thureau-Dangin. *Tablettes d'Uruk.* Paris: Musée du Louvre, 1922 |
| *TUAT* | O. Kaiser et al., eds. *Texte aus der Umwelt des Alten Testaments.* Gütersloh: Gütersloher Verlaghaus, 1982– |
| *TuL* | E. Ebeling, *Tod und Leben nach den Vorstellungen der Babylonier.* Berlin: de Gruyter, 1931 |
| *UBL* | *Ugaritisch-Biblische Literatur* |
| *UF* | *Ugarit Forschungen* |
| *Urk.* | *Urkunden des Ägyptischen Altertums* |
| *Urk. IV* | K. Sethe and W. Helck, *Urkunden der 18. Dynastie. 22 fascicles.* Leipzig: Hinrichs, 1906–1958 |
| Utt. | Utterance from the Egyptian Pyramid Texts. Translations after R. O. Faulkner, *The Ancient Egyptian Pyramid Texts.* 2 vols. Oxford: Clarendon, 1969 |
| VAT | museum siglum of the Vorderasiatisches Museum, Berlin (Vorderasiatische Abteilung Tontafel) |
| VTSup | Supplements to Vetus Testamentum |
| *Wb* | A. Erman and W. Grapow, eds., *Wörterbuch der ägyptische Sprache.* 7 vols. Berlin: Akademie, 1926–1931 |
| *WdO* | *Die Welt des Orients.* Wissenschaftl. Beiträge zur Kunde des Morgenlandes |
| WMANT | Wissenschaftliche Monographien zum Alten und Neuen Testament |
| WVDOG | Wissenschaftliche Veröffentlichungen der Deutschen Orientgesellschaft |
| *WZKM* | *Wiener Zeitschrift für die Kunde des Morgenlandes* |
| *ZA* | *Zeitschrift für Assyriologie und Vorderasiatische Archäologie* |
| *ZABR* | *Zeitschrift für altorientalische und biblische Rechtsgeschichte* |
| *ZAW* | *Zeitschrift für die alttestamentliche Wissenschaft* |

# Part 1

# Temples in the Ancient Near East

# CHAPTER 1

# TEMPLES IN THE ANCIENT NEAR EAST:
# AN INTRODUCTION

IN A DANGEROUS AND VOLATILE WORLD, the ancient Near Eastern temple was the primary point of intersection between human and divine. As a principle means of establishing security in an otherwise insecure world, it situated the deity in the midst of human habitation, so that humanity might offer service and gifts in exchange for divine protection and prosperity.[1] The temple was also the divine residence, which intimates that its resident had a vested interest in his residence and the community around it. Thus, through regular and regulated interactions in the temple, people could gain some measure of control over both their own fate and that of the world around them. By influencing the resident deity, they influenced the cosmos it governed, often jointly with the other gods.[2] Furthermore, because it marked the intersection of two otherwise separate spheres, the temple structure also served to mediate contact, facilitating safe and fruitful commerce.[3]

Conceptually, the temple was integrally related to and dependent upon the divine presence and the interaction between that presence and humanity. It had an important role to play, yet one that should not be overestimated. The temple was secondary to both divine presence and ritual action, serving as the setting for both. Without them, it was merely an empty building, a stage bereft of actors and action. However, when all three elements converged, the temple became a place of power, accomplishing specific functions and communicating specific messages.

The temple's complementary relationship may perhaps be understood best via analogy.[4] In a play, the actors and actions are generally regarded as more

---

1. "Architecture is space structured to meet social needs, and the temple is the architectural type that services the social institution of religion" (Gregory J. Wightman, *Sacred Spaces: Religious Architecture in the Ancient World* [Leuven: Peeters, 2007], 898).

2. The term cosmos derives from the Greek κόσμος, representing the antithesis of chaos, and refers here to the ordered universe.

3. Wightman, *Sacred Spaces*, 932.

4. The analogy is used here for its explanatory power in a limited context; it is not meant to be stretched too far. In making it, I am not suggesting that ritual should be understood as a drama (see, e.g., Victor Turner, *Dramas, Fields and Metaphors: Symbolic Action in Human Society* [Ithaca, NY: Cornell University Press, 1974]), only that drama and ritual have points of intersection.

interesting and important than the stage itself. A play, if well-performed, could be effective on nearly any stage. However, the stage and setting possess remarkable power to influence and enhance the play's effectiveness. A successful stage is not only functional, but also successfully conveys the play's message, facilitating the proper emotional and physical response. Furthermore, the stage and the theater have a significant effect on how the actors perform and perceive their performances. For example, an elaborate Broadway or West End set may be far more evocative than a simple stage in a local community center and, as such, not only affects the audience's perception but also influences the actors' performances. Likewise, a priest may perform and perceive his actions differently depending on the form and evocative power of the temple. As the arena of human-divine interaction, the temple structure evokes and enculturates in both the observer and the participant the "correct" emotive and behavioral responses. Like a play, divine presence and human-divine interaction can occur on practically any stage. However, when the deity is permanently or semipermanently resident, boundaries must be carefully established and the rooms appropriately fashioned and adorned. The deity's residence must be properly prepared, both to accommodate the deity's specifications and to communicate the appropriate message to the public.

## ARCHITECTURAL AND SPATIAL THEORY

### Built Environment Studies

The temple's encoded messages have a theoretical basis in built environment studies.[5] Built environment studies builds on psychological and sociocultural anthropological approaches to architectural forms,[6] and focuses on the relationship

---

5. The following analysis builds on the helpful summary of Clifford Mark McCormick, *Palace and Temple: A Study of Architectural and Verbal Icons* (BZAW 313; Berlin: de Gruyter, 2002), 8–16; see also Michael B. Hundley, "Before Yahweh at the Entrance of the Tent of Meeting: A Study of Spatial and Conceptual Geography in the Priestly Texts," *ZAW* 123 (2011): 17–18.

6. McCormick, *Palace and Temple*, 9; see also the various references to nonverbal communication in Amos Rapoport, *The Meaning of the Built Environment: A Nonverbal Communication Approach* (London: Sage, 1982), 48. Its rise also coincides with increasing importance of studies of material culture and environmental psychology. Regarding the former, see, e.g., Thomas J. Schlereth, ed., *Material Culture: A Research Guide* (Lawrence, KS: University Press of Kansas, 1985); Steven Lubar and W. David Kingery, eds., *History from Things: Essays* (New York: Smithsonian Books, 1993); Ian Woodward, *Understanding Material Culture* (London: Sage, 2007). Regarding the latter, see, e.g., Harold M. Proshansky, et al., eds., *Environmental Psychology: People and Their Physical Settings* (2nd ed.; New York: Holt, Rinehart & Winston, 1976); Winifred Gallagher, *The Power of Place: How Our Surroundings Shape Our Thoughts, Emotions and Actions* (New York: Harper, 1994); Paul A. Bell et al., *Environmental Psychology* (5th ed.; Andover, UK: Thomson, 2001); cf. also Mari-

between the "structure and the cultural categories that influence it,"[7] recognizing that buildings are "molded theatres of human activity."[8] Even when the structure lies abandoned, "a trace of this vanished life remains behind in a building to the extent that the purpose is incarnated in the forms of the space."[9] This is an especially helpful insight for examining the structures of the ancient world, which have outlived the cultures that formed and frequented them. The Egyptian temple, for example, is particularly informative as the purpose of the structure is inscribed on the very walls, in the form of reliefs and inscriptions.

Recognizing the communicative power of structures, built environment studies examines the effect the "physical constitution of an environment has on the human activity within it."[10] It analyzes the purpose of the structure (for both designers and users),[11] how its form communicates this purpose, and its power to influence, if not determine, behavior. Instead of (or in addition to) having signs for people to read and obey, a building often communicates unconsciously. When viewing the physical layout of a building, the observer unconsciously makes associations derived from that layout.[12] For example, the structures of a modern cathedral, skyscraper, or an ancient temple often inspire awe. This response is not a conscious decision. Instead, viewing the building itself elicits this emotive reaction without any conscious thought.[13] The temple employs this powerful tool to

---

Jose Amerlinck, ed., *Architectural Anthropology* (Westport, CT: Bergin & Garvey, 2001); Jerome A. Winer et al., eds., *The Annual of Psychoanalysis,* Volume 33: *Psychoanalysis and Architecture* (Catskill, NY: Mental Health Resources, 2005).

7. McCormick, *Palace and Temple,* 9.

8. Paul T. Frankl, *Principles of Architectural Study* (Cambridge, MA: MIT Press, 1968), 159.

9. Ibid., 160.

10. McCormick, *Palace and Temple,* 10, referring to Rapoport, *Built Environment.* See also recent studies on sacred space (Thomas Barrie, *Spiritual Path, Sacred Place: Myth, Ritual, and Meaning in Architecture* [Boston: Shambhala, 1996]; idem, *The Sacred In-Between: The Mediating Roles of Architecture* [New York: Routledge, 2010]; Lindsay Jones, *The Hermeneutics of Sacred Space: Experience, Interpretation, Comparison* [Cambridge, Mass.: Harvard University Press, 2000]).

11. See Frankl, *Principles of Architectural Study,* and Thomas A. Markus, *Buildings and Power: Freedom and Control in the Origins of Modern Building Types* (London: Routledge, 1993).

12. Cf. Rapoport (*Built Environment,* 19–34), who notes two levels to the built environment, the perceptual and associational, where the perceptual notes the physical items perceived by the observer and the associational is concerned with the different associations the user makes with the physical elements.

13. For Richard E. Blanton, the form of a dwelling facilitates and promotes the behavior that inspired its structure. For example, the decoration and levels of elevation provide signals within a culture of the privileged status of older generation over the younger (*House and Households: A Comparative Study* [New York: Plenum, 1994], 102).

reinforce already established cultural messages.[14] For Rapoport, it serves as a cue to inspire the appropriate emotive, interpretive, and behavioral response. In his words, "it is the social situation that influences people's behavior, but it is the physical environment that provides the cues."[15] In other words, the structure provides a behavioral mnemonic that reminds the body how to behave.[16]

The building's message goes beyond implicit prompting. Its beauty lies in its ability to make the appropriate cultural response seem like a truth inherent in nature, which thus cannot be ignored. In Egypt, for example, the ubiquity of the king[17] in the decoration instilled in the observer the idea that the king alone was the mediator between the people and the gods, between order and chaos. Since such "truths" were built into the very fabric of the temple, created to house the deity, they seem to have been built into the very fabric of creation.

Walls and doors are particularly relevant examples of a building's communicative strategy, and, in the ancient Near East, portals between spaces were especially important, evidenced by the overabundance of terms for doors and gates in Egyptian.[18] Walls form an impenetrable barrier between significant spaces and doors serve as the only means of access between those spaces. As such, walls and doors are especially useful in separating spaces and defining access to those spaces. Today, as in the past, people often take these forms for granted, responding to their cues without consciously noticing them.

However, the structure in isolation often contributes an ambiguous message. As with ritual action, in which multiple actions may accomplish the same purpose and the "same" action may accomplish multiple purposes in different contexts, different architectural and decorative features may communicate the same message, while the same features in different settings may express different messages.[19] One must also know something of the cultural context of the building and the actions conducted therein.[20] Rather than focusing exclusively on design, we may also ap-

---

14. These messages are established through enculturation or acculturation; Rapoport, *Built Environment*, 65–70.

15. Ibid., 56–57; cf. Blanton, *House and Households*, 102.

16. Rapoport, *Built Environment*, 67, 80–81.

17. The terms "king" and "pharaoh" refer to the same Egyptian person. While "pharaoh" will be used, "king" will feature for consistency across cultures.

18. Patricia Spencer, *The Egyptian Temple: A Lexicographical Study* (London: Kegan Paul, 1984), 179–216; cf. the important Akkadian terms *daltu* and *bābu*, *CAD* D, 52–55; B, 14–22.

19. Diederik J. W. Meijer, "Ground Plans and Archaeologists: On Similarities and Comparisons," in *To the Euphrates and Beyond: Archaeological Studies in Honor of Maurits N. Van Loon* (ed. O. Haex, H. Curvers, and P. Akkermans; Rotterdam: A. A. Blakema, 1989), 221–36, esp. 223; McCormick, *Palace and Temple*, 25.

20. This last represents Rapoport's third category, nonfixed features, denoting the inhabitants "shifting spatial relations, their body positions and postures, hand and arm

peal to the preserved texts, which provide invaluable evidence about the use of the structures and their elements. Written texts, especially those concerned with the planning and construction of the building, provide important clues as to the intent of the planners and builders.[21] These texts are less open to interpretation as the designers often communicated their intentions explicitly.

Within these texts and within the structure of the building, one also finds elements of an ideological nature. For example, various elements often speak to the underlying rationale of a structure, how it is understood by designers and users, religious authorities and commoners, and where the temple and its ideology fit within the larger cultural worldview (e.g., how is it understood to be an appropriate residence from the deity, different from all others, and what is its cosmic symbolism?). When evidence of an ideological nature is missing or does not explicitly indicate purpose, the interpreter must "rely on his own sensitivity and creativity to offer an explanation that approaches the cultural and social significance of the structure."[22]

From another (similar) perspective, George has recently examined the biblical tabernacle through the lens of spatial theory, or, more particularly, a spatial poetics.[23] Building on the work of Lefebvre[24] and the New Historicism, he posits three categories through which space may be analyzed: spatial practice, conceptual space, and symbolic space. According to George, "social space ... is understood as more than physical reality. It is a combination of interrelated fields: the physical reality of space; the conceptual systems a society creates to explain and think space; and the symbolic meanings a society ascribes and imputes to space."[25]

## Modern Analogs

Even today buildings communicate. Two of the closest modern analogs to the ancient Near Eastern temple are particularly illustrative as points of comparison and contrast, highlighting the two primary aspects of the ancient temple: a cathe-

---

gestures, and even facial expressions, along with other nonverbal behaviors" (quoting McCormick's description, *Palace and Temple*, 11).

21. McCormick, *Palace and Temple*, 15, drawing from the work of Markus, *Buildings and Power*.

22. Ibid., 16.

23. Mark K. George, *Israel's Tabernacle as Social Space* (SBL Ancient Israel and Its Literature 2; Atlanta: SBL, 2009).

24. Henri Lefebvre, *The Production of Space* (trans. D. Nicholson-Smith; Oxford: Blackwell, 1991). Stephen Lumsden ("The Production of Space at Nineveh," *Iraq* 66 [2004]: 187–97) applies Lefebvre's argument for the conceptual unity of physical, mental, and social dimensions to the production of space at Nineveh.

25. George, *Israel's Tabernacle*, 19.

dral[26] (as the temple was the place for encountering the deity) and a private house (as the temple was the home of the deity).

As with an ancient Near Eastern temple, the adornment of a cathedral indicates its relative wealth, and its layout marks access.[27] The elaborate structure and its ornamentation indicate the prestige of the place, while the layout controls access to its various parts. More than that, its sheer presence evokes an emotional response. Rather than consciously analyzing its elements to intuit the proper reaction, one is simply affected by it. As in the temple of old, the observer is awestruck and responds appropriately with reverence.[28] For example, visitors often instinctively lower their voices, even if the building is empty. The architecture thereby unconsciously reinforces and in some ways even creates the impression of divine power and presence.[29]

Nonetheless, there are major differences between a modern cathedral and an ancient Near Eastern temple. Although constructed as a point of contact between human and divine, ancient Near Eastern temples primarily served as the estates of the gods to which people had limited access, not gathering places for a congregation.[30] In ancient Near Eastern contexts, the deity's continued presence was the primary concern, and, as such, the people's role focused on keeping the deity happy so that it would remain at home and positively disposed to its servants. Likewise, personal concerns, which are often primary in a modern context, played

---

26. Cathedral is used here rather vaguely to refer to large, grandiose church structures like Notre Dame in Paris, St. Peter's in Rome, and St. Paul's in London; for a more precise definition of "cathedral," see Jeanne Halgren Kilde, *Sacred Power, Sacred Space: An Introduction to Christian Architecture and Worship* (Oxford: Oxford University Press, 2008), 66 and n. 8.

27. Especially in years past, many Catholic and Orthodox churches were hierarchically divided, separating the common people from the clergy and especially from the divine presence made especially manifest in the elements of the Eucharist, in some cases kept in a niche like ancient Near Eastern statues (see esp. Kilde, *Sacred Power*). As such, they have many parallels with ancient Near Eastern temples that may be profitably explored. Here, analysis will focus on more recent understandings of the cathedral as a gathering place for a worshiping congregation, akin to that of Protestant churches. For as Kilde notes, "Vatican II transformed the house of God into the house of God's people" (*Sacred Power*, 189).

28. Many modern churches meet in nondescript buildings, often as a response to the opulence of the cathedrals, aiming to be more accessible and emphasizing that the building itself is not as important as the believer's internal relationship with the deity; cf. Steven Snape, *Egyptian Temples* (Buckinghamshire, UK: Shire, 1996), 8.

29. Kilde, *Sacred Power*, 58.

30. On Egypt, see, e.g., Alexander Badawy, *A History of Egyptian Architecture: Empire (the New Kingdom)* (Berkeley: University of California Press, 1968), 181; on Mesopotamia, see, e.g., Jean-Claude Margueron, "Temples: The Mesopotamian Temple," in *OEANE* 4: 165.

little role in ancient Near Eastern temples since they did not necessarily contribute to the divine well-being.[31]

Access is an especially important contrast. Although in the ancient Near Eastern temple courts were occasionally accessible and often their size could accommodate large crowds, especially during festivals, access was severely restricted to the temple interior, and one is hard-pressed to find anything resembling pews inside.[32] Furthermore, rather than serving as a refuge like cathedrals and other modern churches where worshipers seek physical and emotional sanctuary, ancient Near Eastern temples often elicited fear and threatened danger. In the ancient Near East, this intersection between human and divine was perceived to be volatile, and a positive divine reception was not assured. In a modern context, although the deity is perceived to be present, especially in Catholic and Orthodox contexts, worshipers often focus more on their internal relationship with the deity. The church is thus used to accommodate their worship and enhance their feelings of intimacy, such that the modern cathedral functions more as a house for God's people than the house of God.[33]

For another analogy, we turn to the private house. Like temples, homes communicate on a general level the prestige of their occupant, their tastes, and the hierarchical divisions within their households. The house and its furnishings communicate wealth or status, while the layout of the house indicates rank within the household and access to its various regions. For example, in a western home, the private domain is often separated from the public world by a front door. Practically anyone from the public sphere may come to the front door, the threshold between public and private worlds. Access to the private world, however, must be given, while those who transgress this boundary may be punished.[34] The entryway (or vestibule in archaeological parlance) often indicates the next level of accessibility, beyond which one typically encounters a room for entertaining guests. Only the privileged few travel further, as we move beyond the category of guest to that of intimate. Graded access becomes especially pronounced when the house has two or more levels. Access to the upper floor, and particularly to its bedrooms and bathrooms, is a special privilege. The master bedroom, frequently the most important room, is often the largest and best-decorated bedroom and the most isolated room in the house—i.e., the farthest from the front door. Likewise, in an ancient Near Eastern temple, the importance of a room was usually proportional

31. See Michael B. Hundley, *Keeping Heaven on Earth: Safeguarding the Divine Presence in the Priestly Tabernacle* (FAT II/50; Tübingen: Mohr Siebeck, 2011), 120–34.

32. As we will see in ch. 5, the benches occasionally lining the walls of sanctuaries in many ways provide a poor parallel.

33. Cf. Kilde, *Sacred Power*, 189.

34. Indeed, in some American states, a violation of this boundary legally permits homeowners to shoot trespassers.

to its distance from the entrance of the temple complex, and the number of walls and portals one must pass through to reach it. With each successive wall and doorway, fewer and fewer people had access, until only a privileged few could enter the divine bedchamber, often found in the most secluded and most protected area of the compound.

More than simply mediating access and marking status, the house provides a powerful impetus to behave according to its rules. Entering an impressive private domain, especially when it is owned by someone of higher social status, naturally evokes a submissive response. One feels privileged to be allowed into another's private space and unconsciously compelled to follow the rules of that space. Indeed, when guests enter a person's domain, wherein they have no authority, they must obey its rules as a condition of their access. Because the space belongs to another, a guest would never think to regulate the inhabitant's rules; he or she would instead follow those rules willingly.[35]

Ancient Near Eastern temples functioned similarly. They were universally referred to as divine residences, and deities were of a higher social, even ontological, standing than everyone else, including the king. As such, ancient Near Eastern and biblical literature on temples and temple protocol often focused on the rules of the house, given to ensure proper conduct in the divine domain and a profitable interchange between the deity and its human servants. Since humans could not presume to understand, regulate, or enumerate divine actions in divine space, divine conduct was commonly mentioned only when it was necessary to ensure that guests behave appropriately.

However, once again, there is an important difference between a human home and a temple, just as there is an important difference between their residents. To differentiate it as an appropriate divine abode, the ancient Near Eastern temple builders, as we will see, often included marks of its otherness in the structure itself and almost always in their textual presentation of it.

In each context, whether the cathedral, home, or temple, the environment itself does not create messages; instead it is created to reinforce, perhaps even enculturate, preexisting messages regarding rank and access. This message is particularly persuasive precisely because the observer often absorbs it unconsciously. Thus, by reinforcing the divisions within the society and within the homes of its members, the structure seems to indicate that the differences are innate.

---

35. For example, a person entering a home and seeing shoes stacked by the door would yield to the owner's preference and defer to his or her wishes, rather than imposing her or his own personal preferences or habits.

## HOW DO WE INTERPRET ANCIENT TEMPLES AS BUILDINGS?

Analyzing ancient temples requires an understanding of their complexity and interconnectedness with divine presence, and the interaction between that presence and humanity. The divine has been understood as the wholly other[36] that stands outside of normal experience and is thus indescribable in its terms; "for all available descriptive terms are grounded in human experience and so fall short."[37] To describe it, one must use analogical language,[38] for although a metaphor cannot and does not encapsulate meaning, it can approximate it. When dealing with the wholly other, approximation is the best one can do. However, no single approximation exhausts meaning, and if taken too far it can even distort meaning. Instead, various metaphors are amassed, each grasping to catch an aspect of the ineffable, together grasping at the whole. Again, one must be careful not to stretch the metaphors too far, thereby producing contradictions that are often more a result of the inadequacy of the description, rather than the inadequacy of that being described.

The ancient Near Eastern temple represented an uneasy symbiosis, a necessary mixing of human and divine spheres. As the house of the divine, the temple had elements of the numinous. As a building in human space, it also had elements of this world. The temple was built in the natural world with earthly materials and was frequented by humans. Because it was a physical, terrestrial abode, we are right to call it a home, but as the home of a god, it was different from all human analogs, requiring elements of analogical representation that point to its otherness.

On a practical level, the design of a temple functionally differentiated it from ordinary buildings, in order to construct an abode suitable for its divine resident.[39]

---

36. In his classic book, Rudolf Otto uses the expression "numinous" to refer to the confrontation between humanity and a power not of this world (*The Idea of The Holy* [trans. J. Harvey; Oxford: Oxford University Press, 1958]). This is not to say, as we will see in the section on divine presence, that the deity does not overlap at all with humanity, only that deities exceed humans in almost every conceivable way, and thus cannot be adequately described in human terms.

37. Thorkild Jacobsen, *The Treasures of Darkness: A History of Mesopotamian Religion* (New Haven, CT: Yale University Press, 1976), 3, describing religion as a universal. Division between the natural and the supernatural is a modern distinction. Nonetheless, this distinction is useful in putting words to the innate understanding of the ancients that the divine is special; and, although present in the ordinary, it is also distinct from it.

38. Thus, the metaphor is central to religious expression; cf. Jacobsen, *Treasures of Darkness*, 3. On the nature of religious language, see, e.g., Janet Soskice, *Metaphor and Religious Language* (Oxford: Clarendon, 1985); for a brief summary, see Hundley, *Keeping Heaven*, 12–14.

39. This is akin to Catherine Bell's ritualization, which refers to a "way of acting that is designed and orchestrated to distinguish and privilege what is being done in relation to other, more quotidian, activities" (*Ritual Theory, Ritual Practice* [Oxford: Oxford University Press, 1992], 74).

In other words, the ancient Near Eastern temple was made similar enough to be meaningful and comprehensible to humans, yet different enough to be appropriate for the deity. In constructing a divine abode, the ancient Near Eastern temple builders were bound to the constraints of physical materials, available resources, and the human imagination. In order to highlight its special status, they were limited to the elements of design, language, and aesthetics to communicate its otherness. In this analysis, we will note both how the temple is differentiated from human analogs and attempt to explain what that differentiation implies about its perceived nature.

## METHODOLOGY

In recognition of the temple's complexity, I adopt a multilayered approach suitable to the multivalent temple, analyzing it using four categories: structure, use, structural communication, and ideology.[40] Although by no means perfect, this fourfold division provides a fuller portrait of the ancient Near Eastern temples by addressing their effects and how they were used and perceived from different angles.

Structure literally refers to the structure of the building, in effect providing its blueprint, including the description of gates, walls, furniture, and adornment. For example, this section addresses the location of the sanctuary and its decoration. Use is also rather straightforward category, referring to what the building was designed and used for, according to textual and archaeological evidence, on both an overall and room-by-room basis. For example, each culture refers to the temple as a "house," thereby employing the same terminology used for human dwellings, while the presence of an altar and animal bones would indicate animal offerings.

As its name suggests, structural communication addresses what the structure itself likely communicated and the effects it elicited from its observers. Whereas the level of structure notes that the Egyptian pylon is large and describes its shape, structural communication describes how the pylon's size highlights the importance of the space it protects and describes the response it likely elicited. At this level, information is communicated largely unconsciously, involving a reaction rather than a cognitive process, one that may be engineered to reinforce already existing cultural messages. For example, the temple structures often unconsciously inspire awe and prompt submission to their codes of conduct.

The level of ideology takes us one step further, examining the underlying rationale of the building, primarily from the perspective of the builders but also of its users, and situating it in the context of the larger cultural worldviews. For example, it asks: why was the temple constructed the way it was constructed? How does it

---

40. For an explication of their relevance to ritual theory, see Hundley, *Keeping Heaven*, 26–37, esp. 34–37.

reflect and reinforce the society's conceptions of the divine and temple space? How is the temple perceived to be suitable for the deity and different from human analogs? To communicate the underlying thoughtworlds, this category incorporates mythology and includes symbolism. For example, many ancient Near Eastern temples were conceptually linked with creation, served as a bridge between heaven and earth, and constituted semidiscrete worlds whose well-being determined the well-being of the human world around them. Because the texts rarely fully articulate their ideological agenda and different texts articulate it differently, ideology may function on many levels, and because it derives from the diverse associations people make, ideological interpretations invariably vary.[41]

Analysis thus moves from the more concrete—describing the temple's layout and function—to the more subjective and abstract—examining the effect of the structure on the observer and the underlying rationale of the building. Viewing temples from multiple angles with multiple perspectives allows for a more robust portrait of ancient Near Eastern temples. The four-pronged format makes room both for the more straightforward structural layout, terminology, and purpose as well as the more theoretical analysis of temple ideology and the effect the structure elicits.

Before proceeding, I must note several limitations of this study. First, since much of the communicative power of a temple comes across as a response to viewing it,[42] the fact that little remains of the once glorious temples to respond to puts the interpreter in a difficult predicament. I will use the structural remains and imagination, hoping to reconstruct both the buildings in their pristine form and the response they likely would have elicited.[43]

Second, a temple is notoriously difficult to identify. When little remains of the original structure and of our understanding of the culture using it, our identification relies on circumstantial evidence. The structure itself, its furniture (e.g., tables and altars), the presence of cult objects (e.g., the divine cult statue[s]) and paraphernalia (e.g., votive vessels and censers), and the remains of cult offerings (e.g., animal bones) provide the best indicators. However, they are often less than foolproof, as statues and an altar may have been present in a person's home as well as a temple.

Third, we must recognize the superficial nature of this survey, which attempts to identify the common features of temples and the ideologies attached to them across millennia and vast, ever-shifting regions. This common pattern must also

---

41. Cf. Martin Modéus, *Sacrifice and Symbol: Biblical Šĕlāmîm in a Ritual Perspective* (CBOT 52; Stockholm: Almqvist & Wiksell, 2005), 128–30, 133–34.

42. Like poetry and ritual action, the temple must be engaged with so that it may evoke a visceral response from its audience.

43. In light of these hurdles, the state of preservation of many Egyptian temples is a welcome boon, as they still evoke a response in the observer.

be derived from the few examples that have survived, most of which are analyzed on the basis of minimal remains. Thus, instead of being an exhaustive examination of ancient Near Eastern temples and their various elements, the present study explores some of the common features and their implications in each ancient Near Eastern culture.[44] In other words, it is an attempt to find unity in the diversity of ancient Near Eastern material, to find the common traits within each culture and the worldviews encoded in the various temples and to analyze their import. I will focus more narrowly on the official (often state) temples, which are often closely allied to the royal interests. However, rather than simply focusing on a comparison with the royal palace, which is often its closest analog, I will examine how it is constructed to be a suitable divine abode, both like and unlike royal palaces. In addition, although the temple is far more than merely a religious institution (as it has economic, political, and social implications), I will focus on its religious aspects, that is, what it communicates about perceptions of the divine and their interaction with humanity in various ancient Near Eastern cultures.

## Order of Analysis

I will analyze the temples of each region separately, beginning with Egypt. Egypt occupies the primary position for several reasons. The temple remains are the best preserved in the Near East and are accompanied by an abundance of textual and pictorial representations. They are likewise the most capable of eliciting a response today similar to that evoked by the temples in their original states. Official Egyptian architecture, especially of a religious nature, was extremely conservative, thus producing great continuity.[45] I will proceed to Mesopotamia, followed by Hittite Anatolia, and finally Syria-Palestine,[46] after which I will offer a synthesis comparing the temples of the various regions.[47]

---

44. The term "culture" refers rather loosely to the people who make up each of the various regions analyzed. It is an inadequate term since it requires a more precise definition and each region was undoubtedly made up of more than one culture. However, it is employed here generally to indicate that the people in Egypt, e.g, are part of a different culture than those in Mesopotamia.

45. Sigfried Morenz, *The Egyptian Temple* (trans. A. Keep; Ithaca, NY: Cornell University Press, 1973), 85.

46. To avoid the unnecessary complications of biblical comparisons, I also will limit my analysis of Syro-Palestinian temples to non-Israelite examples.

47. Although the results may profitably be applied to biblical studies, these results will be compared with the biblical material only incidentally. Instead, the assessed material will be offered in such a way that it invites the reader to make comparisons with analogs from the Bible and from other cultures, both ancient and modern. Indeed, the material amassed in the present study has been the foundation for all of my publications in biblical studies.

Each chapter begins with a general introduction including some of the limitations specific to each region. Analysis follows using the fourfold categories of structure, use, structural communication, and ideology, with occasional subsections. For example, in Syria-Palestine, subsections on the relationship between temple and palace appear at the end of the structural communication and ideology sections.

## A Note on Spatial Terminology

Primary space[48] refers to the immediate locus of divine presence, the cult image, and the space immediately around it that sets it apart from its surroundings. Secondary space refers to the larger space around the primary cult image, either in the same room or adjacent to it. The cult image was set apart from the surrounding secondary space in various ways. Most prominently, it was situated on a pedestal, in a niche in the back wall, a small shrine, or occupied its own small room. In such cases, the pedestal, niche, shrine, or room and the cult image constitute primary temple space, while the space around it is secondary space. Tertiary space refers to the spaces that mediate access to secondary and primary space, such as vestibules and corridors, and to auxiliary rooms, such as storerooms, slaughter rooms, and archives. Quarternary space often appears outside of the primary roofed temple structures (e.g., courts, processional paths, and separate buildings used among other things as workshops and priestly residences) or mark the entryway to those structures (e.g., gates).[49]

The terminology used to describe primary divine space is often employed variously and inconsistently by scholars across and even within disciplines. *Cella* is a Latin term that refers to a small chamber, while *naos* is a Greek term for temple. Both terms are used to refer somewhat inaccurately to the space housing the cult

---

48. The terms "primary," "secondary," "tertiary," and "quarternary" are used in reference to the temple architecture. Given the complexity and uncertainty of temple structure and function, these designators are not problem free and require some comment. The inner sanctuary serves as the point of reference and is designated "primary space," since it is generally the most isolated space and the resting place of the cult image. This is not to say that the cult image always remained in the sanctuary, that it was not moved to other temple spaces for ritual purposes. In such contexts, by virtue of the perceived divine presence, secondary spaces became primary. However, within the structure of the complex and according to normal practice, these spaces remain secondary. Likewise, chapels to other deities, often members of the divine entourage, were present in the temple complex. Although presumably some form of cult image rested within, the cult image of the temple's primary deity was situated elsewhere and the architecture was designed to privilege the sanctuary of the primary deity, such that architecturally the other chapels are secondary.

49. Regarding the labels primary, secondary, tertiary, and quarternary, see further Wightman, *Sacred Spaces*, 932–52.

image in a temple, the former especially for Mesopotamia and Syria-Palestine and the latter especially for Egypt. The *naos* often refers more particularly to the small shrine built to house the cult image. Instead of using *cella* and *naos*, the space housing the cult image will be referred to as the sanctuary.[50] When evidence exists for the separation of the cult image from its surroundings (e.g., through a pedestal or separate room), the separated space will be referred to as the "inner sanctuary" and the space it is separated from the "outer sanctuary," in accord with the designators primary and secondary space.

Moving further out from the center, the "temple core" refers to the area within the temple around the central sanctuary and may include various tertiary spaces like storerooms, secondary chapels, vestibules, and corridors. The "temple complex" refers to the primary temple building and, when its walls extend around them, to the temple court(s). If two courts (e.g., in Mesopotamia) are present, they will be designated "inner" and "outer" court.[51] The divine sphere or sacred precinct (*temenos*) refers to the entire (often walled) compound belonging to the deity in distinction from the mundane world, that is, the rest of the city or surrounding area, and includes various quarternary elements, such as unwalled courts and auxiliary buildings. Processional ways may extend beyond the walled divine sphere and thus extend its influence further into mundane space.

50. This nomenclature too has its limitations, especially since others, like Wightman (*Sacred Spaces*), refer to the entire divine complex as the sanctuary.

51. Multiple pylons occasionally feature in Egypt and will be given numerical values starting from closest to the sanctuary and moving outward (e.g., the first pylon, the second pylon, etc.).

# CHAPTER 2
## EGYPTIAN TEMPLES

ANALYSIS BEGINS WITH SOME of the most magnificent monuments that have survived from the ancient world, namely, the Egyptian temples, which have piqued the interests and inspired the imaginations of generations. Although it will include evidence from earlier and later temples, my examination will focus on the New Kingdom since its temples mark the height of the long tradition of Egyptian religious architecture and some of its most impressive structures remain more or less intact.[1]

Although various factors favor an accurate reconstruction, limits to a complete understanding remain. Few of the original temples remain standing,[2] none of which are entirely intact, and many of which have been altered over the years by successive rulers.[3] In addition, these remains largely hail from "Upper Egyptian sites where the single model is the New Kingdom type at Thebes, taken up in the Ptolemaic period for example at Edfu."[4] This type was built for festival processions, a model not shared by all.[5] Other temples undoubtedly presented different forms

---

1. As a brief overview of Egyptian chronology (after Emily Teeter, *Religion and Ritual in Ancient Egypt* [Cambridge: Cambridge University Press, 2011], xv–xvii; see also Ian Shaw, ed., *The Oxford History of Ancient Egypt* [Oxford: Oxford University Press, 2000], 479–83; see more fully Jürgen von Beckerath, *Chronologie des pharaonischen Ägypten* [MÄS 46; Mainz: von Zabern, 1997]), the Old Kingdom, consisting of dynasties 3–8, lasted from 2686 to 2125 BCE, the First Intermediate period (dynasties 9–11) from 2160 to 2055, the Middle Kingdom (dynasties 11–14) from 2055 to 1650, the Second Intermediate period (dynasties 15–17) from 1650 to 1550, the New Kingdom (dynasties 18–20) from 1550 to 1069, the Third Intermediate period (dynasties 21–25) from 1069 to 664, the Saite period (dynasty 26) from 664 to 525, the Late period (dynasties 27–31) from 525–332, the Ptolemaic period from 332 to 30 BCE, and the Roman period from 30 BCE to 295 CE. Because of its anomalous and short-lived nature, New Kingdom Amarna will not feature in our analysis. This omission is by no means an admission that it played no part in religious formation in the New Kingdom (see, e.g., Jan Assmann, *The Search for God in Ancient Egypt* [trans. D. Lorton; New York: Cornell University Press, 2001], 198–221).

2. Stephen Quirke, *Ancient Egyptian Religion* (New York: Dover, 1992), 76; John Baines, "Palaces and Temples of Ancient Egypt" in *CANE* 1:308; Steven Snape, *Egyptian Temples* (Buckinghamshire, UK: Shire, 1996), 29; Rolf Gundlach, "Temples," in *OEAE* 3:363.

3. Badawy, *History of Egyptian Architecture*, 177; Snape, *Egyptian Temples*, 28–29.

4. Quirke, *Ancient Egyptian Religion*, 76.

5. Ibid.

than those pervasive in the south, yet knowledge of these forms is unfortunately lost with the temples (e.g., the great temples at Memphis and Heliopolis).[6] However, there is some evidence that the southern New Kingdom temples were part of a single architectural strand extending back at least to the Middle Kingdom and through the time of the last pharaohs[7] and into the Greco-Roman period.[8] For example, although little remains of the large temples built in the delta during the reigns of the last pharaohs (eleventh–fourth centuries BCE), enough evidence exists at Tanis to indicate that its general organization differed little from its Theban predecessors.[9]

In addition to the archaeological difficulties, it is also difficult to differentiate cleanly between the mortuary and divine temples (the former primarily was dedicated to the cult of the deceased king and the latter to the cult of the various nonhuman deities of the Egyptian pantheon).[10] Many scholars rightly hold that the traditional distinction, which sharply differentiates between temples of the gods and temples of dead monarchs, is problematic. "The function and symbolic characteristics of all Egyptian temples were both too varied and too intertwined to support this distinction."[11] For example, the worship of (nonhuman) deities fea-

---

6. Ibid.; Baines, "Palaces and Temples," 308, 315.

7. As noted (ch. 1 n. 18), the terms "pharaoh" and "king" will be used interchangeably; the latter will feature for the sake of consistency across cultures.

8. New Kingdom temples had the same basic elements as Middle Kingdom temples, albeit on a grander scale, while later temples carried on and in some ways added to the earlier New Kingdom tradition. The temple of Satet at Elephantine provides especially clear evidence of the gradual expansion of a temple from a tiny sanctuary between two rocks to a large temple centuries later (Werner Kaiser, Günter Dreyer, Robert Gempeler, Peter Grossmann, and Horst Jaritz, "Stadt und Tempel von Elephantine: Siebter Grabungsbericht," *MDAIK* 33 (1977): 64–83). Regarding the continuity, see, conveniently, Wightman, *Sacred Spaces*, 99–104, 126–43. See also, e.g., Dieter Arnold, *Die Tempel Ägyptens: Götterwohnungen, Kultstätten, Baudenkmäler* (Zurich: Artemis & Winkler, 1992); Byron E. Shafer, ed., *Temples of Ancient Egypt* (Ithaca: Cornell University Press, 1997); on the temple of the last pharaohs, see further Arnold, *Temples of the Last Pharaohs* (New York: Oxford University Press, 1999).

9. Wightman, *Sacred Spaces*, 126.

10. Regarding their common ritual stock, see, e.g., Harold Hays, "The Worshiper and the Worshipped in the Pyramid Texts," *SAK* 30 (2002): 153–67. Regarding the problematic term "mortuary" temple and the nature of the structures so designated, see, e.g., Gerhard Haeny, "New Kingdom 'Mortuary Temples' and 'Mansions of Millions of Years,'" in Shafer, ed., *Temples of Ancient Egypt*, 86–126. See more expansively Martina Ullmann, *König für die Ewigkeit: Die Häuser der Millionen von Jahren: Eine Untersuchung zu Königskult und Tempeltypologie in Ägypten* (ÄAT 51; Wiesbaden: Harrasowitz, 2002); Stefanie Schröder, *Millionenjahrhaus: Zur Konzeption des Raumes der Ewigkeit im konstellativen Königtum in Sprache, Architektur und Theologie* (Wiesbaden: Harrasowitz, 2010).

11. Richard H. Wilkinson, *The Complete Temples of Ancient Egypt* (Cairo: The American University in Cairo Press, 2005), 25.

tures prominently in mortuary temples, while mortuary elements were also occasionally present in the divine cult temples.[12] However, the categories may be too entrenched to casually eschew and may remain useful.[13] The signifiers "divine" and "mortuary" temples developed for a reason, and even if the clear-cut differentiation they presume is artificial, real differences remain.[14] The present study focuses primarily on the temples of the Egyptian deities, since god temples and the gods in those temples are our explicit interest. Nonetheless, given the overlap, it also draws from the related mortuary temples.

## STRUCTURE

### The "Standard" Temple Plan

In the New Kingdom, the so-called standard temple plan emerged in the Theban region. From the most elaborate, the sacred precinct of Amon-Re at Karnak (figs. 2.1 and 2.3),[15] to the smaller and more typical temple of Khonsu at Karnak (figs. 2.2 and 2.3),[16] most temples adhered to the same general design. It was characterized by several distinctive features: an entrance pylon, a walled courtyard, a hypostyle hall, an offering room, and a sanctuary, many of which were incorporated into a single, large, direct-axis, and symmetrical structure.[17]

---

12. See, e.g., Teeter, *Religion and Ritual*, 57. The term "divine" temple is also problematic since Egyptian kings were often deified upon death.

13. Quirke proposes to amend "mortuary temple" to "temple of the royal cult" (*Ancient Egyptian Religion*, 81), while Shafer offers the designation "royal cult complex" ("Temples, Priests, and Rituals: An Overview," in *Temples of Ancient Egypt*, 4).

14. Notably, the two temple "types" have different names ("mansion of the god" and "mansion of millions of years") and tenures (though there is little indication that many mansions of millions of years remained in use after their proprietor's death; Wilkinson, *Complete Temples*, 25).

15. Regarding Karnak, see, e.g., Paul Barguet, *Le temple de Amon-Re à Karnak: essai d'exégèse* (Recherches d'archéologie, de philologie et d'histoire 21; Le Caire: Impr. de l'Institut français d'archéologie orientale, 1962); Jean-Claude Golvin and Jean-Claude Goyon, *Karnak, Ägypten: Anatomie eines Tempels* (Tübingen: Wasmuth, 1987); R. A. Schwaller de Lubicz, *The Temples of Karnak: A Contribution to the Study of Pharaonic Thought* (London: Thames & Hudson, 1999); Jean-François Carlotti, "Considérations architecturales sur l'orientation, la composition et les proportions des structures du temple d'Amon-Rê à Karnak," in *Structure and Significance: Thoughts on Ancient Egyptian Architecture* (ed. Peter Jánosi; Untersuchungen der Zweigstelle Kairo des Österreichischen Archäologischen Institutes 25; Vienna: Verlag der Österreichischen Akademie der Wissenschaften, 2005), 169–207; Elizabeth Blyth, *Karnak: Evolution of a Temple* (London: Routledge, 2006).

16. Wightman, *Sacred Spaces*, 116.

17. Badawy, *History of Egyptian Architecture*, 176–80; Snape, *Egyptian Temples*, 29;

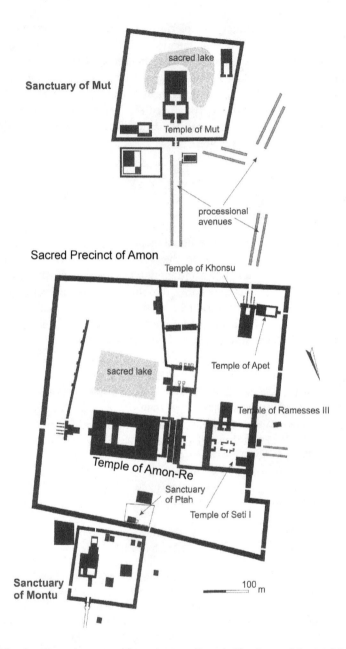

Fig. 2.1. The three prominent sacred precincts at Karnak (for Amun, Mut, and Montu), constructed primarily during the New Kingdom. Processional avenues between precincts were lined with ram-headed sphinxes. In addition, a number of smaller temples to kings and pharaohs appear, including the temple of Khonsu in the top right corner of the Amun precinct. From Wightman, *Sacred Spaces*, fig. 2.18.

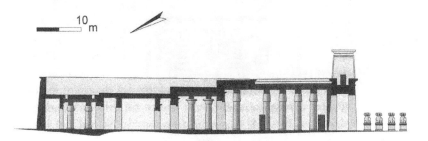

## KARNAK, TEMPLE OF KHONSU

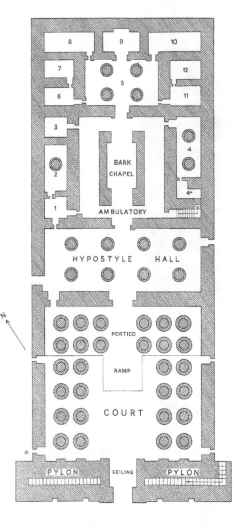

Fig. 2.2. The well-preserved temple of Khonsu at Karnak, which characteristically displays the pylon gateway leading into the court, the small hypostyle hall leading into the temple core, the bark chapel, the vestibule or offering room, and the sanctuary at the rear (room 9). Note how space becomes increasingly smaller as one moves toward the sanctuary. Groundplan from *The Temple of Khonsu*, Vol. 1: *Scenes of King Herihor in the Court* (OIP 100; Chicago: The Oriental Institute of the University of Chicago, 1979), 57. Sideview from Wightman, *Sacred Spaces*, fig. 2.15.

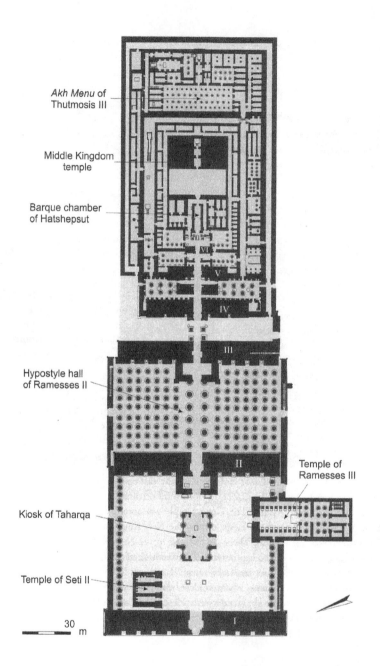

Akh Menu of
Thutmosis III

Middle Kingdom
temple

Barque chamber
of Hatshepsut

Hypostyle hall
of Ramesses II

Temple of
Ramesses III

Kiosk of Taharqa

Temple of Seti II

30 m

Fig. 2.3. Groundplan of the temple of Amon-Re at Karnak, the largest ancient Egyptian temple, which grew by a slow process with the addition of new courts, pylons, and the hypostyle hall westward (with the majority of work completed during Dynasties 18 and 19). From Wightman, *Sacred Spaces*, fig. 2.19.

Fig. 2.4. Ram-headed sphinxes lining the processional path between the Karnak and Luxor temples. Photo by the author.

Many temples also were surrounded by several subsidiary structures or quarternary spaces, such as a sacred lake (fig. 2.1), kitchens, workshops, administrative buildings, magazines, storehouses, and priestly residences.[18] The larger sacred precinct, with temple and auxiliary structures, was often surrounded by mud-brick walls, which were constructed with alternating concave and convex sections (especially in the Greco-Roman period but also presumably in the New Kingdom).[19]

---

Wilkinson, *Complete Temples*, 24. Aside from the later hypostyle hall, each of these elements had already emerged by the end of the Middle Kingdom (Wightman, *Sacred Spaces*, 103). Nonetheless, not all temples adhere to the symmetrical, direct-axis model. See, e.g., the New Kingdom temple at Buhen built by Hatshepsut (Walter Emery et al., *Excavations at Buhen 1, The Fortress of Buhen: The Archaeological Report* [London: Egypt Exploration Society, 1979]).

18. Gundlach, "Temples," 365; Wilkinson, *Complete Temples*, 74–75. However, since they were made of mud-brick instead of the stone of the temples, little survived (Arnold, *Die Tempel Ägyptens*, 29). Regarding the lakes, trees, and flower beds, see Beatrix Gessler-Löhr, *Die heiligen Seen ägyptischer Tempel* (HÄB 21; Hildesheim: Hildesheim Gerstenberg, 1983).

19. Quirke, *Ancient Egyptian Religion*, 80; Snape, *Egyptian Temples*, 30; Baines, "Palaces and Temples," 309; Wilkinson, *Complete Temples*, 57. On Karnak, see Barguet, *Le temple de*

Fig. 2.5. The massive entrance pylon at Luxor with colossi and an obelisk (which would have been one of a pair) flanking the entrance. The twin towers were originally connected above the heads of the colossi. Photo by the author.

In the processional temple model, as at Karnak, the sacred precinct began further out at the Nile or a canal connected to it with a landing quay. The processional paths that connected the landing quay to the main entrance of the temple and occasionally connected temples by land (e.g., Karnak to Luxor) were frequently lined with sculptures. The sphinx, with a leonine body and a human or other animal head, was an especially common form (fig. 2.4).[20]

The pylon is noted as the most distinctive feature of Egyptian architecture.[21] It consisted of a pair of massive trapezoidal towers connected by a bridge decorated with solar images, forming a gateway that marked the entrance to the larger tem-

---

*Amon-Re,* 29–33. Since the walls were constructed of mud-brick, little evidence remains of earlier walls.

20. Wilkinson, *Complete Temples,* 55–56.

21. Baines, "Palaces and Temples," 30; Wilkinson, *Complete Temples,* 60.

Fig. 2.6. View of several columns of the hypostyle hall of the temple of Amon-Re at Karnak, completed by Ramesses II in the thirteenth century. Photo by the author.

ple structure.[22] Flag poles often framed the entrance portal.[23] Especially in larger temples, obelisks were "often erected in pairs before the temple entrance proper [i.e., the outer pylon] and only came to be enclosed within the temple form as the precincts grew and new pylons were added."[24] In several larger temples, these obelisks were accompanied by colossi, gigantic statues of the kings,[25] which together abutted the entrance pylon (as at Luxor; fig. 2.5).[26]

Crossing the threshold of the pylon, one stood within the temple complex, enclosed on all four sides by walls and thus part of a single physical structure. This structure was subdivided into various sections by walls and doors (e.g., the

22. Shafer, "Temples, Priests, and Rituals," 5. Occasionally, as in the Amun temple of Karnak with six pylons in succession, multiple pylons were constructed by successive rulers.

23. Wilkinson, *Complete Temples,* 60–61; Wightman, *Sacred Spaces,* 1010.

24. Wilkinson, *Complete Temples,* 57–58.

25. Ibid., 59–60.

26. Regarding temples from the perspective of the Egyptian observer, see Dieter Kurth, *Edfu: Ein ägyptischer Tempel, gesehen mit den Augen der alten Ägypter* (Darmstadt: Wissenschaftliche Buchgesellschaft, 1994).

Fig. 2.7. Reconstructed cross-section of the hypostyle hall. Note the much larger central columns along the processional path, which "bloomed" in the sunlight coming in through the lattices, unlike the smaller columns with closed bud capitals. From Wightman, *Sacred Spaces*, fig. 2.20.

Khonsu temple at Karnak; fig. 2.2), with all but the court roofed.[27] The first unit was a large open-air court, [28] referred to as the "forecourt" since it stood directly before the roofed temple building and was surrounded on all four sides by the walls of the temple complex. This forecourt was "usually of the same width as the hypostyle hall and on a rectangular plan. [It was] bordered on one or more of its sides with a portico of columns or pillars,[29] with abutting Osiride statues of the pharaoh"[30] and other royal and private statues.[31] The statuary here was smaller and less obtrusive than that outside the pylon.[32]

Progressing inward, the next unit was the hypostyle hall, which lay directly behind the open-air court. Its entrance, and indeed the threshold of the roofed temple building, was marked by another gateway set along the same axis as the pylon, yet smaller and less obtrusive. This hypostyle hall, so designated because of the often larger central columns,[33] was usually covered and broader than it was deep.[34] Inside, the viewer encountered multiple columns arranged symmetrically throughout the hall, except along the central processional axis (figs. 2.6 and 2.7).

Proceeding through another monumental doorway,[35] one would encounter the temple core,[36] incorporating primary, secondary, and tertiary spaces (fig. 2.8). At the heart of the temple core along the central axis lay the sanctuary, which housed the divine statue in the small enclosed shrine, i.e., the inner sanctuary.[37]

---

27. Physical breaks in the larger structure (e.g. in the Amun temple at Karnak) were often the result of additional building phases.

28. In Egyptian the terms used for the court varied depending on architectural style and column type (Patricia Spencer, *The Egyptian Temple: A Lexicographical Study* [London: Kegan Paul, 1984], 63-89; Wilkinson, *Complete Temples*, 62).

29. On the multiple terms for columns, see Spencer, *The Egyptian Temple*, 231–59.

30. Badawy, *History of Egyptian Architecture*, 179.

31. Wilkinson, *Complete Temples*, 62–63.

32. With the continual expansion of the temple precincts, e.g., in the Amun temple at Karnak, the large statues standing in the outer court today once stood outside the temple's first pylon.

33. Wightman, *Sacred Spaces*, 109.

34. Wilkinson, *Complete Temples*, 65. Although not entirely intact, evidence of covering exists in the temple of Amun at Karnak, the temple of Seti I at Abydos, and at the later temple of Khnum at Esna.

35. The doors were made of wood and thus no longer exist. However, there is ample, especially textual, evidence of their existence (see, e.g., Spencer, *The Egyptian Temple*, 179–82, 205–11).

36. The temple core consisted of the area around the temple's central sanctuary, which housed the divine cult image.

37. The shrine consisted of two parts: a stone outer enclosure and a smaller double-doored wooden enclosure within it that housed the cult image. At times, there were multiple sanctuaries for multiple deities, commonly grouped in a triad (e.g., the bark-chapel of Seti

Fig. 2.8. View from the temple core of the sacred precinct of Amon-Re at Karnak looking outward along the central, processional axis of the hypostyle hall. Note the height of the columns and the darkness of the temple core. Photo by the author.

In contrast to the hypostyle hall, the sanctuary was often longer than it was wide. If the cult included a processional element, there was often "a 'bark chapel' with a pedestal to support the 'bark' or ship-shaped litter with its cabin,"[38] which either occupied a separate room or, in smaller (especially later) temples, the same room as the primary cult image (fig. 2.9).[39] The sanctuary was frequently surrounded

---

II at Karnak). Although ostensibly an Osiride temple, the temple of Seti I at Abydos was unique among preserved temples in having seven sanctuaries for the seven deities and one for the deified pharaoh himself (Badawy, *History of Egyptian Architecture*, 214).

38. Gundlach, "Temples," 365.

39. Ibid.; Wightman, *Sacred Spaces*, 127.

Fig. 2.9. The sanctuary of the Ptolemaic temple of Horus at Edfu containing both the bark and the shrine (inner sanctuary). Photo by the author.

by various auxiliary rooms (tertiary spaces), including cult rooms for other deities, offering chambers, storerooms for cultic objects, and treasuries.[40] In several temples, such as the Khonsu temple at Karnak, a vestibule sometimes containing an offering table stood between the bark chapel and the sanctuary.[41]

Finally, elevation played a significant role in several temples. This tendency was more pronounced in later periods yet already existed in the New Kingdom. For example, in the temple of Khonsu at Karnak, a raised platform, leading up to the porch, separated the temple core from the court.[42] In several cases, the aisles narrowed and floors sloped upwards, while the ceiling within the temple complex descended,[43] so that in the sanctuary the ceiling was at its lowest while the floor was at its highest (fig. 2.2).

40. Gundlach, "Temples," 335.

41. Klaus Koch, *Geschichte der ägyptische Religion: Von den Pyramiden bis zu den Mysterien der Isis* (Stuttgart: Kohlhammer, 1993), 286; Wightman, *Sacred Spaces*, 116.

42. See the temple groundplan in fig. 2.2 and *The Temple of Khonsu*, 1:57, and pl. 2.

43. Badawy, *History of Egyptian Architecture*, 177, 182; Koch, *Geschichte der ägyptische Religion*, 287; Gundlach, "Temples," 366.

## Adornment

Although the temple façades now display a monochromatic austerity, in ancient times the Egyptian temple was awash with color.[44] More than mere decoration, color carried rich symbolic associations that could vary according to the context.[45] For example, green was associated with fresh vegetation and by extension vigor and regeneration. Depicting Osiris with green skin thus served to signify his resurrection or regeneration.[46] Likewise, blue was associated with the night sky, the primordial waters from which the sun arose each day, and the especially precious lapis lazuli. Drawing on these associations, from the Eighteenth Dynasty onward Amon-Re was depicted with bright blue skin.[47]

---

44. The adornment was by no means purely decorative. Even the most repetitive scenes served important functions (Wightman, *Sacred Spaces*, 1009). Regarding the relationship between decoration and function, see especially Dieter Arnold, *Wandrelief und Raumfunktion in ägyptischen Tempeln des Neuen Reiches* (MÄS 2; Berlin: Hessling, 1962); see also Betsy N. Bryan, "Designing the Cosmos: Temples and Temple Decoration," in *Egypt's Dazzling Sun: Amenhotep III and His World* (ed. A. P. Kozloff et al.; Cleveland: Cleveland Museum of Art, 1992), 73–115; Dieter Kurth, ed., *Systeme und Programme der ägyptischen Tempeldekoration: 3. Ägyptologische Tempeltagung Hamburg 1.–5. Juni 1994* (ÄAT 33; Wiesbaden: Harrasowitz, 1995); see more briefly Gundlach, "Tempelrelief," *LÄ* 6 (1986): 407–11. See also the organizing role played by dedicatory inscriptions, Silke Grallert, "Pharaonic Building Inscriptions and Temple Decoration," in *Sacred Space and Sacred Function in Ancient Thebes* (ed. P. F. Dorman and B. N. Bryan; SAOC 61; Chicago: The Oriental Institute of the University of Chicago, 2007), 35–49; see more fully idem, *Bauen, Stiften, Weihen: Ägyptische Bau- und Restaurierungsinschriften von den Anfängen bis zur 30. Dynastie* (Abhandlungen des Deutschen Archäologischen Instituts Kairo 18; Berlin: Achet, 2001).

45. Richard H. Wilkinson, "Symbolism," in *The Ancient Gods Speak: A Guide to Egyptian Religion* (ed. D. Redford; Oxford: Oxford University Press, 2002), 341; see further Hermann Kees, "Farbensymbolik in agyptischen religiosen Texten," *Nachrichten der Akademie der Wissenschaften in Göttingen, phil.-hist. Klasse* 11 (1943): 413–79; John Baines, "Color Terminology and Color Classification: Ancient Egyptian Color Terminology and Polychromy," *American Anthropologist* 87 (1985): 282–97; idem, *Symbol and Magic in Egyptian Art* (London: Thames & Hudson, 1999), 104–25; Elisabeth Staehelin, *Von der Farbigkeit Ägyptens* (Leipzig: University of Leipzig, 2000); Robins, "Color Symbolism," in *OEAE* 1:291–94. However, a thorough examination of color is both difficult and beyond the scope of this work. Likewise, comparative use of color in the rest of the ancient Near Eastern world is difficult to reconstruct. For an analysis of the history and use of wall decoration, see, e.g., Peter J. Brand, "Veils, Votives and Marginalia: The Use of Sacred Space at Karnak and Luxor," in Dorman and Bryan, eds., *Sacred Space and Sacred Function*, 51–83 and, more broadly, Gay Robins, *The Art of Ancient Egypt* (2nd ed.; London: Trustees of the British Museum, 2005).

46. In other contexts Osiris had black skin.

47. "The color referred both to the primordial waters of lapis lazuli and to the blue of the

Fig. 2.10. Images of the king smiting his helpless enemies on the pylon at the Greco-Roman Philae Temple. Photo by the author.

Although most remaining shrines, like the temples in which they appear, are austere stone enclosures, in antiquity they were more lavishly adorned befitting their divine resident. For example, "one is described as having a ceiling and walls of gold, a floor of 'pure silver,' door leaves of hammered copper, and 'figured images in fine gold,'" while another from Dynasty 26 is described as "one block of granite, [with] the august shrine of electrum, ornaments, divine amulets, [and] all sacred objects were of gold and silver, and all precious stones."[48]

Reliefs and inscriptions were practically ubiquitous in the Egyptian temple complex.[49] For example, from the time of Thutmose III, observers of the pylons were often met by an enormous relief of the pharaoh smiting his helpless enemies

---

sky across which the sun travels. The lapis lazuli blue skin set the god apart from the other deities, emphasizing his status as 'king of the gods': the most important god was given a body of the most precious stone"; Gay Robins, "Color Symbolism," *OEAE* 1:293.

48. See Teeter, *Religion and Ritual*, 43 and the references cited therein.

49. There is also some evidence that reliefs were plated with precious metals (see briefly Golvin and Goyon, *Karnak, Ägypten: Anatomie eines Tempels*, 125).

before the god of the temple (fig. 2.10).[50] Ramesses II expanded on this theme at Luxor, displaying in relief a "full pictorial and textual account of his prowess in the battle of Qadesh."[51] In addition, although not present on the pylon itself, ritual scenes become more prominent on the outer walls from the time of Ramesses II onward.[52] These scenes were likely connected with popular worship, serving as access points to the deities who were otherwise off limits in the heart of the temples.[53]

Although they may seem unduly repetitive to the modern observer, a closer examination reveals that each detail in the reliefs was purposeful,[54] often relating to the function of the various rooms and arranged with respect to locational markers:[55]

> Upper Egyptian gods, symbols, and crowns appear in the southern half of the temple, and Lower Egyptian elements are found in the northern half. Scenes of processions, boating, or wars follow the same geographical direction as their actual prototypes. Asian enemies are attacking from the north of the temple entrance, African enemies from the south. Offering bearers move from the entrance to the sanctuary, the divine barque is carried from inside to the court. Outside walls were often used for public statements, such as offering and festival lists and royal immunity edicts ... Barque processions and feasts for the gods, such as the Luxor festival in the Luxor temple, appear properly oriented in the courts and hypostyle halls. Representations of offering bearers marching from the temple gate into the sanctuary supply the altars with offerings. Scenes of the daily maintenance of the cult image surround the walls of the statue sanctuary.[56]

---

50. Baines, "Palaces and Temples," 313. See further Sylvia Schoske, "Das Erschlagen der Feinde: Ikonographie und Stilistik der Feindvernichtung im alten Ägypten" (2 vols.; Ph.D. diss., Heidelberg University, 1982); Emma Swan Hall, *The Pharaoh Smites His Enemies: A Comparative Study* (MÄS 44; Munich: Deutscher Kunstverlag, 1986).

51. Quirke, *Ancient Egyptian Religion*, 78. Ramesses III even went so far as to emblazon pictures of himself fighting the enemies of his namesake, Ramesses II, which Ramesses III himself never fought. Inscriptions accompanied the battle reliefs, indicating that the campaigns were carried out for the sake of the king of the gods and not the kings themselves (see, e.g., the annals of Thutmose III; Lichtheim, *AEL* 2:29–35). For other examples, see Dagmar Stockfisch, "Bemerkungen zur sog. 'libyschen Familie,'" in *Wege öffnen: Festschrift für Rolf Gundlach* (ed. M. Schade-Busch; ÄAT 35; Wiesbaden: Harrasowitz, 1996), 315–25.

52. Constance S. Heinz, *Die Feldzugsdarstellungen des Neuen Reiches: Eine Bildanalyse* (Vienna: Verlag der Österreichischen Akademie der Wissenschaften, 2001).

53. See, e.g., Brand, "Veils, Votives and Marginalia," esp. 57–64.

54. Quirke, *Ancient Egyptian Religion*, 80.

55. See esp. Arnold, *Wandrelief und Raumfunktion*.

56. Arnold, "Egyptian Temples," in *OEANE* 4: 177.

Fig. 2.11. Painted stars on the ceiling of the Eighteenth Dynasty mortuary temple of Hatshepsut at Deir el-Bahri. Photo by the author.

Within the sanctuary, reliefs of the king faced inward presenting offerings to the god(s), who faced outward toward the king. In several cases, pictures and inscriptions represented the gods returning blessings to the offering pharaoh. Within the storerooms, walls often depicted the kinds of offerings stored therein, and slaughter-rooms were designated by scenes of slaughter.[57] Even seemingly mundane royal epithets were often purposeful. At Karnak, for example, the inscription that the king "is beloved of Ptah" marked the route taken by the offerings from the main complex to the small sanctuary of Ptah.[58] Symmetry also played a key role, as in the hypostyle hall of Seti I and Ramesses II at Karnak, where the scenes followed a careful pattern in which "each scene must complement those around it and those facing it directly and diagonally across the hall."[59]

In addition to the ubiquitous reliefs and inscriptions, various architectural elements were artistically crafted. For example, natural elements predominated in the hypostyle hall, such as the forests of papyrus or lotus columns and the stars adorning the ceiling,[60] while offering scenes featured in the sanctuary (fig. 2.11).

---

57. Cf. Badawy, *History of Egyptian Architecture*, 182.

58. Quirke, *Ancient Egyptian Religion*, 80.

59. Ibid.

60. The stars were especially prevalent in the Ptolemaic temples, yet were still present in

## Use

On a basic level, the temple was "intrinsically the 'house of god' and not a gathering place for the congregation."[61] This was reflected in the terms used to describe the temples.[62] *Pr* can be roughly translated as "estate."[63] When referring to the divine estate, *pr* designated the totality of the deity's possessions, both in terms of the land and the people who made their livings from it.[64] Thus, it included everything within the outer wall of the divine sphere as well as various elements owned by the deity, both in the temple vicinity and further afield. *Ḥwt nṯr* refers more specifically to the god's house,[65] the temple complex, within which the deity's image was kept.[66] Both terms intimate that the temple was the deity's house, its residence amid its larger estate, much akin to that of a contemporary monarch.[67] As the god's residence in the midst of human community, the temple was the point of contact between human and divine and the locus of divine service, performed by the kings in the reliefs but primarily by the priests in reality.

From the temple structure, we may also identify the function of some of its constituent parts. In addition to serving as an impressive introduction to divine space, the sphinxes outside of the divine compound extended divine space, forming a clear passage along which processing deities could travel without ever leaving

a New Kingdom context (Badawy, *History of Egyptian Architecture*, 182; Snape, *Egyptian Temples*, 30).

61. Badawy, *History of Egyptian Architecture*, 181; see also Françoise Dunand and Christiane Zivie-Coche, *Gods and Men in Egypt: 3000 BCE to 395 CE* (trans. D. Lorton: Ithaca, NY: Cornell University Press, 2004), 83.

62. The Egyptian temple was unique in that the purpose of the structure and its various rooms were inscribed on the walls of the temple. Thus, much of the "use" section is explicitly dictated by the structure and may be somewhat repetitive.

63. Spencer, *The Egyptian Temple*, 14–20, 27.

64. This included the priests as well as peasants, shepherds, miners, and artisans (Assmann, *The Search for God,* 28–29).

65. Perhaps it could be more accurately rendered "cult center." *Ḥwt* likely originated in the mortuary sphere to refer to the cult center of the king (Spencer, *The Egyptian Temple*, 21–27, 43–55).

66. Ibid., 46, 55; Assmann, *The Search for God,* 28–29. See also *r-pr* (Spencer, *The Egyptian Temple*, 37–42). Once again, the temple complex refers to the primary roofed temple building and the walled, unroofed court and includes the hypostyle hall and the sanctuary.

67. For further implications of divine anthropomorphism, see the ideology section. The names of the temples and their various parts likewise could express the quality of the building or indicate the primary cultic recipient. For example, the temple of Thutmose III at Deir el Bahri was called "Most Splendid," while the northern part of the hypostyle hall at Karnak built by Seti I was called "Temple of the Son of Mernamon in the house of Amun" (Badawy, *History of Egyptian Architecture*, 155-6).

divine space. The walls and gateways throughout the complex served respectively to separate the divine sphere into significant spaces and to grant access to those spaces.[68] Each of the other structures in the divine precinct contributed to divine service and/or appropriate contact with the divine and together they indicated the broader scope of the temple. In addition to their protective and propagandistic role, statues and the reliefs of deities and of the king also served as objects of veneration. Visible from the gate and on the exterior walls, they functioned as access points to the hidden deities or as accessible manifestations of deities themselves because the common person could get no closer to them.[69]

The open-air court, which seems to have been a liminal zone, carried its own purpose.[70] In processional temples like Karnak and Luxor, courtyard reliefs are dominated by festival scenes, which include processions of the divine bark, indicating that festivals were the court's primary purpose.[71] As such, it was likely a gathering place for the common people, at least during festive occasions.[72] In addition, several New Kingdom inscriptions on the walls and statues in the courts indicate that petitions of people were heard at these locations.[73] Furthermore, Gee suggests that a term used for the forecourt (wb3) implies that the area was open to the public, instead of the common conception of being open to the sky.[74] It also seems to have been a gathering place for the statues of prominent private individu-

---

68. See Spencer, *The Egyptian Temple*, 179–220, 260–92 for the multiple terms used to describe doors and walls.

69. Wolfgang Helck, "Torgötter," *LÄ* 6 (1986): 637; Brand, "Veils, Votives and Marginalia," 60; see further below. See also, e.g., Waltraud Guglielmi, "Die Funktion von Tempeleingang und Gegentempel als Gebetsort: Zur Deutung einer Widder- und Gansstelen des Amun," in *Ägyptische Tempel – Struktur, Funktion und Programm: Akten der Ägyptologischen Tempeltagungen in Gosen 1990 und in Mainz 1992* (ed. R. Gundlach and M. Rochholz; HÄB 37; Hildesheim: Gerstenberger, 1994), 55–68; Brand, "Veils, Votives and Marginalia."

70. Regarding terms for court, of which *wsḫt* is perhaps the most frequent, see Spencer, *The Egyptian Temple*, 4–13, 63–98.

71. Hosam Refai, "Notes on the Function of the Great Hypostyle Hall in the Egyptian Temple: A Theban Approach," in *Egyptology at the Dawn of the Twenty-First Century: Proceedings of the Eighth International Congress of Egyptology, Cairo 2000, Vol. 1: Architecture* (ed. Z. Hawass; Cairo: American University in Cairo Press, 2003), 394.

72. Lanny Bell, "The New Kingdom Divine Temple: The Example of Luxor," in Shafer, ed., *Temples of Ancient Egypt*, 163–72. There is also some indication in the inscriptions of the temple of Amun at Karnak that the common people had some access to the hypostyle hall (Barbara S. Lesko, "Private Cults," in Redford, ed., *The Ancient Gods Speak*, 78).

73. Carolyn Routledge, "Parallelism in Popular and Official Religion in Ancient Egypt," in *Text, Artifact, and Image: Revealing Ancient Israelite Religion* (ed. G. M. Beckman and T. J. Lewis; BJS 346; Providence: Brown Judaic Studies, 2006), 230–32.

74. John L. Gee, "The Requirements of Ritual Purity in Ancient Egypt" (Ph.D. Diss., Yale University, 1998), 29–32; cf. the qualifications in Spencer, *The Egyptian Temple*, 7–8, 27.

als, whose inscriptions often implored passersby to pronounce their names and to recite the appropriate offering formula.[75] The presence of these statues indicated that the individual represented was in some way present. In fact, texts such as the Harris Papyrus indicated that statues depicting or describing daily offerings were functionally equivalent to an individual presenting them himself.[76] The presence of scenes of procession and a wayside chapel, as at Karnak, also suggest that the procession of the divine bark passed through the courtyard.

Although wall reliefs and inscriptions abound in the hypostyle hall, it remains difficult to identify precisely the purpose of the hypostyle hall beyond its role as mediating space.

Quite dissimilar architectural backgrounds and building concepts defined the variety of forms brought forth and whereas the function of each room of the Egyptian temple can normally be determined from its name and from the scenes on its walls, the hypostyle hall has no specific name, nor is there a specific repertoire of scenes.[77]

Despite these difficulties, the wall reliefs allow for a general reconstruction, which predominantly portray offering and ritual scenes focusing on the royal cult.[78] Processional scenes also appear in the Great Hypostyle Hall of Karnak and perhaps also in the festival hall of the Akhmenu at Karnak.[79] However, although often associated with processionals, none of the other Theban hypostyle halls depict processions in their reliefs. Instead, processional scenes, as noted above, feature in the open courts.[80] In fact, since the later roofed festival hall of the Akhmenu and the Great Hypostyle Hall were originally open courts, "it becomes evident that scenes of barque processions belong to the open court and not to the hypostyle

---

75. Wilkinson, *Complete Temples*, 62–63. By placing their statues in the courts, individuals were careful to situate them where they received the most traffic, especially during festival times (Arnulf Schlüter, *Sakrale Architektur im Flachbild: Zum Realitätsbezug von Tempeldarstellungen* [ÄAT 78; Wiesbaden: Harrasowitz, 2009], 485). For evidence from the Old and Middle Kingdoms, see Alexandra Verbovsek, *"Als Gunsterweis des Königs in den Tempel gegeben...": Private Tempelstatuen des Alten und Mittleren Reiches* (ÄAT 63; Wiesbaden: Harrasowitz, 2004).

76. Gertie Englund, "Offerings," in Redford, ed., *The Ancient Gods Speak*, 285.

77. Refai, "Great Hypostyle Hall," 393. See further idem, *Untersuchungen zum Bildprogramm der großen Säulen in den thebanischen Tempeln des Neuen Reiches* (BzÄ 18; Vienna: Afro-Pub, 2000), 25–32.

78. Refai, "Great Hypostyle Hall," 393.

79. See respectively Harold Hayden Nelson, *The Great Hypostyle Hall at Karnak 1*, Part 1: *The Wall Reliefs* (OIP 106; Chicago: Oriental Institute, 1981), pls. 37, 38, 53, 76, 151, 152, 178, 180, 197, 226 and Barguet, *Le temple de Amon-Re*, 175. See also Claude Traunecker, *La chapelle d'Achôris a Karnak II: Texte* (Paris: ADPF, 1981), 82–84.

80. Refai, "Great Hypostyle Hall," 393.

hall."[81] Thus, it would seem that the hypostyle hall was especially associated with exalting the king and in the case of the Amun temple of Karnak was also an assembly point for the divine barks as they waited to process.[82]

The bark chapel served as the resting place for the bark when it was not in transit, while the bark itself served both as the means of divine transport and as a protective shield around the deity as it traveled, as indicated by its name *sšm-ḥwi* ("protected image").[83] The vestibule before the sanctuary with its table likely served as a primary place for presenting offerings.

The sanctuary[84] served as the abode of deity and the locus of daily service, clearly represented by the presence of the cult statue and the wall reliefs. "The subject of the [wall] scenes was almost invariable: the king offered to a god or gods, while they gave him gifts symbolic of life, prosperity, and power."[85] In short, this room embodied the purpose of the temple, to house and serve the gods in order to receive divine blessing. The auxiliary rooms that surrounded the sanctuary served as complements to the sanctuary and the temple complex itself. The wall scenes often indicated their specific use (e.g., scenes of slaughter decorated a slaughter area and scenes of various items being stored designated a storeroom).[86]

## Structural Communication

As noted, Egyptian temples are unique among ancient Near Eastern temples in that their reliefs communicate through word and image the function of the various rooms, the proper behavior in them, and even access. In addition to being

---

81. Ibid.; see also Arnold, *Wandrelief und Raumfunktion*, 106–7.

82. Regarding the latter, see Refai, "Great Hypostyle Hall," 395–96. For a helpful three-dimensional reconstruction of bark processions, see Elaine A. Sullivan, "Visualizing the Size and Movement of the Portable Festival Barks at Karnak Temple," *BMSAES* 19 (2012): 1–37.

83. In the New Kingdom, it seems that veils also were used to partially shield the cabin shrines from view (Christina Karlshausen, "L'évolution de la barque processionelle d'Amon à 18e dynastie," *RdE* 46 (1995): 119–37; idem "L'iconographie de la barque processionelle divine en Égypte au Nouvel Empire" [Ph.D. diss., Université Catholique du Louvaine, 1997], 305–10). The bark chapel likewise served as mediating space within the temple, further distancing the sanctuary from the outer entrance and mediating access to it.

84. Regarding terms for sanctuaries, see Spencer, *The Egyptian Temple*, 99–146, of which *k3r* is especially prominent in referring to a temple sanctuary, portable shrine, or bark shrine. On the daily service, see ch. 8.

85. Baines, "Palaces and Temples," 313.

86. A word of caution is necessary at this point. Although wall scenes often indicated the function of the particular rooms, there is no one-to-one relationship between scene and action. In other words, the presence of a wall scene does not always mean that the action it depicts took place in that location.

functional, the architecture of Egyptian temples made an impression that can still
be felt today. As today, in ancient times it would have immediately elicited awe, an
appropriate response given the nature of the temple as the home of the deity. In addition to being evocative, temple architecture gave shape to divine space, creating
a home, and physically and emotionally mediating contact between the resident
deity and its human visitors.

Walls, portals, and their adornments in particular demarcated the temple
complex into clear zones, whose functions were made known on the wall reliefs. At
the same time, these features heightened the importance of the overall space and
of the hierarchical importance of its parts, which increased as one moved beyond
boundaries and ever closer to the center. The importance of these thresholds may
be underscored by the overabundance of terms meaning "door" or "gate."[87] Indeed,
the temple was masterfully created to express in physical form the ideology of the
temple builders, to communicate subconsciously to the observers the appropriate behavior and emotional response, and to impress on them the importance of
compliance. Again, the divisions were likely communicated unconsciously by the
structure itself, thereby reinforcing in the observers the boundaries and behavior
expected of them and providing powerful impetus to behave appropriately.[88]

The wall surrounding the divine sphere visually and viscerally communicated
the separation of divine space from its surroundings. The doorway marked the
liminal zone, the meeting point of two distinct areas and the threshold over which
the other could be accessed. Although the enclosure wall was constructed of the
same material as mundane dwellings, its special status was indicated by its undu-
lating form and association with the deity. The auxiliary structures surrounding
the temple complex indicated that divine space included more than a home; in
some contexts, it was even a self-sufficient world unto itself, in practice as well as
in theory. Since these structures stood within the outer enclosure, they were associated with the divine sphere and thus shared in its special status. However, since
they remained outside the temple complex and its pylon gateway, they were only
secondarily important.[89]

Next, the pylon gateway, as the most impressive (and thus seemingly primary)
boundary, separated the temple complex emphatically from everything around
it, even the subsidiary structures within the divine sphere.[90] As the most visibly

---

87. Spencer, *The Egyptian Temple*, 179–216. The "profusion of terms for walls in the
Egyptian language" likewise testifies to their importance in dividing spaces (p. 283; see
further 260–92).

88. It is also interesting to note that the decoration on doors related to the interior rooms to
which they granted ingress, in effect serving as an introduction to the space they protected
(Friedhelm Hartenstein, personal communication).

89. Cf. Gundlach, "Temples," 357.

90. The presence of purification basins, scenes, and chapels as well as the scenes adorning

massive and arresting element of the Egyptian temple, the pylon functioned as an appropriate introduction to the deity's house. The prominence of this boundary is especially fitting since, as the most visible element in the entire divine sphere, the entrance to the temple complex was in many ways the face of the divine abode, indicating like no other element the importance of the space it protected. It must also be noted that the primary temple route was not meant for humans, as evidently no priest ever penetrated through this succession of doorways from the outside to the inside (except when carrying the divine image). Outer doors were usually shut, while the priests were on duty. After purifying themselves in the sacred lake, they would enter through the side door. When the temple doors opened on festival days, it was the deity who made its way through them as it left the temple in procession and returned.[91]

In addition to the prominent pylon portal, the architecture itself and its adornment, clustered around the entrance portal, highlighted both the threshold and the importance of the zone beyond it. For example, the obelisks adjacent to the pylon served as towering markers for all to see, proclaiming the special nature of the place,[92] while the reliefs of the king demonstrated his prominence and potency, suggesting his role as both protector of the divine sphere and as mediator between human and divine. As such, the architecture visually and viscerally reinforced the appropriate response and the appropriate behavior, indicating that only the ritually pure could be granted access.[93] In addition, the temple complex was constructed largely of stone, quarried elsewhere and often brought from great distances. The stone likely indicated the strength and permanence of the temple,[94] and served effectively to differentiate it from the both the mundane sphere, including the royal palace, and the auxiliary elements within the divine sphere.[95]

Once through the pylon, the portal flanked by the twin towers, the scene changed again, indicating a new zone. The court was open to the sky, bounded by pillars and often containing smaller, less obtrusive statues of the king and select private individuals. The court served as a transitional area attached to the temple

---

the entrance of Amun's Karnak temple showing purification at the beginning of the ritual sequence further enhanced the special nature of the place, indicating that entering required special measures (see Gee, "Requirements of Ritual Purity," 28).

91. Assmann, *The Search for God*, 31.

92. Regarding the obelisks as boundary markers, see Gundlach, "Temples," 368, 371. It seems that these obelisks were located only within the sacred precinct yet originally constructed outside of the main temple complex.

93. Koch, *Geschichte der ägyptische Religion*, 287; Gee, "Requirements of Ritual Purity," 28.

94. Incidentally, it also facilitated the use of reliefs and ensured their preservation (Assmann, *The Search for God*, 30).

95. Egyptians also used different kinds and colors of stones in temple construction (Friedhelm Hoffmann, personal communication).

structure yet separated from its roofed core.⁹⁶ It mediated between inside and out-side spaces by distancing the sanctuary from the enclosure entrance and allowed some access to inside the temple complex (in its court) without really being inside the temple (indoors).

Through another occasionally raised entrance, the hypostyle hall as a domed structure with a forest of thick columns with floral capitals marked a new zone, with distinct structural markers to delineate its boundaries.⁹⁷ With the floor slop-ing gradually upward while the ceiling descended, one would have felt like he was ascending into a different realm. The air would be darker; the ceiling had stars; statuary was at a minimum. No longer consumed with militarism and displays of power and protection, the wall scenes were more intimate in nature, suggesting the increasing intimacy and importance of the space. In these reliefs, the king was always present with the primary deity and its divine compatriots, making offerings to the gods and receiving their blessing in return (e.g., via the symbol for life [ankh (ꜥnḫ)]).⁹⁸ The scenes here as elsewhere were animated with life; the images and inscriptions were arranged in sequence signifying motion.

Another doorway marked the transition between the hypostyle hall and the temple core, which was itself divided into various rooms. In many New Kingdom temples, the bark chapel was appropriately situated before the sanctuary to begin the deity's procession outward and to further isolate the sanctuary from the out-side. When a vestibule appeared between it and the sanctuary (e.g., in the Khonsu temple), it like the court served to mediate space by isolating the core of the divine residence, the sanctuary, from the rest of the temple building.

By far the most important room, the divine sanctuary emerged at last. Several factors converged to herald its special status. The room was shrouded in the deep-est darkness, and often surrounded by a ring of corridors and support chambers.⁹⁹ When illuminated, here and nowhere else one would discover the shrine contain-

---

96. Rather than surrounding the temple, the court preceded the main building and formed a single architectural unit with it (see ch. 4 for the importance of this connection).

97. The multitude of columns did not serve to conceal the sanctuary from view [contra Snape (*Egyptian Temples*, 36) and others], for there was a clear passageway along the central axis from the entrance through the pillars to the sanctuary (Wilkinson, *Complete Temples*, 65). Instead, the closed doors likely served as visual and physical barriers.

98. See ch. 8 for a fuller analysis of ritual activity and the ritual scenes. The ubiquity of the king in this and all other temple spaces stressed his primary role as mediator between human and divine.

99. These isolating spaces ensured that although the spaces grew increasingly smaller toward the sanctuary, the proportions remained the same, such that the temple was often rectangular in shape (Wightman, *Sacred Spaces*, 993). This separation and isolation grew more pronounced in the Ptolemaic temples, descendants of the standard temple type, as the sanctuary was isolated by both corridors and layers of wall (Assmann, *The Search for God*, 30–33).

ing the resident deity. The ceiling likewise reached its lowest point while the floor was at its peak. The wall scenes at this stage were intimate and purposeful, focusing on the ruler's presentation of offerings to the resident god, frequently reciprocated with divine blessing. The room also was situated along the central axis, on a line from the pylon gateway, practically at the farthest point from that gateway.[100] As the heart of the temple, the cult statue lay nestled in the deep darkness, in the smallest room, in the most remote and well-protected area of the entire massive complex.

The entire temple complex highlighted the importance of this sacred core. Each unit and each boundary communicated to the observers their progression further and further from the mundane sphere and into the divine sphere, into the very residence of the gods on earth. This feeling was only heightened by the symmetry of the direct axis temple, which suggested order and perfection. As such, one would feel increasingly privileged to access increasingly important and intimate space and increasingly compelled to follow the rules of the divine residence. The structures in the divine sphere thus effectively reinforced the already entrenched importance of the divine sphere over the rest of the world and the relative importance of its various zones. By giving shape to it with stone, the Egyptians likewise communicated that the temple and its boundaries were inviolate.

## Ideology

In a dangerous and volatile world, where order was constantly under threat on a local and cosmic scale,[101] the Egyptians constructed temples both to bring divine presence and favor to their world and to have some measure of agency in the divine world. The gods' preferred abode was the sky or heaven, while the underworld was the home of the deity's body to which his *ba* (*b3*)

---

100. Other rooms occasionally appeared behind the sanctuary, yet they were clearly secondary, serving the needs of the sanctuary as storerooms, treasuries, slaughter rooms, etc., as well as smaller shrines to other deities.

101. Erik Hornung, *Conceptions of God in Ancient Egypt: The One and the Many* (London: Routledge, 1983), 172–85, 195, 212–16; Quirke, *Ancient Egyptian Religion*, 70; Vincent A. Tobin, "Myths," in Redford, ed., *The Ancient Gods Speak*, 239–46; Gay Robins, "Cult Statues in Ancient Egypt," in *Cult Image and Divine Representation in the Ancient Near East* (ed. Neal H. Walls; ASOR Books 10; Boston: ASOR, 2005), 1. In the divine realm, for example, Re had to nightly overcome the serpent Apep (Apophis), his chief enemy, who was one of the primary threats to order (Tobin, "Myths," 242–43, 245).

For the rich ideological import of the late temple of Edfu, see E. A. E. Reymond, *The Mythological Origin of the Egyptian Temple* (Manchester: Manchester University Press, 1969); Ragnhild Bjerre Finnestad, *Image of the World and Symbol of the Creator: On the Cosmological and Iconographical Values of the Temple of Edfu* (Wiesbaden: Harrasowitz, 1985); Kurth, *Edfu*.

(translated roughly as "soul") was united nightly.[102] The gods had little natural contact with the human realm, appearing at times only at the periphery.[103] The temple and, more precisely, the cult statue within it was the Egyptian solution to divine absence,[104] a way to localize the deity within the human sphere, at the heart of human community. Although not always so neatly presented, Egyptian theologians systematized the divine presence as threefold: the god's *ba* was in the sky, his corpse was in the underworld, and his cult statue was on earth.[105] Since divine presence and blessing could not simply be assumed, the temple was constructed to be as enticing an abode as possible, with lavish offerings and some degree of separation from the mundane world.[106] With the temple functioning as intended, regular presence and regular and regulated service enabled contact and communication between the human and divine spheres, granting humanity some degree of security and agency in an otherwise insecure world. In fact, successful cult service was considered absolutely necessary for prosperity on individual, corporate, and cosmic levels.[107]

In the temple as heaven on earth, the king, imbued with the divine *ka*-spirit, was the primary human actor (in theory if not in practice). The king's gifts and services to the gods were often classified as the "eye of Horus" and as *maat* (*m3ʿt*). In Egyptian mythology, Thoth recovered, healed, and returned to Horus the eye he lost to Seth. Offerings equated with this "sound eye" (*wḏ3t*) of Horus, like the eye itself, thus represented the reestablishment of order after the incursion of chaos, or more generally "embodiment of every alleviation of lack or need."[108] Offerings equated with *maat*, cosmic order, naturally served to strengthen the cosmic order.[109] Together the "eye of Horus" and *maat* repre-

---

102. Regarding the *ba* as "soul," cf. the qualifications of James P. Allen, "Ba," in *OEAE* 1:161–62; see further chapter 8. Regarding the divine connection to heaven and the underworld, see Hornung, *Conceptions of God*, 229.

103. Hornung, *Conceptions of God*, 128.

104. On the relationship between the deity and its image, see ch. 8.

105. The Leiden Hymn to Amun; see Jan Zandee, *De Hymnen aan Amon van Papyrus Leiden I 350* (Leiden: Brill, 1948), pl. IV, 16–17; Siegfried Morenz, *Egyptian Religion* (trans. A. E. Keep; Ithaca, NY: Cornell University Press, 1973), 151; Hornung, *Conceptions of God*, 228. For an updated translation, see *TUAT* 2:827–28.

106. Cf. Hornung, *Conceptions of God*, 229.

107. Thompson, "Cults," in Redford, ed., *The Ancient Gods Speak*, 64. Although the king had other civic duties, such as ruling in accordance with *maat*, appropriate divine service in the temple was absolutely necessary for any prosperity.

108. Assmann, *The Search for God*, 50; see also Englund, "Offerings," 279.

109. See further Assmann, *Maʾat: Gerechtigkeit und Unsterblichkeit im Alten Ägypten* (Munich: Beck, 1990); Teeter, *The Presentation of Maat: Ritual and Legitimacy in Ancient Egypt* (SAOC 57; Chicago: The Oriental Institute of the University of Chicago, 1997).

sented two sides of the same process, reestablishing lost order and strengthening existing order.[110] By presenting both to the gods, pharaoh played his part in upholding cosmic order.

The king was presented in more guises than as a mere obeisant. Nonetheless, in each he fulfilled his role as the preserver of *maat* on earth. Throughout the temple, the pharaoh featured prominently. However, as one moved outward from the center, representations of the king became increasingly larger and more militaristic. His statuary too, absent from the sanctuary, became more pronounced as one moved outward. Giant colossi of the pharaoh adjoined the pylon and an even larger relief of the king smiting his enemies adorned it. Such martial images were consonant with the tenor of the pylon. Its imposing exterior proclaimed both power and protection, and the prominence of a pugilistic pharaoh there ensured that all observers recognized him as the powerful protector, the preserver of divine order. The giant colossi demonstrated his prowess, and their seated position may have indicated his watchfulness and even his rest after conquering all opposition. The image of the king smiting his enemies was emblazoned upon the face of the pylon, showing his power over his enemies, seen as the forces of chaos, which were antithetical to the upkeep of *maat*.[111] At the same time, the presence of a deity to witness the slaughter indicated both divine protection of the pharaoh and reciprocal royal protection of the divine and the temple complex. Thus, to outsiders the king was an indomitable force holding chaos at bay, while within he was a tender and beloved servant of the gods.

In addition to being propagandistic, the varied portrayal of the king was consonant with the larger Egyptian worldview. Outside of the temple, as the representative of the gods and with their support, the king upheld *maat* on earth and protected the temple from the encroachment of chaos. Thus, the pharaoh as ever-present pugilist was a suitable image for the face of the temple complex. Within the temple, however, the gods held sway.[112] Rather than defending *maat* with his god-given might, as the only suitable servant of the gods, the king presented *maat* as an obeisant in the form of an offering; thus his images featured in all contact between human and divine, in procession and especially in intimate service.

Although constructed of elements of the terrestrial world, the temple was nonetheless made suitable for its divine resident. As the home of the deity who defied explanation, the temple shared in its ineffability. The temple represented a

110. In Egyptian terms, together they signified what is "sound and perfect" (Englund, "Offerings," 279–80; see, e.g., Quirke, *Ancient Egyptian Religion*, ch. 3, entitled "Preserving the Universe: Kingship and Cult").

111. As already noted, the statuary and decoration also served an intercessory function, stressing the king's role as mediator between human and divine.

112. Nonetheless, the transition was apparently gradual as the hypostyle hall stresses divine support of the king.

meeting of disparate worlds, with elements of each commingled to form a place somewhat unnatural to both. Since no sufficient human analog existed, figural representation abounded to approximate the essence of the divine abode and the reality enacted therein.[113] Temple builders incorporated into the temple structure elements from their worldview, particularly their mythology, available to us primarily in the preserved texts.[114] In addition, although not as prevalent as in Mesopotamia and Hittite Anatolia, there is some late evidence that the temple itself was considered alive, animated through the opening of the mouth ritual.[115]

On a fundamental level, the Egyptians pictured their gods as human-like with human-like needs. As such, Egyptians crafted their temples and temple service to meet the deities' human-like needs and appetites. In the temple, the gods served as the "lords of cities and proprietors of huge landed estates"[116] governed by various servants who made their livings from them.[117] The temple resembled a contemporary home in terms of the structure[118] and the basic needs of its inhabitant. Like humans, the deity required and received more than words of adoration. It too had

---

113. In addition, the structure carried a political agenda, as the king sought to paint himself, his kingdom, and the patron deity in the best possible light.

114. For a summary, see Tobin, "Myth," 239–45. However, the Egyptian textual record is somewhat problematic. "Despite its obvious importance in religion of ancient Egypt, [myth] appears to have belonged largely to the domain of oral literature (Jacobus van Dijk, "Myth and Mythmaking in Ancient Egypt," in *CANE*, 3:1697)." Instead myths were "often alluded to in various non-narrative texts, such as hymns to the gods or ritual texts" (ibid). Van Dijk plausibly suggests myths were largely absent from the early written record because they were "originally transmitted orally, perhaps because knowledge of them was restricted to those directly involved in the state cult: the king and the fairly small group of high officials that later developed into the professional priesthood (p. 1698)." See also Katja Goebs, "A Functional Approach to Egyptian Myth and Mythemes," *JANER* 2 (2002): 27–59, who argues that the nature and purpose of myths lay in their flexibility. See further Assmann, "Die Verborgenheit des Mythos in Ägypten," *Göttinger Miszellen* 25 (1977): 7–43; Jürgen Ziedler, "Zur Frage der Spätentstehung des Mythos in Ägypten," *Göttinger Miszellen* 132 (1993): 85–109; H. Roeder, "'Mit dem Auge sehen': Ägyptisches und Ägyptologisches zum 'Auge des Horus,'" *Göttinger Miszellen* 138 (1994): 37–69.

115. Assmann, *The Search for God*, 45.

116. Ibid., 27.

117. Ibid., 28–29.

118. Bell, "The New Kingdom Divine Temple," 133. The role of the temple as the physical home of the god was reflected in the appearance of a New Kingdom temple; the open courtyard, pillared hall and hidden sanctuary might be said broadly to coincide with the parts of an ordinary Egyptian house, with the semi-public space for entertaining visitors and the more private areas, such as the bedroom, at the rear of the house (Snape, *Egyptian Temples*, 10).

physical needs which were met by physical means, such as food, drink, bathing, and clothing.[119]

Nonetheless, the deity was not simply envisioned as one of humanity. The temple was thus crafted to suit the divine otherness, often carrying cosmic significance. Creation was mirrored, even present, in the temple construction. For example, the columns in the hypostyle hall represented the aquatic marsh plants that sprang up around the primeval mound of creation.[120] The large number and variety of column types reflected the diversity of the vegetation in the primordial swamp at creation.[121] The lower registers of the walls repeated this motif in various ways.[122] The floor sloped upward to the sanctuary, the highest point, which served as the primeval mound of creation, the first land to emerge from the watery abyss. As the divine chamber, the sanctuary and especially the shrine within it marked the beginning of the created world. In some cases, the Nile's annual flooding served to enhance this motif as "some of the floors in many temples would have been covered with water, and there the inclined path to the sanctuary would literally have risen up out of the waters."[123]

Although part of this world, the temple was also a special world unto itself. The outer walls surrounding the divine sphere set the borders for the differentiated, hierarchically divided world of order within.[124] Indeed, in Egypt separation itself was seen as the hallmark of creation, such that the creator god was commonly said to have divided himself into millions in the act of creation.[125] By clearly separating the temple complex into ideal spaces and setting those separations in stone, the temple builders and the gods continually represented and reenacted the initial act of creation and the ideal world it created.

The massive pylon appropriately granted entrance to the world of order within. The temple's floor and the lower parts of the walls were the earth, highlighting

---

119. Quirke, *Ancient Egyptian Religion*, 70.

120. For a summary of the creation myths see, e.g., Griffiths, "Myths: Creation Myths," in Redford, ed., *The Ancient Gods Speak*, 249–55.

121. In the great hypostyle hall of Karnak alone, there were at least 134 columns (Snape, *Egyptian Temples*, 31–32; Wilkinson, *Complete Temples*, 67). Forms include the palmiform, lotiform, papyriform, and campaniform columns (Wilkinson, *Complete Temples*, 66–67).

122. Baines, "Palaces and Temples," 313.

123. Shafer, "Temples, Priests, and Rituals," 8 n. 56; cf. Hornung, *Conceptions of God*, 123–24 n.18. See also Martin Bommas, "Schrein unter: Gebel es-Silsilah im Neuen Reich," in *Grab und Totenkult im Alten Ägypten* (ed. H. Guksch, E. Hofmann, and M. Bommas; Munich: Beck, 2003), 88–103.

124. In Egypt, unity was an undesirable quality that refers to the undifferentiated mass (the "nonexistent") from which creation emerged and which continued to threaten the ordered world (Hornung, *Conceptions of God*, 170–85).

125. See, e.g., Hornung, *Conceptions of God*, 170 and the references cited therein.

their role in vitalizing everything upon them.[126] The ceiling was the sky, appropriately decorated with stars, constellations, or flying birds,[127] often held aloft by the columns, which represented both plants and cosmic pillars.[128]

The temple as a whole and the pylon in particular served as the *akhet* (*3ḫt*), the "horizon" or "radiant place."[129] Indeed, the hieroglyph for *akhet* bears a striking similarity to the pylon when the sun would alight between its two towers. The pylon, and thus the temple by extension, marked "the horizon over the eastern mountains where the sun rose in the morning and over the western mountains where it disappeared at night, the land to which the blessed dead journeyed."[130] As such, heaven, earth, and the netherworld met in the temple, where the divine brushed up against the earth in its daily tour of the cosmos.[131]

At the heart of the temple, the shrine in the sanctuary represented heaven itself.[132] In addition to being the divine dwelling place, which brought heaven to earth, the shrine was a portal to heaven, the heavenly deity's entry point into the terrestrial realm.[133] As such it was appropriately shrouded in mystery, described in contemporary texts as "more inaccessible than what happens in

---

126. Thus, it was often painted black or bore long processions of fecundity figures (Grallert, "Building Inscriptions," 39). In addition, the stones used to construct the wall bases were occasionally made of black granite (Hoffmann, personal communication).

127. Wilkinson, *Complete Temples*, 76; Grallert, "Building Inscriptions," 39.

128. For example, Amenhotep III referred to these pillars in Karnak as reaching to "heaven like the four pillars of heaven" (Wilkinson, *Complete Temples*, 65).

129. Wilkinson, *Complete Temples*, 77–78.

130. Shafer, "Temples, Priests, and Rituals," 8.

131. Hellmut Brunner, "Die Sonnenbahn in ägyptischen Tempeln," in *Archäologie und Altes Testament: Festschrift für Kurt Galling zum 8. Januar 1970* (ed. A. and E. Kutsch; Tübingen: Mohr, 1970), 31–33.

132. The description of the sanctuary reflected this reality, as it was "simply called 'heaven,' or or with an eye to its doors 'the doors of heaven'" (Morenz, *Egyptian Religion*, 88). This distinction also applied to the temple as a whole as evidenced by some of the temple titles (e.g., Karnak was "heaven on earth" and Heliopolis was the "heaven of Egypt"; Othmar Keel, *The Symbolism of the Biblical World: Ancient Near Eastern Iconography and the Book of Psalms* [trans.T. J. Hallett. London: SPCK, 1978], 172).

133. Indeed, the shrine was conceived of as the inner heavens, where the deity dwelt (Koch, *Geschichte der ägyptische Religion*, 288). In addition, the opening of the double door of the shrine in the daily cult ritual was accompanied by words—"the double door of heaven is opened, the double door of earth is unclosed"—and signified the opening of the "cosmic 'double door,' that is, the point at the horizon where heaven and earth meet through which the sun emerges at dawn" (David Lorton, "The Theology of Cult Statues in Ancient Egypt," in *Born in Heaven, Made on Earth: The Making of the Cult Image in the Ancient Near East* [ed. M. B. Dick; Winona Lake, IN: Eisenbrauns, 1999], 139). See also Christiane Gräfin von Pfeil-Autenrieth, *Der Gotteslohn für die Pharaonen: Untersuchungen zu den Gegengaben in ägyptischen Tempeln der griechisch-römischen Epoche* (SRaT 6; Dettelbach: J. H. Röll, 2009).

the heavens, more veiled than the state of the other world, more revered than the inhabitants of the Primeval Ocean."[134] In addition, no inscription within the shrine itself labeled it until the Twenty-Second Dynasty,[135] suggesting that it was too mysterious to be named.[136]

The temple was more than a replica of the world; it was an ideal world in itself. In the reliefs, the relationship between the king and the gods was perfect. In an intimate exchange, the king presented the gods with the appropriate offerings and the gods blessed the king in turn.[137] Priests rarely appeared in the scenes, nor were they needed, as the king was the sole mediator between human and divine.[138] This was especially the case since, to the Egyptian mind, an image and the reality it depicted were often inextricably linked.[139] Thus, the reliefs that depicted the king making offerings to the deity and receiving blessing in return in some way made the images a reality.[140]

On a grander scale, the temple recorded the victory of order over chaos.[141] The outer enclosure wall with its wave-shaped walls may have marked the boundary between the ordered world within and the chaotic waters of Nun without.[142] More than merely building a larger temple than his predecessor, the

---

134. *Urk. IV*, 99, ll. 15–17; Dimitri Meeks, *The Daily Life of the Egyptian Gods* (trans. G. M. Goshgarian; London: Pimlico, 1999), 126.

135. However, other texts referred to the sanctuary by several terms, depending on the context (Spencer, *The Egyptian Temple*, 99–146).

136. Badawy, *History of Egyptian Architecture*, 180. Similarly, although known by many names, in "The God and His Unknown Name of Power" Re's true name and form remained secret (see conveniently *ANET* 12–14; *COS* 1.22:33–34).

137. This ideal was not even realized in the temple as the king himself did not perform all, or even most, of the offerings.

138. See, e.g., Quirke, *Ancient Egyptian Religion*, 80–81.

139. Assmann, *The Search for God*, 83; Wilkinson, "Symbolism," 340–41. Thus, a person's name, whether written or spoken, "identified and represented the person as an individual and was a veritable part of the person's being to the extent that to deface or destroy the name helped to destroy the existence of the person named" (ibid., 340–41).

140. See further ch. 8 on the relationship between an image and its referent.

141. In Egyptian terms, the preservation of order (*maat*) over against lack (*isft*) was the chief responsibility of the king. The former expressed the form of the world intended by its creator, a form to which the contemporary world no longer corresponded. The latter represented the dissolution of order: "sickness, death, scarcity, injustice, falsehood, theft, violence, war, [and] enmity." To the ancient Egyptian, the way forward was to look backward, to restore the "original plenitude of meaning" and thus ensure prosperity (Assmann, *The Search for God*, 3–5; see also Michael Hundley, "The Way Forward is Back to the Beginning: Reflections on the Priestly Texts," *Remembering and Forgetting in Early Second Judah* (ed. E. Ben-Zvi and C. Levin; FAT 85; Tübingen: Mohr Siebeck, 2012), 209–24.

142. See, however, the caution of Dunand and Zivie-Coche (*Gods and Men in Egypt*, 88–

king's expansion of the sacred precinct likely served as an expansion of the ordered world. As the limits of the gods' domain began at the frontier of chaos, the extension of order further into this world, increased the scope of order and thus the gods' kingdom.[143] The sanctuary, resting atop the primordial hill, represented and in some ways was the heart of the ordered world.

On the one hand, this world was strictly separated from the external chaos; on the other, it preserved a degree of chaos within. However, this internal chaos was carefully controlled and overcome so that the temple modeled the victory of order over chaos. The hypostyle hall purposely modeled the primeval swamp amid the chaos waters. However, chaos held no sway within the temple. The floor ascended, rising out of the swamp until it met the closed portal of the sanctuary area, effectively sealed off from the chaos without. The sanctuary stood at the center of this sequestered region at the highest point. Atop the primeval hill, the embodiment of the victory of order over chaos, the sanctuary showed no hint of the chaos features. While the hypostyle hall was awash with elements of the chaotic swamp (e.g., multiple columns alluding to aquatic marsh plants), the sanctuary was devoid of such elements.[144] Instead the reliefs depicted idealized offering scenes where the king and gods coexisted in harmony as the king offered the gods *maat* (life-sustaining order) in return for the fullness of life (*ankh*) and blessing. Because of the close association between an image and its referent,[145] the temple did far more than model the victory; within the ideal world of the temple, the triumph of order was continually (re)enacted. This world functioned as intended, full and ordered, without lack. By both being carefully shut off from the chaos without and by overcoming the chaos within, the temple stood as the ultimate symbol of order. Thus, it is no wonder that when this small world functioned appropriately, the greater world around it would prosper.

---

89). Rather than representing waves, which in art were depicted differently (e.g., with wavy vertical lines), the alternating concave and convex lines may have been so constructed for a more practical purpose, i.e., to withstand earthquakes (Friedhelm Hoffmann, personal communication). On Nun as the nonexistent, see Hornung, *Conceptions of God,* 172–83.

143. See, e.g., Hornung, *Conceptions of God,* 169; Meeks, *Daily Life of the Egyptian Gods,* 92.

144. Cf. Baines, "Palaces and Temples," 313.

145. See further ch. 8.

# CHAPTER 3
# MESOPOTAMIAN TEMPLES

IN COMPARISON WITH THE Egyptian temples, ancient Mesopotamian temples are little understood. In turn, sweeping generalizations about "the" Mesopotamian temple are especially problematic. Egypt was relatively isolated and stable; its official architecture and decoration were very conservative, so that one may refer to a "common" Egyptian temple with some degree of success. Made of stone, several Egyptian temples remain relatively intact. Mesopotamia, however, was far from isolated, representing a hodgepodge of people groups and nations always influencing and being influenced by those around them. Thus, the standard forms changed over time and across regions. The predominant building material, mud-brick, provides yet another obstacle to reconstructing the "standard" Mesopotamian temple, as few temples remain intact.[1] Nonetheless, the Mesopotamian preoccupation with the past ensured that there was some continuity of form to which ample textual representation attests.[2] From this data, we may then present a serviceable, if

---

I would like to thank Michael Roaf for reading an earlier version of this chapter and preventing many a misstep.

1. Roaf laments:

    Despite the large number of buildings which have been excavated, most excavations have produced only fragmentary ground plans and there are regions of Mesopotamia and long periods for which there is little or no architectural information. Furthermore elevations of buildings are unknown except for a very few exceptionally well preserved structures and for a limited number of examples illustrated on bas-reliefs or on seals" ("Palaces and Temples in Ancient Mesopotamia," *CANE* 1:423).

2. Regarding Mesopotamian religious conservatism in general, see Wilfred G. Lambert, who contends that "no major changes [to Mesopotamian religion] took place over history except in the organization of the gods into a pantheon, and except where cities completely died out and ceased to be inhabited" ("Ancient Mesopotamian Gods: Superstition, Philosophy, Theology," *RHR* 207 [1990]: 123). Regarding the Mesopotamian view of the past, see further Blahoslav Hruška, "Das Verhältnis zur Vergangenheit im alten Mesopotamien," *ArOr* 47 (1979): 4–14; Claus Wilcke, "Zum Geschichtsbewusstsein im Alten Mesopotamien," in *Archäologie und Geschichtsbewusstsein* (ed. H. Müller-Karpe; Munich: Beck, 1982), 31–52; Dietz Otto Edzard, "La vision du passé et de l'avenir en Mésopotamie: Période paléobabylonienne," in *Histoire et Conscience dans les Civilizations du Proche-Orient ancien: Actes du Colloque de Cartigny 1986* (ed. A. de Pury; Les Cahiers du CEPOA 5; Leuven: Peeters, 1989), 157–66; Paul-Alain Beaulieu, "Antiquarianism and the Concern for the Past in the Neo-Babylonian Period," *BCSMS* 28 (1994): 37–42; Stefan M. Maul, "Die altorientalische

not full, portrait of Mesopotamian temples, providing us with the general contours that may be filled in with greater details for specific times and places.

## Structure

In the past, Mesopotamian temples have been classified "according to means of access and the shape of the cella,"[3] that is, whether one accessed the deity on a straight line from the outer doorway (direct approach) or had to turn along the way (indirect approach or bent-axis), and whether the sanctuary was wider than it was long (broad room) or longer than it was wide (long room). Structural variations are particularly notable over time and between regions. For example, until 2400 BCE, indirect-approach temples prevailed throughout Mesopotamia, after which time direct-approach temples became increasingly prominent.[4] In the south, a broad sanctuary and vestibule remained the most common blueprint across the millennia, whereas in the north, a T-shaped temple with broad vestibule and long sanctuary began to feature during the middle of the second millennium and remained the most common form until the end of the Iron Age.[5] While dif-

---

Hauptstadt - Abbild und Nabel der Welt," in *Die Orientalische Stadt: Kontinuität, Wandel, Bruch. 1. Internationales Colloquium der Deutschen Orient-Gesellschaft, 9.–10. Mai 1996 in Halle/Saale* (ed. G. Wilhelm; CDOG 1; Saarbrücken: SDV Saarbrücker, 1997), 109–24; idem, "Altorientalische Schöpfungsmythen," in *Mythos und Mythologie* (ed. R. Brandt and S. Schmidt; Berlin: Akademie, 2004), 43–53; idem, "Walking Backwards into the Future: The Conception of Time in the Ancient Near East," in *Given World and Time: Temporalities in Context* (ed. T. Miller; Budapest: CEU, 2008), 15–24; Hundley, "The Way Forward is Back to the Beginning: Reflections on the Priestly Texts," in *Remembering and Forgetting in Early Second Temple Judah* (ed. E. Ben-Zvi and C. Levin; FAT 85; Tübingen: Mohr Siebeck), 209–24. Regarding the textual evidence, see Richard S. Ellis, *Foundation Deposits in Ancient Mesopotamia* (Yale Near Eastern Researches 2; New Haven: Yale University Press, 1968) and esp. Mark J. Boda and Jamie Novotny, eds., *From the Foundations to the Crenellations: Essays on Temple Building in the Ancient Near East and Hebrew Bible* (AOAT 366; Münster: Ugarit-Verlag, 2010).

3. Roaf, "Palaces and Temples," 426. Cella here refers to the sanctuary where the cult image was housed.

4. Wightman, *Sacred Spaces*, 35. Although more direct, northern temples retained an element of indirectness. While the cult statue could be directly accessed from the temple vestibule, which stood before the sanctuary, portals between courts or between the court and the temple were set slightly off-axis (ibid. 41, 56).

5. Ibid. 37, 43–44, 57, 60, 993; see also Roaf, "Palaces and Temples," 426. In addition, Assyrian temples were relatively small in comparison with their Babylonian counterparts, likely due to the different economic functions of the northern and southern temples. In the south, temples were a vital component of the economic infrastructure that rivaled the royal institutions, while in the north they played a more minor role (Roaf, personal communication).

ferent orientations undoubtedly contributed to the temples' effect, we will focus instead on the commonalities: the shared areas, rooms, architectural features, and furniture, regardless of their shape and axiality. Likewise, rather than examining all times and all places, analysis will focus on the second millennium to the first half of the millennium BCE.[6]

In spite of temporal and regional differences and the diversity of evidence, "a general analysis permits the recognition that the same three elements and an identical organizing principle unify all the temples that can be recognized as such: an inner sanctuary, outer sanctuary, and vestibule, to which a court or annexes may be added as accessories."[7] In describing the structure of the temple, our analysis will begin with the cult statue and move progressively outward to the outer gate of the sacred precinct.[8]

The inner sanctuary refers to the temple's primary space, where the deity was present in the form of a cult statue. This primary space was usually either located within its own small room (e.g., in the Neo-Assyrian temple of Nabu at Kalhu [modern Nimrud] and the Neo-Assyrian temples associated with the royal palace at Dur Sharrukin [modern Khorsabad])[9] and/or set off in some way from a larger room (in a niche in the back wall [e.g., the Middle Assyrian Assur temple at Kar Tukulti-Ninurta and the Kassite Ningal temple at Dur Kurigalzu] and/or in an elevated position [e.g., the old Assyrian Sin-Shamash temple at Assur and the late Babylonian Ninmakh temple in Babylon]; fig. 3.1).[10] Whatever its precise location,

---

6. Thus, Sumerian evidence will largely be excluded from our evaluation. Nonetheless, both later and (especially) earlier evidence will also be adduced to expand and sharpen our portrait.

7. Jean-Claude Margueron, "The Mesopotamian Temple," 4:165. See further idem, "Sanctuaires semitiques," *Supplement au dictionnaire de la bible* 11 (1991): 1104–1257.

8. This progression also makes the most sense of the terminology employed here to describe these spaces: primary, secondary, tertiary, and quarternary. Regarding these labels, see Wightman, *Sacred Spaces*, 932–52.

9. Ernst Heinrich, *Die Tempel und Heiligtümer im alten Mesopotamien: Typologie, Morphologie und Geschichte* (2 vols.; Denkmäler antiker Architektur 14; Berlin: de Gruyter, 1982), 250–51, 259, 266–72 and diagrams 349, 352–55, 357–58; Wightman, *Sacred Spaces*, 56–57. On the Kalhu temple, see further M. E. L. Mallowan, *Nimrud and Its Remains I* (London: Collins, 1966), 231–88. On the temple of Nabu at Dur Sharrukin, see further Gordon Loud and Charles B. Altman, *Khorsabad, Part 2: The Citadel and the Town*, (OIP 40; Chicago: The University of Chicago Press, 1938), 56–64 and plates 2, 44, 70–71, 79–85.

10. For an example of a niched inner sanctuary, see fig. 3.7, where the niche was carved into the adjoining ziggurat. For another example of a raised inner sanctuary, see fig. 3.14, where the twin inner sanctuaries at either side of the temple complex were elevated above the outer sanctuaries. Regarding the aforementioned temples, see Heinrich, *Tempel und Heiligtümer*, 19, 182, 200–202, 225–27, 235–37, 285, 294–96, 313–14 and figs. 286, 290, 292, 325–26, 400, 402; Wightman, *Sacred Spaces*, 43–45, 62–63. See further regarding the Assur temple Walter Andrae and Walter Bachmann, "Aus den Berichten über die Grabungen in

Fig. 3.1. Plan of the Neo-Assyrian temple of Nabu at Dur Sharrukin (modern Khorsabad). Room 21 was the outer sanctuary, with isolating corridors surrounding it, and room 22 was the raised inner sanctuary with a raised pedestal for the cult image. The courts, which formed a single architectural unit with the temple, had portals set off-axis, while within the temple core the cult image could be approached directly. From Loud and Altman, *Khorsabad*, Part 2, pl. 79.

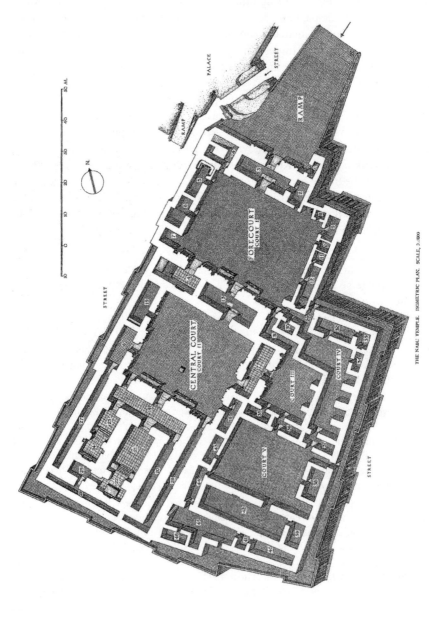

the sanctuary was almost always situated at the furthest point from the temple's entrance and was relatively dark.[11]

The larger room around the inner sanctuary constituted the outer sanctuary, or secondary temple space, and often served as the primary point of intersection between the priest(s) and the deity. In it, one occasionally found a table for the presentation of divine gifts, an incense altar, and statues of prominent citizens.[12] The often smaller vestibule, or lobby, was tertiary space, standing between the sanctuary and the outside world. Other tertiary spaces were commonly present within the temple. For example, service areas and other areas with no apparent practical function frequently surrounded the sanctuary.[13] Finally, a gate, which ranged from simple to complex and imposing, was often attached to the vestibule, both granting and restricting access to this temple core (for the complex, see, e.g., fig. 3.2).[14] While these three zones formed the core of the temple, other elements were often attached to the temple, extending temple space (*temenos*) further. One or two courts served as the most common temple appendage, or quaternary space, each commonly with its own, often imposing walls, gate, and vestibule.[15] The courts are especially noticeable and definable when they are of single architectural unit with

---

Tulul Akir (Kar Tukulti-Ninib)," *MDOG* 53 (1914): 41–57; regarding the Ningal temple, see Leonard Woolley, *Ur Excavations, V: The Ziggurat and its Surroundings* (London: Oxford University Press, 1939), pl. 73; regarding the Ninmakh temple, see Robert Koldewey, *Das Ištar-Tor in Babylon* (WVDOG 15; Leipzig: Deutsche Orient-Gesellschaft, 1911), 4–17, fig. 1–19 and pl. II–III.

11. Margueron, "The Mesopotamian Temple," 165–66. The room was often called the "dark room" (itima=*kiṣṣumu*) which "knows not daylight" (The Fall of Agade, l. 131), and whose ritual vessels "no eye is to see" (Lamentation over the Destruction of Sumer and Ur, l. 450) (Jacobsen, *Treasures of Darkness*, 16).

12. Regarding incense altars, see, e.g., Kjeld Nielsen, *Incense in Ancient Israel* (VTSup 38; Leiden: Brill, 1986), 32. Regarding statues, see Henri Frankfort, *The Art and Architecture of the Ancient Orient* (Middlesex: Penguin Books, 1977), 45; F. A. M. Wiggermann, "Theologies, Priests and Worship in Ancient Mesopotamia" in *CANE* 2:1863; Margueron, "The Mesopotamian Temple," 169; Jean Bottéro, *Religion in Ancient Mesopotamia* (trans. T. L. Fagan; Chicago: The University of Chicago Press, 2001), 126; Peter Machinist, "Kingship and Divinity in Imperial Assyria," in Beckman and Lewis, eds., *Text, Artifact, and Image*, 176.

13. This does not suggest the rooms were not used; rather, architecturally they served an isolating purpose. See fig. 3.1, in which various corridors surround and isolate the sanctuary area.

14. Once again, the "temple core" refers to the area within the temple in and around the central sanctuary and may include various tertiary spaces like storerooms, secondary chapels, vestibules, and corridors.

15. On quaternary space, see Wightman, *Sacred Spaces*, 947–52.

Fig. 3.2. Reconstruction of the façade of the temple core in the temple of Nabu at Dur Shar-rukin, viewed from the central court. Of the various impressive portals within the divine precinct, this entryway was the most imposing. From Wightman, *Sacred Spaces*, fig.1.25.

the temple[16] (e.g., the temple at Tell Rimah and the Nabu temple at Dur Sharrukin [see figs. 3.1 and 3.8]).[17] In several instances, the portals to both the temple core and to the larger temple complex were guarded by twin towers (figs. 3.3 and 3.8), and, when the complex contained two courts, these too were separated by substan-tial portals (e.g., the temples of Ishtar-Kititum in Neribtum of Eshnunna [modern Ischali] [fig. 3.3] and Nabu at Dur Sharrukin [figs. 3.1 and 3.2]).[18] Often an altar (e.g., in the Ur III temple of Shu-Shin at Eshnunna and the Ninmakh temple in Babylon [fig. 3.4])[19] and occasionally a well (e.g., in the Neo-Assyrian Anu-Adad

16. Seton Lloyd, *The Archaeology of Mesopotamia: From the Old Stone Age to the Persian Conquest* (2nd ed.; London: Thames & Hudson, 1984), 181.

17. See also figs. 3.3, 3.7, and 3.14. Wightman, *Sacred Spaces*, 31, 39, 57–59. Regarding the Tell Rimah temple, see David Oates, "The Excavations at Tell al Rimah, 1964," *Iraq* 27 (1965): 62–80; idem, "The Excavations at Tell al Rimah, 1965," *Iraq* 28 (1966): 122–39; idem, "The Excavations at Tell al Rimah, 1967," *Iraq* 29 (1967): 70–96; idem, "The Excavations at Tell al Rimah, 1967," *Iraq* 30 (1968): 115–38; Heinrich, *Tempel und Heiligtümer*, 181–22, 200, 259 and figs. 287, 291, 293.

18. Regarding the Ishtar-Kititum temple, see Heinrich, *Tempel und Heiligtümer*, 20, 171, 188–89, 268–70 and figs. 253, 352–55; Wightman, *Sacred Spaces*, 41–42, 57–59; see further Frankfort, *Progress of the Work of the Oriental Institute in Iraq, 1934/35: Fifth Preliminary Report of the Iraq Expedition* (OIC 20: Chicago: The Oriental Institute of the University of Chicago, 1936), 74–87.

19. Wightman, *Sacred Spaces*, 37–38, 62–63; regarding the Shu-Shin temple, see Henri Frankfort, Seton Lloyd and Jacobsen, *The Gimilsin Temple and the Palace of the Rulers at*

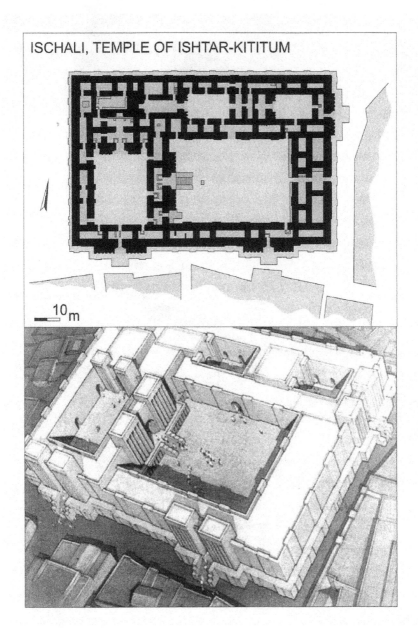

ISCHALI, TEMPLE OF ISHTAR-KITITUM

10 m

Fig. 3.3. The temple of Ishtar-Kititum in Neribtum of Eshnunna (modern Ischali). Note the prominent entryways, each with stairs and substantial twin-towered portals, at the entrance to the temple complex, between the two courts, and at the entrance to the temple core. The elevated sanctuary was located in the northwestern corner of the temple complex. From Wightman, *Sacred Spaces*, fig.1.18 (watercolor by W. Suddaby from Lloyd, *The Archaeology of Mesopotamia*, fig. 109).

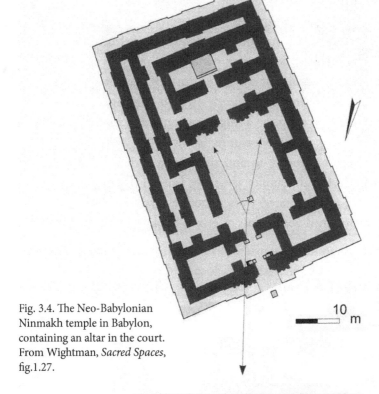

Fig. 3.4. The Neo-Babylonian
Ninmakh temple in Babylon,
containing an altar in the court.
From Wightman, *Sacred Spaces*,
fig.1.27.

10 m

BABYLON, NINMAKH TEMPLE

temple at Assur)[20] were also present in the court, along with stelae especially concentrated at portals.[21]

Like royal palaces and the major Egyptian complexes, other structures were at times present in the temple complex and the surrounding space for the benefit of the deity and the upkeep of its temple such as storerooms, servants' quarters, workshops, kitchens, secondary temples, and chapels.[22] In some major complexes, like the Esagil ("house whose top is high") in Babylon,[23] an outer wall with portals surrounded the sacred precinct or divine estate (akin to the Egyptian *pr*), thereby sequestering a much larger space.[24] Indeed, major temples were often separated from the rest of the city (sometimes at a distance from it) into a walled sacred neighborhood of sorts, called simply "holy city" (iri-kù/*ālu ellu*).[25] Unfortunately, "archaeological exploration has not always extended far enough to uncover the relationship between built space and open space," namely, between the temple complex and the surrounding space, especially when that space was not enclosed by walls.[26]

Finally, the most distinctive element of Mesopotamian religious architecture, the ziggurat (Akk. *ziqquratu*), deserves special mention. Its precise function is difficult to pinpoint. Minimally, ziggurats were massive platforms upon which small temples presumably rested, which were distinct from and often located at

---

*Tell Asmar* (OIP 43; Chicago: The University of Chicago Press, 1940), 9–27, pl. 2; Heinrich, *Tempel und Heiligtümer*, 149–50, 163–64 and figs. 239, 244.

20. Heinrich, *Tempel und Heiligtümer*, 248, 265–66 and figs. 346, 348; Wightman, *Sacred Spaces*, 56. See further Walter Andrae, *Der Anu-Adad-Tempel in Assur* (WVDOG 10; Leipzig: Deutsche Orient-Gesellschaft,1909), 39–78, pl. 5 and 9.

21. Wightman, *Sacred Spaces*, 1009.

22. See, e.g., Stefan M. Maul, "Das Haus des Götterkönigs: Gedanken zur Konzeption überregionaler Heiligtümer im Alten Orient," in *Tempel im Alten Orient: 7. Internationales Colloquium der Deutschen Orient-Gesellschaft 11.–13. Oktober 2009, München* (ed. K. Kaniuth et al.; CDOG 7; Wiesbaden: Harrasowitz, 2013), 311.

23. Contained within a larger walled *temenos*, the temple core of the Esagil was of a single architectural unit with two courts (Heinrich, *Tempel und Heiligtümer*, 20, 181, 284, 287–88, 310–12 and figs. 387–88, 391, 393; Wightman, *Sacred Spaces*, 60–62). See further Koldewey, *Das Ištar-Tor in Babylon*, 37–49, figs. 59–85, and pl. VIII–XI.

24. In the case of the Esagil, the sacred precinct was located near another even larger sacred precinct, the Etemenanki, such that the heart of the city served as a city of the gods.

25. Hanspeter Schaudig, "The Restoration of Temples in the Neo- and Late Babylonian Periods: A Royal Prerogative as the Setting for Political Argument," in Boda and Novotny, eds., *From the Foundations to the Crenellations*, 142. Cities themselves, were often thought to be divinely constructed, and especially their walls and gates were considered sacred, viewed as protecting the cities from the chaos without (ibid.). Thus, the temple compound often formed a city of the gods within a larger city built by and for the gods.

26. Margueron, "The Mesopotamian Temple," 166.

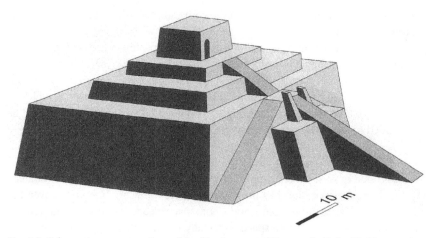

Fig. 3.5. Schematic reconstruction of the Ur ziggurat of Nannar, built by Ur-Nammu (ca. 2100 BCE), which rose in three stages upon which a small summit temple presumably rested. From Wightman, *Sacred Spaces*, fig. 1.12.

a distance from the ground-level temples (figs. 3.5 and 3.6).[27] Taking the form of a stepped pyramid with either a square or rectangular plan,[28] ziggurats often towered over their surroundings, including the rest of the sacred precinct. At times, the ziggurats of the major sacred areas were the centerpiece of their own sacred precinct, distinct from the lower level temple and at some distance from the palace. At other times, ziggurats were located near the royal palace, and ziggurats

---

27. Although this is a general assumption of Assyriology and has textual warrant, no remains of such a temple have been found yet (Harriet Crawford, *Sumer and the Sumerians* [New York: Cambridge University Press, 1993], 73; Roaf, "Palaces and Temples," 430), since, with few exceptions, little of the upper levels remain. See, however, Wilfrid Allinger-Csollich ("Gedanken über das Aussehen und die Funktion einer Ziqqurrat," in Kaniuth et al., eds., *Tempel im alten Orient*, 1–18), who suggests based on the archaeological record that the ziggurat temple was divided over different levels of the ziggurat rather than resting on the top; see also Allinger-Csollich, "Birs Nimrud II: 'Tieftempel' – 'Hochtempel': Vergleichende Studien Borsippa – Babylon," *BaM* 29 (1998): 95–330. For a different and more traditional approach, see most recently Andrew R. George, "A Stele of Nebuchadnezzar II [Tower of Babel Stele]," in *Cuneiform Royal Inscriptions and Related Texts in the Schøyen Collection* (ed. Andrew R. George; CUSAS 17, Manuscripts in the Schøyen Collection, Cuneiform texts 6; Bethesda, MD: CDL, 2011), text 76, 153–69.

28. "Although the distribution of well-understood ziggurats over time and space is very uneven, they appear to have come in two varieties: the generally earlier and Babylonian one had a rectangular base with stairs providing access to the top; the later one, more often found in Assyria, is square in plan and had more variable access, sometimes including a ramp that spirals up the building" (Elizabeth Stone, "Ziggurat," in *OEANE* 5:390).

Fig. 3.6. Photo of the reconstructed Ur ziggurat of Nannar. Source: Wikipedia.

and temples abutted each other, such that the inner sanctuary of one ground level temple was carved into the base of its adjacent ziggurat (the Assur temple at Kar Tukulti-Ninurta; figs. 3.7 and 3.8).[29]

The most famous and perhaps most enigmatic[30] of these structures is the ziggurat in Babylon, called Etemenanki, "house, foundation platform of heaven and earth,"[31] the centerpiece of a walled sacred area that was situated to the north of the smaller temple complex, the Esagil. Thought to have been built around the time of Hammurabi and restored by Nebuchadnezzar in the sixth century,[32] this tower was one of the largest and most awe-inspiring of Mesopotamian ziggurats.

## Other Notable Features: Decoration and Elevation

In comparison with the Egyptian temples teeming with imagery and architectural adornments, or the Neo-Assyrian palaces guarded by massive human-headed bulls or lions with eagles wings, the remains of Mesopotamian temples

---

29. Wightman, *Sacred Spaces*, 44–45. Neo-Assyrian temples more often fall into the second category; perhaps because of their minor economic role relative to Babylonian temples, monarchs more readily assimilated them into the royal compound. See further regarding the Assur temple, Andrae and Bachmann, "Die Grabungen in Tulul Akir" 41–57. See also fig. 3.8, where the sanctuary stood before the ziggurat.

30. Although its name and its descriptions are informative, little remains of the actual structure. See further Hansjörg Schmid, *Der Tempelturm Etemenanki in Babylon* (BaF 17; Mainz: von Zabern, 1995).

31. George, *House Most High: The Temples of Ancient Mesopotamia* (Winona Lake, IN: Eisenbrauns, 1993), 149.

32. Roaf, "Palaces and Temples," 431.

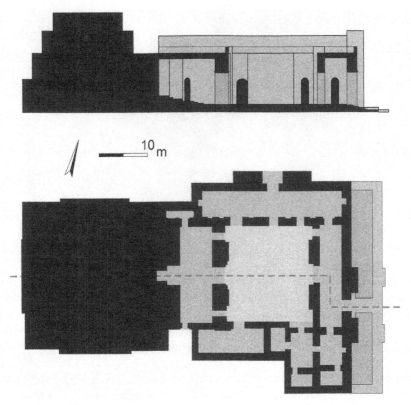

Fig. 3.7. The Middle Assyrian Assur temple at Kar Tukulti-Ninurta (late thirteenth century BCE). The niche in back wall of the sanctuary was carved into the base of the adjacent ziggurat. Note the direct approach from the court, while the entrance to the temple complex was set off-axis. From Wightman, *Sacred Spaces*, fig.1.20.

appear especially reserved. Since little has survived of the Mesopotamian temples,[33] it should come as little surprise that even less has survived of their decoration.[34]

The archaeological record suggests that adornment within the temple interior was rather sparse.[35] The outer walls of both the temple core and temple

---

33. For example, no temple entrance survived to the lintel (Ursula Seidl, "Bildschmuck an mesopotamischen Tempeln des 2. Jahrtausends v. Chr.," in Kaniuth et al., eds., *Tempel im alten Orient*, 478).

34. For example, mural iconography, such as that found in the so-called Painted Temple at Tell 'Uqair, was likely "more common than it appears, since most Mesopotamian temples have been reduced to their foundations" (Wightman, *Sacred Spaces*, 1009). See, e.g., Seidl, "Bildschmuck an mesopotamischen Tempeln," for a survey of second-millennium temple decoration.

35. See, e.g., Seidl, "Bildschmuck an mesopotamischen Tempeln," 14.

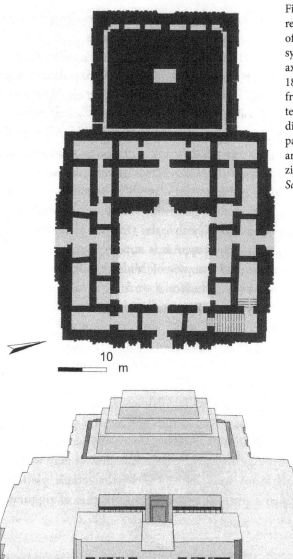

Fig. 3.8. Groundplan and reconstructed schematic of the well-preserved, symmetrical, direct-axis Tell Rimah temple (ca. 1800 BCE). Twin towers framed the portal to the temple complex, the façade displayed recessed-niche paneling, and the sanctuary abutted the attached ziggurat. From Wightman, *Sacred Spaces*, fig.1.13.

10
m

complex were made up of alternating niches (*ḫipšu*) and projections (*dublu*) (fig. 3.8).[36] The rest of the preserved decoration was especially concentrated at the portals.[37] The temple gateways themselves were often "flanked by a pattern of narrow vertical steps, an effect achieved by staggering the brickwork so that the wall recedes into the gateway," also known as rabbeting,[38] and frequently abutted in major temples by ornamental twin towers. Statues of various fierce and sometimes hybrid creatures also adorned the gateways.[39] For example, near life-sized lions were discovered guarding the portals at Tell Harmal, Mari, and Nimrud (see figs. 3.9 and 3.10),[40] while at Tell Rimah the head of the hybrid creature Huwawa from the Gilgamesh epic and a bull-man were found on either side of the door (fig. 3.11).[41] In addition to the fierce creatures, interceding goddesses were also found (e.g., at Tell Rimah).[42] There is even evidence from the Kassite Ishtar temple in Uruk of several paired hybrid divine figures situated in the niches (fig. 3.12). The females have an anthropomorphic upper body and a wavy skirt as a lower body, suggesting water, while the males have anthropomorphic upper bodies and scale-patterned skirts, resembling mountains, each of which carries a vase of overflowing water.[43] One also finds palm trees and twisted posts (e.g., at Tell Rimah).[44]

---

36. Andrew R. George, "The Bricks of E-Sagil," *Iraq* 57 (1995): 181–83; idem, *Cuneiform Royal Inscriptions*, 157. Regarding this architectural feature in ancient Mesopotamia, see further Muayad Said Basim Damerji, *The Development of the Architecture of Doors and Gates in Ancient Mesopotamia* (trans. T. Takase and Y. Okada; Tokyo: Institute of Cultural Studies of Ancient Iraq, 1987), 71–74.

37. Wightman, *Sacred Spaces*, 994. See more extensively the evidence culled by Novotny ("Temple Building") and Seidl ("Bildschmuck an mesopotamischen Tempeln"). In some cases, the portals seem to have been more impressively adorned the further one progresses into the divine sphere (see, e.g., the Temple of Nabu at Dur Sharrukin [figs. 3.1 and 3.2; Loud and Altman, *Khorsabad,* Part 2, 64 and pl. 2].

38. George, "The Bricks of E-Sagil," 182. See further Damerji, *Doors and Gates,* 68–70.

39. For a study of apotropaic statues, see Burkhard J. Engel, *Darstellungen vom Dämonen und Tieren in assyrischen Palästen und Tempeln nach den schriftlichen Quellen* (Mönchengladbach: Hackbarth, 1987). For animals used in architectural contexts, see Chikako E. Watanabe, *Animal Symbolism in Mesopotamia: A Contextual Approach* (Wiener Offene Orientalistik 1; Vienna: University of Vienna, 2002), 111–25.

40. Lloyd, *Archaeology of Mesopotamia,* 171.

41. Seidl, "Bildschmuck an mesopotamischen Tempeln," 11.

42. Ibid.

43. Ibid., 6. Regarding the mountainous skirts, see further Peter Calmeyer, "Wandernde Berggötter," in *Languages and Cultures in Contact: Proceedings of the 42nd RAI* (ed. K. van Lerberghe and G. Voet; OLA 96; Leuven: Peeters, 1999), 1–32.

44. Seidl, "Bildschmuck an mesopotamischen Tempeln," 2. See also the Nabu temple at Dur Sharrukin, which lacked the twisted poles, but had twin trees (fig. 3.2; Wightman, *Sacred Spaces,* 59; cf. Keel, *Symbolism of the Biblical World,* 123). Water and palm forms

Fig. 3.9. One of a pair of reconstructed lion statues guarding the portal to temple from Old Babylonian Tell Harmal (Iraq National Museum, Baghdad).

The written evidence tells a slightly different story. There is enough textual evidence, particularly in royal inscriptions, to suggest that, although likely not as extensive as in Egypt, at least some Mesopotamian temples were lavishly decorated.[45] Several inscriptions described lavish decoration in rather generic terms. For example, Assurnasirpal II used the stock expression, "I decorated (the

---

were largely abandoned in the first millennium to be replaced by the simpler array of seven pilasters (slightly projecting columns built into the face of a wall) on outer and court walls (Seidl, "Bildschmuck an mesopotamischen Tempeln," 5), such as at the temples of Sargon II at Dur Sarrukin (Loud, *Khorsabad I* [OIP 38; Chicago: University of Chicago Press, 1936], fig. 98, 100, 103, 104) or the Nabu temple in Borsippa of Nebuchadnezzar II (Allinger-Csollich, *Birs Nimrud II*, figs. 26–30).

45. For written evidence of temple decoration by Assyrian monarchs, see Jamie Novotny,

Fig. 3.10. One of a pair of colossal lions flanking the entrance of the Ishtar temple in Nimrud (ca. 883–859 BCE). Courtesy of the Trustees of the British Museum.

temple) more splendidly than before,"[46] while Tiglath-pileser I used more elaborate but little more descriptive terminology, claiming to have made the inner rooms of the Anu-Adad temple of Assur "like the interior of the heavens" and its walls "as splendid as the brilliance of rising stars."[47]

Other royal inscriptions were more specific. For example, Assurnasirpal II boasted of decorating the inner sanctuary of Ninurta in Kalhu with gold and lapis lazuli and to have placed "wild ferocious gold dragons (*ušumgallū*) by his seat."[48]

---

"Temple Building in Assyria: Evidence from Royal Inscriptions," in Boda and Novotny, eds., *From the Foundations to the Crenellations*, 131–35.

46. See, e.g., A. Kirk Grayson, *Assyrian Rulers of the Early First Millennium BC I (1114–859 BC)* (RIMA 2; Toronto: University of Toronto, 1991), 332, A.0.101.57 3; Novotny, "Temple Building," 131–32.

47. RIMA 2, 28–29, A.0.87.1 vii 97–101; Novotny, "Temple Building," 131.

48. RIMA 2, 291, A.0.101.30 69–73; Novotny, "Temple Building," 131.

Fig. 3.11. The head of the hybrid Huwawa from the Gilgamesh epic on either side of door at the Tell Rimah temple. From Carolyn Postgate, David Oates, and Joan Oates, *The Excavations at Tell al Rimah: The Pottery* (Iraq Archaeological Reports 4; Warminster, England: Aris & Phillips, 1997), pl. 7b (Mosul Museum).

Esarhaddon likewise boasted of adorning the inner sanctuary of Assur's temple in Assur with gold and installing in it gold-plated long-haired heroes and *kūribu-genii*. In the room before the sanctuary, he set up gold-plated statues of creatures from the watery abyss.[49] Textual evidence from the Kassite period also indicates that the doors to the sanctuaries of Marduk and Sarpanitum were adorned with fantastical creatures.[50] The principle item within the temple was undoubtedly the divine cult statue, made of the finest materials available.[51]

---

49. Rykle Borger, *Die Inschriften Asarhaddons, Königs von Assyrien* (AfO Beiheft 9; Graz: E. Weidner, 1956), 87; Novotny, "Temple Building," 133.

50. See Wayne Horowitz, *Mesopotamian Cosmic Geography* (Mesopotamian Civilizations 8; Winona Lake, IN: Eisenbrauns, 1998), 108 and references in n. 2. In addition, texts mention a protective deity (*kāribu*) beside the gate of a temple's inner sanctuary (*papāḫu*) and an *anzû* bird standing before the inner sanctuary (*CAD* P, 103, 104).

51. See ch. 9.

Fig. 3.12. The façade of the Kassite Ishtar temple in Uruk with several paired hybrid divine figures situated in the niches. All have anthropomorphic upper bodies and carry vases of overflowing water. The females (e.g., second from left) have watery skirts carved with wavy lines, while the males (e.g., far left) have scale-patterned lower bodies, suggesting mountains. Courtesy of the Staatliche Museen zu Berlin, Vorderasiatisches Museum. Photo by J. Liepe.

Hybrid and fierce natural creatures like bison (*kusarikkū*), fish-men (*kulīlū/kulullû*), goat-fish (*suḫurmāšū*), wild dogs (*uridimmū*), wild bulls (*rīmū*), scorpion-men (*girtablilū*), lions (*urmaḫḫū*), long-haired heroes (*laḫmū*), *kūribu*-genii, and lion-headed eagles (*anzû*) also are attested at portals, many of which were adorned with precious materials like gold, silver, and bronze.[52] As protective and intercessory deities, female *lamassū* and their male counterparts *šedū* stood at prominent portals, presumably taking the same form as the massive winged human-headed bulls prevalent in Neo-Assyrian palace gateways (fig. 3.13).[53]

---

52. See with references Novotny, "Temple Building," 131–35. For example, Sennacherib adorned the gateways of the temple of Assur with creatures of mixed form (*Mischwesen*) (Paul-Alain Beaulieu, *The Pantheon of Uruk During the Neo-Babylonian Period* [CM 23; Leiden: Brill, 2003], 356).

53. See, e.g., D. Foxvog, W. Heimpel and D. Kilmer, "Lamma/Lamassu A. I. Mesopotamien.

Fig. 3.13. A winged human-headed bull (*aladlammû*) from Nimrud, palace of Assurnasirpal II. Courtesy of the Trustees of the British Museum.

Two other features are worth noting: 1) the height of the temple and the zig-gurat and 2) the elevation of their constituent parts. First, although most tem-ples have been reduced to their foundations, enough written and archaeological evidence exists to suggest that some Mesopotamian temples rose to a uniform height of approximately 15–20 meters, except the towers flanking the entrance portal(s) which were approximately 20–25 meters tall (see esp. the remarkably well-preserved temple at Tell Rimah; fig. 3.8).[54] Although it is difficult to know precisely, the ziggurat at Babylon may have risen to between 60 and 90 meters. Second, builders elevated key elements of Mesopotamian temples. Naturally, the small temples atop the ziggurats enjoyed a privileged vantage point. Nevertheless, the use of elevation was not always so obvious. For example, the sacred complex of the Ishtar-Kititum temple of Neribtum and the temple core were both elevated above the surrounding terrain.[55] The inner sanctuary, housing the cult statue, also often rose above the outer sanctuary (e.g., the Sin-Shamash temple in Assur, the Nabu temple in Dur Sharrukin, and the Ningal temple at Ur; see figs. 3.1, 3.14).[56]

## *The Visibility of the Cult Image*

Much of the interest in the axiality of Mesopotamian temples revolves around the issue of the visibility of the cult image.[57] Presumably, an axial temple granted a direct view of the deity from the outer gate. By contrast, a disaxial temple, in which the cult statue was approached indirectly, did not grant a direct view of the statue until one stood directly before it. Rather than corresponding to either approach in the extreme, many temples combined the two approaches, such that the portals between courts were set distinctly off-axis, while the core of the temple embodied a direct approach (e.g., the temples of Assur in Kar Tukulti-Ninurta and the Neo-Assyrian Sin-Shamash temple in Assur).[58] However, the contrast between direct and indirect axes may not be as strong as it first appears. As in Egypt, doors

---

Philologisch.," *RlA* 6 (1980–1983): 447–48. Regarding the archaeological record, see A. Spycket, "Lamma/Lamassu. B. Archäologisch," *RlA* 6 (1980–1983): 453–55.

54. Wightman, *Sacred Spaces*, 31, 39, 994.

55. Heinrich, *Tempel und Heiligtümer*, 188–89 and fig. 253; Lloyd, *Archaeology of Mesopotamia*, 161–62; Wightman, *Sacred Spaces*, 41–42. Note that the temple core was elevated along with its inner court. See also the temple of Nabu at Dur Sharrukin, which, along with the adjoining priestly residence, was built on a high, buttressed platform (Wightman, *Sacred Spaces*, 59).

56. Wightman, *Sacred Spaces*, 60.

57. See, e.g., Wightman, *Sacred Spaces*, 35 and *passim*. There is also interest in finding analogs to Solomon's temple.

58. See figs. 3.1, 3.3, 3.4, 3.7, and 3.14. Wightman, *Sacred Spaces*, 41, 56.

provided the appropriate screens between zones in the direct approach temples.[59] Only when the doors stood open could one behold the cult image.[60]

## USE

Although the functions of the various rooms were not inscribed on the walls as in Egypt, their purposes may nonetheless be deduced with some degree of certainty from the texts and architecture. The word É=*bītu* provides a major clue. *Bītu*, the word for house, was the primary term used for the temple.[61] The Sumerian and Akkadian speakers apparently found no need to create a new term, since for them the temple was simply the terrestrial house of the deity.[62] As the home of the god, the temple was the primary locus of service and, as the votives and statues indicate, the place to come to make contact with the deities. Although they took different forms, both service and contact shared a common goal. In exchange for gifts and good service, the people individually and corporately hoped to be rewarded (on the principle *do ut des*, "I give that you may give"). For example, on the statues of private individuals in the temple, "the dedicatory hymns and inscriptions named the gift givers and reminded the god of what they expected in return: prosperity

---

59. See the various references to temple doors (*daltu*) in *CAD* D, 52–55; see also the brief summary of doors in Assyrian temples in Novotny, *Temple Building*, 129–30; see further Damerji, *Doors and Gates*; cf. *bābu* (gate) in *CAD* B, 14–22; cf. *CAD* P, 102; see also the remains of door jambs found at various sites (e.g., the temple of Nabu at Dur Sharrukin [Loud and Altman, *Khorsabad*, Part 2, 59]). There is also evidence of curtains (*gidlû*) hanging at the inner sanctuary of temples (*papāḫu*) (e.g., in the NB temple of Ishtar at Uruk; Beaulieu, *Pantheon of Uruk*, 139; see more generally the description in Michael B. Dick, "The Mesopotamian Cult Statue: A Sacramental Encounter with Divinity," in *Cult Image and Divine Representation in the Ancient Near East* [ed. Neal H. Walls; Boston: ASOR, 2005], 27).

60. The importance of these doors, which along with the gateways served as the "neuralgic contact zones between the building and the outside world," was made evident in the ritual performed after the installation of the doorframes (*sippū*) (Claus Ambos, "Building Rituals from the First Millennium BC: The Evidence from the Ritual Texts," in Boda and Novotny, eds., *From the Foundations to the Crenellation*, 223).

61. See *CAD* B, 282–95; with cognates in West Semitic (see ch. 5). Regarding the names of the temples themselves, see esp. George, *House Most High*.

62. Jacobsen, *Treasures of Darkness*, 15; Wiggerman, "Theologies, Priests and Worship," 1861; Bottéro, *Religion in Ancient Mesopotamia*, 115. More broadly, the Mesopotamian temple "was seen as the god's 'house' or perhaps better 'estate,' and was run along the lines of a secular institution" (J. Nicholas Postgate, *Early Mesopotamia: Society and Economy at the Dawn of History* [London: Routledge, 1992], 114).

and a long life for themselves, for their loved ones, or for the ruler, their representative before the god."[63]

Each specific area likely also had a specific use, yet a lack of concrete evidence has rendered these uses speculative. Walls and gates had the obvious function of dividing the larger space into specific smaller spaces, and granting and controlling access to those spaces. Workshops, storage and service areas, and servants' quarters, whether attached to the temple or not, facilitated the divine service and the business of running the "holy city."

Courts seem to have been the appropriate place to prepare offerings,[64] to wash to ensure ritual purity before engaging with the deity, and for the community to gather for festive occasions. When set within a temple housing two gods, a single courtyard also served to neatly separate the two spheres (see, e.g., the Sin-Shamash temple at Assur; fig. 3.14). As in a palace or large residence, a temple with a dual-courtyard system (e.g., the Esagil in Babylon and the Nabu temple of Dur Sharrukin; fig. 3.1) differentiated the courts by name, *bābānu* and *bītānu*, which reflected their respective roles. The latter, related to the *bītu* (house), was reserved for priests, while the former, related to the *bābu* (gate), was used for public ceremonies officiated by the priests.[65]

The vestibules, like the entryway in a modern home or the lobby in a modern business, served as mediating spaces. They stood between the exterior and interior worlds as liminal zones, ensuring that access to the interior was gradual. The sanctuary[66] served as the principal living quarters of the deity and could be conveniently divided into inner and outer sanctuaries. The presence of a table, an incense burner, and other similar installations in the outer sanctuary imply that it was the place to carry out the daily ritual, especially the divine meals.[67] The inner sanctuary, whether attached to the outer sanctuary or as its own room, served as a bedchamber of sorts, where the deity in the form a cult statue rested and where more intimate care probably occurred (e.g., bathing and dressing).

The ziggurat (Akkadian *ziqquratu*) was likely derived from *zaqāru*, meaning something like "highly built."[68] Each ziggurat was also given its own descriptive name (e.g., the ziggurat of the Enlil sanctuary at Nippur was called Duranki, the "house, bond of heaven and earth").[69] In general, the ziggurat seems to have

---

63. Wiggermann, "Theologies, Priests and Worship," 1861.

64. A single court may have served several temples as the example at Mari suggests (Margueron, "The Mesopotamian Temple," 166).

65. *CAD* B, 7 and 274–76; Wightman, *Sacred Spaces*, 42.

66. For the various Akkadian terms that can be used for sanctuary, *aširtu, papāḫu*, and *parakku*, see respectively *CAD* A/2 436–39; *CAD* P 102–5, 145–52.

67. Margueron, "The Mesopotamian Temple," 165. For the daily cult ritual, see ch. 9.

68. See *CAD* Z, 55–56, 129–32.

69. George, *House Most High*, 80; Wightman, *Sacred Spaces*, 25. See further Hermann

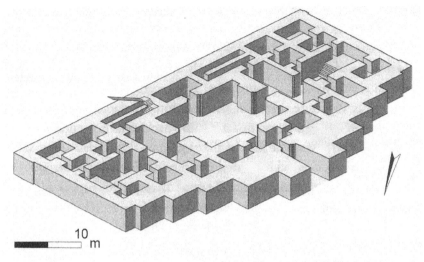

ASSUR, SIN-SHAMASH TEMPLE

Fig. 3.14. The Middle Assyrian Sin-Shamash temple with twin raised sanctuaries connected by a single court, which was part of a single architectural unit with rest of temple complex. From Wightman, *Sacred Spaces*, fig.1.19.

been a large stepped-structure that rose from earth to approach heaven with a small temple likely situated atop it.[70] Unlike the lower temples and the ziggurats themselves, which bore their own names, the summit temple was referred to with the descriptors *gigunû, nuḫar, šaḫūru* (alternatively *šuḫūru*), or simply *bīt ziqrati* ("the ziggurat temple").[71] The reference to the ziggurat temple as a *šaḫūru*, which was also used to refer to the vestibule in the ground-level temples, leaves open the possibility that the summit temple was simply a vestibule, while heaven itself

---

Vollrat Hilprecht, *Die Ausgrabungen der Universität von Pennsylvania am Bêl-Tempel zu Nippur* (Leipzig: Hinrichs, 1903); Heinrich, *Tempel und Heiligtümer*, 101, 147, 158–59 and figs. 233–36.

70. Since no such summit temple has survived and so little has survived from the written record, we can make no firm conclusions. Although certainly possible, Allinger-Csollich's proposal that, like the ziggurat itself, the ziggurat temple was a stepped temple with the sanctuary on its summit ("Ziqqurat") seems slightly less likely since any buildings on the lower levels would have to be small and would thus less likely form part of the main temple at the top.

71. See respectively *CAD* G, 67–70, N/2, 313, Š/1, 108–9 and George, *Cuneiform Royal Inscriptions*, 157. As George suggests, the name of the ziggurat itself may have referred most particularly to its summit temple.

was the sanctuary.[72] Thus, the priest may have waited in the summit temple for an epiphany of the gods in their celestial forms. However, this proposal too has potential shortcomings, namely, that there is some textual evidence that at least some summit temples had a sanctuary or sanctuaries.[73] Likewise, rather than referring to a vestibule, *šaḫūru* in the Esagil tablet seems instead to refer to a rooftop structure or penthouse on the second floor of the summit temple.[74] What little evidence remains suggests that the summit temple resembled the lower temple, albeit on a much smaller scale.[75] Nonetheless, if it was simply a smaller version of the lower sanctuary, one wonders why two were necessary. Although the Esagil tablet refers to a bed and a throne in the summit temple (l. 35), was there a cult image? Was regular divine service or other ritual activity conducted? In the end, while we may suppose that the summit temple resembled the lower temple, it remains a mystery what went on inside it.

## Structural Communication

Reflecting its status as the divine abode, the built environment of the temple communicated its importance and that of its resident. Although the remains of Mesopotamian temple no longer elicit the same visceral response as the temples did in their pristine form, they divulge enough that we can approximate the response it would have evoked while in use. From what we can reconstruct, its structure differed from that of the Egyptian temple. Nonetheless, it likely would have produced a similar emotive response. The imposing buildings with especially prominent portals both in terms of height and decoration, the occasional presence of fierce creatures at the entrances, the massive ziggurats, and the sacred precinct's prominent (and often elevated) position in the cities no doubt inspired awe. In addition, the nondescript "niche and projection" temple architecture (see figs. 3.3 and 3.8) would have appeared to be constantly shifting and shimmering in the

72. Wightman, *Sacred Spaces*, 25.

73. For example, *CAD* N/2, 313 lists a *nuḫar* with 6 sanctuaries (*papāḫāni*), while the Esagil tablet refers to six sanctuaries in the summit temple of Etemenanki (l. 25; for the text, see George, *Babylonian Topographical Texts* (OLA 40; Leuven: Peeters, 1992), 109–19, and for commentary, see ibid., 414–34). In addition, a stele of Nebuchadnezzar II displays a groundplan of what seems to be a summit sanctuary with a groundplan resembling the lower temple, including a central courtyard and various sanctuaries (see esp. George, *Cuneiform Royal Inscriptions*).

74. George, *Topographical Texts*, 433.

75. After George, *Cuneiform Royal Inscriptions*. However, this summit temple lacked a chain of rooms surrounding and protecting the sanctuary as was common in lower temples. Their absence may be attributed to limited space or to the elevated position of the summit temple, which rendered it far removed from polluting influences below.

strong sunlight.[76] As such, constructed temple spaces served to unconsciously and effectively reinforce the entrenched cultural message that they housed the deities and were worthy of the utmost respect.

The individual elements of the sacred precinct divided spaces and offered cues as to the function of the spaces and the appropriate responses to them. Walls and portals, respectively, separated significant spaces and allowed and controlled access to those spaces. The presence of doors at the portals in particular provided a visible and physical barrier between spaces at their thresholds. Portals set on a single axis provided a symmetry befitting the order of the divine realm, while those set off-axis provided an additional layer of shielding, appropriate for protecting the divine realm from unwanted (visual) intrusions.[77] When the doors stood open in the direct-axis temple, the statue would have been an impressive site to behold, indicating that the deity was both tantalizingly close in its lavishly crafted image and beyond the reach of all but the most privileged servants.[78]

As in Egypt, the outer walls marked and indeed created the boundary between the outside and inside worlds, between the temple complex (and in some cases the larger divine estate) and the city around it. The height of these walls relative to the surrounding buildings and their "alternating buttresses and recesses"[79] clearly marked this boundary and the importance of the divine space it protected. The fortress-like portal and its decoration drew onlookers' attention, serving as the face of the sacred sphere and the only means of entering it.[80] Fearsome creatures standing beside the portals protected the temple complex from unwanted influences and highlighted the importance of both the divine abode and its master. Intercessory figures mediated between human and divine, welcoming those worthy of access into the temple complex, the temple core, and potentially into the divine presence itself. While each portal served as a focal point of architectural activity relative to its surrounding walls, there is some evidence that the portals

---

76. With such a flickering structure, exterior decoration was less necessary to evoke an awed response (Seidl, "Bildschmuck an mesopotamischen Tempeln," 1).

77. See, e.g., Margarete van Ess, "Babylonische Tempel zwischen Ur III- und neubabylonischer Zeit: Zu einigen Aspekten ihrer planerischen Gestaltung und religiösen Konzeption," in Kaniuth et al., eds., *Tempel im Alten Orient*, 74, who notes that the precision of temple design and construction stood in stark contrast to that of human houses.

78. Regarding access, see with references Caroline Waerzeggers, "The Babylonian Priesthood in the Long Sixth Century BC," *BICS* 54 (2011): 64–66.

79. Beate Pongratz-Leisten, "Sacred Places: Mesopotamia," in *Religions of the Ancient World: A Guide* (ed. S. I. Johnston; Cambridge, MA: Harvard University Press, 2004), 253.

80. As the temple's most visible areas, portals naturally attracted the most architectural attention in order to highlight the importance of the temple itself and its portal as a liminal space between interior and exterior worlds. Stelae were purposely placed at these boundaries so that those who frequented the temple would notice them.

became increasingly elaborate as one approached the divine presence.[81] Thus, the portals and their adornment highlighted the importance of the areas to which they granted entry and stressed that these areas became progressively more important as one neared the deity.[82]

Once through the initial portal, larger complexes had several auxiliary structures, indicating that, like a palace, the sacred sphere included more than a dwelling. Although open to the sky, the court(s) was often bounded by walls and connected to the core of the temple, such that it was part of the temple complex.[83] However, the presence of an additional wall, gate, and vestibule separating the court from the temple core clearly distinguished between the two zones. Within the sacred precinct, gates and vestibules separated spaces into concentric sections, at the heart of which rested the divine presence. In an especially large complex (e.g., the Esagil at Babylon), portals separated the sacred precinct from the mundane, the walled temple complex from the rest of the sacred precinct, the outer court from the inner court, and the inner court from the temple core.

Such divisions also worked on the vertical plane. Indeed, like its ziggurat, the base of the ground-level Mesopotamian temple complex was not unlike a stepped pyramid upon whose platforms the temple's major sections progressively rested. The sacred precinct was often elevated above the mundane sphere on a platform, while in Neribtum, for example, the primary sanctuary and its inner court stood on higher ground than the rest of the already raised temple complex. In most cases, the cult statue was raised above the rest of the sanctuary, indicating its prime importance (see fig. 3.1).[84] Thus, the relative elevation of a zone in the divine sphere unconsciously communicated to the observer its relative importance.[85] The ziggurat served as a more conspicuous example of the vertical dimension. Each platform climbed progressively skyward with few architectural features to divert the observer's gaze from moving ever upward, until at its highest point, the summit temple stood at what seemed to be the threshold of heaven.[86]

---

81. See, e.g., the temple of Nabu at Dur Sharrukin (Loud and Altman, *Khorsabad,* Part 2, 56–64 and pl. 2). As indicated above, the written record also indicates the increasingly valuable materials used to adorn the temple interiors.

82. The spaces' importance increased because of the increasing seclusion and restricted access of the rooms to which they granted access.

83. For the implications of its structural connection to the temple building, see further ch. 4 under "Structural Communication."

84. The elevation of the cult statue had both a practical and aesthetic function. As today, it was logical to keep valuables elevated both for protection and display.

85. Nonetheless, this progressive architectural privileging was not always obvious, as the elevation of the platform upon which the various sections were built was somewhat muted by the massiveness of the very structures they elevated. In other words, because the temples were so massive, one was less likely to notice the relative elevation of their constituent parts.

86. The ziggurat was especially prominent in the south, where it presumably originated, as

In each temple, the sanctuary rested in the most isolated position, commonly at the furthest point from the outer entrance both horizontally and vertically. In at least one instance (the Kassite Esagil in Babylon), the door to the sanctuary was also covered in fantastical creatures, indicating that the space beyond was special and ruled by a power that ruled over such impressive creatures.[87] In other cases, progression toward the sanctuary was marked by the increasing value of the adornments, such that unadorned (colored) bricks gave way to gold and lapis lazuli in the sanctuary, rendering it "like the interior of the heavens."[88] Progress toward the sanctuary was marked by several major and minor boundaries. In addition to walls and gates, service and mediating spaces also served to surround the sanctuary, further isolating it from the outside world. In fact, in some temples it seems that walls and gates grew thicker as one approached the sanctuary, indicating their relative importance and seclusion from the outside world.[89]

As in a domestic dwelling, access was progressively restricted as one moved from the exterior to the interior,[90] a feature that the architecture was sure to reinforce unconsciously. At the same time, the structured space reinforced the firmly entrenched message that the temple was no ordinary house, thereby reinforcing the belief that its occupant was especially important and its space especially inviolate.

Thus, the temple builders encoded their spatial hierarchy into the structures that shaped sacred space. The structures thereby unconsciously reinforced to the observer the importance of the entire sacred precinct over the rest of the city and the relative importance of its various regions. In fact, these divisions were built into the temple design in such a way that they appeared to be built into the very fabric of creation and therefore beyond question.

---

it towered over the relatively flat terrain around.

87. In other instances, such fantastical creatures flanked the divine throne, inspiring awe and suggesting the deity's potency over such fearsome creatures (e.g., in Assurnasirpal II's description of the temple of Ninurta in Kalhu [Novotny, "Temple Building," 131]).

88. In reference to Tiglath-pileser I's description of the Anu-Adad temple of Assur (Novotny, "Temple Building," 131).

89. See, e.g., the Nabu Temple at Dur Sharrukin (Loud and Altman, *Khorsabad*, Part 2, 64 and pl. 2). See fig. 3.1.

90. See above n. 82. The presence of statues, votives, and altars in the sanctuary indicate the intersection of human and divine spheres, and the architecture reinforced the human privilege and responsibility of such a close encounter.

## Ideology

The Mesopotamians shaped temple space in such a way that it effectively served as the divine abode.[91] As we have seen, they encoded the importance of the temple, its resident, and its spatial hierarchy into the buildings themselves. More than simply communicating the temple's importance, the Mesopotamians also communicated its otherness and some of the nature of this otherness.

In groping for means of representing the divine presence and the building that enclosed and mediated access to it, the Mesopotamians naturally turned to their own culture for analogs. The temple was designed and equipped like a household, requiring a "staff, organization and management."[92] As in a human household, the primary need was food, for which the temple was equipped with a table (altar), kitchens, storing and serving vessels, and servants to prepare and serve the food.[93] However, it was much more than a mere manor house; as the home of the deity, it shared in the numinous.[94] In fact, in some cases, the temple was addressed as if it were alive.[95] In addition, various elements of the temple, including ziggurats, temple doors, door locks, platforms for cult statues, temple pipes, and hybrid guardians, were deified, such that not only the deity but also the elements of its environment were considered divine.[96] The deification of the divine environs likewise enhanced the potency of the deity by suggesting that even the realm in which it dwelt and over which it ruled was in some sense divine.

---

91. As van Ess notes, in comparison with Egypt, we stand only at the beginning of a deeper understanding of the Mesopotamian temple (van Ess, "Babylonische Tempel," 80–81). However, even from such a limited vantage point the view is quite impressive.

92. Jacobsen, *Treasures of Darkness*, 16. Like human royalty, the deities lived with their families and were surrounded by a court of subordinates. Like palaces, their houses were sometimes equipped with thrones, reception rooms, living rooms, bedrooms, clothes, jewelry, vehicles, furniture, and a staff that even included a hairdresser. They were also surrounding by workshops, storage rooms, kitchens, bakeries, breweries, and butchers (Maul, "Das Haus des Götterkönigs," 311).

93. Wiggermann, "Theologies, Priests and Worship," *CANE* 3:1861.

94. It carried both "the awesome aura" (ní) and "awesome nimbus" (me-lám; Jacobsen, *Treasures*, 16).

95. Schaudig ("Restoration of Temples," 141; cf. Ambos, "Building Rituals," 236), e.g., suggests that the temple was understood to be a living being with a name that could "rejoice at its divine owner, convey prayers to him/her, and it could suffer and mourn in times of destruction and desecration."

96. See, e.g., Barbara Nevling Porter, "Blessings from a Crown, Offerings to a Drum: Were there Non-Anthropomorphic Gods in Ancient Mesopotamia?," in *What Is a God? Anthropomorphic and Non-Anthropomorphic Aspects of Deity in Ancient Mesopotamia* (ed. Barbara Nevling Porter; Transactions of the Casco Bay Assyriological Institute 2; Winona Lake, IN: Eisenbrauns, 2009), 156, 165, 168, 171.

As several temple names attest, the Mesopotamian temple served as the link between heaven and earth.[97] As heaven on earth, the welfare of the temple and its resident was deemed absolutely essential for the welfare of the nation and its residents. Indeed in mythology the very purpose of humanity was to serve the gods,[98] relieving the discontented lower gods, in order to ensure "that the [higher] gods led an opulent and worry-free life."[99] Since the temple was the primary locus of this service, the quality of human service determined the quality of divine care, primarily in terms of agricultural fertility and protection.[100] In other words, the welfare of the state depended on the maintenance of the temple.

Since to meet the gods' needs was the primary purpose of the state and the justification for its survival, to do so was an obligation that could not be avoided. Avoidance was akin to high treason; it jeopardized peace, prosperity, and life. It was the cult, supervised by the ruler, that met this obligation. The cult provided the gods with food and shelter or, in cultic terms, with offerings and a temple.[101]

Because the state existed to serve the gods, angering the gods invited disaster, potentially resulting in the divine abandonment of the temple (e.g., the image being destroyed or plundered).[102] Instead of recognizing the superior might of a plundering foe, the military defeat of a nation and the plundering of its temple instead suggested to its inhabitants the resident god's wrath.[103] On the other side of the spectrum, kings attributed their prosperity, especially in warfare, to good relations with the deity.[104] Thus, the king's care of the gods, especially in his upkeep of the temple, was considered primarily responsible for his success in both war and

---

97. For example, Enlil's sacred precinct in Nippur was named Duranki, "the connection (between) heaven and earth."

98. The fullest portrait is found in the Atrahasis Epic. The *Enuma elish* offers a similar description, with the major difference being that Marduk was the one who decided to create instead of his father Enki/Ea (cf. Bottéro, *Religion in Ancient Mesopotamia*, 97–105, 114).

99. Ibid., 114. As the divine representative, it was also the king's primary responsibility to protect the world as it had been ordered by the gods during creation and to restore it to that condition when it deviated from the original ideal (Maul, "Die altorientalische Hauptstadt," 110).

100. See, e.g., Pongratz-Leisten, "Sacred Spaces," 253.

101. Wiggermann, "Theologies, Priests and Worship," 1861.

102. Oppenheim, *Ancient Mesopotamia*, 184; Daniel I. Block, *The Gods of the Nations: Studies in Ancient Near Eastern National Theology* (Grand Rapids, MI: Baker, 2001), 134–35.

103. Alternatively, the conquering army would interpret the victory as reflecting the superiority of their god over that of their foes. For example, the Assyrian conquest portrayed the "abandonment of the enemy by his own gods in submission to the superior might of Assyria's god, Ashur" (Mordecai Cogan, *Imperialism and Religion: Assyria, Judah and Israel in the Eighth and Seventh Centuries B.C.E.* [Missoula, MT: Scholars Press, 1974], 40).

104. The victory texts overflow with such language, as a perusal of the pertinent *ANET* texts reveals.

peace. More expansively, the well-being of this small world—achieved by keeping the gods happy in their temples—was necessary for the well-being of the larger world around it.

To ensure the deity's blessing and thus a successful reign, Mesopotamian kings often devoted their "energy and resources to embellishing the house of the god" with the finest materials available.[105] Nonetheless, with so much at stake, certain conditions must be met to ensure divine satisfaction.

Because they were built of mud-brick, a more perishable substance than the stone of ancient Egypt, Mesopotamian temples were often in need of renovation, so much so that rebuilding rituals are more commonly preserved than rituals for the initial building process.[106] In the course of the renovation process, rather than updating or expanding upon the previous model, builders often sought to rebuild the temples according to the exact original specifications, "not deviating even a finger's width" (*ūban [ana] lā aṣê [u] lā erēbi*) from the original prototype.[107] In turn, the people believed that deviating from this divine prototype invited divine disfavor. Indeed, it was not uncommon to attribute the collapse of a temple to the deity's dissatisfaction with renovations.[108] To ensure accuracy, kings searched the foundations of the dilapidated temple much like modern archaeologists for evidence of the former structure in such forms as inscriptions and clay tablets,[109] in order to restore the temple to its original condition,[110] without deviating "an eyelash" from the original blueprint.[111]

---

105. Margueron, "The Mesopotamian Temple," 169.

106. Ambos, "Building Rituals," 224, with reference to the first millennium.

107. When a new temple was constructed or an ancient model altered, the kings often were careful to indicate that their innovations were made at the divine behest. For example, "when Tukulti-Ninurta I rebuilt temple of Ishtar in Assur according to completely different ground plan, he stressed that the goddess had asked him for this new temple" (Ambos, "Building Rituals," 225; Grayson, *Assyrian Rulers of the Third and Second Millennium BC to 1115 BC* (RIMA 1; Toronto: University of Toronto, 1987), 255–26, A.0.78.11 82–84). The phrase "not deviating even a finger's width" concerning the exactness of temple restoration became especially prominent in the reign of Nabonidus (Hanspeter Schaudig, *Die Inschriften Nabonids von Babylon und Kyros' des Grossen samt den in ihrem Umfeld entstandenen Tendenzschriften: Textausgabe und Grammatik* (AOAT 256; Münster: Ugarit-Verlag, 2001), 688 s.v. *ūbanu*; Schaudig, "The Restoration of Temples in the Neo- and Late-Babylonian Periods: A Royal Prerogative as the Setting for Political Argument," in Boda and Novotny, *From the Foundations to the Crenellations*, 149–50).

108. Ambos, "Building Rituals," 224–26.

109. Maul, "Walking Backwards into the Future," 18–19.

110. Thereby recreating the condition from "the days of eternity" (*ūm sâti*) (Maul, "Die altorientalische Hauptstadt," 112; see further *CAD* S, 118–19)

111. Maul, "Die altorientalische Hauptstadt," 112. Rather than casting them as improvements, innovations instead had to be couched as a return to the pristine beginning.

Such antiquarian tendencies were firmly rooted in the Mesopotamian mentality, in which the way forward was back to the beginning.[112] In Mesopotamia, creation was often viewed as the ideal, as the time when the gods ordered the world and established their terrestrial temples.[113] Since Mesopotamians credited the gods with constructing the original temples, it was especially important that all future temples were modeled after these original prototypes.[114] In fact, rather than merely serving as copies of the original temple, Mesopotamians actually equated subsequent temples with their divine prototypes.[115] In addition to the various other rituals that separated the temple from imperfection and prepared it for the divine presence,[116] the transfer of the first brick (*libittu maḫrītu*) from the damaged temple to the new temple was an especially prominent means of ensuring continuity.[117] By transferring the first brick, theoretically part of the original temple, to the new temple, the Mesopotamians were in effect equating the new temple with the original. The incantation, "When Anu created the heavens," which described how the gods themselves constructed their temples after they had created—that is, ordered—the world, was addressed to the first brick, such that the whole temple was identified with this original temple and thus the work of the gods, not humans.[118]

As in Egypt, the temple was structurally and conceptually connected to the moment of creation, thereby representing the ordering of the world and, in its

---

112. Cf. Maul's provocatively titled 2008 article, "Walking Backwards into the Future." See more generally Hundley, "Way Forward."

113. I am not asserting that the temples were believed to have been created at the same time as the cosmos took shape. Rather, their establishment served as a culmination of the ordering process, representing the ideal state. See generally Karel van der Toorn, "The Iconic Book: Analogies between the Babylonian Cult of Images and the Veneration of the Torah," in *The Image and the Book: Iconic Cults, Aniconism, and the Rise of Book Religion in Israel and the Ancient Near East* (ed. van der Toorn; CBET 21; Leuven: Peeters, 1997), 238. For greater detail, see the works cited above in n. 2.

114. J. J. A. van Dijk, "Inanna raubt den 'grossen Himmel': Ein Mythos," in *Eine Festschrift für Rykle Borger zu seinem 65. Geburtstag am 24. Mai 1994: Tikip Santakki Mala Bašmu* (ed. Stefan Maul; CM 10; Groningen: Styx, 1998), 9–38; Ambos, "Building Rituals," 223–24, 227; Schaudig, "Restoration of Temples," 141.

115. Schaudig, "Restoration of Temples," 141: "In the same way that a statue is not only a mere image but *is* actually the deity after its purification ritual, a temple is not only a mere brickwork structure where the statue is stored but *is* actually identical with the original, primeval and transcendent, sometimes 'heavenly' abode of the deity after its inauguration."

116. See the various contributions in Boda and Novotny, *From the Foundations to the Crenellations.*

117. For further information on the first brick, see Ellis, *Foundation Deposits*, 26–29; Ambos, *Mesopotamische Baurituale aus dem 1. Jahrtausend v. Chr.* (Dresden: Islet, 2004), 66–67, 77–78, 178–81; idem, "Building Rituals," 227–28.

118. See Ambos, "Building Rituals," 227–28.

contemporary context, connoting an ordered world that functioned as originally intended. Another prominent means of solidifying the connection with creation was the du$_6$-kù, ("pure hill" or "sacred hill"), a pedestal lined with clay bricks, most often situated in the forecourt or vestibule. This pedestal represented the sacred mound upon which creation emerged from the primeval waters.[119] In addition, the gods who were present at creation, and indeed were the powers behind it, were the only remaining soluble link to creation. Thus, the divine presence in the temple and the human interaction with that presence was the primary means of maintaining the connection to creation.

Thus, the temple was of supreme importance; it connected the modern world to its idyllic beginning, the human world to the divine, heaven to earth, thereby making connections that were otherwise unavailable. This ideal world of the gods in miniature, which preserved and mirrored creation, had to be preserved at all costs in order to preserve the all-important link with creation and to bring prosperity to the land that surrounded it and existed to maintain it.

In addition to serving as an ideal world bound to creation, temples also served as cosmic centers. Major cities were considered to be situated at the center of the world. By contrast, the "periphery" was the realm of chaos and inimical to the gods and the state.[120] Temples in particular were cosmic centers, the hearts of the ordered world, where the gods and their representative the king ruled.[121]

As the center of the "king of the gods," the temple of Enlil in Nippur was thus the original *axis mundi*, the center of the world both vertically and horizontally.[122] On the horizontal plane, as the home of the king of the gods, Enlil's temple was the epicenter of the ordered world. Vertically, it united heaven, earth, and the realms under the earth. Nippur's role as the navel of the world was reflected in the

---

119. Maul, "Die altorientalische Hauptstadt," 116. In addition to being the primeval mound, the "pure hill" was also the cosmic seat of the king of the gods in the divine assembly, from which destinies were determined (George, *House Most High*, 77). See also Edzard, "Deep-Rooted Skyscrapers and Bricks: Ancient Mesopotamian Architecture and Its Imagery," in *Figurative Language in the Ancient Near East* [ed. M. Mindlin et al.; London: School of Oriental and African Studies, 1987), 13–24; George, *Topographical Texts*, 286–91; Pongratz-Leisten, Ina šulmi īrub: *Die kulttopographische und ideologische Programmatik der* akītu-*Prozession in Babylonien und Assyrien im I. Jahrtausend v. Chr.* (BaF 16; Mainz am Rhein: von Zabern, 1994), 54–65; Hruška, "Zum 'Heiligen Hügel' in der altmesopotamischen Religion," *WZKM* 86 (1996): 161–75. Especially associated with Nippur and Enlil, this pedestal was also erected in various other Mesopotamian temples.

120. Wiggermann, "Theologies, Priests and Worship," 1996; see further idem, "Scenes from the Shadow Side," in *Mesopotamian Poetic Language: Sumerian and Akkadian* (ed. M. E. Vogelzang and H. L. J. Vanstiphout; CM 6; Groningen: Styx, 1996), 207–20.

121. See, e.g., the Babylonian map of the world (Wayne Horowitz, "The Babylonian Map of the World," *Iraq* 50 [1988]: 147–65).

122. Maul, "Die altorientalische Hauptstadt," 118–19.

name of its ziggurat, Duranki ("the mountain" or "connection between heaven and earth").[123]

With the ascendancy of Babylon, its city god Marduk rose to prominence, causing the cosmic axis to shift from Nippur to Babylon. To be the king of the gods and for Babylon to be the center of the world, Marduk's temple needed to be the cosmic axis. Thus, Babylonians set to the task of promoting this shift.[124] The Code of Hammurabi states simply that Anu, the largely absent god of the upper heavens, and Enlil passed the Enlil-ship—that is, the power and authority of Enlil—to Marduk.[125] Likewise, according to the *Enuma elish*, the gods constructed the Esagil in Babylon for Marduk below Anu's heavenly palace[126] and above the *Apsû*, the subterranean waters, where Ea built his home.[127] Indeed, the terrestrial Esagil was conceived of as a replica of both celestial and underworld palaces,[128] designed to connect the three divine palaces and their divine realms vertically.[129] This connection, and the permanence of the three realms, was established by fastening the tail of Tiamat, the monster whom Marduk defeated to become king of the gods, to

123. George, *House Most High*, 80. Maul, "Die altorientalische Hauptstadt," 118.

124. The Babylonians defended this monumental shift in the *Enuma elish*. The Mesopotamian theistic worldview also supported this shift, as the success of their king demonstrated divine favor and the conquest of other cities indicated that the gods of these cities recognized the rule of Marduk (Maul, "Die altorientalische Hauptstadt," 119).

125. CH I, 11–12. Regarding the phenomenon of Enlil-ship being borne by deities other than Enlil, see Porter, "The Anxiety of Multiplicity: Concepts of the Divine in Ancient Assyria," in *One God or Many? Concepts of Divinity in the Ancient World* (ed. Barbara Nevling Porter; Transactions of the Casco Bay Assyriological Institute 2; Maine: Casco Bay Assyriological Institute, 2000), 245–46.

126. *Enuma elish* V 119–22. In addition, the trapezoidal form of the inner court may reflect the constellation Pegasus, thus further binding the Esagil with the heavenly palace (Maul, "Altorientalische Schöpfungsmythen," 47). For archaeological support for this and other cosmological claims, see van Ess, "Babylonische Tempel," esp. 77–81.

127. *Enuma elish* I 71.

128. Lambert, "Himmel," *RlA* 4 (1972–1975): 410–12; Alasdair Livingstone, *Mystical and Mythological Explanatory Works of Assyrian and Babylonian Scholars* (Oxford: Oxford University Press, 1986), 79–82; Maul, "Die altorientalische Hauptstadt," 114–15; idem, "Altorientalische Schöpfungsmythen," 46–47.

129. Maul, "Die altorientalische Hauptstadt," 115. More expansively, in first-millennium Babylonia, the world was divided into six vertically oriented spheres: 1) the upper heaven, where Anu dwelt; 2) the middle heaven, the home of Enlil and the Igigi-gods; 3) the lower heaven, the realm of the stars; 4) the human plane; 5) the middle earth, the watery Apsu ruled by the god Ea; and 6) the underworld, where the Anunnaki-gods reigned and the dead dwelt (Horowitz, *Cosmic Geography*; Pongratz-Leisten, "Mental Map und Weltbild," in *Das biblische Weltbild und seine altorientalischen Kontexte* [ed. B. Janowski and B. Ego; FAT 32; Tübingen: Mohr Siebeck, 2001], 261–80).

the vertical world axis *Durmaḫ*. It was memorialized in the name of the ziggurat, Etemenanki, "house foundation of heaven and earth."[130]

Like Babylonia, Assyria too laid claim to the cosmic axis.[131] When Shamshi-Adad I of Assur rose to power, his city god, Assur, began to be worshiped in the form of Enlil, making the king "the representative of Enlil" and thus ruler of the world. To cement this connection and to ensure that Assur was understood as the cosmic axis of the world, the city adopted from Nippur the names of its temples and their individual elements. The name of Assur's ziggurat further solidified this connection; Earattakisarra ("house, mountain of the entire world")[132] emphasized that the "connection between heaven and earth" (Duranki)—the name given to the ziggurat in Nippur—had shifted to Assur. From the second millenium until the end of their respective existences, such claims remained central to Babylonian and Assyrian identities and their struggle for supremacy over Mesopotamia.[133]

As empires with aspirations of world dominion, Babylonia and Assyria needed their primary temples to be *axes mundi*, and thus in multiple and different ways tried to establish Babylon and Assur respectively as the legitimate heirs of Nippur. Once these axes were established inside national borders, they were never successfully relocated.[134] Whereas other deities may have had many major sanctuaries in many different locales, the kings of the gods and guardians of the cosmic axis

---

130. Maul, "Die altorientalische Hauptstadt," 115; idem, "Altorientalische Schöpfungsmythen," 46; see *Enuma elish* V 59ff. Here as elsewhere the writers of *Enuma elish* seem to be building on earlier precedents (see generally Ambos, *Mesopotamische Baurituale*). For example, Löhnert suggests that *"Schwanz-Haupt"* lies behind the etymology of the Sumerian designation for the ascending staircase of the ziggurat, kúg-saĝ/kun$_8$-saĝ (Anne Löhnert, *"Wie die Sonne tritt heraus!" Eine Klage zum Auszug Enlils mit einer Untersuchung zu Komposition und Tradition sumerischer Klagelieder in altbabylonischer Zeit* [AOAT 365; Münster: Ugarit-Verlag, 2009], 218).

131. In rising to prominence, both Marduk and Assur also took on the attributes of other deities, thereby rising from obscure beginnings to become the most powerful gods in Babylonia and Assyria. For example, Assur assumed aspects of Enlil, Marduk, Ea, Šamaš, Ninurta and/or Adad (see esp. Angelika Berlejung, "Die Reduktion von Komplexität: Das theologische Profil einer Gottheit und seine Umsetzung in der Ikonographie am Bespiel des Gottes Aššur im Assyrien des 1. Jt. v. Chr.," in *Die Welt der Götterbilder* [ed. B. Groneberg and H. Spieckermann; BZAW 376; Berlin: de Gruyter, 2007], 9–56).

132. George, *House Most High*, 69.

133. Capturing the cult statue of the rival god is an interesting example of this struggle. By abducting the image of Marduk, thereby depriving Babylon of its god in terrestrial form and assimilating Babylonian cult-tradition into the Assyrian cult, Tukulti-Ninurta I of Assyria attempted to break Babylon's axis-claim and the dominion attached to it (Maul, "Die altorientalische Hauptstadt," 122). Sennacherib's destruction of Esagil and its ziggurat pursued similar ends, yet with equally unsuccessful results (Maul, "Das Haus des Götterkönigs," 318–19).

134. In addition, in contrast to other, especially Neo-Assyrian temples, the palace and

could have only one immovable cult center.[135] While kings had the power to and often did argue that their nation's primary deity was supreme and the keeper of the *axis mundi*, they could not relocate the deity or its axis.

In fact, the primary exception proved the rule. Tukulti-Ninurta I's attempt to shift both his residence and Assur's domain to the newly built Kar Tukulti-Ninurta can only be viewed as a colossal failure. Assur, the god of the mountain peak of Assur, was so intimately allied to that particular physical location that neither he nor the cosmic axis his home represented could be safely moved. As with Akhenaten in Egypt, after the death of Tukulti-Ninurta, his city and its temple were eventually abandoned, sending his successors a powerful message. Subsequent monarchs responded appropriately by shifting their residences without attempting to bring Assur with them. Even after the city lost political prominence, Assur and his sanctuary remained the inviolate religious heart of Assyria.[136]

Although these major religious centers connected the heavens and the earth, humanity for the most part had no access to heaven, and the gods rarely appeared to humans on earth.[137] Both the ground-level and ziggurat temples served to close this gap between heaven and earth in different ways. The lower temples provided a conducive environment for the deity to bring heaven to earth in the form of a cult image (see part 2). By contrast, the temple above brought earth to heaven, or at least as close to heaven as possible.[138] The ziggurat itself was a stairway toward

---

the sacred sphere of the major deity were separated in Nippur, Babylon, and Assyria, and indeed the temple and the ziggurat rested some distance from each other.

135. In fact, in Neo-Assyrian times, there is no evidence of shrines of Assur outside of the city of Assur (Steven W. Holloway, *Aššur is King! Aššur is King! Religion in the Exercise of Power in the Neo-Assyrian Empire* [Leiden: Brill, 2002], 65–68, 160–93; Eva Cancik-Kirschbaum, *Die Assyrer: Geschichte, Gesellschaft, Kultur* [Munich: Beck, 2003], 53). Such, however, is not the case for Marduk, whose presence was felt throughout the Mesopotamian world. This could have been one reason for the indomitable potency of Marduk that Assyrian hegemony seemed unable to undermine (Maul, "Das Haus des Götterkönigs," 318–19).

136. Maul, "Die altorientalische Hauptstadt," 122. Likewise, as long as it remained the cultic center of the world, Nippur had to be similarly preserved even though it was never a major seat of royal power.

137. Etana and Adapa are the most notable exceptions of human ascension to heaven (Horowitz, *Cosmic Geography*, 319–20); see further the survey in Esther J. Hamori, *"When Gods Were Men": The Embodied God in Biblical and Near Eastern Literature* (BZAW 384; Berlin: de Gruyter, 2008), 128–44. The gods did, however, appear in or as the elements of nature and in signs left behind for humans to interpret (e.g., in sheep entrails) (see the comprehensive summary of Maul, "Omina und Orakel. A. Mesopotamien," *RlA* 10 [2005]: 45–88).

138. Strictly speaking, like mountains, the ziggurat was still part of the earthly plane and, thus, not in heaven (Horowitz, *Cosmic Geography*, 319–20). However, it was as close to heaven as humanity could reach.

heaven, while perhaps its sanctuary remained even more mysterious than the lower sanctuary, itself referred to as the "secret house."[139]

The blending of human and divine worlds that resulted was a complicated admixture, in some ways unnatural to both realms. The lower temple and its cult image were situated on earth and crafted from terrestrial elements, yet were inhabited by the celestial divine presence. Despite their best efforts, Mesopotamians could only distance the human connection, not dissolve it. Because of its location, building materials, and servants, earth continually encroached upon "heaven on earth," human imperfection encroached upon the perfect divine world of the temple. Although in residence as a semipermanent theophany, the deity was sequestered in the deepest recesses of the temple to secure this unnatural incursion of heaven onto earth. Through this unnatural symbiosis, Mesopotamians were able to bring the presence and blessing of the gods into the human sphere, to influence the gods with their service and thus gain some measure of control over their lives and cosmic events, both of which were governed by deities.

The ziggurat and its temple served as a sanctioned intrusion of earth into heaven, a human-made bridge between heaven and earth. Although built of terrestrial materials, the ziggurat provided a platform for the deity to intersect with humanity further from the human environment and as close to its own environment as possible. Unfortunately, in the summit temple, we have minimal evidence of what form the deity took, if any, or how the priest(s) may have interacted with it. Perhaps, while the lower temple provided regulated access to the divine, contact in the summit temple was more ephemeral even to the Mesopotamian people.

---

139. Jacobsen, *Treasures of Darkness*, 16.

# CHAPTER 4

# HITTITE TEMPLES

HITTITE TEMPLES ARE DIFFICULT TO IDENTIFY, let alone analyze. Hittite records, profuse in so many ways, provide few details regarding the type and design of temple buildings.[1] Instead, we are left with the archaeological remains,[2] which are less extensive than their Egyptian and Mesopotamian counterparts and limited primarily to the temples in the Hittite capital, Hattusa. Little remains of Hittite buildings beyond the foundations, while few religious objects have been found in situ.[3] In turn, archaeologists have identified temples primarily on the basis of common structural elements.[4] Likewise, given the state of preservation, they can only make limited comments about these buildings. Nonetheless, with the archaeological record and some textual clues, we can begin to meaningfully discuss the Hittite temples in their ancient Near Eastern context.

## STRUCTURE

Of the various cultic locations identified between 1800–1200 BCE, we will focus on "large temple complexes with many rooms, representing an individual architectural style"[5] and smaller temples with many shared elements that seem to be constructed to fit into their surroundings rather than being isolated from them.[6] These temple types appear to have been the primary official temples with a perma-

---

1. Kurt Bittel, "Hittite Temples and High Places in Anatolia and North Syria," in *Temples and High Places in Biblical Times* (ed. A. Biran; Jerusalem: The Nelson Glueck School of Biblical Archaeology of Hebrew Union College-Jewish Institute of Religion, 1981), 63.

2. Ibid.

3. See, e.g., Gary Beckman, "Sacred Times, Sacred Places: Anatolia," in Johnston, ed., *Religions of the Ancient World*, 261.

4. Regarding the difficulty of differentiating between temples and palaces, see, e.g., Wulf Schirmer, "Stadt, Palast, Tempel: Charakteristika hethitischer Architektur im 2. und 1. Jahrtausend v. Chr.," in *Die Hethiter und ihr Reich: Das Volk der tausend Götter: Kunst- und Ausstellungshalle der Bundesrepublik Deutschland (Bonn 2002)* (ed. Tahsin Özgüç; Darmstadt: Wissenschaftliche Buchgesellschaft, 2002), 204–17.

5. Bittel, "Hittite Temples and High Places," 65.

6. See, e.g., the four types of cultic locations identified by Bittel, "Hittite Temples and High Places," 65.

nent priesthood and regular service. We will focus more specifically on the sacred precincts at the capital of Hattusa (modern Boğazköy, Turkey) since these have received the most archaeological attention.[7] Although every sizable town likely had at least one temple,[8] few have been properly excavated. With more than thirty excavated temples, Hattusa is the primary exception to this trend and provides the bulk of our data.[9] Recent excavations at Sarissa (modern Kuşaklı) have unearthed

---

7. The Hittite city of Hattusa was subdivided into two sections by an interior wall, the first mostly on higher ground. Thus, the sections are conveninetly labeled the Upper City and the Lower City. The major temple (temple 1) and the royal palace were situated in the Lower City, while the Upper City had many more temples. Regarding the temples, see further Peter J. Neve, "Boğazköy-Ḫattuša: New Results of the Excavations in the Upper City," *Anatolica* 16 (1989): 7–20; idem, "Hattusha, City of Gods and Temples: Results of the Excavations in the Upper City," *Proceedings of the British Academy* (1991 Lectures and Memoirs) 80 (1993): 105–32; idem, *Ḫattuša-Stadt der Götter und Tempel: Neue Ausgrabungen in der Hauptstadt der Hethiter* (2nd ed.; Mainz am Rheim: von Zabern, 1996); idem, "Der Große Tempel (Tempel 1) in Boğazköy-Ḫattuša," *Nürnberger Blätter zur Archäologie* 12 (1996): 41–62; idem, Die Oberstadt von Ḫattuša: Die Bauwerke II: Die Bastion des Sphinxtores und die Tempelviertel am Königs- und Löwentor (Boğazköy-Ḫattuša: Ergebnisse der Ausgrabungen 23; Mainz: von Zabern, 2001); idem, "The Great Temple in Boğazköy-Ḫattuša." Pages 77–97 in *Across the Anatolian Plateau: Readings in the Archaeology of Ancient Turkey* (ed. D. Hopkins; Annual of ASOR 57; Boston: ASOR, 2002), 77–97; Itamar Singer, "A City of Many Temples: Ḫattuša, Capital of the Hittites," in *Sacred Space: Shrine, City, Land: Proceedings of the International Conference in Memory of Joshua Prawer* (ed. B. Z. Kedar and R. J. Z. Werblowsky; Basingstoke: Macmillan, 1998), 32–44; Jürgen Seeher, *Hattuscha-Führer: Ein Tag in der hethitischen Hauptstadt* (3rd ed.; Istanbul: Ege, 2006); idem, "Hattusa - Tuthalija-Stadt? Argumente für eine Revision der Chronologie der hethitischen Hauptstadt," in *The Life and Times of Hattusili III and Tuthaliya IV: Proceedings of a Symposium Held in Honour of J. de Roos, 12–13 December 2003, Leiden* (ed. Th. P. J. van den Hout, Leiden: Brill, 2006), 131–46; idem, "Chronology in Hattusa: New Approaches to an Old Problem," in *Strukturierung & Datierung in der hethitischen Archäologie: Voraussetzungen - Probleme - Neue Ansätze: Internationaler Workshop Istanbul, 16.–27. November 2004* (ed. D. P. Mielke, U.-D. Schoop and J. Seeher; BYZAS 4; Istanbul: Ege, 2006), 197–214; idem, *Die Lehmziegel-Stadtmauer von Hattusa: Bericht über eine Rekonstruktion* (Istanbul: Ege, 2007); idem, "Die Techniken der Steinbearbeitung in der hethitischen Architektur des 2. Jahrtausends v. Chr.," in *Bautechnik im antiken und vorantiken Kleinasien. Internationale Konferenz vom 13.–16. Juni 2007, DAI Istanbul* (ed. M. Bachmann; BYZAS 9; Istanbul: Ege, 2009), 119–56; Andreas Schachner, *Hattuscha: Auf der Suche nach dem sagenhaften Großreich der Hethiter* (Munich: Beck, 2011).

8. Billie Jean Collins, *The Hittites and Their World* (SBL Archaeology and Biblical Studies 7; Atlanta: SBL, 2007), 160; cf. Hans G. Güterbock, "The Hittite Temple According to Written Sources," in *Perspectives on Hittite Civilization: Select Writings of Hans G. Güterbock* (ed. H. A. Hoffner, Jr.; Anatolian Studies 26; Chicago: The Oriental Institute of the University of Chicago, 1997), 82, for some qualifications.

9. See, e.g., Singer, "A City of Many Temples," 33.

two additional temples, one built before most in Hattusa and the other seemingly contemporaneous with the Upper City temples.[10]

Though limited, all the excavated structures share a common architectural style (see figs. 4.1 and 4.2).[11] Whether the centerpiece of a religious quarter or situated cheek-by-jowl with adjacent structures, each temple featured a primary gateway, leading to a large enclosed courtyard open to the sky, usually with pillared halls on one or two sides (often before the sanctuary).[12] The sequence began with a gate structure. The entrance, itself often consisting of a symmetrical double-leafed door adjoined on either side by small guard rooms, always entered into the court. The court was surrounded by various rooms, most of indeterminate function.[13] Rather than immediately preceding the temple interior as in Egypt, the court served as the central element around which the various flat-roofed rooms were situated.[14] Located along the outer wall, the primary sanctuary appeared either at the opposite end of the court, farthest from the entryway as was common in

---

10. Regarding Kuşaklı and its temples, see Andreas Müller-Karpe, "Untersuchungen in Kuşaklı 1992–1994," *MDOG* 127 (1995): 5–36; idem, "Untersuchungen in Kuşaklı 1995," *MDOG* 128 (1996): 69–94; idem, "Untersuchungen in Kuşaklı 1992–1996," *MDOG* 129 (1997): 103–42; idem, "Untersuchungen in Kuşaklı 1997," *MDOG* 130 (1998): 93–172; idem, "Untersuchungen in Kuşaklı 1998," *MDOG* 131 (1999): 57–113; "Untersuchungen in Kuşaklı 1999," *MDOG* 132 (2000): 311–53; idem, "Untersuchungen in Kuşaklı 2000," *MDOG* 133 (2001): 225–50; idem, "Untersuchungen in Kuşaklı 2001," *MDOG* 134 (2002): 331–51; idem, "Untersuchungen in Kuşaklı 2002," *MDOG* 136 (2004): 103–35; idem, "Untersuchungen in Kuşaklı 2004," *MDOG* 137 (2005): 137–72; idem, "Untersuchungen in Kuşaklı 2004 and 2005," *MDOG* 138 (2006): 15–42; idem, "Ein Großbau in der hethitischen Stadtruine Kuşaklı: Tempel des Wettergottes von Sarissa? Alter Orient aktuell " 1 (2000): 19–22; idem, "Kuşaklı-Sarissa: A Hittite Town in the 'Upper Land'" in *Recent Developments in Hittite Archaeology and History: Papers in Memory of Hans G. Güterbock* (ed. K. A. Yener and H. A. Hoffner Jr.; Winona Lake, IN: Eisenbrauns, 2002), 145–55; idem, "Kuşaklı-Sarissa: Kultort im oberen Land," in *Die Hethiter*, 176–89; Michael Zick, "Sarissa - die Heimat des Wettergottes," *Bild der Wissenschaft* 6 (2000): 34–38; Wightman, *Sacred Spaces*, 228, 231. Later Syro-Hittite evidence, most prominently regarding the temples of 'Ain Dara and Tell Tayinat, will be considered in the Syro-Palestine section.

11. See, e.g., Neve, "Hattusha, City of Gods and Temples," 109: "all temples [in Hattusa] were designed and built according to an almost uniform plan."

12. Bittel, "Hittite Temples and High Places," 68; Neve, "Hattusha, City of Gods and Temples," 109; Charles A. Burney, *Historical Dictionary of the Hittites* (Oxford: Scarecrow Press, 2004), 277; Beckman, "Sacred Times, Sacred Places," 261; Wightman, *Sacred Spaces*, 226.

13. Müller-Karpe, "Zu einigen archäologischen sowie archäoastronomischen Aspekten hethitischer Sakralbauten," in Kaniuth et al., eds., *Tempel im alten Orient*, 337–38. The entranceway could be expanded by doubling or even tripling the gates and the flanking guard rooms (ibid., 337). See fig. 4.3 for a double gateway.

14. Ibid.

Temple 3

Temple 6

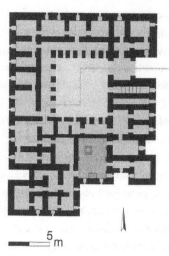

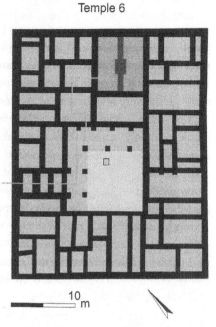

5
m

HATTUSHA, UPPER CITY TEMPLES

10
m

Fig. 4.1. Temples 3 and 6, each of which comprised a single architectural unit with an emphatically indirect axis to the sanctuary, which was located adjacent to the entrance of the court along the outer wall. From Wightman, *Sacred Spaces*, fig. 4.10.

Egypt and Mesopotamia (e.g., temples 1, 4, and 5; see fig. 4.2),[15] or adjacent to the entryway, forcing a right-angled turn (e.g., temples 3 and 6, as well as the primary temple at Sarissa; see figs. 4.1 and 4.3).[16] When rectangular in shape, the shorter side of the sanctuary was always located along the outer wall, while the cult image was most often located toward the back of the sanctuary near the outer wall.[17] Between the sanctuary and the court stood one or more chambers, conveniently termed vestibules or tertiary spaces.[18] As in Mesopotamia, most temples were fully

15. Temple 1 is distinct in that it has two sanctuaries, presumably for the Weather God and Sun Goddess.

16. Wightman, *Sacred Spaces*, 226. As a point of clarification, adjacent here does not mean right next to the entrance, but rather distinctly off-axis, usually along one of the sides of the temple in an especially isolated location . Thus, rather than being located on a direct line from the entrance at the back of the structure, the sanctuary could be located at the far right or far left of the temple.

17. Schachner, *Hattuscha*, 177.

18. Wightman, *Sacred Spaces*, 226; Müller-Karpe, "Aspekte hethitischer Sakralbauten," 337.

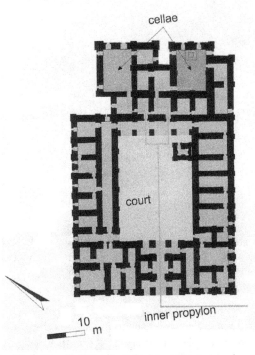

Fig. 4.2. The Great Temple (Temple 1) had two sanctuaries located at the furthest points from the temple entrance, which could only be accessed through a series of twists and turns. From Wightman, *Sacred Spaces*, fig. 4.8.

integrated—that is, all of the various rooms and even the court itself formed part of a single, walled architectural unit. The court, support chambers, and primary chambers also were located within a roughly square or rectangular superstructure (e.g., Temple 6 and the primary temple at Sarissa).[19] Nonetheless, although closer to Mesopotamian architecture in that the court was often integrated into the temple structure, the layout of Hittite temples remained distinct. While in Mesopotamia the court was often surrounded by auxiliary rooms, the temple core including the principle sanctuary predominantly lay behind it, usually on a more or less straight line from the entrance. In contrast, in Hatti the sanctuary often lay significantly off-axis, at times at a ninety degree angle along one of the temple's short sides, and was accessed through various twists and turns (figs. 4.1, 4.2, and 4.3).

They are labeled "vestibules" because of their location between the court and the sanctuary and because their m1ore immediate functions remain unknown.

19. Burney, *Historical Dictionary*, 277; Wightman, *Sacred Spaces*, 226–28.

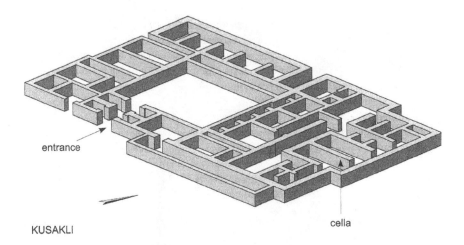

entrance

cella

KUSAKLI

Fig. 4.3. One of the excavated Kuşaklı (ancient Sarissa) temples, partially reconstructed, with the sanctuary at a right angle from the entrance to the court, which was accessed by following a circuitous path. From Wightman, *Sacred Spaces*, fig.4.11.

Various auxiliary structures also have been found around the primary temple complex. Temple 1, the main temple at Hattusa located in the Lower City, resembled a fortress,[20] situated within a substantial walled compound. Multiple large rooms surrounded the temple and the presence of large storage jars and cuneiform tablets suggests that many were used to store food and archives. In the southern section of the precinct, situated across the paved street, various rooms—which may have been servants' quarters, secondary shrines, and workrooms—filled out the temple quarter (see fig. 4.4).[21] Although none of the other excavated temples in the Upper City had so extensive a network of supporting structures, various annex buildings have been unearthed in the vicinity of these temples.[22]

### Location, Decoration, Furnishings, and Elevation

Like their Egyptian and Mesopotamian counterparts, Hittite temples tended to be larger than the surrounding structures. Although not as prominent as in Egypt and Mesopotamia, elevation was a factor in Hittite temple design, especially of the larger sanctuaries. For example, the temenos of Temple 1 was situated in a

---

20. Henri Frankfort, *The Art and Architecture of the Ancient Orient* (Middlesex: Penguin Books, 1977), 217. See further Neve, "Boğazköy-Ḫattuša"; idem, "Great Temple."

21. Cf. Burney, *Historical Dictionary*, 274; Wightman, *Sacred Spaces*, 224; for a diagram, see Schachner 185, abb. 85.

22. Singer, "Ḫattuša," 39.

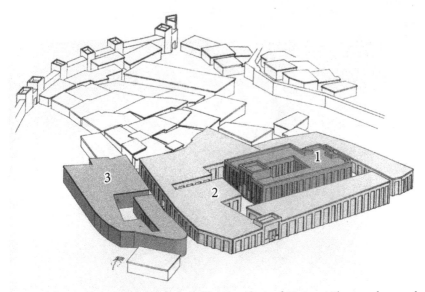

Fig. 4.4. Reconstruction of the fortress-like Temple 1 of Hattusa. The temple complex (1) was situated in the Lower City within a substantial, elevated walled compound surrounded by various storage magazines (2). In the southern section of the precinct, situated across the paved street, multiple rooms (3) filled out the temple quarter. Courtesy of the Bogazköy-Archive, Deutsches Archäologisches Institut.

prominent position, on an artificial terrace, such that it towered over its surroundings, while the primary gateway to Temple 5 was accessed via a staircase.[23] The sanctuary of Temple 1 was also elevated above the surrounding temple space.[24] In addition to building upward, Hittite temples also featured subterranean levels, especially where space was limited. For example, basements beneath the sanctuaries and the auxiliary rooms may have housed treasuries and archives.[25] Furthermore, temples were often constructed on a slope, in which case the sanctuary always lay toward the base of the hill, under which basements were erected to ensure the temple's roughly uniform height. Hittite architects thereby maximized sanctuary space.[26]

As in much of the ancient Near East, preserved temple decoration is minimal.[27] There is some evidence for alternating niches and projections in the temple

23. Burney, *Historical Dictionary*, 273; Wightman, *Sacred Spaces*, 221, 225.

24. Schachner, *Hattuscha*, 185.

25. Burney, *Historical Dictionary*, 277; Wightman, *Sacred Spaces*, 227.

26. Schachner, *Hattuscha*, 177.

27. This is not to say that Hittite temples were minimally decorated, only that we know

Fig. 4.5. Lion head found in Temple 2 (height 45 cm [18"]). Courtesy of the Bogazköy-Archive, Deutsches Archäologisches Institut.

façades as in Mesopotamia.[28] Regarding the architectural details, temples 2 and 3 in Hattusa provide the bulk of the remaining decoration in the form of low-relief lions and sphinxes of greenish stone resembling granite, presumably located at the portals (fig. 4.5).[29] The remains of wall paintings have also been found in Temple 9.[30] Unlike in Egypt and Mesopotamia, the preserved Hittite sculptures were not freestanding; rather, they were joined intimately to the structure itself (fig. 4.6).[31] In Temple 3, for example, columns were placed on the backs of lions.[32]

---

little of their decor (cf. Schachner, *Hattuscha*, 188). As in Mesopotamia, "other forms of decoration almost certainly adorned these temples" (Burney, *Historical Dictionary*, 277), especially when compared with the abundant decoration in the rock sanctuary at Yazılıkaya (see figs. 10.3 and 10.5). Yazılıkaya stands outside our purview because it is unlikely that it held regular cultic service and had its own regular priesthood. Nevertheless, despite these differences, the Yazılıkaya temple had a similar structure to the ones under investigation (Schachner, *Hattuscha*, 98 abb. 39, 177).

28. Müller-Karpe, "Aspekte hethitischer Sakralbauten," 340.

29. Neve, "Hattusha, City of Gods and Temples," 118; Burney, *Historical Dictionary*, 277; Wightman, *Sacred Spaces*, 226; Schachner, *Hattuscha*, 190.

30. Schachner, *Hattuscha*, 190.

31. Frankfort, *Art and Architecture*, 221.

32. Ibid., 220.

Fig. 4.6. Sphinx gate at Alaca Höyük with the sculptures built into the gate structure. Photo courtesy of Billie Jean Collins.

Another element of adornment, shallow pilasters (*šarḫulli*), served as "a defining characteristic of Hittite sanctuaries."[33] Color also seems to have been used to distinguish temple zones. For example, in Temple 1, the large socles or foundation stones of the sanctuary and a small separate building in the court were constructed of darker greenish stone not found in Hattusa itself, as were the lions and sphinxes found in other temples, contrasting with the white limestone walls of the rest of the buildings.[34] Once again, the textual record presents a more lavish portrait of the temples. The cult statue was crafted of the finest materials, including silver, gold, and semi-precious stones.[35] Other texts report that elements of the temple

---

33. Beckman, "Sacred Times, Sacred Places," 261. Pilasters are slightly projecting columns built into the face of a wall.

34. Singer, "A City of Many Temples," 34; Wightman, *Sacred Spaces*, 221; Schachner, *Hattuscha*, 183. The pilasters may also have been decorated with colored panels (Burney, *Historical Dictionary*, 275).

35. See briefly the description of the statue for the Deity of the Night (for a convenient translation, see, e.g., Beckman, "Temple Building Among the Hittites," in Boda and Novotny, eds., *Foundations to the Crenellations*, text 6, 80–85, esp. 81 §§2–4); see ch. 10 for further analysis.

itself, especially its foundations, contained similar elements (e.g., silver, gold, and lapis lazuli).[36]

Pedestals in the sanctuaries, upon which the divine statues presumably stood, and basins for ablutions and perhaps also for libations (e.g., inside the temenos gate and in the court of Temple 1 and in the court of Temple 5)[37] have also been preserved. Written sources indicate that other more portable furnishings were present, at least in some cases, such as a throne, an offering table, cult utensils, a brazier, and a cult statue.[38] There is also evidence for additional sacred vessels either in the sanctuary or auxiliary rooms: spears, bags, axes, bows and arrows, quivers, clothes, musical instruments, and vases.[39]

The evidence is mixed regarding the temples' proximity to the palace. On the one hand, none of the preserved temples in Hattusa appear near a palace, with the possible exception of Temple 5, whose western side may have been a palace of sorts integrated into the temple proper.[40] Temple 1, for example, occupies its own significant space and is located some distance away from the primary palace. On the other hand, written records often mention a *halentuwa* house, translated as "palace," in connection with major Hittite temples.[41] Perhaps, since overseeing the cult was one of the kings' primary responsibilities, royal structures may have been attached or adjacent to major temples to facilitate this function. However, the kings' primary administrative center and residence may have been located elsewhere.

Finally, we must comment on the most enigmatic element of Hittite sacred architecture, windows in the sanctuary, and the possibility of viewing the cult image.[42] Whereas Egyptian and Mesopotamian sanctuaries were located in the dark heart of the sacred complex with no contact with the outside world, some Hittite sanctuaries had large windows, admitting the light, noise, and aromas of the human world. It would seem then that the cult image was visible to passersby.

---

36. E.g., *CTH* 413; Nilüfer Boysan-Dietrich, *Das hethitische Lehmhaus aus der Sicht der Keilschriftquellen* (Heidelberg: Winter, 1987), 43–60; see Beckman, "Temple Building," text 7, 85–87, esp. §9.

37. Wightman, *Sacred Spaces*, 221, 226.

38. Beckman, "Sacred Times, Sacred Places," 261; see further Güterbock, "Hittite Temple."

39. Schachner, *Hattuscha*, 190.

40. Neve, "Hattusha, City of Gods and Temples," 113–15; Wightman, *Sacred Spaces*, 225. Temple 5 and the other buildings within the surrounding *temenos* may have been a sacred district created by Tudhaliya IV with a temple and royal residence (Neve, "Hattusha, City of Gods and Temples," 115).

41. Burney, *Historical Dictionary*, 275.

42. There is some evidence in the archaeological record for windows (e.g., in Temple 1). Nevertheless, it is hard to know how common they were given the incomplete remains and ongoing excavations.

However, as elsewhere in the ancient Near East, the passersby were restricted to the most elite. In Temple 1, for example, only those who had access to the sacred precinct would have been able to peer through the windows, thus excluding all but the most privileged. In addition, a Hittite oracle from Alalakh forbids looking upon the deity, even through a window.[43] In fact, Hittite windows could be shut when necessary with lattices or shutters.[44] Thus, despite the presence of windows, viewing the deity was both a privilege and a danger.

## USE

On a basic level, we can reconstruct the temple's function from Hittite texts. The texts refer to the temple as the "house of the god" (Hittite *šiunaš per*, or more simply *per* or *parn* ["house"]), yet more often with the Sumerogram É, or to specify that the house belongs to a god É-DINGIR-*LIM* or more specifically É + the name of the god).[45] As in Egypt and Mesopotamia, the Hittite god's house was the primary locus of divine service and the place to come to make contact with the divine,[46] each for the purpose of receiving divine blessing.

The gate structure (*ḫilammar*)[47] and the walls surrounding it separated the divine estate from the surrounding world. Additional walls and doors divided the larger space into specific smaller spaces, and granted and controlled access to those spaces. Workshops, archives, storage and service areas, and servants' quarters in Temple 1 facilitated divine service and indicated the broader scope of this temple, perhaps also used to control the local agricultural supply, and the greater power wielded by its caretakers. By contrast, the lack of such facilities in the other temples indicated their more limited functions. Nonetheless, enough evidence of annexes to the temple, consisting of residences, workshops, and industrial institutions ex-

---

43. AT 454; Gurney, "A Hittite Divination Text," in *The Alalakh Tablets* (ed. D. J. Wiseman; Occasional Publications of the British Institute of Archaeology at Ankara 2; London: The British Institute of Archaeology at Ankara, 1953), 116–18; Singer, "A City of Many Temples," 35.

44. Kay Kohlmeyer, "The Temple of the Storm God in Aleppo during the Late Bronze and Early Iron Ages," *NEA* 72 (2009): 195.

45. See *CHD* P 273-91. Regarding the Sumerogram, see Güterbock, "Temple," 81; Beckman, "Temple Building," 711: "This term might designate divine accommodations of any size, from a large independent building with many internal subdivisions, such as the Great Temple at Hattusa (Boğazköy), to the more modest establishments recently excavated in Hattusa's Upper City and the single rooms ('chapels') devoted to a minor god or goddess within a large complex belonging to a major divinity."

46. As indicated by the presence of votive vessels, i.e., objects deposited in temples as gifts in the hopes of securing divine favor (Neve, "Hattusha, City of Gods and Temples," 112).

47. Singer, "A City of Many Temples," 34; Beckman, "Sacred Times, Sacred Places," 261.

ists to suggest that "each temple was conceived of as an independent economic unit, providing its own means for the cult and maintenance of the personnel."[48]

The court (ḫila),[49] situated inside the gate and bounded on all sides by walls, seem to have been the appropriate place for the presentation of offerings, large gatherings, and purification before entering the temple core.[50] By placing the court in the middle of the enclosed structure, the temple also served to organize and regulate access to divine space. If nothing else, the so-called vestibules served as mediating spaces. They mediated access to the court and thereby separated the temple interior from the exterior world and ensured that access to the interior was gradual. It would seem that primary service, such as regular meals, occurred in the sanctuary (tunnakeššar),[51] likely at the offering table. More intimate care likely took place closer to the pedestal, where the divine presence was located, such as bathing and adornment of the statue (see further chapter 10). As noted above, the basements may have functioned as treasuries and archives.[52] The specific functions of the other rooms in the temple are more elusive. Some are identified as chapels largely because of the presence of pilasters.[53] The flat roof, which could be accessed by a stairwell, also served as a venue for ritual action.[54]

The function of the most enigmatic feature, the windows, continues to defy interpreters. Some scholars explain their presence as an import from palace architecture or from open sanctuaries.[55] Although by no means certain, it is also possible that if Temple 1 was dedicated to the Weather God as is often assumed, the windows may have functioned like the "rift in the clouds" in Baal's palace from the Ugaritic Baal epic, through which he controlled the weather;[56] alternatively,

---

48. Singer, "A City of Many Temples," 39.

49. Singer, "A City of Many Temples," 34; Beckman, "Sacred Times, Sacred Places," 261.

50. For example, the small building in the court of Temple 1 seems to have been a wash-house for the king (Schachner, Hattuscha, 185).

51. Singer, "A City of Many Temples," 34.

52. Burney, Historical Dictionary, 277; Wightman, Sacred Spaces, 227. Müller-Karpe ("Aspekte hethitischer Sakralbauten," 337 and 340 diagram 6) suggests that since some sanctuaries were located on a slope, basements served primarily to raise the floor level so that sanctuary was on the same horizontal plane as the entrance and court.

53. Beckman, "Sacred Times, Sacred Places," 262.

54. Müller-Karpe, "Aspekte hethitischer Sakralbauten," 340. See, e.g., the ritual for installation of the Goddess of the Night into a new satellite temple (for a recent English translation, see Beckman, "Temple Building," 80–85).

55. See respectively Wightman, Sacred Spaces, 221, and Ewa Wasilewska, "Sacred Space in the Ancient Near East," Religion Compass 3 (2009): 402.

56. Regarding the Baal epic, see esp. Mark S. Smith, The Ugaritic Baal Cycle: Vol. 1: Introduction with Text, Translation & Commentary of KTU 1.1–1.2 (VTSupp 53; Leiden: Brill, 1994); Smith and Wayne T. Pitard, The Ugaritic Baal Cycle, Vol. 2: Introduction with Text, Translation and Commentary of KTU/CAT 1.3–1.4 (VTSupp 114; Leiden: Brill, 2009).

they may have been constructed simply to resemble such a divine palace. Another Ugaritic textual parallel (*KTU* 1.109 and 1.41 11), which states that windows were used for the presentation of offerings to various deities, suggests that the Hittite windows may have been similarly employed.[57] This parallel may also suggest that the windows in the Hittite temples allowed a larger audience to participate in the presentation of the offerings, with the priests with more immediate access to the deities distributing them to the appropriate cult image(s) in the sanctuary. In addition, the placement of the cult statue on a pedestal at the base of the slope also theoretically gave the deity access to the sunlight and a view of its land.[58]

## STRUCTURAL COMMUNICATION

As in Egypt and Mesopotamia, the temple structure communicated its importance and that of its resident. Its physical and associational prominence inspired awe. More specifically, the temple's size, location, elevation, and adornment indicated its importance and reinforced the firmly established message that the temple was divine space and worthy of respect and reverence.

Walls, doorways, decoration, and furnishings divided spaces both literally and conceptually, encoding the Hittite spatial hierarchy into the structure that shaped sacred space. As in both Egypt and Mesopotamia, the walls and doorways divided the various areas of the temple complex, and the logical progression of rooms suggested increasingly privileged access as one approached the deity in its sanctuary. Walls formed literal boundaries between spaces, thereby reinforcing the divisions within the sacred precinct and the privilege of crossing boundaries. Portals both controlled and allowed access between spaces. Decoration clustered at the portals naturally drew attention to the portals, highlighting their importance and the importance of the spaces which they protected and to which they granted access. The fearsome creatures in particular communicated the importance of the temple and especially of its master.

Auxiliary rooms and structures highlighted that the sacred sphere was more than a mere dwelling place. For example, Temple 1 appears to have been the heart of a sacred city within the larger city, itself divided by walls and gates into three primary regions: the temple complex, the surrounding storerooms, and the smaller complex to the south (see fig. 4.4).[59] The walled temple and its gate separated the temple complex with court, vestibules, auxiliary rooms, and sanctuaries inside

---

57. See Dennis Pardee, *Les textes rituels* (Ras Shamra-Ougarit 12; Paris: Editions recherche sur les civilisations, 2000), 148–52 and 688; idem, *Ritual and Cult at Ugarit* (SBLWAW 10; Atlanta: SBL, 2002), 29–31 and 56–65.

58. Schachner, *Hattuscha*, 177.

59. Although the other sacred precincts were less grandiose, they too had auxiliary elements indicating the nature of the sacred sphere.

from the surrounding storerooms outside. The walls around the storerooms and the paved street separated the northern part of the compound from the southern. Finally, these three sections comprising the sacred precinct were separated from the rest of the Lower City by their elevation and substantial walls.

By placing the court within the single, self-contained architectural unit with the rest of the temple, as in Egypt and Mesopotamia, the architects associated the court with the temple core, thereby enhancing its status.[60] Entering any impressive building, especially one with such a lofty standing as the divine abode, evokes an awed response. One often feels privileged to be on the inside, in another's impressive domain, and implicitly compelled to follow the rules of that space, whatever they may be. By placing the court on the inside, the builders thereby inspired awe and elicited the proper behavior within the court. Rather than surrounding the temple, the court formed part of the temple structure; it rested at the heart of the enclosed temple complex, mediating access within instead of to the temple. Indeed, the Hittite court served as the central element around which the other rooms were situated and through which they were accessed.[61] With an enclosed court, the temple caretakers also may have regulated access and behavior by limiting court space (e.g., by surrounding it with walls) and limiting access (e.g., by controlling who may enter the gate). Such regulation privileged and isolated whatever activities took place therein. In contrast, if unwalled and thus outside of the temple complex, it would have been more difficult to delineate the boundaries of the court and regulate behavior within it and the viewing of it. Thus, the court's location with the walls of the temple complex significantly enhanced its status and the privilege of entering it, and served as a powerful (subconscious) motivator to follow proper protocol.[62]

---

60. Rather than being part of the core, the court served as the access point to the temple core.

61. This contrasts with Egypt and Mesopotamia. In Egypt, the court was part of a single walled structure, yet it stood before rather than in the middle of the temple core. In Mesopotamia, while rooms surrounded the court as in Hatti, the temple core, including the sanctuary, generaly lay behind the court. The Hittite court was thus closer both spatially and conceptually to the temple interior and its privileged resident(s) and activities.

62. A modern example may help to elucidate the impact of a walled court. King's College Cambridge is a prestigious and well-preserved space with a world-renowned chapel that attracts tourists' attention. It is sequestered from the rest of the city behind walls and accessed through an ornamental entrance, where a guard regulates access. Catching a glimpse of interior space through the entrance also enhances the privilege of entering, a privilege that would be far diminished without a wall. Beyond this gate stands a courtyard, which only some may access and only the privileged few may tread upon the grass. Once inside the court, people's behavior changes (e.g., while the outside bustles with noise and energy, on the inside, people are far quieter and behave more sedately). They often feel privileged to be allowed entrance and thus willing to follow the rules. In fact, the walls

Locating the divine statue in the least accessible region of the sacred complex was likewise evocative. By situating the divine presence in the most secluded spot, often accessed through what seemed a labyrinth of rooms and corridors, the Hittite architects reinforced the already enculturated message that the room housing the divine presence was of primary importance and must be protected from unwanted elements. Similarly, as in a modern home, the location of the master (divine) "bedchamber" relative to the outer portal, indicated that spaces became increasingly important and intimate, while access became increasingly privileged, as one passed through portals on the way to the heart of the divine complex. In turn, as one approached the deity, one's awe intensified as did the compulsion to behave correctly. Making the path to the most important space somewhat circuitous likewise reinforced both the importance of seclusion and the privilege of entering secluded space. The nondescript portals to the Temple 1 sanctuary also seem to have hidden its location while indicating the importance of divine seclusion.[63] In turn, accessing the sanctuary was in some cases not unlike navigating a maze.

At first glance, the windows seem to run counter to the Hittite and ancient Near Eastern tendency to isolate and protect their sanctuaries, a deviation likely prompted by the desire to provide the deity with some access to the wider world. Nonetheless, as indicated in the structure section, view of the divine presence was limited and at times prohibited. Since few had permission to peer into the windows, beholding the luminous beauty of the deity in the sunlight was a privilege. Likewise, although it was perhaps possible to see the deity from outside of the temple, one had to pass through a maze of chambers to the most inaccessible spot in the temple to gain direct access. Thus, although the deity was present on earth and partook of its light, aromas, and sounds, its nearness was elusive, as its presence remained tantalizingly out of reach to all but the most privileged and then only under special circumstances.

## Ideology

Hittite temples, like their Egyptian and Mesopotamian counterparts, were the socially constructed and controlled spaces used to bridge the mundane and divine spheres, bringing divine presence and blessing to bear in the human world and giving humanity a greater role in cosmic events. As a bridge between two worlds, temples mixed elements of both. Temples were constructed of mundane materials and functioned much like grand households, equipped with a service staff to cater to the deities' primary anthropomorphic needs. For example, in the "divine house" (šiunaš per), the deity, like its royal counterpart, was bathed, fed, and clothed.

---

and rules mutually reinforce and in some ways create the specialness of King's College and impel the proper behavior in such privileged space.

63. Wightman, *Sacred Spaces*, 221, 223.

At the same time, in order to be a suitable divine abode, the temple had to transcend the mundane in various ways. However, unlike in Egypt and Mesopotamia, neither the preserved structure itself nor the texts seem to develop the cosmic significance of the Hittite temple or its link with creation.[64] Instead, the temple was infused with the divine in other ways. Rather than merely adorning the temple, the imagery was part of the structure itself. This structural design made the lions and sphinxes seem less like decoration and more like indelible fixtures, intertwined with the structure itself. Thus, the building would be imbued with the attributes of its statuary, sharing in the strength and otherworldliness of the lions and sphinxes, respectively (fig. 4.6).

In addition to being imbued with various potencies, the temple was also treated as animate in several contexts. For example, in a Hittite ritual from the late fifteenth to early fourteenth century BCE, the temple received offerings and the ritualist implored it to be loyal to its new master and to deny entry to another deity or evil influence.[65] More than simply being alive, the temple and many of its parts, like the hearth, window, and door bolt, were also treated as divine.[66] Each element was marked with the divine determinative (DINGIR), behaved in ways characteristic of the gods, such as conferring blessings or receiving prayers, and was treated like a god, for example, by being presented with offerings. Although we cannot entirely rule out the possibility that these elements simply served as appropriate channels to the deity,[67] it remains more likely that they were treated as divine in their own right or alternatively as controlled by specific divine powers charged with their care.[68] In addition to being presented with offerings and marked with

---

64. The absence of such connections undoubtedly is affected by the lack of written evidence (there is little preserved indigenous cosmology or cosmogony [see, e.g., Collins, *Hittites and Their World*, 191–92]). In turn, it is difficult to assess whether the connections have been lost or never existed at all. For the relation of the temple to astral phenomena and its potential role as a miniature cosmos, see Müller-Karpe, "Sakralbauten."

65. CTH 415; Boysan-Dietrich, *Das hethitische Lehmhaus*, 60–79; for a convenient translation, see Beckman, "Temple Building," text 5, 78–80, §§ 1′, 2′, 6′, 7′.

66. E.g., ᵈḪašša, "hearth" (Maciej Popko, *Kultobjekte in der hethitischen Religion* (Warsaw: Wydawnictwa Uniwersytetu Warszawskiego, 1978], 51–52). See further Alfonso Archi, "Trono regale e trono divinizzato nell'Anatolia ittita," *SMEA* 1 (1966): 83–202; Popko, *Kultobjekte*, 14–28; Volkert Haas, *Geschichte der hethitischen Religion* (HO 1/15; Leiden: Brill, 1994), 262–93, 297–98; Piotr Taracha, *Religions of Second Millennium Anatolia* (DBH 27; Wiesbaden: Harrasowitz, 2009), 62, 128.

67. Beckman, "Sacred Times, Sacred Places," 262.

68. Regarding the division of divine labor, i.e., the divine supervision of specific elements deemed necessary, cf. Gerd Steiner, "Gott. D. Nach hethitischen Texten," *RlA* 3 (1957): 570–571; Haas, *Geschichte der hethitischen Religion*, 299; Manfred Hutter, "Religion in Hittite Anatolia: Some Comments on 'Volkert Haas: Geschichte der hethitischen Religion,'" *Numen* 44 (1997): 78; Beckman, "Pantheon. A. II. Bei den Hethitern," *RlA* 10 (2004): 312.

the divine determinative, they were also implored to behave like gods, fully inde-pendently from the deities they housed, for example, by being loyal to the resident deity and conferring blessings.

More tellingly, many of the same elements like the door, doorbolt, and hearth were also deified in domestic dwellings[69] without any connection to the major gods of the temples. It would seem instead that these elements, whether in the temple or the home, were deified out of a perceived necessity. The Hittites thought it necessary to protect the temple, like the private home, from various evils. To do so, they had to appeal to powers stronger than the unwanted influences. They thus pragmatically envisioned that the very elements protecting the primary entrance points were themselves divine or were controlled by benevolent divine spirits po-tent enough to repel evil and protect the divine or human home.

Such deification of the divine environment was especially appropriate for the temple. The temple served as the divine sphere in the midst of the human sphere not only because it housed the deity, but also because this structure that demarcated and protected divine space was itself divine. Deifying or assigning divine powers to the access points as guardians demonstrates the importance of dividing divine spaces and mediating access to those spaces. In addition, since most people presumably did not have access to the temple interior (as in Egypt) they accessed the deity through the elements that were available to them, such as those that stood at the boundary of divine space. Even for those with access, there nonetheless would be a tendency to approach the major deity of the temple, like a king, through its lesser divine servants, in this case the divine doors, windows, and hearths.[70] Likewise, in addition to eliciting awe, the various fierce creatures that adorned the boundaries may also have been considered animate protectors of di-vine space and perhaps even as intercessors, as in Mesopotamia. Thus, the deified elements of the temple served both protective and intermediary roles, exalting, protecting, and granting access to the divine sphere and its resident deity.

Although temple buildings were clearly constructed by humans from human materials, the Hittite texts also take pains to stress the divine role in their construc-tion, even going so far as to deny human involvement. For example, a Hittite ritual text from the Empire period states: "This temple that we have just built for you, O deity—it was not we who built it, (but) all of the gods (who) built it."[71] Thus,

---

69. Haas, *Geschichte der hethitischen Religion*, 249–93; Hutter, "Religion in Hittite Anatolia," 83–84.

70. E.g., the author of a prayer implores the members of the Sun Goddess' staff from the vizier to the chief cosmetician (*CTH* 371; Singer, *Hittite Prayers*, 24; Beckman, "Pantheon," 312). Like the divine staff, modeled after the royal staff, the deified elements functioned as divine servants.

71. *CTH* 413; translation after Beckman, "Temple Building among the Hittites," text 7, 87, §7. See further ibid., texts 2 §43; 3 §8; 4 §§2–3; and 7 §§7–8.

although clearly terrestrial, the temple itself contained enough elements of the divine to make it a suitable divine abode.

In order to successfully bridge human and divine spheres, temple space was constructed to mediate contact. While the deity remained present on earth with access to its light, sounds, and smells, it was kept at a safe distance from it so that its imperfection would not pollute it.[72] Its access to the sky, and the smells and noises of the world around even may have implied a deeper connection between the deity and this world, making its sanctuary less otherworldly than the dark Egyptian and Mesopotamian sanctuaries which resembled the womb of primordial creation.[73] However, the Hittite deity's access to the terrestrial world does not suggest that its sanctuary was somehow less important, more accessible, or more vulnerable. Its prominence and seclusion find ample expression in the fact that it is the best protected and often most isolated room, accessed via a circuitous path from the outer gateway. Likewise, only privileged human servants could enter divine space and only if appropriately pure.[74] Thus, the deity remained in this world so that it could be contacted to elicit blessing, yet was kept from its unsavory elements to prevent punishment.

It is even possible that the window served a mediating function, especially if as in Ugarit the window functioned as a means of delivering offerings to deities without entering their immediate presence. Especially if connected with monthly rites as at Ugarit,[75] the window afforded more people the opportunity to participate in or at least view the presentation of offerings to the deities without any having to set foot in their sanctuaries or even in the temple complex. Thus, the window paradoxically allowed both more and less access to the deity. At the same time, while suitably protected from the outside world, the window provided the deity some access to it. Rather than sequestering the deity in the dark as in Egypt and Mesopotamia, windows provided a vantage point from which the deity could view its land and estate.

As in both Egypt and Mesopotamia, the king was concerned with and responsible for properly serving the gods.[76] As noted, the texts present mixed evidence about the role of the palace vis-à-vis the temple. Nonetheless, it would seem that

---

72. On the purity of the gods, see, e.g., *CTH* 264; *COS* 1:83.217–21.

73. Indeed if understood to be a means through which the deity controlled the elements, the window hints at a cosmological function for the resident deity not otherwise attested in terrestrial temples, i.e., it served as the means by which the deity controlled cosmic elements like rain.

74. The need for purity is evident in the both the archaeology (e.g., the basins in the courtyard) and the texts (e.g., Texts for Temple Personnel [*CTH* 264; *COS* 1:83.217–21]).

75. Pardee, *Ritual and Cult*, 26.

76. On the role of the king in the cult, see esp. Hoffner, "The Royal Cult in Ḫatti," in Beckman and Lewis, eds., *Text, Artifact, and Image*, 132–51.

most Hittite kings held the divine sphere in great esteem, and were not willing to subsume its temples into palace space or under palace control. Indeed, archaeological and textual data indicate the king's preoccupation with serving the divine. All extant Hittite reliefs and sculptures seem to be of a religious nature, and the king, as the primary actor, always appeared in ritual garb even when one finds his likeness in newly conquered lands.[77] The king also featured prominently in ritual texts,[78] and attributed both weal and woe to his relationship with the deities.[79] Thus, as in Egypt and Mesopotamia, proper divine service was considered foundational to domestic success.

---

77. Frankfort, *Art and Architecture*, 224–25, 231.

78. See, e.g., Pulisa's Ritual Against Plague (*COS* 1:62.161), where the Hittites used humans as a kind of "scapegoat" to stand in the king's stead, who was held responsible for the divine disfavor.

79. See, e.g., the plague prayers of Muršili II (for the basic edition, see Goetze, "Die Pestgebete des Muršili," *KlF* 1 [1929]: 161–251; for an English translation, see, e.g., Singer, *Hittite Prayers* [SBLWAW 11; Atlanta: Scholars Press, 2002], 47–69; for an abbreviated translation see *COS* 1:60.156–60).

# CHAPTER 5
# SYRO-PALESTINIAN TEMPLES

As in Mesopotamia and Hittite Anatolia, generalizations about Syro-Palestinian temples are problematic.[1] Syria-Palestine too served as the home for diverse and interconnected people groups. However, unlike Mesopotamia and Anatolia, empires did not readily form inside the region, especially in the south.[2] In turn, the smaller city-states were often governed by the nearest empire (e.g., the Hittites, Egyptians, and Mesopotamians), which undoubtedly influenced their architecture both in terms of style and resources devoted to building. Some temples incorporated Egyptian elements (e.g., at Beth Shean and Lachish), others Hittite elements (e.g., 'Ain Dara, Aleppo, and Hazor Area H), and still others Mesopotamian elements (e.g., Aleppo).[3] Reflecting the relative weakness of Syro-Palestinian

---

1. The term "Syria-Palestine" functions as a sort of catch-all category, encompassing the diverse and ever-shifting people groups and small kingdoms that were situated between and often subject to the great powers: Egypt in the south, Hittite Anatolia to the northwest and the Mesopotamian empires to the north and east. Syria and Palestine, as the northern and southern territories, formed the most distinct divisions within Syria-Palestine. The northern kingdoms tended to be richer and more powerful than their southern counterparts. Despite the diversity, temples and what we can reconstruct of the divine presence in them shared various common features distinct from the temples of their more powerful neighbors.

2. In Syria, exceptions include Yamhad, an Amorite kingdom centered in Aleppo, which was especially potent from around 1800–1600 BCE and Mitanni, a loosely organized state with a substantial Hurrian element in north Syria and southeast Anatolia prominent from approximately 1500–1300 BCE (see, e.g., Marc Van den Mieroop, *A History of the Ancient Near East, ca. 3000–323 BC* [Malden, MA: Blackwell, 2004]).

3. Regarding Beth Shean and Lachish, see Beth Alpert Nakhai, *Archaeology and the Religions of Canaan and Israel* (ASOR Books 7; Boston: ASOR, 2001), 136–38, 148–50 and the references cited therein. Like Nahkai's work, Wolfgang Zwickel (*Der Tempelkult in Kanaan und Israel. Ein Beitrag zur Kultgeschichte Palästinas von der Mittelbronzezeit bis zum Untergang Judas* [FAT 10; Tübingen: Mohr Siebeck, 1994]) provides a helpful overview of the evidence for a German audience. The present study instead refers to Nakhai for the sake of English readers and because it is slightly more recent. Regarding 'Ain Dara, see Ali Abu Assaf, *Der Tempel von 'Ain Dara* (Mainz: von Zabern, 1990); Paul Zimansky, "The 'Hittites' at 'Ain Dara," in *Recent Developments in Hittite Archaeology and History: Papers in Memory of Hans G. Güterbock* (ed. K. A. Yener and H. A. Hoffner Jr.; Winona Lake, IN: Eisenbrauns, 2002), 177–91; John Monson, "The 'Ain Dara Temple and the Jerusalem

states, temples also were relatively small in the Late Bronze Age.[4] Syro-Palestinian temples, especially those in the lower cities, exercised a much greater flexibility over time at a single site than their Egyptian and Mesopotamian counterparts.[5] In addition, although many temples have been uncovered in the region, few have been preserved above the foundations and significant gaps exist in the archaeo-

---

Temple," in Beckman and Lewis, eds., *Text, Artifact, and Image*, 273–99. Regarding Aleppo, see Kay Kohlmeyer, *Der Tempel des Wettergottes von Aleppo* (Münster: Rhema, 2000); J. Gonnella, W. Khayyata, and Kohlmeyer, eds., *Die Zitadelle von Aleppo und der Tempel des Wettergottes: Neue Forschungen und Entdeckungen* (Münster: Rhema, 2005), esp. 88 for a provisional groundplan; Kohlmeyer, "Der Tempel des Wettergottes von Aleppo," in Kaniuth et al., eds., *Tempel im alten Orient*, 179–218. For a convenient summary of the results in English, see idem, "The Temple of the Storm God in Aleppo during the Late Bronze and Early Iron Ages," *NEA* 72 (2009): 190–202. Regarding the LB IIA temple at Hazor Area H, see Yigal Yadin, *Hazor: The Head of All Those Kingdoms* (London: Oxford University Press), 1972; idem, *Hazor: The Rediscovery of a Great Citadel of the Bible*. London: Weidenfeld and Nicolson, 1975; Amnon Ben-Tor, ed., *Hazor III–IV: An Account of the Third and Fourth Seasons of Excavations, 1957–1958, Text* (Jerusalem: Israel Exploration Society, 1989), 212–13; Nakhai, *Archaeology and the Religions of Canaan and Israel*, 127; regarding the Hazor temples, see now Sharon Zuckerman, "The Temples of Canaanite Hazor," in *Temple Building and Temple Cult: The Architecture and Cultic Paraphernalia of Temples in the Levant (2nd–1st Millennium BCE)* (ed. J. Kamlah; Tübingen: Institute of Biblical Archaeology, 2012), 99–126.

4. William G. Dever, "The Contribution of Archaeology to the Study of Canaanite and Early Israelite Religion," in *Ancient Israelite Religion: Essays in Honor of Frank Moore Cross* (ed. P. D. Miller, Jr., P. D. Hanson, and S. D. McBride; Philadelphia: Fortress, 1987), 229. The relatively meager resources were further depleted by regional overlords. For example, "Egyptian suzerainty did have the effect of sapping Canaanite resources, with the result that temples newly-built in Canaan during the Late Bronze Age tended to be smaller and thinner-walled than their predecessors" (Wightman, *Sacred Spaces*, 166). The most prominent exception to the comparatively spartan temples is that of the Weather God of Aleppo, about which Daniel Schwemer remarks, "The most important transregional sanctuary of the weather god in all ANE periods was without doubt in Ḫalab, modern Aleppo" (*Die Wettergottgestalten Mesopotamiens und Nordsyriens im Zeitalter der Keilschriftkulturen* [Wiesbaden: Harrasowitz, 2001], 108, translated from German).

5. Wightman, *Sacred Spaces*, 149. See, e.g., the transformations of the temple of the Weather God of Aleppo, largely determined by changing cultural influences. In the Middle Bronze era, the cult niche, where the statue was kept, lay on a direct axis with the entrance of the temple (similar to the level VII temple at Alalakh [Kohlmeyer, "Tempel des Wettergottes von Aleppo," 194]). Under Hittite sovereignty, the temple was rebuilt with a bent-axis scheme so that one had to turn when entering the sanctuary to access the divine presence. Later, after the end of Hittite dominion, the temple was once again realigned to allow direct axis to the cult image (see conveniently ibid.). The temple of Alalakh seems to follow a similar trajectory (Woolley, *Alalakh: An Account of the Excavations at Tell Atchana in Hatay, 1937–1939* [Oxford: Oxford University Press, 1955], 33–90; Wightman, *Sacred Spaces*, 166–67; Kohlmeyer, "Tempel des Wettergottes von Aleppo," 195).

logical record.[6] For example, there are almost no data on the major Aramean and Phoenician temples.[7] We have little knowledge of the activities conducted in and around the temples, and excavations have given significantly less attention to the open spaces around the temples than to the temple structures themselves.[8] The textual evidence is also minimal, derived mostly from Ugarit and Emar.[9] Thus, it is difficult to identify a common Syro-Palestinian temple and more difficult still to understand its use and ideology. Nonetheless, the available evidence reveals surprising commonalities.[10]

## STRUCTURE

Although varied, Syro-Palestinian temples of the Middle Bronze to the Iron Age shared several features,[11] allowing archaeologists to speak meaningfully about a "common" temple of the time.[12] Mazar, for example, divides the temples into two categories: symmetrical, direct-axis temples and other anomalous temples.[13] The "common" symmetrical, direct-axis temples were often located centrally, especially

---

6. Wightman, *Sacred Spaces*, 150, 178. Dever ("Contribution of Archaeology," 229) also laments the lack of careful excavation.

7. See briefly Wightman, *Sacred Spaces*, 178. Excavated Philistine temples generally fall into Mazar's "other anomalous temples" category (see n. 13) and thus will only be discussed peripherally (see ibid.).

8. Cf. Adelheid Otto, "Gotteshaus und Allerheiligstes in Syrien und Nordmesopotamien während des 2. Jts. v. Chr.," in Kaniuth et al., eds., *Tempel im alten Orient*, 355.

9. See, e.g., Wayne T. Pitard, "Temple Building in Northwest Semitic Literature of the Late Bronze and Iron Ages," in Boda and Novotny, eds., *From the Foundations to the Crenellations*, 91–108.

10. Analysis focuses on temples from the Middle Bronze to the Iron Age, though comparatively few major Iron Age temples have been unearthed (Syro-Hittite temples are the most prominent exception). Given the incomplete evidence available, any common pattern posited must remain tentative.

11. Close parallels between the temple of Hazor Area H (in Galilee) and Alalakh (in northern Syria) over their various stages of development provide an example of such continuity (Amihai Mazar, "Temples of the Middle and Late Bronze Ages and the Iron Age," in *The Architecture of Ancient Israel: From the Prehistoric to the Persian Periods* [ed. A. Kempinski and R. Reich; Jerusalem: Israel Exploration Society, 1992], 172).

12. Mazar, "Temples of the Middle and Late Bronze Ages," 187. Alternatively, we may refer to common temple types. Our classification naturally depends on the specificity of our criteria. For example, subdivisions within a single category could alternatively be viewed as separate categories. For an alternative scheme, see, e.g., A. Kuschke, "Tempel," *Biblisches Reallexikon* (ed. K. Galling; HAT 1; Tübingen: Mohr Siebeck, 1977), 333-42.

13. Mazar, "Temples of the Middle and Late Bronze Ages," 187, with reference to Palestine. This division serves his purposes in focusing on possible Solomonic temple analogs.

near royal palaces, and represented the cities' primary temples and loci of official religion. By contrast, the temples with variable arrangements were often less central and official, appearing most frequently in lower towns and outside defensive walls.[14] Syrian temples also tended to be located at the edge of settlements or at breaks in the terrain. For example, in Emar the primary temples were situated next to each other on a cliff above the Euphrates Valley, and in Ekalte three temples appeared side-by-side on the edge of the Euphrates Valley.[15] Unlike their Mesopotamian and Hittite counterparts, Syro-Palestinian temples were often isolated from surrounding structures, since they were frequently surrounded by (occasionally walled) open spaces.[16] Since the present study is concerned primarily with official temples, it will focus on the symmetrical temple category.

Within the direct-axis temple category, there was some variability (see fig. 5.1).[17] Some temples (types 1 and 2), especially common in lower towns,[18] had a single room, sometimes with a walled façade. The popular type 3 temple (e.g., at Emar and Tell Tayinat)[19] added a shallow porch in front of the enclosed sanctuary, which, in larger temples, was supported by two columns. Type 4 temples convert-

---

14. Mazar, "Temples of the Middle and Late Bronze Ages," 187; Wightman, *Sacred Spaces*, 147–50, 178.

15. Otto, "Gotteshaus und Allerheiligstes," 359.

16. Ibid., 360, referring to northern Mesopotamian and Syrian temples.

17. For the following types, see Wightman, *Sacred Spaces*, 150–51. An especially common temple type in Syria in the MB and LB periods was the antis temple, defined as a free-standing long room structure with strict axial orientation, which consisted in the rule of one room, and more seldom of a series of two or more rooms, in which the long walls extended beyond the lateral, creating antenna, which bordered the roofed open porch (Peter Werner, *Die Entwicklung der Sakralarchitektur in Nordsyrien und Südostkleinasien vom Neolithikum bis in das 1. Jt. v. Chr.* [Munich: Profil, 1994], 15). Indeed, such temples were common from the EB to Iron ages (ibid., 94–115). Since they are defined by their protruding antennae and not by their interior structure, antis temples had variable internal structures (Otto, "Gotteshaus und Allerheiligstes," 359) that fall into several of Wightman's types, employed here.

18. "Lower towns" generally refers to the areas of a town or city that do not rest on the tel or tell, the often artificial hill created by the accumulation of settlements.

19. Regading Tell Tayinat, see Richard C. Haines, *Excavations in the Plain of Antioch*, Vol. II: *The Structural Remains of the Later Phases: Chatal Hüyük, Tell Al-Judaidah, and Tell Tayinat* (OIP 95. Chicago: The Oriental Institute of the University of Chicago, 1970); see more recently the ongoing excavations of the University of Toronto (http://www.utoronto.ca/tap/) and Timothy P. Harrison and James F. Osborne, "Building XVI and the Neo-Assyrian Sacred Precinct at Tell Tayinat," *JCS* 64 (2012): 125–43; Harrison, "West Syrian Megaron or Neo-Assyrian Langraum? The Shifting Form and Function of the Tayinat Temples," in Kamlah, ed., *Temple Building and Temple Cult*, 3–22. Regarding Emar, see Margueron, "Meskene (Imar/Emar)," *RlA* 8 (1993–1997): 84–93; Margueron and Veronica Boutte, "Emar, Capital of Aštata in the Fourteenth Century BCE," *BA* 58 (1995): 126–38.

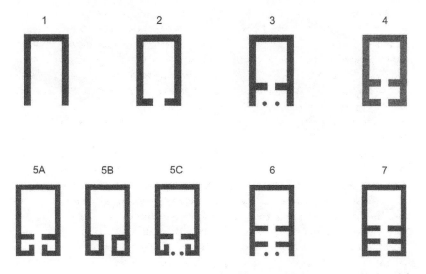

Fig. 5.1. Groundplans of the different types of direct-approach temples (second and first millennium). From Wightman, *Sacred Spaces*, fig. 3.1.

ed the porch into a broad vestibule, while type 5 temples inserted walls on both sides of the vestibule to form a central atrium between two tower-like chambers.[20] Because of their thick walls, up to five meters wide, which are believed to have supported a tall superstructure, these temples have been called fortress or tower temples (e.g., Temple 2048 at Megiddo, the Fortress Temple at Shechem, and the temple of the Weather God in Aleppo; see fig. 5.2).[21] Perhaps the most common form, especially for the primary temples, type 6 temples included a broad porch

20. The atrium could also have been broadened to form a porch with one or two columns (Wightman, *Sacred Spaces*, 151).

21. In addition to the thick walls, the Aleppo temple also has a partially preserved staircase, suggesting that it had at least one upper story (Kohlmeyer, "Temple of the Storm God in Aleppo," 194). Regarding Megiddo, see Gordon Loud, *Megiddo II, Seasons of 1935–1939, Text* (OIP 62; Chicago: The Oriental Institute of the University of Chicago, 1948); Graham I. Davies, *Cities of the Biblical World: Megiddo* (Cambridge: Lutterworth, 1986); Aharon Kempinski, *Megiddo: A City-State and Royal Centre in North Israel* (Materialien zur Allgemeinen und Vergleichenden Archäologie 40; Munich: Beck, 1989). Regarding Shechem, see Robert J. Bull, "A Re-examination of the Shechem Temple." *BA* 23 (1960): 110–19; Lawrence E. Toombs, "The Stratification of Tel Balâtah (Shechem)," *BASOR* 223 (1976): 57–59; George E. Wright, "Shechem," in *Encyclopedia of Archaeological Excavations in the Holy Land* (ed. M. Avi-Yonah and E. Stern; Englewood Cliffs, NJ: Prentice-Hall, 1978), 4: 1083–94; Edward F. Campbell, "Shechem: Tel Balâtah," in *The New Encyclopedia of Archaeological Excavation in the Holy Land* (ed. Stern; Jerusalem: Israel Exploration Society, 1993), 1345–54.

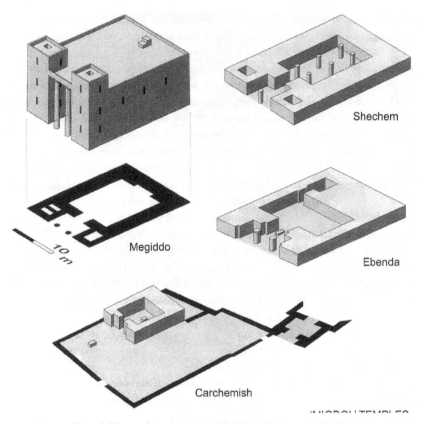

Fig. 5.2. Tower ("migdol") temples, characteristic of Middle Bronze Age (seventeenth–sixteenth centuries) Palestine and Syria. The thick walls presumably supported a tall superstructure, leading to their designation "fortress" or "tower" temples. From Wightman, *Sacred Spaces*, fig. 3.8.

(with two columns), a broad vestibule, and a long sanctuary (e.g., the ʿAin Dara temple [see fig. 5.3] and the Ebla Temple D).[22] Finally, type 7 temples included two broad vestibules in front of the sanctuary (e.g., the Hyksos sanctuary at Tell El-Dabʿa in the Egyptian Delta [ancient Avaris]).[23]

22. ʿAin Dara is interesting and anomalous in that giant, meter-long footprints appear on the porch, one footprint close by at the threshold of the vestibule and another at the threshold of the sanctuary approximately ten meters away (for a discussion, see further ideology). Regarding Ebla, see Paolo Matthiae, *Ebla: An Empire Rediscovered* (London: Hodder & Stoughton, 1980), 114, fig. 30; Nakhai, *Archaeology and the Religions of Canaan and Israel*, 88–89; Wightman, *Sacred Spaces*, 159–60.

23. Manfred Bietak, "Avaris and Piramesse: Archaeological Exploration in the Eastern Nile

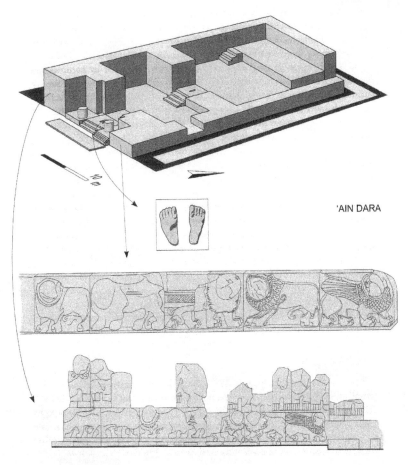

'AIN DARA

Fig. 5.3. The temple at 'Ain Dara in northwestern Syria (type 6) with a broad porch with two columns, a vestibule, an outer sanctuary, and an inner sanctuary. Note the raised entrance to each area of the temple, the abundant decoration, and especially the oversized footprints. From Wightman, *Sacred Spaces*, fig. 3.20.

Despite the variety of forms, the differences were often superficial. In most temples, the sanctuary was the largest room, usually long or square in shape, while the space before it served primarily to mediate access to it from the outside world. Within the sanctuary, one often found an inner sanctuary, that is, a separate space

Delta," *Proceedings of the British Academy* 65 (1979): 247–53, figs. 8–9; Nakhai, *Archaeology and the Religions of Canaan and Israel*, 99–100. Regarding Avaris, see more fully, Bietak, *Avaris, The Capital of the Hyksos: Recent Excavations at Tell el-Dab'a* (London: British Museum, 1996).

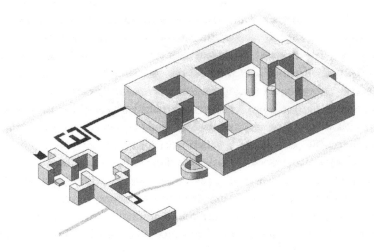

Fig. 5.4. The Late Bronze I Hazor Area H temple with a preserved altar and basin, an inner sanctuary forming a separate room, and a court wider than and not attached to the temple. It is one of the few temples where excavations extended into the open space beyond the temple core. From Wightman, *Sacred Spaces*, fig. 3.10.

where the cult image was kept. The inner sanctuary occasionally appeared as its own separate room (e.g., the LB I and II Hazor Area H temple [see fig. 5.4], the LB Pella Fortress temple, the Tell Tayinat temple [see fig. 5.5], and the 'Ain Dara temple [see fig. 5.3]),[24] but more often as a niche in the back wall (e.g., MB Hazor Area H temple, MB Aleppo, Tell El-Dab'a, and Alalakh Stratum IV) and/or a raised platform (e.g., Ebla temple D, Tell Deir 'Alla, Hazor Area A, Tell Tayinat, and the

---

24. At Hazor Area H, the LB I temple inner sanctuary was enclosed by a narrow wall (see fig. 5.4), while the inner sanctuary in the LB II temple could be sequestered by a curtain (Mazar, "Temples of the Middle and Late Bronze Ages," 171–72; Nakhai, *Archaeology and the Religions of Canaan and Israel*, 127). The LB Pella temple also had a separate chamber for the inner sanctuary (Stephen Bourke, "The New Pella Bronze Age Temple: The Largest 'Migdol' Ever Found," *Occident & Orient* 192 (1999): 57–58; idem, "The Six Canaanite Temples of *Ṭabaqāt Faḥil*: Excavating Pella's 'Fortress' Temple (1994–2009)," in Kamlah, ed., *Temple Building and Temple Cult*, 159–202; Wightman, *Sacred Spaces*, 163–64. At Tell Tayinat, the inner sanctuary had its own room with a raised platform (see fig. 5.5), while the Iron Age 'Ain Dara temple used a partition to separate the inner sanctuary with its podium from the outer sanctuary (Wightman, *Sacred Spaces*, 193–97). Regarding MB Aleppo, see Kohlmeyer, "Temple of the Storm God in Aleppo," 194.

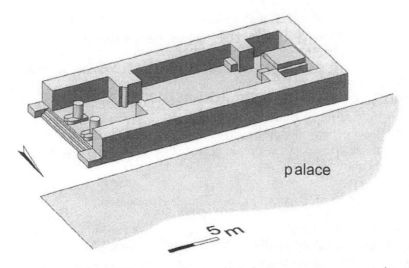

Fig. 5.5. One of the Tell Tayinat temples, in which the inner sanctuary occupied its own room and a raised pedestal further isolated the cult image. From Wightman, *Sacred Spaces*, fig. 3.16.

Late Bronze Age Shechem Fortress temple IIa).[25] Although none have been found conclusively in situ, the divine image presumably rested in the inner sanctuary.

A wall occasionally surrounded the temple compound, marking the boundary of the sacred sphere (e.g., LB I Hazor Area H, thirteenth-century Alalakh, and thirteenth-century Megiddo temple 2048).[26] Unlike their Egyptian, Mesopotamian, and Hittite analogs, Syro-Palestinian portals to the larger divine precinct were often rather pedestrian. Whether or not the precinct was walled, a courtyard and occasionally auxiliary structures surrounded the temple building (e.g., at Tell Deir 'Alla).[27] Since it rarely formed a single architectural unit with the temple core,

---

25. The inner sanctuary of the Megiddo fortress temple was even changed from a niche to a platform (Mazar, "Temples of the Middle and Late Bronze Ages," 171). Regarding Tell Deir 'Alla, see H. J. Franken, *Excavations at Tell Deir 'Alla* (Leiden: Brill, 1969); Gerrit van der Kooij, "Deir 'Alla, Tell," in *NEAEHL*, 338–42; Nakhai, *Archaeology and the Religions of Canaan and Israel*, 139–40; Regarding Hazor Area A, see Ruhama Bonfil, "Area A: Analysis of the Temple," in *Hazor V: An Account of the Fifth Season of Excavation, 1968* (ed. Ben-Tor and Bonfil; Jerusalem: Israel Exploration Society, 1997), 85–101.

26. Nakhai, *Archaeology and the Religions of Canaan and Israel*, 126, 134; Wightman, *Sacred Spaces*, 167. Unfortunately, it is difficult to determine how extensive these enclosure walls were, since excavations do not always extend beyond the temple to include the open spaces around them (cf. Otto, "Gotteshaus und Allerheiligstes," 355).

27. Nakhai, *Archaeology and the Religions of Canaan and Israel*, 139. LB I Hazor Area H is anomalous in that its temple court was bisected by a wall and gate (Mazar, "Temples of the

the court was often wider than the temple, even when walled (e.g., the LB 1 Hazor Area H temple; see fig. 5.4). In other words, rather than being incorporated inside the temple complex, the court surrounded it. By contrast, in Egypt, Mesopotamia, and Hittite Anatolia, the court was part of a single architectural unit with the temple and thus either of the same width or narrower than the temple core. Identifiable auxiliary structures include workshops, storerooms, and servants' quarters (i.e., priestly residences), which were often built into or as annexes to the enclosure wall.[28] Instead of adjoining the sanctuary within the same building, the service rooms were unattached, at a respectful distance from the temple core, often situated around the court.[29]

## Location, Elevation, Decoration, and Temple Paraphernalia[30]

Syro-Palestinian temples were generally located in prominent position, clearly visible, and often near the royal palace.[31] Besides the palace, which was often larger, the temple was the largest structure in most cities.[32] Some temples, especially the major ones, were elevated above the rest of the city. For example, the primary temples at Ugarit and Emar were in the most elevated parts of their cities, the Bazi temple was situated on a peak sixty meters above the Euphrates Valley, the MB IIC Megiddo 2048 temple was built on a one-meter-high platform, and the Fortress temple at Shechem was constructed on a thick stone base.[33] Elevation also occasionally was used to set off the temple's constituent parts, especially the inner sanctuary.[34]

---

Middle and Late Bronze Ages," 171; Nakhai, *Archaeology and the Religions of Canaan and Israel*, 126).

28. Wightman, *Sacred Spaces*, 149; Otto, "Gotteshaus und Allerheiligstes," 365.

29. Wightman, *Sacred Spaces*, 149; Otto, "Gotteshaus und Allerheiligstes," 365.

30. The latter term (from Dever, "Contribution of Archaeology," 225) consists of furniture and movable objects.

31. Wightman, *Sacred Spaces*, 147.

32. Ibid.; Otto, "Gotteshaus und Allerheiligstes," 359. For example, the typically 2 to 3-m-thick walls of Syrian temples compared to the approximately 1-m-wide walls of domestic dwellings suggests that the temples towered over the surrounding architecture (ibid.).

33. Nakhai, *Archaeology and the Religions of Canaan and Israel*, 102–3; Wightman, *Sacred Spaces*, 162, 177; Otto, "Gotteshaus und Allerheiligstes," 359. Even in some non-central temples, i.e., those located in the lower city, the temple building was elevated. For example, the Hazor Area H temple stood partly above the rampart and partially above the artificial fill on the slope (Mazar, "Temples of the Middle and Late Bronze Ages," 165).

34. In the Lachish summit temple, steps separated the entrance hall from the main hall/ sanctuary, and the outer sanctuary from the inner sanctuary (ibid., 176). At 'Ain Dara, stairs separated the temple entrance from nontemple space, the sanctuary from the vestibule, and

Fig. 5.6. One of the two lions framing the entrance of the thirteenth-century Hazor Area H temple. Photo by the author.

Compared with the gate granting ingress to the divine precinct, some temple entrances were rather elaborate. For example, with twin towers flanking the entrance portal, the façades of the fortress temples resembled city gates.[35] The bulk of the minimal decoration[36] was likewise concentrated at these portals, and the concern for symmetry often meant that it was found in pairs. Twin columns and, more occasionally, twin lions framed the temple entrance (e.g., Ebla temple D, thirteenth-century Alalakh, thirteenth-century Hazor Area H, and Tell Tayinat) (see fig. 5.6).[37] There is also some evidence for "relief-carved wooden panels at-

---

the inner sanctuary from the outer sanctuary (Wightman, *Sacred Spaces*, 194; see fig. 5.3). As indicated above, many temples also elevated the divine cult image on a pedestal.

35. Mazar, "Temples of the Middle and Late Bronze Ages," 166; Wightman, *Sacred Spaces*, 165.

36. In terms of both the state of preservation and in comparison with other regions.

37. Nakhai, *Archaeology and the Religions of Canaan and Israel*, 88, 127; Wightman, *Sacred Spaces*, 160, 167–68, 196–97. Tell Tayinat combines the two features, as lions formed the base of the twin columns that supported the façade of the porch (Wightman, *Sacred Spaces*,

Fig. 5.7. The orthostat blocks lining the pedestal wall of the Iron Age temple of the Weather God of Aleppo (900 BCE) were decorated with depictions of the Weather God and his entourage. From Kohlmeyer, "The Temple of the Storm God," *NEA* 72 (2009): 198.

tached to both interior and exterior walls" and low-relief imagery, especially at the portals of major temples.[38] With an abundance of carved reliefs, the Syro-Hittite 'Ain Dara and Aleppo temples are especially anomalous in both their state of preservation and in the amount of decoration (see figs. 5.3, 5.7, and 5.8).[39]

Like the decoration, furniture and accessories were rather spartan, of which altars, benches, basins, and cisterns were especially characteristic.[40] Altars and benches ocasionally featured inside the sanctuary,[41] while large stone altars were commonly found in the central courtyards (e.g., at LB I Hazor Area H, the Baal

196–97). Although only one lion has been found at Ebla, it would seem by comparison with other ancient Near Eastern evidence that there were originally two.

38. Wightman, *Sacred Spaces*, 1011. It is difficult to assess the prevalence of mural iconography, given the little that remains and the generally poor state of temple preservation (ibid., 1012).

39. See respectively Abu Assaf, *Der Tempel von 'Ain Dara*, and the summaries of Kohlmeyer, "Temple of the Storm God in Aleppo" and "Tempel des Wettergottes von Aleppo." Regarding the footprints at 'Ain Dara, see "Ideology" (p. 128).

40. Dever, "Contribution of Archaeology," 225–26, 229; Nakhai, "Temples: Syro-Palestinian Temples," in *OEANE* 4: 168; Wightman, *Sacred Spaces*, 149.

41. Dever "Contribution of Archaeology," 225. Low benches were especially common in the less prominent temples (George R. H. Wright, *Ancient Building in South Syria and*

Fig. 5.8. Reliefs from the Hittite-period sanctuary (fourteenth–thirteenth centuries BCE) of the Weather God of Aleppo depicting a bull man, false window, and the Weather God (second figure from right) facing King Taita (who was added in the eleventh century). From Kohlmeyer, "The Temple of the Storm God," *NEA* 72 (2009): 192.

temple at Ugarit, and Tell El Dab'a).[42] Smaller altars also occasionally appeared near or in front of the cult image.[43] Whereas furniture and decoration were likely minimal, an abundance of movable objects have been unearthed in both Syria and Palestine.[44] These include pottery, votive vessels, stone vessels, cylinder seals, cult stands, small altars, weapons, jewelry, as well as the remains of livestock, agricul-

---

*Palestine* [Leiden: Brill, 1985]); cf., however, Alalakh Stratum VII (Woolley, *Alalakh*, 62) and LB Hazor Area H (Nakhai, *Archaeology and the Religions of Canaan and Israel*, 127).

42. Nakhai, *Archaeology and the Religions of Canaan and Israel*, 100, 124, 126.

43. Magnus Ottosson, *Temples and Cult Places in Palestine* (Boreas 12; Uppsala: Acta Universitatis Upsaliensis, 1980), 29, 32, 118; see Eric Gubel, *Phoenician Furniture: A Typology Based on Iron Age Representations with Reference to the Iconographical Context* (Studia Phoenicia 7; Leuven: Peeters, 1987), pls. IV, VI–VIII, X–XI, for incense stands before divine thrones in Phoenician art.

44. Dever, "Contribution of Archaeology," 225–26. Such an abundance has either not been found or featured more minimally in the archaeological records of Egypt especially and also Mesopotamia. This may stem from the focus on large, well-preserved structures at these sites at the expense of smaller finds (e.g., pottery). In Syria-Palestine, the structures are less absorbing, leaving space for an examination of the auxiliary items.

tural products, and luxury items.[45] As elsewhere, the primary cult image seems to have been constructed of the finest materials.[46]

As in Hittite Anatolia, there is some evidence for windows in the temples. In addition to the well-known window in Baal's palace in the Baal cycle and the false windows in Aleppo (fig. 5.8),[47] an Akkadian building report from Ugarit describes Ea's appearance and command to build a window in the superstructure, which presumably was a temple.[48] As noted in the previous chapter, Pardee argues that the temples of Baal and El at Ugarit had windows used for sacrificial purposes.[49] *KTU* 1.109 explicitly mentions a window (*urbt*) in the temple of Baal at which offerings were made to various deities (ll. 19–31), and in *KTU* 1.41, describing the temple of El, *urbt* in line 11 may plausibly be restored.[50]

## USE

Although the structures of Syro-Palestinian temples differed from their larger neighbors, the temples nonetheless seem to have performed similar functions. As in the rest of the ancient Near East, the Syro-Palestinian people conceived of their temple as a house of god (Ugaritic and Aramaic *bt*, Hebrew and Aramaic *byt*, Akkadian *bītu*).[51] As the house of god in the midst of human community, the temple

---

45. Dever, "Contribution of Archaeology," 225–26; Nakhai, "Syro-Palestinian Temples," 168.

46. For example, divine statues in Emar were made of gold and silver and were decorated with precious stone (Joan Goodnick Westenholz, *Cuneiform Inscriptions in the Collection of the Bible Lands Museum Jerusalem: The Emar Tablets* [CM 13; Groningen: Styx, 2000], nos. 25–26).

47. The windows were false in the sense that, although they were made to look like windows, they were simply an embellished part of the wall and granted no access to the outside world. Regarding the Aleppo windows, see Kohlmeyer, *Tempel des Wettergottes*, 19.

48. RS 94.2953 in Daniel Arnaud, *Corpus des textes de bibliothèque de Ras Shamra-Ougarit (1936–2000) en sumérien, babylonien et assyrien* (AuOrSup 23; Barcelona: AUSA, 2007), 201–2 + pl XXIV; see also Gregorio del Olmo Lete, "Una 'ventana' en el temp de Baal," *AuOr* 20 (2006): 177–88; Pitard, "Temple Building in Northwest Semitic Literature," 101–5. Although possible, this window is likely unrelated to that in the mythological temple of Baal (ibid., 102–3, contra Arnaud, *Corpus des textes de bibliothèque*, 202).

49. Dennis Pardee, *Le textes rituels* (Ras Shamra-Ougarit 12; Paris: Editions Recherche sur les Civlizations, 2000), 148–52 and 688; English translation in idem, *Ritual and Cult at Ugarit* (SBLWAW 10; Atlanta: Society of Biblical Literature, 2002), 29–31 (*KTU* 1.109 and RS 24.253) and 56–65 (*KTU* 1.41 and RS 1.003).

50. Ibid.

51. See conveniently Hoffner, "bayit," *TDOT* 2 (1975): 107–11; Hundley, "Before YHWH," 19–20 n. 28. Regarding the term "temple," Otto suggests that the entire divine sphere in Syria-Palestine, including the open space surrounding the temple building, should be

was the primary locus of both service and supplication, both intended to elicit a favorable divine response. The textual and archaeological remains suggest that service and supplication primarily took the form of food and drink offerings, animal sacrifices, and votives.[52]

As in the Hittite and Mesopotamian temples, the functions of the specific areas are somewhat enigmatic. Nonetheless, the furniture, cultic remains, and ritual texts provide substantial fodder for interpretation.[53] Here as elsewhere, when present the gates and walls served to separate and control access to spaces, separating the divine sphere from the human sphere and the temple complex from the rest of the divine sphere. The auxiliary buildings, some of which have been identified as workshops, storerooms, and servants' quarters, facilitated the upkeep of the temple and appropriate interaction with the deity.[54] For example, the potter's workshop at Hazor Area H seems to have both produced and sold votives for temple suppliants.[55]

The courtyard was the appropriate place for the presentation, slaughter, and burning of sacrifices,[56] preparation to approach the deity, and for larger gatherings.[57] Major festivals where the entire population gathered could not be celebrat-

---

referred to as the "temple," while the "temple" building itself may be more aptly referred to as a "sanctuary" ("Gotteshaus und Allerheiligstes," 375). However, it seems perhaps better to refer to the building housing the sanctuary as the "temple" or "temple complex," akin to the Egyptian *ḥwt nṯr* ("god's house"), and refer to the surrounding space including its open spaces and auxiliary structures and perhaps even the associated spaces outside the city (e.g., standing stones used among other things for festival processions) as the divine estate, akin to the Egyptian *pr* ("estate").

52. Dever, "Contribution of Archaeology," 228–29. For the various offerings and rituals at Ugarit, see, e.g., Jean-Michel de Tarragon, *Le Culte a Ugarit: D'apres les textes de la pratique en cuneiformes alphabetiques* (CRB 19; Paris: Gabalda, 1980); Pardee, *Textes Rituels*; idem, *Ritual and Cult at Ugarit*; David M. Clemens, *Sources for Ugaritic Ritual and Sacrifice: Ugaritic and Ugaritic Akkadian Texts* (AOAT 284; Münster: Ugarit-Verlag, 2001).

53. On the relationship between the Emar temple and the text describing the installation of Baal's high priestess, see esp. Otto, "Gotteshaus und Allerheiligstes," 365–68; regarding the archaeology, see esp. Uwe Finkbeiner, "Emar 2001 – Bericht über die 4. Kampagne der syrisch-deutschen Ausgrabungen," *BaM* 33 (2002): 111–46; idem, "Emar 2002 – Bericht über die 5. Kampagne der syrisch-deutschen Ausgrabungen," *BaM* 34 (2003): 9–100; idem, "Neue Ausgrabungen in Emar, Syrien: Kampagnen 1996–2002," in *Colloquium Anatolicum IV* (Istanbul: Türk Eskiçağ Bilimleri Enstitüsü, 2005), 43–65; for the text, see Daniel E. Fleming, *The Installation of Baal's High Priestess at Emar: A Window on Ancient Syrian Religion* (HSS 42; Altanta: Scholars Press, 1992).

54. Cf. Otto, "Gotteshaus und Allerheiligstes," 368.

55. Dever, "Contribution of Archaeology," 229.

56. Ibid.; Nakhai, "Syro-Palestinian Temples," 170; Otto, "Gotteshaus und Allerheiligstes," 368.

57. Cf. Dever's qualifications ("Contribution of Archaeology," 228–29).

ed within the court because of size restrictions and were thus relocated to areas outside of the city.[58]

Within the temple itself, the vestibule and/or porch, when present, served as mediating spaces, separating and mediating access to the sanctuary from the court. The relatively small size of the sanctuaries allowed space only for intimate encounters with the deity, especially its care and feeding.[59] The presence of a platform and/or benches within the sanctuary in particular suggests that the sanctuary was the venue for regular service and the presentation of various gifts.[60] The occasional presence of small altars located in front of or near the cult object as well as the burn residue on some of them suggests that these altars may have served as incense altars.[61] The inner sanctuary—i.e., the often segregated space within the sanctuary where the divine image rested—represented the god's primary quarters and presumably was the setting of more intimate care, such as washing and anointing the statue.[62] Thus, although structurally distinct, Syro-Palestinian temples' constituent parts functioned similarly to those of their more illustrious neighbors: the sanctuary served as the locus of the divine presence and its more immediate care, other rooms served auxiliary and mediating functions, the open space around the temple hosted larger rituals such as slaughter, presentation, and shared consumption of offerings, while certain open spaces outside of the city served as an extension of divine space and the site of especially large public rituals.[63]

As noted, in *KTU* 1.109 the windows explicitly served as a means of presenting offerings to the deities within the temples without actually entering those temples. The windows may also have performed a mediating function, allowing some access to the gods in the sanctuary for a larger number of people than could set foot within the sanctuary, without anyone actually setting foot in the sanctuary. At

---

58. Otto, "Gotteshaus und Allerheiligstes," 375. In the case of the major *zukru* festival from Emar, the city's deities and its people processed to standing stones outside of the city (Fleming, *Time at Emar: The Cultic Calendar and the Rituals from the Diviner's House* [Mesopotamian Civilizations 11; Winona Lake, IN: Eisenbrauns, 2000], 82; regarding this festival, see further ibid., 48–140, 234–67).

59. Cf. regarding the Baal temple of Emar, Otto, "Gotteshaus und Allerheiligstes," 368. Regarding textual evidence, see, e.g., the presentation of various offerings to the deities in the Ugaritic temple of Baal (Pardee, *Ritual and Cult*).

60. Cf. Dever, "Contribution of Archaeology," 225–26, 229.

61. From a practical point of view, it makes sense that incense was burned here not only to perfume the air around the god's room, but also as an air freshener of sorts, to overpower the scent of animal remains and to shroud the divine presence in the sanctuary with a divinely suitable scent. It has been suggested that the general lack of burn residue may be because incense was burned in another vessel on top of the altar.

62. For more details, see ch. 11.

63. Cf. Otto, "Gotteshaus und Allerheiligstes," 375.

the same time, rather than secluding them in the dark, windows afforded the deities some access to the world around.

## STRUCTURAL COMMUNICATION

When juxtaposed with some of their ancient Near Eastern analogs, the Syro-Palestinian temples, including the so-called tower temples, appear rather unremarkable.[64] However, in their own context, where the architecture generally was less grandiose and its adornment less elaborate, the temples were certainly impressive. Similarly, in a modern context, a two-story building appears miniscule next to a skyscraper, yet massive in a place where every building only has one story. The relatively small size of the temples was also partially offset by their prominent locations, elevated above and isolated from their surroundings, often situated in topographical locations that reinforced their monumentality.[65] Situated prominently, arranged symmetrically, larger than all but the palace, comparatively well-decorated, and associated with the resident deity, Syro-Palestinian temples like their ancient Near Eastern counterparts thus would have elicited an appropriate reverence.

Walls, portals, decoration, furniture, and elevation served to divide spaces and/or highlight the divisions of those spaces.[66] When present, a wall separated the divine estate from the world around it, marking the interior as significant space. The walls of the temple itself segregated the temple from the rest of the sacred sphere, and, if more than one interior room existed, they too were separated by walls. Portals naturally granted and controlled access to these walled spaces.

Compared to the gate to the divine estate, the gate to the temple core was often especially impressive, indicating that, of the two major boundaries, that of the temple complex was the most prominent. For example, with twin towers framing the portal, the façade of the fortress temple resembled that of a city gate. The strength and prominence of the façades indicated the importance of the protected area and of the boundary between inside and outside spaces.[67] The bulk of the minimal decoration was also clustered around the temple gate, drawing attention to this important boundary marker. In addition, with minimal decoration, more

---

64. The cultures' respective temples no doubt reflected their relative stability and resources. Egypt, Mesopotamia, and Anatolia were ruled by large empires that were both affluent and relatively stable. By comparison, Syro-Palestinian states were small, unstable, and often relatively poor.

65. Cf. Werner, *Entwicklung der Sakralarchitektur*, 177.

66. The items of furniture also indicated the function of the spaces in which they were situated.

67. Cf. Nakhai, *Archaeology and the Religions of Canaan and Israel*, 110–11; Wightman, *Sacred Spaces*, 165.

subtle changes in architecture were evocative. For example, dressed stones were confined mainly to portals, altars, and the lower parts of larger temples.[68] Finally, temple builders further differentiated temples from their surroundings by founding them on elevated terrain or elevating them above the surrounding terrain. Each feature thereby drew attention to the temple portal as the primary liminal zone and highlighted the supreme importance of the space it protected.

In the Syro-Palestinian sacred precinct, court-space often bounded by walls communicated as much as the walls and portals themselves, indicating that the temple and its relationship to the space around it were different in Syria-Palestine than in Egypt, Mesopotamia, and Hittite Anatolia. In these neighboring regions, the courts and various auxiliary rooms were often incorporated into the temple building. The temple walls extended to encompass the court that either fronted the temple building or formed the centerpiece around which the many other rooms were situated, such that the temple core—i.e., the sanctuary and its immediate environs—were but one small part of the larger constructed temple space. This core was often nestled at the rear or isolated in a corner of this substantial temple complex.

By contrast, rather than forming part of the massive temple complex, the Syro-Palestinian court and auxiliary spaces were not connected to the freestanding temple core, and hence served different mediating functions. Instead, the court consisted of open space that often surrounded the temple on all sides, and few temples had (significant) auxiliary rooms within their walls.

In Egypt, Mesopotamia, and Hittite Anatolia, attaching the temple core structurally to the court and fronting the entire temple complex with massive gates suggested that these gates marked a major boundary and indicated that the courts rested on the inside of this prominent barrier.[69] Thus, the court mediated between spaces inside the larger temple complex, namely, between the temple core and the portal (and auxiliary rooms) of the temple complex.[70] By contrast, since the Syro-Palestinian court stood outside and was structurally distinct from the temple core, it mediated between temple space and the space around it. In other words, rather than being part of the larger temple complex, the Syro-Palestinian court isolated the smaller temple core—that is, the temple building with sanctuary and mediating space(s)—from all surrounding structures both physically and visually.[71] Thus, what in Egypt, Mesopotamia, and Hatti was the temple core, in Syria-Palestine was

---

68. Wightman, *Sacred Spaces*, 150.

69. In some Mesopotamian temples, gateways to the temple core were equally impressive, and served to bisect the larger temple structure.

70. In Hittite and some Mesopotamian temples, the court even functioned as the centerpiece of the temple, around which the various individual rooms were situated.

71. Within the temple, vestibules and porches, when present, served the complementary function of increasing the space between the most protected inside space, where the deity

simply the temple, since no human structures shared its space.[72] The function of the Syro-Palestinian court marked the temple as especially distinct and especially important by isolating it, so that it stood alone in space as it stood alone in status.[73]

Whereas in Egypt, Mesopotamia, and Hittite Anatolia the massive temple complex allowed no visual access to the temple core, isolating the temple core in Syria-Palestine from surrounding structures rendered it more visible and potentially more accessible. In these neighboring ancient Near Eastern regions, few had visual or physical access to the temple core. By contrast, in Syria-Palestine, with a more open court with a more porous outer boundary,[74] more people presumably could approach the temple core and all could view it. When the doors stood open or where they were absent,[75] the direct axis even may have afforded direct visual access to the divine image.[76] In addition, since the court was outside of temple space architecturally, it did not co-opt its status in the same way as Mesopotamian and Hittite courts. In turn, it did not have the same gravitas to effect behavior, especially when unwalled; the nearby temple alone compelled obedience.

As in Egypt, Mesopotamia, and Hittite Anatolia, the Syro-Palestinian sanctuary, and more specifically the divine presence within it, was located in the most isolated region, behind the most walls and doors, and farthest from the entrance of divine space. As in Egypt, Mesopotamia, and Hittite Anatolia, the logical progression of spaces as one moved inward suggested the increasing importance of those spaces and the privilege of accessing them. Likewise, inward progress would have elicited an increasingly reverent response and provide an increasingly greater impetus to follow proper protocol. Nonetheless, in contrast to its larger ancient Near Eastern neighbors, Syro-Palestinian gods had more modest dwellings, often more like a monumental main room than an elaborate divine palace.[77] Syro-Palestinian temples also used elevation to mark the different zones; a zone's relative elevation unconsciously communicated to the observer its relative importance. In Syria-Palestine, the elevation of the inner sanctuary was especially common and especially

---

was present, and outside space, thereby highlighting the prominence of the primary divine space and the privilege of accessing it.

72. In other words, in Syria-Palestine, the temple complex was the temple core.

73. It is unclear if this isolation was intentional. However, its effect cannot be denied.

74. The courts were either unwalled, surrounded by service structures, or surrounded by often unimpressive walls.

75. Evidence for doors exists at such places as Alalakh Stratum VII (Woolley, *Alalakh*, 60), 'Ain Dara (Wightman, *Sacred Spaces*, 193), Tell Tayinat (ibid., 197), and Hazor Area H (Mazar, "Temples of the Middle and Late Bronze Ages," 166).

76. The degree and ease of physical access remain open questions. However, it would seem that access was hierarchically determined with purity as a requisite, especially in the larger temples.

77. Otto, "Gotteshaus und Allerheiligstes," 375.

prominent, functioning as the temple's major vertical division and thereby indicating the major distinction in status between the locus of the divine presence and the next most intimate and important space.

By surrounding the court with service structures, the builders not only communicated that the temple was more than a single-roomed residence,[78] they also hemmed in the divine precinct with structures of secondary religious importance. Thus, whether or not there was a surrounding wall, there was often primarily a threefold division within city space: 1) inside the temple core, 2) outside the temple core within the ring of auxiliary structures or the divine precinct, and 3) outside of divine space, in the human sphere.

The windows in (some) Syro-Palestinian sanctuaries, like those in Hittite Anatolia, seem to run counter to the ancient Near Eastern tendency to isolate and protect sanctuaries. However, in contrast to Hittite Anatolia, with the temple isolated from other structures, it would seem that anyone with access to the divine estate could have viewed the cult image. Thus, the deity itself in its richly decorated splendor may have been at once visible yet remained out of reach to all but the most privileged divine servants, suggesting both divine accessibility and the need to maintain a safe distance. However, it is possible that the windows may have been shuttered, thereby allowing only occasional visual access to the deity (e.g., in the context of a special monthly offering ceremony).[79]

### Relationship between Palace and Temple

Although cities almost always had a temple, they did not always have a palace (e.g., LB I Megiddo).[80] Thus, in such cases, city architecture suggested that the temple was the most powerful city institution. However, when both were present, they were commonly juxtaposed and the palace was often larger, thereby suggesting the relative power[81] and interconnectedness of the two institutions.[82]

## IDEOLOGY

Like their ancient Near Eastern counterparts, Syro-Palestinians endeavored to shape temple space in such a way that it served as a suitable divine residence.

---

78. E.g., the builders indicated the necessity of secondary service structures.

79. Pardee, *Ritual and Cult*, 26.

80. Nakhai, *Archaeology and the Religions of Canaan and Israel*, 133.

81. Even the most pious kings constructed larger palaces than temples unless the temple institution was strong enough to prevent them. Since the palaces were built larger than temples, we may tentatively conclude that the monarchy was a more powerful institution.

82. Nakhai suggests that the sacral and secular leadership were largely undifferentiated (*Archaeology and the Religions of Canaan and Israel*, 111).

Like their ancient Near Eastern analogs, Syro-Palestinian temples aimed to mix worlds, situating the divine in the midst of human habitation and appropriately mediating human access to the resident deity. However, given the more limited resources at their disposal, the nature of this symbiosis is not as clear in the architecture itself.[83]

There is little hint in the architectural remains of any cosmic significance or link to creation. The temple window seems to provide the best, albeit tenuous, evidence. Since the temple of Baal in Ugarit is the only clearly attested instance of a window in Syro-Palestinian religious architecture, the window may have been constructed to resemble or perhaps even to function as Baal's mythological window in his temple. In the temples of Baal of Ugarit and Baal of Ugaritic mythology, the window served as a point of contact with the surrounding world, in particular the human world. As Baal controlled the weather from his mythological palace, so too might he have controlled the weather from his terrestrial temple. Minimally, the presence of the window implies that the Baal present in the temple was the same Baal who controlled the weather. As Baal controlled the weather from his mythological palace (and terrestrial temple) without leaving it, so too could he exert his influence in the human sphere without ever leaving his terrestrial abode.

Like other ancient Near Eastern temples, Syro-Palestinian temples were made of human materials in the human sphere. The divine residence was nonetheless isolated from human space by walls and doors, thereby safeguarding the divine presence within it. In particular, the temple complex's otherness was indicated by the massive portal (of the fortress temples), like the Egyptian pylon serving as a clear boundary.[84] When present, potent animal and hybrid guardians marked the specialness of the place and the strength and importance of their divine master. While in many ways equipped like a human household, several of the temple's elements indicated that it was something more. For example, instead of a bed, the deity's resting place was often a pedestal; and, instead of a human body, the deity used a cult image as its physical embodiment.

As in Mesopotamia and Hittite Anatolia, there is also some indication at Ugarit that the temple itself and some of its parts were considered divine. For example, the steps of the altar, the stairs, and the architrave were presented with offerings.[85] Thus, more than simply marking off divine space, the temple itself was in some way divine and thus especially suitable for its divine resident.

---

83. Evidence for temple ideology is especially meager because of the dearth of texts and absence of major decorative elements.

84. Even when not massive by other ancient Near Eastern standards, the regular Syro-Palestinian temple portals were massive in comparison to domestic architecture.

85. Marjo A. Korpel, *A Rift in the Clouds: Ugaritic and Hebrew Descriptions of the Divine* (UBL 8; Münster: Ugarit-Verlag, 1990), 376. It is unclear if these elements were considered divine in their own right or simply imbued with or controlled by divine powers (it is even

The larger conceptual context also helps to fill out our picture of the Syro-Palestinian temple as mixing and meeting point. The nature of divine residences portrayed in Ugaritic mythology in particular helps to illumine the nature and ideology of the terrestrial temple.[86] The Ugaritic texts describe most divine dwellings in realistic detail. Like a human palace, divine palaces were constructed of the finest natural resources, with similar elements (e.g., with various rooms, gates, and courts), and were often localized on earth.[87] For example, Baal's palace was made of the finest cedar, silver and gold bricks, and lapis lazuli on Mt. Sapan with a window and storehouses (*KTU* 1.4 v–vi).[88]

However, lest we equate the mythological divine residence with a royal residence, the text bursts the confines of this anthropomorphic language, describing, for example, Baal's window as a "rift in the clouds" (*bdqt 'rpt*)[89] and his storehouses as containing thunder, lightning, and snow.[90] Although constructed of mundane materials, the construction process likewise partook of the supramundane, as a seemingly divine fire built his palace, effectively molding silver and gold respectively into sheet and bricks.[91] Thus, as a divine residence Baal's palace defied adequate description, portrayed as a hybrid structure of sorts, seeming to be both a human-like palace and an otherwordly castle in the clouds.[92] Syro-Palestinian temples like their ancient Near Eastern counterparts aimed to recreate some of the otherness of the divine abode in its natural habitat so that the god would profitably dwell amid human community. At the same time, because it was within the human sphere and thus accessible to humanity, it could not be so fantastically described or constructed.[93] Given the resources available, it must instead have been constructed to be similar to a human dwelling, yet with enough divine elements to indicate

---

possible, though less likely, that they merely served as portals to the resident deity). In either case, they served as access points to the divine sphere.

86. See briefly Korpel, *A Rift in the Clouds*, 370–76.

87. Ibid., 374–75, 383–86.

88. Ibid.

89. *KTU* 1.4 vii 19, 27–28.

90. *KTU* 1.101 3–4; 1.4 vii 59–60. The house also has exaggerated dimensions (a thousand acres, ten thousand hectacres) befitting the greatness of the divine resident (*KTU* 1.4 v 118–19).

91. Korpel, *A Rift in the Clouds*, 384–5; cf. Pitard, "Temple Building in Northwest Semitic Literature," 98.

92. Cf. Korpel, *A Rift in the Clouds*, 389–90. Similarly, while described as human-like, Anat's sanctuary appears to have been the high heavens (ibid., 375 n. 75, 389).

93. In other words, when situated in realms (or times) inaccessible to contemporary humanity, a place can be imagined in the most elaborate and imaginative terms. However, when situated amid human community, a place can be elaborately adorned, but it cannot transcend its realistic human surroundings.

that it was not the same as a human dwelling. Since these elements only minimally inhered in the structure, they had to be made by association.[94]

In Syria-Palestine, as in Mesopotamia, the center seems to have represented the cultivated, ordered world, while the periphery, or in some cases beyond the periphery, represented the uncultivated, chaotic world.[95] Within the center, benevolent deities often dwelt (e.g., Baal on Mt. Sapan and Anat on Mt. Inbub), while cosmic enemies, such as Yamm and Mot, dwelt beyond the bounds of human habitation, in the sea and underworld respectively.[96] Similarly, the council of the (benevolent) gods met on a mountain to decide the fertility of the land and the fate of the people.[97]

Although the benevolent gods dwelt in the center and in the earthly sphere,[98] they were largely beyond reach. Since, as servants, Syro-Palestinians could not compel their masters to do their bidding,[99] they sought instead to provide luxurious environments for the gods to dwell in the midst of human community. In other words, they sought to bring heaven to earth, or, more precisely, the gods from their natural habitats to the center of human habitation. By contrast, they hoped to keep the gods who dwelt beyond the periphery, Yamm and Mot, safely beyond the periphery. Thus, there is little indication that they were given temples

---

94. Nonetheless, although considered a suitable terrestrial residence, *KTU* 1.13 10–18 indicates that "Ugaritic worshippers were acutely aware of the fact that such an earthly abode could in no way be compared to the splendour of the heavenly dwelling of the deities" (Korpel, *A Rift in the Clouds*, 373).

95. Mark S. Smith, "The Structure of Divinity at Ugarit and Israel: The Case of Anthropomorphic Deities versus Monstrous Divinities," in Beckman and Lewis, eds., *Text, Artifact, and Image*, 38–63, reproduced and expanded from Mark S. Smith, *The Origins of Biblical Monotheism: Israel's Polytheistic Background and the Ugaritic Texts* (Oxford: Oxford University Press, 2001), 27–40.

96. Korpel, *A Rift in the Clouds*, 372–74; Smith, "Structure of Divinity," 38–45. Located in a palace at the head of the two rivers, El lived at "the horizon of the habitable cosmos" (Korpel, *A Rift in the Clouds*, 371; cf. Smith, "Structure of Divinity," 44). Such a dwelling seems appropriate for the powerful yet distant deity, while the active Baal naturally dwelt in the thick of the human sphere.

97. Richard J. Clifford, *The Cosmic Mountain in Canaan and the Old Testament* (Cambridge, MA: Harvard University Press, 1972), 190–91; Smith, "Structure of Divinity," 44–45. In an area where rainfall was essential, the gods' decision to grant or withhold it was a matter of life and death, thus the special importance of the weather god Baal, similar to his Hittite counterpart.

98. Although high and often isolated, mountains were nonetheless still part of earth, at least by Mesopotamian standards.

99. David P. Wright, "Histories: Syria and Canaan." in *Religions of the Ancient World: A Guide* (ed. S. Johnston; Cambridge, MA: Belknap Press of Harvard University Press, 2004), 175; cf. Frauke Gröndahl, *Die Personennamen der Texte aus Ugarit* (Studia Pohl 1; Rome: Päpstliches Bibelinstitut, 1967), 150; Korpel, *A Rift in the Clouds*, 306.

or a cult.[100] In a dangerous and unstable world, where even the great Baal was constantly challenged by Mot,[101] Syro-Palestinians built temples so that they could gain some degree of control and certainty. With a sustained and accessible meeting point, the people could serve the gods and offer them gifts so that they could receive divine blessing and, more expansively, influence cosmic events.[102] Thus, in their minds, the welfare of the small world of the temple and their appropriate actions in it were necessary to ensure the welfare of the larger world and their places in it.

Even with the larger context in place, there is no clear link to creation in the structure or ideology, perhaps because, as in Hittite Anatolia, a creation account is not evident in its mythology.[103] Nonetheless, the cosmic significance of the temple is apparent, derived from the benevolent cosmic presence that it housed. The significance of the temple is expressed in a striking way at ʿAin Dara (see fig. 5.3). Giant footprints impressed into the floor (ca. 1 m or 3 ft in length) are situated in the center of the porch, followed shortly by a single left footprint at the threshold of the vestibule and a right footprint some ten meters or thirty feet later at the threshold of the sanctuary. These footprints give the impression that a massive deity once strode into the sanctuary.[104] Since there are no return footprints, one could infer that a deity entered the sanctuary long ago without ever leaving, suggesting continued divine presence and approval of the temple. Indeed, since the cult image is the most common locus of terrestrial presence, one could also infer that the giant deity in some way resided in that image, thereby highlighting the potency of the resident deity, a potency that belied its sculpted form. At the same time, the footprints suggest that the deity was too great to be encapsulated by the cult image.[105] In other cases, even when decoration is less ostentatious and/or when other

---

100. Smith, "Structure of Divinity," 41, 47.

101. Ibid., 51–53.

102. By influencing the deities in the temples who controlled the cosmos, by extension, the people gained some control over cosmic events.

103. We may perhaps explain the structural variability of the temples in this way. Although there is some effort to mimic natural prototypes in order to provide a suitable environment (e.g., Baal's mountain palace [see Gregorio del Olmo Lete, *Canaanite Religion: According to the Liturgical Texts of Ugarit* (Winona Lake, IN: Eisenbrauns, 2004), 27]), there is no known primeval prototype to be scrupulously recreated.

104. There is no corroborating textual evidence and the physical evidence can be interpreted in multiple ways. Thus, any conclusions must be tentative.

105. This phenomenon may be compared to the hand- and footprints outside the Chinese Theatre along the Hollywood Walk of Fame. Both the ʿAin Dara footprints and the Hollywood handprints leave behind an imprint of a deity or person, serving as a reminder that they were once present at these very spots, a mark of their greatness, and an opportunity to experience that greatness through the marks they have left behind.

cosmic associations are lacking, signs of divine presence indicate the otherness and significance of temple space.

## Relationship between Palace and Temple, King and God

As indicated by their proximity, the palace and temple were often interconnected spheres. Based on size, the palace generally seems to have had more power. However, the texts from Ugarit and Emar present an ambivalent picture of the king's role in the divine cult. At Ugarit, the king featured prominently in the preserved rituals[106] and in the cult in general.[107] At Emar, however, the king played a more minimal role;[108] he was in fact absent from the rituals of the central *zukru* festival,[109] although he supplied much of the raw materials for the festival.[110] Perhaps this ambivalence was reflected in the complications of religious formation. The rites in Ugarit may have derived from an urban setting where the king was the prominent power, while the *zukru* festival may have had older, premonarchic origins.[111] Wherever the truth may lie, this discrepancy illustrates the religious complexity of the region and the difficulty inherent in analyzing its architecture. Thus, although the two spheres were interconnected and the palace appears to have been more powerful, we should not simply view the major temples as state appendages. Indeed, the monarchy was only more "powerful" within a limited sphere, namely, the institution of the monarchy had more wealth and perhaps more practical power to influence the city's people and events. Nonetheless, as elsewhere in the ancient Near East, the person of the king was beholden to the gods, and his primary contact point with them was in the temple. Thus, although the cult likely depended on the king, the king likewise depended on the cult. Especially with the continual tumult in Syria-Palestine, the king's maintenance of the temple was deemed essential for his continued good relations with his patron deity and thus foundational to his and his people's welfare.[112]

---

106. See, e.g., The Rites of the Vintage (*KTU* 1:41).

107. Del Olmo Lete, *Canaanite Religion*, 31, 166–212.

108. Fleming, "The Israelite Festival Calendar and Emar's Ritual Archive," *RB* 106 (1999): 21.

109. For a more extensive treatment of this festival, see Fleming, *Time at Emar*, 48–140, 234–67.

110. Fleming, "The Israelite Festival Calendar," 16–17, 21–23.

111. Ibid., 22–23; see more fully, idem, "A Limited Kingship," *UF* 24 (1992): 59–71.

112. Like their Mesopotamian counterparts, Syro-Palestinian texts especially boast of their temple building activities. See, e.g., the inscription of Yehimilk, king of Byblos (KAI no. 4; see COS 2:29, for a recent English translation) and Akish of Ekron (Seymour Gitin, Trude Dothan, and Joseph Naveh, "A Royal Dedicatory Inscription from Ekron," *IEJ* 47 [1997]: 1–16), who boasted of rebuilding temples and seemingly as a result pleaded for divine blessing.

# CHAPTER 6
## TEMPLES: SYNTHESIS

THE ANCIENT NEAR EASTERN TEMPLE served as a built environment crafted to house the deity in the heart of the human sphere and to allow limited access to its sheltered presence, for the benefit of all parties involved.[1] The temple represented the form and forum for divine-human communication, while the deity, humanity, and their interactions provided the content. Although only a stage, the temple was not without communicative power as the locus of presence and interaction with that presence. It was constructed to reflect and reinforce the importance of the space it shaped as the meeting point between heaven and earth.

The temple communicated its own message and elicited its own response, yet in doing so it bolstered and reinforced the already existing message of the actors and actions, of gods on earth and their interaction with humanity. It communicated the sanctity of the temple structure, its otherness and separateness, especially of the room that housed the divine presence. It expressed the concomitant privilege of accessing divine space and the necessity of following the proper protocol when one did. The structure itself and the ideology undergirding it conveyed that the temple was a mixing of worlds—in effect, heaven on earth—with elements of both built into the architecture itself. The degree to which it communicated this message varied, depending on the strategy of its designers and the success of their design.

### STRUCTURE

When examining the various temples of the ancient Near Eastern world, a remarkable continuity of form and its communicated message emerges, both within and across regions.[2] Axis, the shape of the rooms, and the complexity of the sacred

---

1. While the individual chapters have demonstrated the differing configurations of ancient Near Eastern temples, the present synthesis focuses on points of intersection, to see what may be said of the "common" ancient Near Eastern temple.

2. One may attribute this phenomenon to the shared ancient Near Eastern conservatism. Whereas the modern western, and especially American, mind hungers for innovation, thinking newer is almost always better, the ancient mind lauded tradition and looked upon change with a skeptical eye. As we have seen in the individual chapters, to the ancient Near Eastern mind, the way forward was often a return to the glorious past.

precinct varied, yet many constituent parts remained similar. The presence of a wall surrounding the sacred precinct and a gate to access it was a common feature, especially of the major urban temples, present in the massive Egyptian, Mesopotamian, and Hittite temples as well as the more modest Hazor Area H temple. In the larger sacred precincts, auxiliary buildings joined the main temple building and in most a courtyard appeared, either enclosed within the primary temple structure (as in Hittite Anatolia) or surrounding it (as in Syria-Palestine). The temple buildings themselves were often separated from the rest of the divine sphere by an exterior wall and gateway, from the imposing Egyptian pylon to the more modest Syro-Palestinian gateways, within which one could often find a vestibule or outer sanctuary. Further in, in the most isolated space and often in the dark,[3] dwelt the cult image, either at the end of a larger room or as the centerpiece of its own. The use of elevation was another common factor, both of the entire divine sphere in relation to the city around it (e.g., the primary temples in Ugarit and Emar were situated in the most elevated parts of their cities) and within that sphere itself (e.g., the raised platform for the cult image).

## USE

The temple structures themselves (and often supporting texts) also communicated the purpose of the building and of its various constituent parts with varying degrees of success. In Egypt, the purpose of the temple structure was inscribed on the very walls, in the form of reliefs and inscriptions. By contrast, in Syria-Palestine, the function of the various areas often must be inferred by analogy, from the few texts and from the remains of various moveable and nonmoveable elements (e.g., animal bones, votive vessels, altars, and washbasins).

Nonetheless, although the temples communicated their functions differently, the functions that they communicated were strikingly similar. On the whole, temples, as attested in the texts of each region, were the homes of the gods in the midst of human community, whom the people served in hopes of eliciting divine benevolence. In fact, each culture used the same word for human and divine dwellings, adding additional modifiers to distinguish them.

Although variable, the purposes of the temples' individual areas were likewise similar. In each, the walls and gates separated significant spaces. The outer gate separated the divine compound from the mundane world, the temple gate separated the divine residence from the larger divine estate, and (when present) the walls and doors inside the temple complex separated its significant spaces. Within the sacred precinct, the various auxiliary structures seem to have primarily supported the cult (e.g., a storage shed or a pottery workshop for making votive vessels).

---

3. With the possible exception of temples with windows in the sanctuary in Hittite Anatolia and Syria.

In other cases, structures seem to have appeared in the temple precinct because they wished to be associated with the sacred area and the deity who inhabited it (e.g., burial plots and small mortuary temples in Egypt). The court appears to have been a place for communal gathering, and, because it was open to the sky, animal slaughter.[4] The function of the rooms within the temple apart from the sanctuary is more difficult to pin down, especially when concrete clues and a written record are lacking. Those closer to the entrance appear to have been transitional space, akin to a modern lobby or reception hall. Consistently, the sanctuary was the home the home of the cult image and the place of regular, often anthropomorphic divine care and feeding (see part 2). Thus, the temple's built environment was created to regulate access to and highlight the importance of temple space as the home of the deity, who through its presence brought heaven to earth.

## Structural Communication

Beyond the shared form, the temples communicated similar messages. They highlighted the separateness and otherness of the temple[5] and simultaneously communicated something of the nature of this otherness.[6] Depending on the skill and resources of the builders, ancient Near Eastern temples expressed to a greater or lesser extent the ideology of the temple and all that was done therein, simultaneously eliciting the appropriate physical and emotional responses. Where present, the massive entry structures (e.g., the Egyptian pylon) projected strength and elicited awe, subconsciously informing observers that they were in a special space and had to follow its rules. Indeed, the temple structure and the people's conceptions of that space worked together to ensure unconscious reverence and acquiescence. When less grandiose, as in Syria-Palestine, these structures separated the exterior from the interior, the mundane world from the world of the gods, and communicated to some extent the otherness and separateness of the divine compound, even in muted form. Even when relatively unremarkable and unadorned, entry portals communicated the importance of the space to which they granted ingress because they were among the area's most imposing structures.

Within the temple complex, the structure continued to speak, and one would have subconsciously listened and responded appropriately. The architecture and

4. Since the courts of esp. Syro-Palestinian temples were often too small for large festival gatherings, sacred areas outside of the city, such as the standing stones of Emar, were constructed for this purpose.

5. The temple structure differentiated itself from other structures and thus identified itself as special and worthy of attention.

6. Here, the builders communicated analogically, groping for a way to display the temple, the divine abode and the arena for human interaction with the god, with the mundane forms at their disposal.

adornment separated the various rooms and often provided cues as to their uses. This communicative power is especially evident in the Egyptian temples, in which the structure and adornment of the various sections differed significantly, distinguishing between spaces and proclaiming their unique rules. Even in less elaborate structures, walls and doors physically divided spaces and granted access to those spaces, communicating concretely and silently the division of space. Adornment, even in the relatively unadorned temples, was often clustered around the portals, highlighting their importance in separating spaces and the boundaries between significant spaces. In addition, temple walls and doors with their adornment, as in a modern home, unconsciously communicated the increasing privilege of moving further from the exterior and closer to the most secluded area of the built environment, the (divine) bedchamber. Likewise, progressive ingress informed entrants that they were moving progressively further from public space and further into private space and, as such, were beholden to its rules.

While significant spaces were separated in different ways in the different Near Eastern temples, almost all clearly distinguished the deity's room—either a room set apart from the rest or, more often, a space set apart from the sanctuary, such as a pedestal or niche—from the rest of the complex. In each, we presumably would have found the cult image, most often an ornate statue, in the most secluded area of the entire compound.

## IDEOLOGY

The structure of the temple communicated its architects' ideology to some extent. When joined with relevant texts, especially of a mythological nature, this ideology emerges more clearly. The texts inform us of the underlying mythology of the culture, which the temple structure often built upon and enhanced. The names of the temples themselves and the texts describing them are also informative, often providing native interpretations that fill out the picture. When such textual representation is insufficient, as in much of the Syro-Palestinian and Hittite world, our reconstruction is both more tentative and more general.

Like the structures themselves, there is both a remarkable general commonality in ideology and remarkably different ways of expressing that shared ideology in different cultures. Most fundamentally, the temple was crafted to house the divine and mediate human access to it, to bring heaven to earth so that the powers of heaven could be brought to bear on the people's behalf to bring security in an otherwise insecure world. In short, the temple regularized contact with the deity by creating a home for it to dwell in the midst of human community. In fact, while contact was important, the mere presence of the deity signaled blessing. In order to ensure this blessing, as part 2 will elucidate, contact primarily took the form of service so that the resident deity remained resident and favorably disposed to bless the community around it. As such, the temple design represented a mixing of worlds, suitable for its otherwise inaccessible divine resident and for limited human access to him. The temple was created to be functional, and thus not too dissimilar from the most opulent known structure, the royal residence. At the same time, it must be appropriate for its unique divine resident, and thus bear marks of its otherness suitable to its deity to differentiate this residence from all human analogs. Thus, more than simply communicating the importance of the structure, builders and architects sought to communicate its otherness and some of the nature of its otherness. Given the limits of the human imagination and mundane resources, they communicated this numinous otherness primarily through figural representation and association.

In its varied expression, the temple relied on anthropomorphisms.[7] In groping for means to express the divine abode, the ancient Near Eastern world naturally turned to anthropomorphic representations, either assuming that the gods were human-like and as such required human-like accommodations and services, or simply using anthropomorphisms since they were the most appropriate media of communication available. In the latter case, although the people knew that their gods were not human, they nonetheless envisioned and represented them as such because anthropomorphism would be the closest approximation of their ineffable reality. Much akin to feudal lords, the gods were depicted as living in houses, often surrounded by landed estates, where their (quasi-)physical needs were met by a team of servants.

Within this anthropomorphically envisioned world, various architectural and associational elements communicated the otherness of divine space, often mirroring creation and the victory of order over chaos and stressing the temple's role as link between heaven and earth. In some cases in Mesopotamia, Hittite Anatolia, and Syria-Palestine, the temple itself was even considered divine. More than simply bringing heaven to earth (and ontologically belonging to a different sphere of existence), the temple created heaven on earth. Thus, ancient Near Eastern people took great pains to communicate that their temple, as the Christian refrain expresses, was "in the world but not of it."[8] As the individual chapters indicate, the config-

---

7. We may also speak of sociomorphisms, in which the divine is interpreted according to the patterns of social reality (Friedhelm Hartenstein, *Das Angesicht JHWHs: Studien zu seinem höfischen und kultischen Bedeutungshintergrund in den Psalmen und in Exodus 32–34* [FAT 55; Tübingen: Mohr Siebeck, 2008], esp. 15–26, building on the work of Jean-Pierre Vernant in particular [e.g., *Mortals and Immortals: Collected Essays* (ed. F. I. Zeitlin; Princeton: Princeton University Press, 1991]).

8. This concept, derived largely from John 17:11–17, indicates that the Christian by nature belongs to another world yet continues to inhabit this one. This connection is reinforced by the biblical understanding of the Christian as a temple of God (1 Cor 3:16; 2 Cor 6:16). Christians, like the ancient temples, would then carry within themselves the divine and as such be connected with the heavenly realm, yet continue to dwell on earth. Like the temple, they too would be a piece of heaven on earth.

uration of heaven on earth varied across regions and over time, while the tension between expressing presence and maintaining divine distance was also articulated in different ways, from the massive Mesopotamian ziggurat to the more modest one room temple. While it allowed minimal access, the deity was also safely sequestered from the mundane world in its sacred abode. Thus, the temple both prevented the irruption of a meeting of worlds and uniquely embodied their (semi-) permanent intersection.

As the meeting point of heaven and earth—and in some contexts the vertical and horizontal cosmic axis, the very center of the world around which all else revolved—the temple was in some ways a miniature world of its own. Often self-sufficient and set apart from the mundane sphere, the temple was the ideal, embodying the perfection to which the rest of the world could only aspire and hope to absorb by association. As a self-contained ideal world inhabited by the powers who ruled the cosmos, and indeed the primary human access point to the divine world, the welfare of this small sacred area and its divine resident determined the welfare of the community around it.

# Part 2

## Divine Presence in Ancient Near Eastern Temples

# CHAPTER 7

## INTRODUCTION TO DIVINE PRESENCE IN ANCIENT NEAR EASTERN TEMPLES

IN THE ANCIENT NEAR EAST, deities seem to have been envisioned as primarily anthropomorphic,[1] yet, rather than being cast as bigger and better humans, they transcended the human model in various ways.[2] In addition to the vast differences in power and spheres of influence,[3] a primary difference lay in a deity's ability to adopt multiple forms (e.g., anthropomorphic, theriomorphic, and celestial) and to move fluidly between forms as the need arose.[4] Deities even seem to have been able to occupy multiple forms in multiple places simultaneously and, in some cases, multiple forms in the same place. In turn, the relationship between a "single" deity's various manifestations was complex.[5] For present purposes and in anticipa-

---

1. Again, with Hartenstein (Angesicht JHWHs), we also may refer to conceptions of deity as sociomorphic, i.e., reflecting the social realities of the human world.

2. Ronald Hendel speaks of a "transcendent anthropomorphism" ("Aniconism and Anthropomorphism in Ancient Israel" in van der Toor, *Image and the Book*, 207 and passim), whereby gods were generally predicated on a human model, yet transcended that model in every conceivable way. Hendel's use of the term is to be differentiated from that of Hamori (*When Gods Were Men*, 32), who instead uses "transcendent anthropomorphism" to refer to an anthropomorphic description of deity without mention of a concrete body. "Transcending" is perhaps a better term than "transcendent" since the gods did not wholly abandon anthropomorphisms, but transcended them in various ways (ibid.).

3. E.g., the gods were thought to control the very elements that humanity could not control, like rain.

4. For example, in Ugarit, deities often took mammalian form for the purpose of mating and bird form for travel (Korpel, Rift, 524–32, 544–49). In first millennium Mesopotamia, however, there is less evidence of deities switching forms. Instead they seem to have simultaneously occupied various different forms (e.g., an anthropomorphic form, heavenly bodies, and several statues). This stands in contrast to classical Greece, wherein it would seem that rather than occupying several different bodies simultaneously, a deity occupied a single body that could change form at will (Benjamin D. Sommer, *The Bodies of God and the World of Ancient Israel* [Cambridge: Cambridge University Press, 2009], 30–36; regarding the relationship between statue and deity, see esp. Tanja S. Scheer, *Die Gottheit und ihr Bild: Untersuchungen zur Funktion griechischer Kultbilder in Religion und Politik* [Zetemata 105; Munich: Beck, 2000]).

5. Evidence for this assertion will be outlined in each section. Here, I speak in generalizations as a point of orientation and entry into the complex subject of divine presence in the ancient

tion of the contextually differentiated discussions in each chapter, suffice it to say that each was in some way connected, yet also treated as distinct.

Although deities could adopt multiple forms, it is striking that they appeared rarely in the human sphere in one of their "natural" forms[6] and, especially in Egypt and first millennium Mesopotamia, rarely on earth.[7] When they did occasionally appear to humanity, such encounters were ephemeral, often occurring on the periphery or through such tenuous media as dreams. Except in rare instances, humanity could not access the divine realm.[8] To elicit a meeting with the divine, people had to coax the deities to come into the human realm, to bring heaven to earth. The temple and its cultic apparatus were the primary ancient Near Eastern solution to this divine absence, constructed to bring the divine world concretely to earth, by providing the deity with a residence in the heart of human community. In short, the temple was the site of a semi-permanent theophany, one that would remain as long as the deity remained content. It was the controlled and isolated environment that enabled divine presence on earth and mediated contact between the resident deity and its human servants. By serving the deity in this consistent and controlled environment, people could bring divine power to bear on their lives and even influence cosmic events. Thus, in a dangerous and volatile world, people could gain some measure of control and security.

Since there was no way to capture, copy, or control the divine in all of its perceived glory, divine presence was further concretized and localized in the form of a cult image.[9] More than simply living in a space marked off as sacred, the deity was persuaded, often through elaborate rituals, to in some way inhabit a tangible, human-made form, its cult image. The connection between statue and deity was perceived to be so strong that when the image was present, the deity was often assumed to be present as well. This remained the case even when the image left the sacred precinct, primarily during processions on festive occasions. Not only was the deity present in the image, but the well-being of the image also seems to

---

Near East. Analysis will focus on the primary manifestation of the deity in the human sphere: divine presence in cult images within the various ancient Near Eastern temples. While fascinating, ancient Near Eastern conceptions of the divine in other locales, such as in their heavenly abodes and as celestial bodies, will feature only as they illuminate our main point of inquiry.

6. By "natural," I mean forms not constructed by humanity.

7. Instead, as we will see, the primary access point to deity in the human sphere was the human-made cult image.

8. For a helpful summary, see, e.g., Hamori, *When Gods Were Men*, 129–49.

9. Cult image refers to the primary human-made locus or loci of divine presence in the temple, which may be an anthropomorphic, theriomorphic, or hybrid statue or a symbol like the spade of Marduk.

have been connected to that of the deity.[10] Thus, it follows logically that how the worshipers treated their deity in the form of its image determined how the deity treated them and their nation.

Although the perceived connection between deity and image spanned the ancient Near East, the form of the cult image and the understanding of its relationship to the deity varied within and across regions. This complex and wide-ranging expression is understandable, reflecting the complexity of presencing the deity in a human-made statue in the human sphere.

As in the temple, with divine presence temple tradents were grasping at something beyond their reach, faced with the classic problem of trying to define and describe the supernatural divine in natural, human terms that it by definition transcended.[11] To elucidate this problem, we may point to a dimensional analogy. When a three-dimensional sphere touches down in two-dimensions, it becomes a circle. This two-dimensional representation has no way of adequately portraying the fullness of a three-dimensional sphere. It can merely use the language at its disposal, two-dimensional language, which in no way encapsulates but in some way approximates and represents a sphere. While a circle is truly a piece of a sphere, it is flat, lacking the dimensionality of a circle, and is limited to its two-dimensional reality.

Similarly, as humans we can only perceive the three spatial dimensions: up/down, left/right, and forward/backward. However, string theory, an increasingly prominent theory of particle physics, suggests that there are extra-spatial dimensions that we cannot see.[12] M-theory, for instance, suggests that there are eleven dimensions operating in our world. It posits that in addition to the three known dimensions of space and the dimension of time, the world consists of an additional seven imperceptible spatial dimensions. Naturally, when we lack the appropriate descriptors to describe reality in its multidimensional plenitude, we may only approximate that reality. Although accurate, our approximation is nonethtless as flat as a two-dimensional slice of a three-dimensional sphere, only a small sliver of the complete figure. For example, a four-dimensional cube, called a tesseract, looks like "two cubes with interconnecting lines to us—that is, one 3-D intersection, just as a circle is one intersection of a [sphere] within a 2-D world."[13] In other words,

---

10. The nature of this connection will be examined in each chapter.

11. On the complexity of religious language, see, e.g., Soskice, *Metaphor and Religious Language*.

12. See, e.g., Brian Greene, *The Fabric of the Cosmos: Space, Time, and the Texture of Reality* (New York: Knopf, 2004); Katrin Becker et al., eds., *String Theory and M-Theory: A Modern Introduction* (Cambridge: Cambridge University Press, 2007).

13. Jaron Lanier, "Jaron's World: Shapes in Other Dimensions," *Discover Magazine*, April 2007. Online: http://discovermagazine.com/2007/apr/jarons-world-shapes-in-other-dimensions.

our visual perception of a four-dimensional cube is only a three-dimensional sliver of its four-dimensional reality, just as a circle is a two-dimensional sliver of a three-dimensional sphere. Likewise, when a divine being, perceived to be multidimensional, touches down in a three-dimensional world, humans lack adequate descriptors. They too may genuinely approximate but in no way encapsulate divine presence.

Indeed, the concept and application of divine presence is far more ineffable even than the temple itself. The temple combined elements of two worlds. Built in and of this world, it was an earthly home, yet a home whose occupant was not of this world, thus rendering this home different than any imaginable residence. If this home lacked adequate human descriptors, how much more so the presence of the god who inhabited it in an unnatural symbiosis of the unmediated divine with a human-made image? The symbiosis of deity and image was all the more unnatural than that of a deity and a terrestrial residence since it merged the most powerful beings in the universe with inert matter.

Faced with this difficulty, ancient Near Easterners often adopted a cumulative approach that tended to eschew classifications of the divine.[14] Each attempt to grasp at meaning used analogical language,[15] both verbal and visual, some of which could capture an aspect of divine presence yet fail to grasp the whole. Thus, they combined these attempts to portray the deity from different angles, hoping that different perspectives would provide a fuller picture of the whole.[16] In addition, rather than trying to fit all perspectives into a unified picture, they seemed content to accumulate and juxtapose the different perspectives and live with the inherent tension between them.

The modern mind often views the ancient perspective with its fluid approach as frustratingly inconsistent or, worse yet, embarrassingly primitive. However, the ancient Near Eastern thinker would find modern categorizations maddeningly restrictive or, worse yet, the height of hubris. Although modern scholars are careful in their classifications, they often end up categorizing the divine in binary terms with consistent abstract principles. These careful divisions consistently limit the deity so carefully described, and thus are consistently distant from the complex ancient Near Eastern portrait. Realizing that any representation was merely an approximation, ancient Near Easterners instead piled on approximates in the hopes

---

14. See, e.g., regarding Egypt, Hornung, *Conceptions of God*, 99: "It is evidently unnatural for Egyptians gods to be strictly defined. Their being remains a fluid state to which we are not accustomed; it escapes every dogmatic, final definition and can always be extended or further differentiated."

15. See further Hundley, *Keeping Heaven*, 12–14 and the references cited therein.

16. They were also pragmatic in that they approached the deity from the particular perspective that suited their need.

of approaching plenitude.[17] For them, inconsistencies, which are often the result of the limits of human cognition, were far preferable to consistent yet consistently restrictive categories.[18] In other words, for them, it was better to allow the deity to be practically limitless even if that limitlessness baffled the mind, rather than confine the deity to the limited boundaries that are a necessary product of the human mind. Returning to our previous analogy, when one consistently portrays a three-dimensional sphere as a two-dimensional circle, one might imply that a sphere is nothing more than a circle. Instead, by portraying a sphere in multiple ways, one communicates that a circle is a "true" representation of but not identical with a sphere. Similarly, when one employs fixed binary categories to describe a deity, one implicitly limits the deity to the categories so described. By contrast, using many different analogs indicates that the deity is more than the sum of its perceived parts, that no approximation is sufficient yet together all approximations may approach the divine plenitude.

Because of their general reticence to categorize and because of their generally different conceptions, ancient Near Eastern perspectives are notoriously difficult for the modern scholar to comprehend. Selz notes that the ancient conception of divine presence "seems problematic, even contradictory to us, but evidently was not to the mind of ancient man."[19] However, a more apt diagnosis is that ancient Near Eastern thinkers recognized the difficulty inherent in conceptualizing and concretizing the divine presence, yet approached the problem in a very different way than their modern interpreters. Ancient theologians, like their modern counterparts, understood the complex nature of the issue and composed complicated and not always consistent theories and rituals to explain it, all the while showing their relative unease with divine presence in human-made form. Thus, rather than being entirely comfortable with the issues, ancient Near Easterners addressed them from different angles, with different strengths and weaknesses.

---

17. Cf., e.g., Vincent Arieh Tobin, *Theological Principles of Egyptian Religion* (New York: Lang, 1989), 23–25, regarding Egyptian versus modern perspectives.

18. For example, "the Egyptians place the tensions and contradictions of the world beside one another and live with them" (Hornung, *Conceptions of God*, 97). Regarding Mesopotamia, cf., Barbara Nevling Porter, "Blessings from a Crown, Offerings to a Drum: Were There Non-Anthropomorphic Deities in Ancient Mesopotamia?", in What is a God? Anthropomorphic and Non-Anthropomorphic Aspects of Deity in Ancient Mesopotamia (ed. Porter; Transactions of the Casco Bay Assyriological Institute 2; Winona Lake, IN: Eisenbrauns, 2009), 187–88; cf. with caution, regarding modes of ancient perception, Emma Brunner-Traut, *Frühformen des Erkennens: Am Beispiel Altägyptens* (Darmstadt: Wissenschaftliche Buchgesellschaft, 1990).

19. Gebhard J. Selz, "'The Holy Drum, the Spear, and the Harp': Toward an Understanding of the Problems of Deification in Third Millennium Mesopotamia," in *Sumerian Gods and Their Representations* (ed. Irving J. Finkel and Markham J. Geller; Groningen: Styx, 1997), 183.

In the past, scholars have denigrated ancient Near Eastern perceptions and practice as primitive, largely derived from a particular reading of the biblical prophets and from the different way of conceptualizing the divine. Recently, a scholarly vogue has been to correct this extreme portrait, and rightly so, yet in the process some have gone to the other extreme. In their efforts to rehabilitate iconic worship, some scholars have idealized it. In their vigor to overturn the caricature of the past, they have in some ways produced a caricature of their own. Scholars have even placed ancient Near Eastern conceptions of divine presence and divine images in the realm of complex figural language, thereby denying the real corporeal presence so stressed in the ancient Near Eastern world.[20] Their theoretical, and even mystical,[21] portrait may be warranted at times by texts, yet in no way encapsulates the whole ancient Near Eastern landscape, especially not the mindsets of the pragmatically minded populace.[22] The reality, as always, was more complex than either extreme would allow, lying somewhere and somewhat uneasily between the poles.[23]

Ancient expressions of the divine, which were by no means simple barbarisms, were limited by the ineffable nature of the object of their inquiry. Both then and now, humanity lacks adequate descriptors to describe the supernatural divine and its perceived presence on earth. In the ancient Near Eastern world, as in the world of today, descriptions and depictions of deity were by necessity somewhat anthropomorphic.[24] Xenophanes, a sixth century pre-Socratic Greek philosopher,

---

20. Richard E. Friedman, e.g., suggests that the cult statue only reminds the worshiper of the divine presence, much like an icon in a Christian church (*Who Wrote the Bible?* [Englewood Cliffs, NJ: Prentice Hall, 1987], 35).

21. Karel van der Toorn refers to this view as "spiritualizing" ("Worshipping Stones: On the Deification of Cult Symbols," *JNSL* 23 [1997]: 2).

22. For a similar analysis, see van der Toorn, "Worshipping Stones"; idem, "Book," 229–48; cf. William H. C. Propp, *Exodus 19–40* (AB 2A; New York: Doubleday, 2006), 168.

23. Several recent studies have presented a more balanced perspective; see, e.g., the various articles in Neal H. Walls, ed., *Cult Image and Divine Representation in the Ancient Near East* (ASOR Book Series 10; Boston: ASOR, 2005).

24. "It seems that human imagination is somewhat limited and that even when men and women wished to allude to the supernatural they could not transcend their realistic surroundings" (Tallay Ornan, *The Triumph of the Symbol: Pictoral Representation of Deities in Mesopotamia and the Biblical Image Ban* [OBO 213; Fribourg: Academic Press, 2005], 168). For example, modern Christians continue to use anthropomorphic language to describe God (referring to him as father, to his heart, hands, etc.; cf. Andreas Wagner, *Gottes Körper: Zur alttestamentlichen Vorstellung der Menschengestaltigkeit Gottes* [Gütersloh: Gütersloher Verlaghaus, 2010]). It seems natural to Christian interpreters because it is part of their cultural vocabulary (i.e., because it is not foreign), not because it is a natural or an adequate descriptor. Anthopomorphisms refer more broadly to the various kinds of human-likeness, whether in form, emotions, or description (see further the clarifications in Hamori, *When Gods Were Men*, 26–34, with special reference to the biblical text).

astutely noted that if horses had gods, they probably would have a horse's form.[25] In other words, in describing the divine, it is difficult for humans to entirely escape human-like description.[26] Indeed, although ancient Near Eastern gods were depicted in many different forms—including as animals, hybrids, and as natural phenomena—ancient Near Easterners nonetheless primarily refered to and conceptualized them in anthropomorphic terms.[27] Anthropomorphisms render deities understandable, sentient, and approachable. Using approximate human terms to describe them renders them more understandable than would any other descriptors. Since humans are the most sentient beings in their natural environments, the human model is the only sensible archetype for depicting sentient deities. Since they are conceived of as like humans, deities also may be approached and communicated with far more than with an animal, a river, or a storm, and may even be persuaded to provide divine assistance. In addition, a potent yet mindless force like a storm becomes the source of greater reverence when it is controlled by a human-like being. Divine anthropomorphisms likewise render the cosmos more understandable and consistent, and thus more secure. When human-like divine beings control it, people may begin to understand it, predict and even influence its behavior, rendering the world a safer and more comprehensible place. Finally, as attested in Egypt and Mesopotamia, humanity was conceived of as theomorphic. In other words, rather than imagining gods as like us, the gods crafted us like them. By bearing a likeness to the supreme deities, humans thus garnered greater dignity and perhaps warranted more of the gods' concern than, e.g., a squirrel.

Both ancient and modern expressions are limited by more than mere anthropomorphisms; humans often fail to escape the cultural confines of their particular anthropocentric world. For example, the western world has depicted Jesus as a western man for centuries, often with blond hair and blue eyes, a portrait that says far more about the biases of the artists than about the reality of a first-century Jew. Thus, humans often cannot see beyond their own environment. As interpreters, we can never entirely escape our biased perspectives, yet by being aware of our shortcomings we may avoid more egregious errors. With these limitations in mind, we may begin to understand how the ancients perceived and presented the gods as like themselves but much more, especially within the temple realm.

25. Henk S. Versnel, "Thrice One: Three Greek Experiments in Oneness" in Porter, ed., *One God or Many?*, 92.

26. Ornan argues this position with respect to Mesopotamia most vehemently and, with qualification, persuasively (idem, *Triumph of the Symbol*; idem, "In the Likeness of Man: Reflections on the Anthropocentric Perception of the Divine in Mesopotamian Art," in Porter, ed., *What Is a God?*, 93–151); see also Hamori, *When Gods Were Men*, 35–64, esp. 46–50, under the heading "All Theism is Anthropomorphic."

27. There are of course exceptions, such as deified rivers and divine furniture with no apparent human-like form or emotions.

It is natural and valuable to use modern cultural analogies to "familiarize"[28] ourselves with aspects of a foreign world, to show that complicated alien concepts are not so alien after all. However, we must be careful not to take the analogies too far[29] and be aware that our analogies often say as much about us and our interpretations as about what we are interpreting.[30]

Perhaps the closest modern parallel lies in the Hindu religious culture in India.[31] Hindu deities, like their ancient Near Eastern counterparts, often in some way inhabit statues constructed for them in temples. As with ancient Near Eastern deities, Hindu deities can be present in multiple locales without diminishment and their presence in a cult image may be interpreted in different ways. As in ancient Mesopotamia, the materials used to craft the deity are also treated as a deity in the making[32] and are transitioned into a fully functioning divine presence through elaborate ritual action.[33] Finally, like the ancient Near Eastern cult statues, Indian perceptions of divine presence have been much criticized and misunderstood.[34]

Another prominent modern analogy for understanding the divine presence in a statue is the Eucharist.[35] First, it can account for the real presence of the deity in more than one form and one locale at once. As the real body and blood of Jesus in Roman Catholic and Orthodox theology, Jesus may be simultaneously present without diminishment in various churches throughout the world, even within several chapels in the same church, while continuing to be present simultaneously in

---

28. Dick, "Mesopotamian Cult Statue," 44.

29. Modern analogies are merely analogies. They are meant to approximate but not encapsulate the object they hope to elucidate. When we equate the analogy with the concept it seeks to approximate, or we simply begin to extend it too far (e.g., by making the ancient data fit our modern analogy), we begin to confuse and distort the issue instead of illuminating it.

30. Michael Ann Holly provides a similar caution with regard to interpreting artifacts: "We may be talking about an artifact, but we are also talking about ourselves" ("Past Looking," *Critical Inquiry* 16 [1990]: 390).

31. On the complicated nature of the Indian image, see, e.g., Joanna Punzo Waghorne and Norman Cutler, eds., *Gods of Flesh/Gods of Stone: The Embodiment of Divinity in India* (New York: Columbia University Press, 1985).

32. For Hindu images, see, e.g., Richard Davis, *Lives of Indian Images* (Princeton: Princeton University Press, 1999), 34–35; for Mesopotamia, see, e.g., Victor A. Hurowitz, "What Goes in is What Comes Out: Materials for Creating Cult Statues," in Beckman and Lewis, eds. *Text, Artifact, and Image*, 3–23.

33. For an example from South India, see Waghorne, "The Divine Image in Contemporary South India: The Renaissance of a Once Maligned Tradition," in Dick, ed., *Born in Heaven*, 211–43.

34. Waghhorne, "The Divine Image."

35. This position has been argued most extensively by Dick ("Mesopotamian Cult Statue") but also noted by others (for these references, see ibid., 43–44).

heaven.[36] Second, one may interpret both the Eucharistic elements and the divine cult statue as: a) a god; b) a god in (but distinct from) the image or elements; or c) merely a reminder or symbol of a god.

The Christian concept of the Trinity is yet another analogy, which in some way approximates ancient Near Eastern divine presence.[37] As with the Eucharist, the deity may be present in more than one locale without diminishment (as God the father, YHWH dwells in heaven; Jesus the son corporeally inhabits human flesh and, upon resurrection, resides with YHWH in heaven; while the Holy Spirit is active in the world and mysteriously indwells the hearts of Christian believers). Again, the mystery may be interpreted in different ways. The various aspects of the divinity (Father, Son, and Holy Spirit) are either a) one and the same; b) connected yet distinct; or c) or the latter two are merely manifestations of God the father, akin to an Indian avatar, a partial manifestation of the heavenly deity on earth.[38] Many Christians identity the aspects of the Trinity as separate individuals who are fully God, while at the same time affirming that there is only one God. This parallel also may help to explain how each statue could be a god in its own right, while at the same time be part of the one original god[39] (e.g., in Mesopotamia, Ishtar of Arbela is in some way distinct from Ishtar of Nineveh, yet each is also in some way Ishtar[40]).

Another possible analogy comes from the secular sphere. Ancient Near Eastern divine manifestations, especially temple cult images, may be understood to function like clones. Although clones essentially reproduce the original and are

---

36. Cf. ibid., 54.

37. Cf. Sommer, *Bodies of God*, 132–33. We may also appeal to the conceptualizations of Mary in certain Roman Catholic traditions, where local manifestations of Mary are given different epithets and treated as distinct by local worshippers, though officially recognized as derived from a single prototype, the biblical Mary (see, e.g., Spencer L. Allen, "The Splintered Divine: A Study of Ištar, Baal, and Yahweh Divine Names and Divine Multiplicity in the Ancient Near East" [Ph.D. diss., University of Pennsylvania, 2011], 87–97; forthcoming as idem, *The Splintered Divine: A Study of Ištar, Baal, and Yahweh Divine Names and Divine Multiplicity in the Ancient Near East* (SANER 5; Berlin: de Gruyter).

38. Recently popularized (and somewhat inaccurately portrayed) in James Cameron's film, Avatar. On the avatar, see, e.g., David Kinsley, "Avatāra," in *Encyclopedia of Religion* (ed. Mircea Eliade et al.; 16 vols.; New York: MacMillan, 1987), 2:14–15; Alain Daniélou, *The Myths and Gods of India: The Classic Work on Hindu Polytheism from the Princeton Bollingen Series* (Rochester, VT: Inner Traditions, 1991), 164–87; Sommer also draws the comparison between the ancient Near Eastern image and an avatar (*Bodies of God*, 15).

39. See also the various local manifestations of Mary in Roman Catholicism (see, e.g., Allen, "Splintered Divine," 87–97).

40. Regarding the distinction between Ishtar of Arbela and Ishtar of Nineveh, see, e.g., Porter, "Ishtar of Nineveh and Her Collaborator, Ishtar of Arbela, in the Reign of Assurbanipal," *Iraq* 66 (2004): 41–44.

clearly connected to it, they are nonetheless in some ways distinct entities. For example, although each clone is born essentially the same as the original, i.e., with the same DNA, it will develop its own distinct personality and experiences.[41] Each divine manifestation in the form of an image is also both essentially the same as the original and distinct from it. Likewise, the fullness of the original entity is found not only in that original, but also in all its various copies. For example, in Mesopotamia, Ishtar is manifest at least to some degree as the divine goddess, the planet Venus, the cult images in Nineveh and Arbela, the number 15, lapis-lazuli, and lead.[42] Each is (fully) Ishtar, yet each is not the fullness of Ishtar in all her plenitude, for her fullness lies in the accumulation of all of her manifestations, names and attributes. Therefore, treaties, ritual texts, and some iconography appeal to each manifestation so that the deity in all its fullness is brought to bear.

Having employed the biology of cloning, we may also make positive comparisons with physics, more specifically quantum mechanics.[43] Quantum mechanics contends that on the atomic and sub-atomic levels "matter" functions in bizarre ways, which are not obviously compatible with the observable universe around us.[44] Most notably, physicists have demonstrated that (sub-)atomic particles may manifest themselves in more than one place at the same time and that the various manifestations may act synchronously while far apart although they have no apparent way to communicate. Likewise, although it has no place in our mundane experiences, a deity may be perceived to mysteriously manifest itself in multiple locales at once and act in concert, at least to some degree, in each of those locales.

Each analogy helps us to situate this alien concept from an alien world in concepts of the modern world. Each is useful in "familiarizing" the modern in-

---

41. See, e.g., Aaron D. Levine, *Cloning: A Beginner's Guide* (London: Oneworld, 2007); Ian Wilmut and Roger Highfield, *After Dolly: The Promise and Perils of Cloning* (New York: W. W. Norton, 2007).

42. Porter, "The Anxiety of Multiplicity: Conceptions of Divinity as One and Many in Ancient Assyria," in Porter, ed., *One God or Many?*, 244. In fact, in addition to Ishtar of Nineveh and Arbela, Ishtar/Inanna was worshiped in at least one hundred cult places (Birgitte Groneberg, "Aspekte der 'Göttlichkeit' in Mesopotamien: Zur Klassifizierung von Göttern und Zwischenwesen," in *Götterbilder, Gottesbilder, Weltbilder, I: Ägypten, Mesopotamien, Persien, Kleinasien, Syrien, Palästina* [ed. R. G. Kratz and H. Spieckermann; FAT II/17; Tübingen: Mohr Siebeck, 2006], 139–40.

43. For an introduction to quantum mechanics, see, e.g., Roland Omnès, *Understanding Quantum Mechanics* (Princeton: Princeton University Press, 1999); Richard L. Liboff, Introductory Quantum Mechanics (Reading, MA: Addison-Wesley, 2002); Jeremy Bernstein, Quantam Leaps (Cambridge, MA: Belknap Press of Harvard University Press, 2009).

44. See, e.g., Tim Folger's provocatively titled article, "If an Electron Can Be in Two Places at Once, Why Can't You?," *Discover Magazine*, June 2005. Online: http://discovermagazine.com/2005/jun/cover.

terpreter with the ancient world, as one of many lenses through which we may examine the issue at hand, yet none should be used too freely or to the exclusion of other fruitful avenues.

The following study in part 2 is an attempt to view the multivocal ancient Near Eastern portrait of divine presence in the temple in its complexity, recognizing all the while that the ancient world is only partially preserved and must be viewed through a biased lens.[45] In our analysis, we will attempt to look at the picture through various lenses, using various analogies in an attempt to let the disparate ancient voices speak, so that we may begin to understand the various ways ancient Near Easterners conceptualized god on earth.

In the modern western world, the relationship between sign and referent, in our case between a deity and its image, is often one of mimesis.[46] The image is merely a copy of the original, which points to the real but contains none of its es-

---

45. "The original context is not simply formed by data, found by the scholar. It also is produced through an entire set of interpretive decisions and assumptions that are often left unstated" (Zainab Bahrani, *The Graven Image: Representation in Babylonia and Assyria* [Philadelphia: University of Pennsylvania Press, 2003], 3).

46. The following theory builds on the work of Bahrani, *Graven Image*, with reference to ancient Mesopotamia and applies it more broadly and provisionally to the rest of the ancient Near East. In particular, it builds on her assertion that an image is a partial presence. Although her analysis is at times problematic (see, e.g.. Marian Feldman, Review of Zainab Bahrani," *JAOS* 124 [2004]: 599–601; Brigitte Groneberg, review of Zainab Bahrani, *The Graven Image*, BMCR, 2004, online: http://bmcr.brynmawr.edu/2004/2004-02-06.html) and her approach to an image and its referent is not altogether original, her general approach to divine images and the language used to describe them, with qualifications, seems persuasive even if some of the details and applicability of her argument are less so. Most notably, Dominik Bonatz has recently demonstrated that the meaning and use of *ṣalmu* is variable and that *tamšīlu* refers to mimetic aspects that Bahrani rejects ("Was ist ein Bild im Alten Orient?: Aspekte bildlicher Darstellung aus altorientalischer Sicht," in *Bild—Macht—Geschichte: Visuelle Kommunikation im Alten Orient* [ed. Maries Heinz and Dominik Bonatz; Berlin: Reimer, 2002], 9–20, esp. 11–16; cf. earlier Irene J. Winter, "Art in Empire: The Royal Image and the Visual Dimensions of Assyrian Ideology," in *Assyria 1995: Proceedings of the 10th Anniversary Symposium of the Neo-Assyrian Text Corpus Project, Helsinki, September 7–11, 1995* [ed. Simo Parpola and Robert M. Whiting; Helsinki: The Neo-Assyrian Text Corpus Project, 1997], 359–81). Nonetheless, although an image is not always a "simulacram," a repetition or doubling, of its referent, official cult images seem to have been intimately allied with their divine referents; cf. with reference to Mesopotamia, Angelika Berlejung, "Washing the Mouth: The Consecration of Divine Images in Mesopotamia," in van der Toorn, ed., *The Image and the Book*, 46: "A cultic statue was never solely a religious picture, but was always an image imbued with a god, and, as such, it possessed the character of both earthly reality and divine presence." Rather than taking Bahrani's revised hypothesis as a given, we will use it as a working hypothesis, ready to be altered according to the dictates of the data.

sence. In other words, although it looks like the original and reminds one of it, it is of a different order entirely.

In the ancient Near Eastern world, images often seem to have been something entirely different, something much more than mere imitation.[47] The image in particular was frequently considered part of the real, partaking of its essence yet doing so without diminishing that of the original.[48] In a divine cult image, one encountered a deity not just as a resemblance but also in reality, without in any way diminishing the deity in all its heavenly plenitude. In fact, the image enhanced the divine plenitude by extending the deity's sphere of influence to the city and increasing cultic veneration.

In addition, the entity was frequently linked to its image in such a way that what affected the image affected the entity as well. Nonetheless, although the image captured some of the essence of the original, it did not capture all of it. It was similar to a "metonymy of presence" that fell short of the full presence.[49] Thus, once crafted, a divine image was in a real sense the god, but only partly so. For example, at the beginning of the mouth-washing ritual in Mesopotamia, before any ritual manipulation, the divine cult statue was already addressed as a god, yet did not become a fully functioning locus of divine presence until the end of the ritual.[50] To arrive at a plenitude of divine presence, one accumulated metonymic representations of the divinity.[51] As a metonymy of presence, the image alone was

---

47. See the qualifications made in the previous note and those in each chapter below.

48. This concept resembles the modern belief of certain people who do not want their pictures taken because they believe a photograph captures some of the essence of what it depicts (Propp, *Exodus 19–40*, 168). In the ancient Near East, however, the original was undiminished.

49. Bahrani, *Graven Image*, 205. In speaking of a metonymy of presence, I realize that "metonymy," which refers to the use of a single characteristic of an object to describe the entire object (e.g., the White House for the American presidential administration), is an inadequate term. However, it seems to be the best available term (the closely related "synecdoche," in which a part is used for the whole or the whole for a part, is perhaps the next closest inadequate category).

50. Berlejung, "Washing the Mouth," 71; idem, "Geheimnis und Ereignis: Zur Funktion und Aufgabe der Kultbilder in Mesopotamien," in *Die Macht der Bilder* (ed. I. Baldermann; JBTh 13; Neukirchen: Neukirchen Verlag, 1999), 110–11.

51. Bahrani (*Graven Image*, see esp. 129–30) uses the example of the substitution ritual for the king when omens predicted an ill fate for him. In it, four metonymic elements (i.e., ways of encountering some part of the person) were combined—a garment, the written and spoken name, and the image (a man)—to transform the substitute into the king. In the transformation ritual, the metonymic elements were manipulated through metonymic actions (i.e., ritual actions) to transform the image into the king. At the end of the process, the double was the king and was referred to as such. The original king then was freed from his fate, while the "new" king suffered in his place. In Egypt as well, as we will see, image and name were metonymic expressions of an individual.

insufficient to encapsulate divine presence. It had to be combined with other elements and actions, on the principle that amassing metonymic aspects approaches fullness.[52] Ritual itself, which has the power to transcend the mundane and transform it into something miraculous, added to the efficacy. Thus, under the auspices of ritual, metonymic elements of divine presence were combined with metonymic actions to arrive at a plenitude of presence.[53] With this working hypothesis as a general frame of reference, we may begin to examine how the cultures in each region understood and approached the divine presence in their midst.

We will proceed with analysis of the following in each region: 1) the perceived nature of the gods and their relationship to humanity;[54] 2) the forms and implications of divine cult images;[55] 3) the rituals for installing a cult image and maintaining the divine presence; 4) the relationship of a deity to its statue(s); 5) the relationship between different manifestations of a deity; 6) the consequences of conquest and/or improper divine service; 7) the divine consumption of human offerings.[56]

Before beginning, we pause to discuss our methodology for interpreting rituals, since installation and maintenance rituals occupy an especially prominent position in our analysis. To accommodate ritual multivocality, a fourfold ritual analysis is employed, using the same categories as in part 1, amended for the ritual context for which they were originally formulated.[57] First, structure describes ritu-

---

52. Like the various elements, actions alone were insufficient and so must be combined, even repeated, in order to approach sufficiency; see, e.g., Hundley, *Keeping Heaven*, 65–70, for a survey of ancient Near Eastern material.

53. This hypothesis raises further questions: if each enlivened image represented a plenitude of presence, why were there so many different images, even within the same sanctuary, and what was the relationship between them and the gods in or as them? These questions will be addressed where appropriate.

54. The broader conceptions of deity and divine presence in the ancient Near East and the non-Priestly Pentateuch, especially outside of the temple realm, are the subject of a new project, which overlapped with the completion of this book. In turn, some of the conclusions posited in the present work, especially about the nature of the divine, will be expanded upon in the forthcoming publication(s). For Mesopotamian conceptions of deity, see more fully Hundley, "Here a God."

55. Regarding the complexity of interpreting images, see, e.g., Michael Leicht's aptly named, "Die erste Pflicht der Bildwissenschaft besteht darin, den eigenen Augen zu misstrauen," in Heinz and Bonatz, eds., *Bild—Macht—Geschichte*, 21–36.

56. Removal rites will largely be excluded from analysis since individual and communal removal rites often occured outside of the temple cult and removal rites for the deity and temple were embedded in regular and special rites (e.g., festivals) (see briefly Hundley, *Keeping Heaven*, 120–34). Festivals too have been omitted since, although important, they were not a fundamental element of securing and safeguarding the divine presence.

57. The methodology for the present study was developed for biblical studies in Hundley,

al activity, i.e., the ritual words and actions described in the ritual texts. Second, in contrast to structural communication, which in the temple section analyzed what the structure communicated and the effect it elicited from its observers, structural interpretation analyzes the relationships between people, places, and objects that can be derived (verifiably) from the rituals themselves. Thus, it is built on more empirical foundations. For example, in the Egyptian Opening of the Mouth ritual, the priest's physical contact with the cult statue indexes a connection between himself and the statue, while in the Hittite expansion of the Goddess of the Night, the *ulihi* (presumably some kind of wool) indexes a connection between the statues in the new temple and old temple by making contact with both.[58] Third, use examines what participants expected ritual action to accomplish, often instrumentally, by analyzing the *causa* that prompts ritual and the various purpose statements assigned to ritual actions. Fourth, ideology explores the text's ideological import, theoretical underpinnings, and rhetorical implications. For example, it addresses how multiple, often repeated actions contribute to ritual efficacy and how a single action can work on multiple levels: instrumentally, mythologically, and by association (in Egypt often through wordplay).

---

*Keeping Heaven*, 17–37; regarding ritual multivocality as well as ambiguity and condensation of meaning, see, e.g., David I. Kertzer, *Ritual, Politics, and Power* (New Haven, CT: Yale University Press, 1988), 11.

58. An index is a sign that is existentially related to its signifier. Rather than being a matter of convention—e.g., with a symbol—the connection is a matter of fact (Nancy B. Jay, *Throughout Your Generations Forever: Sacrifice, Religion and Paternity* [Chicago: Chicago University Press, 1992], 7; see further Charles Sanders Peirce, e.g., Justus Buchler, *The Philosophical Writings of Peirce* [New York: Dover, 1955]).

# CHAPTER 8

# DIVINE PRESENCE IN EGYPTIAN TEMPLES

HAVING ESTABLISHED THAT THE TEMPLE was designed to provide a terrestrial home for the deity, we turn to the locus of terrestrial divine presence, the cult image, to discuss its nature, form, and function. In order properly to understand the cult image, I begin with the conceptual background, addressing briefly the nature of Egyptian deities and their relation to the world and its inhabitants. Then, I examine the textual and archaeological evidence for the cult images themselves, their enlivening and installation in the temples, and their daily care and feeding before assessing the nature of the cult image and its relationship to the deity and other cult images. The following analysis will concentrate on the evidence from the New Kingdom with some attention to the Late period and Greco-Roman times.[1]

## THE GODS AND THEIR RELATION TO HUMANITY AND THE WORLD

In many ways, Egyptian deities were like their human servants. Like humans, deities were sentient beings with a body, name, human-like families, emotions, behavior, and, especially in cultic contexts, needs. They were capable of the full gamut of human emotions and behaviors, from the most noble to the most petty, and were by no means immune to infighting.[2] In the cult, deities, like their royal human counterparts, had a body, a house, and a realm, properly equipped with servants to ensure that every need be met, including feeding, bathing, and clothing.

However, although similar, the gods were greater than their human counterparts in practically every capacity. In addition to the vast difference in power and spheres of influence, the gods primarily distinguished themselves in their accumulation of manifestations, names, and epithets.[3] Most major deities are labeled

---

1. See ch. 2 n. 1 for Egyptian chronology.

2. See, e.g., the conflict between the brothers Horus and Seth (J. Gwyn Griffiths, *The Conflict of Horus and Seth from Egyptian and Classical Sources: A Study in Ancient Mythology* [Liverpool: Liverpool University Press, 1960]; Herman te Velde, "Relations and Conflicts between Egyptian Gods, Particularly in the Divine Ennead of Heliopolis," in *Struggles of Gods: Papers of the Groningen Work Group for the Study of the History of Religions* [ed. H. G. Kippenberg; Berlin: de Gruyter, 1984], 239–57).

3. For an exhaustive list of divine iconography, manifestations, names, epithets, and

"rich in manifestations (*ḫprw*)" or "lord of manifestations,"[4] which is borne out by
the iconography, such that "a deity shows many faces to an Egyptian and presents
himself in many forms,"[5] including physical phenomena, various cult statues of
different forms, and animals.[6] For example, Thoth appeared in human form, as the
moon, an ibis, a baboon, or as a mixture of these elements.[7] As elsewhere in the
ancient Near East, Egyptians adopted the additive approach,[8] such that a deity displayed its potency and potential in its many manifestations, each of which embodied a particular power or attribute. Thus, the more manifestations a deity had, the
more potent and important it became.[9] Nonetheless, no single manifestation or
even an accumulation of all manifestations could capture a deity's plenitude, since
a deity always had the potential to adopt more and different forms.[10] Although a
deity showed many faces to Egyptians, none represented its "true form (*ḫprw*),"

---

attributes see Christian Leitz, ed., *Lexikon der ägyptischen Götter und Götterbezeichnungen*
(8 vols; OLA 110–116, 129; Leuven: Peeters, 2002–2003). For the expansive profile of Amun
in particular, see Ivan Guermeur, *Les cultes d'Amon hors de Thèbes: Recherches de géographie
religieuse* (Bibliothèque de l'école des hautes etudes sciences religieuses 123; Turnhout,
Belgium: Brepolis, 2005).

4. Hornung, *Conceptions of God*, 126; John Baines, "Egyptian Deities in Context:
Multiplicity, Unity, and the Problem of Change," in Porter, ed., *One God or Many?*, 27.
"Parallel epithets refer to the multiplicity of 'faces' (*ḥrw*) which gods have at their disposal;
the most varied gods are termed 'many face' or are 'lord of faces'" (Hornung, *Conceptions
of God*, 126).

5. Hornung, *Conceptions of God*, 126.

6. See with illustrations R. V. Lanzone, *Dizionario di Mitologia Egizia* (Turin: Litografia
Fratelli Doyen, 1885). For the textual evidence, see esp. Leitz, *Lexikon der ägyptischen Götter*.

7. Hornung, *Conceptions of God*, 126.; see also Brunner-Traut, *Frühformen des Erkennens*,
117. For the multiple ways of expressing Hathor and Amun, see, e.g., Izak Cornelius, "The
Many Faces of God: Divine Images and Symbols in Ancient Near Eastern Religions," in van
der Toorn, *The Image and the Book*, 23–26. On Hathor, see more fully Hornung, *Conceptions
of God*, 110–14. See also Brunner-Traut, *Frühformen des Erkennens*, 117–18, regarding
Thoth, Horus, Isis, Osiris, and Hathor. Most deities could also in some sense combine with
other deities further multiplying the range of possible manifestations (see briefly Hornung,
*Conceptions of God*, 91–99).

8. See, e.g., Brunner-Traut, *Frühformen des Erkennens*, 115–19 and *passim*; Friedhelm
Hoffmann, "Zum Körperkonzept in Ägypten (P. Berlin P. 10472 A + 14400)," in
*Menschenbilder und Körperkonzepte im alten Israel, in Ägypten und im alten Orient* (ed. A.
Berlejung, J. Dietrich, and J. F. Quack; ORA 9; Tübingen: Mohr Siebeck, 2012), 481–500.

9. Hornung, *Conceptions of God*, 125–26; cf. Baines, "Egyptian Deities in Context," 28. As
they entered the divine realm, deceased humans likewise aspired to multiple forms and
names (Hornung, *Conceptions of God*, 98).

10. Ibid., 126. "Their being remains a fluid state to which we are not accustomed; it escapes
very dogmatic, final definition and can always be extended or further differentiated" (p. 99).

which humans could only view when they are dead.[11] In addition to expressing divine complexity and potency, each manifestation also represented the deity's visible face. However, rather than being restricted to a single face, a deity could simultaneously adopt multiple forms in multiple locales.[12]

Similarly, worshipers addressed their deities with multiple names and epithets[13] in order to extend the nature and sphere of influence of a deity[14] and to appeal to various aspects of the deity. Names expressed the complexity and potency of the name bearer, such that complex and important beings required multiple names, since their potency and potentiality could not be expressed in a single word.[15] For example, kings bore at least two names and at least five throne names, while deities, reflective of their greater status, "must have many names."[16] Like each manifestation, each name and epithet highlighted a particular form, function, attribute, or potency, which when accumulated approached but did not equal divine plenitude.[17] Likewise, although deities could be addressed with many names, no one, not even the other gods, could know a deity's true name.[18] These gods

---

11. Spell 491 of the Coffin Texts; Adriaan de Buck, *The Egyptian Coffin Texts*, Vol. 6: *Texts of Spells 472–787* (OIP 81; Chicago: The Oriental Institute of the University of Chicago, 1956), 69c, 72d; translations in Raymond O. Faulkner, *The Ancient Egyptian Coffin Texts* (3 vols., Warminster: Aris & Phillips, 1973–1978); Hornung, *Conceptions of God*, 124; Tobin, *Theological Principles*, 36. Texts also continually stressed that the divine form was "hidden" and "mysterious" (Hornung, *Conceptions of God*, 117).

12. Baines, "Egyptian Deities in Context," 26; Robins, "Cult Statues in Ancient Egypt," 2.

13. See, e.g., Helmut Brunner, "Name, Namen und Namenlosigkeit Gottes im alten Ägypten," in *Der Name Gottes* (ed. H. v. Stietencron; Dusseldorf: Patmos, 1975), 33–49; Hornung, *Conceptions of God*, 86–91; Assmann, *The Search for God*, 83–87. Osiris and Isis in particular were referred to as "multinamed" (Brunner-Traut, *Frühformen des Erkennens*, 189 n. 24), while Re was addressed with seventy-five appellations (Hornung, *Das Buch der Anbetung des Re im Westen* [2 vols.; Aegyptiaca Helvetica 2/3; Geneva: Faculté des Lettres de l'Université de Genève, 1975/1976]; Brunner-Traut, *Frühformen des Erkennens*, 189 n. 24). The longest name lists may be found in the Book of Hours (Faulkner, *An Ancient Egyptian Book of Hours (Pap. BM 10569)* [Oxford: Griffith Institute, 1958]; Brunner-Traut, *Frühformen des Erkennens*, 189 n. 24).

14. Hornung, *Conceptions of God*, 90.

15. Koch, *Geschichte der ägyptische Religion*, 37.

16. *RÄRG*, "Name," 502, translated from German. Regarding pharaonic names, see von Beckerath, *Handbuch der ägyptischen Königsnamen* (2nd ed.; MÄS 49; Mainz: von Zabern, 1999), 1–9 and *passim*.

17. Cf. Brunner-Traut, *Frühformen des Erkennens*, 19–20.

18. In a text labeled "The God and His Unknown Name of Power" in *ANET*, Isis must trick Re in order to discover his secret name (Alexandre Piankoff, *The Litany of Re: Texts Translated with Commentary* [Egyptian Religious Texts and Representations 4; New York: Bollingen Foundation, 1964], 56–59; see conveniently *ANET* 12–14; *COS* 1.22:33–34).

controlled the very elements of nature and society that humans could not control and that they often needed to survive. Thus, by associating these necessary yet uncontrollable elements with human-like beings who may be approached, reasoned with, and influenced, humans gained some understanding and indeed some measure of control over the otherwise dangerous and volatile world around them.

However, contact with the divine and divine consent to human demands was by no means a given. In order to explain the disarray on earth, Egyptian mythology claims that although human and divine originally dwelt together, evil in creation (attributed to human rebellion or Seth) precipitated the gods' withdrawal from the human sphere.[19] The newly demarcated universe contained three realms: the celestial realm (*pt*), the underworld (*dw3t*), and the earth (*t3*). Deities (and the dead) inhabited the first two realms, while the third was the realm of living human beings.[20] Thus, the gods "ultimately dwelt outside of the human world and the realm of human experience."[21] Although the gods dwelt in realms inaccessible to living humanity, they remained part of the created world, and thus subject to its vicissitudes.[22] They remained embroiled in the struggle to maintain world order against the various chaos forces that encroached upon it. Although powerful and perspicacious, none of the gods were omnipotent or omniscient.[23] Indeed, each was vulnerable.[24] As part of the cosmos, its fate determined their own. As part of a polytheistic hierarchy, preserving the cosmos was a constant and joint venture,

---

19. Meeks, *Daily Life of the Egyptian Gods*, 120; Assmann, *The Search for God*, 6, 17–19, 113–16.

20. Robins, "Cult Statues in Ancient Egypt," 2. In the Old Kingdom, the texts seem to indicate that the gods inhabited the sky, which was also the setting for the afterlife (Hornung, *Conceptions of God*, 227). In the Middle and New Kingdoms the world in the sky found a complement in the netherworld, both of which were the realm of the divine (p. 228). In later periods, distinctions between gods and their presence in the three realms became increasingly blurred (p. 230).

21. Robins, "Cult Statues in Ancient Egypt," 12.

22. Hornung, *Conceptions of God*, 166–70, 186–96. Only chaos could truly be called transcendent, since it dwelled outside of the ordered cosmos and ever sought to infiltrate it (see also p. 195).

23. Baines, "Egyptian Deities in Context," 26. Although hymns and litanies praised individual deities in such a way that it seems that they each represented an ultimate being that transcended the created world, the focus of such hymns lay more in "developing ever more elaborate formulations of praise than on expressing radically new ideas about the nature of deities" (Baines, "Presenting and Discussing Deities in New Kingdom and Third Intermediate Period Egypt," in *Reconsidering the Concept of Revolutionary Monotheism* [ed. B. Pongratz-Leisten; Winona Lake, IN: Eisenbrauns, 2011], 68–69).

24. Hornung, *Conceptions of God*, 151–66. In addition, there was no need to justify the gods in the face of evil. The gods could not be said to be responsible for evil. Instead they were the very powers that combatted it (p. 213).

one in which humans had a role to play. In Egypt, chaos was the ever-present enemy of human and divine alike threatening to topple world order.[25] In the divine realm, for example, Re had nightly to overcome the serpent Apep (Apophis), his chief enemy, who was one of the primary threats to order.[26] Within the human sphere, the king helped to preserve order by serving the gods and presenting them with the eye of Horus and *maat*, both representing what is "sound and perfect."[27]

Although spatially separated, humanity maintained a link with the gods and the ability to influence cosmic events. The gods left the divine *ka*-spirit in the living king.[28] With the establishment of the temple, its cult, and the divinely imbued priest-king as the sole intermediary between human and divine,[29] humanity successfully brought or persuaded the deities to return to earth. The primary locus of their presence was the cult statue, which represented a (semi)permanent theophany in the human sphere. Through divine presence on earth and human cultic interaction with it, humans were able to bring divine power to bear on their lives and more broadly to influence cosmic reality and help preserve cosmic order.[30]

25. Hornung, *Conceptions of God*, 172–85, 195, 212–16; Quirke, *Ancient Egyptian Religion*, 70; Robins, "Cult Statues in Ancient Egypt," 1.

26. Tobin, "Myths," 242–43, 245.

27. Englund, "Offerings," 279–80; see also Quirke, *Ancient Egyptian Religion*, ch. 3, "Preserving the Universe: Kingship and Cult."

28. See esp. Lanny Bell, "Luxor Temple and the Cult of the Royal *Ka*," *JNES* 44 (1985): 251–94; idem, "The New Kingdom Divine Temple," 137–44; cf. regarding other humans, Andrey O. Bolshakov, *Man and His Double in Egyptian Ideology of the Old Kingdom* (ÄAT 37; Wiesbaden: Harrasowitz, 1997). Although the king was consistently associated with a deity, the identity of the deity changed based on time and circumstance. For example, the king was most often associated with Horus, the sun god, and in the afterlife with Osiris, yet could also be identified with other deities, such as Montu, Khnum, and Sekhmet (Hornung, *Conceptions of God*, 141). The closest modern analogy to the dual nature of the king might be that of the pope, who is human yet carries the divine in his papal office; so too "it can be shown that an astonishingly consistent distinction was drawn between the divine character of the royal office and the human nature of the person holding it" (Morenz, *Egyptian Religion*, 37).

29. In some way, the king existed in a perpetual liminal state. As a semidivine being, he ruled over and served the gods on behalf of the people. However, as a mere man, even a man with the royal *ka*-spirit, he had to kneel before and worship the gods (ibid., 41).

30. Cf. Assmann, *The Search for God*, 53.

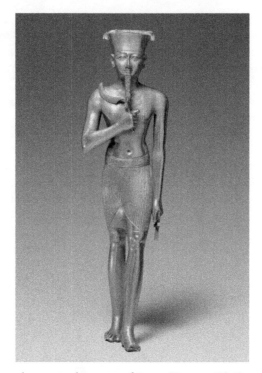

Fig. 8.1. A bronze anthropomorphic statue of Amun (Dynasty 22). Courtesy of the Metropolitan Museum of Art.

## CULT IMAGES

Evidence for the construction and composition of Egyptian cult statues is minimal.[31] Few, if any, remain.[32] Likewise, although occasionally grandiose, the textual descriptions often fail to note the specifics.[33] Nonetheless, various clues allow for possible reconstructions.

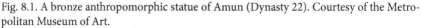

31. Cult statue refers here to the main statue of the god situated in the inner sanctuary and, if distinct, to the statue used in festival processions.

32. For a discussion and possible examples of cult statues, see, e.g., Lorton, "Theology of Cult Statues," 127–29; Robins, "Cult Statues in Ancient Egypt," 4–6.

33. The Greco-Roman temple of Dendara provides the best evidence. In its crypts, there are hundreds of depictions of divine statues, many with inscriptions indicating the material composition and height of the statues (see Sylvie Cauville, "Les statues cultuelles de Dendera d'après les inscriptions pariétales," *BIFAO* 87 (1987): 73–117; Hoffmann, "Measuring Egyptian Statues," in *Under One Sky: Astronomy and Mathematics in the Ancient Near East* [ed. J. Steele and A. Imhausen; AOAT 297; Münster: Ugarit-Verlag, 2002], 109–19; for the images, see Émile Chassinat, *Le Temple de Dendara*, Vol. 5 [Cairo: Institut Français

First, the sizes of their resting places suggest that the cult statues were rather small. The remaining stone shrines tend to be no more than 19 to 23 inches tall (50–60 cm).[34] Inside one would have found an even smaller wooden shrine, which housed the divine statue. From this, we may infer that most cult statues would have been at most little more than a foot (30 cm) tall (see fig. 8.1).[35] Although there is some debate regarding whether or not the statue in the processional bark was the same as the primary cult statue,[36] the dimensions of the cabin inside the bark shrine where the deity rested were likely equally small. Thus, regardless of whether there were one or two statues in a single temple, most cult statues were probably small.[37]

Although the cult statue's form and the consistency of that form across temples and time remain somewhat unclear,[38] it is evident that they were made of materials

---

d'Archéologie Orientale, 1947]. However, in addition to being late (though one would expect the late images to be similar to earlier images), the numbers likely do not represent the real heights of statues, but rather the ideal heights, written for theological purposes (Hoffmann, "Measuring Egyptian Statues," 113).

34. Dietrich Wildung, "Naos," *LÄ* 4 (1982): 342; Lorton, "Theology of Cult Statues," 128; Herman te Velde, "Theology, Priests and Worship in Ancient Egypt," in *CANE* 3:1732; cf. Wolfgang Helck, "Kultstatue," *LÄ* 3 (1980): 861. Nonetheless, there may have been some variability as the wooden doors for the shrine of Thutmose III and Hatshepsut measured 75 cm in height, the interior of the shrine of Shabako (25th Dynasty) measured 92 cm, while that of one dedicated to Nectanebo (30th Dynasty) was 1.43 m (Günther Roeder, *Naos: Catalogue Général du Musée du Caire* [Catalogue général des antiquités égyptiennes du Musée du Caire 75; Wiesbaden: Breitkopf & Härtel, 1914], CG 7001A, 70007, and 700019 respectively; Teeter, *Religion and Ritual*, 43).

35. Lorton, "Theology of Cult Statues," 128. Cf., however, the exceptions in the previous note. *Pace* Lorton (ibid.), it is likely that the statues in the shrines did not wear their headdresses (Hoffmann, "Measuring Egyptian Statues," 117).

36. Robins ("Cult Statues in Ancient Egypt," 10, after Jean-Marie Kruchten, "Oracles," *OEAE* 2:609) is likely correct that the two were distinct. If the main cult statue was out on procession, the daily rituals in the temple and, in effect, the temple itself would have been inoperative during the duration of the long and frequent festivals while the resident deity was absent. For a similar distinction regarding Hindu temples, see C. J. Fuller, *The Camphor Flame: Popular Hinduism and Society in India* (Princeton, NJ: Princeton University Press, 1992), 58.

37. Although this may seem counterintuitive, the diminutive divine statue reflected the relative size of the sanctuary and the shrine within it. Although the distinction was not absolute, spaces tended to get smaller the closer one came to the statued presence of deity. This minimization in turn expressed the relative importance (and sacredness) of the various spaces. Thus, it makes sense that the divine statue, the most important item in the temple, would itself have been small.

38. "Some may have been solid cast metal with or without inlays, while others would have been made of wood or built round a wooden core, probably with fittings in other materials"

Fig. 8.2. Isis and Osiris in anthropomorphic form (Dynasty 21). Adapted from the Greenfield Papyrus in the British Museum. Drawing by Susan Hundley.

highly valued by the Egyptians.[39] The texts indicate that they were constructed of "gold, silver, lapis lazuli, turquoise, and other highly valued materials."[40]

There is also ample evidence for the visual renderings of the gods (e.g., other divine statues, stelae, wall reliefs, drawings, as well as various textual descriptions).[41] From these we may deduce that Egyptian deities were primarily displayed in one of three forms: 1) human (figs. 8.1 and 8.2); 2) animal (fig. 8.3); or 3) a mixture of the two (figs. 8.4–8.6).[42] The mixed form, with a human body and an animal head,

---

(Robins, "Cult Statues in Ancient Egypt," 6). The wooden core made the statues more affordable and more transportable.

39. Helck, "Kultstatue," 861; Robins, "Cult Statues in Ancient Egypt," 6.

40. Robins, "Cult Statues in Ancient Egypt," 4; see also Pierre Grandet, *Le papyrus Harris I (BM 9999)* (vol. 1; Bibliothèque d'Étude 109; Cairo: Imprimerie de l'Institut français d'archéologie orientale du Caire, 1994), 227, 228, 229, 259; William J. Murnane, *Texts from the Amarna Period in Egypt* (SBLWAW 5; Atlanta: Scholars Press, 1995), 213, 233. For example, one of the earliest texts describing a divine statue refers to a statue of Osiris of gold, silver, lapis lazuli, amethyst, *sesnedjem*-wood, and true cedar (Kei Yamamoto, "The Materials of Iykhernofret's Portable Shrine: An Alternative Translation of Berlin 1204, lines 11–12," *Göttinger Miszellen* 191 [2002]: 101–6; Teeter, *Religion and Ritual*, 52–53). In addition, the Restoration Stele of Tutankhamun describes Amun's statue as constructed of "electrum, lapis lazuli, turquoise and every precious stone" (Murnane, *Texts from the Amarna Period*, 213; Teeter, *Religion and Ritual*, 53).

41. It must be noted that it is often difficult to tell whether various visual media depict a cult statue or the deity itself.

42. Cornelius, "The Many Faces of God," 24; Hornung, "Ancient Egyptian Religious

Fig. 8.3. Hathor in her bovine form protecting the high official Psamtik (Dynasty 26). Courtesy of the Egyptian Museum, Cairo.

figured prominently yet by no means fully usurped the other forms. The symbol and the so-called aniconic representation are also attested.[43]

These visual representations varied from god to god, while many of the "same" gods were presented differently in different contexts. In most cases, there were several ways of displaying the same god,[44] sometimes in multiple ways in the same

---

Iconography," in *CANE* 2:713–16; Robins, "Cult Statues in Ancient Egypt," 2.

43. Symbols often appeared on standards and staves (Cornelius, "The Many Faces of God," 26; see further Matthias Seidel, "Götterstäbe," *LÄ* 2 [1977]: 711–13; Wildung, "Götterstandarte," *LÄ* 2 [1977]:713–14; Winfried Barta, "Göttersymbole," *LÄ* 2 [1977]: 714–16), likely as a divine shorthand. On the aniconic in general, see Tryggve N. D. Mettinger, *No Graven Image? Israelite Aniconism in Its Ancient Near Eastern Context* (CBOT 42; Stockholm: Almqvist & Wiksell, 1995) and 49–56 with regard to Egypt centered on the figures of the Aten and Amun.

44. "There is an astonishingly rich variety of possibilities; only to a very limited extent can one speak of a canonically fixed iconography of a god" (Hornung, *Conceptions of God*, 110). As noted, the multiplicity of images played a similar role to the multiplicity

Fig. 8.4. Thoth, represented as a man with an ibis head standing before the enthroned Re-Horakhte, represented as a man with a falcon head (Third Intermediate period; ca. 950 BCE; Greenfield Papyrus sheet 52). Courtesy of the Trustees of the British Museum.

Fig. 8.5. The God Khepry with a male anthropomorphic body and a beetle head (from the tomb of Nefertari, during the reign of Ramesses II, 1290–1222 BCE). Courtesy of UNI DIA Verlag München.

place and even the same image. For example, Mahes appeared as both a lion and a man with the head of a lion on the Hildesheim stela,[45] while a group statue at the Louvre brought together the various forms of Hathor: a cow, a lion-headed goddess, uraeus serpent, and a goddess with a sistrum on her head.[46] Other renderings from the Late period onward went even further, combining various representa-

---

of divine epithets, indicating the potency and complex nature of the deity itself and of its manifestation on earth (ibid., 125–26).

45. Cornelius, "The Many Faces of God," 25.

46. Jacques Vandier, "Un don des amis du Louvre au départment des antiquités égytiennes," *La revue du Louvre et des musées de France* 19 (1969): 49–54; Hornung, *Conceptions of God*, 113. In some contexts, Hathor was even depicted with multiple faces simultaneously (Philippe Derchain, *Hathor quadrifons: Recherches sur la syntaxe d'un mythe égyptien*

tions into one composite form. "Just as hymns usually endowed a divinity with as many epithets as possible, so these depictions combined as many attributes as possible, not even stopping short at the monstrous"[47] (i.e., monstrous according to modern aesthetic sensibilities). Such later images had clear antecedents in earlier periods. For example, from the New Kingdom the Devourer of the Dead appeared as an amalgam of the lion, hippopotamus, and crocodile (fig. 8.7).[48] The sphinx was both a partaker of the divine and of composite form, often a winged lion with a human, ram, or falcon head. In others, the same symbol represented several gods. For example, a staggering number of deities were associated with the sun and the lion,[49] while the image of the so-called tree goddess could also refer to various deities, including, Isis, Nephtys, Nut, Hathor, and Maat.[50] As noted, rather than representing the true form of the deity, each depiction served merely as an attempt to highlight an aspect of the deities' complex nature.[51] None captured the true essence or even the true form of the deity, one which was often inaccessible to humanity.[52]

Of these approximate forms, the mixed form is the most intriguing and distinct and, as such, deserves further comment.[53] The principle of the common

---

[Uitgauen van het Nederlandsch Historisch Archaeologisch Instituut te Istanbul 28; Istanbul: Nederlands Instituut voor het Nabije Oosten, 1972], pls. 1–2).

47. Hornung, "Ancient Egyptian Religious Iconography," 1716.

48. Ibid.; See further Christine Seeber, *Untersuchungen zur Darstellung des Totengerichts im alten Ägypten* (MÄS 35; Munich: Deutscher Kunstverlag, 1976).

49. Hornung, *Conceptions of God*, 126.

50. Cornelius, "The Many Faces of God," 25.

51. See generally Hornung, *Conceptions of God*, 109–35; Tobin, *Theological Principles*, 35–36; David P. Silverman, "Divinity and Deities in Ancient Egypt," in *Religion in Ancient Egypt: Gods, Myths, and Personal Practice* [ed. B. E. Shafer; Ithaca: Cornell University Press, 1991], 16–17; cf. Ann Macy Roth ("Buried Pyramids and Layered Thoughts: The Organisation of Multiple Approaches in Egyptian Religion," in *Proceedings of the Seventh International Congress of Egyptologists* [ed. C. J. Eyre; OLA 82; Leuven: Peeters, 1998], 991–1003; idem, "The Representation of the Divine in Ancient Egypt," in Beckman and Lewis, eds., *Text, Artifact, and Image*, 24–37), who posits that mixed forms represents a nesting of forms in which older forms were preserved alongside newer ones even in the same image. On Hathor in particular, see Hornung, *Conceptions of God*, 113. According to Hornung, the mixed form is a hieroglyph of sorts, a way of writing "the nature and function of the deity in question" (p. 124). Or, it is an "ideogram," a pictorial sign that conveys but does not exhaust meaning (Frankfort, *Ancient Egyptian Religion: An Interpretation* [New York: Columbia University, 1949], 12). Although the attributes presented in the various forms could allude to the deity in question, they did not encapsulate it (cf. Hornung, *Conceptions of God*, 117).

52. Hornung, *Conceptions of God*, 117, 124–25, 128–35.

53. The mixed form (see, e.g., figs. 8.4–8.6) is often taken as the most characteristic depiction, yet it was by no means the sole one (Hornung, *Conceptions of God*, 109–10, 123).

Fig. 8.6. A rope-headed god in the Amduat (tomb of Seti I; 1304–1290 BCE). From Hornung, *Conceptions of God*, pl. V.

mixed form seems to have associated a single deity with the attributes and potencies of generally an animal and a human, thereby differentiating the deity from the mundane realm. Since each form represented a manifestation, the mixed form represented a mixing of manifestations. This does not imply that the deity really appeared in such a hybrid form (outside of the statue).[54] Rather, the hybrid form combined two or more manifestations in one, stressing at least two aspects of the deity, while simultaneously distancing it from humans and from the deity's true form.[55]

---

54. For example, rather than expressing that the anthropomorphic deity actually had a rope head, the Amduat presents it that way to express its function, i.e., to bind the damned in the underworld (Hornung, *Conceptions of God*, 118–21). See fig. 8.6.

55. Many of these images were so well crafted that they even appear "natural." "If today one stands before the figure of such a god in human form with animal head, it requires some time before one becomes aware that such a figure represents something unnatural" (Morenz, *Egyptian Religion*, 21). The long tripartite wig worn by most gods facilitated the

The deity's nonhuman head was thus a divine marker of sorts,[56] distinguishing one deity from the next and highlighting the aspects of the deity's nature embodied in the animal. Additional attributes of divinity often appeared on the deity's head,[57] adding to the divine descriptors, often with a specific type of head and various symbols on top of the head.[58]

The nature of the visual representation as an approximation of the deity did not necessarily give the artist freedom of expression, since divine representation was marked by a strong conservatism.[59] Although there was some variety in expression, each form, including the materials used,[60] emerged through the approved channels and corresponded to the deity's "exact" form.[61] It was thus imperative that the "statue was recognizable and appropriate to the deity who was supposed to manifest in it."[62] Each deity in turn had its own recognizable physical form(s).[63]

Although these representations included a combination of human and animal attributes, in the New Kingdom, they consistently stopped short of the monstrous forms that emerged in the Late period,[64] thereby suggesting that the New Kingdom

---

often seamless transition between human and animal form by disguising it (Hornung, *Conceptions of God*, 115).

56. In the New Kingdom, this divine attribute occasionally took the iconographically bold form of a symbol. For example, Osiris appeared with a symbolic *Dd*-column, and Re was given a solar disk as a head (Hornung, "Ancient Egyptian Religious Iconography," 1714).

57. As a general rule, universal attributes of divinity appeared in the hands, while the attributes specific to a deity appeared on the head. Instead of unique attributes, divinities often carried in their hands the symbols of life and power, which they would bestow on the king. From the Amarna period, various goddesses also had wings, likely highlighting their protective roles (Hornung, "Ancient Egyptian Religious Iconography," 1714–15). However, some deities did indeed hold their charateristic attributes in their hands; Ptah carried a distinctive staff and Osiris held the crook and flail (see, e.g., fig. 8.2).

58. Hornung, "Ancient Egyptian Religious Iconography," 1714–15; Cornelius, "The Many Faces of God," 26.

59. This deviates from modern artistic representation, where diversity of expression in approximating reality is laudable, while traditional conservatism is often considered less valuable.

60. Texts assert that the bones of deities were silver, their flesh gold, and their hair lapis lazuli (Lichtheim, *AEL* 2:198; Hornung, *Conceptions of God*, 134; Robins, "Cult Statues in Ancient Egypt," 6).

61. Cf. Robins, "Cult Statues in Ancient Egypt," 2. Rather than representing the "true" form, the exact form refers to statue's exact correspondence to the model employed, such that it met the divine specifications, whether it is anthropomorphic, zoomorphic, or mixed.

62. Robins, "Cult Statues in Ancient Egypt," 2.

63. "Animal, human or mixed; male, female; anthropomorphic, mummiform, ithyphallic," each "with typical items of insignia" (ibid.).

64. Hornung, *Conceptions of God*, 116–18.

Fig. 8.7. The Devourer of the Dead, located on the far right of the weighing of the heart scene from The Book of the Dead of Any (Dynasty 19; ca. 1275 BCE; EA 10470.3). If the deceased's heart was not lighter than a feather, he would be devoured by this aptly named composite creature. Courtesy of the Trustees of the British Museum.

aesthetic was not entirely dissimilar from our own. For the Egyptians, the deity, like its abode, was often represented in an orderly and beautiful way—in other words, in a way not too distinct from accepted human or animal form.[65] In addition to the concern for aesthetics, such forms and the human-like beings that inhabited them rendered the potent deities more understandable and approachable, giving humanity greater agency.

The exceptions are especially illustrative, as figures of a more hybrid nature were primarily reserved for secondary deities and the potent forces they embodied.[66] Many of these figures need not be approachable, in fact quite the opposite. As divine foes or in tamed form as protective figures, their multidimensionality elicited fear and/or stressed their ability to ward off danger. For example, in its composite form, the "monster," the Devourer of the Dead, was especially suitable to protect the entrance into the afterlife (fig. 8.7), while the sphinx, despite its mixed form,

65. With the waning power of the monarchy and the influx of foreign influence, depictions in the Third Intermediate period and beyond sacrificed such aestheticism (ibid., 118). They turned to a multiform approach, sacrificing the beauty of the deity for an amalgam of attributes that better approximated the deity's essence.

66. E.g., such deities rarely had their own temples or received cultic care.

remained orderly and beautiful as befit the divine space that it protected (fig. 2.4).[67] Nonetheless, its mixed form was suitably other and potent enough to protect that space from unwanted intruders. The sphinx's form, often with a human head and mixed animal body, differentiated it from the major deities[68] and suggests that, unlike the Devourer of the Dead, the sphinx remained somewhat human-like and approachable, suitable for its potential role as an intermediary figure. In addition, while major deities did not deviate too far from human or animal forms, the fact that the obviously potent mixed and monstrous did their bidding indicates that the primary gods were far more potent than their exterior forms would suggest.

## PRIMARY RITUAL TEXTS

We have minimally established that a deity was not coterminous with its various forms, including its cult images. We now turn to the ritual texts to more precisely determine the relationship between the deity and its image(s) and the nature of the divine installation and maintenance in its terrestrial temple. The Opening of the Mouth ritual seems to have been created to answer the question, "How does an inert statue house (some part of) the divine essence?" The daily cult ritual takes the answer one step further, addressing how the divine presence, once installed, may be maintained. An analysis of each ritual will follow according to the categories of structure, structural interpretation, use, and ideology. After the fourfold analysis of each ritual, we will discuss specific questions these rituals help to answer, such as the divine statue's perceived origin, the relation of the deity to its statue(s), the necessity of divine nourishment, and the permanence of divine presence in the statue.

### 1. THE OPENING OF THE MOUTH RITUAL[69]

The Opening of the Mouth ritual (*wpt-r3* or *wn-r3*) was performed on all newly formed divine statues in order to prepare them to be fully functioning loci

---

67. For a general examination of the sphinx, see Heinz Demisch, *Die Sphinx: Geschichte ihrer Darstellung von den Anfängen bis zur Gegenwart* (Stuttgart: Urachhaus, 1977).

68. "Major deities" refers to the deities with the most prominent cultic and mythological presence. While major deities in hybrid form generally had animal heads and human bodies, the sphinx had a mixed animal body with a human or animal (often ram's) head.

69. For primary studies with translations and commentary, see E. A. Wallis Budge, *The Book of Opening the Mouth: The Egyptian texts with English Translations* (Books on Egypt and Chaldaea 26–27; London: Kegan Paul, 1909); Eberhard Otto, *Das ägyptische Mundöffnungsritual* (2 vols; ÄA 3; Wiesbaden: Harrasowitz, 1960); Jean-Claude Goyon, *Rituels funéraires de l'ancienne Égypte: Le Rituel de l'ouverture de la bouche, les Livres des respirations* (Paris: Cerf, 1972). For other helpful studies, see, e.g., Wolfgang Helck, "Einige

of divine presence (fig. 8.8). The ritual, however, was by no means exclusive to divine cult statues; it was performed on mortuary statues, divine barks, coffins, mummies, and, at least in the Late period, entire temples as well as other prominent ritual objects.[70] Although performed on divine statues, most extant examples come from the funerary sphere.[71] Lest we despair at the lack of direct evidence, it is likely that this ritual, or something quite like it, was performed on divine cult statues;[72] for it seems that "shared problems found shared solutions."[73] Namely, in both spheres, inanimate objects had to be (re)animated, giving them the ability to communicate cultically, such as by consuming offerings.[74]

---

Bemerkungen zum Mundöffnungsritual," *Mitteilungen des Deutschen archäologischen Instituts Abteilungs Kairo* 22 (1967): 27–41; Svein Bjerke, "Remarks on the Egyptian Ritual of 'Opening the Mouth' and Its Interpretation," *Numen* 12 (1965): 201–16; Finnestad, "The Meaning and Purpose of *Opening the Mouth* in Mortuary Contexts," *Numen* 25 (1978): 118–34; Petra Barthelmess, *Der Übergang ins Jenseits in den thebanischen Beamtengräbern der Ramessidenzeit* (SAGA 2; Heidelberg: Heidelberger Orientverlag, 1992), 93–114; Ann Macy Roth, "The *psš-kf* and the 'Opening of the Mouth' Ceremony: A Ritual of Birth and Rebirth," *JEA* 78 (1992), 113–47; idem, "Fingers, Stars, and the 'Opening of the Mouth': The Nature and Function of the *nrwj*-Blades," *JEA* 79 (1993): 57–79; Hans-Werner Fischer-Elfert, *Die Vision von der Statue im Stein* (Schriften der Philosophisch-historischen Klasse der Heidelberger Akademie der Wissenschaften 5; Heidelberg: Winter, 1998); Lorton, "Theology of Cult Statues," 147–79; Jan Assmann, *Tod und Jenseits im alten Ägypten* (Munich: Beck, 2001), 408–31; idem, *Death and Salvation in Ancient Egypt* (trans. D. Lorton; Ithaca, NY: Cornell University Press, 2005), 310–29; Joachim Friedrich Quack, "Ein Prätext und seine Realisierungen: Facetten des ägyptischen Mundöffnungsrituals," in *Text und Ritual: Kulturwissenschaftliche Essays und Analysen von Sesostris bis Dada* (ed. B. Dücker and H. Roeder; Hermeia 8; Heidelberg: Synchron, 2005), 165–85; idem, "Fragmente des Mundöffnungsrituals aus Tebtynis," in *The Carlsberg Papyri 7: Hieratic Texts from the Collection* (ed. K. Ryholt; Copenhagen: Museum Tusculanum Press, 2006, 69–150); idem, "Bilder vom Mundöffnungsritual – Mundöffnung an Bildern" in *Bild und Ritual: Visuelle Kulturen in historischer Perspektive* (ed. C. Ambos, P. Rösch and S. Weinfurter; Darmstadt: Wissenschaftliche Buchgesellschaft, 2010), 18–28.

70. Quack, "Ein Prätext und seine Realisierungen," 166.

71. As the primary exception, there is papyri evidence of the Opening of the Mouth for a divine cult image from Tebtynis (Quack, "Fragmente des Mundöffnungsrituals aus Tebtynis"). Although the Opening of the Mouth ritual itself is not attested until the New Kingdom, the term "Opening of the Mouth" appears with no special explanation in the tomb of an official in the Fourth Dynasty, and first refers to a temple statue with the words, "fashioning and opening the mouth in the workshop," from the sun temple of Nyuserre in the Fifth Dynasty (Lorton, "Theology of Cult Statues," 148).

72. Lorton, "Theology of Cult Statues," 149–51.

73. Ibid., 181; see also 132–33.

74. Ibid., 133; cf. William Kelly Simpson, "Egyptian Sculpture and Two-Dimensional Representation as Propaganda," *JEA* 68 (1982): 267. Or, more expansively, the shared

Fig. 8.8. Scene depicting the Opening of the Mouth of a mummy from The Book of the Dead of Hunefer (Dynasty 19; EA 9901). Courtesy of the Trustees of the British Museum.

The preserved ritual texts and accompanying images may be divided into scenes, each of which normally include two components, typical of all Egyptian ritual texts, an action and a recitation, both of which were considered essential for ritual efficacy.[75] Of the seventy-five Opening of the Mouth scenes identified by Otto in his composite edition, the first forty-eight appear essentially the same in each extant version, while the remaining scenes are more variable.[76] Some versions have altered, abbreviated, or eliminated some of the remaining scenes to fit

purpose could be to make the object cultically operative (Finnestad, "Meaning and Purpose of Opening the Mouth," 121).

75. Quack, "Ein Prätext und seine Realisierungen," 166–67. The Tomb of Rekhmire provides an especially thorough example of both text and image (for texts and images, see conveniently "Contents of the Ritual for 'Opening the Mouth': The selection of 51 episodes in the tomb-chapel of Rekhmira, in the sequence in which they occur." Online: http://www. digitalegypt.ucl.ac.uk/religion/wpr2.html).

76. Ibid., 168, 170; except when present in abbreviated form in tombs (Barthelmess, *Übergang ins Jenseits*, 93–114; Quack, "Ein Prätext und seine Realisierungen," 168).

the context in which they appear. For example, in some instances scenes involving dressing may have been abbreviated or omitted because they were inappropriate for mummies, coffins, and barks.[77] The common presence of an offering table with an offering list in tombs with nearly identical offerings also occasionally rendered the Opening of the Mouth offering scenes redundant.[78] Likewise, scenes involving craftsmen are unnecessary for mummies since they were not crafted.[79]

Given this variability and the difference between mortuary and nonmortuary spheres, we may expect the Opening of the Mouth for divine statues to deviate from this general pattern.[80] However, since no full texts remain from the Opening of the Mouth of divine cult statues, it is impossible to identify definitively any such deviations. Thus, we will follow the composite ritual from the mortuary realm as outlined by Otto. Rather than interpreting each action and each utterance, analysis will focus on the elements that seem most important and most appropriate for examining divine presence.

### Structure[81]

The ritual begins with the purification, awakening, and dressing of the *sem*-priest (*sm*),[82] followed by the artisans appearing before the statue. In the following stage,[83] the *sem*-priest changes clothes, donning a panther skin, followed by the presentation of the foreleg and the heart of a slaughtered bull. Next, the priest touches the mouth of the statue with various instruments that seem to be artisans' tools as well

77. Quack, "Ein Prätext und seine Realisierungen," 172–73.

78. However, when the Opening of the Mouth is visually depicted, offering scenes often remain unabridged (ibid., 173).

79. Barthelmess, *Übergang ins Jenseits*, 94–97; Fischer-Elfert, *Die Vision von der Statue*, 78–79; Quack, "Ein Prätext und seine Realisierungen," 173.

80. Indeed, it is not improbable that different temples employed slightly different rituals. This is especially the case if we take into account the diachronic perspective, in which the ritual likely grew and adapted over time (see conveniently Roth, "Opening of the Mouth," in *OEAE* 2:605–9).

81. As noted in the introduction, in order to understand the larger ritual and its many individual actions and utterances, it must be situated in its proper context, which is the task of the following analysis.

82. The meaning of the title "*sem*-priest" remains obscure (Lorton, "Theology of Cult Statues," 149).

83. A "stage," which may include various scenes, refers to a conceptual unit of the ritual identified by structural markers, which may be inferred from, but is not explicitly enumerated in the ritual words and images.

as his little finger.[84] The "loving son" then enters and opens the mouth (and eyes)[85] of the statue with an instrument, a finger of electrum, and his little finger and presents the statue with various items that have life-endowing, mouth-opening effects, such as a knife, grapes, an ostrich feather, and water.[86] After the "loving son" leaves, the priest brings the leg and heart of another slaughtered bull before the statue and opens its mouth again with an adze. He then burns incense, presents cloth strips and clothing, anoints the statue, offers green and black eye paint, presents scepters, censes the statue in various ways, performs an act of homage with jars, a libation and censing, and prepares and presents an elaborate food offering, interspersed with censing and libation. Finally, the statue leaves the workshop and is installed in its shrine in the temple.[87]

These ritual actions are accompanied by a series of utterances, which by comparison to other ritual texts, including the daily cult ritual, are brief and rather cryptic.[88] Rather than attempt to interpret all such expressions, we will mention some of the most pertinent.[89] The section involving the artisans is highlighted by the priest's statements and rhetorical questions regarding the statue. As such, the statements are particularly important in uncovering the native interpretations of

---

84. The little finger was typically used to indicate the application of ointment (Hoffmann, personal communication).

85. It is unclear what exactly opening the mouth and eyes involve. Minimally, it seems to include touching the various elements to the statue's mouth and eyes respectively as well as the recitiation of the various utterances.

86. As this ritual derives from the funerary context, it is natural that the "loving son" would appear as the one responsible for easing his (soon-to-be) deceased father into the afterworld. During the Opening of the Mouth of the father's statue, the father would likely have been still alive, as individuals secured their tombs and furnishings, including their statues, during their lifetimes whenever possible (Andrey O. Bolshakov, "The Moment of the Establishment of the Tomb-Cult in Ancient Egypt," *AoF* 18 [1991]: 204–18; Lorton, "Theology of Cult Statues," 169; Teeter, *Religion and Ritual,* 123). Of course, for the Opening of the Mouth of the mummy, the father would have been deceased. Since the father–son roles do not seem appropriate to the opening of the mouth for a divine statue, presumably they were either excluded or adapted to fit the divine context.

87. If any fanfare for the installation of the statue into the temple existed, it is not present in the preserved ritual text. However, this does not exclude the possibility of some ceremony. Since the preserved text is from the mortuary sphere, the installation of the statue in the tomb likely would not have been anywhere near as grand an occasion as the installation of the divine statue in its temple.

88. Lorton, "Theology of Cult Statues," 149.

89. Other utterances—like "How *heneg* is your mouth! I weigh your mouth over against your bones!"—recur and seem important. However, as their meanings remain obscure, they will not be addressed here (see Otto, *Das ägyptische Mundöffnungsritual,* 2:94; Helck, "Bemerkungen zum Mundöffnungsritual," 34–35; Lorton, "Theology of Cult Statues," 172–74).

the ritual.[90] In this section, the priest remarks on the crafting of the statue, exclaiming, "Made perfect for me is my father [the cult statue]! Who has made him perfect for me?"[91] In the ensuing scene, the questioning continues, but in a different tone: "Who has smitten my father? Who has seized his head?" Soon thereafter, the priest remarks, "Lo, my father has been smitten!"[92] The artisans then reply, "Lo, may those who might smite your father be exempt!"[93] In the section involving the bull, the great falcon speaks in the statue's ear, "I have brought you your enemy, for him to be offered beneath you. Atum has slaughtered him for you. Do not approach that god! Receive the foreleg, the eye of Horus; the heart is brought to you with it. Do not approach that god!"[94] As he presents the foreleg, the *sem*-priest declares four times, "I have opened your mouth for you with the foreleg, eye of Horus." As he uses the various implements, he utters, "Horus has opened your mouth for you, he opens your eyes for you (with) the *ntrty*-blade, with the Great-of-Power blade, with which the mouth of every god is opened."[95] In addition, the presentations of the ostrich feather, grapes, water, and various food offerings are all declared to be "the eye of Horus."

### Structural Interpretation[96]

Structurally, this ritual bridges the gap between the crafting of the statue in the workshop and its installation in the temple as a fully functioning locus of divine presence. The ritual establishes a clear connection between several of the elements and the statue, suggesting that in some way the use of these elements brings about the necessary transition. Both the bull's foreleg and heart are indexically connected

---

90. Although unfamiliar to modern ears, these meanings will become clear when contextualized in the following analysis.

91. Lorton, "Theology of Cult Statues," 154.

92. Or, alternatively, again "Who has smitten my father?," evidencing the textual difficulties inherent in this passage (ibid., 155).

93. The verb translated as "exempt" has a basic meaning to "protect" and appears frequently "in legal contexts with the meaning of 'exemption' from taxes or obligations to perform duties that assume the character of taxes. In the present context, this nuance is clearly applied to the possibility of prosecution or punishment for those who would do harm to the statue" (ibid.). This verb is adapted from casuistic law: "As for anyone who might do such-and-such …," with the apodosis specifying the punishment (Lorton, "The Treatment of Criminals in Ancient Egypt through the New Kingdom," *JESHO* 20 [1977]: 53–54).

94. Episode 23 from the 18th Dynasty tomb-chapel of Rekhmire (see Norman de Garis Davies, *The Tomb of Rekh-Mi-Rēʿ at Thebes* [New York: Plantin, 1943]). The following translations as well are taken from the Rekhmire edition.

95. The *sem*-priest makes similar statements when applying the other implements.

96. In interpreting the ritual, we must realize that we are dealing with textual and pictorial representations that do not necessarily reflect actual practice.

with the statue as they are presented to it and touched to its mouth.[97] The various tools are likewise indexically bound to the statue, particularly its mouth.

The ritual also establishes hierarchical relationships among the participants. The privileged role of the *sem*-priests over both the ritualist (*ẖry-ḥb*) and the artisans emerges clearly, while the common people bear no mention at all.[98] The artisans, who had the essential and most intimate role in the crafting stage, have a minimal role after their craftsmanship is complete. The priest inspects their handiwork, yet their only active role is asking for exemption for those who smote the god, presumably themselves. In addition, they are only present for the first part of the ritual. The ritual thus seems to tie up any loose ends relating to the artisans so that they may be removed from the picture entirely.[99] In other words, it functionally limits their role to the crafting and inspection of the deity and limits it from the rest of the ritual process. Although more central than the artisans, the ritualist also seems to play a secondary role. He does not appear to perform any ritual action relating to the statue and his major role seems to be to instruct and assist the *sem*-priest.[100]

The *sem*-priest is the main actor and is indexically connected to the statue. He alone seems to come into direct contact with it, twice touching its mouth with his little finger.[101] He is likewise the only character who changes his attire, an action that, because of the fixed setting, helps to mark the transition from one section to the next.[102] In addition, the *sem*-priest conducts all the important ritual acts and utters many of the ritual recitations.

It seems then that the ritual transitions the statue from one realm to the next, from the workshop to the temple and from a potential to an actual receptacle of the

---

97. An index is a sign that is existentially related to its signifier. Rather than being a matter of convention—e.g., with a symbol—the connection is a matter of fact (Nancy B. Jay, *Throughout Your Generations Forever: Sacrifice, Religion and Paternity* [Chicago: Chicago University Press, 1992], 7; see further Charles Sanders Peirce, e.g., Justus Buchler, *The Philosophical Writings of Peirce* [New York: Dover, 1955]). In this instance, the explicit presentation of the bull's foreleg and heart to the statue and contact between them indexes their relationship.

98. Other figures emerge in the course of the ritual (e.g., the female greater and lesser falcons), who play a brief yet specific role. Their hierarchical status is difficult to determine.

99. For an examination of these "loose ends," see the ideology section.

100. For example, his statements seem to be directed toward the priest: "I brand for you your eye, that you may be a *ba* by means of it!" (Lorton, "Theology of Cult Statues," 158) and "*Sem*-priest, extend your arm…" (p. 161). Even when the ritualist appears to be addressing the statue, the instructions specify that he is facing the *sem*-priest (p. 162).

101. The "loving son" also makes such intimate contact. However, because he seems more suited to the mortuary role, his role will be omitted from analysis.

102. The presence of many of the separate stages presented in different scenes in the wall reliefs serves as another way to subdivide the ritual (Lorton, "Theology of Cult Statues," 148).

divine. At the same time, the ritual marks a transition between primary caretakers, moving from the artisans, who play the essential role in crafting the statue, to the priests, who will now play the essential role of caring for the deity in its temple.[103]

As a prelude to the statue's installation, the ritual occurs outside of the primary sanctuary, that is, in the workshop. Nonetheless, the ritual in no way eschews careful protocol. As an encounter with the divine, the ritual elicits awe, engenders intimacy, and requires clearly delineated actions and preparations.[104]

## Use

Functionally, the ritual serves as an intermediate though no less central stage, standing between the finished statue and its taking up residence and rule in the temple. The title of the ritual identifies its purpose as the Opening of the Mouth of the statue.[105] Individual interpretive statements also appear throughout the ritual, especially in the utterances accompanying the actions.[106] For example, the presentation of the bull's foreleg and heart as well as the cultic use of the various instruments are explicitly said to open the statue's mouth, while each offering as well as the bull's foreleg is identified as the eye of Horus. In order to understand these interpretive statements, we now turn to ideology.

## Ideology

I begin with some general points of orientation, which will inform the following discussion of the individual elements and their place in the larger whole. Rather than commenting on every detail, analysis will focus on those deemed most pertinent and interesting.

In the Opening of the Mouth ritual, as elsewhere, the Egyptians adopted a comprehensive approach to ritual. Rather than adopting a single solution that best

---

103. As noted above, the role of the "loving son" will be largely ignored because it does not seem to fit the divine sphere.

104. The various actions and exclamations are precisely enumerated and given to specific actors. To play a role, ritual purity was essential, as the purification of the *sem*-priest precedes any of the other ritual actions.

105. Instead of playing a significant role, the actual installation of the statue in the temple seems to be done without fanfare, a mere aftereffect of the "Opening of the Mouth" ritual.

106. The importance of interpretive statements has been noted by Roy E. Gane and applied to the biblical text (*Ritual Dynamic Structure* [Gorgias Dissertations 14; Piscataway, NJ: Gorgias, 2004]; idem, *Cult and Character: Purification Offerings, Day of Atonement and Theodicy* [Winona Lake, IN: Eisenbrauns, 2005]). Incorporating the insights of systems theory, especially that of Brian Wilson (*Systems: Concepts, Methodologies, and Applications* [Chichester: Wiley, 1984]), Gane contends that ritual, like other nonritual systems, finds meaning in the goals attributed to it by the authority who commands the ritual (*Ritual Dynamic Structure*, 18–23, 50–60; *Cult and Character*, 7, 13).

fits their agenda, the Egyptians employed "a multiplicity of approaches,"[107] amassing and juxtaposing various ritual words and actions designed to achieve the same
result, the Opening of the Mouth.[108] Although these approaches do not always
logically cohere, at least according to the dictates of Western logic, they were graft-
ed into the ritual with care.[109] As we will see, the approaches are complementary
and add to the ritual's comprehensive efficacy, which is especially important in
rituals where the achievement of the goal often cannot be tangibly verified.

In addition to adopting multiple approaches, many of the approaches were
employed repeatedly (e.g., the central presentation of the bull's foreleg and heart).
Rather than being redundant, these too were purposeful, adding new meaning
through nuanced differences and their presence in different settings. Strictly
speaking, repetitive statements or actions in a new setting are not repetitive at all.
More simply, performing a single action multiple times was considered to be more
effective than a single performance.[110]

There is also some evidence that the ritual itself was repeated, that a single
Opening of the Mouth was insufficient. For example, in the mortuary sphere, it
seems that additional Opening of the Mouth rituals were performed on statues at
the annual mortuary festival, the Feast of the Valley.[111] This need not suggest that
the enlivened statue had somehow died. Rather, on special occasions the statue required a revitalization or perhaps an increased vitalization to prepare it to partici-

---

107. John A. Wilson, "The Nature of the Universe," *The Intellectual Adventure of Ancient
Man* (ed. H. Frankfort *et al.*; Chicago: Chicago University Press, 1946), 32–33.

108. Roth ("Buried Pyramids and Layered Thoughts," 991–1003; idem, "Representation of
the Divine," 24–37) posits the concept of nesting to explain the likely gradual accumulation
of alternative approaches. She contends that, instead of viewing each explanation as
equally valid, multiple explanations "represent a layered hierarchy, in which the oldest
explanation or manifestation is retained, embedded in a sequence of later interpretations"
("Representation of the Divine," 28). "Supplementary metaphors, either borrowed from
related rituals or invented afresh, infused new meaning into older forms, forms that were
themselves the result of an endless sequence of such infusions and reinterpretations. Old
metaphors were rarely discarded; instead, they were embedded in successive new versions,
intensifying the ritual's effectiveness, deepening and enriching its meaning, and preserving
the authority conferred by its age" (idem, "Fingers, Stars," 79). "The entire amalgam thus
combined the power and advantages of these and all the intervening nested stages" (idem,
"Representation of the Divine," 28).

109. Roth, "*psš-kf*," 147; idem, "Fingers, Stars," 79; Quack, "Ein Prätext und seine
Realisierungen," 169; *pace* Otto, *Das ägyptische Mundöffnungsritual*. In some cases, multiple
means of achieving the same end were part of the ritual from the beginning.

110. In ritual terms, repetition is also a central method used to ritualize an event, i.e.,
identify it as especially important. According to Catherine Bell, ritualization is a "way of
acting that is designed and orchestrated to distinguish and privilege what is being done in
relation to other, more quotidian, activities" (Bell, *Ritual Theory*, 74).

111. Finnestad, "Meaning and Purpose of *Opening the Mouth*," 125.

pate cultically in the important festivities.[112] It is likewise possible that in the divine sphere additional Opening of the Mouth rituals were performed on special occasions not to resurrect the god in the statue, but rather to enhance the divine statue's cultic vitality, above and beyond the vitalizing effects of the daily cult ritual.

Furthermore, many of the multiple complementary and repeated approaches to Opening the Mouth function simultaneously on multiple levels.[113] First, some ritual activities produce instrumental effects (e.g., burning incense makes the room smell nice). Second, throughout the ritual, the various recitations appeal to mythic precedents, equating the actors, objects, or activities with their mythic counterparts.[114] For example, the ostrich feather, grapes, water, and various food offerings are identified as "the eye of Horus." Rather than following a single myth through the course of the ritual, utterances draw from a variety of myths and thereby connect, and indeed seem to equate, a ritual element with an analogous element in the mythic sphere in order to increase its ritual efficacy. For example, while a grape remains a grape, through mythic associations it also becomes "the eye of Horus,"

---

112. Cf. ibid., esp. 125–26; see also Aylward M. Blackman, "The House of the Morning," *JEA* 5 (1918): 160. This accords with Egyptian cyclical thinking in which, e.g., the sun had to be daily reborn or the cult statue had to sleep and eat daily to maintain its vitality. An additional Opening of the Mouth also ritualized or marked the importance of the festival, since it warranted such an important activity.

113. Ritual activity in general and ritual signs in particular are characterized by a condensation of meaning, multivocality, and ambiguity (Kertzer, *Ritual, Politics, and Power*, 11). Ritual can condense a rich diversity of meanings into a single sign (see esp. Turner, *Forest of Symbols* [Ithaca, NY: Cornell University Press, 1967]), e.g., a bull's foreleg may be interpreted as a vitalization of inert matter, a meal, or the biological equivalent of the craftsmen's tools (see further below). Multivocality suggests that the same sign "may be understood by different people in different ways" (Kertzer, *Ritual, Politics, and Power*, 11, drawing on the works of Turner, *Forest of Symbols*, 50 and Nancy D. Munn, "Symbolism in Ritual Context: Aspects of Symbolic Action," in *Handbook of Social and Cultural Anthropology* [ed. J. Honigmann; Chicago: Rand McNally, 1973], 580), in different ways in different contexts, and especially in our case, in different ways in the same context by the same person (e.g., on literal and symbolic levels). Ritual ambiguity indicates that an individual sign has no precise meaning when contextless (cf. Frits Staal, "The Meaninglessness of Ritual," *Numen* 26 [1979]: 2–22; idem, *Rules Without Meaning: Ritual, Mantras and the Human Sciences* [New York: Peter Lang, 1989], 127–29, 131, 134, 330; Gane, *Cult and Character*, 4–6). Rather, meaning is assigned to it only in context (e.g., severing a bull's foreleg alternatively may be interpreted as a necessary and effective means of enlivening inert matter or as a sadistic episode of animal cruelty).

114. See esp. Assmann, "Die Verborgenheit des Mythos in Ägypten," *Göttinger Miszellen* 25 (1977): 7–43; see also Bjerke, "'Egyptian Ritual of 'Opening the Mouth'," 205; Jørgen Podemann Sørensen, "Redundans og abstraktion i det ægyptiske daglige tempelritual," *Chaos* 1 (1982): 52 and *passim*; Lorton, "Theology of Cult Statues," 135.

associated with "every alleviation of lack or need."[115] Third, Egyptian ritual makes various analogous associations such that a ritual element or activity is symbolically identified and in some sense equated with other elements, activities, and potencies.[116] For example, the Opening of the Mouth seems to be associated with birth, while one of its central elements—the bull's foreleg—is identified with strength.[117] One of the primary ways of making such associations is through wordplay. Rather than being playful, "wordplay was regarded as a highly serious and controlled use of language."[118] Punning plays an especially significant role as a meaningful way of making connections between words and the objects they refer to and in some ways embody.[119] Similarly, the Egyptian texts seem to use the multiple meanings of a word's semantic domain in one space in order to add layers of meaning.[120]

## Ideology of Individual Elements

Direct rites of purification, which seem to be an essential component of all Egyptian divine rituals, appear only at the beginning and end of the Opening of the Mouth.[121] By bookending the ritual with purifications, which are elsewhere associated with rituals involving deities, the writers stress the importance of the ritual as a means of contacting the divine and of the statue as the locus of this contact, while highlighting the importance of purity throughout and, by extension, the standards of perfection necessary for the ritual to be successful.[122] Rather than serving as a simple repetition, the anointing associated with the final purification adds a new

---

115. Assmann, *The Search for God*, 50. See esp. Günter Rudnitzky, *Die Aussage über "Das Auge des Horus": Eine altägyptische Art geistiger Äusserung nach dem Zeugnis des alten Reiches* (Analecta Aegyptiaca 5; Copenhagen: Ejnar Munksgaard, 1956). For further interpretation, see below.

116. Teeter ("Temple Cults," in *The Egyptian World* [ed. T. A. H. Wilkinson; London: Routledge, 2007], 312) characteristically refers to the actions and recitations as symbolically awakening the statue's senses. Nonetheless, it must be stressed that the relationship between the symbol and its referent is not simply one of association. Rather, through the medium of ritual the symbol in some sense becomes what it symbolizes.

117. See further below.

118. Assmann, *The Search for God*, 87.

119. See generally Morenz, *Egyptian Religion*, 9–10; Waltraud Guglielmi, "Wortspiel," *LÄ* 6 (1986): 1287–91; Lorton, "Theology of Cult Statues," 134–35. See especially Helck "Bemerkungen zum Mundöffnungsritual," 33–36 on the puns relating to this ritual. Although not necessarily homophones, given the complexity of reconstructing Egyptian vowels, homographs do appear in these texts for the purpose of punning (Lorton, "Theology of Cult Statues," 134–35).

120. Ibid., 134.

121. Bjerke, "'Egyptian Ritual of 'Opening the Mouth'," 209–11.

122. In addition, purifications clearly demarcate the beginning and the end of the ritual.

element.[123] Alongside the statue's adornment and investment with a ruler's insignia, anointing signifies the deity's installation into office.[124]

The use of incense to purify the air warrants further comment. Incense removes any olfactory impurity, surrounding the deity, its space and its priests with the divine aroma. Alongside radiance, aroma is a primary sign of divinity.[125] For example, when the god Amun approaches the sleeping Queen Ahmose in order to beget Queen Hatshepsut by her, his divine aroma gives him away even though he takes the form of her husband, Thutmose I.[126] "Like that of (the incense land) Punt," the divine aroma seems to be associated with the incense burned in the temple.[127] By burning incense in the sanctuary, the room smells like the divine sphere and is thus a suitable place for divine manifestation. Similarly, by shrouding himself in incense, the priest becomes god-like and thus fit to enter the divine presence. Egyptian wordplay demonstrates this reality, as "burning 'incense' (*sntr*) for the god could 'deify' (*sntri*) the king."[128]

In the artisan scene,[129] the various statements regarding the perfection of the statue and the smiting necessary to perfect it gain clarity when the statue is understood analogically as a body.[130] In order to be suitable for its divine resident, the body had to be perfectly crafted, yet the very actions required to craft it would be a serious assault on a human body.[131] The craftsmen, indeed their craftsmanship it-

---

123. Bjerke, "'Egyptian Ritual of 'Opening the Mouth,'" 211.

124. Ibid. In the ancient Near East in general as in the Hebrew Bible, anointing with oil "ceremonializes an elevation in legal status" (Jacob Milgrom, *Leviticus 1–16* [AB 3; New York: Doubleday, 1991], 553–55).

125. Hornung, *Conceptions of God*, 133.

126. Ibid.

127. Ibid.

128. Bell, "The New Kingdom Divine Temple," 174; cf. Nielsen, *Incense in Ancient Israel*, 9. In the Egyptian pyramid texts, incense also ensures that, upon death, the king takes his place among his divine brethren since his "scent is as their scent, [his] sweat is as the sweat of the Two Enneads" (Utt. 412). Similarly, the king says, "my sweat is the sweat of Horus, my odor is the odor of Horus" (Utt. 508).

129. The preceding vision, preserved from a mortuary context, in which the form of the statue is revealed, may be unnecessary, since in the case of the divine image, the artisans may simply reproduce the previous statue. However, theoretically if the statue is damaged or if the deity desires a new form, consulting the deity ensures that the statue conforms to the deity's wishes, serving as the deity's "exact shape" (for this phrase of Horemheb, see Murnane, *Texts from the Amarna Period*, 233; cf. Mesopotamia and Hatti).

130. Or, perhaps, even before it has been crafted, the statue already is the divine body, which must be perfectly crafted to make it suitable. See, e.g., the reference to the statue as the divine body in the Memphite theology (ll. 59–60; see Assmann, *The Search for God*, 45–46; Lorton, "Theology of Cult Statues," 187).

131. Even in the mortuary realm, preservation of the body was essential.

self, thus play an ambivalent role. They are both applauded for their craftsmanship of the divine statue and must be exempted from the potential damage it causes.[132] The artisans' plea for exemption and the very possibility of harm are expressed indirectly, as the perceived violent assault is cast in the hypothetical future. "Lo, may those who *might* smite [the cult statue] be exempt!"[133] The artisans thereby implicitly deny that they have participated in the assault and that any retribution due should be withheld since such violence is necessary in creating the statue.[134]

The donning of the panther skin, which follows, does more than simply indicate a change of scene; it also serves as a highly productive pun. The word *ba* translates as both "panther" and "manifest power."[135] By donning the panther skin, the priest himself becomes manifestly powerful,[136] likely manifesting the power—that is, physical strength—of the panther whose skin he wears, and is thus equipped to perform the ritual effectively.[137]

In the next scene, the bull's foreleg and heart occupy primary position,[138] together endowing the statue with physical strength and consciousness respectively.[139] Like the panther skin, the foreleg also serves as a meaningful pun, such that the foreleg (*ḫpš*) may be associated with physical strength (*ḫpš*).[140] Beyond

---

132. This approval occurs both within the ritual itself ("Made perfect for me is my father!") and is amply attested in other sources; there is substantial evidence that the Egyptians both acknowledged and celebrated the physical aspect of the statue and its manufacturing process. In the textual realm, "kings and officials proudly recorded their role in the manufacture of cult statues, sometimes including the material of which they were made" (Lorton, "Theology of Cult Statues," 157).

133. The verb is as clear in the Egyptian as it is in English (ibid., 156).

134. Ibid., 156–57.

135. Regarding *ba* as "manifest power," see Lorton, "Theology of Cult Statues," 134.

136. As declared by the accompanying ritualist who claims that the *sem*-priest will be "manifestly powerful" or "manifest power" (ibid., 159).

137. Goyon, *Rituels funéraires*, 120 n. 4; Helck, *Untersuchungen zur Thinitenzeit* (ÄA 45; Wiesbaden: Harrasowitz, 1987), 51; Lorton, "Theology of Cult Statues," 159–61.

138. From both the pictorial representations and the accompanying words, it is clear that the presentation of the foreleg and the heart of the bull are the primary elements of the ritual. We may also be able to distinguish between these two elements, as the text makes it clear that the foreleg itself serves to "open the mouth" (Lorton, "Theology of Cult Statues," 164). Thus, it would seem to play a more prominent role than even the heart. However, this need not be the case, as the reference to the foreleg may imply the presence of the other elements, most notably the heart but also perhaps the goat and goose (which are also slaughtered and presented to the deity).

139. Ibid., 165.

140. Ibid., 159; cf. Peter Munro, "Die Nacht vor der Thronbesteigung—zum ältesten Teil des Mundöffnungsrituals," in *Studien zu Sprache und Religion Ägyptens zu Ehren von Wolfhart Westendorf* (vol. 2; ed. F. Junge; Göttingen: Hubert, 1984), 924.

the obvious punning, the foreleg likely carries additional freight. The freshly severed foreleg of a bull exhibits spontaneous muscle contractions and tremors for up to twenty minutes, which may continue to be induced artificially for up to two hours.[141] Attaching this twitching mass of live flesh spurting the bull's life blood to the statue indexically connects the two elements and suggests a transfer of the potent life energies and potency of the bull. In addition, the hieroglyph for "foreleg" resembles the adze, the instrument used to carve the statue and literally open its mouth and the instrument ritually employed in the following scenes.[142] Thus, the association with the adze reinforces the textual reference to the foreleg opening the mouth, suggesting that it is the biological equivalent to the craftsmen's tools. On the mythic plane, the accompanying recitation also explicitly identifies the foreleg as the eye of Horus, suggesting that it serves to make the statue whole and without lack.

The heart carries a more straightforward yet no less important meaning. The Egyptian heart was perceived as the body's emotional and cognitive center, the self-consciousness.[143] As such, it endowed the statue with consciousness, which together with physical strength makes up the essential attributes of a human life.[144] The heart's red appearance and the likelihood that it continued to spurt blood also seem to suggest a connection with life, taken from the bull and imparted to the statue.[145]

Before moving on, it bears mentioning that here, as elsewhere in Egyptian ritual, the slaughter of the sacrificial animal is also associated with the destruction

---

141. Results derived from laboratory experiment; see Calvin W. Schwabe, "Bull Semen and Muscle ATP: Some Evidence of the Dawn of Medical Science in Ancient Egypt," *Canadian Journal of Veterinary Research* 50 (1986): 150; idem et al., *"Live Flesh": Rudiments of Muscle Physiology in Ancient Egypt* (Working Paper Series 54; Davis: Agricultural History Center, University of California, 1989), 9–11.

142. Assmann, *Death and Salvation*, 315.

143. Claude Traunecker, *Les Dieux de l'Égypte* (Paris: University of France Press, 1992), 40; Lorton, "Theology of Cult Statues," 140. "*Ib* is the world used for 'heart' in the daily cult ritual, while the Opening of the Mouth ritual employs *haty*. Both terms can be used for the heart as the seat of emotions, while of the two, it is *haty* that tends to be employed to express the specific connotation of the heart as a physical organ, which is essentially appropriate to the sacrificial context here" (Lorton, "Theology of Cult Statues," 165 n. 64). On the nuances of meaning of the words for "heart" see Piankoff, *Le "Coeur" dans les textes égyptiens depuis l'Ancien jusqu'à la fin du Nouvel Empire* (Paris: Geuthner, 1930), 10–13; Bernard Long, "Le *ib* et le *ḥ3ty* dans les textes médicaux de l'Égypte ancienne," in *Hommages à François Daumas* (vol. 2; ed. A. Guillaumont; Montpellier: University of Montpelier, 1986), 484–85.

144. Lorton, "Theology of Cult Statues," 165.

145. This impression is reinforced by the fact that the heart and leg are hastily delivered to the statue (Assmann, *Death and Salvation*, 325), perhaps to visually and conceptually maximize the transferral of life.

of the deity's enemies.[146] Thus, in a single and interpretively supple act, the heart and foreleg bring victory over the deity's foes and the mythic return to wholeness. They simultaneously function as the biological counterparts to the artisans' tools, which serve to open the statue's mouth by endowing it with the vital strength and consciousness still visibly pulsing through the foreleg and heart.

The next episode involving the application of the artisan's tools to the statue's mouth, like the presentation of foreleg and heart, explicitly serves to open the statue's mouth, yet approaches the problem from a different angle. In this context, the priestly activities and recitations seem to "*transvalue* the manufacturing process into something of ritual effectiveness in quickening the statue by endowing it with its faculties, especially the ability to open its mouth."[147] In other words, the ritual seems to employ the very same or similar tools used by the artisans for the purpose of enlivening the divine statue, thereby connecting the crafting of the statue with its enlivening and the artisans' tools with both important elements.

The ritual accomplishes this transvaluation through the creative use of language, both in the names ascribed to the tools and the use of puns.[148] Through wordplay, the tools are made to transmit various potencies that contribute to enlivening the divine statue. The instrument, an adze called a *ntrty*, recalls the root for god (*ntr*), and as such alludes to the statue's infusion with divinity.[149] In fact, the scene with the adze was considered so central that it was used as shorthand for the entire ritual.[150] The next implement, called Great-of-Power, co-opts and applies to the statue *ḥk3*, the "all-pervading coercive power"[151] characteristic of deities and responsible for creating and maintaining the world. Another tool, the *psš-kf*, together with the goose (*smn*) and goat (*ʿr*)[152] presented in the offering scene, seems

---

146. Assmann, *Death and Salvation*, 324; Quack, "Ein Prätext und seine Realisierungen," 170; see further, idem, "Opfermahl und Feindvernichtung im altägyptischen Ritual," *Mitteilungen der Berliner Gesellschaft für Anthropologie, Ethnologie und Urgeschichte* 27 (2006): 67–80.

147. Lorton, "Theology of Cult Statues," 173, italics his.

148. Otto (*Das ägyptische Mundöffnungsritual*, 2.22) notes that the names given to the artisan's tools are mostly not attested outside of the ritual and thus seem to be either special names applied to the ritual or ancient names no longer in use.

149. Lorton, "Theology of Cult Statues," 149.

150. Otto, *Das ägyptische Mundöffnungsritual*, 2.83. As noted, its visual association with the hieroglyph for the bull's foreleg serves as a conceptual link between the two episodes.

151. Assmann, "Prayers, Hymns, Incantations, and Curses: Egypt," in Johnston, ed., *Religions of the Ancient World*, 350. Such coercive power in Egypt and elsewhere is often translated as "magic." Here, we avoid such a term because of its different and often negative modern connotations and the problematic dichotomy commonly drawn between ancient religion and magic.

152. In its more immediate context, the goat is connected with a pun on the word *ʿr*, "approach" (Lorton, "Theology of Cult Statues," 170) or "ascend."

to form a productive pun that elucidates its purpose. The accompanying utterance states, "I make firm (smn) for you your jaws (ˁrty), they being split (psš)."[153] With this gesture, the transvaluation of the manufacturing process seems to be complete, confirmed by the utterance that appears to ensure that the statue's mouth will be able to open and close (split).[154]

In addition, some of the elements seem to allude to childbirth, suggesting that the statue is not only made but also born.[155] For example, the verb for making a divine cult statue is msi 'to give birth,'[156] the psš-kf seems to mimic childbirth, as it serves to cut the umbilical cord of a newborn baby, while the use of the little fingers and perhaps also the finger of electrum seem to mimic the clearing of a newborn's mouth.[157] More simply, since before the ritual began the statue was not alive with the divine presence and the faculties necessary to communicate cultically, opening its mouth marks the birth of this particular symbiosis of statue and deity.[158]

The grapes and the ostrich feather are also linguistically evocative. The presentation of the grapes reinforces several of the ritual's main purposes, while in some ways forming a microcosm of it. "Since the function of the statue's mouth is to consume cult offerings, the presentation of the grapes can be seen as encapsulating two main purposes of the ritual: it endows the statue with its ability to perform (iri) this function, while the grapes" (i3rrt) approximate the purpose of "the offerings (iret [irt], ritual 'act' …, also mythologized as iret 'Eye' of Horus)."[159] The utterance accompanying the ostrich feather (šwt) explains its purpose: "Take for yourself the Eye of Horus! Your face will not be empty/deprived (shu [šw]) because of it!"[160]

Although seemingly repetitive, the second presentation of the foreleg and heart occurs in a new setting with new elements and is thus not redundant.[161] The endowment with physical strength and consciousness likely continues to be pres-

---

153. Translation after Lorton, "Theology of Cult Statues," 170.

154. Ibid.

155. As we will see, other texts suggest that in addition to being humanly contructed and born, a cult statue was also created by the deity who inhabited it.

156. Wb II 138 12; Roth, "psš-kf;" 146; Rainer Hannig, Großes Handwörterbuch Ägyptisch-Deutsch: Die Sprache der Pharaonen (2800–950 v. Chr.) (2nd ed.; Mainz: von Zabern, 2003), 382.

157. See Roth, "psš-kf"; idem, "Fingers, Stars,"

158. See further below.

159. Lorton, "Theology of Cult Statues," 171.

160. Ibid.

161. Cf. Lorton, "Theology of Cult Statues," 174–75, though it is possible that the ritual may not have involved the slaughter of a second bull (Otto, Das ägyptische Mundöffnungsritual, 2.103; Lorton, "Theology of Cult Statues," 175).

ent in this new context, reinforced by the repetition of the mouth-opening process after the use of the artisans' tools. In addition, various elements differ from the previous rite and serve to enhance the mouth opening. First, instead of the great falcon, the lesser falcon speaks in the ear of the sacrificed animals, which together with the great falcon in the first slaughtering scene, establishes a mythological link to Isis and Nephtys, the sisters of Osiris, who mourned their slain brother in this particular bird form.[162] In the Opening of the Mouth ritual context, their utterances associate the slaughtered animal(s) with the enemy, stereotypically Seth, who murdered Osiris and snatched Horus' eye, such that its slaughter brings an end to divine opposition and restores divine fullness through the presentation of the foreleg as the eye of Horus.[163] The term used to designate the second bull (*sšr*) is especially evocative, as it seems to pun *sš* "to open," which figures prominently in the falcon's question, "Is your mouth open (*sesh* [*sš*]) now?"[164] By delaying the pun to this point, the ritual implies that only now can an affirmative answer be given.

With the completion of the Opening of the Mouth process, it is now possible that the presentation of the foreleg and heart involves a first meal, a possibility enhanced by its position before the elements of the daily cult ritual and the feeding inherent in it.[165] Since the statue has now been enlivened, it may now properly draw strength from these essential elements in a new way as a special first meal, accompanied by the elements of the daily ritual that will soon make up its daily care and feeding regimen.[166] Rather than dwelling on them here, the analysis of these elements will be addressed in the analysis of the daily ritual. Suffice it to say that these elements invigorate the now-living statue as material sustenance—that

---

162. However, for the divine cult image, they would likely not function as mourners since no one has died (cf. Lorton, "Theology of Cult Statues," 174).

163. In addition to the two falcons, the bulls themselves seem to be distinguished in that one is associated with Upper Egypt and the other with Lower Egypt (ibid.).

164. Ibid.

165. Lorton, "Theology of Cult Statues," 174–75; *pace* Assmann, who states emphatically that it has "nothing to do with the ordinary food offering" (*Death and Salvation*, 326). Although it serves to transfer the bull's vital energies to the statue, there is no reason that it cannot simultaneously serve as a first meal, a position strengthened by the presentation of a foreleg in the daily offering meal, where it serves both as an element of the daily meal and as the strength of the eye of Horus (LACMA Ostrakon; Kathlyn M. Cooney and J. Brett McClain, "The Daily Offering Meal in the Ritual of Amenhotep I: An Instance of the Local Adaption of Cult Liturgy," *JANER* 5 [2006]: 54).

166. On the similarity of the concluding elements of the Opening of the Mouth and the daily cult ritual, see Lorton, "Theology of Cult Statues," 149. In some cases, an additional opening of the mouth rite with an adze follows, adding to the efficacy of the mouth opening by repeating the activity with the instruments after the second presentation of bull's foreleg and heart and completing the doublet.

is, care and food—with heightened potencies derived from mythic associations and wordplay and thus serve as a fitting end to the enlivening process.

### Enlivening as a Joint Effort

The Opening of the Mouth brings the statue to life and charges it with the appropriate divine powers. While the ritual serves to open the mouth of the statue, it gives no indication of when or how the divine presence enters the statue, whether it is there from the beginning and/or appears only in increments. Some texts, according to Junker, refer to the divine "indwelling" or "installation" (*Einwohnung*), in which the divine *ba* descends from the celestial sphere to indwell its terrestrial cult image.[167] Nonetheless, although it seems clear that (some part of) the divine essence installs itself in the cult image, it remains unclear how and when the deity does so, especially in the context of the Opening of the Mouth. Such an omission need not concern us overmuch, for ritual texts tend to stress the human role, the human preparation for and ritual activity necessary to induce divine indwelling.[168] Since divine indwelling falls outside of the human purview, it need not be thoroughly described. Human servants must prepare, protect, and empower the deity's home and its body for divine presence, in essence getting the house in order so that its divine resident will indeed take up residence and bring divine blessing to the community responsible for its care. As we will see, the deity itself must decide to move into and stay in its terrestrial home.[169] In this joint venture, it would seem

---

167. The term "indwelling" is especially appropriate to the Greco-Roman period. However, the concept appears at least as early as the 18th Dynasty in the mortuary sphere, where the *ba* of the deceased descends from heaven to indwell images and the mummy (Assmann, *The Search for God*, 431). Similar conceptions also appear earlier in the divine sphere (see, e.g., ibid., 42–47). E.g., the Memphite theology (to be dated anywhere between the reign of Ramesses II to that of Shabaka of Dynasty 25 [Lorton, "Theology of Cult Statues," 187; regarding the problem of dating, see further Friedrich Junge, "Zur Fehldatierung des sog. Denkmals memphitischer Theologie oder der Beitrag der ägyptische Theologie zur Geistesgeschichte der Spätzeit," *Mitteilungen des Deutschen Archäologischen Instituts Abteilung Kairo* 29 (1973): 195–204; Hans Goedicke, "727 vor Christus," *WZKM* 69 (1977): 1–19; James P. Allen, *Genesis in Egypt: The Philosophy of Ancient Egyptian Creation Accounts* (Yale Egyptological Studies 2; New Haven: Yale Egyptological Seminar, 1988), 43]) refers to the gods as "entering" their bodies (Assmann, *The Search for God*, 46).

168. The recitations more often directly address the deity, yet rather than describing the deity's activity, they often serve to explain and empower human activity or to entreat the deity to partake of the elements being proffered.

169. Cf. Cooney and McClain, "The Daily Offering Meal," 70: "Liturgical practice *waits* for divinity to manifest itself by creating the conditions for the god to appear. The ritual meal, the sacred space, the magical incantations, and the offerings that symbolically become what they need to be all create the necessary conditions, but in the end, the human element must simply wait for the divine element to become manifest."

that priests enliven the image and make it a suitable divine vessel, all the while appealing to deities and divine energies, while the deity fills the living body with its divine essence.[170]

## Origin of the Divine Statue

Indwelling the statue seems to be primarily a divine endeavor, while enlivening it appears to be a joint effort. What about the statue itself? Who is responsible for its creation? In the ritual text, although their role is minimized and sanitized, the artisans nonetheless are clearly responsible for the construction of the divine statue. Various inscriptions likewise proudly stress the human role in crafting the divine image.[171] However, hymns and mythological texts tend to assert that it is divinely created, not humanly crafted.[172] In fact, in some cases, the statue is described as self-created—that is, created by the deity who will indwell it. For example, in the Leiden hymn, Amun is described as he who "built his images, who himself created himself."[173] Even within the Opening of the Mouth ritual itself, as we have seen, the statue is born in addition to being made. How are we to reconcile these claims? In the Egyptian world, each was an equally valid means of overcoming the inherent uneasiness with identifying a deity with its statue, while together they served as a more valid means of achieving the desired end than any one means could alone. Although they might not logically cohere, at least according to modern standards, the Egyptians juxtaposed alternate claims to add to the cumulative effect.[174] Ritual efficacy requires divine-human cooperation, yet the various texts often opt to highlight the aspect of that process that is most appropriate to their context. Wishing to highlight their piety, kings tended to stress their role in crafting the divine

---

170. See further below under "Relationship of the Deity to Its Statue(s)."

171. For example, Horemheb declares that he "created [the gods'] statues, each in their exact shape" (Murnane, *Texts from the Amarna Period*, 233).

172. Lorton, "Theology of Cult Statues," 185. For example, in the Memphite Theology, Ptah "made their (the deity's) bodies according to their wishes" (l. 59; Assmann, *The Search for God*, 46). This is also the case in some historical texts. For example, an inscription of Ramesses II describes how the god as cult statue was already waiting in the mountain for the king to discover (Cairo CGC 34504; Kenneth A. Kitchen, *Ramesside Inscriptions: Historical and Biographical: Ramesses II, Inscriptions* [vol 2. Oxford: Blackwell, 1979], 361 l. 1–362 l. 12; idem., *Ramesside Inscriptions: Translated & Annotated: Ramesses II, Royal Inscriptions* [vol. 2; Oxford: Blackwell, 1996], 193–95).

173. Translation after Lorton, "Theology of Cult Statues," 185.

174. Here, they posit different claims, all which, to the Egyptian mind, could be true, yet none of which possessed a monopoly on truth. Rather than try to reconcile conflicting claims, writers often pragmatically chose the expression that best fit their current need and rhetorical purposes.

image according to the divine wishes and of the finest materials. Wishing to exalt the deity, hymns instead highlight the divine element.

## 2. Daily Cult Ritual

Once the statue has been fully endowed with the divine and placed safely in the temple, how do the people safeguard this presence? The daily cult ritual provides the answer to this question and further discloses the nature of the divine presence as well as the proper human response to it.

The daily cult ritual involves two primary elements: the care and the feeding of the deities in their various temples.[175] These elements are often attested separately and mirror the final elements of the Opening of the Mouth ritual and the king's daily care.[176] The daily care of deities is attested on the wall scenes in the temple of Seti I at Abydos, the Great Hypostyle Hall at Karnak, the temple of Horus at Edfu, and on several papyri (Papyrus Berlin 3055 from the 22nd Dynasty describing the daily care of Amun and 3014 and 3052 describing the care of Mut).[177] Wall

---

175. The elements related to divine care have been misleadingly referred to as the daily cult ritual (see, e.g., Alexandre Moret, *Le Rituel du culte divin journalier en Égypte, d'après les papyrus de Berlin et les textes du temple de Séti Ier, à Abydos* [Paris: Leroux, 1902]), without mention of the elements involving daily divine feeding. The elements related to divine care have also been called the cult image ritual (*Kultbildritual*), which is likewise imprecise, as only part of the ritual directly involves the cult image (Harold Hays, "The Ritual Scenes in the Chapel of Amun," in *The Epigraphic Survey, Medinet Habu IX: The Eighteenth Dynasty Temple, Part I: The Sanctuary* [OIP 136; Chicago: University of Chicago, 2009], 3 n. 17). Hays refers to the elements related to divine care more generally as the "temple sanctuary ritual" (ibid., 3). One may loosely refer to them as the divine care ritual, since they involve elements of intimate care that do not involve feeding. In addition, since the two papyrus exemplars feature Amenhotep I as either the donor or beneficiary, the daily feeding ritual has been referred to as the ritual of Amenhotep I, which has wrongly conjured up connotations of a ritual for the royal ancestors (ibid., 8). It also has been also referred to as the offering ritual (*Opferritual*), which is far more appropriate. I have opted to refer to it as the daily feeding ritual, so that it may form the pair care and feeding, classically posited for the daily cult of Mesopotamian gods (A. Leo Oppenheim, *Ancient Mesopotamia: Portrait of a Dead Civilization* [2nd ed.; Chicago: University of Chicago, 1977], 183–96). In addition, several texts refer to the offerings as 'meals' for the god (Utt. 273–274; Uvo Hölscher, *The Mortuary Temple of Ramses III, Part 1: The Excavation of Medinet Habu*, Vol. 3 [OIP 53; Chicago: University of Chicago Press, 1941], pl. 138 col. 45; Ben J. J. Haring, *Divine Households: Administrative and Economic Aspects of the New Kingdom Royal Memorial Temples in Western Thebes* [Egyptologische Uitgaven 12; Leiden: Nederlands Instituut voor het Nabije Oosten, 1997], 47; Teeter, "Temple Cults," 315). However, I recognize that offering ritual is perhaps a more appropriate title, since not every element involves feeding the deity.

176. Winfried Barta, "Kult," *LÄ* 3 (1980): 843–44.

177. Teeter, "Temple Cults," 315; *Religion and Ritual*, 47; Hays, "Ritual Scenes in the Chapel

scenes in the hypostyle hall of the temple of Amun at Karnak, Abydos, and the temple of Ramesses III at Medinet Habu as well as papyri from Cairo (CG 58030), Turin (CGT 54041), the British Museum (Papyrus British Museum 10689), and Tebtynis provide our primary evidence for divine feeding.[178] Although evidence for the daily care appears in separate sources from the daily feeding ritual, Nelson has demonstrated that the daily feeding ritual in the morning followed the daily care ritual such that the two together formed the daily cult ritual.[179] With relatively small variations, the same ritual was shared by temples throughout the land.[180] The meal element of the daily ritual occurred thrice daily, corresponding to human meals.[181] While there remains no scholarly consensus on the extent of the afternoon and evening services, all agree that the morning was the most substantial and the one represented primarily in the extant evidence.[182] Like the Opening of the Mouth ritual, the larger ritual was conveniently subdivided into various stages, each often with its own name (e.g., "lighting the fire," "taking the censer," and "opening the face").[183]

---

of Amun," 2–3. For an extensive list of references, see ibid., 3 n. 17.

178. Nikolaus Tacke, "Das Opferritual des ägyptischen Neuen Reiches," in *Rituale in der Vorgeschichte, Antike und Gegenwart; Studien zur vorderasiatichen, prähistorischen und klassischen Archäologie, Ägyptologie, alten Geschichte, Theologie und Religionswissenschaft; interdisziplinäre Tagung vom 1.-2. Februar 2002 an der Freien Universität Berlin; Internationale Archäologie; Arbeitsgemeinschaft, Symposium, Tagung, Kongress; 4*; (ed. C. Metzner-Nebelsick; Rahden: Leidorf, 2003), 27–29; Hays, "Ritual Scenes in the Chapel of Amun," 7–8. Temple walls are also covered with inventory lists enumerating the requirements for daily service (Harold H. Nelson and Uvo Hölscher, *Work in Western Thebes, 1931–1933* [OIC 18; Chicago: University of Chicago Press, 1934], 42–63; Haring, *Divine Households*, 39–51, 399–410; Teeter, "Temple Cults," 315). In addition, several economic texts detail the source of the materials and the record of their transfer from one temple to another (Teeter, *Religion and Ritual*, 47). For the papyri from Tebtynis, see Jürgen Osing and Gloria Rosati, *Papiri geroglifici e ieratici da Tebtynis* (Florence: Istituto Papirologico, 1998).

179. Harold H. Nelson, "Certain Reliefs at Karnak and Medinet Habu and the Ritual of Amenophis I," *JNES* 8 (1949): 202; Barta, "Kult," 844; Hays, "Ritual Scenes in the Chapel of Amun," 11–12.

180. Lorton, "Theology of Cult Statues," 132. However, there is some variability, especially in the elements related to divine care (Hays, "Ritual Scenes in the Chapel of Amun" 3), as the care could be adapted to suit the differing needs and characteristics of the specific deities (Holger Hussy, *Die Epiphanie und Erneuerung der Macht Gottes: Szenen des täglichen Kultbildrituals in den ägyptischen Tempeln der griechisch-römischen Epoche* [Studien zu den Ritualszenen altägyptischer Tempel 5; Dettelbach: Röll, 2007], 159).

181. Teeter, "Temple Cults," 315.

182. Ibid., 316. See, e.g., Utt. 273:4: "Their big ones are for his morning meal; their middle-sized ones are for his evening meal; their little ones are for his night meal" (translation after Teeter, "Temple Cults," 324 n. 1).

183. Regarding the latter, see esp. Angelika Lohwasser, *Die Formel "Öffnen des Gesichts"*

## Structure

In theory, only the king could interact directly with the gods in the cult (e.g., as seen in temple reliefs). However, in practice, the king could not be always and everywhere present to perform rituals. In turn, he often, if not always, had priestly stand-ins who repeatedly proclaimed that they came in the name of the king. As in the Opening of the Mouth ritual, each priestly activity is accompanied by a recitation. However, the utterances are fuller and more comprehensible in the daily cult ritual.[184]

After the royal representative is ritually purified with water, he lights a fire and burns incense on a censer over the flame. He then advances to the shrine, breaks the cord and clay seal that bind the door bolt, and removes the bolt that holds the double door of the shrine shut.[185] The ritual continues with opening the doors of the shrine and seeing the god.[186] Acts of worship follow, including anointing the statue with honey and censing it with incense, during which time the priest assures the deity he has not come to harm it. The priest also declares, "I bring you your heart in your body, set in its place" and that the perfume serves to bind the god's "bones, [to] join for him his limbs."[187] Next, the priest enters the "house" and the "shrine," presumably the larger stone shrine and the smaller wooden double-doored shrine within it, to embrace the statue.[188] Thereupon the divine presence is finally identified: "oh living *ba* who smites his enemies, your *ba* is with you and your *sekhem* is at your side."[189] The officiant then closes the doors of the shrine, only to reopen them with repeated cultic acts and exclamations.[190] After a series of repeated actions, the section ends with a presentation of the goddess Maat to the resident deity in the form of a statue.

In preparation for the daily removal of the deity from its shrine, the priest scatters pure white sand on the floor of the sanctuary. He then recites a liturgy

---

(BzÄ 11; Vienna: Afro-Pub, 1991).

184. Lorton, "Theology of Cult Statues," 149. Only a few of the utterances will be mentioned explicitly. In the text, however, they occupy by far the most space, as each scene consists of a brief heading and a detailed recitation.

185. This bolt is called the "finger" (Lorton, "Theology of Cult Statues," 136).

186. Referred to as the "opening (i.e., revelation) of the face" and "seeing the god" respectively (ibid., 139).

187. Ibid., 140.

188. Given that these areas are too small to enter, it seems that the officiant is merely extending his arms inside.

189. The terms *ba* (*b3*) and *sekhem* (*sḥm*) roughly translate as "manifestation" and "power" respectively (ibid., 141).

190. At the beginning of this section, *ba* and *sekhem* reappear: "Your manifestation (*ba*) is powerful (*sekhem*)...." (ibid, 142).

entitled "laying hands upon the deity" before removing it from the shrine.[191] Following additional purifications with water and incense, the priest removes the deity's outer garment and jewelry and wipes away the previous day's unguents. Once suitably cleansed, the priest presents the deity with strips of red, white, and green cloth and green and black eye make-up. The priest adorns the deity with bracelets, a collar, and anklets and presents it with scepters and a headdress suitable to its office. The statue was then wrapped in its "great garment."[192]

After being dressed for the occasion, the deity is presented with a sumptuous meal, which has been prepared in the room with the offering table preceding the sanctuary during the course of the divine care.[193] Thus the feeding portion of the care and feeding of the deity begins, consisting of offerings of substantial quantities of high-quality food and drink accompanied by censing.[194] After the deity is sated, the food is taken away and the deity is prepared for sleep. Following suitable purifications, the deity returns to its shrine and the doors are again closed and sealed. As an exit ritual, the priest performs the "Bringing of the Foot" rite, in which the priest backs out of the sanctuary, sweeping away his footprints and all traces of his presence.[195] Finally, after returning the deity to its shrine, the priest performs the reversion of offerings, by taking the divine leftovers first to lesser deities and enlivened statues within the sacred precinct, then to the necropolis, and finally dividing them among the priests and temple staff.[196]

### Structural Interpretation

The daily cult ritual indexes a connection between the deity and various elements in the ritual, including clothing, food, and purifications, suggesting that each is essential for ritual efficacy and the satisfaction of the deity. The role of the priests in presenting these elements throughout the course of the ritual likewise highlights their special status.[197] The priests are indexically connected to the king, as they explicitly perform the rituals in his name. Although not overtly denying

---

191. Teeter, *Religion and Ritual*, 48.

192. Ibid.

193. Barta, "Kult," 843.

194. For a fuller account of the ritual sequence, see Nelson, "Certain Reliefs," 229–32. The beginning of the offering sequence is lost (ibid., 229; Hays, "Ritual Scenes in the Chapel of Amun," 9).

195. Teeter, *Religion and Ritual*, 48. See more fully Harold H. Nelson, "The Rite of 'Bringing the Foot' as Portrayed in Temple Reliefs," *JEA* 35 (1949): 82–86.

196. Englund, "Offerings," 281–82.

197. Ritual texts mention various priestly actors, such as *wab*-priests, lector priests, and "God's Fathers" (Teeter, *Religion and Ritual*, 47), though the chief *wab*-priest is the primary actor, especially in the more intimate divine care.

access to others, their prominence suggests a special relationship between the king with his priestly surrogates on the one hand and the various Egyptian deities on the other, a relationship highlighted by privileged access and behavior and indexed by direct contact.[198] Since the performance of the cult is requisite for divine blessing and since all deities in their various cultic manifestations must be served, the king delegates his function as sole divine intermediary to the various local priests who carry out the cult in the name of the king.[199]

The detailed ritual intimates that the deity must be approached with care, according to a strict formula.[200] The priest must first undergo purification and continually profess his purity during the ritual.[201] He also must assure the deity that he comes in the name of the king and to do no harm. A striking intimacy appears alongside the necessary caution. For example, in addition to various scenes showing the king and the gods in intimate commerce, the priest may enter the deity's innermost chamber and embrace, bathe, and clothe its statue.

Unlike the Opening of the Mouth ritual, this ritual occurs solely within the sacred confines of the temple. As a result, there is no transfer of roles of the participants or a transfer of the nature or location of the cult statue. As we will see, the ritual instead seems to be a preservation of the deity in its current state, involving its awakening from its nightly slumber.

There also seem to be structural elements that both link the daily cult ritual to and distinguish it from the Opening of the Mouth ritual.[202] Although the rituals begin differently, suggesting that they have different *causae*, they end on similar notes, suggesting similar goals.[203] The actors and activities likewise suggest some ritual progression from the Opening of the Mouth to the daily cult ritual. For example, after completing and sanitizing their craftsmanship, the artisans disappear

---

198. This special connection is enhanced by the fact that the king bears the divine *ka*-spirit and the priests come in the name and as servants of the king (see Bell, "Cult of the Royal *Ka*"). Since the king possesses a divine element and the priests come in his name, rather than presenting ritual activity as human contact with the divine, all speech and activity occurs in the divine realm as the king and priests take on various divine personas as they perform cultic service (Assmann, *The Search for God*, 49).

199. Cf. Hussy, *Epiphanie und Erneuerung*, 159.

200. The text lists the exact words to be recited, undoubtedly accompanied by precise actions.

201. Regarding purification in the daily offering ceremony, see esp. Brigitte Altenmüller-Kesting, *Reinigungsriten im ägyptischen Kult: Dissertation zur Erlangung der Doktorwürde der Philosophischen Fakultät der Universität Hamburg* (Hamburg: Lüdke bei der Uni, 1968), 175–211.

202. Lorton, "Theology of Cult Statues," 153.

203. Although such a parallel is suggestive, it is not conclusive, as similar actions can have significantly different meanings in different settings.

from the stage, never to appear in the course of the daily cult.[204] Having completed the crafting stage, the statue is instead addressed with continual priestly care.

## Use

Once the divine image has been properly enlivened, the deity may take up residence in the temple.[205] The daily cult ritual serves to maintain and renew the divine presence through the daily care and feeding, which consists of awakening, feeding, bathing, anointing, clothing, embracing, and enlivening various elements (*ba, sekhem,* and *ka*).

As in the Opening of the Mouth ritual, the texts abound with individual interpretive statements. For example, Papyrus Berlin 3055 equates every offering with *maat*: "that which you (the god) eat is *maat*, your beverage is *maat*, your bread is *maat*, your beer is *maat*, the incense that you inhale is *maat*."[206] Throughout the course of the ritual, many of the offerings are likewise identified as the eye of Horus, including such diverse elements as the offering meal of Nun, various jars and pots of water, natron, bread, cake, the foreleg, wine, and bee-honey.[207] In addition, various liquids are associated with opening the deity's mouth (e.g., *mtt*-vessels of water, red pots of water, and cups of wine),[208] establishing a connection with the Opening of the Mouth ritual.

## Ideology

The daily cult service has much in common with the care of a human monarch and is thus rightly referred to as anthropomorphic.[209] The servant priests seem to awaken the deity from its slumber, to bathe, clothe, and perfume it, and to feed and praise it, all with appropriate pomp and self-abasement. However, far more is involved than simple care.[210] Like the Opening of the Mouth ritual, the daily cult

---

204. They may only reappear when the statue is in need of repair or a new cult image is necessary.

205. Interpretive statements for the constituent elements of the ritual may be derived from the individual incantations. However, for the sake of space and the scope of the present topic, we will focus on the purpose and function of the larger ritual as a whole.

206. Moret *Le Rituel du culte divin*, 142; Teeter, "Temple Cults," 310.

207. The list is derived from an ostracon in the LACMA collection (see Cooney and McClain, "The Daily Offering Meal." For a discussion of the many offerings usually associated with the eye of Horus in various rituals, see Rudnitzky, *Auge des Horus*, 25–28.

208. See previous note.

209. Cf. Assmann, *The Search for God*, 48.

210. One of the primary differences is the nature of the participants. Whereas in the royal realm, human servants serve their king, in the daily cult ritual the priest adopts various divine personas, such that the human role is minimized and deity interacts with

ritual employs a multiplicity of means to achieve a single end, the daily renewal and satisfaction of the resident deity.

In addition to functioning on a literal level (e.g., ritual activities literally care for and feed the deity in a manner akin to its royal counterpart), mythic precedent and wordplay establish complementary connections with the divine sphere and various other potencies throughout the ritual. Purposeful repetition again features, both within the ritual itself and as it is reenacted daily.[211] Such repetition is especially consonant with the cyclical worldview, prominent in the journey of the sun across the sky and through the netherworld only to reemerge and repeat the cycle.[212] More than simply being fed and cared for, the deity, like the sun, requires daily rejuvenation so that it may maintain both its divine potency and order in the world. As we will see, the various words and deeds of the daily cult ritual bring about this divine revitalization in multiple ways on multiple levels.[213]

## Ideology of Individual Elements

Following the requisite priestly purifications, the lighting of the fire serves a dual function, literally enabling the priests to see, while simultaneously driving off divine enemies, that is, the hostile powers of darkness.[214] The opening of the shrine is likewise evocative. Drawing back the door bolts is equated with removing the finger of Seth from the eye of Horus.[215] On the literal level drawing back the door bolt serves as a prelude to opening the doors of the shrine so that the deity may see out, while on the mythic plane removing Seth's finger serves as a prelude to the restoration of Horus' sight.[216] "Opening of the face" and "seeing the god"—that is, opening the shrine doors—enable the priest to see the deity face-to-face, while simultaneously awakening the deity. In addition, this action causes heaven to brush up against earth and serves as a divine rebirth.

---

deity. Thus, in some way, Horus interacts with Horus, and in doing so, the two exchange mutual blessings. The priest may also adopt other divine personae (e.g., Thoth and Anubis), indicating the complexity of the interaction (Assmann, *The Search for God*, 49).

211. In the case of the feeding portion, thrice daily.

212. On the Egyptian conceptions of time, see, e.g., Assmann, *The Search for God*, 74–75; idem, *The Mind of Egypt: History and Meaning in the Time of the Pharaohs* (Cambridge, Mass.: Harvard University Press, 2003), 18.

213. See, e.g., Hussy's aptly titled monograph on the daily cult ritual, *Die Epiphanie und Erneuerung der Macht Gottes*, which stresses the daily renewal of the divine potency. For example, Hussy notes that divine renewal is the primary benefit of the daily cult ritual (63).

214. Lorton, "Theology of Cult Statues," 136.

215. Ibid., 136–37; Teeter, *Religion and Ritual*, 48.

216. Lorton, "Theology of Cult Statues," 137.

At least in the form of its cult statue, the deity, like a human, is cyclically rejuvenated by its nightly slumber. Thus, one may be tempted to conclude that the deity leaves the statue at night only to rejoin it in the morning, thereby "awakening" or reanimating it.[217] In Greco-Roman times, some texts assert continual presence (e.g., stating that Horus "sleeps in Edfu daily"),[218] while other texts suggest the daily reunification of the divine *ba* and cult image (e.g., Re's "living *ba* comes from heaven and rests upon his cult statue every day").[219] However, the title of the ritual sequence itself—"awakening the god"—coupled with the fact that there are no rituals for attracting the divine *ba* to the statue suggest a more permanent presence.[220] Nonetheless, while continually connected with the image, the deity also remains present in the sky, from which it daily renews its *ba* in its cult statue in the same way that priestly ritual action daily renews the vitality of the statue.

Patterned on the cyclical journey of the sun, opening the shrine's double doors also unites heaven and earth and signals divine rebirth. First, the act is referred to as opening the "double doors of heaven," equated on the cosmic plane with opening the cosmic double door, "that is, the point at the horizon where heaven and earth meet and through which the sun emerges at dawn."[221] Thus, by opening the double doors of the shrine, the priest causes heaven (the interior of the shrine) and earth (the temple) to meet.[222] Second, as the sun emerges daily from the underworld into the sky and is in this sense reborn, so too does the deity arise from its nightly slumber to new life.[223]

The following ritual activities are engineered to bring the deity new life and bring it to the full. After the statue awakens to the light, the presiding priest arouses the divine self-consciousness, especially with the declaration, "I bring you your heart in your body, set in its place, as Isis brought the heart of her son Horus to

---

217. This theory may offer some justification for the need for daily renewal, as the daily symbiosis of deity and image would require supporting rites to ensure the vitality of such a union.

218. Lorton, "Theology of Cult Statues," 176–77; Teeter, *Religion and Ritual,* 45.

219. Louis V. Žabkar, *A Study of the Ba Concept in Ancient Egyptian Texts* (SAOC 34; Chicago: University of Chicago Press, 1968), 40; Teeter, *Religion and Ritual,* 45; cf. Lichtheim, *AEL* 3:105.

220. Teeter, *Religion and Ritual,* 45; cf. more (and perhaps too) emphatically Lorton, "Theology of Cult Statues," 176–77.

221. Lorton, "Theology of Cult Statues," 139. The priest also appropriately greets Geb, the earth god, from whom the sun daily emerges.

222. As noted in ch. 2, when inside the shrine, the deity on earth always remains in heaven.

223. Cf. Teeter, "Temple Cults," 315–16. The double doors may also be associated with the vulva of Nut, the sky god, whose body separates heaven from earth. Bursting forth from the underworld, (governed by) Geb, through the birth canal of the sky goddess, the sun is daily reborn in its journey through heaven (ibid.).

him."[224] As the seat of emotion and thought,[225] the heart is necessary for the restoration of one's faculties, whether from sleep or in rebirth.[226] The following application of perfumed honey to the statue serves as an adhesive of sorts that assures
the deity of the physical integrity of its statue, as it "binds for him (i.e., Amun) his
bones, it joins for him his limbs."[227]

With the embrace of the statue and the placement of the headdress with a
uraeus serpent on its head, the deity seems to be empowered to act.[228] With this
action, "the divine essence is fully identified: 'oh living *ba* who smites his enemies, your *ba* is with you and your *sekhem* is at your side.'"[229] The *ba* is "essentially
an [immaterial] element of mobility that enabled passage from one realm to the
other,"[230] which may manifest itself in various perceivable and often visible forms,
including natural elements like water and animate beings like a ram, and thus
becomes "the deity's visible face."[231] The closest modern translation seems to be
"manifest power," while *sekhem* seems to roughly correspond to "power."[232] With
its faculties fully active, the deity becomes fully manifest and thus its statue becomes an image of power.[233]

---

224. Lorton, "Theology of Cult Statues," 140.

225. Traunecker, *Les Dieux de l'Égypte*, 40.

226. See Emil Buzov, "The Role of the Heart in the Purification," in *Proceedings of the First
International Conference for Young Egyptologists, Italy, Chianciano Terme, October 15–18,
2003* (ed. A. Amenta; Egitto antico 3; Rome: L'Erma di Bretschneider, 2005), 281, who notes
that the return of consciousness in the form of the heart is compulsory for revival; see also
Hellmut Brunner, "Herz," *LÄ* 2: 1158–68.

227. Lorton, "Theology of Cult Statues," 140–41.

228. Ibid., 141.

229. Ibid.. A precise differentiation between the two words is difficult. *Ba* seems to roughly
connote 'manifestation' and *sekhem* implies 'power.' However, as we have seen in the
Opening of the Mouth ritual, the former also connotes power (ibid., 134, 141).

230. Claude Traunecker, *The Gods of Egypt* (trans. D. Lorton; Ithaca, NY: Cornell University
Press, 2001), 22. Beginning with the 18th Dynasty, the *ba* was represented as a human-
headed bird, "an eloquent image for expressing both its mobility and its status as an element
of the personality" (ibid., 23).

231. Ibid., 33. As deities could animate multiple objects and entities, so too could they have
more than one *ba*, at least in the Late period (see, e.g., the ten *bas* of Amun [ibid., 88]).

232. Lorton, "Theology of Cult Statues," 134; regarding *sekhem*, see also Traunecker, *Gods
of Egypt*, 34–35. Although literally "power," *sekhem* may also refer more expansively to the
object in which power is manifested, e.g., the cult image (cf. Assmann, *The Search for God*,
42).

233. See also Traunecker, *Gods of Egypt*, 34, who notes that "from the New Kingdom on,
the cult statue inhabited by the divine *ba* was a *sekhem*, an image of power." In referring to
himself as a *ba* and as the goddess Sekhmet as he embraces the statue, the priest may be
signaling the deity's full and powerful manifestation through creative wordplay. It is also

Like the donning of the panther skin in the Opening of the Mouth, the closing and opening of the shrine signals a new ritual section. In the following section, many of the cultic actions and recitations are repeated, yet the important concept of the *ka* (*k3*), loosely translated as "vital force," is stressed for the first time in tandem with offerings (*kau* [*k3w*]).[234] Rather than being an abstract universal force that pervades nature, the *ka* seems to be the vital force of particular forms.[235] In the present context, the *ka* is the vital force enlivening the statue, which like that of a human, is sustained through food (*kau*).[236] With the deity fully alert and intact with its various faculties and *ba*, *sekhem*, and *ka* present and active, the section concludes with the presentation of a statue of the goddess Maat, the personification of order. The accompanying recitations recap what has been accomplished to this point and stress that all is right and ordered with the deity and in the world. The presentation of Maat emphasizes that the king has done his part in upholding *maat*, exemplified in his care of the deity. It also foreshadows the offerings to come that are themselves *maat* and serve to strengthen the divine presence, especially in the terrestrial realm, and thus cosmic order.[237]

In the following section, the more intimate care and feeding begins. Initial contact with the deity stresses the sensitive nature of such contact. Rather than dare to touch the deity himself, the priest is careful to assert that his body parts that make contact with the deity are also divine; his arms are Horus, his hands Thoth, and his fingers Anubis.[238] Similarly, rather than focusing on the removal of the deity's clothes and ointments, the accompanying recitations focus on the

---

possible that the embrace of the priestly *ba* mimics that of the divine *ba* and the statue mentioned in texts of the Ptolemaic period (regarding the latter, see Lorton, "Theology of Cult Statues," 141–42, 196–97).

234. Ibid., 142–43. E.g., the first utterance of the section stresses offerings, while another makes repeated reference to the *ka* in relation to the deity Maat. Regarding *ka*, see further Ursula Schweitzer, *Das Wesen des Ka im Diesseits und Jenseits der alten Ägypter* (Glückstadt: Augustin, 1965); Bolshakov, *Man and His Double*.

235. See further below. In noting its association with a particular form, Teeter has gone so far as to equate the *ka* with a physical form, in the context of the cult, the statue itself (*Religion and Ritual*, 44; "Temple Cults," 311).

236. In fact, there is abundant evidence indicating that food offerings were presented to the *kas* of dead humans, and there is even some evidence from the New Kingdom onwards that such offerings were presented to the divine *kas* (Lorton, "Theology of Cult Statues," 179–81). There is also some evidence that worship in general was directed to the divine *ka* (ibid.; for examples, see Lichtheim, *AEL* 2:91–109).

237. See further Guglielmi, "Bemerkungen zum Maatopfer im Amunsritual," *Göttinger Miszellen* 40 (1980): 23–28.

238. A. Rosalie David, *Religious Ritual at Abydos (c. 1300)* (Warminster: Aris & Phillips, 1973), scene 13, 99; Hussy, *Epiphanie und Erneuerung*, 37.

future, on the benefits of new clothes and ointments.[239] As the utterances attest, the clothes and ointment are more than simple comforts; they are also associated with various necessary potencies, such that by removing them the deity becomes vulnerable.[240] Instead of stressing this vulnerability, the recitations stress the resultant potency that makes the indignity of human contact and vulnerability acceptable, in order to convince the deity that the end justifies the means.[241] In fulfillment of these forward-looking utterances, the subsequent purifications and clothing function together to renew the divine statue to its full potency.[242]

Once properly prepared, the deity may then partake of the various offerings presented to it. Analogous to but far more than human nourishment, the food offerings are charged with divine potencies through the medium of ritual, both to protect and empower the divine image.[243] The dominant mythic archetype in the feeding portion of the ritual, the eye of Horus, represents divine perfection or the alleviation of all lack. In order for the deity to attain such divine perfection, it must "partake of offerings from the human realm, of food and drink,"[244] which through the medium of ritual also impart to the deity necessary divine powers.

---

239. Ibid., 37–38.

240. Hussy (*Epiphanie und Erneuerung*, 37) contends that removing the various elements signifies the removal of part of the god's divinity. Circling the unclothed deity thus serves to protect the deity from all unwanted influences. In Egypt, circumambulation was "perhaps the most common ritual technique" used to "enclose and defend sacred space" (Robert K. Ritner "Magic," in Redford, ed., *The Ancient Gods Speak*, 197; see further idem, *The Mechanics of Ancient Egyptian Magical Practice* [SAOC 54; Chicago: The Oriental Institute of the University of Chicago, 1993], 57–67).

241. The *nms*-cloth used to wipe away the ointments is the same one used to wipe away any remaining impurities in the Opening of the Mouth ritual (Otto, *Das ägyptische Mundöffnungsritual*, 1.117, 2.110; Hussy, *Epiphanie und Erneuerung*, 37; cf. Quack, "To clothe or to wipe? On the semantics of the verb *nms*," in *Lexical Semantics in Ancient Egyptian* [ed. E. Grosman, S. Polis, and J. Winand; Lingua Aegyptia Studia Monographica 9; Hamburg: Lingua Aegyptia, 2012], 379–86). Thus, the ritual seems to stress that the removal of divine potencies also accomplishes the removal of impurity. The claim is reinforced by the result. Once the remnants of the previous day's ritual have been removed, the deity is sparkling clean. Like a newly polished floor, the brilliance of the statue's surface signifies the absence of all imperfections.

242. Cf. Hussy, *Epiphanie und Erneuerung*, 41, who contends the preparations for purification, the purification, and the clothing function to renew the divinity of the cult image.

243. Cf. Cooney and McClain, "The Daily Offering Meal," 57, who assert that "the offering of food or drink, in and of itself, was not the element that allowed the god to reawaken. Rather the transformative elements are found in the charged powers symbolized in the food or drink—magical powers created through the act of ritualizing." Regarding the mythic precedents in this portion of the ritual, see ibid.

244. Cooney and McClain, "The Daily Offering Meal," 69.

For example, as in the Opening of the Mouth ritual, the utterance equates the presentation of a foreleg (ḥpš) with the strength (ḥpš) that is in the eye of Horus.[245] In the first part of the LACMA Ostrakon (ll. 1–15), offerings are repeatedly associated with Horus's wound and the violence that caused it, serving a defensive role, "granting him ownership over the wound and the violence that caused it." For example, "when the god is offered symbols of blood, of cutting, or of tears, the ritualists provide him with the means to gain control over his wound, and to overcome it."[246] Rather than protecting against weakness, offerings in the latter part of the ostrakon (from l. 16) are associated with strength and rejuvenation (e.g., the presentation of the foreleg empowers the deity with divine strength).[247] The last word in the ostrakon, "to make content" (sḥtp), refers back to the title of the daily meal ritual—dbḥt-ḥtp or "required offerings"—such that the "name of the ritual itself, as with every other ritual offering, anticipates the desired outcome—the contentment (ḥtp) of the god."[248] The ritual concludes where it began, with the deity safely shut inside its shrine in heaven on earth. To ensure the divine safety, the priest sweeps away his footprints and all traces of the human presence in the sanctuary, thereby repelling all evil, presumably by eliminating any trail to follow.[249]

In sum, the daily cult service serves to revitalize the deity in the statue through a multiplicity of means such that it possesses the full complement of divine potencies. The ritual words and actions transform a common care and feeding ritual into the investiture of the divine statue with various divine powers that rejuvenate it and allow it to serve as the fully functioning deity on earth. In fact, the daily cult service throughout the land of Egypt serves to revitalize all cult statues so that all of the deities may be fully functional and fully satisfied. In return for such royal largesse mediated by priestly stand-ins, the gods choose to remain in the terres-

---

245. "Amen, take to yourself the strength in the eye of Horus" (LACMA Ostrakon l. 16; Cooney and McClain, "The Daily Offering Meal," 57, 67.

246. Ibid., 67. E.g., "in line 7, two red pots of water are associated with 'what is in the eye of Horus, it being red,' alluding to the blood of the wound through word play between the redness of the pots and the redness of the eye (dšr.t)" (ibid., 66; for the redness associated with blood, see Rudnitzky, Auge des Horus, 29; see also Griffiths, The Conflict of Horus and Seth, 38).

247. Cooney and McClain, "The Daily Offering Meal," 67.

248. Ibid., 68; see also Goyon, Le rituel du sḥtp šḥmt au changement de cycle annuel: d'après les architraves du temple d'Edfou et textes parallèles, du Nouvel Empire à l'époque ptolémaïque et romaine (Le Caire: Inst. Français d'Archéologie Orientale, 2011). Line 4 also connects the offering meal (dbḥ-ḥtp) of Nun with the eye of Horus and his contentment (ḥtp) at having received it. In addition, the divine renewal is associated with the abundance brought about by the rising Nile's floodwater of the Nun (ibid., 66; for the ḥtp meal in the Pyramid Texts and its association with the eye of Horus, see Rudnitzky, Auge des Horus, 41–42).

249. Teeter, "Temple Cults," 316; idem, Religion and Ritual, 48.

trial sphere and with their presence bless the king, his land, and his people, thus maintaining cosmic order.

## How Do the Opening of the Mouth and the Daily Cult Ritual Relate?

The rituals have different settings and the majority of the actions seem to serve different though complementary purposes. The Opening of the Mouth ritual is a necessary prelude to the daily cult ritual. It serves an essential transitory function, spanning the gap between the workshop and the temple. In essence, the ritual makes the statue more than merely a statue; it brings it to life and fills it with various divine potencies so that it is fit for the divine. Once the statue has been appropriately endowed with divinity and installed in the temple, the daily cult ritual serves to maintain that presence through constant cultic renewal. Thus, instead of bringing the statue to life, it serves to arouse and reinvigorate it. Although they initially serve different purposes, the rituals end on similar notes, the care and feeding of the deity, with remarkably similar activities and accompanying recitations. The Opening of the Mouth ends with a supernaturally charged care and feeding ritual that endows the newly enlivened statue with the potencies it needs to function as the divine locus, while the daily cult ritual, in accord with the cyclical course of the sun, serves to continually reinvigorate the cult image so that the deity remains present, content, and fit to serve as god on earth. Thus, the rituals begin differently with the quickening of the divine statue and the reinvigoration of the already enlivened divine statue respectively, yet both end similarly with the care and feeding of the appropriately quickened divine statue. Once dressed in proper regalia and charged with the powers associated with that regalia, the deity is ready to fulfill its role as the living god in the midst of human community, and the statue's daily supernaturally charged meal prepares it for the task.[250]

## Relationship of the Deity to Its Statue(s)

How is (some part of) the divine essence present in a statue and how are a deity's various statues related? On a simple level, the statue gives the deity a physical body and thus "a fixed location within the human world where the divine cult and ritual activities for the deity could be focused."[251] Rather than being merely a copy of

---

250. Like anointing, donning the clothing appropriate to an office signals that the person is taking up the role appropriate to that office.

251. Robins, "Cult Statues in Ancient Egypt," 12. Regarding the identification of the statue as the divine body, see esp. the Memphite theology, which states, "The gods entered their bodies ... in which they took form" (l. 60; Assmann, *The Search for God*, 46). Such a clear differentiation, not attested elsewhere in the ancient Near East, seems to be a result of the

the celestial divine body, the cult statue is the deity's terrestrial body.[252] In addition to referring to statues as gods' "bodies," the Memphite theology also asserts that the gods "become" (*ḫpr*) their bodies; namely, by entering their cult statues, the gods in some way "become" those statues.[253] Thus, rather than being an inanimate vessel in which the immaterial potencies of a deity manifest themselves, the statue symbiotically joins with the divine essence such that the body and all it contains is the deity.[254] Although the relationship between a deity's immaterial elements and the statue remains difficult to define, we may nonetheless approximate it. The deity's *ba*, its mobile power, joins with and indwells its cultically enlivened body (statue), endowing it with the divine *ka* (vital force) and making it a place of power (*sekhem*). The divine servants direct subsequent cultic attention, especially worship and food offerings (*kau*), to the divine *ka*, which must be sustained and daily renewed.

Having established that the cult statue serves as the terrestrial divine body, we now turn to the question of how much of the divine essence inhabits the statue. In other words, does the deity leave heaven (or the underworld) to indwell the statue? If instead it remains in heaven, how much of its essence does it transfer to the statue? What about its multiple statues? Here as elsewhere in the ancient Near East, deities with heavenly manifestations do not leave heaven to take up residence on earth. In fact, divine withdrawal from nature would signal chaos. For example, in the Prophecies of Neferti when Re withdraws himself from the sun, "though the hour of his rising will still exist, one will no longer know when it is noon."[255] In Egypt, as in the rest of the ancient Near East, there is also no evidence that deities are imagined to possess a fixed amount of power, such that each manifestation receives a diluted portion of divinity. As immaterial substances, it would seem that the divine *ba* and *ka* may be divided or multiplied infinitely without losing any potency, such that the deity in heaven and in the cult image may each possess the

---

relationship of the divine to the mortuary sphere and the Egyptian preoccupation with that sphere. The image of the deceased is not simply equated with the deceased. Rather it serves as a body into which the person's immaterial elements, which survive the death of the physical body, may be transferred. Likewise, rather than simply being equated with the god, the cult image, in addition to divine animals, the king, and celestial phenomena (see below), serves as a body for the deity who is described as "rich in manifestations."

252. "*The statue is not the image of the deity's body, but the body itself*" (Assmann, *The Search for God*, 46, italics his).

253. Lorton, "Theology of Cult Statues," 187 and n. 88; see also Allen, *Genesis in Egypt*, 44.

254. This does not mean that the deity is immaterial (*pace* Hornung, *Conceptions of God*, 135). Rather a single deity consists of multiple parts, many of which are immaterial and require a material form, i.e., a body, to be made manifest, of which the cult statue is but one aspect.

255. Helck, *Die Prophezeiung des Nfr.tj* (Kleine Ägyptische Texte 2; Wiesbaden: Harrasowitz, 1970), 42–43; Assmann, *The Search for God*, 72–73.

full complement of divine potencies.[256] In fact, in accord with the idea that multiple manifestations make a deity greater, deities have multiple *ka*s and in later periods multiple *ba*s, each of which possesses full divine potency. For example, Re in the 19th Dynasty is assigned fourteen *ka*s, which in later, especially Greco-Roman, times are given names, each of which corresponds to elements of the daily offering ritual.[257] Thus, it would seem that since the *ka* refers to the embodied form of the divine life force and the divine *ka* in the statue is sustained by offerings (*kau*), the fourteen *ka*s refer to fourteen separate cult images, which together form a representative sample of all of the cult images of Re throughout the land.[258] Nonetheless, while fully imbued with the deity, it is also clear that the statue is not the fullness of the deity, since the deity's fullness lies in the accumulation of its multiple manifestations, names, and potencies. This principal finds pictorial representation in the case of the fourteen *ka*s of Re, as the *ka*s, like the deities of the nomes, appear in procession scenes bringing gifts to the god himself.[259] In turn, each cult statue has its own divine life force (*ka*) and is thus fully the deity, yet each represents only an aspect of the larger deity. In addition, a deity's multiple *ba*s are associated with the deity's various faculties, such that the more *ba*s a deity possesses, the greater the deity. Thus, for example, Amun's ten *ba*s express his potency, as each animates a sector of the universe (e.g., the sun, moon, water, fire, cattle, aquatic creatures, plant growth, and humanity [i.e., the king]).[260] Similarly, another text makes an initial distinction between the cult image and the hidden god, which it then clarifies by comparing these divine aspects respectively to an artificial pond and a living stream that cannot be dammed.[261] In sum, "the god who is present, dwelling in the cult statue, reigns everywhere in his hiddenness and can at any time burst forth from this 'channeled' form in which he dwells like a river that overflows its dam."[262]

---

256. Cf. Robins, "Cult Statues in Ancient Egypt," 2.

257. Benedikt Rothöhler, "Die vierzehn Kas des Re," in *Mythos & Ritual: Festschrift für Jan Assmann zum 70. Geburtstag* (ed. Rothöhler and A. Manisali; Religionswissenschaft: Forschung und Wissenschaft 5; Münster: LIT, 2008), 187, 201.

258. Ibid., 201. In light of the presence of sun courts in the New Kingdom, where the cult was performed directly before the sun, one may wonder if Re had any cult images at all. However, the use of sun courts as a particular medium of terrestrial interaction with the deity in no way speaks against the other more common medium, the presence of cult images in shrines (ibid., 205).

259. E.g., in Greco-Roman Dendara (ibid., 202).

260. Traunecker, *Gods of Egypt*, 33, 88.

261. Instruction for Merikare, which appears in the 18th Dynasty, but likely originated in the Middle Kingdom (Assmann, *The Search for God*, 46–47); for the relevant text, see Lichtheim, *AEL* 1:97–109; Stephen Quirke, *Egyptian Literature 1800 BC: Questions and Readings* (London: Golden House, 2004), 112–20; see also Assmann, *The Search for God*, 46–47.

262. Ibid., 47. This differentiation, by no means present nor preserved everywhere in the

Rather than being limited to statues, deities may adopt multiple other bodies, including celestial elements like the sun, certain animals, the king, and even various wall reliefs in the various temples. As noted, the sun is neither equated nor coterminous with Re. Instead, it is merely one of his many bodies that he may renounce at any time.[263] Likewise, certain animals are associated with the deity in such a way that they serve as possible divine hosts.[264] In particular, the Apis bull in Memphis is understood to be a "living cult image," an embodiment of Ptah.[265] Like the Apis bull and cult image, the human body of the king is a vessel for the divine *ka*, the divine life force that passes from one legitimate king to the next.[266] Finally, various wall reliefs also seem to be imbued with some form of the divine essence, serving as popular access points to the otherwise distant deity.[267] For example, Hathor of Dendara is described as "she (who) alights on her forms that are carved on the wall."[268]

Each statue, like the king and each related natural element, animal, or relief, thus serves as a bodily manifestation of the deity, which together form the divine fullness. Rather than being limited to a fixed number of forms, each deity is always

---

ancient Near East (this distinction may not even be continually and consistently applied in ancient Egypt), likely draws strength from parallels in the funerary realm, where an individual is present in, yet clearly not coterminous with, his mortuary statue (cf. Assmann, *The Search for God*, 45).

263. Lines 51–53 of the Prophecies of Neferti (Helck, *Prophezeiung des Nfr.tj*, 42–43; Assmann, *The Search for God*, 72–73); see also ll. 24–25 (Helck, *Prophezeiung des Nfr.tj*, 21–25; Assmann, *The Search for God*, 72–73).

264. This does not mean that every animal of the species is a divine body, but that each possesses the potential to be a divine body (Hornung, *Conceptions of God*, 137).

265. Hornung, *Conceptions of God*, 136–37; on the phrase, "a living cult image," see Meeks, *Daily Life of the Egyptian Gods*, 129.

266. Bell, "Cult of the Royal Ka."

267. See, e.g., Guglielmi, "Funktion von Tempeleingang," 55–68; Brand, "Veils, Votives and Marginalia." Brand notes that not all divine images on wall reliefs receive special cultic attention (p. 59). Those that are especially venerated seem to have been embellished to mark their special veneration and/or enshrined or veiled (evidenced by drill holes used to support veils; pp. 59, 61–64). Beyond this distinction, it is unclear what sort of ritual enlivening they underwent, if any; an (abbreviated) Opening of the Mouth(-like) ceremony is certainly possible. Likewise, it is also unclear whether such forms were understood to be imbued with deity or simply channels to deity. Indeed, it is unlikely that the worshipers made such a distinction. Whether the images were understood as the god or merely as conduits to the god, they would have been treated in the same manner since they were the (only) access points the common people had to the deities. However, the people would likely have differentiated between these images on the walls and the statue in the sanctuary, which they probably would have viewed as somehow more divine.

268. Morenz, *Egyptian Religion*, 318 nn. 60–61; Assmann, *The Search for God*, 42.

capable of more manifestations.[269] In fact, it would seem that a deity may inhabit more than one image in the same temple (e.g., the bark statue and the primary image used for the daily cult). According to the additive approach, such divine multiplicity highlights the divine prestige, demonstrating the divine capacity to show many faces. Multiple statues likewise also serve practical purposes, as the various statues may perform different functions simultaneously. For example, while the bark statue is out on procession, the primary cult image can remain in its shrine so that the daily cult can continue uninterrupted and the temple and its environs will not be left unprotected.[270]

Nonetheless, although each manifestation is part of the larger deity, each may also be treated as distinct in certain contexts. For example, although they together represent the fullness of Amun, when given names, his various *bas* are treated as independent entities.[271] This apparent paradox may be clarified by aspective theory.[272] In order to present the whole, especially when it is complex, ancient Egyptians frequently amassed and juxtaposed various individual elements, most often without systematically attempting to fit those elements into a consistently articulated, all-encompassing organic unity. In fact, they focused on the individual aspects or elements to such an extent and with such an attention to capturing them in all their fullness that they were often conceived of as (semi-)independent.[273] In other words, an Egyptian deity may be understood as the accumulation of its vari-

---

269. Including combinations with other deities (see the classic study of Hans Bonnet, "On Understanding Syncretism," *Or* 68 [1999]: 181–98).

270. In addition, various kings and other notables may have donated divine images to the temple in order to demonstrate their piety or enhance their position. Although unlikely to replace the primary statue, many such donations likely were considered somewhat divine and as such may not be discarded, leaving a single temple with many (enlivened) divine bodies.

271. See also the four *bas* of Re in the New Kingdom (Traunecker, *Gods of Egypt*, 33, 88). Regarding the independence of the *bas*, see ibid., 33.

272. Brunner-Traut, *Frühformen des Erkennens*. In positing the theory, Brunner-Traut builds on the work of her mentor, Heinrich Schäfer, *Von ägyptischer Kunst: Eine Grundlage* (4th ed.; Wiesbaden: Harrasowitz, 1963). In the present analysis, only an aspect of her aspective theory is promoted, namely, her assertion that the ancient Egyptians focused especially on individual aspects. Other elements of her presentation are more questionable. For example, her evolutionary model of development and the association of ancient Near Eastern people with children, the mentally ill, and the untrained are problematic, as is her general exclusion of the Egyptian understanding of the parts as part of the whole (regarding the latter, see the critique of Assman [*Tod und Jenseits*, 34–36]). See briefly Hundley, "Divine Fluidity? The Priestly Texts in Their Ancient Near Eastern Contexts," in *Reading Leviticus in Its Contexts* (ed. Francis Landy and Leigh M. Travaskis; Sheffield: Sheffield Phoenix Press, in press).

273. This is not to say that there is no room for systematic thinking, only that there is a tendency to isolate individual elements even when presenting the larger whole.

ous aspects, each of which was treated in such detail and often in such isolation from the other elements that it could be understood (semi-)independently. A locally manifested deity, like a clone, could develop its own context-specific identity and experience and thus be different although it possessed the same DNA. More practically, the local populace likely viewed the local manifestation of the deity as the deity, which although related remained distinct from all other local manifestations.

## EGYPTIAN RITUAL AND THE ADDITIVE APPROACH

As we have seen, ancient Egyptians adopted an additive approach. Although not every image was necessarily imbued with some of its referent's essence,[274] ritual texts establish that the statue was clearly a component part of the deity, without which it could not be made manifest in the temple. Thus, the Opening of the Mouth and daily cult rituals support Bahrani's contention that an image was connected to and was in some way a living copy of its referent. Furthermore, as asserted by Bahrani, in order to approach and maintain divine plenitude, a deity's physical form had to be combined and charged with various other divine attributes and potencies including the divine name, attire, and immaterial *ba* and *ka*. In short, ancient Egyptians combined multiple divine aspects through the medium of ritual, many of which simultaneously functioned on multiple levels so as continually to render the statue–deity symbiosis more fully divine and thus a more fitting locus of the deity on earth.

## NECESSITY OF DIVINE NOURISHMENT?

Did the deity need its daily care, especially the food, to survive? Ancient Egyptians clearly understood the daily offerings as a meal of sorts that the deity was thought to consume. It is equally clear that to provide such a meal was an obligation and the failure to do so could have dire consequences.[275] However, it is not clear within the ritual itself whether such a meal was necessary for divine survival. On one level, since anthropomorphization of the deity is inevitable, people undoubtedly assumed that the human-like deity required food in the same way that they themselves did. The question of whether it would have starved if they neglected it probably never entered their minds; for to neglect the deity would have been unconscionable since its contentment was understood to be essential for human prosperity.

---

274. For example, as noted, only certain reliefs seem to be charged with divinity.

275. See, e.g., the Restoration Stela of Tutankhamun (see, e.g., Baines, "Presenting and Discussing Deities," 46–55 and references below).

Nonetheless, the texts give enough hints to suggest that cult offerings were considered necessary for the survival of the statue, but not the deity itself. As noted, offerings sustained the divine *ka*, without which the deity as statue would be left in a weakened state, as would a human without food.[276] The Restoration Stela of Tutankhamun laments Akhenaten's neglect of the traditional temples, such that the gods "turned their backs" on the land, precipitating disaster.[277] With the reestablishment of the temples and the cult, the gods joyfully returned to "protect Egypt."[278] Thus, rather than themselves dying of starvation, the gods absented themselves from their statues since they were malnourished. With the loss of their cultic bodies, the deities and their divine *ba*s had other manifestations to fall back on and even without them could continue to exist as various immaterial elements (e.g., the *ba*). In turn, at least according to this depiction, feeding the deity seems to have been a service that was required to maintain a terrestrial cultic presence and to avoid calamity, rather than a requirement to keep the god alive.

## THE DURATION OF DIVINE PRESENCE

What would happen if a deity was improperly served? Could it leave the statue it indwelt? Just as a human could leave his body upon death or a deity could leave an animal form it temporarily inhabited, even its natural form (e.g., Re as the sun)[279] or any other of its multiple bodies, so too could a deity leave its cult image.[280] Thus, kings had to make the temples and temple service as enticing as possible to keep the resident deity happily resident and the blessings flowing.[281] As indicated above, the Restoration Stele of Tutankhamun suggests that with neglect the gods could at any time absent themselves from their cult statues. Because of

---

276. Here, it must be stressed that the offerings were not simply divine food; they also imparted various essential divine potencies to the deity through the medium of ritual.

277. Lorton, "Theology of Cult Statues," 167 n. 66; te Velde, "Theology, Priests and Worship," 1731; for the text, see John Bennett. "The Restoration Inscription of Tutʿankhamūn," *JEA* 25 (1939): 8–15; *Urk. IV* 2025–32; translations in *ANET* 251–52; Murnane, *Texts from the Amarna Period*, 212–14.

278. Lorton, "Theology of Cult Statues," 167 n. 66. "The gods and goddesses who are in this land, their hearts are joyful.... Life and dominion proceed from them to the nose of the victorious king" (*Urk. IV*, 2030; translation after Murnane, *Texts from the Amarna Period*, 214).

279. See the above-mentioned (at nn. 255 and 263) Prophecies of Neferti.

280. A deity could also dissolve a temporary connection or the indwelling of another deity (e.g., Amun of Amon-Re theoretically could separate from the amalgamated form) (see esp. Bonnet, "Syncretism").

281. Robins, "Cult Statues in Ancient Egypt," 2–3; Hornung, *Conceptions of God*, 229; on the danger of divine cruelty and the united human-divine pursuit of *maat*, see ibid., 197–216.

Akhenaten's neglect, "the gods were ignoring this land ... if one prayed to a god, to ask something from him, he did not come at all; and if one beseeched any goddess in the same way, she did not come at all."[282] The Bentresh Stele, which recounts the international loan of a statue of the god Khonsu that was capable of "expelling disease demons," provides yet another example. When the foreign king failed to return the statue to Egypt, in a dream the deity, presumably in the form of its *ba*, withdrew from the statue and flew "as a falcon of gold" toward Egypt.[283] Thus, with the neglect of their homes and their care, the gods could withdraw themselves, precipitating disaster.[284] On a more fundamental level, if the king did not play his role by presenting the deity with *maat* (i.e., order), creation itself could unravel.[285] To avert such disaster, it behooved the king to serve the gods appropriately.

---

282. Murnane, *Texts from the Amarna Period*, 213.

283. Teeter, *Religion and Ritual*, 45–46.

284. Including the dissolution of the state, defeat at the hands of enemies, and illness and premature death of Egypt's people (te Velde, "Theology, Priests and Worship," 1731).

285. See, e.g., Hornung, *Conceptions of God*, 197–216, esp. 213–16.

# CHAPTER 9
# DIVINE PRESENCE IN
# MESOPOTAMIAN TEMPLES

As IN EGYPT, THERE IS a remarkable consistency of religious expression across the millennia.[1] As such, the study of Mesopotamian divine presence is open to meaningful generalizations. Nonetheless, the Mesopotamian picture of divine presence is far from simple. The physical and, at times, literary evidence are spotty. For example, while we can assume some continuity with earlier periods, primary evidence for the installation of the cult image comes from the first half of the first millennium and later, and the evidence for the daily cult is even later, from the late first millennium. Although consistent on a general level, there is also a good deal of flexibility in the particulars.[2] The following study will, in some places, seek to account for the diversity of expression, while in other places, especially in the analysis of ritual, it will stress the commonalities. Rather than consider all of the data on cult statues, the following presentation focuses on the second half of the second millennium onward.

## PERCEPTIONS OF DEITY

Before examining the temple's divine images, it is profitable to trace the general contours of Mesopotamian conceptions of deities, with special attention to the major Mesopotamian deities.[3] The Mesopotamian portrait of the divine (labeled

---

1. See Lambert, "Ancient Mesopotamian Gods," 123: "No major changes took place over history except in the organization of the gods into a pantheon, and except where cities completely died out and ceased to be inhabited."

2. See esp. below the move away from anthropomorphic to symbolic representations of deity.

3. Other elements, like beds, boats, chariots, musical instruments, crowns, weapons, city gates, and various temple elements associated with the deities, were deified as distinct deities (for a survey, see Porter, "Blessings from a Crown"). For example, Assur's crown, "Lord Crown," "was venerated in his company but recognized as an independently powerful divine entity" (ibid., 185–86). Although they possessed neither anthropomorphic form nor fully developed personalities, many of these elements were marked with the divine determinative DINGIR and presented with temple offerings, clearly identifying them as "gods" (cf. Porter, "Blessings from a Crown," 161 and *passim*). Although such divine elements were included

with the Sumerian DINGIR or the Akkadian *ilu*[4]) is frustratingly complex, and the Mesopotamians themselves rarely attempted to systematically unravel its complexities.[5] Rather, realizing that any representation is merely an approximation, they instead piled on approximates in the hopes of approaching plenitude. For them, inconsistencies, which are often the result of the limits of human cognition, were far preferable to consistent yet consistently restrictive categories. In other words, for them, it was better to allow the deity to be practically limitless even if that limitlessness baffled the mind than to confine the deity to the limited boundaries that are a necessary product of the human mind.[6] With this perspective in mind, we now move to a survey and synthesis of the data.

Mesopotamian gods were understood to be vastly superior to humans in most respects. However, rather than abandoning the anthropomorphic model in their descriptions, Mesopotamians elevated the divine by transcending anthropomorphic categories.[7] Like a human, the gods often were embodied in human-like form and expressed human-like emotions, not all of which were positive.[8] They possessed corporeality,[9] sharing with humanity "size, age, gender, attractiveness, and even in rare cases mortality."[10] The gods required "nourishment, drink, clothing, jewelry, cleansing, travel, music, perfume and sex"[11] and were often grouped into family units with a home in their sacred realm much like a king in his royal realm.[12] However, the gods differed from humanity in that they could adopt mul-

---

in the cult, they did not serve as primary cult images in the sanctuaries and, as such, will not be addressed.

4. See esp. the helpful analysis by Porter ("The Anxiety of Multiplicity: Concepts of the Divine in Ancient Assyria," in Porter, ed., *One God or Many?*, 243–48; see further idem, "Blessings from a Crown") on the Assyrian evidence.

5. This is not to say that there was no room for systematic thinking in ancient Mesopotamia (see, e.g., the god list An = Anum).

6. In making this claim, I am not arguing that ancient Mesopotamians were aware of the implications of their perceptions. Rather, I am putting what I understand their rationale to have been in modern terms and a modern context.

7. See ch. 7 n. 1.

8. See, e.g., Enlil's attempt to destroy humanity for disturbing his sleep and Ishtar's lascivious and capricious behavior toward Gilgamesh for which he chastised her (cf. Bottéro, *Religion in Ancient Mesopotamia*, 66–67).

9. Burkhard Gladigow, "Gottesvorstellungen," *Handbuch religionswissenschaftlicher Grundbegriffe*, Vol. 3: Gesetz-Kult (Stuttgart: Kohlhammer, 1993), 32–49.

10. Dick, "Mesopotamian Cult Statue," 46. On the latter, the best-known examples come from Atrahasis and *Enuma Elish*, where a lesser god was killed to create humanity (Bottéro, *Religion in Ancient Mesopotamia*, 61).

11. Dick, "Mesopotamian Cult Statue," 47; cf. Bottéro, *Religion in Ancient Mesopotamia*, 66, 136.

12. Bottéro, *Religion in Ancient Mesopotamia*, 68. Large temples required large bureaucratic

tiple forms. In fact, it would seem that they could manifest themselves in multiple forms in multiple locales all at the same time, many of which were not conceived anthropomorphically.[13]

Anthropomorphically understood divine personages manifested themselves in and were in charge of such visible and tangible elements as celestial bodies, natural phenomena, qualities, and perhaps more distantly numbers, stones, and metals. For example, Ishtar was simultaneously identified as a divine person who dwelled in heaven, yet was localized in various terrestrial temples (most prominently Arbela and Nineveh); identified with the planet Venus, the number 15, the semiprecious stone lapis lazuli, and the mineral lead; and understood as the embodiment of such qualities as love and war.[14]

The exact relationship between elements was not always clear or consistently articulated. However, on the whole, the data seems to suggest that all of these elements were substantially connected, such that together they constituted the deity in all its plenitude,[15] and in some measure each individual element partook of the divine essence enough to be called by the divine name and associated with the primarily anthropomorphically conceived divine personage.[16] However, each element was in various contexts treated as distinct, such that, for example, Ishtar of Arbela and Ishtar of Nineveh, Ishtar of mythology and Ishtar as Venus, were not coterminous and in many ways were understood as distinct entities.[17] For example,

---

institutions with various groups of servants, including priests, farmers, shepherds, millers, bakers, cooks, weavers, woodworkers, metalworkers, stonecutters, architects, cleaners, courtyard sweepers, doormen, and scribes (Wiggermann, "Theologies, Priests and Worship," 1864).

13. Nonetheless, as noted (ch. 7 n. 4), there is minimal evidence of divine shapeshifting in the first millennium. In other words, although a god could theoretically manifest itself in multiple places in multiple forms, there is little indication that a particular manifestation changed its form, e.g., from a human to a star.

14. Porter, "Anxiety of Multiplicity," 243–44.

15. Here, as elsewhere in the ancient Near East, the fullness of a being lay in the accumulation of its names, attributes, and manifestations. For example, treaty and ritual texts appealed to different deities with the same forename (e.g., multiple localized Ishtars and different deified aspects of Ishtar) so that Ishtar in all her plenitude was brought to bear. In the context of a treaty, the fullness of Ishtar was appealed to in order to ensure fidelity to the terms of the contract.

16. Though, as in Egypt, a deity could have multiple names. See, e.g., Marduk's fifty names, which serve as the climax of *Enuma Elish* (see, e.g., Bottéro, "Les noms de Marduk," in *Essays on the Ancient Near East in Memory of Jacob Joel Finkelstein* [ed. M. de Jong Ellis; Memoirs of the CT Academy of Arts & Sciences 19; Hamden, CT: Archon, 1977], 5–28). The *Enuma Elish* is especially reliant on An = Anum (Stephanie Dalley, "Statues of Marduk and the Date of *Enūma eliš*," *AoF* 24 [1997]: 167).

17. See esp. Porter, "Ishtar of Nineveh," 41–44; Allen, "Splintered Divine," esp. 283–339.

a hymn of Assurbanipal addresses the distinct Ishtars of Nineveh and Arbela,[18] while the treaty between the Assyrian king Esarhaddon and Ramataya, king of Urakazabanu, includes in the witness list Ishtar of Arbela, Ishtar of Nineveh, and the planet Venus, often associated with Ishtar, and in divine curses invokes Venus alongside Ishtar Lady of Battle, Ishtar who resides in Arbela, Ishtar of […], and Ishtar [… of] Carchemish.[19] In the Assyrian *tākultu* ritual texts, various Ishtars in the form of cult images are venerated separately, including an unmodified Ishtar, Ishtar of the Šibirri Staff, Ishtar of the Stars, Assur-Ishtar, Ishtar the Panther, and Lady of Nineveh.[20]

How can we explain such phenomena? In general, it would seem that a deity could be characterized as an interconnected divine network composed of many distinct elements, which may be referred to as a divine constellation.[21] More precisely, each major god consisted of a constellation of aspects, which could act and be treated (semi-)independently or as a unity depending on context.[22] Given this divine fluidity,[23] it is striking that, although they had multiple forms in multiple locales, deities rarely appeared in the human sphere in the first millennium and rarely communicated directly with humanity.[24] Instead they mostly manifested themselves in their dealings with each other. While they generally were separate from humanity and the human sphere, they nonetheless manifested their presence

---

See also Sommer, *Bodies of God*, 13–15. As the following examples attest, such divine "fragmentation" (ibid., 13) was especially characteristic of (but not limited to) Ishtar.

18. K. 1290; Livingstone, *Mystical and Mythological Explanatory Works*, 10–13; for analysis, see esp. Porter, "Ishtar of Nineveh."

19. For a convenient English translation, see *ANET*, 534–41; see more fully D. J. Wiseman, "The Vassal-Treaties of Esarhaddon," *Iraq* 20 (1958): i–ii, 1–99; see also Sommer, *Bodies of God*, 13.

20. Porter, "Ishtar of Nineveh," 43–44. Regarding the texts, see Rintje Frankena, Tākultu: *De Sacrale Maaltijd in het Assyrische Ritueel met een Overzicht de in Assur Vereerde Goden* (Leiden: Brill, 1954); Brigitte Menzel, *Assyrische Tempel* (vol. 2; Rome: Biblical Institute Press, 1981), no. 54 (K. 252), T 113-25 and 61 (VAT 10126), T 138-44.

21. This use of the term is to be differentiated from Jan Assmann's use of constellation (e.g., [Stuttgart: Kohlhammer, 1984], 117–35), which refers to iconic representations of myths.

22. For a fuller explanation, see Hundley, "Here a God"; see more briefly ibid., "Divine Fluidity?"; cf. Beate Pongratz-Leisten, "Divine Agency and Astralization of the Gods in Ancient Mesopotamia," in Pongratz-Leisten, ed., *Reconsidering the Concept*, 138–52. Although interesting and important, the relationship between a deity's multiple parts will be addressed only as it illuminates relationship between divine statues.

23. Porter, "Anxiety of Multiplicity," 243–48; idem, "Blessings from a Crown," 187–88; Sommer, *Bodies of God*, 12–24.

24. See, e.g., Hamori's survey of primarily mythological texts (*When Gods Were Men*, 129–49). Regarding means of divine communication, see esp. the comprehensive survey of Maul, "Omina und Orakel," 45–88.

in, or perhaps more distantly their presence was mediated by, elements that could be perceived and encountered.[25]

Although visible and in some sense communicative, stars and other natural forces remained distant both spatially and conceptually.[26] Such elements were visible from yet not situated on earth, anthropomorphized yet not anthropomorphic and could not be suitably approached. Given this divine distance, Mesopotamians presumably felt a need to bring heaven to earth, to bring the deity to the heart of human community in a form that could be accessed, cared for, and influenced, so that the otherwise distant deity could be present and persuaded to act on the people's behalf. The cult image situated in the temple provided that form.

Nonetheless, divine presence on earth was not simply a divine condescension. Rather, the human-divine relationship was characterized by functional interdependence.[27] As noted in ch. 3, various texts suggest that the temples were created by the gods themselves in primordial times, while the responsibility for their upkeep was given to humanity. In fact, humans were created solely to serve the gods and meet their basic needs.[28] Humans thus existed and indeed strove to keep the gods happy so that the gods would in turn withhold suffering and extend blessing.[29]

---

25. They manifested themselves in natural phenomena, celestial bodies, and statues, and communicated through omens and oracles. Pongratz-Leisten differentiates between primary agents, the deities themselves, and secondary agents, such as cult images that presenced the otherwise absent deity ("Divine Agency and Astralization," 144–52). This is helpful in that it distinguishes between the anthropomorphically envisioned core of the divine constellation and the various other elements through which the deity made itself visible. However, it is perhaps better to situate the various ways of manifesting deity along a continuum, so as to not too sharply differentiate between the primary and secondary agents and to more strongly distinguish between secondary agents (such as a statue and a standard).

26. On the ambivalent relationship between the gods and the stars, see Francesca Rochberg, "'The Stars Their Likenesses': Perspectives on the Relation Between Celestial Bodies and Gods in Ancient Mesopotamia," in Porter, ed., *What Is a God?*, 41–91.

27. "While human existence depended on the satisfaction of the gods, the gods depend on their human servants for their leisured life, whose performance they closely monitored" (Wiggermann, "Theologies, Priests and Worship," 1860); cf. Bottéro, *Religion in Ancient Mesopotamia*, 37.

28. This position finds abundant expression in "hymns, prayers, historical texts, royal inscriptions, and art, but it appears most unequivocally in a number of Sumerian and Akkadian myths" (Wiggermann, "Theologies, Priests and Worship," 1859; see briefly ibid., 1860–61; Bottéro, *Religion in Ancient Mesopotamia*, 38). In fact, the creation of humanity was a secondary solution, initiated to relieve the lesser gods of the burdens for which they went on strike (see, e.g., the summaries in Wiggermann "Theologies, Priests and Worship," 1859–61; Bottéro, *Religion in Ancient Mesopotamia*, 97–103).

29. The removal of suffering was a more prevalent theme than the extension of blessing. To

Like the Egyptian gods, none of the Mesopotamian gods were omnipotent or omniscient, but rather jointly maintained the ordered world.[30] It would seem that the Mesopotamians associated specific deities with the areas of the cosmos they deemed important, from nature to culture or government.[31] Divine rule was especially contested beyond the national borders of Assyria and Babylonia by such inimical forces as demons, monsters, rebellious mountains, dangerous seas, and barbarians.[32] Although there was room for significant strife in the Mesopotamian divine community,[33] too much upheaval of the divine hierarchy had cosmic consequences.[34] Humans, and in particular the state apparatus led by the king, played

---

meet the gods' needs and anticipate (and avert if unfavorable) their desires, humanity had to discern their will, which often was understood to be written into the fabric of creation. In the same way that people communicate through writing, the gods were understood to communicate through the writing of creation, leaving behind various signs for humans to decipher via such media as extispicy and astrology (see briefly Bottéro, *Religion in Ancient Mesopotamia*, 178–79; see more fully Maul, "Omina und Orakel").

30. Even the most extreme statements of a single deity's power must be understood in their polytheistic context. For example, hymns exalt various deities by ascribing to the exalted god the praise, powers, and celestial bodies of the other deities. However, as in Egypt, this in no way suggests that the exalted god was omnipotent or that the other gods were impotent (see esp. Porter, "Anxiety of Multiplicity"; Hundley, "Here a God").

31. Walther Sallaberger, personal communication; cf. Walther Sallaberger, "Pantheon A. I. In Mesopotamien," *RlA* 10 (2004): 297. For example, brewing and woodworking were considered important enough to have their own patron deities Ninkasi and Siraš, and Ninduluma respectively (Sallaberger, "Pantheon," 297, 306).

32. See, e.g., Wiggermann "Theologies, Priests and Worship," 1857; on the issue of and interchange between gods of the center and inimical forces of the periphery, see further idem, "Scenes from the Shadow Side," 207–30. Although the threat of monstrous enemies in Mesopotamia, like Tiamat, largely had been averted in the past (unlike Mot in the Ugaritic Baal Cycle, who continued to plague Baal), some danger nonetheless remained from these divine foes and especially from internal strife. Indeed, while victory over chaos was often presented as occurring in primeval times, it was not a one-time event. Rather, it had to be cyclically repeated as in Egypt. For example, during the *akītu* Festival, the *Enuma Elish* was recited recounting Marduk's rise to prominence and establishment of world order. Rather than simply celebrating Marduk's prominence, the text and the ritual activity accompanying it indicated that during the course of the ritual Marduk's victory and cosmic ordering were renewed. The text appeals to Marduk to defeat Tiamat anew and adjures Tiamat to "remain distant without being held back; may she go far away forever" (VII 133–134). "The point is that cosmic order is not an automatic given: it must be regularly renewed, and the enemies of order, the Tiamats, if defeated once, must be defeated again and again" (Peter Machinist, "How Gods Die, Biblically and Otherwise: A Problem of Cosmic Restructuring," in Pongratz-Leisten, *Reconsidering the Concept*, 234).

33. Such strife is the subject of many Akkadian myths.

34. Excessive turmoil naturally invited encroachment by divine enemies. Disaster from within, however, was perhaps the greater threat (see esp. the myth of Erra and Ishum [*COS*

their part in the cosmic struggle by preserving the idealized state of creation as much as possible.[35] Thus, instead of being a boon, progress was often viewed as a distortion or deterioration to be avoided at all costs.[36] Because of this prevailing view, the culture, especially the official religious culture, remained relatively static and, as such, open to fruitful generalizations.[37]

## CULT IMAGES

Like the Egyptians, Mesopotamians made their statues of precious materials. They were made from a core of wood with the body sumptuously dressed, face and hands plated with gold, and the eyes and beard of precious stones.[38] Their size is difficult to determine, as the available texts do not describe the statues' dimensions, cult statues have rarely (if ever) been found, and the pictorial representations vary.[39] From the images, the statues often seem to have been human-sized

---

1:113.404–16], in which Erra's rebellion threatened to unsettle the world order [cf. the title given by Benjamin R. Foster, *From Distant Days: Myths, Tales, and Poetry of Ancient Mesopotamia* (Bethesda: CDL, 1995), 132: "How Erra Wrecked the World"]).

35. "Kingship was lowered from heaven" as a measure to ensure that humanity, in its large and unruly state, appropriately served the deities (Wiggermann, "Theologies, Priests and Worship," 1861, 1863). See further Machinist ("Kingship and Divinity," 152–88), regarding the mingling of human and divine elements in the king. On creation as the ideal, see ch. 3 and Hundley, "Way Forward."

36. See, e.g., van der Toorn, "Iconic Book," 238 (see further in ch. 3).

37. Of course, there were also times and rulers who challenged the prevailing model (see, e.g., the innovations of some of the Neo-Assyrian kings). However, the mere fact that we can speak of such a model and make generalizations about the concept of divine presence in Mesopotamia testifies to the effectiveness of the prevalent mindset.

38. J. Renger, "Kultbild A. Philologisch (in Mesopotamien)," *RlA* 6 (1980–1983): 310–11; Livingstone, *Mystical and Mythological Explanatory Works*, 175–87; Wiggermann, "Theologies, Priests and Worship," 1862; Porter, "Introduction," in Porter, ed. *What Is a God?*, 25–26; see more fully Angelika Berlejung, *Die Theologie der Bilder: Herstellung und Einweihung von Kultbildern in Mesopotamien und die alttestamentliche Bilderpolemik* (OBO 162; Fribourg: University Press, 1998), 35–61.

39. There are no detailed descriptions of cult statues as found, e.g., in Hittite Anatolia (Renger, "Kultbild," 311). No free-standing statues of deity have been found in either Assyria or Babylonia (Ursula Seidl, "Babylonische und assyrische Kultbilder in den Massenmedien des 1. Jahrtausends v. Chr.," in *Images as Media: Sources for the Cultural History of the Near East and the Eastern Mediterranean (1ˢᵗ millennium BCE)* [ed. C. Uehlinger; Fribourg: University Press, 2000], 106). Matsushima similarly contends that, to his knowledge, we have "no indisputably genuine cult statue of a god who was worshiped as a main god in a large sanctuary in Babylonia or in Assyria" and also laments that written materials are not particularly informative (Eiko Matsushima, "Divine Statues in Ancient Mesopotamia: Their Fashioning and Clothing and Their Interaction with the Society," in *Official Cult and*

and occasionally larger or smaller.[40] However, there is no way to discover to what extent these pictures reflected reality or whether the image depicted was the deity itself or the statue.[41] From the little evidence available, we may tentatively suggest that cult images varied from 30 to 60 cm (12–24 inches) for peripheral and lower deities to life size for primary cult images in major temples, that is, human size (figs. 9.1 and 9.2).[42]

## Form

Mesopotamian gods were depicted primarily either in human-like form or as symbols (figs. 9.3–9.7). The anthropomorphic statues of the primary deities venerated in the temple resembled the human form in most respects, yet could be differentiated by their skin of gold or silver, and blue hair as well as their identifying supernatural paraphernalia and attributes.[43] In addition, radiance as a defining characteristic of divinity was also attributed to divine cult statues.[44] In fact, texts

---

*Popular Religion in the Ancient Near East: Papers of the First Colloquium on the Ancient Near East: The City and Its Life Held at the Middle Eastern Culture Center in Japan (Mitaka, Tokyo) March 20–22, 1992* [ed. Matsushima; Heidelberg: Winter 1993], 210); cf. Herman Vanstiphout , "Die Geschöpfe des Prometheus: Or How and Why Did the Sumerians Create Their Gods?," in Porter, ed., *What Is a God?*, 27 n. 60. On the few statuettes that have been found, see Seidl, "Kultbild Archäologisch," 314–15; Berlejung, *Theologie der Bilder*, 35 n. 191; see also Dominique Collon, "Iconographic Evidence for Some Mesopotamian Cult Statues," in *Die Welt der Götterbilder* (ed. B. Groneberg and H. Spieckermann; BZAW 376; Berlin: de Gruyter, 2007), 57–84. In addition, unlike in Egypt, small shrines did not enclose the statues and thus offer little clue as to the size of these statues.

40. See the illustrations in Ornan, *Triumph of the Symbol*, 227–84.

41. Seidl, "Kultbild," 316. See, e.g., the image of Shamash in the Sippar tablet of Nabu-apla-iddina (fig. 9.4) and the cylinder seal from the time of Naram-Sin (Louis Delaporte, *Musée du Louvre, Catalogue des cylindres, cachets et pierres gravées de style oriental* [Paris: Hachette, 1920], T. 103; Dick, "Mesopotamian Cult Statue," 54, fig. 3.3).

42. Berlejung, *Theologie der Bilder*, 58. This does not mean that the deity itself was perceived to be the same size as its statue. When the two were pictured together (e.g., in cylinder seal mentioned in the previous note), the deity was significantly larger than the statue.

43. Berlejung, *Theologie der Bilder*, 54–55, 58–60. This description resembles that of Egypt where the bones of deities were silver, their flesh gold, and their hair lapis lazuli (Lichtheim, *AEL* 2:198; Hornung, *Conceptions of God*, 134; Robins, "Cult Statues in Ancient Egypt," 6). Regarding anthropomorphic cult images, see further, e.g., F. Köcher, "Der babylonischen Göttertypentext," *MIO* 1 (1953): 57–107; Berlejung, *Theologie der Bilder*, 35–61 for their appearance and 80–177 for their construction.

44. For example, in the *Enuma Elish*, Tiamat "endowed (certain beings) with radiance [*melammū*], (and thus) turned (them) into gods" (I 138, II 24). For a discussion of the matrix of the terms, e.g., *melammu, pulḫu, pulḫutu,* and *namrirru,* see esp. Elena Cassin, *La splendeur divine: introduction à l'étude de la mentalité mésopotamienne* (Civilisations et

Fig. 9.1. Foreign cult statues carried away by Assyrian soldiers (from the Southwest Palace of Nineveh). After Barnett, Turner, and Bleibtreu, *Sculptures from the Southwest Palace*, pl. 451. Drawing by Susan Hundley.

Fig. 9.2. The removal of the statue of Marduk (carried by Assyrian soldiers, far left) and a bird of prey statue from Babylon (relief from the central palace of Nimrud). After Layard, *Monuments of Nineveh*, pl. 67a. Drawing by Susan Hundley.

Fig. 9.3. Old Babylonian fragment of a terracotta statue from Ur of an anthropomorphic deity wearing a horned crown (ca. 2000–1750 BCE). Courtesy of the Trustees of the British Museum.

Fig. 9.4 (facing page). The Shamash tablet of Nabu-apla-iddina from Sippar, depicting Shamash in anthropomorphic form (far right) and a sun disk (ca. 887–855 BCE). Courtesy of the Trustees of the British Museum.

---

sociétés 8; Paris: Mouton, 1968), 17–51; see further Shawn Zelig Aster, "The Phenomenon of Divine and Human Radiance in the Hebrew Bible and in Northwest Semitic and Mesopotamian Literature: A Philological and Comparative Study" (Ph.D. diss., University of Pennsylvania, 2006), 29–176, now updated and published as idem, *The Unbeatable Light: Melammu and Its Biblical Parallels* (AOAT 384, Münster: Ugarit Verlag, 2012).

The same language was also applied to the other major visible manifestation of the divine, the astral bodies, which shone with a divine radiance (Rochberg, "The Stars Their Likenesses," 49). Shamash is the most obvious example: "you, Šamaš, have covered the heavens and all the countries with your radiance (*melammu*)" (Stephen Langdon, *Babylonian Penitential Psalms* [Oxford Editions of Cuneiform Texts 6; Paris: Geuthner, 1927], 51:9–10, cited in Rochberg, "The Stars Their Likenesses," 49).

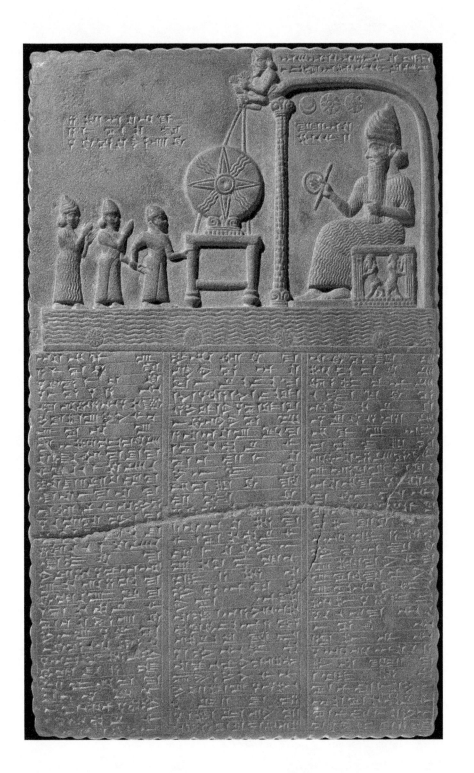

Fig. 9.5. A lapis lazuli cylinder depicting the anthropomorphic Marduk alongside his hybrid animal (the *mušḫuššu*). After E. Klengel-Brandt, ed., *Mit Sieben Siegeln versehen*, fig. 99.

Fig. 9.6. The spade of Marduk alongside his *mušḫuššu*. After the *kudurru* in King, *Babylonian Boundaries Stones*, pl. L. Drawing by Susan Hundley.

Fig. 9.7. A pedestal of Tukulti-Ninurta I, with the repeated figure of the king standing and then kneeling before the pedestal with a stylus or staff and a tablet atop it (from the Ishtar temple in Assur; ca. 1243–1207 BCE). Courtesy of the Staatliche Museen zu Berlin, Vorderasiatisches Museum. Photo by J. Liepe.

apply the same terms (*melammu*, *pulḫutu*, and *namurattu*) to statues as they do to the otherwise inaccessible divine beings.[45] For example, an incantation from the mouth-washing ritual describes the statue as "clothed in splendor, … he is surrounded with radiance (*melammu*), he is endowed with an awesome radiance, he shines out splendidly, the statue appears brilliantly."[46]

---

45. Elena Cassin, "Forme et identité des hommes et des dieux chez les Babyloniens," in *Le temps de la réflexion 7: Corps des dieux* (ed. C. Malamoud and J.-P. Vernant; Paris: Gallimard, 1986), 74; Dick, "Mesopotamian Cult Statue," 50; Sommer, *Bodies of God*, 20–21. See also Hurowitz, "What Goes In," 9.

46. STT 200:1–10 (IT 3 B 49ab–53ab); translation after Christopher Walker and Michael B. Dick, "The Induction of the Cult Image in Ancient Mesopotamia: The Mesopotamian *mīs pî* Ritual," in Michael B. Dick, ed., *Born in Heaven Made on Earth: The Creation of the Cult Image in the Ancient Near East* (Winona Lake, IN: Eisenbrauns, 1999), 98; see also the translation in Walker and Dick, *The Induction of the Cult Image in Ancient Mesopotamia: The Mesopotamian* mīs pî *Ritual* (SAALT 1; Helsinki: University of Helsinki, 2001), 149–50.

Symbols refer to non-anthropomorphic objects of various forms that functioned roughly as an emblem standing for the deity.[47] Rather than literally depicting a particular divine form, symbols were associated elements that did not literally depict the deity. For example, Marduk could be depicted in anthropomorphic form alongside his associated hybrid being, the *mušḫuššu* (see fig. 9.5). Alternatively, he could be represented by means of a symbol. In fig. 9.6, the spade, alongside Marduk's hybrid pet, served as a shorthand for Marduk. This does not imply that Marduk looked like a spade or took the form of a spade. Rather, the spade was a shorthand for him. Such symbols could also

> take the form of an inanimate object, such as the wedge-like reed stylus of Nabu (*qan ṭuppi*); of an animal, such as the lion of Ishtar; of a composite fantastic creature, such as the *mušḫuššu* of Marduk; of the stylized image of a natural phenomenon, such as the crescent moon of Sin (*uskaru*) and the star of Ishtar; or of a floral motif, like Šala's ear of corn.[48]

## EXCURSUS: SYMBOLS

Since it encompasses such an array of elements and is a somewhat problematic designator, "symbol" requires further clarification before discussing its various exemplars. It is a common assumption that anthropomorphic forms were truer to their divine prototypes than "symbols" and even that the deities were somehow more present in them. However, this assumption is problematic for several reasons.

Since a symbol is by definition something that represents something else, it would seem that a divine "symbol" representing a divine entity was not that entity itself nor even its body, but rather a visual cue pointing away from itself to the (absent) deity. Nonetheless, a divine symbol could at least theoretically be understood to be the deity itself in its terrestrial form or its cultic body.[49] If used as a primary cult image (see, e.g., the image of the bird of prey that appears as a primary cult image alongside the anthropomorphic image of Marduk[50] [fig. 9.2]), which had been

---

47. "When they are shown carried by a (human-shaped) deity or depicted in his immediate proximity, they are to be understood as identifying attributes; when shown without a godly figure in human form, they are to be understood as emblems standing for their signified divine entity" (Ornan, "In the Likeness of Man," 100; see further Seidl, *Die Babylonischen Kudurru-Reliefs: Symbole Mesopotamischer Gottheiten* (OBO 87; Fribourg: University Press, 1989), 120–21, 125).

48. Ornan, "In the Likeness of Man," 100.

49. Unlike in Egypt, Mesopotamian language made little effort to distinguish between the two possibilities.

50. The bird of prey could alternatively be understood as a depiction of a deity in animal form or a symbolic representation of a deity using an associated animal.

enlivened by the mouth-washing ritual (practiced, e.g., on Sin's moon crescent), it could be just as suitable a receptacle of divine presence as the anthropomorphic statue. In other words, anthropomorphic statues and symbols were simply different ways of visually representing a deity. This form itself did not necessarily indicate the kind or quantity of presence. Presence was instead determined by the deity itself, ritual activation, ritual use, and most pragmatically by the cultic authorities. Thus, a visual object that was not a portrait of a deity, but rather a visual cipher, theoretically could be understood as the deity's chosen terrestrial form.

The form and the likeness of that form to its divine/mythic prototype did not in themselves determine what made a suitable divine image or the quality of the connection between deity and image. In fact, the "truer" anthropomorphic image that represented the presumably anthropomorphic deity was likely not intended to be an exact replica of the divine body in its celestial habitat. Like the symbol, it too was merely a representation of that form that presumably represented the deity through resemblance rather than association. For example, assuming that each deity had different physical features, the statues did not realistically portray the face and physical features of the deity in question. Rather, the divine statue depicted a stereotyped face and body that was the same as all other faces and bodies of deities of the same gender. Indeed, the observer could only differentiate between deities based on their characteristic attributes and accessories.[51]

Nonetheless, the mere fact that a cult image did not look exactly like a deity's "true" form does not mean that it was not the god itself or, more precisely, the divine-image symbiosis. Although clearly not the moon itself, a stylized moon crescent would be as appropriate a terrestrial form of the moon god Sin as an anthropomorphic image is of a deity in anthropomorphic form.[52] In short, a divine symbol was not prima facie a more distant representation than an anthropomorphic image.[53]

* * *

---

51. Thus, when these attributes and accessories were ambiguous, it is often difficult to identify the deity in question. On the generic form of deity in representation and their differentiation through paraphernalia, attributes, and inscriptions, see, e.g., Berlejung, *Theologie der Bilder*, 54–55.

52. However, as will be elucidated in the next section, although not necessarily more distant, symbolic representations of deity were often so understood. On the occasional divinity of the celestial bodies, see Rochberg, "The Stars Their Likenesses;" Hundley, "Here a God."

53. Despite the possible shortcomings, I retain symbol as a designator for lack of a better option. The precise relationship between it and the deity as well as the anthropomorphic statue and the deity will be assessed further in the course of and after the analysis of the mouth-washing and daily-cult rituals.

Fig. 9.8. A procession of anthropomorphic deities astride various natural and hybrid animals (Maltai rock relief from the time of Sennacherib). From F. Thureau-Dangin, "Les sculptures rupestres de Maltaï," *RA* 21 (1924): 187.

The animal form appeared primarily in divine attributes, such as the bull of the Weather God or Ishtar standing on a lion, rather than in depictions of the deity itself (fig. 9.8).[54] The mixed form, so prevalent in Egypt, was largely absent

54. Cornelius, "Many Faces of God," 31. There is nonetheless some evidence of a deity portrayed in purely animal form. For example, an Assyrian wall relief from the Central Palace at Nimrud depicts what seems to be a primary cult statue in the form of a large bird of prey (A. H. Layard, *Monuments of Nineveh I* [London: John Murray, 1849], pl. 67A). The relief pictures the removal of two large captured statues from Babylon (identified because of the fallen date palm and in accordance with Tiglath-pileser III's campaign to Babylon in 731) by Assyrian soldiers. The first seemingly life-sized statue depicts an anthropomorphic figure, identified with Marduk because he holds a spade (*marru*), Marduk's primary divine attribute. The second, as indicated, portrays a large bird of prey, which may perhaps be identified as Ninurta. The prominence of the portrait and the size of the statues suggest that both were primary cult statues (Richard D. Barnett and Margarete Falkner, *The Sculptures of Aššur-nasir-apli II, 883–859 B.C. Tiglath-Pileser III, 745–727 B.C. [and] Esarhaddon, 681–669 B.C., From the Central and South-West Palaces at Nimrud* [London: Trustees of the British Museum, 1962], xvi, 17, pl. 7; Hayim Tadmor, *The Inscriptions of Tiglath-Pileser III, King of Assyria: Critical Edition, with Introductions, Translationss and Commentary* [Jerusalem: The Israel Academy of Sciences and Humanities, 1994], 239–40, 272; Ornan, "In the Likeness of Man," 122 and fig. 21). Another text refers to the taking of an oath before Ninmar's bird, which is marked with the divine determinative (Charles-Francis Jean, *Tell Sifr: Textes cuneiformes conserves au British Museum* [Paris: Geuthner, 1931], 58:21; Dominique Charpin, *Archives familiales et propriété privée en Babylonie ancienne: Étude des documents de "Tell Sifr"* [HEO 12; Geneva: Droz, 1980], 243; *šurinnu, CAD* Š/3, 345 1.a). A lion deity is also marked with the divine determinative and presented with offerings (Menzel, *Tempel* II, no. 54 [K. 252]).

Fig. 9.9. A bronze statue of Pazuzu (early first millennium) (15 x 8.60 x 5.60 cm [6" x 3.4" x 2.2"]). Courtesy of the Louvre.

from Mesopotamia. When it appeared it took a different form than that of the major Egyptian deities, instead resembling the protective figures like the Egyptian sphinx. Whereas the major Egyptian deities often had a human body with an animal head, the mixed Mesopotamian deities often had a human head on an animal body (fig. 3.13). Such hybrid forms, often containing more than one animal form, did not often represent the major deities. Instead, one finds them portraying so-called monsters, demons, protective beings, and divine accessories.[55] For example, Lamashtu, who belonged to the "demon" category, was described as having the head of a lion, the teeth of a donkey, naked breasts, a hairy body, stained hands, long fingers and nails, and bird talons, while Pazuzu had a canine-

55. Although not absolute, monsters and demons may be generally differentiated by their functions and areas of activity. Monsters served as cosmic agents, who interacted primarily with the gods in the divine world, while demons were especially active within the human or natural world, afflicting or protecting human beings (see further, Karen Sonik, "Daimon-Haunted Universe: Conceptions of the Supernatural in Mesopotamia" [Ph.D. diss., University of Pennsylvania, 2010]).

like face with bulging eyes, a scaly body, a snake-headed penis, bird talons, and wings (fig. 9.9).[56] Anzu, a "monster" associated with the clouds, was presented as a bird-lion hybrid, representing prominent aspects of the storm, air, and roaring respectively.[57] *Aladlammû*,[58] the well-known protective and intercessory *lamassu* and *šēdu* figures that stood on either side of entryways to palaces and presumably also temples, were depicted as often winged, colossal human-headed bulls or lions (see fig. 3.13).[59]

Such hybrid beings in particular highlight a theological tension in the Mesopotamian understanding of the major gods. On the one hand, in order to make them understandable and approachable, the gods were perceived to be like humans. Awesome, uncontrollable forces and those necessary to sustain life were largely incomprehensible unless predicated on the human model.[60] In order to make these deified forces more understandable, approachable, and manageable, they were often thought to be, or be controlled by, personified deities. Since many of the gods were understood primarily as human-like beings, humans could meaningfully communicate with them.[61] Since many of the gods were understood to be both comprehensible and approachable,[62] their favor could be secured and their powers brought to bear on peoples' behalf. Likewise, since humans were understood to be created in the image of the gods at least to some extent,[63] they had

---

56. Regarding Lamashtu, see, e.g., W. Farber, "Lamaštu," *RlA* 6 (1980–1983): 439–46. Wiggermann, "Lamaštu Daugher of Anu: A Profile," in *Birth in Babylonia and the Bible: Its Mediterranean Setting* (ed. M. Stol; CM 14; Groningen: Styx, 2000), 217–52. Regarding Pazuzu, see, e.g., Wiggermann, "Pazuzu," *RlA* 10 (2004): 372–81; Nils P. Heeßel, *Pazuzu: Archäologische und Philologische Studien zu einem altorientalischen Dämon* (Ancient Magic and Divination 4; Leiden: Brill, 2002); idem, "Evil against Evil: The Demon Pazuzu," *SMSR* 77 (2011): 357–68.

57. Wiggermann, "Mischwesen A. Philologisch. Mesopotamien," *RlA* 8 (1994): 225.

58. Although not attested in syllabic writing, for the sake of convenience I follow Landsberger in rendering ᵈALAD.ᵈLAMMA.MEŠ as *aladlamû* or the Sumerian logographic equivalent of ᵈšēdu and ᵈlamassu.

59. Foxvog, Heimpel, and Kilmer, "Lamma/Lamassu," 446–53. See also *ANEP*, 646.

60. Ornan, *Triumph of the Symbol*; idem, "In the Likeness of Man"; Hamori, *When Gods Were Men*, 26–64.

61. Mountains and rivers, e.g., with no clear anthropomorphic form could still be anthropomorphized, which as loosely understood refers to far more than physical form (e.g., anthropomorphization may include human[-like] emotions or actions). Namely, they could be presented with offerings suggesting that they could eat or at least in some way enjoy them.

62. The gods were by no means simply equated with humans externally or internally. Their superiority rendered them somewhat ineffable, while their similarities to humanity rendered them somewhat understandable, far more so than, e.g., an abstract storm.

63. See, e.g., *Enuma Elish* in which humanity was created from slain body of the god Qingu.

greater dignity and a greater affinity to the gods. Thus, humanizing the divine was both unavoidable and profitable.[64]

On the other hand, by associating the gods so closely with humanity, it was sometimes difficult to differentiate between them, especially visually.[65] To distinguish deities from humanity, they were presented as superhuman in size and wearing horned crowns upon their heads.[66] It would seem that humans, both modern and ancient, cannot escape perceiving the gods as human-like and likely would be uncomfortable depicting their gods in forms too deviant from themselves.[67] Thus, instead of depicting the major gods as freakish beings, composed of an odd assortment of other powerful beings and forces, ancient Mesopotamians depicted them as superior to such freakish beings, and thus far superior to humans.[68]

---

64. In making this claim, I am saying nothing of the evolution of deities, whether they were originally conceived of as potent forces or abstract qualities that later were humanized and/or humanized deities absorbed several potent forces and abstract qualities into their divinity. In addition, although not all Mesopotamian deities were humanized, Mesopotamians often appealed to the more humanized deities to deal with those that were less understandable and approachable, more primal and thus more dangerous.

65. This is particularly the case when images lack the color that differentiated divine image from human (i.e., the gold or silver skin and blue hair of cult statues).

66. Regarding their size, see, e.g., Jeremy A. Black and Anthony Green, *Gods, Demons and Symbols of Ancient Mesopotamia: An Illustrated Dictionary* (Austin: University of Texas, 1992), 93; for a representative survey, see Hartenstein, *Angesicht JHWHs*, 41–47. Regarding the horned crowns, See, e.g., R.M. Boehmer, "Hörnerkrone," *RlA* 4 (1975): 431–34; Wiggermann, "Mischwesen," 233; Julia M. Asher-Greve, "Reading the Horned Crown (A Review Article)," *AfO* 42 (1995–1996): 181–89; Cornelius, "Many Faces," 31; Ornan, *Triumph of the Symbol*, 168. The other primary marker distinguishing deity from human was the flounced skirt or garment (Edward M. Curtis, "Images in Mesopotamia and the Bible: A Comparative Study" in *The Bible in the Light of Cuneiform Literature* [eds. W. W. Hallo; Lewiston, NY: The Edwin Mellen Press, 1990], 40).

67. Ornan, *Triumph of the Symbol*, 168. "It seems that human imagination is somewhat limited and that even when men and women wished to allude to the supernatural they could not transcend their realistic surroundings" (ibid.). As Xenophanes, a sixth-century pre-Socratic Greek philosopher, astutely noted, if horses had gods, they would probably have a horse's form (Versnel, "Thrice One," 92).

68. Wiggermann appropriately refers to so-called monsters as "supernatural freaks" (*Mesopotamian Protective Spirits: The Ritual Texts* [CM 1; Leiden: Brill, 1992], 151–52). However, while visual depictions rarely entered the realm of the monstrous, literary depictions stretched the boundaries of anthropomorphic expression to render the gods more superior. In literary texts designed to exalt specific gods, the more the deity transcends the human form, the greater the deity becomes. For example, the *Enuma Elish* extends the common adage that the god's mind is inscrutable to Marduk's body (the mind's inscrutability appears frequently in wisdom literature [Jean Bottéro, *Mesopotamia: Writing, Reasoning and the Gods* (trans. Z. Bahrani and M. van de Mieroop; Chicago: University of Chicago, 1992), 211, 264–65; Hendel, "Aniconism and Anthropomorphism," 207]).

While the major anthropomorphic gods were at the heart of and responsible for the ordered cosmos, so-called monsters[69] dwelled outside of and threatened that order.[70] While the major anthropomorphic gods were more or less clearly differentiated and had their own spheres of activity in the ordered cosmos, monsters

---

Marduk's appearance is "impossible to understand" (I 94; VI 37), with four eyes and ears (I 95). Marduk is thus distinct from the other gods insofar as he is distinct from human form (Hendel, ibid.). Another text (STT 118 rev.; Bottéro, *Religion in Ancient Mesopotamia*, 235–36; Benedikt Hartmann, "Monotheismus in Mesopotamien?," in *Monotheismus in Alten Testament und seiner Umwelt* [ed. O. Keel; BibB 14; Fribourg: University Press, 1980], 61–62; Livingstone, *Mystical and Mythological Explanatory Works*, 101–2; Hendel, "Aniconism," 207–8; Porter, "Anxiety of Multiplicity," 240–51; for a translation, see Benjamin R. Foster, *Before the Muses: An Anthology of Akkadian Literature* [3rd ed.; Bethesda: CDL, 2005], 713–14) contends that Ninurta's body parts are both other gods and features of the cosmos (Hendel, "Aniconism and Anthropomorphism," 207–8). Ninurta's transcendence, even if transcendent hyperbole, expresses clearly that "the god is superior to other gods insofar as his body is 'other' from human form" (ibid., 208). There is a similar description of Ningursa on the Gudea cylinder (Livingstone, *Mystical and Mythological Explanatory Works*, 93; Hendel, "Aniconism and Anthropomorphism," 208). Each text uses literary artistry to express the greatness and otherness of the gods, emphasizing "the ineffable nature of the divine by offering descriptions which are only barely conceivable" (Livingstone, *Mystical and Mythological Explanatory Works*, 93). These texts differentiate the form of the exalted god from human shape, thereby distinguishing the exalted god from the other gods who took human shape. However, although acceptable in some literary compositions (as a scholarly exercise in divine exaltation; cf. Hendel, "Aniconism and Anthropomorphism," 209), such representations would likely not be acceptable in visual form. Texts and images have different effects on their intended audience. While such textual descriptions render a deity ineffably complex and thus superior, such an image would simply appear monstrous, transgressing the aesthetic sensibilities that a text may more safely extend, and thus would not engender the intended reverence. Indeed, figurative language and hyperbole do not often translate well from concept to canvas; an elegant idea often yields an inelegant portrait. In addition, a text often has greater flexibility of expression; it can compare and qualify various means of expression, such that it is clear how they are intended to be understood (e.g., literal or analogical), in a way that is difficult to express visually.

69. Wiggermann distinguishes monsters from both the gods and demons, since, unlike gods, monsters did not appear in the god-lists, were only sporadically listed with the divine DINGIR determinative, and generally did not wear the horned crown of divinity. Unlike demons, they were not listed among the *utukku lemnu* (roughly translated as evil demons; see *CAD* U–W, 339–42), nor were they demons of disease listed in the medical texts ("Mischwesen," 231). Although they could be generally distinguished from gods and demons, there is no generic Sumerian or Akkadian term to describe "monsters" as a category. Monsters in general were presented as hybrid beings, who combined various potent natural elements into one form. For example, as noted, Anzu, associated with the clouds, was presented as a bird-lion hybrid, representing air and roaring, prominent aspects of the storm (Wiggermann, "Mischwesen," 225).

70. See Wiggermann, "Mischwesen;" idem, "Scenes from the Shadow Side," 207–30.

were largely undifferentiated in terms of identity and function.[71] As a general rule, these hybrid creatures were considered the anthropomorphic gods' closest rivals, who were defeated in the ancient past and later served as divine servants, pets, mounts, and emblems.[72] Thus, portraying these beings as defeated foes and servants both demonstrated their lesser status and exalted the anthropomorphically conceived deities.

As an amalgam of potent creatures, *aladlammû* were the ideal supernatural bouncers, potent enough to protect against any manner of intruder (see fig. 3.13).[73] However, although mixed, they appeared majestic, befitting the sphere they protected, like the sphinx in Egypt. Given their imposing presence and prime position, they also served two related functions. First, in the context of the temple, they were appropriate boundary markers, indicating the importance of the space they protected and the potency of the deities, who, though represented in anthropomorphic form, were capable of controlling such majestic beasts.[74] Second, in their function as gatekeepers, they both protected the divine sphere from unwanted attention and introduced appropriate guests to the deity.[75] Thus, the protective deities (*lamassū*) of the various deities, who were the same as the protective deities (*lamassū*) of their temples, were important divine servants, whose otherness

---

71. Monsters were only individualized under specific conditions and not for their own intrinsic value, but rather as a vehicle for exalting a particular god. For example, in the combat myth of Ninurta and the *Enuma Elish*, Ninurta and Marduk defeated monsters with clear identities, Anzu and Tiamat respectively. In both cases, Anzu and Tiamat were used to explain the power and cult of the emergent gods (in fact, the *Enuma Elish* is dependent on and adopts the same strategy as the Anzu myth [Wiggermann, *Protective Spirits*, 163]). In other words, Ninurta and Marduk were powerful and important because they had defeated powerful monstrous foes, in Ninurta's case indicating how he rather than Enlil was the master of Anzu (Wiggermann, *Protective Spirits*, 151–64). More expansively, as both myths were concerned with the setting up of the cosmos in its present ordered form (Livingstone, *Mystical and Mythological Explanatory Works*, 170), Anzu and Tiamat were used as a means to this end.

72. Wiggermann, "Mischwesen," 225–29.

73. Esarhaddon described their function in the palace context as those who "because of their appearance, turn back an evil person, guard the steps and secure the path of the king who fashioned them" (Borger, *Die Inschriften Asarhaddons*, 62–63).

74. In the palace context, Neo-Assyrian kings borrowed from the prestige of the divine sphere, using such gatekeepers to indicate their importance and power and also to strike appropriate fear in all who visited the royal precincts.

75. This introductory function likely derived from their presence at doorways, and in some ways allowed them to usurp the divine vizier's (*sukkallu*) role in this respect (Wiggermann, "The Staff of Ninšubura: Studies in Babylonian Demonology, II," *JEOL* 29 [1985–1986]: 18, 26).

marked the otherness of the divine realm and the extreme otherness of the major deities that belied their generally anthropomorphic form.[76]

## Anthropomorphic versus Symbolic Representation

Of the two major forms of the divine, human-like and symbolic, evidence is split over which form predominated. The texts rarely refer to the divine symbols,[77] yet such symbols dominated the archaeological record from the second half of the second millennium to the first millennium.[78] How can we explain such a discrepancy?

Although any conclusion is speculative, it seems that anthropomorphic portrayals of deity were primarily consigned to the temple, while symbolic representations were employed everywhere else.[79] It is clear from the archaeological record that symbols generally replaced anthropomorphic representations of deity in the second half of the first millennium BCE to the first millennium. However, this evidence does not necessarily indicate that representations of deity in the cult changed with the general trend. In fact, the available evidence seems to indicate that the anthropomorphic form of deity remained prominent in the temple.[80]

---

76. Regarding the identity of the protective deity (lamassu) of the deity and of the temple, see Foxvog, Heimpel, and Kilmer, "Lamma/Lamassu," 450–51.

77. Many of these sources go one step further in implying that deities had a human form (see, e.g., William W. Hallo, "Cult Statue and Divine Image: A Preliminary Study," in Scripture in Context 2 [ed. Hallo et al.; Winona Lake: Eisenbrauns, 1983], 9–14; Lambert, "Ancient Mesopotamian Gods," 122–23; Hendel, "Aniconism," 206–7; Ornan, Triumph of the Symbol, 176–77). When they referred to the various elements used as divine symbols, they did not usually refer to the cult symbols themselves, but rather their counterparts in nature (e.g., the stars in astronomical or astrological texts). In many cases, these elements were themselves referred to as divine (Rochberg, "The Stars Their Likenesses"). In cultic contexts, various objects, many of which were likely symbols, were deified alongside the regular anthropomorphic cult images in that they were marked with the divine determinative, were entreated as deities, and received offerings (see, e.g., Porter's survey, "Blessings from a Crown").

78. Ornan, Triumph of the Symbol, 170. This is especially true of Babylonia (ibid., 170–71). In Assyria, there is some evidence of anthropomorphic portrayals, especially during the reign of Sennacherib (Ornan, "In the Likeness of Man," 134–42). On the general disconnect between text and image, see, e.g., Ornan, Triumph of the Symbol, 10–12.

79. Ornan, Triumph of the Symbol, 171–74. There are without doubt many exceptions to both elements of this proposal, which as a whole do not invalidate it, but rather suggest caution in employing it unilaterally.

80. Ornan in particular has gathered the evidence for the anthropomorphic conception of deities and their anthropomorphical portrayal of primary cult images (Triumph of the Symbol; idem, "Likeness").

First, while divine iconography in general was fluid and subject to change, cultic iconography, conceptions, and activity were remarkably conservative.[81]

> The characteristics of art valued by modern onlookers, such as change, innovation, expressiveness and creativity, were probably not appreciated by the ancient beholders. On the contrary, an artisan who would fashion the god's image or even his accessories in a new form or shape, unknown to previous renderings, would be considered as having committed a cultic offense – not unlike a scribe making a sudden, unexplained alteration in the words of a prayer.[82]

In other words, in a cultic context, deviation from the original was often considered a distortion. Instead, each new image had to be a "renewal" (*tēdištu*) of the original.[83] Any alteration, even one for the better, was often discouraged. For example, there is a story in which Nabonidus sought to make a larger and more elaborate crown for the statue of the sun god, Shamash. However, the people would not accept it, arguing that the crown had to be "exactly like the old one" (*kīma labīrimma*)[84]; if it was changed, the statue would no longer be Shamash.[85]

---

81. However, the Mesopotamian preoccupation with the past does not mean that their culture was impervious to change. Rather, in order to be acceptable, change was often presented as a return to the glorious past, a renewal of what had been lost, and/or made at the divine behest. For example, a change in the form of the divine image had to be presented as a renewal of the original divine image, forged, it would seem, at the beginning of time. Although the form of a divine image likely did not remain static, it was essential that the divine image always be presented officially as unchanging—the same as the original, divinely authorized prototype—in order for it to be palatable (van der Toorn, "Iconic Book," 238).

82. Ornan, *Triumph of the Symbol*, 9.

83. Van der Toorn, "Iconic Book," 236. The most prominent counterexamples come from the Neo-Assyrian kings, who, with their imperialistic tendencies, generally sought to make everything bigger and better than their predecessors, often including the temples. See, e.g., Esarhaddon's claim to have made the statues "even more artistic than before" (Borger, *Die Inschriften Asarhaddons*, 83, § 53; translation after Walker and Dick, "Induction of the Cult Image," 66).

84. Langdon, *Neubabylonischen Königsinschriften* (Vorderasiatische Bibliothek 4; Leipzig: Hinrichs, 1912), 264 i 41–ii 1; van der Toorn, "Iconic Book," 238. We should, however, handle this Nabonidus example with care, since it was likely a polemic against him, i.e., his inability to make the crown the right size stressed his incompetence. However, such a polemic is nonetheless suggestive, since a change in the size of the cult statue or its paraphernalia (in this case making it bigger rather than smaller) demonstrated his incompetence. In other words, he tried to do something that simply was not done, at least in an official capacity.

85. The anthropomorphic nature of Nabonidus's cult image also could be inferred from the anthropomorphic elements used to adorn it, most notably the crown.

This beholdenness to the prototype proved especially problematic when the divine image was captured or destroyed. When an enemy plundered a statue, one could not simply make a new one without having an exact model of the original and divine approval to form it. For example, on the well-known Sippar tablet of Nabu-apla-iddina (fig. 9.4), the Babylonian king indicates that his predecessors could not replace Shamash's cult statue after its capture because they had no appropriate model and Shamash did not reveal his face to them (*pānīšu lā iddinšu*).[86] Instead, they constructed a sun disc (*niphu*) as a cultic stand-in, which was presented as inferior to the anthropomorphic prototype.[87] During Nabu-apla-iddina's reign, however, Shamash was said to have revealed a clay model of the divine image with its insignia, giving Nabu-apla-iddina a model and divine license to make a renewed divine statue—that is, to fashion a new one based on the primeval prototype.[88]

Second, although evidence for symbolic representations abounds outside of temple contexts, there is very little to indicate that temple iconography and especially the cult statues were symbols. In fact, the minimal archaeological evidence remaining for the temple cult and its primary cult statues suggests that cult statues remained predominantly anthropomorphic.[89] In addition to the Nabu-apla-iddina tablet, the images of captured divine statues on Assyrian wall reliefs are predominantly anthropomorphic.[90] Although the majority stem from conquered territories across the Euphrates and outside of the Mesopotamian heartland, one such image pictures the capture of an anthropomorphic statue of Marduk from Babylon

---

86. L. W. King, *Babylonian Boundary Stones and Memorial Tablets in the British Museum* (London: Trustees of the British Museum, 1912), no. 36 i 8–17.

87. Nonetheless, as in the case of Nabonidus, there remains some debate over whether Nabu-apla-iddina's preference for an anthropomorphic image was the norm or a rhetorically driven anomaly, i.e., whether the anthropomorphic form should be considered superior or Nabu-apla-iddina's assertion of its superiority simply served his own purposes.

88. King, *Babylonian Boundary Stones*, no. 36; Walker and Dick, "Induction of the Cult Image," 58–63. Regarding the king's claims, it seems unlikely (though not impossible) that a priest conveniently found the image of the original. Perhaps more likely, Nabu-apla-iddina simply wanted to replace the sun disc in the sanctuary with an anthropomorphic model and justified the innovation by labeling it a divinely sanctioned return to the ideal, original state. He further suggested that only with the reinstitution of the anthropomorphic Shamash statue was Shamash really present.

89. See, e.g., Berlejung, *Theologie der Bilder*, 35–61.

90. Layard, *Nineveh I*, pl. 65; idem, *The Monuments of Nineveh II* (London: John Murray, 1853), pls. 30, 50. Barnett and Falkner, *The Sculptures*, xxiv–xxv, 29–38, pls. XCII–XCIII. Barnett et al., *Sculptures from the Southwest Palace of Sennacherib at Nineveh* (London: British Museum, 1998), 13, 25–26, 36, 74, 128, pls. 143, 451–53; Jutta Börker-Klähn, *Altvorderasiatische Bildstelen und vergleichbare Felsreliefs* (BaF 4; Mainz: von Zabern, 1982), 43-44; John Malcolm Russell, *Sennacherib's Palace without Rival at Nineveh* (Chicago: The University of Chicago, 1991), 53, 169–70, fig. 35.

Fig. 9.10. A winged deity in sun disk (from Assur, Northwest Palace slab 3). After Layard, *Monuments of Nineveh*, pl. 13. Drawing by Susan Hundley.

(see fig. 9.2).[91] A wall relief of Tiglath-pileser III from the Central Palace at Nimrud depicts the monarch's removal of a human-sized standing anthropomorphic Marduk statue, which appears alongside a similarly large bird of prey statue from Babylon in 731. In a time when there was little evidence of anthropomorphic divine representation in Babylonia, this image of the primary cult image of Marduk demonstrates that cult images within the temple nonetheless remained anthropomorphic.[92] In addition, a deity from the Northwest Palace at Nimrud appears as a fusion of the winged sun disc, an anthropomorphic figure, and a tail-like lower body (fig. 9.10).[93] Although presented as a hybrid of sorts, this figure is primarily anthropomorphic, differentiated from fully human analogs by transcending the human form. In addition, while major deities were generally rendered pictorially in nonanthropomorphic guise, lesser deities like those on the façade of the Eanna temple in Uruk more often continued to be depicted anthropomorphically (see, e.g., fig. 3.12).[94] For Ornan, this presentation "reconfirms the premise of the anthropomorphic perception of the major deities in Mesopotamia because it seems highly unlikely that at a time when lesser divinities were considered anthropomorphic, their divine masters would have been conceptualized differently."[95]

91. Ornan, "In the Likeness of Man," 121–22.

92. However, the presence of the large bird of prey, presumably also a primary cult image, suggests that primary cult images need not always be anthropomorphic. Theoretically, any image could serve as a divine host. Regarding the bird of prey, it remains unclear if this image is to be understood as a representation or emblem, i.e., a stand-in image for an otherwise anthropomorphic deity or, as in Egypt, one of the deity's many possible manifestations.

93. Layard, *Nineveh I*, pl. 13, 21, 25. Although Shamash remains more likely, for the identification of the figure as Assur, see Ornan, "A Complex System." See also the image of a deity within a winged disc on a glazed tile of Tukulti-Ninurta II (Walter Andrae, *Coloured Ceramics From Ashur* [London: K. Paul, Trench, Truebner, 1925], 27, pl. 8). See further, e.g., Ruth Mayer-Opificus, "Die geflügelte Sonne: Himmels- und Regensdarstellungen im alten Vorderasien," *UF* 16 (1984): 189–236; Ornan, *Triumph of the Symbol*, figs. 107–11.

94. Ornan, "In the Likeness of Man," 130–34.

95. Ibid., 134.

Third, the occasional anthropomorphic representations of deity outside of the temple context are also suggestive. For example, Sennacherib's depiction of major deities anthropomorphically may suggest that he simply chose to portray the common perception of deity and common cultic reality that for some reason otherwise had been withheld from public consumption.[96] It is far less likely, and indeed with the textual record all but impossible, that Sennacherib (re)invented the idea that the gods were anthropomorphic in form.

Fourth, we must not forget that the texts continued to describe deities in anthropomorphic terms. These texts, which are most often concerned with the official cult (e.g., temple building inscriptions) or the mythological portrait of deities, refer to anthropomorphic deities and divine representations.[97] Thus, when texts about the cult describe anthropomorphic deities, we have every reason to expect that primary cult images remained anthropomorphic.

Fifth, a primary anthropomorphic cult image is most consonant with a primarily anthropomorphic cult. The divine cult seems to have been primarily modeled after the king's court. In it, the deity was bathed, clothed, fed, entertained, and entreated. Such a cult is far more appropriate for an anthropomorphic image than various symbols like a divine sun disk.[98] The anthropomorphism of the cult is further confirmed by many of the deified nonanthropomorphic elements associated with temples such as divine crowns, beds, chariots, weapons, and musical instruments. As possessions of an anthropomorphic deity, which make little sense

---

96. Some such depictions (e.g., the rock relief from Maltai) betray Syrian influences (Ornan, "In the Likeness of Man," 140). Ninth- to eighth-century Assyrian cylinder seals also aberrantly portray deities anthropomorphically (Kazuko Watanabe, "Seals of Neo-Assyrian Officials," in *Priests and Officials in the Ancient Near East: Papers of the Second Colloquium on the Ancient Near East—The City and its Life, held at the Middle Eastern Culture Center in Japan (Mitaka, Tokyo), March 22–24, 1996* [ed. Watanabe; Heidelberg: C. Winter, 1999], 313–66; Irene Winter, "Le Palais imaginaire: Scale and Meaning in the Iconography of Neo-Assyrian Cylinder Seals," in Uehlinger, ed., *Images as Media*, 68–74; Ornan, "In the Likeness of Man," 138). "Their very existence shows approval, however, of the underlying anthropocentric concept that governed Mesopotamian thinking regarding the nature of the divine" (Ornan, "In the Likeness of Man," 138).

97. Instead of addressing how the deities were portrayed, the mythological, hymnic, and prayer texts simply testify to the primary conception of deity as anthropomorphic (Ornan, *Triumph of the Symbol*, 171, 175–76) or perhaps the conception of humans as theriomorphic (Dick, "Mesopotamian Cult Statue," 47 n. 13).

98. The nature of the cult even supports Nabu-apla-iddina's claims for cultic improvement in transferring primary cultic attention from such a sun disk to a divinely sanctioned anthropomorphic statue. Regardless of the hierarchical relationship between divine representations, the anthropomorphic statue is more appropriate to the anthropomorphic cult and as such would seem to be more cultically efficacious.

apart from such a deity, these elements seem to have been deified by association with that deity.[99]

Sixth, conceptions of deities tended to be predicated on the human model.[100] Although deities were far more than anthropomorphic in that they transcended the anthropomorphic model in multiple respects, they were not less than anthropomorphic. Namely, they had a human-like form and human-like emotions, which seem to have made up the core of their being from which the other conceptions and representations emerged (e.g., astral). Thus, while deities were certainly more than humans writ large,[101] they nonetheless seem to have been predicated on the human model, which they transcended to establish their superiority. At the same time, the evidence suggests a general reticence to display this anthropomorphic form outside of the temple context and a general tendency to replace it with nonanthropomorphic alternatives.

Thus, it would seem that primary cult images, as well as other images within a temple context, were anthropomorphic because this form most resembled primary divine conceptions and cult practices. As noted above, a Mesopotamian deity was a network of several connected parts, at the heart of which was an anthropomorphic core that functioned generally as the network's epicenter.[102] For example, Ishtar was a mythological person, resident in various terrestrial temples, associated with the planet Venus, the number 15, love, and war.[103] As the heart of this divine constellation, the internally and externally anthropomorphic core was

---

99. Porter speaks of their deification by "contagion" ("Blessings from a Crown," 191): these associated elements "became deities by 'contagion,' by a transfer of divinity to them from the inherently numinous gods that owned them and with whom they were in frequent contact."

100. Ornan, *Triumph of the Symbol*; idem, "In the Likeness of Man"; Hamori, *When Gods Were Men*, 26–64.

101. See Porter, *What is a God?*; Hundley, "Here a God"; *pace* Georges Roux, *Ancient Iraq* (Middlesex, England: Penguin Books, 1964), 88, 190; Jacobsen (*Treasures of Darkness*, 9); Wolfram von Soden, *The Ancient Orient: An Introduction to the Study of the Ancient Near East* (trans. D. Schley; Grand Rapids, MI: Eerdmans, 1994), 175; Black and Green, *Gods, Demons and Symbols*, 93; Bottéro, *Religion in Ancient Mesopotamia*, 44; and to a lesser extent Lambert ("Gott. B. Nach akkadischen Texten," *RlA* 3 (1957): 544; idem, "Mesopotamian Gods," 125–27); Regarding the (previous) scholarly consensus, see further Porter, "Introduction," 1–13.

102. Although most often connected to the divine person, the various nonanthropomorphic elements of deity were only occasionally deified, while the major anthropomorphic core, as the essence of deity, was always deified (see further Hundley, "Here a God").

103. Porter, "Anxiety of Multiplicity," 243-4. Ishtar could also be alternatively presented as male and female (Groneberg, "Die sumerisch/akkadische Inanna/Ištar: Hermaphroditos?," *WdO* 17 [1986]: 25–46; however cf. Bahrani, *Women of Babylon: Gender and Representation in Mesopotamia* [London: Routledge, 2001], 141–60).

the quintessence of divinity. Since the epicenter of the vast divine network was anthropomorphically envisioned, we may expect the same of the primary cult image in the temple, the epicenter of the deity's heavenly presence on earth.[104]

## EXCURSUS: THE FUNCTION OF DIVINE SYMBOLS

Before addressing potential reasons for the exclusion of anthropomorphic images from the public eye and the inclusion of divine symbols, we will address the function of such symbols. In general, the symbol seems to have been a type of shorthand that presenced the otherwise distant deity.[105] While present in the heavens as celestial bodies and in the temples as cult images,[106] deities were made manifest outside of the temple in the human sphere as divine emblems (e.g., standards, weapons, and symbols).[107] Although the extent of the connection between the emblem and the deity is debatable, the emblems nonetheless served as differ-

---

104. Ornan ("In the Likeness of Man," 148) refers to the anthropomorphic form as the "true" form of deity and thus equates the anthropomorphic cult statue with this true form. However, there is little evidence that a deity's true form was anthropomorphic. The anthropomorphic form seems rather to have been situated atop a hierarchy of various forms, such that rather than being the true form it was the privileged form. Furthermore, as noted, the anthropomorphic cult statue represented a stereotyped divine form differentiated from other such divine forms by divine accessories, such that, however a deity's "true" anthropomorphic form was understood, it likely differed from its anthropomorphic cult image. Even if one does not accept the argument for anthropomorphic priority, it is hard to deny that the anthropomorphic form was most suited to the terrestrial temple and service similar to the king in his court.

105. Mettinger, *No Graven Image*, 47. In literary terms, it functioned like metonymy: part, in this case an attribute, substituting for and representing the whole (Hendel, "Aniconism and Anthropomorphism," 206–7). Following Peirce, Mettinger elsewhere refers to the symbol as an index of the divinity (Mettinger, *No Graven Image*, 21), where a symbol as an attribute of divinity referred to that deity by association and implication.

106. Although they could depict stars, none of the various terrestrial emblems were themselves stars. Rather, they merely depicted the stars and referred to the deity who manifested itself as or controlled the stars. As luminous celestial bodies, stars made the invisible and inapproachable deities visible and approachable (regarding stars, in *Enuma Elish* V 1–2, the stars are referred to as the likenesses of the great gods, which seems to indicate that the "images of the gods are made visible in the stars" [Rochberg, "The Stars Their Likenesses," 65]; cf. regarding stars, Sallaberger, "Pantheon," 297). Mesopotamians could interact with the gods by discerning their will through observation of the activity of the celestial bodies and respond appropriately to ensure a good omen or avert a bad omen (see, e.g., Rochberg, *The Heavenly Writing: Divination: Divination, Horoscopy, and Astronomy in Mesopotamian Culture* [Cambridge: Cambridge University Press, 2004]).

107. Groneberg, "Aspekte der 'Göttlichkeit,'" 141; Ornan, "In the Likeness of Man," 142–43; see also processions (e.g., Pongratz-Leisten, *Ina šulmi īrub*, 193–95).

ent kinds of divine access points.[108] Battle standards, for example, were treated in much the same way as primary cult images (e.g., they were presented with offerings and incense was burned before them).[109]

Listed with the divine determinative, for example, *durigallu*, the divine standard, was both associated with and distinct from the deity it represented. A common trope in royal inscriptions, "the gods who go before me (in battle)," is functionally equivalent to the phrase, the divine "standard that goes before me (in battle),"[110] which seems to intimate that the presence of the standard was functionally equivalent to the presence of the deity. However, another inscription states that the king fought "with the support of Aššur my great lord, and the divine standard (*durigallu*) that goes before me ... with the supreme might of the divine standard that goes before me,"[111] suggesting that Assur was to be differentiated from his divine standard, which also bore significant divine power. Whether the standard was a deity in its own right or simply an extension of Assur, Assur's power was brought to bear by means of his standard. Namely, the standard was a means of presencing Assur, more particularly, his power, outside of the temple sphere.[112] In addition to being an extension of the divine power and potentially presence in the context of battle, when the presence of the divine cult image was impractical, a standard (*šurinnu*)[113] or a weapon (*kakku*) could also serve as suitable surrogates for the deity in witnessing oaths, effectively binding the god depicted to punish the oath takers if they broke their oath.[114] Thus, such emblems simultaneously made

---

108. Cf. Berlejung, "Reduktion von Komplexität," 37; Groneberg, "Aspekte der 'Göttlichkeit,'" 141.

109. Karlheinz Deller, "Götterstreitwagen und Götterstandarten: Götter auf dem Feldzug und ihr Kult im Feldlager," *BaM* (1992): 291–98.

110. Holloway, "The *giš Kakki Aššur* and Neo-Assyrian Loyalty Oaths," in *Proceedings of the XLV Rencontre Assyriologique Internationale,* Part 1: *Historiography in the Cuneiform World* (ed. T. Abusch et al.; Bethesda. MD: CDL; 2001), 260–61; regarding the latter statement, see also A. Kirk Grayson, *Assyrian Rulers of the Early First Millennium BC* (RIMA 2; Toronto: Toronto University Press, 1991), 134, A.0.98.1 48.

111. RIMA 2, 203, A.0.101.1 ii 25–28; translation after Holloway, "Neo-Assyrian Loyalty Oaths," 260.

112. The divine standard seems to have been deified by association. It appears to have possessed its own (semi-)independent numinous power that had to be placated with offerings to ensure its favor, or, alternatively, the deity himself had to be placated from afar to ensure that the standard remained charged with divine power. Either way, the effect was the same; the standard had to be presented with offerings to ensure that it brought its power to bear on the people's behalf.

113. Although not a human-shaped statue, *šurinnu* standards sometimes bore small anthropomorphic forms (Ornan, "In the Likeness of Man," 121).

114. With the absence of Assur shrines outside of Assur, the weapon of Assur seems to have served this function (Holloway, "Neo-Assyrian Loyalty Oaths," 265) and, given its power,

the deity more accessible and extended its power in the terrestrial sphere, since it and its terrestrial power were not bound to its home city.

Although there is little indication that the symbols on entitlement *narûs*,[115] seals, or victory monuments were animated with the divine presence or received offerings,[116] such symbols nonetheless served as access points to the deity. The presence of the divine symbol invoked the protection of the deity depicted, in an apotropaic capacity, and/or to enforce one's claim to territory or some other entitlement and the benefits derived therefrom (serving as, e.g., the pictorial equivalent of listing the names of multiple divine witnesses in treaties).[117] Instead of being the deity, divine symbols in such contexts served as an appeal to or mark of divine support, and thus an effective means of accessing the deity.[118] Like the weapons and battle standards mentioned above, such symbols extended the divine influence beyond the city and temple.

* * *

served as an effective enforcer. Indeed, rather than take oaths before an anthropomorphic cult image, there is evidence that standards and weapons were kept in temples and used for oath taking purposes in court contexts, on the premise that no one would swear a false oath and risk the consequences of divine censure (Kathryn A. Slanski, "Representation of the Divine on the Babylonian Entitlement Monuments (*kudurrus*): Part I: Divine Symbols," *AfO* 50 [2003]: 308–23). On the long history of the use of weapons in promissory oaths, see briefly ibid., 253; regarding the use of symbols in court contexts, see further Eva Dombradi, *Die Darstellung des Rechtsaustrags in den altbabylonischen Prozessurkunden* (FAOS 20,1; Stuttgart: Steiner, 1996), esp. 84, 333–34. See also the extensive references to the use of standards (d*šurinnu*) in oath-taking and as a means of enforcing oaths (*CAD* Š/3, 345).

115. On this term, see Slanski, *The Babylonian Entitlement* narûs *(*kudurrus*): A Study in their Form and Function* (ASOR Books 9; Boston: ASOR, 2003).

116. Slanski, "Representation of the Divine," 321.

117. Slanski suggests that rather than representing the deity, the symbols on these monuments represented the symbols in the temple that played a decisive role in the determination and enforcement of justice (Slanski, "Representation of the Divine," 310, 321). Whether or not this was the case makes little practical difference. In each instance, the divine symbols suggested divine sanction and divine enforcement, such that the entitlement (or other benefit) and the monument or seal were protected.

118. Although not necessarily equated with the deity, symbols of the deity were nonetheless part of the divine constellation because they were extensions of the deity that extended its power (and presence) wherever they were depicted. In the case of the victory monument, e.g., the divine symbol buttressed the statement of royal power with divine power and the threat of divine reprisal for rebellion.

How can we explain the different modes of representation? First, representing the deity differently inside and outside the temple drew attention to the different functions of the various representations.[119] As the primary locus of the anthropomorphic deity on earth, the cult image was appropriately anthropomorphic in its form, needs, and desires. It was served and addressed like a king and similarly expected to respond favorably to service and entreaty. As a type of shorthand, the various symbols outside suggested some distance between deity and object, such that although the deity could be present to some extent in the symbol, the two were not equated. Such symbols seem to have been a way to extend divine presence beyond the temple and indeed seem to have mediated the temple presence to more distant environs. It is likewise logical that, since anthropomorphic images were "not always available when divine presence was needed, emblems were used in their stead."[120] Cult statues were likely both too few and too special to be used under most circumstances (e.g., in court). Nonetheless, some sort of divine presence was necessary in the court, e.g., as oaths were taken in the gods' names.[121] When the divine statue was unavailable, the appropriate symbol served in its place.[122]

Second, the different modes of representation served to privilege the temple and its cult image. Since the anthropomorphic form of the deity rested at the heart of the divine constellation, its terrestrial counterpart, the cult statue, was also depicted anthropomorphically. Just as other divine forms including the heavenly bodies could be understood as secondary manifestations of the anthropomorphized deity, so too did the deity's other terrestrial depictions represent secondary manifestations of the primary cult image. By placing the privileged anthropomor-

---

119. The anomalous anthropomorphic depiction of deity on *šurinnu*-standards did not obviate the difference between interior and exterior representations. Depicting the deity in anthropomorphic guise on the standard attached divine power, presence, and authority more firmly to the standard such that it could perform its mediating role outside of the temple. Since the image appeared on a standard and not as a statue, a clear differentiation between the two remained.

120. Ornan, *Triumph of the Symbol*, 176; see also Lambert, "Ancient Mesopotamian Gods," 123–24.

121. Lambert, "Ancient Mesopotamian Gods," 124.

122. Lambert also offers an additional practical reason for the presence of divine symbols. In art, the small scale of the images, particularly on seals, made anthropomorphic representations difficult to distinguish, whereas symbols were more easily engraved and distinguishable (glyptic art was likewise more susceptible to change than the extreme conservatism of the official cultic statuary and their accouterments and, as such, able to incorporate new forms as the times changed [Lambert, "Ancient Mesopotamian Gods," 123–24; cf. Christoph Uehlinger, "Anthropomorphic Cult Statuary in Iron Age Palestine and the Search for Yahweh's Cult Statue," in *Image and the Book*, 111, who comments similarly for Syria-Palestine]).

phic representations exclusively in the temple, Mesopotamians thereby exalted the sacred precinct over all other potential loci of divine presence.[123]

Third, restricting access to the anthropomorphic image privileged the deity itself and its primary anthropomorphic image as well as those people with the privilege to access it. Just as access to the deity in the sanctuary was limited both spatially and visually, so too was access to the anthropomorphic form limited to those with access to the sanctuary. The removal of the anthropomorphic form from public display finds a parallel in the divine realm, where a Sumerian poem expresses Enlil's primacy among the gods by stating that "no god could look upon him."[124] Just as the other gods were barred from beholding Enlil, so too were the majority of humans barred from viewing the deity's primary terrestrial form.[125] Thus, the primary form of deity, like the deity itself, was too special for public display.[126]

The lack of an anthropomorphic image outside of the temple could at once have two conflicting results. On the one hand, coupled with the prominence of the figure of the enthroned king in palace decoration, the absence of portrayals of anthropomorphic deities, especially in the palace, promoted the person of the king.[127] This pictorial propaganda bolstered the already prevalent portrait of the king as the supreme protagonist.[128] It effectively eliminated the deity from the competition for the "eye of the beholder," thereby exalting the monarch.[129]

On the other hand, the same absence of images could serve to distinguish the divine form from the human form of the king, thereby elevating the deity. When both the terrestrial and celestial kings were enthroned in anthropomorphic repose, one naturally connected the two images. Thus, since the political king mirrored the deity in form, one could naturally assume that the likeness extended to the power of the enthroned. Instead of allowing the king to connect himself visually and thus practically to his divine counterpart, the absence of such an anthropomorphic depiction of deity severed any such visual connection, thereby elevating the celestial king at the expense of its earthly counterpart. In other words, it demonstrated that the deity was ontologically other and could not be compared to

123. Cf. Ornan, "In the Likeness of Man," 147–48.

124. Black and Green, *Gods, Demons and Symbols*, 76.

125. Cf. Ornan, *Triumph of the Symbol*, 178; idem, "In the Likeness of Man," 147.

126. Cf. Lambert, "Ancient Mesopotamian Gods," 123–24; Ornan, "In the Likeness of Man," 147.

127. The prominence of royal representations alongside the absence of divine anthropomorphisms in the palace was especially prominent in Assyria from the ninth century onward (Ornan, *Triumph of the Symbol*, 172–73).

128. Ibid.

129. Ibid., 173.

the king, even in form.[130] The similar anthropomorphic representation would then be reserved for the temple where the learned would know the difference between likeness in form and content.[131]

## 1. THE MOUTH-WASHING (*Mīs Pî*) RITUAL

Like the Egyptians, the Mesopotamians were aware of the difficulty of a human-made statue being or housing divinity. The official cult of the gods responded by developing a complex ritual to explain and enable the divine presence in the statue. In Mesopotamia, this ritual is often called the mouth-washing (*mīs pî*) ritual, a name that belies its more complex structure.[132] Mouth-washing and mouth-opening, the ritual's other primary component, occur multiple times in the larger ritual,[133] yet when extracted from the larger ritual the meaning and nature of these acts are elusive. Neither text nor identifiable pictorial representation explicitly mention what these rites entail, nor is the meaning of these specific rites easily extractable from the larger ritual. Perhaps the form and function of the rites was self-evident to the scribes and, as such, omitted. Within the ritual, mouth-washing always precedes mouth-opening[134] and seems to involve the application of water enhanced with various purifying agents to the mouth of the statue, while mouth-opening entails the application of several tasty and fragrant substances (syrup [rather than the traditional honey],[135] ghee, cedar, and cypress).[136] In order

---

130. For roughly the same argument relating to the Israelite aniconism (i.e., the empty divine throne), see Ron Hendel, "The Social Origins of the Aniconic Tradition in Early Israel," *CBQ* 50 (1988): 365–82; idem, "Aniconism and Anthropomorphism," 224–8; William W. Hallo, "Texts, Statues and the Cult of the Divine King," *Congress Volume, Jerusalem 1986* (VTSup 40; ed. J. Emerton; Leiden: Brill, 1988), 54–66.

131. The frequent reference to the king as the "image" (*ṣalmu*) of the god would also be affected (on the reference, see Hallo, "Texts, Statues and the Cult," 64 n. 59; Hendel, "Social Origins," 380; Machinist, "Kingship and Divinity").

132. For an examination of the title of the ritual see Walker and Dick, *The Mesopotamian* mīs pî *Ritual*, 8–10.

133. The mouth washing alone occurrs fourteen times in the Babylonian version and five to seven times in its Assyrian counterpart depending on how one reconstructs the missing text (i.e., whether one posits a mouth-washing in gap between lines 82 and 87 and in the lost section at the end; Berlejung, "Washing the Mouth," 62 n. 73).

134. In the various rituals where mouth opening appears, mouth washing always precedes it in the ritual sequence (Walker and Dick, *The Mesopotamian* mīs pî *Ritual*, 13–14).

135. Maul, *Zukunftsbewältigung: Eine Untersuchung altorientalischen Denkens anhand der babylonisch-assyrischen Löserituale (Namburbi)* [BaF 18; Mainz: von Zabern, 1994], 51 n. 61.

136. Hurowitz, "The Mesopotamian God Image, from Womb to Tomb," *JAOS* 123 (2003): 147. However, the various incantation tablets do not present a unified picture. For example,

to understand these elements more fully, we must first analyze the ritual as a whole before dissecting its various parts.

An analysis of the mouth-washing ritual will follow according to the categories of structure, structural interpretation, use, and ideology. Since evidence is minimal for the daily cult, its analysis will not be subdivided into the four categories. After a comparison of the mouth-washing ritual with the daily cult, we will discuss the relationship between the deity and its statue(s) and the necessity of divine nourishment.

There is ample attestation of the ritual from the first millennium,[137] and some evidence that the ritual existed earlier.[138] First, the fact that the ritual's incantations are written in Sumerian seems to imply that the rituals date to an earlier period.[139] Second, and more concretely, there is evidence from Neo-Sumerian times for the mouth-opening ritual (*pīt pî*; Sumerian ka-luḫ-ù-da)[140] and for the mouth-washing ritual (*mīs pî*; Sumerian ka-duḫ-ù-da) since Middle-Babylonian times.[141] Thus, although our texts date to the first millennium, it is likely that at least part of the ritual existed earlier in some form. As in Egypt, the ritual includes both ritual actions and recitations.[142] However, the two appear on separate

---

IT 5 C 25 indicates that the statue's mouth is to be washed with syrup and ghee (Walker and Dick, *The Mesopotamian mīs pî Ritual*, 14). Mouth washing and mouth opening are prevalent outside of this ritual as well, involving animals, people, and other objects (e.g., a leather bag; see Hurowitz, "Isaiah's Impure Lips and Their Purification in Light of Akkadian Sources," *HUCA* 60 [1989]: 39–89; Berlejung, *Theologie der Bilder*, 182–85, 188–90; Walker and Dick, *The Mesopotamian mīs pî Ritual*, 10–15).

137. Tablets survive from Assur, Nineveh, Nimrud, Babylon, Sippar, Nippur, Uruk, Sultantepe, and Hama (Berlejung, "Washing the Mouth," 48; Walker and Dick, "Induction of the Cult Image," 67).

138. Unfortunately, there is no way of discovering if the earlier rituals shared the same form. For a further examination of the history and possible development of the ritual, see Walker and Dick, *The Mesopotamian* mīs pî *Ritual*, 16–30.

139. Renger, "Kultbild," 313; Berlejung, "Washing the Mouth," 48.

140. Sumerian administrative texts from the Ur III period identify various provisions for the mouth-opening of the statue of the dead and deified ruler, Gudea of Lagash. See Miguel Civil, "Remarks on 'Sumerian Bilingual Texts,'" *JNES* 26 (1967): 200–211; Piotr Steinkeller, "Studies in Third Millennium Paleography, 2: Sign Šen and Alal: Addendum," *OrAnt* 23 (1984): 39–41; Berlejung, "Washing the Mouth," 48; Walker and Dick, "Induction of the Cult Image," 58. The next reference comes from the aforementioned Sippar tablet of Nabu-apla-iddina in the mid-ninth century BCE. (King, *Babylonian Boundary Stones*, 120–27 no. 26 [BM 91000] iv 22–28; Walker and Dick, "Induction of the Cult Image," 58.

141. Jussi Aro, *Mittelbabylonische Kleidertexte der Hilprecht-Sammlung Jena* (Sitzungsberichte der Sächsischen Akademie der Wissenschaften zu Leipzig 115/2; Berlin: Akademie-Verlag, 1970), 18–19 HS 165 22–24; Berlejung, "Washing the Mouth," 48.

142. Once again, it must be noted that we are dealing with textual descriptions of ritual

tablets, such that it is not always easy to coordinate the various actions with their accompanying utterances.[143] Where the link may be clearly established, the incantations are closely associated with the ritual actions and indispensable for their interpretation.[144] "They serve as a sort of running commentary, revealing to a great extent the purpose of the prescribed ritual actions that they accompany. Despite variations in the recensions and the remaining problems, it is now possible to get a good sense of how the ritual worked and what it meant."[145] The following is a synoptic summary of the two primary traditions from Nineveh and Babylon.[146] Since the Ninevite version is fuller in detail, it will serve as the primary source text until it breaks off in the orchard, after which the Babylonian version will be used exclusively. Although there are some differences between versions, most are of a rather superficial nature, such that we may speak of a single ritual with local variations. As in Egypt, rather than interpreting every action and utterance, analysis will be limited to those that seem the most important and interesting.

## Structure

The larger ritual can be divided into various scenes based on the changes in setting and processions between settings:[147] 1) preparations in the city, countryside, and temple (NR 1–54)[148]; 2) the workshop (NR 55–64; BR 1–4)[149]; 3) at the

---

actions and recitations, not actual ritual practice. Regarding recitations, see Berlejung, *Theologie der Bilder*, 197–205.

143. See, e.g., Hurowitz, "Mesopotamian God Image," 149. Evidence suggests that there was a series of six incantation tablets circulating in Babylon and eight at Nineveh, which differ slightly in content to each other and are not fully consistent with the ritual tablets (Walker and Dick, "Induction of the Cult Image," 69).

144. Berlejung, *Theologie der Bilder*, 197; Hurowitz, "Mesopotamian God Image," 149.

145. Ibid., 149.

146. "NR" refers to the Nineveh recension, while "BR" refers to the Babylon recension. For a comparison of the versions and an analysis of their content, see Berlejung, "Washing the Mouth," 51–68 and more fully idem, *Theologie der Bilder*, 212–59. For a transliteration and translation of the various texts, see Walker and Dick, *The Mesopotamian* mīs pî *Ritual* (see also Walker and Dick, "Induction of the Cult Image," 72–97; Berlejung, *Theologie der Bilder*, 422–68).

147. For a fuller summary that includes transitions from one setting to the next, see Berlejung, "Washing the Mouth," 49; idem, *Theologie der Bilder*, 247–50. The various processions serve primarily as links between locales and generally lack their own ritual elements (Berlejung, *Theologie der Bilder*, 210; regarding the processions in general and their relation to festival processions, see ibid., 208–12). As such, they are not listed as separate sections as in Berlejung, "Washing the Mouth," 49.

148. This appears in the Nineveh version but not in the Babylonian one.

149. The Babylonian version commences at the workshop (*bīt mummi*). For its identification

river bank (NR 70–94; BR 6–12)[150]; 4) in the orchard (NR 95–204; BR 12–59); 5) at the temple (BR 60–65).[151]

The ritual tradents begin the ritual sequence by making various preparations, involving the statue's decoration and purification with censer, torch, and holy water basin (*egubbû*).[152] In the workshop, the first mouth-washing (*mīs pî*) and mouth-opening (*pīt pî*) rites (NR 58) are accompanied by censer, torch, and holy water basin (NR 59).[153] After this initial mouth washing and opening, the priest speaks directly to the statue for the first time and asks it three times to go before its father Ea (the god of craftsmanship)[154] with a happy heart (NR 60–64).[155]

The priest then takes the statue by the hand and leads it to the river (NR 65–69).[156] Although neither the river nor the orchards fit the description, line 69 of

---

as a workshop, see Walker and Dick, *The Mesopotamian* mīs pî *Ritual*, 52 and the references cited therein.

150. NR 65–69 and BR 5–6 describe the procession from the workshop to the river.

151. The Nineveh version breaks off in the orchard. The reconstruction of the rest of the ritual relies on the Babylonian version (Berlejung, "Washing the Mouth," 66). The procession from the orchard to the gate of the temple is described in BR 59–60 and the procession from the temple gate to the inner sanctuary is described in BR 60–61. The ritual concludes with the priest cleansing the procession route from the temple to the quay (BR 65–66; ibid., 49, 68).

152. The "holy water basin of mouth-washing" features prominently at this stage of the ritual. It was prepared during the night by mixing various distinct elements with well-known purifying properties, including wood, herbs, semiprecious stones, precious metals, oils, ghee, and treacle (Berlejung, "Washing the Mouth," 51–52). According to the Babylonian version, the holy water basin was prepared at the beginning of the second day (ibid., 52).

153. Mouth washing seems to involve the application of water enhanced with various purifying agents to the mouth of the statue, while mouth opening entails the application of several tasty and fragrant substances (see further at n. 138 above).

154. Ea is also closely associated with purification (see, e.g., Walker and Dick, *The Mesopotamian* mīs pî *Ritual*, 53 n. 43).

155. Before speaking, the priest recites the incantation, "In heaven by your own power you are born" (STT 199:1–12; for translations see Berlejung, *Theologie der Bilder*, 437; Walker and Dick, *The Mesopotamian* mīs pî *Ritual*, 119), which, despite its name, refers primarily to the purity of the priest in preparation for his touching the statue (ibid., 53; idem, *Theologie der Bilder*, 216).

156. Along the way, the priest recites the incantation, "As you go out, as you go out, great …" (STT 199: 13–40; translations in Berlejung, *Theologie der Bilder*, 438–39; Walker and Dick, *The Mesopotamian* mīs pî *Ritual*, 119–20), which names the different woods used in order to confirm the purity and supernatural quality of the materials and mentions the craftsmen's tools and the craftsmen themselves, identifying the tools as pure and the craftsmen as the gods themselves (Berlejung, "Washing the Mouth," 54; idem, *Theologie der Bilder*, 218).

the Nineveh version speaks of the *ṣēru*, the "steppe" or "Jenseitsgelände."[157] Once at the riverbank, the statue meets Ea, its divine father, for the first time. The priests seat the statue on a reed mat, facing the sunset (NR 70; BR 6–7). Here the priest presents offerings to Ea and his son Asalluhi, identified with Marduk (the god of Babylon),[158] and throws the carpenters' tools and a tortoise and turtle, made of silver and gold, into the river bound inside a ram's skin (NR 72–80). Lines 81 to 87 are broken and may include a second mouth washing and opening.[159] The ritual tablet includes a short incantation stating that the statue's mouth is washed and urging the gods, Ea in particular, to count it among the divine community (NR 88–93).

The priest takes the hand of the statue again and leads it to the orchard, where he places it on a reed mat surrounded by reed huts and reed standards. He orients the statue toward sunrise, where it will encounter Shamash (the sun god) for the first time (NR 95–97).[160] The priest then prepares the statue for its first night under the stars, which includes the presentation of offerings to various gods and two additional mouth washings and openings in the Ninevite version (NR 100–108) and ten in the Babylonian version (NR 24–36).

On the second day in the orchard, the priest presents offerings to Ea, Shamash, and Asalluhi, the judges of heaven and earth, who oversee all the cult places (NR 109–21).[161] A series of incantations follow, including a repetition of "Born in heaven by his own power" (NR 133). In "Ea, Shamash, and Asalluhi" the priest asks them to determine the statue's destiny, to set its mouth to food and its ears to hearing, and to make it as pure and brilliant as the heavens (IT 3 B 36–40).[162] After the incantation, another mouth washing, mouth opening, and purification occur (NR 149–152). Five long hand-lifting prayers (*šu-illa*) follow: 1) "On the day when the

---

157. Bernd Janowski, *Sühne als Heilsgeschehen: Studien zur Sühnetheologie der Priesterschrift und zur Wurzel KPR im alten Orient und im Alten Testament* (WMANT 55; Neukirchenen-Vluyn: Neukircherner Verlag, 1982), 51; Berlejung, "Washing the Mouth," 53–54; idem, *Theologie der Bilder*, 217–18.

158. Asalluhi is the patron of exorcism who purifies heaven and earth (Walker and Dick, *The Mesopotamian* mīs pî *Ritual*, 53 n. 43). Identified with Marduk, he also serves as Ea's son and in some ways acts as his apprentice (see, e.g., IT 6/8 where Ea instructs Marduk how to effect purification).

159. Such a hypothesis is supported by the Babylonian version, which includes a mouth-washing before the incantation, "He who comes, his mouth is washed" (BR 11), and the following incantation (NR 88–93).

160. Shamash is also the god of judgment and plays a prominent role in purification.

161. The designators come from IT 3 B 7–11. For translations, see Berlejung, *Theologie der Bilder*, 447; Walker and Dick, *The Mesopotamian* mīs pî *Ritual*, 148.

162. Berlejung, "Washing the Mouth," 61. For a translation, see Berlejung, *Theologie der Bilder*, 447–48; Walker and Dick, *The Mesopotamian* mīs pî *Ritual*, 148–49.

god was created, when the pure statue was completed";[163] 2) "Pure statue, suited to great divine attributes";[164] 3) "As you go out, as you go out, great...";[165] 4) "Statue born in a pure place";[166] and 5) "Statue born in heaven."[167]

As its catchline indicates, the first incantation equates the god with its statue and stresses that it is visible in its brilliance in all the lands and was constructed both in heaven and on earth. Although STT 200 19 (IT 3 B 58ab)[168] suggests that the image was created by both gods and humans,[169] the following lines (STT 200 20–40; IT 3 B 59ab–69ab) stress that the craftsmen gods (e.g., Ea) made the image. STT 200 43–44 (IT 3 B 70–71) offers the important clarifying statement, "This statue without its mouth opened cannot smell incense, cannot eat food, nor drink water," while STT 200 79–80 (IT 3 B 92–93) indicates that humans open the statue's mouth fourteen times with honey, butter, cedar, and cypress. The craftsmen stand before the craftsmen deities, as the priest binds their hands and symbolically "cuts them off" with a tamarisk-wood sword (STT 200 61–76 [IT 3 B 82ab–91a] in tandem with NR 173–75 and BR 49–52). The human craftsmen then swear that they themselves had no part in making the statue; it is instead a product of the divine alone (NR 179–86). Following the prayer, the Nineveh version mentions another mouth washing and opening (NR 161).

The second prayer speaks of the perfection of the statue and mentions that Asalluhi opened the mouth of the statue with cedar, cypress, oil, and syrup (IT 3 B 112–13).[170] Afterward, the priest whispers into the statue's ear that it is counted among its divine brethren and that it is ready to enter the temple (NR 164–72). The

---

163. IT 3 B 49–99; Berlejung, *Theologie der Bilder*, 449–51; Walker and Dick, "Induction of the Cult Image," 98–100; idem, *The Mesopotamian mīs pî Ritual*, 148–51.

164. IT 3 B 100-C 5; Berlejung, *Theologie der Bilder*, 452–53; Walker and Dick, *The Mesopotamian mīs pî Ritual*, 152.

165. BR 53 refers to the incantation as "As you grew up" (IT 4 A 1–20; Berlejung, *Theologie der Bilder*, 454–55; Walker and Dick, *The Mesopotamian mīs pî Ritual*, 184). Regarding the earlier incantation, "As you go out," see above n. 158.

166. This incantation is not preserved.

167. IT 4 A 23–65; Berlejung, *Theologie der Bilder*, 456–58; Walker and Dick, *The Mesopotamian mīs pî Ritual*, 184–85.

168. STT (the Sultantepe Tablets) 200 refers to a specific incantation tablet, while IT (Incantation Tablet) refers to the incantation tablets as they appear in Walker and Dick, *The Mesopotamian mīs pî Ritual*.

169. The Akkadian of the duplicate text (STT 201) instead intimates that the statue has the features of both gods and humans (Walker and Dick, "Induction of the Cult Image," 99 n. 100).

170. Berlejung, "Washing the Mouth," 62. The incantation tablet also mentions another purification rite with a "scapegoat" of sorts (IT 3 B 116) (see Maul, *Zukunftsbewältigung*, 98; David P. Wright, *The Disposal of Impurity: Elimination Rites in the Bible and in Hittite and Mesopotamian Literature* [SBL Dissertation Series 101; Atlanta: Scholars, 1987], 66).

third prayer reaffirms the supernatural origin of the statue (IT 4 A 1–8) and asks the image to be the good *lamassu* of its temple and to remain there permanently (10–11). Unfortunately, only the title of the fourth prayer is preserved, while the fifth recalls the birth of the statue in heaven and in the mountains and seems to give a synopsis of "what could be expected of the divine presence in the temple."[171]

After the *šu-illa* prayers, the incantations address the image's regalia, as the statue is presented with a scepter (?) (NR 191), clothes (NR 192), a crown (NR 193), and a throne (NR 194). Covered with gleaming gold and silver, the divine clothes like the statue itself visually express the divine luminosity (*melammu*).[172] The crown too possesses an awesome splendor (*namrirru*) befitting the deity and its radiance (*melammu*) reaches the heavens.[173] Like the statue, the crown possesses a perfect purity bestowed on it by the gods;[174] it was crafted and its destiny determined by the gods, not the craftsmen.[175] Likewise, the divine throne is perfectly pure and was crafted by the gods.[176]

The priest then leads the statue by the hand to the temple (BR 59–60) as he recites an incantation that describes the threat of impurity and Asalluhi's countermeasures.[177] Along the way, the priest presumably uses holy water to cleanse the city and makes an offering at the temple gate (BR 60). The accompanying incantation announces that the "god will stay in his house where he will receive his daily food (ll. 35–37) and enjoy the company of a good guardian spirit (l. 38)" (*lamassu*).[178] The priest then installs the statue in the inner sanctuary with the final mouth washing and opening (BR 61–63).

---

171. Berlejung, "Washing the Mouth," 64.

172. Regarding the clothes, see the classic study of Oppenheim, "The Golden Garments of the Gods," *JNES* 8 (1949): 172–93; see also with references Berlejung, "Geheimnis und Ereignis," 127–28. Regarding the luminosity of the garments, see ibid.; cf. Thomas Podella, *Das Lichtkleid JHWHs: Untersuchungen zur Gestalthaftigkeit Gottes im Alten Testament und seiner altorientalischen Umwelt* (FAT 16; Tübingen: Mohr, 1996), 39–40, 116–24.

173. IT 5 A 1, 3.

174. IT 5 A 13; B 3–5.

175. IT 5 A 7–9.

176. IT 5 B 8–40.

177. Regarding IT 6/8, see the translation in Walker and Dick, "Induction of the Cult Image," 100–102 and the full text, translation, introduction, and annotation in Walker and Dick, *The Mesopotamian* mīs pî *Ritual*, 210–25.

178. Berlejung, "Washing the Mouth," 67. IT 4 B 31–40; for a translation, see Berlejung, *Theologie der Bilder*, 466; Walker and Dick, *The Mesopotamian* mīs pî *Ritual*, 187.

## *Structural Interpretation*

As in Egypt, the ritual sequence structurally bridges the gap between crafting the statue in the workshop and its installation in the temple as a fully functioning locus of divine presence.[179] The existence of the ritual likewise suggests that more than expert crafting is required to install a statue in a temple properly. The changes of setting divide the ritual into stages, each of which likely accomplishes a different though complementary purpose. The various mouth washings and openings also help to lend structure to the larger ritual.[180] The first mouth washing and opening (NR 58) mark the beginning of ritual activity directed toward the statue and the following transition from workshop to the river. Like the first, the second mouth washing (and opening)[181] (BR 11) mark a transition from the river to the orchard, from Ea as the prime addressee to Shamash. In the orchard, mouth washings (and openings) accompany each encounter with the gods. In the Nineveh version (NR 104, 108), two mouth washings and openings respectively accompany the encounters with (1) Anu, Enlil, Ea, Sin, Shamash, Adad Marduk, Gula, and Ninsianna and (2) Dingirmah, Kusu, Ningirima, Ninkurra, Ninagal, Kusibanda, Ninildu, and Ninzadim. In the Babylonian version there are ten (BR 24, 26, 28–36), accompanying the same encounters as in Nineveh as well as encounters with seven sets of stars and constellations and an initial mouth washing before the various divine encounters. The fourth mouth washing and opening in the Nineveh version (NR 151) mark the encounter with the gods on the second day, while the fifth mouth-washing and opening in the Nineveh version (NR 161) and the thirteenth mouth-washing in the Babylonian version (BR 47) seem to mark the transition from the first divine encounter to the craftsmen scene that follows. The final mouth washing (and opening) (BR 63) accompanies the divine installation in the temple and serves as a sign that the ritual is finally complete. Throughout these stages, the ritual connects various elements and actors to the statue[182] and, in doing so, defines their roles both in enabling the necessary transition and in serving the deity in the aftermath of that transition.

The key figures on the divine level are Ea, Shamash, and to a lesser extent Asalluhi, and on the human level the officiating priests and the artisans.[183] As in

---

179. As in Egypt, one may say that the ritual is indexically connected to the workshop and the temple, the first as the starting point and the second as the endpoint of the ritual process, and thus serves to connect the two areas.

180. The context in which they appear also helps to inform the reader what mouth washing and opening accomplish both on a general level and in each occasion (see ideology).

181. "Mouth-opening" here appears in parantheses because it never appears explicitly in the Babylonian version, and the Ninevite version, which lists both mouth washing and opening, is broken at this point (NR 81–87).

182. For example, the holy water basin, the artisans' tools, and the divine regalia.

183. On the priests of the ritual, see Bottéro, "Magie. A. In Mesopotamien," *RlA* 7 (1990):

Egypt, the common people bear no mention at all. Throughout the ritual, there is a progression toward the various deities, with the focus moving from Ea to Shamash and finally to the statue itself.[184] In fact, this movement also serves as a legitimate way of dividing the ritual into three segments.

The first stage in the workshop and river is dominated by the figure of Ea, to whom the majority of actions and incantations are addressed. In the second stage in the orchard, Shamash is the primary figure, while Ea and Asalluhi also figure prominently, and the majority of incantations address the triad with a special emphasis on Shamash. In this section, the statue also begins to figure prominently. In the third stage at the temple, the statue and its regalia dominate and are the subject of the incantations.[185] Throughout the ritual the statue is connected to the various deities with Ea and Shamash as the primary figures in successive episodes, while in the climax the other deities, although present, largely recede into the background. By contrast, the incantations indicate the statue's increasingly active role until at the end the statue becomes the primary figure.[186] Thus, ritual words and actions suggest that the ritual focuses on integrating the statue into the divine realm and, once this is accomplished, into the cultic realm of the temple.[187]

There is a concomitant movement both toward and away from the human participants. The artisans feature prominently in the ritual. However, as in Egypt, the ritual keeps their contact with the statue to a minimum, one that lacks the intimacy of the priestly participants. When they do appear, they are indexically connected to the statue so that they may be thematically disconnected from its production and further care. This is made abundantly clear when the artisans'

---

225–28; Berlejung, *Theologie der Bilder*, 185–88; Walker and Dick, *The Mesopotamian* mīs pî *Ritual*, 15–16; cf. Graham Cunningham, *"Deliver Me from Evil": Mesopotamian Incantations, 2500–1500 BC* (Studia Pohl 17; Rome: Pontifcio Istituto Biblico, 1997), 13–16.

184. First, and most obviously, the texts explicitly mention Ea, Shamash, and the god's divine brethren. In addition, the rituals in which the deities are invoked occur in settings with clear connections to those gods. The encounter with Ea occurs at the water (the threshold of his domain), while the statue meets Shamash with the sunrise. The repeated refrain that the deity join with his divine brethren in the settings in which such an encounter would be natural (e.g., in the stars; see Erica Reiner, *Astral Magic in Babylonia* [Transactions of the American Philosophical Society 85; Philadelphia: American Philosophical Society, 1995], 139–43) establish the connection between the statue and the realm of the divine.

185. Berlejung, "Washing the Mouth," 68–69; idem, *Theologie der Bilder*, 204–5.

186. A change in the means of address also highlights the changing role of the statue. The priest first speaks into the statue's ear and later stands before the statue (Berlejung, "Washing the Mouth," 63; Walker and Dick, "Induction of the Cult Image," 66 n. 118).

187. For example, NR 88–93 urges Ea to integrate the statue into the divine community, while NR 164–72 indicates the realization of this goal and instead urges the statue to undertake its terrestrial role in relation to the king, temple, and land, which then dominate the proceedings.

hands are bound and symbolically severed; when they disavow their participation in crafting the deity, while simultaneously avowing that the statue was crafted by the divine; and when they are absent from the ritual's conclusion, particularly the procession to the temple and the statue's installation. In this case, the ritual's primary impetus is to transition the statue from the human to divine realm.

However, since the statue abides in the human realm, it must remain connected to humanity. Thus, as the artisans are phased out of the life of the statue, the priests, as servants of the divine, take their place. Throughout the ritual, the priests are the main actors. Instead of moving away and disentangling themselves from the statue, the priests move toward it. They perform all of the major ritual actions and recite the majority of its incantations.[188] They alone come into contact with and address the statue in an intimate way.[189] Thus, the transitional setting of the ritual transfers the deity from the human to the divine realm and its care from the artisans to the priests.

While generally absent in Egypt, there is significant movement in the spatial sphere in the Mesopotamian mouth-washing ritual. The ritual physically transitions the statue from the workshop to the sanctuary, from its temporary home to its permanent residence. In the process, it moves from the interior (the workshop) to the exterior (the river and orchard) and through the city into a new and improved interior space (the temple).

## Use

As the spatial progression indicates, the purpose of the ritual is to transition the statue from workshop to temple, from approved cult statue to fully functioning locus of divine presence. Various utterances accompany this transition, providing the reader with "native" interpretations. Purity is an especially prominent theme in nearly all of the incantations, while other purpose statements appear selectively throughout the course of the ritual and often seem to build on each other. Purity especially features during the first day, while purpose statements regarding the statue's functionality are particularly prominent on the second day. Here, only some of the most pertinent will be highlighted.

As the statue prepares to leave the workshop, the priest informs the statue of its impending encounter with Ea with the wish that the statue and Ea are pleased with each other (NR 61–63). This suggests that the river episode serves as an encounter with Ea and that his and the statue's mutual satisfaction is one of its goals.

---

188. The major exception seems to be the artisans' disavowal of their role, which distances them from the deity.

189. For example, a priest whispers into the statue's ears. However, the intimacy seems less pronounced than that in Egypt, where the statue is embraced. The king is also mentioned at the end of the ritual as the incantations urge the statue to "draw near to the king who knows your voice; approach your temple" (IT 3 C 11–12).

Before transitioning to the orchard, the incantation (NR 88–93) asserts that the statue's mouth is washed and implores Ea to count him with his divine brethren, which likewise suggests that integration into the divine sphere is a central theme of the following section. NR 164–72 suggest the realization of this plea—"From today may your destiny be counted as divinity; with your brother gods you are counted"[190]—and implore the statue to approach the king, its temple, and its land. The incantations, "As you grew up" and "Statue born in heaven,"[191] continue this theme of integration into the deity's terrestrial realm with the plea that the statue be the temple's good protective deity (lamassu) and stay there forever (IT 4 A 10–11; 60–62).

The incantation, "Ea, Shamash, and Asalluhi,"[192] urges the triad to "grant [the statue] the destiny that his mouth may eat, that his ears might hear" in addition to the usual plea for purity, "May the god become pure like heaven" (IT 3 B 36–38). The statue's destiny is thus in some way linked to its ability to eat and hear. In the incantation, "On the day when the god was created,"[193] Asalluhi asserts that "this statue without its mouth opened cannot smell incense, cannot eat food, nor drink water" (STT 200 43–44; IT 3 B 70–71),[194] suggesting that a purpose of the mouth-opening rite is to enable the deity to partake of these human-like functions. "As you grew up" then follows with the realization of the deity's animation process: Ea "has brought your divinity to completion! He has prepared your mouth for eating!" (IT 4 A 18–19). Similarly, while "Ea, Shamash, and Asalluhi" urges the deities who make the divine decisions to grant the statue its destiny, "As you grew up" implores Shamash, as the divine judge par excellence, to uphold the new deity's decisions once its fate has been determined.[195] Finally, NR 179–86 seem to interpret the binding and "severing" of the artisans' hands with a wooden sword (STT 200 61–76 [IT 3 B 82ab–91a] in tandem with NR 173–75 and BR 49–52) as the artisans' disavowal of their role in their crafting process.

---

190. NR 167–68; translation after Walker and Dick, "Induction of the Cult Image," 95; idem, *The Mesopotamian* mīs pî *Ritual*, 65.

191. "As you grew up" is recited in BR 53 and corresponding to NR 188, while "Statue born in heaven" is recited in BR 54 and NR 190.

192. Recited at NR 144.

193. Recited at NR 160.

194. Translation after Walker and Dick, "Induction of the Cult Image," 99. In their follow-up book, Walker and Dick translate line 70 as "this statue cannot smell incense without the 'Opening of the Mouth' ceremony" (*The Mesopotamian* mīs pî *Ritual*, 151).

195. IT 4 A 12: "May Shamash heed your true decision." Berlejung interprets the verse slightly differently as Shamash "taking responsibility for" the deity's "true decisions" ("Washing the Mouth," 63–64; cf. idem, *Theologie der Bilder*, 455).

## *Ideology*

Given that the ritual exists to transition the statue from the workshop to the temple and the appropriate end result is the full divine presence in the sanctuary in the form of the cult statue, how is the ritual structured to bring about this transition? As noted, two elements are especially prominent in the mouth-washing ritual, namely, purity and cultic functionality. Everything associated with the statue must be perfectly pure as the gods are perfectly pure in order for the statue to commune with the gods and itself serve as the locus of divine presence on earth. From beginning to end the incantations stress the need for and pursuit of purity, of the statue and the various elements used to construct, purify, and vitalize it as well as the divine regalia. In addition to being free from physical and olfactory imperfection, the requisite purity also seems to be a divine quality, such that to be suitably pure the statue must be free from more than human imperfection; it must also be freed from its humble human origins.[196] Since these origins cannot be simply denied, they are transformed such that through the power of ritual words and actions the statue becomes divine and divinely crafted from its inception to its present state. Thus, a large part of the ritual is concerned with this very process, with transforming the statue from a largely human to a purely divine product. As will become clear, the ritual uses multiple, repeated, and not always consistent means to achieve this transformation.

In addition to a purity befitting the gods, the statue also must be able to function as god on earth. Fundamentally, since divine service is primarily anthropomorphic, the deity in or as the statue must have human-like needs (or at least preferences) or else all of the elaborate care will be in vain. If the deity cannot taste the offerings, smell the incense, or more expansively enjoy clothing, jewelry, and entertainment proffered for its pleasure, it will not respond favorably with sustained presence and blessing. From the divine side of the equation, as we have seen, the very purpose of humanity is to provide cultic service. Thus, if the deity cannot enjoy this service, it will be denied the very luxuries for which it created humanity. Rather than assume that the deity as or in the statue already possesses these functions, the ritualists realize that it is unnatural for a statue to be able to enjoy such human pursuits. Thus, it must be ritually activated, to be filled with positive potencies so that it can fulfill and enjoy its cultic role.[197] Although, as we will see, the statue is always divine, it is like a newborn at the beginning of the ritu-

---

196. Although present in Egypt, there is a greater emphasis in Mesopotamia on eliminating the human element, of making the cult image a purely divine product.

197. Such activation remains necessary even if the primary cult image is not anthropomorphic, so that the image may partake of human offerings. For example, K 63a and K 3367 transfer verbatim the assertion that the statue cannot eat, drink, or smell incense until its mouth is open to the lunar crescent of Sin (*askaru*) (Walker and Dick, *The Mesopotamian mīs pî Ritual*, 14).

al sequence that must be brought to maturity before it can function as an adult.[198] It must gain mastery over the basic human functions—eating, drinking, and smelling—so that it may enjoy human offerings. More expansively, the statue must be assimilated into its divine community and know and be empowered to fulfill its divine role as the ruler and protector of the land and its people, in short as god on earth. Like purification, this ritual activation occurs multiple times and multiple ways throughout the course of the ritual.

Thus, as in Egypt, one action is insufficient. Instead, the mouth-washing ritual for a cult statue employs a multiplicity of means (both word and deed) to ritually accomplish the desired ends.[199] In fact, the very complexity of the ritual indicates its importance.[200] For example, of the various mouth washings and mouth openings described in the Mesopotamian texts, the "duration, expenditure and complexity" of the mouth washing of the cult statue set it apart as especially important.[201] Instead of positing a single solution, this ritual puts forth multiple solutions; realizing that no single solution will do, it uses as many as possible to cover all the bases.[202] To produce such a cumulative effect, repetition appears as a way of enhancing the meaningfulness of the words and actions (e.g., the statue's mouth is washed and opened multiple times in multiple contexts throughout the mouth-washing ritual, while many incantations are repeated threefold [e.g., NR 59, 60–64, 88–95, and 137]). Instead of indicating sloppy writing or editing, the repetitions appear to bolster the ritual's effectiveness, on the premise that repeating words and actions in different settings somehow makes what is said and done more of a reality. Individual activities often have more than one function. In particular, the various incantations serve to translate various human activities into the divine sphere, thus transforming the mundane into the supramundane. Rather than simply providing a running commentary, such ritual words have a power of their own,

---

198. In Egypt, by contrast, there is little hint of maturation.

199. Thus, searches for primary and secondary means of transformation are often misguided.

200. The multiple means ritualize the activity, setting it apart from both normal activities and other less elaborate rituals.

201. Berlejung, "Washing the Mouth," 45; see further Hurowitz, "Impure Lips," 48-51, 53-57; Berlejung, *Theologie der Bilder*, 182–85; Walker and Dick, *The Mesopotamian mīs pî Ritual*, 10-15.

202. Although it is difficult to positively identify the ritual's diachronic development, after Walker and Dick (*The Mesopotamian mīs pî Ritual*, 16–20) it seems reasonable to assume that the ritual started rather simply (e.g., following the pattern of STT 200) and in accord with the cumulative approach accrued multiple, complex, and not always consistent elements that comprise the current version of the mouth-washing ritual. Likewise, the ritual seems to have developed along similar yet nonetheless distinct trajectories in Babylonia and Assyria.

capable of enacting ritual transformation. For example, Ea encourages Asalluhi to "purify (the holy water) by your pure incantation" (IT 6/8 43).

Together, the effort, expenditure, and exactitude serve as an attempt to elicit, perhaps even to guarantee, that the gods respond appropriately and fully endow the statue with divinity. Indeed, when the result cannot be easily verified, when the ritualists cannot empirically prove that the statue is the fully functioning locus of divine presence, such complexity is necessary to cover all the bases and maximize the chances of ritual efficacy.

This ritual approach also accords with the general aspective approach, which often presents an object, person, or deity as an assemblage of parts that may be presented (semi-)independently and need not perfectly cohere.[203] Ritual too as a whole consists of an accumulation of complex and not always consistent parts that together produce a more comprehensive effect. By contrast, logical and unified rituals with simple and often single means of achieving the desired end may be considered insufficient.

### Ideology of Individual Elements

After the initial preparations, the ritual proper begins on what at first seems an unremarkable note.[204] NR 55 simply indicates the current location and origin of the statue, "in the house of the craftsmen, where the god was created" (*banû*). However, in the context of the larger ritual, the statement is important; it speaks of the present and obvious condition of the statue that cannot be denied, yet through the power of ritual can be changed. It addresses the perceived condition of the statue before the ritual, as the product of human handiwork and human materials in a human workshop, which the ritual seeks to overcome multiple times in multiple ways in order that the statue may be purely a product of the divine sphere.

The following libation and fumigation, sweeping, and sprinkling pure water before the statue begins this transformative process, serving respectively as the first devotionary gift to the new image[205] and as a means of creating perfectly pure

---

203. See generally with reservations, esp. concerning her evolutionary theories, Brunner-Traut, *Frühformen des Erkennens* (see further ch. 8 n. 272); see more specifically with regard to Mesopotamia Hundley, "Here a God."

204. The purifications with censer, torch, and holy-water basin mark the initial purifications in preparation for the upcoming ritual (NR 41). Regarding the cleansing efficacy of the holy water basin, torch, and censer, see Maul, *Zukunftsbewältigung*, 41–46, 62, 94–97; Giovanni Conti, "Incantation de l'eau bénite et de l'encensoir et textes connexes," *MARI* 8 (1997): 253–54. Regarding the censer in particular, see Piotr Michalowski, "The Torch and the Censer," in *The Tablet and the Scroll: Near Eastern Studies Honor of William W. Hallo* (ed. M. Cohen, D. Snell and D. Weisberg; Bethesda: CDL, 1993), 152–62; Maul, *Zukunftsbewältigung*, 52; Conti, "Incantation de l'eau bénite."

205. Berlejung, "Washing the Mouth," 52.

space befitting a deity in the workshop. Sweeping the ground and sprinkling pure water (*mê ellûti*) remove all material impurities,[206] while the fumigation removes all olfactory impurity. As in Egypt, fumigation with a censer purifies the air,[207] cloaking the area in the appropriate divine aroma[208] and thereby cleansing it of the impure odors of the mundane world.[209] Over the course of the ritual, fumigation, libation, and often offerings occur any time a deity is approached outside of the temple sphere, in effect creating a bubble of divine space in the midst of the human world so that the deity may safely manifest itself.[210]

From the beginning of the ritual the statue is addressed as a god (*ilu*).[211] Thus, rather than being an inert object of human craftsmanship that must be deified, the statue is always a god that must instead be vitalized or rendered cultically operative.[212] As an approved image, the statue from the beginning partakes of the divine essence.[213] However, in order to arrive at divine plenitude—that is, in order to be a fully functioning locus of divine presence—the deity must undergo an enlivening ritual, which imbues the statue with the other essential elements of divinity, culminating with its investiture with ritually charged divine regalia. Only then is the

---

206. On the purifying effect of sweeping, see Maul, *Zukunftsbewältigung*, 48.

207. In addition, IT 1/2 C 9 explicitly states that swinging the censer over the statue makes it "clean and bright."

208. Or at least an aroma acceptable to and appropriate for the deity.

209. Divine air must be pure and, in order to enter the divine presence, so too must the priestly aroma (cf. Nielsen, *Incense in Ancient Israel*, 31). Thus, it is little wonder that "incense burners always are placed between the deity and the suppliant" (ibid., 32).

210. Regarding fumigation, see NR 57 for Ea, Asalluhi, and the god, 77 for Ea and Asalluhi, NR 102 for Anu, Enlil, Ea, Sin, Shamash, Adad, Marduk, Gula, and Ninsianna, NR 107 for Dingirmah, Kusu, Ningirima, Ninkurra, Ninagal, Kusibanda, Ninildu, Ninzadim, and the cult statue, NR 116 for Ea, Shamash, and Asalluhi, NR 148 for Kusu, Ningirima, Ninkurra, Ninagal, Kusibanda, Ninildu and Ninzadim and perhaps also in the broken line NR 157.

211. See, e.g., BR 2 "the god" (*ilu*) and NR 55–56 "the god" (*ilu*) twice. On the identification of the statue as divine from the outset, see Berlejung, *Theologie der Bilder*, 214 and *passim*; idem, "Washing the Mouth," 52 and *passim*; Hurowitz, "Mesopotamian God Image," 150; *contra* Manfried Dietrich and Oswald Loretz, *'Jahwe und seine Aschera': Anthropomorphes Kultbild in Mesopotamien, Ugarit und Israel: Das biblische Bilderverbot* (UBL 9; Münster: Ugarit-Verlag, 1992), 36; Dietrich, "Der Werkstoff wird Gott: Zum mesopotamischen Ritual der Umwandlung eines leblosen Bildwerks in einem lebendigen Gott," *MARG* 7 (1992): 124; Peggy Jean Boden, "The Mesopotamian Washing of the Mouth (*Mīs Pî*) Ritual: An Examination of the Social and Communication Strategies Which Guided the Development and Performance of the Ritual Which Transferred the Essence of the Deity Into Its Temple Statue" (Ph.D. dissertation, Johns Hopkins University, 1998), 222; Walker and Dick, "Induction of the Cult Image," 114.

212. See similarly regarding the Egyptian Opening of the Mouth Finnestad, "Meaning, and Purpose" 121.

213. Bahrani, *Graven Image*.

deity as statue able to take up residence in its temple and fulfill its role as protector of its realm.

More than simply being an approved likeness (*ṣalmu*) and, as such, in some way divine, the very natural elements that are used to craft the deity are themselves divine.[214] For example, the Erra epic refers to the *mēsu*-wood used to craft divine images as the "flesh of the gods" (*šīr ilī*),[215] while elsewhere the tamarisk wood, used in the mouth-washing ritual, is labeled "bones of divinity."[216] In the course of the mouth-washing ritual, the incantation, "Tamarisk pure wood,"[217] identifies the tamarisk tree as the substance from which gods are made, which is also tended and purified by the gods.[218] Regarding the precious stones, Esarhaddon suggests that Ea himself designates the stones for use in the cult image, which like the gods, are characterized by radiance (*melammu*). Rather than naturally inhering in these elements, their radiance is assigned to them by Ea himself.[219] Thus, rather than becoming a god, the statue is considered a god ever since its elements were planted in nature by the gods.[220] Nonetheless, although a god, the statue is essentially a newborn that must be purified, vitalized, and taught its place in the world. In effect, the mouth-washing ritual serves to bring about the divine maturation.

After the initial purifications, the mouth-washing and mouth-opening rituals follow.[221] As in Egypt, mouth washing and opening, whether performed on a cult statue, a person, a hunting bag, torch, or even a river, enable each element to

---

214. See esp. Hurowitz, "What Goes In."

215. Hurowitz, "What Goes In," 5–6, 11–12.

216. *Šep lemutti* 81–82: "Bones of divinity, holy tamarisk, pure wood" (Walker and Dick, *The Mesopotamian* mīs pî *Ritual*, 100 n. 70). Likewise, the *bīnu*-tree is designated "bone of divinity" (*eṣemti ilī*) (Wiggermann, *Mesopotamian Protective Spirits*, 81; Hurowitz, "What Goes In," 6) or "bone of the Igigi-gods" (*eṣemti Igigi*) (*Maqlu* VI 5) (Hurowitz, "What Goes In," 6).

217. Mentioned in BR 9; IT 1/2 B 1–4; translated in Berlejung, *Theologie der Bilder*, 443; Walker and Dick, *The Mesopotamian* mīs pî *Ritual*, 100–101.

218. See also "Statue, Born in Heaven" (NR 190; BR 54; IT 4 A 23–65; translated in Berlejung, *Theologie der Bilder*, 456–68; Walker and Dick, *The Mesopotamian* mīs pî *Ritual*, 184–85).

219. Borger, *Die Inschriften Asarhaddons*, 83, § 53, AsBbA rev. 30–32; Hurowitz, "What Goes In," 9. See further Berlejung, *Theologie der Bilder*, 127–43.

220. In Egypt, it is also possible that at least in some circumstances the statue was perceived as divine from the beginning. For example, an inscription of Ramesses II describes how the deity in the form of its cult statue was already waiting in the mountain for the king to discover (Cairo CGC 34504; Kitchen, *Ramesside Inscriptions 2*, 361 l. 1–362 l. 12; English translation in Kitchen, *Ramesside Inscriptions: Translated 2*, 193–95).

221. Although they are clearly an integral element in the ritual, the ritual nowhere states explicitly the words or actions necessary to effect mouth washing or opening.

fulfill its intended, often cultic role—in essence bringing it to maturation.[222] As the primary means of maturing the statue, that is, of separating it from all unsavory influences (including its human origins) and filling it with the necessary divine potencies, mouth washing and opening occur periodically over the course of the ritual.[223] Mouth washing, which serves as a prerequisite for mouth opening,[224] seems to effect perfect purity in the statue.[225] Once the statue is properly purified and, as such, able to commune with its divine brethren,[226] the mouth opening seems to activate the divinity's faculties,[227] in effect making the deity in or as the statue cultically operative. In line with the maturation metaphor, mouth opening with ghee and honey may even be related to an ancient child-rearing practice. Like an infant, the statue is perhaps being trained to distinguish between different tastes and odors. Since honey is sweet and ghee is sour, an animate statue that partakes of offerings, like a child, should learn to distinguish between them.[228]

---

222. For example, the mouth opening of a river (Egbert von Weiher, *Spätbabylonische Texte aus Uruk* II [ADFU 10; Berlin: Mann, 1983], no. 5 rev. 46–48) explicitly empowers it to regain its former function (rev. 71; Berlejung, *Theologie der Bilder*, 189).

223. However, mouth washing and opening should not be understood entirely incrementally, as if the incremental effect of each mouth washing and opening can be quantified until enough mouth washings and openings are performed for the statue to take up residence in its temple. Rather, each mouth washing and opening likely functions in tandem with the various other ritual words and actions to produce a cumulative effect.

224. As noted, in the rituals where mouth opening appears, mouth washing always precedes it in the ritual sequence (Walker and Dick, *The Mesopotamian* mīs pî *Ritual*, 13–14).

225. Berlejung, "Washing the Mouth," 45; Walker and Dick, *The Mesopotamian* mīs pî *Ritual*, 12; Hurowitz, "Mesopotamian God Image," 147; for comparative material, see Hurowitz, "Impure Lips."

226. Hurowitz, "Impure Lips," 52; Berlejung, *Theologie der Bilder*, 182–85; Walker and Dick, *The Mesopotamian* mīs pî *Ritual*, 13.

227. Berlejung, "Washing the Mouth," 45; idem, *Theologie der Bilder*, 190; Walker and Dick, *The Mesopotamian* mīs pî *Ritual*, 14–15; Hurowitz, "Mesopotamian God Image," 147. As noted, this purpose is explicit in the incantation tablets, as "this statue without its mouth opened cannot smell incense, cannot eat food, nor drink water" (STT 200 42–44, translation from Walker and Dick, "Induction of the Cult Image," 99; so also IT 3 70–71 in Walker and Dick, *The Mesopotamian* mīs pî *Ritual*). Similarly, since the completion of the ritual and the very fate of the deity lies with the great gods (Ea, Shamash, and Asalluhi), the priest implores them to grant the statue the ability to eat and to hear (IT 3 6–25, 33–37; Walker and Dick, *The Mesopotamian* mīs pî *Ritual*, 148–49).

228. Hurowitz, "Mesopotamian God Image," 152 and n. 18; cf. H. M. Y. Gevaryahu, "Ghee and Honey He Will Eat (Isaiah 7)," in *Sepher Eliyahu Auerbach* (ed. A. Birarn; Jerusalem: Kiryat Sepher, 5715), 169–74 (Hebrew).

## Excursus: A Comparison of Versions

The discrepancy between the Nineveh and Babylon versions, where the former always lists a mouth washing and opening together and the latter refers only to mouth washing, must be shortly addressed. Walker and Dick contend that it is more logical to expect one or the other rite and thus reconstruct their expected sequence: mouth washing in BR 2, NR 58; BR 11, 24; BR 26; NR 104, 108; mouth opening in NR 150; BR 47, and NR 161; mouth washing in BR 63 (IT 5 C 25).[229] Along these lines, they suggest that day one focuses on mouth washing, while day two focuses on mouth opening.[230] In support of their reconstruction, they note that the Babylonian recension provides the expected order in every case except for line 47.[231] However, this evidence does not have much explanatory value since the Babylonian version always uses mouth washing, and BR 47 is the only time they instead suggest a mouth opening.

It seems more likely that at least in the literary understanding of both ritual versions, mouth washings and openings were performed together and repeatedly. As Walker and Dick note, the Sippar tablet of Nabu-apla-iddina, like the Babylonian version, only mentions mouth washing.[232] Nonetheless, in light of STT 200, where the mouth washing precedes the mouth opening, Walker and Dick suggest that a mouth opening was likely also performed such that the reference to mouth washing "would seem to be early evidence for the naming of the whole ritual 'mouth washing' (pars pro toto)."[233] In accord with the cumulative perspective, the Babylonian version would seem to work on the same principle, such that each time mouth washing is mentioned, mouth opening as in the Nineveh version should also be assumed. Rather than being pure conjecture, this finds support in STT 200 79–80 (IT 3 B 92–93), which mentions opening the mouth fourteen times with honey, butter, cedar, and cypress, corresponding to the fourteen mouth washings listed in the Babylonian recension. Although the focus shifts from purification to empowerment and as such from mouth washing to mouth opening, elements of purification and empowerment are present throughout. For example, the initial focus on purification seems to be accompanied by a ritual activation of the statue's perceptual functions such that it may respond to the priest's address.[234]

---

229. Walker and Dick, *The Mesopotamian mīs pî Ritual*, 17. They also note that, if the Ninevite ritual reflects actual practice, it "seems to have moved a long way from the original concept of the ritual" (ibid.), moving from simple to increasingly complex.

230. Ibid., 14.

231. Ibid., 17.

232. Ibid.

233. Ibid.

234. Admittedly, mouth opening is not absolutely necessary since mouth washing likewise serves to facilitate communication. Making the mouth pure in effect enables it to speak.

Thus, depending on the context, one or the other rite was prominent, yet both were likely performed together for the cumulative effect.

\* \* \*

The holy-water basin, associated with mouth washing, is especially appropriate to the task of washing the statue's mouth. On a mundane level, it is filled with various elements with known purifying properties.[235] By amassing them all in one place and applying them to the statue, the Mesopotamians seem to envisage a more thorough and thus more effective purification. At the same time, each of the elements included in the basin (BR 16–20) is in some ways associated with a particular god in a cultic commentary, such that by including these elements the powers of their associated gods are brought to bear.[236] In other words, by increasing the number of purifying agents, the ritual tradents increase the number of participating gods and the potency and efficacy of the purificatory act.[237] In addition, the only "evil" gods mentioned, such as Anzu, have been defeated, such that the holy-water basin itself reenacts the victory of good over evil. Thus, the water may at once remove all impurities and overcome all evil forces hypothetically arrayed against the statue.[238]

With the initial mouth washing, mouth opening, and associated purifications, it would seem that the statue's perceptual functions have been activated, such that it may respond to the priest's address to go with a happy heart before Ea its father.[239] In other words, through ritual activation the deity's ears and heart now function. Likewise, mouth washing ensures a heightened state of purity necessary for an encounter with deity.[240] The introduction of Ea marks another important stage in the ritual, hinting that as the divine craftsman Ea may also have a role to play in the image's construction and activation. With the reference to Ea as its father, the text suggests that Ea's role may have a biological as well as mechanical

---

235. Reiner, *Šurpu: A Collection of Sumerian and Akkadian Incantations* (AfO Beiheft 11; Graz: E. Weidner, 1958), IX; Maul, *Zukunftsbewältigung*, 41–46; Berlejung, "Washing the Mouth," 52. STT 198 rev. i 63 (IT 1/2 B) contains the incantations for tamarisk, soapwort, reed, and horned alkali, which through the incantations are imbued with the power to purify the god's mouth (ibid., 52 n. 30).

236. Livingstone, *Mystical and Mythological Explanatory Works*, 176–79; Berlejung, *Theologie der Bilder*, 224–27; cf. idem, "Washing the Mouth," 59. The cultic commentary makes the associations without anywhere explaining them (idem, *Theologie der Bilder*, 225).

237. Ibid., 226.

238. Ibid.

239. Idem, "Washing the Mouth," 52; idem, *Theologie der Bilder*, 214–15. Ea is considered so important in the crafting process that he could be named father (idem, "Geheimnis und Ereignis," 110).

240. As we will see, the following incantation likewise stresses the purity of the statue.

component.[241] In addition, it marks the beginning of the next major stage in the ritual, in which Ea and the craftsmen gods are the dominant figures.

Taking the hand of the god signals a change in scene.[242] The destination of the procession is conspicuously identified as the ṣēru, which on the horizontal plane denotes the wild, uncultivated, and sometimes demonic land, while on the vertical plane it serves as the transition from the world of the living to the world of the dead.[243] As such, it is the location of both mythological and political adversaries and the place where impurities can be disposed of without affecting anything of consequence.[244] Thus, it would seem that in order to become the fully functioning god on earth the statue must leave the safe confines of the workshop to pass through the dangers of the wilderness. However, the ritual locale and preparations minimize any danger. The term ṣēru is unsuitable to both the river and the orchard, doubly so since the river and orchard like the workshop presumably rested within the safe confines of the Mesopotamian temple compound and were only accessible to temple personnel.[245] Thus, as in Egypt, the Mesopotamian temple

---

241. The incantation mentioned in BR 3, "Born in heaven by your own power," following the mouth washing, may even suggest that, in addition to being made and born (Sumerian tu[d]), the statue might also be self-created—i.e., the deity in heaven created his statue on earth. However, the Akkadian version suggests rather that the "heavens were created (banû) by their own power," while the incantation itself addresses the purity of the priest, which would seem to be requisite for touching the now perfectly pure divine statue (Berlejung, "Washing the Mouth," 53; idem, Theologie der Bilder, 215–16). Nonetheless, as we will see with regard to the lamentations during the daily cult, a recitation may be included because it includes a key phrase that establishes a desired connection, especially when that phrase is found in the incipit (see esp. Uri Gabbay, "The Performance of Emesal Prayers within the Regular Temple Cult: Content and Ritual Setting," in Kaniuth et al., eds., Tempel im Alten Orient, 103–22). Not every detail of the incantation need make the same connection or even be relevant to the ritual in which it is recited. In this case, although the incantation primarily addresses other relevant issues, we should not dismiss the connection with birth made in the incipit. For translations, see Berlejung, Theologie der Bilder, 437; Walker and Dick, The Mesopotamian mīs pî Ritual, 119. For an analysis of the allusions to birth, see further below.

242. For the expression "taking the hand," see Pongratz-Leisten, Ina šulmi īrub, 171–74.

243. See the diagram in ibid., 32, 18–19. For the contrasting terms ālu and ṣēru, see ibid., 18–19.

244. Berlejung, "Washing the Mouth," 53; idem, Theologie der Bilder, 217–18. Regarding the wild as a place of purification, see Maul, Zukunftsbewältigung, 48, 124–25; Wright, Disposal of Impurity, 255–56.

245. Berlejung, "Washing the Mouth," 50–51; Theologie der Bilder, 206–8. The river quay and the orchard belonged to the temple of Ea and are known as Ekarzagina ("House of the Quay of Lapis Lazuli" [alternatively "Quay of Splendor" (Walker and Dick, The Mesopotamian mīs pî Ritual, 24 n. 70)]) in historical inscriptions (George, Topographical Texts, 300–303; Maul, "Herzberuhigungsklagen": Die Sumerisch-akkadischen Eršahunga-

contained carefully controlled chaos that could be safely and easily overcome in the heart of the ordered world.

Along the way, the recitation "As you go out, as you go out, great…" builds on the connection with Ea and begins to separate the statue from its human origins, instead contending that the various woods used for the statue are pure and of supernatural quality, the tools are also pure, and the craftsmen are in fact the gods rather than human artisans. Thus, as the statue leaves the workshop, the ritual begins to divest it of its human and mundane qualities.[246]

The riverbank serves as a "cosmic quay," where Ea's underwater realm of the Apsu meets earth, and thus the most appropriate place for a first meeting with the statue's divine father. [247] At the riverbank, the image is further protected from any potential dangers by being seated on a reed mat so that it does not touch the ground, which is connected to the underworld.[248]

The tools and gold and silver tortoise and turtle, which are among Ea's sacred animals,[249] serve to further distance the statue from its human origins by eliminating the last material evidence of human craftsmanship.[250] As the craftsman god and the god of water, each element already is under Ea's divine jurisdiction. The presentation of the tools affirms his primary role in the craftsmanship process, while the silver and gold turtles sweeten the deal.[251]

Another mouth washing and opening follow,[252] which like the first, mark a ritual transition, from the river to the orchard, and from Ea to Shamash as the prime addressee. The setting of the mouth washing and opening after the presentation of the tools and animals and the addresses to Ea may suggest that Ea is present as witness to the mouth-washing proceedings and as the divine father lends his support to enhance their efficacy.[253] With the second mouth washing, the priest may now

---

*Gebete* [Wiesbaden: Harrasowitz, 1988], 123:9). However, the mouth-washing texts do not mention the Ekarzagina.

246. Cf., Berlejung, "Washing the Mouth," 54; idem, *Theologie der Bilder*, 218.

247. On the Apsu as cosmic quay, see George, *Topographical Texts*, 300.

248. Berlejung, "Washing the Mouth," 55 n. 46; idem, *Theologie der Bilder*, 219 n. 1171.

249. E. Ebeling, "Enki," *RlA* 2 (1938): 379; Seidl, "Göttersymbole und -attribute. A. Archäologisch. I. Mesopotamian," *RlA* 3 (1969): 488; Walker and Dick, "Induction of the Cult Image," 75 n. 60.

250. Cf., Berlejung, "Washing the Mouth," 55; idem, *Theologie der Bilder*, 219.

251. The ram-skin wrapping likely serves as a means of ensuring that the offerings stay together and arrive at their intended destination and also may be an offering in its own right.

252. Preserved in Br 11 and potentially in the lacuna between 81–87 of the Nineveh version.

253. Although the Nineveh version mentions both mouth washing and opening, the stress seems to be on the mouth-washing purification, especially in light of the incantations that precede (NR 59) and follow it (NR 88–93), stressing the purity of the statue.

affirm that the statue comes with his mouth washed and implore Ea to integrate him into the divine community, "with his (divine) brothers count him" (NR 93).

Once again led by hand, the statue is situated on another reed mat for the night in the middle of a circle of reed huts and standards and wrapped in linen cloth, and thereby carefully sequestered from his terrestrial surroundings and the hypothetical dangers associated with the "steppe."[254] His eyes are oriented toward the east so that he can see the sunrise and meet Shamash, the sun god, who is the dominant addressee in the orchard phase of the ritual. Here in the orchard the priest's plea to Ea becomes a reality, as the deity is introduced to his divine counterparts.[255]

The Babylonian version follows with the preparation of the holy water and its placement in a trough (*buginnu*), which is placed upon the brick of Dingirmah, a mother goddess. This passage in particular has occasioned some debate about whether or not these elements refer to birth. While Berlejung accepts some allusions to birth in the birthing brick of the mother goddess and repeated use of the number nine for the nine months of gestation,[256] she denies that there is any "evidence for the hypothesis that the mouth-washing ritual enacts the procreation and birth of the statue in the different stages of its evolution."[257] Although no doubt

---

254. Berlejung, *Theologie der Bilder*, 221. The *urigallu* were bundles of reeds grouped in a circle to enclose sacred space (Wiggermann, *Protective Spirits*, 70–71). For an example, see Collon, *First Impressions: Cylinder Seals in the Ancient Near East* (London: British Museum, 1987), 173 seal 803.

255. Berlejung suggests that the statue is "treated like a new-born child which had to be integrated to its own social environment" ("Washing the Mouth," 57; cf. idem, *Theologie der Bilder*, 222–23).

256. The brick has been connected to birth since Old Babylonian times (Livingstone, *Mystical and Mythological Explanatory Works*, 187). See further Anne D. Kilmer, "The Brick of Birth," *JNES* 46 (1987): esp. 211–13; Lambert and Alan R. Millard, *Atra-ḥasīs: The Babylonian Story of the Flood* (Oxford: Clarendon, 1969), 153.

257. Berlejung, "Washing the Mouth," 58–60; see more fully, idem, *Theologie der Bilder*, 135–41; *contra* Erich Ebeling, *Tod und Leben nach den Vorstellungen der Babylonier* (Berlin: de Gruyter, 1931), 100–101; Jacobsen, "The Graven Image," in *Ancient Israelite Religion: Essays in Honor of F. M. Cross* (ed. P. D. Miller, P. D. Hanson and S. D. McBride; Philadelphia: Fortress, 1987), 25–26, 28; Dietrich and Loretz, *Jahwe und seine Aschera*, 31; Dietrich, "Der Werkstoff wird Gott," 115–20; Boden, "Washing the Mouth," 222; Walker and Dick, "Induction of the Cult Image," 116–17; Hurowitz, "Mesopotamian God Image," 151–53; Dick, "Mesopotamian Cult Statue," 62–66. In particular, she denies the association of the trough (*buginnu*), placed upon the brick, with a womb filled with Ea's semen, i.e., the holy water ("Washing the Mouth," 58–60). She is certainly correct in asserting that the holy water basin and its contents are repeatedly and explicitly associated with purification, not birth, and that the association of the trough and its contents with a womb and Ea's semen is a bit of an interpretive stretch. However, granting that the holy water is primarily a "purification elixir" (ibid., 58), there is no reason to deny the possibility that the holy water

secondary, such allusions should not be dismissed and suggest that, in addition to the ritual's various other ways of overcoming the statue's humble origins, it uses birthing language to add a mytho-biological element.

Several texts use the Akkadian verb (w)alādu, "to give birth," "to beget," to refer to the manufacture of cult statues.[258] A text from Esarhaddon is especially telling as it refers to the statues of the great gods Bel, Beltiya, Belet-Babili, Ea and Madanu as being "truly born,"[259] labels Ea not their "father" (abu), but as their more corporeal "inseminator" (zārû) and proceeds to speak of their "birth and the physical growth as part of the maturation process."[260] In addition, the Sumerian equivalent tu(d) to (w)alādu, used elsewhere of divine statues, even appears in the incantation, "Born in heaven by your own power" (NR 59, 133; BR 3; STT 199), which begins "born in heaven by your own power, born in earth by your own power."[261] As noted, Ea is identified as the statue's divine father (NR 61, 63; BR 4). Later, the incantation, "Statue born in heaven," also employing the Sumerian tu(d), refers to the statue being raised by the goddesses like an infant (NR 190; IT 4 27, 29, 31, 58).[262] The verb kunnû "to tend with care," a verb often applied to the

---

can function on two levels at once, as both a "purification elixir" and an inseminated womb (Dick, "Mesopotamian Cult Statue," 62, notes here another possible allusion to birth in the blood in the three troughs [Nineveh l. 116] as referring to birth blood). More importantly, whether we accept this interpretation or not, it is important to acknowledge that the ritual intentionally functions on multiple levels at once. While the allusions to birth may be secondary in most cases, in aggregate they seem to be a secondary theme, functioning as one of the many means through which the ritual overcomes the statue's humble origins.

258. See the debate between Borger (Die Inschriften Asarhaddons, 83, n. 35; idem, "Review of Brief des Bischofs von Esagila an König Asarhaddon," BiOr 29 [1972]: 36) and Benno Landsberger (Brief des Bischofs von Esagila an König Asarhaddon [MKNAW Nieuwe Reeks 28/VI; Amsterdam: Noord-Hollandsche Uitg. Mij., 1965], 24–25, n. 38), summarized in Dick, "Mesopotamian Cult Statue," 62–63; Hurowitz ("Mesopotamian God Image," 151–53) and Dick ("Mesopotamian Cult Statue," 63–66) rightly follow Landsberger.

259. Porter, Images, Power, and Politics: Figurative Aspects of Esarhaddon's Babylonian Policy (Philadelphia: American Philosophical Society, 1993), 124; followed by Hurowitz, "Mesopotamian God Image," 152.

260. Hurowitz, "Mesopotamian God Image," 152.

261. Ibid.; Dick, "Mesopotamian Cult Statue," 63–64. As noted, this association is somewhat mitigated by the alternate rendering in the Akkadian, "the heavens were created by their own power, the earth was created by its own power" and the absence of any further reference to the statue in the incantation. It is even possible that the Akkadian translator opted for this alternate translation because he found references to the statue's birth and/or self-creation unpalatable.

262. IT 3 B 56 likewise suggests that the statue grew up in the forest (translation after Walker and Dick, The Mesopotamian mīs pî Ritual, 150, reading Sumerian è as Akkadian šāḫu).

care of children, is used in reference to Ninzadim's tender care of the statue (IT 4 30b).[263] As noted, the statue also seems to be treated as a newborn.[264]

At the outset, the ritual acknowledges the statue as a material construction made in the workshop by humans as a starting point that must be overcome. Through the power of ritual, the statue is made to be more than what it was at the outset, especially by transposing the mundane construction onto the mythic plane so that the image can transcend its humble beginnings. This emerges clearly regarding the materials used to construct the statues. Texts, including the mouth-washing ritual, proclaim the unused and untouched nature of the elements, which were tended by the gods and designated by them for this special use. For example, Esarhaddon boasts that only virgin materials were used, which had not been used for another purpose or been touched by human hands. Instead, Ea had designated them for this purpose and imbued them with the divine radiance (*melammu*).[265] In reality, however, although always of the highest quality, the materials used to construct statues had much humbler origins; they were "acquired from any available source."[266] For example, Esarhaddon's elaborate and expensive work on Babylon, restoring temples and repairing cult statues, followed his Egyptian campaigns

---

263. Hurowitz, "Mesopotamian God Image," 152.

264. Victor Hurowitz ("Mesopotamian God Image," 153) has noted some other possible effects of the birth allusions that merit being quoted in full:

> The interest in birth may, in fact, add an intertextual and mythological dimension to the ritual, in the form of parallels with the first tablet of Enūma Eliš. In that myth, the first gods are born of intercourse between Tiamat and Apsû. Tiamat is given the title mummu Tiamat (Mommy? Tiamat), and the gods are engendered (*ibbanû*) within her and Apsû (*qerebšum*). Birth of the first gods inside Mummu Tiamat certainly echoes cult statues being manufactured (or birthed) in the *bīt mummi* (Mommy's house). Later on, when Apsû is slain, Ea builds his abode on top of his corpse, incorporating it into his own domain. Marduk is born in Apsû (Ee I 81–82). This parallels the stage in the *Mīs pî* ritual at the riverbank, which is the domain of Ea and where incantations relating to the Apsû are recited (BR 10, 14). Moreover, Marduk is raised and suckled by goddesses (Ee I 84, 85), as is the cult statue (IT 4 A 23ab–33ab, 58ab). In other words, in its own gestation and growth into a god the cult statue passes through the two stages of evolution of the divine species in general. With the statue following in the footsteps of its mythological forebears, divine ontogeny recapitulates divine phylogeny. These parallels reflect an underlying belief that gods are born and develop in places called mummu and Apsû and are fathered, nurtured, and raised by divine beings. While the myth applies this belief to the mythological figures, the *Mīs pî* ritual applies it to the cult statue.

265. Borger, *Die Inschriften Asarhaddons,* 83, §53, AsBbA rev. 30-32; Hurowitz, "What Goes In," 9.

266. Hurowitz, "What Goes In," 11.

and likely was financed by its plunder.[267] Such a rewritten script, especially when read in the course of ritual, reimagines and thus transforms the statue's origins from the mundane to the supramundane, from the common to the perfectly pure. Although secondary, allusions to birth likewise serve this purpose by adding a mytho-biological element to the various other means of transformation.[268] Even if not always so overt, as in the case of the references to birth, such allusions form part of the transvaluation process, such that through the power of ritual the statue is reinvented, if not reborn, and made perfectly pure as the gods are perfectly pure.

In addition to the various allusions to the birth of the statue, there are also some references to the statue's self-creation, which serves as another way of overcoming the human role in the construction process. As noted, the twice repeated "born in heaven by your own power" refers to the statue's self-genesis.[269] In effect, the text seems to stress that the deity itself made, perhaps even "birthed," its image and thus approves of it. While not overtly denying human involvement, any human activity is thus reinterpreted as guided and empowered by the deity.[270]

---

267. Grant Frame, *Babylonia 689–627 B. C.: A Political History* (Istanbul: Nederlands Historisch-Archaeologisch Instituut te Istanbul, 1992), 76; Hurowitz, "What Goes In," 11; cf. John A. Brinkman, *Prelude to Empire: Babylonian Society and Politics, 747–626 B.C* (Occasional Publications of the Babylonian Fund 7; Philadelphia: University Museum, 1992), 76–77 n. 368.

268. Against reading the ritual as a birthing process, Berlejung contends that "the god was born in the workshop and not the Ekarzagina, orchard or riverbank. Once seated in the orchard (where some of the most prominent birth allusions appear), the image had already left the place of its birth." Thus, the workshop would have been more appropriate than the orchard for the "*mise en scène* of the procreation of the image" ("Washing the Mouth," 60). However, in making such a claim, she seems to be overlooking a crucial purpose of the ritual, namely, to acknowledge the initial state of the image so that it can be rewritten in various ways, including through birth allusions. As an ideal birthplace, which contrasts with the human workshop, the orchard in the sacred precinct and before the gods is thus the ideal place for the rewritten script to be rehearsed.

269. See further Hurowitz, "Mesopotamian God Image," 153–54. Note also the qualifications above in n. 261. The content of the verse need not nullify the thrust of its opening lines (*pace* Berlejung, "Washing the Mouth," 53; idem, *Theologie der Bilder*, 215–16). Instead, the self-created supernatural origin of the statue adds to the perfect purity of the statue enacted through mouth washing, thus necessitating the priest to stress his own purity.

270. See further below regarding the symbolic severing of the priestly hands. Cf. Hurowitz, "Mesopotamian God Image," 154. Elsewhere Sennacherib affirms that Assur is both self-created and that his images were made by the king (Daniel D. Luckenbill, *The Annals of Sennacherib* (OIP 2; Chicago: University of Chicago, 1924), 149 V 1–2, 6–7, 11; VAT 9656 = SAA 12.86 7–12), thereby equating his creation of the statue with Assur's self-creation (Hurowitz, "Mesopotamian God Image," 153–54). "The juxtaposition of the two actions actually equates them. Manufacturing the statue by the king is in fact a rehearsal of the mythological moment when Anšar (=Aššur) created himself and grew to physical maturity

Mouth-washing and -opening rites are especially prolific during the end of the first ritual day in the orchard as the statue is introduced into the divine community. The Nineveh version records a mouth washing and opening associated with the fumigation, offering, and libation before the nine most important gods of the day (NR 100–104) and another associated with the fumigation and offering before the eight gods of purification and craftsmanship and the statue itself (NR 105–108). While the fumigation and offering serve to elicit the divine presence, it seems that the various gods, in addition to integrating the statue into their midst, are called upon to witness and lend their support and potencies to the mouth-washing and -opening rites, thereby adding to their efficacy.[271] Such heightened purity and potency also ensure that the statue is ready for its encounter with the divine fraternity so that they are more apt to accept it into their midst. It is also noteworthy that the statue is included in the second list of nine. Rather than simply filling out the list, the presence of the statue among the other gods indicates the fulfillment of the priest's request to Ea, as the statue has now been integrated into the divine fraternity, an integration enabled by the statue's heightened potency and purity.[272] In accord with the newborn analogy and the mouth-opening's goal of enabling the statue to eat, drink, and smell (STT 200 43–44, 46), the offerings of food, drink, and incense also help to train these very senses of the statue.[273]

In addition to the mouth washings before the same two sets of gods (BR 25–28), in the Babylonian version an additional mouth washing precedes the encounter with divinity after setting up the holy water basin on the brick of Dingirmah (BR 24) and seven additional mouth washings follow it, one associated with each encounter with seven sets of stars and constellations.[274] The accompanying incantation, "Tamarisk, pure wood" speaks of the purity of the wood and makes a plea

---

in Apsû" (ibid., 154). Alternatively, Sennacherib simply could be ascribing to himself the great honor of making the cult image of a god who made himself in his natural form, i.e., while Assur came into being of his own accord, he entrusted the manufacture of his statue to Sennacherib.

271. The Babylonian incantation, "Tamarisk, pure wood" suggests that the focus here is on ritual purity and thus mouth washing, though mouth opening is likely also present.

272. Alternatively or perhaps even additionally, the mouth washing and opening before the different sets of deities may be preparatory, like the fumigation and offering, done to ritually activate the deity for each special encounter, to demonstrate to those gods the statue's suitability, and perhaps as a plea to join the activation process.

273. Cf. Berlejung, *Theologie der Bilder,* 258.

274. It seems that each star is a manifestation of deity or perhaps more distantly a conduit to the deity. It is even possible that Libra, as the star of Shamash, is to be understood as a semi-independent being in its own right, distinguished from Shamash the divine person introduced earlier. More likely, the statue encounters Shamash in his different forms, as an anthropomorphic personage, in the night sky, and as the daylight sun. On the roles of the stars, see Erica Reiner, *Astral Magic,* 139–43.

to the gods to make the statue as pure as the heavens, followed by similar incantations for the other purifying elements in the holy water basin. Thus, it would seem that in each encounter the various deities are implored to lend their potencies to the mouth-washing proceedings, to ensure the statue's perfect purity. Each mouth-washing also serves to heighten the statue's purity for each encounter with deity, so that it will be ready for the encounter and increase its likelihood of being accepted into the divine midst.

With the dawn of the second day, the ritual switches its attention from the gods in aggregate to Ea, Shamash, and Asalluhi, with a special emphasis on Shamash.[275] These three serve as the primary gods of so-called white magic,[276] the use of the supernatural powers in the universe for its good. Here, they are called on to bring their potencies to their task as the judges of heaven and earth, in which they determine the fates and oversee all of the cult places.[277] In particular, the priest requests that they determine the statue's destiny, qualified rather mundanely as the ability to eat and hear and perfect purity.[278] Following this thrice-repeated plea (BR 47), these fate-determining gods presumably lend their potency to the statue's mouth washing and opening (NR 150; BR 47).

The first hand-lifting prayer makes explicit what is already obvious, equating the god with the statue by placing the two in apposition, "On the day when the god was created, the pure statue was completed." Beyond this simple equation, the text reveals the statue's role as the visible manifestation of the otherwise distant deity resplendent with the divine radiance (*melammu*). The following lines stress that the statue grew up in the forest (STT 200 15; IT 3 B 56ab) and, after affirming that the statue is the creation of both gods and humans,[279] undercut this assertion, instead claiming divine craftsmanship. In effect, the text contends that while humans are present, it is the gods who really do the work.[280] Here, the process of separating the statue from its humble origins continues. Rather than being crafted by humans from the precious elements available to them, the incantation contends that the statue was made in both heaven and earth, that it grew up in the forest

---

275. Nonetheless, although less prominent, the other gods remain present, especially the various craftsmen gods, who will become more prominent with the artisans' oath.

276. Berlejung, *Theologie der Bilder*, 206.

277. The descriptors appear in the incantation, "Ea, Shamash and Asalluhi" (translation in Berlejung, *Theologie der Bilder*, 447–48; Walker and Dick, *The Mesopotamian* mīs pî *Ritual*, 148–49).

278. IT 3 B 36–39.

279. The Akkadian (STT 201) instead refers to the statue as in the form (*bunnannû*) of god and human, perhaps in an attempt to avoid attributing the statue's crafting to humans altogether, stressing instead its primarily anthropomorphic form.

280. It likewise ensures that humans did not work of their own accord, at their own initiative, or add their own innovations.

and came from the pure mountains, and that it was crafted by the craftsmen gods themselves.

Soon thereafter, we are confronted with one of the central problems facing the divine statue: "this statue without its mouth opened cannot smell incense, cannot eat food, nor drink water" (STT 200 43–44 [IT 3 B 70–71]). Asalluhi observes the insufficient state of the statue and questions his father Ea, who suggests the remedy, the holy water, which has been used to this effect throughout the ritual. Here, the priestly solution is transposed onto the mythic plane, in effect bringing the divine solution passed from divine father to divine son to earth or, perhaps more aptly, by making the human solution divine. The incantation (STT 200 61–76 [IT 3 B 82ab–91a] along with Nineveh 173–75 and Babylon 49–52) then narrates the climax of the statue's quest to overcome its humble origins. The human craftsmen have their hands symbolically severed and affirm what the incantations have been saying all along, that the gods alone made the statue. With their roles rewritten, the artisans leave the set for the last time.[281] STT 200 79–80 (IT 3 B 92–93) end on an odd note, asserting that humans opened the mouth of the statue fourteen times, an assertion undermined by the next incantation.[282] In the presence of the gods, the next mouth washing and opening seem to draw from its mythologically rewritten script to further purify and empower the statue.

Picking up where the last incantation left off, the second hand-lifting prayer instead asserts that Asalluhi opened the statue's mouth (IT 3 B 112–13). Once again, the priests affirm the present and obvious situation of the statue only to ritually rewrite it so that through the power of ritual word and action, human action becomes divine.

Following the second prayer, the officiant whispers into the god's—i.e., statue's—ear the verbal affirmation of the events enacted in the orchard. It is now one of the gods and is ready to fulfill its role in the land where it was "created to be released" (NR 171). Once released into its realm, the deity has ascended into its full divinity, a sign confirmed by the priest's new position before the god instead of at its side.[283]

The third prayer reaffirms the supernatural origin of the statue and urges the deity to become its temple's permanently present protector (lamassu). Although somewhat puzzling, the attribution of mouth opening to the priests after the previous incantation's attribution of the activity to Asalluhi seems to equate the two

---

281. That is, until a new statue must be constructed or an old statue refurbished.

282. Although the general progression from human to divine craftsmanship is clear throughout the ritual, the progression is not always linear or clearly articulated, given the compositeness of the text and the somewhat loose association between ritual and incantation texts.

283. Cf. Berlejung, "Washing the Mouth," 63.

actors, such that Asalluhi/Marduk is the guiding force behind the priestly mouth-opening.[284]

The fifth prayer reaffirms the statue's birth in heaven and the mountains, suggesting that although constructed of earthly materials, the materials were prepared and nurtured by the gods and imbued with divinity from the beginning. Rather than affirming Ea's parental role, the prayer instead addresses the mothers involved, filling out the portrait of divine parentage, before introducing the deity as or in the statue to its new role as ruler of the land from its throne that connects heaven and earth. The text affirms that the temple has been designed for its pleasure in order to make its stay and rule pleasant and long-lasting. After reiterating its plea that the god be the temple's permanent protector, the text pleads to Sin, Enki, and Ninki to love the new deity-statue symbiosis, that is, to not only welcome it into the assembly of the gods, but also to devote themselves to supporting it in its role as temple protector.

Attention then turns to the divine regalia, which is divinely crafted to be suited to the deity's splendor and purity. In addition to being pure and luminous, the divine garments also express certain aspects of a deity. For example, Marduk's *šer'ītu*-garment worn during the *akītu* festival is compared to water,[285] which proclaims Marduk's supremacy established with his victory over Tiamat, the great water goddess.[286] With the statue's investiture with elements befitting its divinity and reflecting its specific divine role, the statue is finally ready to take office, to become the fully functioning resident deity.[287]

The following procession to the temple serves as the new deity's first public appearance. Although on the theoretical level it represents a passage from the

---

284. Since the incantations are not always consistent with the ritual text or each other, such a variant should not be altogether surprising. Having stressed the supernatural origin and empowerment of the deity, the author of the incantation may have felt no need to eliminate priestly activity. Likewise, as a likely conglomeration of different traditions, the ritual text preserves different voices with different emphases.

285. Alasdair Livingstone, *Court Poetry and Literary Miscellanea* (SAA 3; Helsinki: Helsinki University, 1989), 34–53; Berlejung, "Geheimnis und Ereignis," 126.

286. Ibid.

287. Berlejung ("Washing the Mouth," 65) refers to the enthronement and investiture of the statue as "the transfer of 'me' to the new deity." Regarding the difficult to translate concept "me," see Bendt Alster, "On the Interpretation of the Sumerian Myth 'Inanna and Enki,'" *ZA* 64 (1974): 20–34, esp. 33–34 n. 33: where he defines "me" as "1) Any archetype or cultural norm. 2) Any visible manifestation of an archetype. 3) Any process relating to the actualization of an archetype ('function, duty, success, prayer, ritual'). 4) Anything that symbolizes the capability of actualizing an archetype ('emblem, insignia', etc.)."; see further Berlejung, *Theologie der Bilder*, 20–25; cf. G. Farber-Flügge, "Me," *RlA* 7 (1987–1990): 610–13.

danger of the "steppe" to the safety of the ordered world of the city,[288] the reality is quite the opposite. As part of the sacred precinct, the river and the orchard are the steppe in name only. Any real danger is minimal and further minimized by sequestering the statue in the protected confines of the reed circle. Although theoretically ordered, the city teems with people and innumerable potential pollutants that threaten to undermine the statue's elaborate cultic activation. The accompanying incantation provides the divine remedy to such potential pollution, transposing the human purificatory acts to the divine world. In the incantation, upon noticing all of the potential pollutants, Marduk turns to his father Ea, who provides the solution—purifications with the holy water basin along the processional route, in effect creating pure, divine space in the midst of the relatively impure, mundane world.[289] By casting the purificatory activity as the divine remedy, the priests ensure its efficacy and through the power of ritual words hope to equate their purifications with those of Marduk himself.

As the new god reaches its temple and moves ever inward to its inner sanctuary, the incantation, "My king, for your heart's joy,"[290] assures the deity of the suitability of its new abode, which includes daily food (IT 4 B 35–37) and good protective deities to protect it. Thus, in addition to being the temple's good *lamassu*, the new deity now has its own good *lamassū* who protect and serve it in the temple and the land it rules and protects. Once installed, the priest performs a final mouth washing (and opening), presumably to remove any pollutants accrued during the treacherous journey through the city[291] and perhaps also as a final top-up of purity and potency so that the cult statue can truly serve as god on earth.[292]

### Ritual Activation as a Joint Effort

Both humans and deities have a role to play in the activation process. On a human level, the preparation for divine presence occurs in several ways. In general, the human actions (i.e., the various ritual manipulations and accompanying oaths and incantations) serve as an attempt to create an ideal setting for transformation. Although the ritual actions are perceived as efficacious in and of themselves, on another level, they merely seek to provide the deity and its fellow deities with the

---

288. Cf. Berlejung, *Theologie der Bilder*, 244.

289. The sphinxes in Egypt perform a similar role in extending divine space.

290. IT 4 B 31–39.

291. Unlike the "steppe," the "city" seems to be the real city.

292. It also serves as a structural marker. As mouth-washing begins the ritual proper and marks the transitions between its stages, so too does the ritual fittingly end with a final mouth washing as an exit rite.

ideal forum to carry out the divine investiture.[293] In other words, the people's actions provide a conducive environment for the deities to do the real work.[294]

The transformation from statue to fully endowed deity is especially clear in the movement of the actors themselves. This is particularly the case with the artisans who are progressively distanced from the equation until they are entirely eliminated.[295] This absence of human craftsmen fittingly highlights the divine origin of the statue. The prominent presence of the priests in the ritual is at once appropriate and secondary. As a divine king of sorts, the deity requires servants, a role that the priests logically fill. At the same time, the text affirms that the priests are only incidental to the efficacy of the ritual in transforming the statue into the appropriate locus of divine presence. The transformative power comes from the divine realm alone.[296] The priests appear only to provide the appropriate environment and to help direct the proceedings.[297]

Although the priest does not directly empower the statue, in another way, the priestly provision is central. The priest acts as a guide, leading the statue on a journey of self-discovery and empowerment. The priest guides the statue through each stage of the ritual, putting it in situations where it may realize and embrace its identity.[298] As the statue encounters and is empowered by the gods, the priest often serves as an intermediary, addressing both the gods and the statue. However, once

---

293. Berlejung affirms that "divine descent alone enabled the statue to become vivified as an active and effective god" ("Washing the Mouth," 45–46).

294. Cult action in general is a human attempt to influence the divine. Here, it seems to set the mood, enticing the deities to perform the desired actions. This finds a parallel in the temple where the craftsmen make the structure as desirable as possible so that the deity may happily dwell therein.

295. In the first section, they return the tools to the Ea along with accompanying offerings, indicating that he is the true craftsman. In the second, the artisans symbolically lose their hands and swear that the craftsmen gods are the true artisans; they themselves played no part in the crafting of deity. In the third, they are absent entirely, a fitting sign that their role in crafting the deity has been systematically eradicated. Although the disavowal of human involvement in the manufacturing process seems to go against reality, it may serve as an indication that any action by the artisans was directed by the gods (since the gods themselves chose the artisans by lot and allowed them to see and reproduce the primeval form of deity).

296. The texts indicate that the gods perform all ritual actions (IT 1/2 C 15–34; STT 199: 34–39; IT 3 110–113) (Hurowitz, "Mesopotamian God Image," 150).

297. The mention of the king toward the end of the ritual is appropriate given that he is the ruler of this realm and the ultimate caretaker of the divine, especially in the upkeep of the temple and of the statue itself. His actions toward the gods are also perceived to determine the fate of the nation.

298. The priest is even said to "take the hand of the god" and lead it in procession (Nineveh C 65 in Walker and Dick, *The Mesopotamian mīs pî Ritual*, 57). See further Pongratz-Leisten, *Ina šulmi īrub*, 171–74.

the statue-deity symbiosis has been fully empowered, the priest's role changes to that of a mere servant. It is as if the deity has outgrown the need for a guardian; ready to rule, it needs only servants.[299]

In addition to the movement in the human realm, there is also (a more important) progression in the divine sphere. The human actions both avow and elicit divine control of the ritual. The distancing of the craftsmen emphasizes the divine origin and crafting of the statue, while the cultic actions entice the gods to divinely empower it. The parameters of the ritual likewise stress divine control, as the gods choose the artisans, the place of craftsmanship, the time, and the form of the statue.[300]

The encounters with the divine also mark the progress of the ritual from the formation of the statute to its assimilation in the divine community. First, the statue meets Ea, its divine father, and the other craftsmen gods at the river, the threshold of Ea's realm. In this encounter, the priest introduces the statue to its true father, proclaiming to all that the statue is divine handiwork and avowing its place among the gods.[301] The meeting with Shamash carries the integration one step further. As divine judge, Shamash determines the statue's destiny and place among the divine fraternity.[302] Once invested in the divine community and with their power, the statue may serve as divine locus and rule in the temple.

## 2. Daily Cult Ritual

In comparison with its Egyptian counterpart, little is known of the Mesopo-tamian daily cult ritual and most of the data available is late, stemming from the

---

299. The location of address is one example of the shift in emphasis. Whereas before, the priest stood alongside the statue and often whispered in its ear, after the statue has been fully incorporated into the divine community, the priest stands before the statue (Walker and Dick, *The Mesopotamian* mīs pî *Ritual*, 66 n. 118; Berlejung, "Washing the Mouth," 63).

300. Regarding the workers, place, and time, see Walker and Dick, "Induction of the Cult Image," 115–16; Dick, "Mesopotamian Cult Statue," 59–62. Regarding the time, see especially the Nabu-apla-iddina inscription (appears in King, *Babylonian Boundary Stones*, 120–27) in which the making of the Shamash statue had to wait centuries until the deity revealed a replica. In other words, "Humans simply could not make a god on their own! Only the gods could initiate and further the process" (Dick, "Mesopotamian Cult Statue," 58). The form of this statue (as well as most of its enlivening ritual) is also a matter of great secrecy (van der Toorn, "Book," 235–36).

301. It is as if the priest is letting the statue know its true origin as more than mere stone.

302. Shamash, as the sun god, is naturally encountered in the sun itself, particularly in the sunrise, which is associated with "vivification, purification and rebirth in Mesopotamia" (Berlejung, "Washing the Mouth," 56–57). Making sure to cover all the bases, "the irradiation of the god by divine starlight" (NR 102; Hurowitz, "Mesopotamian God Image," 150) is another means of assimilation (Berlejung, "Washing the Mouth," 57).

Hellenistic period.[303] It is nonetheless clear that throughout much of its history, the Mesopotamian cult included a daily ritual[304]—so much so that the function of the cult can be described as "the care and feeding of the gods."[305] Given the relatively static nature of Mesopotamian religious practice, we may surmise with some hope of authenticity that the ritual later described had similar antecedents in earlier periods.[306] The following presentation is cobbled together from multiple sources, foremost of which is TU 38 (AO 6451), which describes the ritual instructions for the daily offerings in the Hellenistic temples of Uruk.[307] Because of the lateness of the texts, the lack of clear interpretive statements, and the lack of a single full exemplar as in Egypt, rather than offering an exhaustive analysis, we will merely sketch the cultic day and offer some interpretive comments.

The major elements of the cultic day include the awakening of the temple ceremony (*dīk bīti*), the opening of the gate ceremony (*pīt bābi*), the serving and clearing of a main meal (*naptanu*) and second meal (*tardennu*) in the morning and another main and second meal in the evening, followed by the closing of the temple gate.[308] Before dawn and before the gates are opened, the *dīk bīti* ceremony

---

303. As such, the fullest examination of the material comes from a book on Hellenistic Uruk and Babylon: Marc J. H. Linssen, *The Cults of Uruk and Babylon: The Temple Ritual Texts as Evidence for Hellenistic Cult Practice* (CM 25; Leiden: Brill, 2004), 25–39, 129–66, 172–83. See also the classic study of Oppenheim, *Ancient Mesopotamia*, 183–96.

304. For example, multiple tablets from the second half of the third millennium onwards describe various aspects of the daily "sacrificial feeding" of the gods (Bottéro, *Religion in Ancient Mesopotamia*, 126). Among these, lists survive from the Old and Neo-Babylonian periods containing large quantities of foodstuffs for use in the sanctuary (Oppenheim, *Ancient Mesopotamia*, 189–90; Bottéro, *Religion in Ancient Mesopotamia*, 126–28).

305. Oppenheim, *Ancient Mesopotamia*, 183.

306. So Bottéro, *Religion in Ancient Mesopotamia*, 128. See also Linssen (*Cults of Uruk and Babylon*, 168) who concludes that "the Babylonian cults practised in the temples of Uruk and Babylon in the Hellenistic period are, as far as we can see in the sources, not different from those in the pre-Hellenistic times. All evidence clearly shows that Babylonians held on to their old Babylonian traditions."

307. See ibid., 132–38, 172–83; cf. F. Thureau-Dangin, *Rituels Accadiens* (Paris: Ernest Leroux, 1921), 62–65, 74–86.

308. Linssen, *Cults of Uruk and Babylon*, 26. Regarding the *naptanu* and *tardennu* as formal main and second meals offered on a stand in front of the statues of gods in temples, see J. J. Glassner, "Mahlzeit," *RlA* 7 (1987–90): 259–67; regarding use of *naptanu* in older periods, see Edwin C. Kingsbury, "A Seven Day Ritual in the Old Babylonian Cult at Larsa," *HUCA* 34 (1963): 22–23; Baruch A. Levine and William W. Hallo, "Offerings to the Temple Gates at Ur," *HUCA* 38 (1967): 46; Frankena, *Tākultu*, 54–57; G. van Driel, *The Cult of Aššur* (Studia Semitica Neerlandica 13; Assen: van Gorcum, 1969), 159–60. There is also evidence of a main and second meal attested in Neo-Babylonian Uruk (LKU 51; Linssen, *Cults of Uruk and Babylon*, 130–31).

opens the cultic day.[309] Although its function and procedure are nowhere explicitly identified, "the 'awakening' or 'arousing' of the temple [probably] refers to both the residents of the temple, the gods, and the priests, who have to wake up the gods to start the new day."[310] Thus, as in Egypt, it would seem that the gods in the form of their cult images sleep in the temple at night and have to be awakened in the morning.[311] However, there is no guarantee that the gods who sleep in their images will awake in them the following morning; they could theoretically for any number of reasons absent themselves during the night. In response, lamentations (*taqribtu* and *eršemakku*) are recited for the most important gods of the pantheon in order to ensure that "any offense (unknowingly) committed against the gods would be neutralized."[312] Although seemingly incongruous with the daily cultic setting, the content of these lamentations, often associated with the destruction of the temples and cities, is actually quite appropriate. Shared problems find shared solutions,[313] and the main concern in both the destruction of temples and cities and the daily cult is the divine presence. Lamentations written for the destruction of temples and cities aiming to redress the perceived absence of the deity may thus be profitably applied to the daily cult ritual to ensure divine presence.[314] In addition to the general concern with divine presence, specific elements in the laments are also especially suited to their present context.[315] For example, the incipit of the Balaĝ prayer "Appear Like the Sun"—dutu-gin₇ è-ta úru-zu ne, "Appear like the Sun! Watch your city!"—reveals a connection with the time of day it was performed and also functions metaphorically.[316] Namely, it serves as a plea to the deity

---

309. Ibid., 27. Evidence for the awakening of the temple ceremony comes from the Neo-Assyrian and Hellenistic periods (ibid.).

310. Ibid.

311. It is also possible that the deity in heaven must daily renew its presence on earth (see further below).

312. Ibid., 28; cf. Mark E. Cohen, *Sumerian Hymnology: The Eršemma* (HUCASup 2; Cincinnati: Ktav, 1981), 48–49. Regarding these lamentations, see more fully, e.g., Cohen, *Eršemma*; idem, *The Canonical Lamentations of Ancient Mesopotamia* (2 vols.; Bethesda, MD: CDL, 1988); Gabbay, "Performance of Emesal Prayers"; see also Anne Löhnert, *Wie die Sonne*. Three balaĝ prayers are recited daily before or during the *dīk bīti* ceremony (Gabbay, "Performance of Emesal Prayers," 104–5): 1) the balaĝ ᵈutu-gin₇ è-ta, "Appear like the Sun!" (Cohen, *Canonical Lamentations*, 95–119; Löhnert, *Wie die Sonne*, 201); 2) the balaĝ u₄-dam ki àm-ús, "It reaches earth like Day" (Cohen, *Canonical Lamentations*, 120–51); and 3) the balaĝ am-e amaš-a-na, "The Bull in his fold" (ibid., 152–74).

313. Gabbay, "Performance of Emesal Prayers," 104, 118–19.

314. Cf. ibid., 118–19. There is no need for an incantation or lamentation to be appropriate in all its details to the ritual for which it is recited; it may be adopted and applied if any part is considered relevant (ibid., 109).

315. Ibid., 104–7.

316. Ibid., 105–6.

to manifest itself as the sun manifests itself to prevent potential catastrophe, especially appropriate since it was recited before the rising of the sun at dawn and thus implored the deity to manifest itself shortly so that the cultic day could begin.[317]

Like the awakening of the temple, little is known about the opening of the gate (*pīt bābi*).[318] Minimally, it seems to indicate the time in the morning when all temple personnel are allowed to enter.[319] After entering the temple, a significant portion of the personnel set themselves to the task of preparing the morning divine meal. Like the mouth-opening ritual, the primary elements of the daily meal are food, drink, and fumigation.[320]

The meal begins by setting up the offering table, setting out water for washing, arranging the table, and performing fumigations and purifications. Two primary tables are mentioned, the *paššūru* table, usually made of gold, and the *paṭīru* table, made of reeds.[321] The table arrangement (*tabnītu*) includes dishes, bowls, and similar items used for serving food and drinks on the offering table.[322] Various foods and beverages are then served. During the meals, gods are presented with

---

317. Cf. ibid., 106; regarding the reference to the heavenly bodies as an allusion to their actual presence in the sky, see also Maul, "Gottesdienst im Sonnenheiligtum zu Sippar," in *Minuscula Mesopotamica: Festschrift für Johannes Renger* (ed. B. Böck, E. Cancik-Kirschbaum and T. Richter; AOAT 267; Münster: Ugarit-Verlag, 1999), 311 n. 131; Ambos, *Mesopotamische Baurituale*, 56.

318. Linssen, *Cults of Uruk and Babylon*, 36. The *pīt bābi* is attested from the Old Babylonian period onward (Landsberger, *Der kultische Kalendar der Babylonier und Assyrer* [Leipzig: Hinrichs, 1915], 3–4, 87, 112; Giuseppe Furlani, *Riti babilonesi e assiri* (Udine: Istituto delle Edizioni Accademiche, 1940); Gilbert J. P. McEwan, *Priest and Temple in Hellenistic Babylonia* (Freiburger Altorientalische Studien 4; Wiesbaden: Steiner, 1981), 165–66; Linssen, *Cults of Uruk and Babylon*, 36.

319. Ibid. Regarding the Babylonian temple personnel, their roles, access, and purification, see esp. Caroline Waerzeggers, "On the Initiation of Babylonian Priests," *ZABR* 14 (2008): 1–38; idem, "The Babylonian Priesthood in the Long Sixth Century BC," *Bulletin of the Institute of Classical Studies* 54 (2011): 59–70; regarding Assyria, see esp. Löhnert, "The Installation of Priests According to Neo-Assyrian Documents," *SAAB* 16 (2007): 273–86; idem, "Reconsidering the Consecration of Priests in Ancient Mesopotamia," in *Your Praise Is Sweet. A Memorial Volume Presented to Jeremy Allen Black by Colleagues, Students, and Friends* (ed. H. D. Baker, E. Robson, and G. Zólyomi; London: British Institute for the Study of Iraq 2010), 183–91.

320. Linssen, *Cults of Uruk and Babylon*, 129.

321. Linssen, *Cults of Uruk and Babylon*, 140–42; see further Armas Salonen, *Die Möbel des alten Mesopotamien nach sumerisch-akkadischen Quellen: Eine lexikalische und kulturgeschichtliche Untersuchung* (Helsinki: Suomalainen Tiedeakatemia, 1963), 174–203, esp. 176–92 regarding the *paššūru*. Rather than both being used in the same ritual context, it seems that either one or the other was used.

322. *AHw* 1299a, I, 2; Linssen, *Cults of Uruk and Babylon*, 142. Purifications and fumigations could occur either before or after food and beverages were served (ibid., 145).

the four elements of a worthy meal in Mesopotamian "society": beverages, grain products, fruit, and meat.[323] Beverages include various beers, wine, and milk, while the foodstuffs include loaves, cakes, dates, figs, raisins, and meat, especially oxen and sheep.[324] Only the best foods and liquids are served,[325] appropriate to the dignity of the gods and the desire to elicit a favorable response. Thus, more common and cheaper products such as pork, goat, and fish are missing.[326] The priest makes recitations behind closed curtains, after which the table is cleared away and the meal ends.[327] Some or all of the meals are accompanied by music.[328]

The food and drink offerings are presented in a secluded site, sequestered from the mundane world and all evil influences. Most often presented before gods in the sanctuary, offerings are also presented in various temple areas and even occasionally outside of the temple.[329] There is also some evidence that curtains (*šiddu*) are set up to ensure safety and secrecy.[330] Through the manipulation of the curtains, "every contact between the world of physical reality and the world of the gods was hidden from human eyes."[331] Linen curtains surround the deity as it

323. Bottéro, *Religion in Ancient Mesopotamia*, 128.

324. These contents are derived from *TU* 38 (Linssen, *Cults of Uruk and Babylon*, 132–38), which, although likely propagandistic (Adam Falkenstein, *Topographie von Uruk, I. Teil: Uruk zur Seleukidenzeit* [Ausgrabungen der Deutschen Forschungsgemeinschaft in Uruk-Warka 3; Leipzig: Harrasowitz, 1941], 8–9), need not be dismissed altogether (Linssen, *Cults of Uruk and Babylon*, 138). Fruit (*inbu*) is only sometimes included, probably because it is not available throughout the year (ibid., 137). It seems to add "an aesthetic touch" (Oppenheim, *Ancient Mesopotamia*, 188).

325. Lambert, "Donations of Food and Drink to the Gods in Ancient Mesopotamia," in *Ritual and Sacrifice in the Ancient Near East: Proceedings of the International Conference Organized by the Katholieke Universiteit Leuven from the 17th to the 20th of April 1991* (ed. J. Quaegebeur; OLA 55; Leuven: Peeters, 1993), 191–201; Linssen, *Cults of Uruk and Babylon*, 137.

326. Linssen, *Cults of Uruk and Babylon*, 137. The menus for the morning and evening meals generally vary in quantity rather than quality, as the morning meal is more expansive. It is also possible that the quality of the first morning meal is slightly higher than the second, since the text mentions first quality sheep and more loaves (however, the second meal offers more variety), while the two evening meals are identical (ibid., 137–38).

327. Linssen, *Cults of Uruk and Babylon*, 130, 139.

328. Wiggermann, "Theologies, Priests and Worship," 1863; cf. Gabbay ("Performance of Emesal Prayers," 104), who remarks that the daily lamentations performed before the god are accompanied by music.

329. Linssen, *Cults of Uruk and Babylon*, 130, 138–40.

330. Ibid., 139–40; Alternatively and/or additionally, heaps of flour, a circle of flour, or the *urigallu*-standards, used in the orchard in the mouth-washing ritual, also serve to set apart offering space and to exclude all unwanted influences.

331. Oppenheim, *Ancient Mesopotamia*, 192; cf. Linssen, *Cults of Uruk and Babylon*, 139.

eats, yet are removed when it finishes its repast. When it washes its hands, they are drawn again.[332] This careful screening preserves divine privacy and the appropriate separation between divine and human spheres necessary for such an intimate act. In addition, it also helps to disguise the fact that the statues cannot move of their own accord, much less wash their hands or eat.[333] Since the leftovers are redistributed to the temple personnel, it seems that they believe the gods partake of the food and drink in an immaterial sense.[334] However, it is more effective to let the people to use their imagination to conceive of the gods' immaterial consumption than to allow them to watch as the statue sits unmoving before an untouched sumptuous repast. The curtains thus afford the deity privacy, while keeping the people's view of the divine consumption mysterious and less open to doubt.

"In order to perform the divine meal successfully the offering site, and also everything which, and everyone who, participated in the meal had to be 'pure.'"[335] Fumigations, already encountered in the mouth-washing ritual, likewise feature in the daily cult ritual and serve both to please the gods with their soothing scents and to purify the atmosphere.[336] In addition to the general purity necessary to officiate, priests also purify themselves by washing their hands,[337] thereby cleansing the body parts that would make contact with the deity and its service. Sweeping the ground and sprinkling it with water, attested also in the beginning of the mouth-washing ritual (NR 42, 56), respectively remove all potential impurities and purify the swept area with pure water.[338] The holy water basin (*egubbû*), so prevalent in mouth washing, also appears in the context of the daily cult and serves to purify everything used in the divine meal.[339]

Regarding regular care, the deity is periodically and ritually washed and arrayed in multiple and magnificent outfits and adorning jewelry.[340] Although not

---

332. Oppenheim, *Ancient Mesopotamia*, 192.

333. Of course, the deities themselves can move or cause people to move their statues.

334. It seems that the redistribution of the food is minimized. For example, especially when performed in a more public place, the curtains disguise the fact that the priest removes the food and drink untouched, instead giving the impression that it is physically consumed by the deities (cf. Linssen, *Cults of Uruk and Babylon*, 139).

335. Ibid., 147.

336. Ibid., 145; cf. Giuseppe Furlani, *Il sacrificio nella religione dei Semiti di Babilonia e Assiria* (Rome: Giovanni Bardi, 1932), 355; Friedrich Blome, *Die Opfermaterie in Babylonien und Israel, Teil I* (Rome: Apud Pont. Institutum Biblicum, 1934), 272–84.

337. Linssen, *Cults of Uruk and Babylon*, 151.

338. Sprinkling the ground with water also helps to make the dust settle (ibid., 149).

339. Ibid., 150; cf. *CAD* E, 49–50; *AHw* 17a and 440b, with many references from earlier periods; regarding the Neo-Assyrian period, see van Driel, *Cult of Aššur*, 167–68.

340. Bottéro, *Religion in Ancient Mesopotamia*, 132–3.

attested daily, the ritual clothing ceremonies of divine statues (*lubuštu*) occur regularly and are accompanied by offerings, especially of sheep.[341]

Although little is known of how Mesopotamians actually interpreted the daily cult, it seems to be more straightforward than its Egyptian counterpart. It lacks obvious mythological associations and the various offerings proffered do not appear to imbue the statue with divine potencies. Instead, the daily cult seems to simply provide for the deity's care and feeding. However, despite its more mundane effect, the ritual is no less essential. In addition to providing the statue with the ability to eat, the mouth-washing ritual also seems to render the statue–deity symbiosis reliant on human offerings. Like its human counterpart, the statue needs food to be fully functional.[342]

## Relationship between Mouth Washing and the Gods' Daily Care and Feeding

The mouth-washing ritual prepares the statue for its role in the temple as fully functioning locus of divine presence and does so in two primary ways. First, it makes the statue perfectly pure and thus suitable for the deity in or as the statue and for the deity to commune with other deities.[343] Second, the ritual functions as a maturation process, which activates the statue's various faculties, especially those necessary to partake of the three primary cult offerings—food, drink, and incense—and empowers the deity to fulfill its role. Perfectly pure and fully enlivened, the statue is then ready to take up residence in the temple. As in Egypt, the daily cult serves to keep the deity happy and healthy through regular care and feeding. Together, they serve to bring the gods to, and keep them on, earth.

---

341. *Lubuštu* ceremonies are attested from the Old Akkadian period onward and are especially prevalent in the Neo-Babylonian and Hellenistic periods. See Linssen, *Cults of Uruk and Babylon*, 51–56; see also Landsberger, *Der kultische Kalendar*, 117–18; Furlani, *Riti babilonesi e assiri*, 161; Matsushima, "Divine Statues," 209–19; idem, "On the Material Related to the Clothing Ceremony," *ASJ* 16 (1994): 177–200; idem, "Eleven Neo-Babylonian Texts Relating to the *lubuštu* (Clothing Ceremony)," in *Essays on Ancient Anatolia and Its Surrounding Civilizations* (ed. H. I. H. Prince Takihito Mikasa; Bulletin of the Middle Eastern Culture Center in Japan 8; Wiesbaden: Harrosowitz, 1995), 235–43; A. C. V. M. Bongenaar, *The Neo-Babylonian Ebabbar Temple at Sippar: Its Administration and Prosopography* (Leiden: Nederlands Historisch-Archeologisch Instituut te Istanbul, 1997), 305–7.

342. See Berlejung, "Geheimnis und Ereignis," 121; see further K. 2401 rev. iii 32–37; Marie-Claire Perroudon, "An Angry Goddess," *SAAB* 6 (1992): 41–43; Simo Parpola, *Assyrian Prophecies* (SAA 9; Helsinki: Helsinki University, 1997), 3.5 (SAA 9.11).

343. As noted, a large part of the process involves the transformation of the statue's human origins to divine.

## WHAT IS THE RELATIONSHIP BETWEEN THE STATUE AND THE DEITY?

The relationship between the statue and deity may be conceptualized in different ways in different contexts. In the majority of cases, the statue is simply identified as the god, that is, the texts generally make no body-soul dichotomy. From the beginning of the mouth-washing ritual, the statue is addressed as the deity. As an approved image (ṣalmu) of the deity, it bears (some of) the divine essence, especially since the elements from which it was constructed were already divine. Through the course of the ritual, through purification and the addition of other necessary divine aspects, the statue becomes the fully functioning god on earth.

As long as it is practical and palatable, such a unity is assumed. The link remains even when a statue is deported. For example, the prophecy of Marduk catalogs his trips (i.e., his statue's trips) with the Hittites, Elamites, and the Assyrians and his ultimate return to Babylon.[344] However, the threat of destruction necessitates a different solution. Since the death of a god is unacceptable, Mesopotamians distance the gods from their statues in the face of their destruction. For example, Esarhaddon boasts that with the destruction of their statues "the gods and goddesses living within (their statues) fled to heaven above like birds," while Assurbanipal's destruction of the Elamite statues renders the gods "ghosts" (zaqiqū).[345] In such cases, the statue becomes something like a body filled with the immaterial divine essence, as in Egypt. Thus, in order to preserve the deity, the statue–deity symbiosis is dissolved and its body, the statue, may be sacrificed, for with the loss of one vessel, another may take its place.[346]

Until the deity is reunited with its image, it has no anchor in and is thus effectively absent from the terrestrial world (unless it has another statue in another temple).[347] Often presented from the human side of the equation as a catastrophic divine absence, from the divine side it may indicate the deity's inability to exert its influence in the the human sphere or a particular part of it. Although clearly

---

344. Borger, "Gott Marduk und Gott-König Šulgi als Propheten: Zwei prophetische Texte," *BiOr* 28 (1971): 3–24. See further Dick, "Mesopotamian Cult Statue," 53; Mark Chavalas, ed., *Historical Sources in Translation: The Ancient Near East* (Malden: Blackwell, 2006), 168–74 with references. Such a deportation could be explained by the conquered as an expression of divine anger, while conquerors often understood their conquest as a sign of the superiority of their gods. Regarding the former, see, e.g., Matsushima, "Divine Statues," 209.

345. Dick, "Mesopotamian Cult Statue," 57.

346. However, as the Sippar tablet of Nabu-apla-iddina and the mouth-washing ritual indicate, not just any body will do. The deity must approve of its image and the image must be ritually activated.

347. The absence of a deity from one statue does not in any way entail its absence from all other statues.

polemical, the purported state of the Elamite gods as disembodied ghosts suggests that without statues the gods cannot function on earth. To maximize their influence, the deities must adopt a concrete form.

Damage to a statue has an effect that appears to fall between that of a deported statue and a destroyed statue. Damage does not dissolve the connection between image and deity; it merely creates some distance between them. Nonetheless, the results are envisaged somewhat differently, depending on the composition. TuL 27 presents the damage from the human perspective, that is, it addresses the repair of a damaged statue. In it, when "the work of the god" (1), that is, the cult image, is in need of repair, it is covered and brought into the workshop at a propitious time in secret, when nobody is watching (2–7). During its restoration process the lamentation priest continually presents offerings and makes intercessions (19–20). Thus, rather than being treated as a piece of damaged equipment, the statue is still treated like the god, covered to protect it from prying eyes, this time perhaps to hide its shame. The accompanying pleas and offerings, as in the daily cult, presumably appease the offended deities in an attempt to facilitate restoration, such that the damaged statue may simply be reinstalled after its refurbishment as god on earth without the need to create a new statue or perhaps even a new deity (see further below). However, because damage has been done, the statue requires ritual activation, at least in the form of a mouth-washing ritual to enact perfect purity (21–22) and perhaps also other elements like mouth opening to reinvigorate the statue, so that the god as statue may accrue enough appropriate divine aspects to function effectively as god on earth. If, however, the cult image cannot be repaired, it must be sent back to Ea, its divine father and creator, bound with precious metals and some divine property and deposited in the river (23–29). Such a procedure is a last resort and a secret that must be carefully guarded since it is an abomination against Anu, Enlil, and Ea (30).[348] The cult image is thereby removed from the terrestrial sphere and with it the deity. In order to for the deity to return, a new approved and ritually activated image is required.[349]

The Erra epic presents the divine perspective.[350] In it, Marduk's terrestrial presence is tied to his cult image in Babylon, the *axis mundi*, "the palace of heaven and earth" (I 124–125). In the distant past, when Marduk left his palace, the world was plunged into chaos. Once his anger abated, he restored his image, which had been damaged in his absence, and built and settled in a new house (I 130–144). On the mythic plane, the later refurbishment of Marduk's statue is understood simi-

---

348. It is even possible that line 30 also refers to the repair of the divine statue mentioned in lines 1–22.

349. In addition to being returned to Ea or repaired, there is some textual evidence for storing damaged statues in a sort of genizah, pending repairs at an opportune time (see Hurowitz, "Mesopotamian God Image," 156–57).

350. For translations, see *COS* 1.113:404–16; Foster, *Before the Muses*, 880–911.

larly. Erra persuades Marduk to have his statue refurbished because it has come into disrepair (I 180; II 1). Thus, Marduk leaves his home, enters the dwelling of the Anunna-gods (II 1), and returns when his statue is refurbished (II 35–36, 49), thereby suggesting that Marduk absents himself from his statue until it is repaired. In other words, the link is not severed, only temporarily suspended.

Even within the same composition evidence from the cultic plane tells a slightly different story. Marduk in the form of his statue simply enters the workshop,[351] where his statue is refurbished, and then returns to the temple, suggesting some kind of continued presence or connection between statue and deity. In sum, it seems that a damaged statue, like a deported statue, must be treated with care like the deity itself and remains in some way connected to the deity. Like a destroyed statue, the connection between statue and deity, the deity–statue symbiosis, is not completely reestablished until the statue is made perfect.

While the statue is often identified as the deity, the deity is not coterminous with its statue. In other words, while fully the god, the statue is not the fullness of the god. Rather, the statue is but one of a deity's many manifestations or aspects. The fullness of the deity lies instead in the accumulation of its various divine manifestations, names, and attributes. Indeed, since a deity may always adopt more manifestations, names, and attributes, no single list is or attempts to be complete.[352] Rather than being coterminous with the heavenly deity, the statue presences heavenly deity in the terrestrial sphere. As a result, a single manifestation (e.g., a single cult statue) may be destroyed without destroying the deity. However, such a destruction would affect the deity by shrinking its sphere of influence. For example, with the destruction of the statue of Shamash of Sippar, Shamash would no longer reign in Sippar until a suitable image is made.[353]

While from one perspective the deity-statue symbiosis is but one element in the larger divine constellation, from another each statue-deity may be treated as

---

351. The text refers to this place as "that house" (I 180), presumably referring to the workshop (bīt mummi), the place where the statue was initially crafted (see the reference in TuL 27 10 [Walker and Dick, The Mesopotamian mīs pî Ritual, 232] to the transfer of a damaged statue to this workshop).

352. "Nowhere do we find the theological profile of a deity really systematized and assembled. The pressure to form a compendium is a modern phenomenon," a pure construct that nowhere lands in the reality of the ancient Near Eastern world (Berlejung, "Reduktion von Komplexität," 10, 32; translated from German). For example, in amassing fifty names for Marduk in the Enuma Elish, the text is not concerned with describing Marduk in his fullness, with delimiting everything that he is. Rather, they use the number fifty to give a sampling of Marduk's aspects, brought together to indicate his power and importance.

353. In accord with this manner of thinking, Nabu-apla-iddina's fashioning of the cult statue of Shamash after "finding" a model of the deity's true form marked Shamash's true return. However, Nabu-apla-iddina's predecessors likely considered the replacement sun disk suitable, if not ideal, enabling Shamash to be present, to receive his cult, and to rule.

(semi-)independent. The focus on treating these individual elements in all of their fullness and sometimes without reference to the larger whole leads to their occasional independence and identification as self-propelled beings. Thus, each new statue is in some way a new god, or according to a modern metaphor, a clone. Although it bears the same DNA, it was born at a different time, in a different place, under different circumstances and, as it matures, becomes a different person. For example, statues in the mouth-washing ritual are effectively treated as newborns, while their heavenly prototypes retain their full faculties. In addition, Nabu-apla-iddina performs the mouth-washing on the Shamash statue "before Shamash" (*maḫar* ᵈŠamaš).[354] Namely, the new Shamash has its mouth washed before the original Shamash in heaven. As a result, each statue–deity symbiosis may be conceived of as a discrete self-propelled deity.

During the course of the mouth-washing ritual, each new cult statue likely receives its own name,[355] which differentiated it from other divine aspects and in some cases points to its particular function. Although in some cases individual manifestations in different locales are treated as different deities, multiple statues in the same locale seem to represent different aspects of the same deity, that is, they may have been used for different functions.[356] For example, when Sennacherib captured the statue of Marduk used in the *akītu* festival from Babylon, the festival could not be performed even though there were multiple other statues of Marduk in the Esagil temple of Babylon.[357] In addition to serving different functions, the various statues in the same location bear different names.[358] Since a name represents but one aspect of a deity and a deity may accumulate aspects by accumulating names (e.g., Marduk in *Enuma Elish*), by giving the various statues in the sanctuary different names and different functions, the Mesopotamians increased

---

354. IV 24; Dick, "Mesopotamian Cult Statue," 53.

355. Walker and Dick, *The Mesopotamian* mīs pî *Ritual*, 30 following Selz, "Holy Drum," 176–78.

356. The multiple Marduk statues also may be referred to as Marduks in the plural or as different manifestations of the single Marduk. As discrete Marduks, each statue–deity symbiosis may act independently, fulfilling a specific cultic role.

357. Berlejung, "Notlösungen – Altorientalische Nachrichten über den Tempelkult in Nachkriegszeiten," in *Kein Land für sich allein. Studien zum Kulturkontakt in Kanaan, Israel/Palästina und Ebirnâri für Manfred Weippert zum 65. Geburtstag* (ed. U. Hübner, E. A. Knauf; OBO 186; Fribourg: Academic Press, 2002), 196–230, esp. 216–18; idem, " Reduktion von Komplexität," 36. Regarding the multiple statues of Marduk and their different names, see further George, "Marduk and the Cult of the Gods of Nippur at Babylon," *OrNS* 66 (1997): 65–70.

358. See, e.g., the *tākultu* ritual texts, which (exhaustively) list temple cult images, often referring to what appear to be the same deities under many different names, many of which appear to be focusing on an aspect or function of the deity (see Porter, "Anxiety of Multiplicity," 230–39).

the range and prominence of their deities.[359] Likewise, regardless of their perceived function, the simple fact that a deity has multiple statues adds to its prestige and marks it as superior to a deity with fewer statues.

These various approaches are a product of the Mesopotamian context-specific presentation of deity.[360] Pragmatically, since the cult statue is the only aspect of the deity within reach, worshippers tend to treat it as the deity in its fullness without reference to the other elements of the divine constellation. Only when placed alongside other cult images in other cities does one have to come to grips with a deity's different manifestations. Rather than offering a theoretical treatise on the relation of the various aspects, Mesopotamian texts simply juxtapose the deities that share a forename and have a distinct local or functional epithet (e.g., Ishtar of Arbela, Ishtar of Nineveh, and Ishtar Lady of Battle). Since in such contexts no single manifestation can be ignored so as not to anger the particular manifestation of deity or the populace who treasures that manifestation, manifestations in a treaty or ritual context, e.g., are simply listed separately without offering any comment on their precise relationship.[361] Returning to the destruction of the cult image, in order to avoid the death of "the" or the "new" god with the destruction of its image, Mesopotamians dissolved the link between statue and deity and associated the deity with its larger constellation, so that when a more favorable time arose the deity could rejoin or be reborn as a new, approved, ritually enlivened cult image.

## NECESSITY OF DIVINE NOURISHMENT?

Did the Mesopotamian gods need the food offered to them in the sanctuary to survive? In other words, were they reliant on material sustenance like humans? Once again, the picture is complex and the answer depends on the context. In the wider cosmos, that is, apart from their cult images, the evidence is mixed. Although hymns do not address the deity's need for human nourishment directly, their language and content suggest that the deities had no such trivial needs. Nonetheless, such texts should not be given undo weight since they are prone to

---

359. One finds evidence for the multiple divine names also, e.g., in lexical lists, royal inscriptions, hymns, and epic poetry (Allen, "Splintered Divine," 205). Through a name, a deity differentiates itself from all others. Through multiple names with multiple functions, it reserves for itself the benefits attached to the multiple functions, which through the multiple names are ascribed to it.

360. See further Hundley, "Here a God."

361. In the context of the hymn to Ishtar of Arbela and Nineveh (for the text, see Livingstone, *Court Poetry*, 10–12), each manifestation is treated as a self-propelled deity who performs a specific and distinct function. However, although probably offering the best evidence of the distinction between manifestations, the hymn offers no theory about their precise relationship. Instead, it simply and pragmatically treats them as distinct without further comment.

flattery, highlighting divine strengths while avoiding potential weaknesses. As a theological exercise, an expression of worship, and an attempt to engender a favorable divine response, hymns were designed to extol the gods in the most glowing of terms. Other texts state more strongly the need for divine nourishment. For example, Atrahasis (III iii 31; iv 21–22) and Gilgamesh (XI 159–161) seem to suggest the potential starvation of the gods without the sacrifices.[362] In the end, it seems most likely that the ancients Mesopotamians believed their gods needed some sort of nourishment.

Whatever they may have thought about what the gods needed for survival, ancient Mesopotamians clearly understood the feeding aspect of "the care and feeding of the gods" as an obligation of the anthropomorphic cult. To this end, mouth opening was especially necessary for the performance of the daily cult, allowing the gods to enjoy their food and humans to influence the gods through alimentary service. More than that, mouth opening seems to have created a need for such offerings that had to be satisfied regularly.[363] Thus, as in Egypt, it seems that the divine presence could not remain in or as the statue unless it was provided with the finest human nourishment. If not fed, the deity–statue symbiosis theoretically could starve, forcing the deity to leave the statue. However, the deity would not ultimately die, since it was not coterminous with its statue. Nonetheless, if the deity–statue symbioses did not receive offerings, they would be forced to abandon their opulent lifestyle and literally work for a living or, as they had done before, create a suitable human replacement.

The mythological texts mentioned above bolster and indeed appear to explain the need for anthropomorphic cultic service. According to these accounts, deities, like all other living beings, required food to live. Humanity was thus created to provide the gods with food and to ensure "that the [higher] gods led an opulent and worry-free life."[364] Humans fulfilled their role by providing the deities, in the form of their cult statues, with regular regal sustenance. In this way, the realm of myth was superimposed onto the world of the cult, as providing statues with food in some way seems to have nourished deities in heaven.

Cultic service did not explain how all elements of the divine constellation, especially the anthropomorphic core of mythology, partook of human offerings. Perhaps feeding one element in the constellation, the statue, nourished all other

---

362. According to these mythological texts, before the creation of humanity to serve the gods, there was also a widespread panic among the deities at the threat of a strike of the lesser gods and the resulting threat of poverty and starvation (Bottéro, *Religion in Ancient Mesopotamia*, 99).

363. See above at n. 344.

364. Bottéro, *Religion in Ancient Mesopotamia*, 114. The fullest portrait of the creation of humanity is found in the Atrahasis Epic. The *Enuma Elish* gives a remarkably similar description, with the major difference being that Marduk is the one who decides to create instead of his father Enki/Ea (see briefly ibid., 97–105, 114).

elements. Although theoretically possible, such thinking likely did not enter the minds of ancient Mesopotamians. For them, how the statue connected to the larger constellation was largely irrelevant. Indeed, as the only divine element readily accessible and understandable, the statue was treated as the deity in its fullness. The people fulfilled their duty by feeding the divine cult statue in the hopes of receiving divine reward. Anything beyond this was not their immediate concern.

# CHAPTER 10

# DIVINE PRESENCE IN HITTITE TEMPLES

AN ANALYSIS OF HITTITE CONCEPTIONS of the divine is a convoluted endeavor. Hittite religion was an amalgam of the beliefs of many different cultures. In fact, the Hittites themselves—that is, "the Indo-Europeans who began to settle in central Anatolia in the second half of the third millennium—added little from their inherited Indo-European religion" to the indigenous Hattic religion, which they co-opted and incorporated into their own.[1] Luwian religious tradition also played a formative role.[2] In addition, from the fifteenth century the influence of Hurrian and Syrian (and Mesopotamian mediated through Hurrian)[3] religious beliefs became especially influential.[4] As it was an ever-shifting amalgam, no survey can

---

1. Manfred Hutter, "Religion in Hittite Anatolia: Some Comments on 'Volkert Haas: Geschichte der hethitischen Religion,'" *Numen* 44 (1997): 77; see also Beckman, "Pantheon," 309–11. Regarding ancestral Indo-European religious tradition, see, e.g., Calvert Watkins, *How to Kill a Dragon: Aspects of Indo-European Poetics* (Oxford: Oxford University Press, 1995), 247–51. Regarding the adopted Hattic tradition, see, e.g., Jörg Klinger, *Untersuchungen zur Rekonstruktion der hattischen Kultschicht* (StBoT 37; Wiesbaden: Harassowitz, 1996), 129–97.

2. Hutter, "Aspects of Luwian Religion," in *The Luwians* (HO 1/68; Leiden: Brill, 2003), 211–80; Beckman, "Pantheon," 311. Luwian is an Indo-European language and the Luwians were a people group of the second and first millennia in central and western Anatolia and northern Syria.

3. See regarding the mediated Mesopotamian religion, e.g., the prominence of Ishtar in Beckman, "Ištar of Nineveh Reconsidered," *JCS* 50 (1998): 1–10; see further Güterbock, "The Composition of Hittite Prayers to the Sun," *JAOS* 78 (1958): 237–45; idem, "Some Aspects of Hittite Prayers," *Acta Universitatus Upsaliensis* 38 (1978): 125–39.

4. Hutter, "Religion in Hittite Anatolia," 77–78; Beckman, "Pantheon," 309–11. Hurrian language and culture were prominent in the second millennium in Syria and Anatolia and especially exerted influence on the Hittites with the decline of the kingdom of Mitanni in the fourteenth century (possibly ruled by an Indo-Aryan elite). Regarding Hurrian beliefs, see, e.g., Marie-Claude Trémouille, "La religion des Hourrites: état actuel de nos connaissances," *SCCNH* 10 (1999): 277–91; see also Haas, "Substratgottheiten des westhurritischen Pantheons," *RHA* 36 (1978): 59–69; Gernot Wilhelm, *Grundzüge der Geschichte und Kultur der Hurriter* (Darmstadt: Wissenschaftliche Buchgesellschaft, 1982), 69–81; Alfonso Archi, "The Former History of Some Hurrian Gods," in *Acts of the IIIrd International Congress of Hittitology, Çorum, September 16–22, 1996* (ed. S. Alp and A. Süel; Ankara: Anit Matbaa, 1998), 39–44; idem, "Formation of the West Hurrian Pantheon: The Case of Išḫara," in

present an accurate picture of "Hittite" religion at all times and in all places, nor can it confidently claim to capture all the complexity at any one time or in any one place.[5] Rather than attempting to be exhaustive, the following survey traces the general contours of Hittite conceptions of the divine presence in the temple.[6]

## Perceptions of Deity

As in Egypt and Mesopotamia, Hittite gods seem to have been predicated on the human model. According to Bryce, "by and large the gods ... were human beings on a grand scale. They were subject to the same range of emotions, like love, anger, fear, jealousy; they sometimes neglected their responsibilities, they could deceive and be deceived, they enjoyed the pleasures of the flesh, and they liked a variety of entertainment."[7] They were characterized by gender and family relationships,[8] whose activity, as in human families, normally extended only three generations.[9] In the cult in particular, deities, like their royal counterparts, had bodies, houses, and cadres of servants who lavishly catered to their every need and desire including food, bathing, clothing, and entertainment.[10] For example, during festivals the gods were often regaled with music, singing, dancing, and acrobatics as well as athletic contests and cult drama.[11] In fact, Hittite texts explicitly testify to their similarity: "Are the desire of the gods and men different? In no way! Do their natures differ? In no way!"[12]

However, rather than simply being conceived of as humans writ large, Hittite deities transcended the human model in nearly every capacity.[13] Most noticeably,

---

*Recent Developments in Hittite Archaeology and History: Papers in Memory of Hans G. Güterbock* (ed. K. A. Yener and H. A. Hoffner; Winona Lake, IN: Eisenbrauns, 2002), 21–33.

5. Cf. Beckman, "Religion. B. Bei den Hethitern," *RlA* 11 (2007): 334.

6. It also generally excludes analysis of the evidence from the Neo-Hittite states.

7. Trevor Bryce, *Life and Society in the Hittite World* (Oxford: Oxford University Press, 2002), 139, followed by Taracha, *Religions of Second Millennium Anatolia*, 80.

8. Beckman, "Pantheon," 312.

9. Three generations of the gods were considered living and active, while older deities were relegated to the underworld and thereby rendered inactive (Wilhelm, "'Gleichsetzungstheologie', 'Synkretismus' und 'Gottesspaltungen' in Polytheismus Anatoliens," in *Polytheismus und Monotheismus in der Religionen der Vorderen Orients* [ed. M. Krebernik and J. van Ooorschot; AOAT 298; Münster: Ugarit-Verlag, 2002], 59).

10. See, e.g., Billie Jean Collins, "A Statue for the Deity: Cult Images in Hittite Anatolia," in Walls, ed., *Cult Image and Divine Representation*, 13.

11. Taracha, *Religions of Second Millennium Anatolia*, 58–59 and references cited therein.

12. *KUB* 13.4 i 21–22; translation after Bryce, *Life and Society*, 139.

13. Even so, no Hittite deity could be characterized as omniscient, omnipotent, or omnipresent (Wilhelm, "'Gleichsetzungstheologie,'" 59–68). See also Gregory McMahon,

Hittite deities could change form and were capable of reproducing beyond their species. For example, in the mythological text, "The Sun God, the Cow, and the Fisherman," the Sun God changes into a young man to speak to a cow, which he then impregnates, presumably in the form of a bull.[14] In the "Song of Ulikummi," the god Kumarbi impregnates a huge cliff to create a stone monster Ulikummi to challenge the rule of the Weather God.[15]

Fanciful tales aside, *parā ḫandandatar* was a defining characteristic of Hittite deities that intimated divine power and control and set them apart from their human analogues.[16] Like their Egyptian and Mesopotamian counterparts, Hittite deities could also have multiple names, manifestations, and attributes. Weather gods in particular[17] had profiles expansive and fluid enough to be characterized as constellations of aspects, which were in some cases treated as distinct deities and in other cases as part of a single weather god, depending on the context. For example, the various local IŠKURs[18] frequently were identified and treated as distinct entities,[19] yet in other cases, most prominently mythological texts, a single

---

"Theology, Priests, and Worship in Hittite Anatolia," in *CANE* 3:1989: "As in all polytheistic conceptualizations of the universe, no one god could be completely universal in his power or the allegiance owed him because of the existence of so many other deities."

14. Hoffner, *Hittite Myths* (SBLWAW 2; Atlanta: Scholars, 1990), 85–86. The text leaves unspecified the Sun God's original form. Perhaps it was the sun itself.

15. Hoffner, *Hittite Myths*, 55–65, esp. 57.

16. Its precise meaning is difficult to pinpoint. Literally, it seems to mean "prior arrangement" (*HED* 8 [2011]: 105–6) or "arranging, ordering forth/out" (Jared Miller, personal communication). Gerd Steiner ("Gott. D. Nach hethitischen Texten," *RlA* 3 [1957]: 565) refers to it as "divine might," Beckman suggests that it is often best rendered "providence" ("Religion," 334), and *CHD* translates it as both "divine guidance" and "divine power" (*CHD* P, 130). *CHD* elaborates, referring to it in all contexts as an "outworking of divine power, almost always to bring help or deliverance" (*CHD* P, 131). For examples of its uses, see *CHD* P, 130–33. Although it was an inherent quality of deities, *parā ḫandandatar* could also be divinely gifted to humans (Steiner, "Gott," 565).

17. See, e.g., the profile presented in Haas, *Geschichte der hethitischen Religion*, 322–39; for the weather gods of the ancient Near East, see more expansively Schwemer, *Wettergottgestalten Mesopotamiens*; idem, "The Storm-Gods of the Ancient Near East: Summary, Synthesis, Recent Studies: Part I," *JANER* 7 (2007): 121–68; idem, "The Storm-Gods of the Ancient Near East: Summary, Synthesis, Recent Studies: Part II," *JANER* 8 (2008): 1–44. Regarding Hatti in particular, see "Storm-Gods II," 3–8, 17–27.

18. IŠKUR is a Sumerogram used to refer to the general category of weather gods. The Hittite texts tend to use Sumerograms to refer to deities of a similar type, thereby obscuring their individual names and identities.

19. For example, the divine witness list of the treaty between Hattušili III of Hatti and Ulmi-Teššup of Tarhuntassa lists separately fifteen different IŠKURs, including IŠKUR of Lightning, IŠKUR of Hatti, IŠKUR of Nerik, and IŠKUR of Heaven (Beckman, *Hittite Diplomatic Texts*

entity was addressed.[20] In addition, išкur's characteristic qualities and attributes were treated alternatively as distinct entities or as part of his person. For example, while in some contexts treated as descriptors of the Weather God, Respect and Reverence were also addressed as distinct deities who accompanied him as part of his entourage.[21] Likewise, in the Song of Ullikumi, the Weather God arms himself for battle with Downpours and Storms, which are treated as independent, animate extensions of himself.[22] In some contexts, various divine aspects also were listed as independent deities, such as the deity's many attributes, characteristics, and roles. For example, as a function of the Weather God's control over the various aspects of weather, we find the Weather God of Heaven, of Rain, of the Storm, of Clouds, of Thunder, and of Lightning. In accord with his responsibility for the vegetation, we find the Weather God of Growth, of the Vineyard, of Farmland, and of the Meadow. In his function as protector of the king and the state, we find the Weather God of the Palace, of the House, of the Head (of the king), of the Scepter, and of the Camp. In his role as personal protector of the king, we find the Weather God of the (auspicious) Day and of Well-Being, and in his role as helper, the Weather God of the Appeal. As the head of the pantheon, the Weather God was also responsible for upholding justice and was thus referred to as the Weather God of Justice, of Peace, and of the Oath.[23] Various divine epithets were also deified in their own

---

[2nd ed.; Writings from the Ancient World 7; Atlanta: Scholars, 1999], treaty no. 18B, 111–12).

20. For example, the Hurrian Kumarbi cycle refers to a single weather god, Tessub, whose line struggles with that of Kumarbi for supremacy among the gods (here, there is some debate as to how these Hurrian texts were received in the Hittite heartland [Beckman, e.g., contends that they were merely belletristic ("Mythologie A. II. Bei den Hethitern," *RlA* 8 [1993–1997]: 565); cf., however, Carlo Corti, "The So-called 'Theogony' or 'Kingship in Heaven': The Name of the Story," in *Acts of the VIth International Congress of Hittitology* (ed. A. Archi and R. Francia; Studi Micenci ed Egeo-Anatolici 49; Rome: CNR, 2007), 109–21; Amir Gilan, "Epic and History in Hittite Anatolia: In Search of a Local Hero," in *Epic and History* (ed. D. Konstan and K. A. Raaflaub; Oxford: Wiley-Blackwell, 2010), 60.

21. *KUB* 35.145; *KUB* 31.127; Haas, *Geschichte der hethitischen Religion*, 313. These forces were distinct deities in the sense that they were not the Weather God himself, but animate forces controlled by him. As Wilhelm notes, these characteristic qualities of deities were thought of as alive and served as divine companions ("'Gleichsetzungstheologie,'" 59–60).

22. Haas, *Geschichte der hethitischen Religion*, 296. In addition, the male warrior form of Šauška was venerated with various kinds of weapons perceived to be independent divine beings (Ilse Wegner, *Gestalt und Kult der Ištar-Šawuška in Kleinasien* [AOAT 36; Neukirchen-Vluyn: Neukirchener Verlag, 1981], 95–99; Taracha, *Religions of Second Millennium Anatolia*, 122).

23. Haas, *Geschichte der hethitischen Religion*, 313, 325, 327, 337–38 with references; Beckman, "Pantheon," 313; Cem Karasu, "Why Did the Hittites Have a Thousand Deities?," in *Hittite Studies in Honor of Harry A. Hoffner Jr. on the Occasion of His 65th Birthday* (ed. G.

right (like Piḫaimmi and Piḫammi).[24] Furthermore, rather than simply being a defining characteristic of deities, *parā ḫandandatar* was itself occasionally deified.[25]

In most cases, an anthropomorphized being existed at the heart of and exercised control over these separable aspects. The anthropomorphic core thus rendered, for example, the storm, and more generally weather, more understandable, approachable, and subject to influence.[26] In short, like the Mesopotamian gods, the Hittite Weather God consisted of multiple aspects that, like LEGOs, could be taken apart and put back together again.[27]

In addition to gods with detachable aspects, the Hittite divine sphere also included god-groups with detachable gods.[28] This is especially true of the Hittite weather god(s). Since Hittite Anatolian agriculture and economic life depended on rain, most major and many minor towns appear to have had their own weather god, upon whom they relied for rain and protection. Rather than assimilating all of the multiple localized weather gods into a single weather god, it seems that the various weather gods often were viewed as distinct divine entities that instead could be grouped together into a single category of similar, yet independent beings (e.g., the Weather God of Aleppo and the Weather God of Nerik).[29] Thus, we may

---

Beckman, R. Beal and G. McMahon; Winona Lake, IN: Eisenbrauns, 2003), 225; Schwemer, "Storm-Gods II," 21.

24. *CHD* P, 253; Schwemer, "Storm-Gods II," 22.

25. Steiner, "Gott," 565.

26. "Subject to influence" does not mean that weather gods allowed people to control the weather. Instead, anthropomorphized deities in charge of the weather allowed humans to influence them and thus the weather. Regarding their anthropomorphization, see, e.g., Hutter, "Religion in Hittite Anatolia," 78; Beckman, "Pantheon," 312. Regarding anthropomorphization as a means of making deities more understandable, see Wilhelm, "'Gleichsetzungstheologie,'" 59

27. Not all deities were characterized by such fluidity and none to the same degree as the Weather God.

28. Regarding god groups in Hatti, see, e.g., Steiner, "Gott," 551, 553; Haas, *Geschichte der hethitischen Religion*, 311; Itamar Singer, "'The Thousand Gods of Hatti': The Limits of an Expanding Pantheon," in *Concepts of the Other in Near Eastern Religions* (I. Alon, I. Gruenwald and I. Singer, eds.; Israel Oriental Studies 14; Leiden: Brill, 1994), 90. In some instances, the weather gods were organized into a family of weather gods (e.g., many local ᴵŠᴷᵁᴿs [weather gods] were considered to be sons of the great ᴵŠᴷᵁᴿ of Heaven, including ᴵŠᴷᵁᴿ of Nerik and ᴵŠᴷᵁᴿ of Zippalanda, rather than considered manifestations of the main weather god himself [Schwemer, "Storm-Gods II," 21]).

29. The difference between individual and group constellations is admittedly not always apparent, as in many cases it is hard to tell if the texts speak of a single deity who splits into multiple (semi-)independent aspects or various independent deities who are united in a god group. Whatever the connections may be, the relationships may be classified as divine constellations, whether as a constellation of aspects or a constellation of deities. Such constellations demonstrate the ancient Near Eastern divine fluidity in which a deity's

speak of a kind of constellation in which individual deities were grouped together into a collective and could be treated as part of the collective or as individuals depending on the context. Individual deities in this collective could even have their own constellations.[30]

In addition to treating the individual weather gods as distinct entities, the Hittites tended to agglutinate the deities of conquered peoples into their pantheon, especially in the Empire period.[31] As a result, originally foreign deities often retained their local identities, even when they overlapped significantly with others in the Hittite pantheon (e.g., the Weather God of Aleppo was differentiated from other weather gods in the Hittite pantheon).[32] Thus, while Mesopotamian gods collected attributes, the Hittite empire collected gods, often boasting of the "thousand gods of Hatti."[33]

This Hittite approach to multiplying deities is a rather extreme expression of the general ancient Near Eastern comprehensive mentality,[34] in which one attempted to cover all the bases so as not to neglect any single element and thereby face the effects of its displeasure.[35] For example, in order effectively to conquer an

---

multiple parts could be integrated into an organic unity or as "fragmented" into several (semi-)independent aspects.

30. See, e.g., the Weather God of Aleppo, who maintained his own constellation with various local manifestations throughout the Hittite empire, including in the capital, as well as his various detachable attributes (cf. Itamar Singer, "'The Thousand Gods of Hatti': The Limits of an Expanding Pantheon," in *Concepts of the Other in Near Eastern Religions* [I. Alon, I. Gruenwald and I. Singer, eds.; Israel Oriental Studies 14; Leiden: Brill, 1994], 87).

31. Singer, "Thousand Gods," 85; Beckman, "Pantheon," 308. However, there is some evidence of divine consolidation, most notably in Queen Puduhepa's equation of Sun Goddess of Arinna with the Hurrian Hebat, who despite their obvious differences were equated because they were married to weather gods (Taracha suggests that their equation marked an attempt to unite the dynastic and state pantheons [*Religions of Second Millennium Anatolia*, 91]). Nonetheless, this equation was limited since separate cults were maintained for both deities, even in the same place (Singer, "Thousand Gods," 90; Schwemer, "Storm-Gods II," 22).

32. Bryce, *Life and Society*, 135.

33. Regarding the thousand gods, see Singer, "Thousand Gods;"; Cem Karasu, "Why Did the Hittites Have a Thousand Deities?," in Beckman, Beal, and McMahon, eds., *Hittite Studies in Honor of Harry A. Hoffner, Jr.*

34. Regarding ritual, see, e.g., Hundley, *Keeping Heaven*.

35. Cf. Taracha, *Religions of Second Millennium Anatolia*, 80: "This new religiosity [in the Empire period] found reflection in multiplying divine beings through the deification of all entities associated with the gods and their attributes, as if the god's anger could be aroused by unintentional omittance of any especially favored aspect of his nature or attribute. The concept of divinity grew to encompass weather phenomena like winds, clouds, lightning and thunder (all treated as if they were beings associated with the gods), as well as some abstract concepts like goodness, law and order, wisdom, joy, health and others."

enemy city, the Hittites seem to have believed they had to secure the permission of the local deity by supplication rather than by force.[36] In the case of Aleppo, the Hittite takeover was not fully accomplished until the resident weather god acknowledged his "satisfaction with the respect bestowed on him by the conquerors."[37] In order to ensure this acknowledgment, the weather god, his wife Hebat, and their son Sarruma were given a distinct place in Hatti, without being (fully) assimilated by the Hittite weather god(s).[38] Thus, instead of becoming a trophy in the conquering god's temple, the weather god of Aleppo was incorporated into the Hittite pantheon and achieved a prominent status in it.[39] In essence, the Hittites convinced him that he was better off under their care than under that of his previous caregivers.

## Relation to Humans and to the World

The gods were imagined to control everything necessary for human survival. For example, the rainfall necessary for human sustenance was under the purview of the various weather gods.[40] Thus, in order for humanity to survive and thrive, it was necessary to curry divine favor. However, direct appearance of deities to humans was rare and unpredictable in the human sphere. Since gods traditionally dwelt in the heavens or the underworld,[41] evidence of direct contact was generally limited to mythology.[42] The cult served as the primary access point, the means of bringing heaven to earth, of situating the gods in the midst of human society in a

---

36. Singer, "Thousand Gods," 87. However, one should not make too much of this isolated incident, in which the conquest of a major city was involved. Hittite kings likely did not take such care at all times and in all places.

37. Ibid.

38. Ibid.

39. Ibid., 86.

40. Cf. Hutter, "Religion in Hittite Anatolia," 75; Schwemer, "Storm-Gods I," 129–30.

41. Steiner, "Gott," 571.

42. Hittite epic literature is practically nonexistent (Gilan, "Epic and History," 60) and as such does not present contact between the Hittites and their gods. The mythological texts mention exceptional and often fanciful meetings between humans and deities (see Hoffner, *Hittite Myths*). For example, both versions of the old Anatolian Illuyanka myth, concerned with the conflict between the Weather God and an evil reptile, involve direct divine–human contact. In the first, the daughter of the Weather God, Inara, enlists the help of a human, Hupasiya, by sleeping with him, to defeat the serpent. In the second, the Weather God marries the daughter of a poor man and has a son, who marries the daughter of the serpent in return for the captured heart and eyes of the Weather God. In addition, In the tale of Appu and his two sons, the Sun God comes down to earth and transforms himself into a man in order to question Appu.

controlled and accessible environment.[43] In the resulting human–divine relationship, the deity was the master and the humans were the servants.[44] Humans served the deity in the cult, while the deity in turn blessed and protected humans in the interest of continued service.[45]

The gods, who ruled the cosmos,[46] also had expectations of both morality and piety.[47] Any breach invited retribution upon both the offender and his family.[48] Correct behavior was especially important for the king and queen, who served as high priests[49] and, as such, officiated at most of the major festivals.[50] One may even argue with some degree of confidence that the king's ritual responsibilities were his most important duties; for, "in the Hittite mind, the most direct path to political stability lay in maintaining harmonious relations with the gods."[51]

---

43. Deities also communicated through omens and oracles. Omens refer to various forms of contact initiated by the deity, while oracles were initiated by humans (Beckman, "Religion. B. Bei den Hethitern," *RlA* 11 [2007]: 336).

44. See Oliver R. Gurney, *Some Aspects of Hittite Religion* (The Schweich Lecture 1976; Oxford: Oxford University Press, 1977), 2; Popko, *Religions of Asia Minor* (Warsaw: Academic Publications Dialog, 1995), 131–32; Beckman, "The Tongue is a Bridge: Communication Between Humans and Gods in Hittite Anatolia," *ArOr* 67 (1999): 531; McMahon, "Theology, Priests, and Worship," 1988–89; Collins, *Hittites and Their World*, 177; Taracha, *Religions of Second Millennium Anatolia*, 80–81. This relationship is especially clear in the Plague Prayers of Mursili II and the Instructions for Temple Personnel.

45. Taracha, *Religions of Second Millennium Anatolia*, 80–81.

46. In the Hattic understanding, the gods ruled jointly, whereas the Hurrian model was more one of conquest, wherein the supreme god won his place in the pantheon (which may derive from the Mesopotamian mythical texts upon which the Hurrian are patterned) (McMahon, "Theology, Priests, and Worship," 1989).

47. Ibid. In the Hurrian texts, the gods seem more oblivious to humanity (ibid.).

48. The most common breaches related to the temple personnel were theft from gods' stores, violation of purity standards, and neglect of the gods, for which the death penalty was often imposed (ibid., 1988).

49. "As priest, the king stood at the point of contact between the sphere of the gods and that of humans" (Beckman, "Tongue is a Bridge," 530). As such, he was "subject to special standards of purity" (ibid).

50. The god's *parā ḫandandatar* protected the king and people, but only if the king was in the right. Thus, Hittite historiography provides both a chronicle of events and the king's self-justification (McMahon, "Theology, Priests, and Worship," 1989). For a fuller summary of the 'ideal of kingship,' see Beckman, "Royal Ideology and State Administration in Hittite Anatolia," *CANE* 1:529–32. Regarding kingship as a divine gift, see, e.g., Taracha, *Religions of Second Millennium Anatolia*, 46, 72.

51. McMahon, "Theology, Priests, and Worship," 1990; cf. Johan de Roos, "Hittite Prayers," *CANE* 3:1997. The importance of this role finds clear expression in several places, especially in texts of the royal library that "reveal how conscientiously the kings of the later empire discharged their duties on behalf of the nation" (Gurney, *Some Aspects*, 1).

Cultic care also had cosmic implications. Each deity had a necessary role to play in the cosmos, such that the absence of any one deity could throw the world of humans and the gods into turmoil.[52] Disappearing god myths, in which the world was brought to the brink of chaos when any one of the many deities vacated its post, were prevalent, and various different gods served as their subjects, including various weather gods—a generic Weather God, the Weather God of Queen Asmunikkal, of Queen Harapsili, of the scribe Pirwa, of the city Kuliwisna, and in Lihzina. In turn, several deities, even of the same type, could overlap without being redundant, such that the dissatisfaction of any one deity could have cosmic consequences. Thus, for their own and the world's well-being, humans sought to appease any deity that absented itself in order for it to return to its post and provide renewed favor and protection.[53]

## CULT IMAGES

Unlike in Mesopotamia, descriptions of cult images abound in the texts, especially from the reign of Tudhaliya IV in the late thirteenth century.[54] However, few, if any, of the many cult inventories provide details about statues in the major temples of the Hittite capital, Hattusa, instead offering extensive information about the generally less wealthy local cults.[55] As expected, the cult inventories indicate the statues were made of precious materials, most commonly of "precious metal on an armature of wood."[56]

The cult inventories reveal that the divine statues were small, ranging from 22 to 44 centimeters (9–18 inches) (see fig. 10.1).[57] Various similarly sized statues have been found, one of which has hints of gold overlay.[58] Nonetheless, their

---

52. Beckman, "Mythologie," *RlA* 8 (1993–1997): 566–67.

53. See generally Taracha, *Religions of Second Millennium Anatolia*, 77–78, 155–56.

54. See, e.g., Carl-Georg von Brandenstein, *Hethitische Götter nach Bildbeschreibungen in Keilschrifttexten* (MVAeG 46/2; Leipzig, 1943); Liane Jakob-Rost, "Zu den hethitischen Bildbeschreibungen. I. Teil," *MIO* 8 (1961): 161–217; idem, "Zu den hethitischen Bildbeschreibungen. II. Teil," *MIO* 9 (1963): 175–239; Charles W. Carter, "Hittite Cult Inventories" (Ph.D. Dissertation, University of Chicago, 1962); Joost Hazenbos, *The Organization of the Anatolian Local Cults During the Thirteenth Century B.C.: An Appraisal of the Hittite Cult Inventories* (CM 21; Leiden: Brill, 2003). See briefly Collins, "A Statue for the Deity," 15–18 with references.

55. Collins, "A Statue for the Deity," 16, 18.

56. McMahon, "Theology, Priests, and Worship," 1990; see also Collins, "A Statue for the Deity," 16; Taracha, *Religions of Second Millennium Anatolia*, 60, 129.

57. Gurney, *Some Aspects*, 26; Collins, "A Statue for the Deity," 16; cf. Taracha, *Religions of Second Millennium Anatolia*, 60, 129.

58. Sedat Alp, "Eine hethitische Bronzestatuette und andere Funde aus Zara bei Amasya,"

Fig. 10.1. A gold statue of an anthropomorphic god (3.8 x 1.3 x 1.3 cm [1.5" x .5" x .5"]) (fourteenth–thirteenth centuries). Note the characteristic pointed hat and turned-up toes. Courtesy of the Louvre.

identification as divine cult statues remains only a possibility, largely relying on their size.

There is some evidence that cult statues were not universally small. First, relief scenes of a cultic nature seem to portray life-sized statues (see fig. 10.2). However, these scenes need not be taken literally.[59] It is unclear whether the images were meant to depict the deity itself or its statue. The relief may simply be representing the life-sized god who was present in or accessible through the diminutive statue, expressing that the god in the small image was the same as the god who ruled the cosmos. It thereby warned the onlooker that the god was indeed (present in) the statue and, as such, the statue had to be approached with care. Second, and more tellingly, the size of the statue bases in the excavated temples at Hattusa suggests

---

*Anatolia* 6 (1961/62): 217–43; Bittel, "Einige Kapitel zur hethitischen Archäologie," in *Neuere Hethiterforschung* (ed. G. Walser; Historia, Einzelschriften 7; Wiesbaden: Steiner, 1964), 123–30; A. İlaslı, "A Hittite Statue Found in the Area of Ahurhisar," in *Aspects of Art and Iconography: Anatolia and Its Neighbors: Studies in Honor of Nimet Özgüç* (ed. M. Mellink, E. Porada, and T. Özgüç; Ankara: Türk Tarih Kurumu Basımevi, 1993), 301–8; Collins, "A Statue for the Deity," 16.

59. Ibid., 17.

Fig. 10.2. A depiction of a life-sized weather god presented with libations with another image of the weather god in a chariot pulled by the divine bulls Seri and Hurri behind it (Malatya relief). From E. Akurgal, *The Art of the Hittites*, fig. 105.

that the cult statues they supported were life-sized.[60] Although no inventories remain in Hattusa to confirm our suspicions, such large statues, probably made of precious metals, would have been appropriate for the wealth and prestige of the Hittite capital city.[61] In addition to being the political capital, the plethora of cultic texts found at Hattusa, many of which detail cultic activity in the city's temples, and the multiple temples discovered in that city indicate that it was the religious capital as well and thus the most prominent seat of the official cult.[62] In turn, our present picture may better reflect the peripheral regions of the state or at least the state's perception of them.

The diversity of Hittite gods was expressed using a diversity of forms, of which none clearly predominated.[63] As in Mesopotamia and Egypt, divine representations bore some attributes that were universal signs of divinity and others that distinguished one deity from the next. Anthropomorphic images were characterized by a "peaked cap with horns and typical Hittite dress with turned-up shoes, kilt, and often a sword in the belt."[64] Such deities were commonly depicted astride

---

60. Bittel, "Einige Kapitel," 126; Gurney, *Some Aspects*, 26; Collins, "A Statue for the Deity," 17–18. This possibility is bolstered by the evidence for life-sized statues of kings (Collins, "A Statue for the Deity," 18).

61. Gurney, *Some Aspects*, 26.

62. McMahon, "Theology, Priests, and Worship," 1992.

63. There is also some difficulty in distinguishing between depictions of primary deities and those of their often deified aspects, such as their "personified attributes, weapons, symbols, epithets, forces of nature, etc." (Taracha, *Religions of Second Millennium Anatolia*, 61, 128).

64. McMahon, "Theology, Priests, and Worship," 1990.

Fig. 10.3. The central panel at Yazılıkaya depicting the Weather God, Tessub, astride mountain gods and his consort, Hebat, astride a panther with their son, daughter, and a granddaughter. Photo courtesy of Billie Jean Collins.

their associated animals. For example, war gods were pictured with lions and tutelary deities with stags, while the reliefs from the great rock sanctuary of Yazılıkaya picture the Hurrian weather god Tessub standing on the napes of two mountain gods, while his consort Hebat stands opposite on a panther (fig. 10.3).[65] In addition to his depiction astride mountains, Tessub is also depicted in a chariot drawn by two deified bulls, Seri and Hurri (see fig. 10.2).[66] In general, the presentation of the gods astride various potent creatures depicted their potency that belied their anthropomorphic guise. In other words, when depicted anthropomorphically, their mastery over such dangerous creatures distinguished them from their hu-

---

65. Taracha, *Religions of Second Millennium Anatolia*, 60, 94. On the iconography of Tessub on two mountains, see further Meindert Djikstra, "The Weather God on Two Mountains," *UF* 23 (1991): 127–40; Robert L. Alexander, "The Storm-God at Yazılıkaya: Sources and Influences," in Mellink, Porada, and Özgüç, eds., *Aspects of Art and Iconography*, 1–13; Martin Klingbeil, *Yahweh Fighting from Heaven: God as Warrior and as God of Heaven in the Hebrew Psalter and Ancient Near Eastern Iconography* (OBO 169; Fribourg: University Press, 1999), 247–49.

66. For the divine bulls associated with Tessub, see Schwemer, *Wettergottgestalten*, 477–87.

man counterparts. In addition to distancing deities from humans, the variety of associated animals distinguished between individual deities and highlighted certain primary characteristics of these deities. For example, the bull of the Weather God, like the storm, was characterized by superhuman strength and fertility.[67] Deities also bore other divine attributes that distinguished them from each other and further distinguished them from their human counterparts. For example, "the storm-god usually carries a mace and may hold a bolt of lightning as well, Ishtar has wings, and the moon-god has a crescent moon on his hat."[68]

As in Egypt, deities also could be displayed in animal form;[69] most notably the Weather God took the form of a bull as at Alaca Höyük (fig. 10.4).[70] Thus, in addition to being pulled by bulls, the Weather God was also depicted as a bull.[71] As in Mesopotamia, symbolic or aniconic divine images figured prominently.[72] For example, various kurša-bags were venerated as tutelary deities, while the throne goddess Halmasuit was appropriately venerated as the ceremonial throne.[73] Sun goddesses were most often represented as sun disks, while mountain gods were represented by an assortment of weapons or various vessels (fig. 10.5).[74] Present from the earliest times and prevalent through Hittite history, the ḫuwaši-stone is of particular interest (fig. 10.6).[75] Located predominantly outside of town, often in

---

67. Wilhelm, "'Gleichsetzungstheologie,'" 58.

68. McMahon, "Theology, Priests, and Worship," 1990.

69. Regarding theriomorphic and symbolic forms, see, e.g., Güterbock, "Hethitische Götterbilder und Kultobjekte," in Beiträge zur Altertumskunde Kleinasiens: Festschrift für Kurt Bittel (ed. R. M. Boehmer and H. Hauptmann; Mainz: von Zabern, 1983), 203–17; Popko, "Anikonische Götterdarstellungen in der altanatolischen Religion," in Quaegebeur, ed., Ritual and Sacrifice in the Ancient Near East, 319–27; Hazenbos, Organization of the Anatolian Local Cults, 173–90; Collins, "A Statue for the Deity," 24–29, 38–42.

70. Güterbock, "Hethitische Götterbilder," 211–12; Haas, Geschichte der hethitischen Religion, 302–4; Collins, "A Statue for the Deity," 40–41 (fig. 2:12); Taracha, Religions of Second Millennium Anatolia, 60.

71. As in Egypt, live animals also played a role in the cult. For example, the sacred bull of the Weather God "was kept in a special enclosure and was led in a ceremonial procession during some festivals" (Taracha, Religions of Second Millennium Anatolia, 60; see further Taracha, "Bull-Leaping on a Hittite Vase: New Light on Anatolian and Minoan Religion," Archeologia 53 [2002], 13–16).

72. Regarding Hittite material aniconism, see esp. the references in Collins, "A Statue for the Deity," 14–15 n. 6. Like symbols, "aniconic images" refers to images associated with but not visually depicting the deity.

73. Taracha, Religions of Second Millennium Anatolia, 48, 57–58.

74. Collins, "A Statue for the Deity," 24–25; Taracha, Religions of Second Millennium Anatolia, 61, 130; cf. KUB 38.23 obv. 10–11; KUB 38.29 obv. 24'–25'; Hazenbos, Organization of the Anatolian Local Cults, 174, 176.

75. Regarding the early evidence, see Popko, Kultobjekte, 135; idem, "Aniconische

Fig. 10.4. An orthostat relief from the city gate of Alaca Höyük depicting the king worshipping before the Weather God represented in bull form. From K. Bittel, *Die Hethiter*, fig. 214.

a grove, near a spring or on a mountain, i.e., "any location imbued with a sense of the sacred," ḫuwaši-stones could also be found inside temples either in addition to or in the place of another cult image.[76] While small towns may have had a ḫuwaši in place of a temple, cities had a mixture of ḫuwaši-s and temples.[77] Each stele belonged to a specific deity and functioned much like a cult statue in a temple.[78]

---

Götterdarstellungen," 325. Regarding ḫuwaši-stones in general, see Haas, *Geschichte der hethitischen Religion*, 507–9; Collins, "A Statue for the Deity," 26–29 and the references in n. 6; Taracha, *Religions of Second Millennium Anatolia*, 61–63. In exceptional cases, ḫuwaši-stones were constructed of wood or precious metal (Taracha, *Religions of Second Millennium Anatolia*, 61 and references cited in n. 320).

76. Collins, "A Statue for the Deity," 26. In such cases, it is possible that the temples were built secondarily to enshrine the ḫuwaši-stones previously exposed to the elements (personal communication Jared Miller); cf., however, Haas, *Geschichte der hethitischen Religion*, 508, followed by Fleming, *Time*, 85, who contend that ḫuwaši-stones in temples were smaller models of the larger original, made of precious materials, and made to bring rural worship (in the form of ḫuwaši-stones) into the newer urban sanctuaries.

77. Ibid., 26–27. For example, Karahna had 26 deities, 9 of which had temples and 17 of which had ḫuwaši-s (*KUB* 38.12 iii 22'–23'; Güterbock, "Yazılıkaya: À propos a New Interpretation," *JNES* 34 [1975]: 127). However, the juxtaposition of ḫuwaši and temple in cities does not imply that the ḫuwaši required other architectural features around it to function as a temple (Collins, "A Statue for the Deity," 27; *pace* Hazenbos, *Organization of the Anatolian Local Cults*, 175).

78. Hutter, "Kultstellen und Baityloi: Die Ausstrahlung eines syrischen religiösen

Fig. 10.5. The so-called dagger god from Yazılıkaya, made up of an amalgam of animate (e.g., anthropomorphic and leonine) and inanimate elements. From K. Bittel, *Die Hethiter*, fig. 254.

Although deities were conceived primarily according to the anthropomorphic model, "theriomorphic and symbolic representations continue to dominate the inventories" until the end of the Empire period.[79] Although Tudhaliya IV's restoration of the cult displayed a certain predilection for anthropomorphic images,[80] the majority of replacement images were theriomorphic, while mountain gods were almost exclusively presented in the form of a mace decorated with the sun disk and

Phänomens nach Kleinasien und Israel," in *Religionsgeschichtliche Beziehungen zwischen Kleinasien, Nordsyrien und dem Alten Testament: Internationales Symposion Hamburg, 17.-21. März 1990* (ed. B. Janowski, K. Koch and G. Wilhelm; OBO 129; Fribourg: University Press, 1993), 91–95, 103; Collins, "A Statue for the Deity," 27.

79. Collins, "A Statue for the Deity," 40–41.

80. Gurney, *Religion*, 25; Emmanuel Laroche, "La réforme religieuse du roi Tudḫaliya IV et sa signification politique," in *Les syncrétismes dans les religions de l'Antiquité* (ed. F. Dunand and P. Lévêque; Leiden: Brill, 1975), 92–93; Collins, "A Statue for the Deity," 40.

Fig. 10.6. A standing stone (*ḫuwasi*) from Karahöyük with a Luwian inscription. From Özgüç and Özgüç, *Karahöyük*, pl. X.2.

crescent, with an associated anthropomorphic statue.[81] There also seems to have been a differentiation in presentation according to the sex of the deity. While male deities were often represented symbolically or theriomorphically, goddesses were almost always depicted anthropomorphically.[82] Thus, even with the opportunity to upgrade and contemporize the cult images, the Hittites made no attempt to get rid of theriomorphic and symbolic forms. Instead, although still represented in the inventories, there was a tendency to replace *ḫuwaši*-stones with a smaller more mobile image.[83] According to one ritual text, it would seem that the deity itself could choose which of the various possible images it wanted in any given context.[84]

---

81. Ibid., 40.

82. Güterbock, "Hethitische Götterbilder," 204; Collins, "A Statue for the Deity," 40 n. 99.

83. Collins, "A Statue for the Deity," 41. Nonetheless, it must be noted that the lack of physical and textual evidence for cult statues in the Hittite capital renders our portrait incomplete.

84. Collins, "A Statue for the Deity," 24 n. 41; Taracha, *Religions of Second Millennium Anatolia*, 130.

"He will come and worship the goddess (Uliliyassi). In addition if she prefers a pithos, he will make her stand as a pithos. But if not, then he will make her stand as a ḫuwaši-stone or he will make her (as) a statue."[85] It would also seem that a deity could at least in some instances choose the gender of its anthropomorphic representation: "If you, O god, are refusing the statue of a woman; if you, O god, are seeking the statue of a man, but you do not seek the statue of a woman, let the flesh oracle be favorable."[86]

In addition, "there is ample evidence that the gods in Hittite Anatolia were no more limited in quantity of forms than they were in variety."[87] For example, "during a festival at Tahurpa, the queen offered sacrifices to eight Sun Goddesses of Arinna in the form of three statues and five sun disks, which had been donated by six of her predecessors."[88] Thus, the thousand gods of Hatti had a multitude of options, in both form and quantity, for presencing themselves.

Having surveyed the various forms of divine cult representations, we will now examine the induction of images into the temple and their daily care and feeding. The chapter will conclude with a discussion of the perceived nature and function of cult images and the relation between various images.

## 1. THE EXPANSION OF THE CULT OF THE DEITY OF THE NIGHT

The ritual for establishing a new (i.e., satellite) temple for the Goddess of the Night[89] provides the closest parallel to Egyptian and Mesopotamian installation

---

85. *KUB* 7.5 iv 11–16, edited by Hoffner, "Paskuwatti's Ritual against Sexual Impotence (*CTH* 406)," *AuOr* 5 (1987): 276, 279; translation after Collins, "A Statue for the Deity," 24 n. 41.

86. *KUB* 50.89 iii 5'–7', edited in *CHD* L-N, *markiya-*; translation after Collins, "A Statue for the Deity," 24 n. 41.

87. Collins, "A Statue for the Deity," 28; see also Gurney, "Hittite Kingship," in *Myth, Ritual, and Kingship: Essays on the Theory and Practice of Kingship in the Ancient Near East and in Israel* (ed. S. H. Hooke; Oxford: Clarendon, 1958), 120; Gurney, *Religion*, 26; Taracha, *Religions of Second Millennium Anatolia*, 62.

88. *KUB* 25.14 i 10–31; Shoshana R. Bin-Nun, *The Tawannanna in the Hittite Kingdom* (Texte der Hethiter 5; Heidelberg: Winter, 1975), 197–202; Collins, "A Statue for the Deity," 28.

89. Translation after Jared L. Miller, *Studies in the Origins, Development and Interpretation of the Kizzuwatna Rituals* (StBoT 46; Wiesbaden: Harrassowitz, 2004), 259, *pace* Heinz Kronasser's earlier *Die Umsiedlung der schwarzen Gottheit: Das hethitische Ritual KUB XXIX 4(des Ulippis)* (Graz: Verlag der Österreichische Akademie der Wissenschaften, 1963). Miller alternatively refers to the ritual as "The Adlocation of the Cult of the Deity of the Night" (Miller, *Kizzuwatna Rituals*, 259). The authors themselves refer to the ritual as "When someone erects the Deity of the Night separately," a shorter version found in the colophon and in the catalogue entries *KUB* 8.71 edge 16'–rev. 1 and *KUB* 30.64 obv. 1'–4'

rituals of the divine statue.[90] Unfortunately, the text is both incomplete and of uncertain relevance to the Hittite heartland. Only one of two tablets, describing the
first seven days of the ritual, is preserved (*KUB* 29.4+ [*CTH* 481]).[91] In addition,
the text comes from Kizzuwatna in southeastern Anatolia and is coauthored by a
Babylonian and Kizzuwatnean priest.[92] Although incomplete, it nonetheless provides detailed and important information on the expansion of a deity's cult to a
new temple, including the statue's crafting and installation. Likewise, the Kizzuwatnean provenance and the presence of originally foreign elements[93] do not in
themselves render the ritual peripheral. Rather, various other texts refer to "split-
ting" a deity and worshipping it "separately" in a second temple suggesting that the
preserved ritual or something quite like it was practiced widely in the Hittite realm
in the Empire period.[94]

Like other ancient Near Eastern ritual texts, the expansion ritual offers various interpretive problems. "The composition as it stands could by no means serve
as a complete script for someone who was attempting to establish the cult anew."[95]
Since it was likely composed as an outline or memory tool for the cultic offici-

---

of the longer more unwieldy title (ibid.). See Miller, *Kizzuwatna Rituals*, 263–96 for the
identity and character of the Goddess of the Night.

90. On the presence of the mouth-washing ritual among the Hittites and its relation to
the *itkalzi* ritual (*CTH* 471), see Rita Strauß, *Reinigungsrituale aus Kizzuwatna: Ein Beitrag
zur Erforschung hethitischer Ritualtradition und Kulturgeschichte* (Berlin: de Gruyter, 2005),
181–88.

91. The existence of the second tablet is inferred from a catalog text (*KUB* 30.64 obv. 1'–
4'; *COS* 1.70:173; Miller, *Kizzuwatna Rituals*, 259). Two fragmentary duplicates are also
preserved (regarding the manuscripts, see Miller, *Kizzuwatna Rituals*, 262–68, 272). On the
date and provenance of the ritual, see ibid., 362.

92. Ibid., 362, 397–98; Collins, "A Statue for the Deity," 29.

93. See, e.g., the use of the Hurrian designators for pit (*api*) and burnt offering (*ambašši*)
(Strauß, *Reinigungsrituale*, 49, 113).

94. See, e.g., *KUB* 32.133 obv. i 2–3: "When my forefather, Tudhaliya, Great King, split the
Deity of the Night from the temple of the Deity of the Night in Kizzuwatna and worshipped
her separately in a temple in Samuha" (translation after Miller, *Kizzuwatna Rituals*, 312).
On the identification of the king as Tudhaliya I (I/II), see ibid., 350–56. Although similar,
this text is to be distinguished from the ritual text (*CTH* 481; ibid., 357–62). Regarding the
Goddess of the Night, see also *KUB* 8.71 16'–rev. 1 and *KUB* 30.64 obv. 1'–4' (ibid., 383);
cf. *KBo* 24.45+ (ibid., 430–32). See also Hattusili III's statement that he divided Ishtar of
Samuha and made her a new temple in Urikina (*KUB* 21.17 ii 5–8; see *CHD* P, 279–80) and
the oracle text *KUB* 5.6+; *KUB* 35.54 ii 70–72, iii 27 (Richard H. Beal, "Dividing a God," in
*Magic and Ritual in the Ancient World* (ed. P. Mirecki and M. Meyer; Leiden: Brill, 2002),
198–99 and nn. 11–12).

95. Miller, *Kizzuwatna Rituals*, 398.

ant, the SANGA-priest, many of the necessary actions are left undescribed.[96] Other ritual tablets or experienced cultic personnel would have been necessary to fill in the gaps.[97] In addition, the text provides few purpose statements for the various ritual activities. No accompanying incantation tablet has been found and the ritual tablet presents no list of incantations, in which many of the purpose statements may be found, as in Egypt and Mesopotamia. Although extensive, the inventory of necessary cultic paraphernalia is also not exhaustive. For example, the all-important *uliḫi* (presumably some sort of wool) is not mentioned.[98] Like the Mesopotamian mouth-washing ritual, the Hittite expansion is a composite text and as such does not always logically cohere.[99] In addition, compared to its Egyptian and Mesopotamian counterparts, the ritual has received fairly minimal scholarly attention.[100] However, this relative dearth is somewhat offset by the more thorough treatment of various of the ritual elements that feature in other Hittite and particularly Kizzuwatnean rituals.[101] Despite our limitations, much can nonetheless be said that offers an important glimpse into Hittite conceptions of divine presence in the temple. Rather than interpreting the ritual in all its complexity and noting its various inconsistencies like Miller, the following analysis, like Beal's, aims to be more synthetic and selective in its attention. It analyzes the ritual according to the categories of structure, structural interpretation, use, and ideology. After turning briefly to evidence for the daily cult, it will examine the relationship between the deity and its statue(s), the possibility of destruction and deportation, and the necessity of divine nourishment.

---

96. Ibid., 398, 401, 422; cf. Klinger, "Reinigungsriten und Abwehrzauber: Funktion und Rolle magischer Rituale be den Hethitern," in *Die Hethiter und ihr Reich: Das Volk der 1000 Götter – Begleitband zur Ausstellung der Kunsthalle der Bundesrepublik Deutschland* (ed. T. Özgüç; Bonn: Kunst- und Ausstellungshalle Der Bundesrepublik Deutschland, 2002), 146.

97. Miller, *Kizzuwatna Rituals*, 404.

98. Miller, *Kizzuwatna Rituals*, 401. "The most common pattern is an often extensive listing of what items are needed for a certain ritual, then the statement that the ritual is to be performed, whereby it is often the case that some of the items demanded in the very brief ritual prescriptions are not found in the preceding lists. Indeed, it is striking that hardly any description of the ritual performances is to be found in the entire composition, in stark contrast to the sometimes voluminous lists" (ibid., 401–2).

99. Cf. Miller, *Kizzuwatna Rituals*, 421–22.

100. See esp Beal, "Dividing a God," 197–208; Miller, *Kizzuwatna Rituals*, and the survey of scholarship in ibid., 261–62.

101. See esp. Haas, *Materia Magica et Medica Hethitica: Ein Beitrag zur Heilkunde im Alten Orient* (2 vols.; Berlin: de Gruyter, 2003); Strauß, *Reinigungsrituale*. For the text's various parallels and sources, see Miller, *Kizzuwatna Rituals*, 422–37.

*Structure*[102]

After the initial preparations, ritual action revolves around two primary locales, the old temple and the new temple, occupying respectively and consecutively four and two days of ritual activity, with slight detours to the house of the ritual patron,[103] the storehouse, and the riverbank. The following sketch traces these activities as described in the text.

The tablet begins by stating the occasion for the ritual, the establishment of a second temple on the basis of the original temple and the installation of the deity "separately" or "independently."[104] Day one[105] begins with instructions for fashioning the deity's image (§2), furniture and accoutrements (§§3–7), and garments for both sexes (§8). Constructed of gold and adorned with various precious materials, the new image is crafted like its prototype. On day two, the first day of the ritual proper, the ritual actors draw the "waters of purification" (*šeḫelliya[š] wātar/widār*) and place them on the roof of the original temple for the night. They also attract the "old"—i.e., original—deity using colored strands of wool and fine oil "along seven roads and seven paths from the mountain, the river, the plain, Heaven and Earth"[106] into the old temple and bind an *uliḫi* to her, that is, to her statue (§9–12).[107] On day three (§§13–17), the ritualists bring down the waters in the predawn light. After the ritual patron bows to the deity, he and the SANGA-priest each pull up the deity from a pit (*api*) seven times. After entering the storehouse, they perform the *dupšaḫi*-ritual. At dusk, they perform the ritual of blood (*zurki*) with a fish and a kid or a lamb in the old temple, this time without bowing. The praise ritual (*šarlatti*) with a sheep follows, and, after they treat the ritual patron and the deity with silver and the *gangati*-plant, they burn a lamb as a burnt offering (*ambašši*). The ritual patron then bows before going home. That night the waters of purification are returned to the roof, accompanied by various items to be used in the following day's offering to Pirinkir.[108] On the evening of day four (§§18–19),

---

102. See Miller, *Kizzuwatna Rituals*, 272–310, for transliteration, translation, and commentary. Unless otherwise noted, translations follow Miller. Cf. Beckman, "Temple Building among the Hittites," in Boda and Novotny, eds., *From the Foundations to the Crenellations*, 80–85. As a word of caution, it must be noted that the paragraph numbering of Miller and Beckman are not always consistent.

103. The ritual patron is the person responsible for the construction of the new temple, i.e., the person funding it.

104. Beckman ("Temple Building," 81) opts for the translation "independently."

105. The initial "day" undoubtedly refers to more than a single calendar day. It instead encompasses the time necessary to make preparations and construct both the temple and the divine image (see Miller, *Kizzuwatna Rituals*, 399, 417).

106. Translation after Collins, "A Statue for the Deity," 30.

107. Regarding the enigmatic *uliḫi*, see further below.

108. Although related, Pirinkir seems to be distinct from the Goddess of the Night.

the ritual actors perform the ritual of well-being (*keldi*) for Pirinkir on the roof and scatter bread crumbs and fruit before her as they carry her into the temple. Inside they present the well-being offering to the deity, that is, its statue, before the ritual patron bows and returns home. Day five (§§20–23) concludes the rites in the old temple. At dawn, they perform the *tuḫalzi*-ritual. Following the rite, fine oil is poured into a *tallai*-vessel and the deity is implored to "preserve your being, but divide your divine manifestation (*šiuniyatar*)! Come to that new house, too, and take yourself the honored place! And when you make your way, then take yourself only that place!" Thereafter they evoke the deity from the wall with red wool seven times and place the *uliḫi* into the *tallai*-vessel of refined oil, which is then deposited in the new temple apart from the deity in the form of its new statue. They swing [a kid? and] a lamb over the new temple and install the new golden deity and its equipment.

At the discretion of the ritual patron, the first day in the new temple (§§24–29) may overlap with the last day in the old temple. At the riverbank, they draw the deity "from Akkade, from Babylon, from Susa, from Elam, from ḪUR.SAG.KALAM.MA (=Kish) in the city that you love, from the mountain, from the river, from the sea, from the valley, from the steppe, from the spring, from the sky, from the earth, from the seven roads and from the seven footpaths." After they finish evoking the deity, a tent is erected at the riverbank and another *uliḫi*, this time associated with the "new" deity, is placed inside. The ritual of blood with a kid, the ritual of praise with a lamb, and the burnt offering with a lamb follow. The deity, presumably in the form of the *uliḫi*,[109] is then presented with a meal and transferred to the ritual patron's house. The ritualists scatter bread, crumbled cheese, and fruit beneath her, wave some *ḫusti*-mineral substance over her, and then place the deity in the storehouse and present another burnt offering. The new *uliḫi* is attached to the new statue.[110] The day ends with the placement of the waters of purification on the roof of the new temple, where they will remain overnight "beneath the stars."

On the second day in the new temple (§§30–33),[111] they open the *tallai*-vessel brought from the old temple, mix its oil with the waters of purification and wash

---

Regarding Pirinkir, see Beckman, "The Goddess Pirinkir and Her Ritual from Ḫattuša (CTH 644)," *Ktema* 24 (1999): 25–39.

109. So Collins, "A Statue for the Deity," 30; Yitzhaq Feder, *Blood Expiation in Hittite and Biblical Ritual: Origins, Context, and Meaning* (SBLWAW Supplement Series 2; Atlanta: SBL, 2011), 26–27.

110. The text also notes that the blood and praise rituals are not performed.

111. Beckman ("Temple Building," 84) alternatively attributes the events of §29 (§28 according to Beckman's enumeration) including placing the waters of purification on the roof to an additional day such that the following events would take place on the third day in the new temple. Beckman (ibid., 85) also attributes the reference to the "evening of the second day" in §33 (§32 after Beckman) to an additional day, such that there are four days preserved in the new temple.

the walls with the mixture "so that the temple is purified."[112] The old *uliḫi* is removed and bound to the red *kureššar*-garment of the new deity. At dusk, the ritual patron enters the temple and bows to the deity. The ritual actors then dig an offering pit and offer a sheep to the deity for reconciliation (*enumašši*).[113] The sheep's blood is used to smear the wall, the golden image of the deity, and all of the paraphernalia, "and the new deity and the temple become pure." The preserved ritual ends with the burning of the fat.

### Structural Interpretation

The Hittite ritual is broader in scope than the corresponding Egyptian and Mesopotamian rituals. Instead of merely bridging the gap between the crafting of the statue and its installation as a fully functioning divine locus in the temple, the Hittite ritual bridges the gap between the plan to build a new temple and its execution, including the installation of the cult image and some consecratory rites. The ritual focuses on the activities involved in installing a new fully functioning cult image of the Goddess of the Night in her new temple. Since the ritual has been created to bring about this result, it would seem that the activities it prescribes are deemed necessary to ensure the proper presence of the deity. In other words, the expansion ritual is necessary in order to ensure that the new temple functions as intended.

The ritual indexically connects the two temples and their resident deity (or deities),[114] especially via the *uliḫi*-s associated with the old and new deities. In §10, an *uliḫi* is bound to the old deity in the old temple, i.e., her statue, thereby indexically connecting the deity in the form of its statue with the *uliḫi*. In §28, another *uliḫi* is connected to the new deity, indexing a connection between the new deity and the new *uliḫi*. In §32, the *uliḫi* from the old temple is attached to the new deity in the new temple, thereby indexing a connection between the old and new temples and the old and new deities.[115] By means of the *uliḫi*-s, the deity may be indexically transitioned from one temple to the next without leaving the original temple. The *uliḫi*-s thus serve as a way of connecting deities and their statues without ever moving the statues.

---

112. Translation after Beckman, "Temple Building," 84.

113. In contrast to the first temple, the text mentions that there is no ritual of drawing the deity from the wall in the new temple.

114. It remains to be seen whether the two statues represent different deities or two manifestations of the same deity.

115. The use of the *tallai*-vessel and more particularly the fine oil it contains further cement the connection between temples as the vessel is brought from the old temple to the new and its oil is applied to the walls of the new temple. The waters of purification are likewise transported from the old to the new temple.

As in Mesopotamia, the change of setting from the old temple to the new temple via the riverbank divides the ritual,[116] of which the scenes in the old and new temple occupy the bulk of space. Throughout these stages, ritual actions connect various elements and actors to the deity (or deities) and, in the process, help to delimit their roles in enabling the divine installation. However, since the actions themselves are rarely described, only the materials necessary to perform them,[117] it often cannot be said how the elements and actions are related to the deity. For example, the text states that the old deity is evoked with red wool and fine oil without describing how the wool and oil are used.[118] The most prominent exception is the prescription to apply the sheep's blood to the deity, the wall, and the deity's equipment in the new temple.[119]

The primary actors include the craftsmen, the priest, and the ritual patron.[120] Once again, the common people are entirely absent from the described ritual. In the text, movement toward and away from the craftsmen defines their roles. They are indexically connected to the statue as they craft it,[121] yet their role ends when it is fashioned. Thus, their role is structurally limited to the crafting of the deity and excluded from the rest of the proceedings.

---

116. The ritual also makes stops at the ritual patron's house (§27) and the storehouse along the way (§§13, 27).

117. As noted, although extensive, such lists are not exhaustive.

118. Similarly, the text indicates that the deity is evoked at the river, without indicating how this is to be achieved (§25). Earlier (§24), the text mentions a long list of items including red wool, a red garment, fine oil, and various foodstuffs without any reference to their specific use. Cf. the ritual of evoking upwards in §§9–10.

119. Perhaps this action is described because it deviates from normal protocol, the ritual activity is so important that it merits elaboration, and/or the activities surrounding the sheep cannot be subsumed under a single-word ritual descriptor (e.g., *tuḫalzi*, *dupšaḫi*, burnt, praise, or well-being rituals). Conversely, in the other cases, the list of necessary elements and the single-word descriptor provide sufficient information for the ritual actor, who was likely familiar enough with the ritual to perform it from memory or ritual activity was prescribed on a separate ritual tablet. Given the variability in preserved ritual texts (see, e.g., Haas, *Materia Magica*), it is also possible that ritual performance was somewhat flexible.

120. The text also mentions the presence of the *katra*-priestess (§8), yet the ritual does not mention her role (see further "*katra-*, *katri-*," *HED* 4: 136–38; Miller, "The *katra/i*-Women in the Kizzuwatnean Rituals from Hattuša," in *Sex and Gender in the Ancient Near East: Compte Rendu de la XLVIIe Rencontre Assyriologique Internationale, Helsinki 2001* [S. Parpola and R. M. Whiting, eds.; Winona Lake, IN: Eisenbrauns, 2002], 423–31). In the divine sphere, both the Goddess of the Night and Pirinkir are mentioned. Since the text omits most utterances, it is impossible to discern the role of the other gods.

121. In addition, they craft the deity's furniture and her accouterments (culminating in the fashioning of her wardrobe; Collins, "A Statue for the Deity," 30).

The priest and the ritual patron, on the other hand, feature prominently until the end of the preserved ritual text and, presumably, until the end of the ritual.[122] The ritual structurally introduces the role of the priests, which begins in earnest when the artisans exit the scene. Within the ritual, it is their role to oversee and enact the ritual[123] and, in so doing, come into contact with the new deity.[124] Structurally, the ritual thus transfers primary care of the statue from the craftsman to the priests and ritual patron.[125]

## Use

As the introduction and colophon indicate, the text describes the ritual component of the establishment of a new temple for the Goddess of the Night and setting up the deity separately or independently. Although often laconic in its description and largely without interpretation, a few purpose statements emerge that help the reader to pinpoint more precisely the function of the ritual and some of its various constituent elements. Most prominently, following the *tuḫalzi* ritual and before drawing the deity from the wall and placing the *uliḫi* in the *tallai*-vessel, the ritual actor requests that the deity "preserve your being, but divide your divine manifestation (*šiuniyatar*)! Come to that new house, too, and take yourself the honored place! And when you make your way, then take yourself only that place!" (§22). In addition, after drawing the deity to the river, various foodstuffs are presented to the deity "to eat" (§27), thus highlighting their alimentary purpose. The waters of purification are explicitly placed on the roof "so that they remain beneath the stars" (§29; cf. §§9, 16). The mixture of fine oil from the *tallai*-vessel and the waters of purification[126] are used to wash the wall so that "the wall is pure" (§31). They slaughter a sheep into the pit "to the deity for reconciliation," and apply its

---

122. The priest emerges to instruct the artisans and emerges more prominently after their construction work is completed. The ritual patron likewise emerges and features prominently once the artisans finish their work.

123. In most cases, the text uses the impersonal "they," thereby obscuring the identity of the ritual actor and indicating that various roles are not fixed.

124. The priest and the ritual patron are the ones who attract the deity to the temple and presumably attach the *uliḫi* to and purify her. Although it is far from explicit (and may change significantly in the unpreserved second tablet), it seems that their contact with the deity in the form of the two statues is minimal. The surrogates (*uliḫi*-s) take the prominent role, while the statues themselves remain in the background.

125. After the installation ritual, it is likely that the priest takes the primary role in caring for the deity, while the ritual patron may continue to sponsor the cult.

126. Which presumably are the same waters as "the water with which they wash the temple wall" (§31).

blood to "the golden deity, the wall and all the paraphernalia of the new deity" so that "the new deity and the temple become pure" (§32).[127]

The names given to the ritual elements likewise seem to be informative. The designator "waters of purification" suggests that purification is a primary use of the waters. The designators "ritual of blood" and "burnt offering" indicate that the manipulation of blood and the burning of the animal as an offering are especially important components of these rites, while the rituals of praise and well-being imply the goals of these rites, namely, for divine praise and to secure divine well-being.

Although they by no means exhaust ritual purpose, these goal statements are nonetheless suggestive of the goals of the larger ritual and its individual elements. As the single recorded ritual utterance and in line with the overall goal of the ritual, the request that the goddess divide her person is especially important. To ensure that this division goes smoothly, various subrites in the larger ritual process serve to (re)establish good relations with the deity. Present throughout the ritual (e.g., through the waters of purification), purity is an especially important goal in and for the newly constructed temple and the newly constructed statue. Indeed, drawing the waters of purification is the first ritual activity described after initial preparations, such that references to purification bookend the ritual and highlight its prominence throughout. Finally, lest we spiritualize or abstract it, the various foodstuffs are explicitly identified as divine food.

## *Ideology*

The Hittite bent for comprehensiveness finds clear expression in the expansion ritual, which abounds with overlapping ritual activity and repetition. Such a comprehensive approach is most apparent in the various evocation rites, where the deity is evoked on different occasions from many different locales and even many times from the same locale on a single occasion (e.g., when the priest and ritual patron each pull up the deity seven times from a pit).[128] As in Egypt and Mesopotamia, the multiple actions and repetition are simply part of the nexus of ritual. The various actions serve as a multiplicity of means to accomplish the desired end ritually. In other words, since no single action is sufficient; the Hittites seem to employ every means at their disposal to ensure that the new temple functions as intended. Repetition naturally appears alongside these multiple actions to produce a cumulative effect, enhancing the function of any one action.[129] The concentration

---

127. Although not explicitly stated, we may presume that the sheep's blood is the blood used since no other blood or animal is in view.

128. See also the multiple and repeated purification, blood, burnt offering, and praise rituals and the repeated use (or at least mention) of the waters of purification.

129. By repeating the same actions in different settings, these repetitions seem to make what is done more of a reality.

of actions and the repetition of those actions in various settings mark the ritual as important and the desired effect as difficult to attain. Likewise, since the efficacy of the ritual—i.e., the satisfied presence of the Goddess of the Night in her new statue in her new temple— is difficult to confirm, multiple and repeated actions serve as a means of thoroughly covering the bases. Like a deity, the ritual is an assemblage of not always consistently articulated parts that together produce a more comprehensive whole.

As in Egypt and Mesopotomia, these multiple means likely forge similar and similarly multiple connections that function on various levels simultaneously. However, given the dearth of descriptive, much less interpretive statements, such connections are more difficult to identify concretely. Likewise, whereas Egyptian and Mesopotamian texts abound with utterances and incantations, the Hittite expansion ritual includes only one, the plea to the Goddess of the Night to divide her divinity or divine manifestation.[130] In Egypt and Mesopotamia and elsewhere in the Hittite ritual corpus, myths are closely associated with rituals and serve as a means of bolstering their efficacy and authority, transposing human activity onto the divine sphere and enlisting divine support to ensure efficacy. For example, in certain evocation rites, mythological material concerned with appeasing an angry and absent god dominates over the description of actual ritual practice.[131] By contrast, the expansion ritual does not explicitly mention any mythological connections or even divine connections apart from Pirinkir and the Goddess of the Night.

While prominent in its Egyptian and Mesopotamian analogs, there is little mention of cultic functionality in the Hittite expansion ritual, such as assigning the new statue its cultic roles and empowering it with the potencies necessary to fulfill them. We may reasonably suspect that, had the various utterances been preserved, they would address such issues. Alternatively, the overall purpose of the ritual seems to be cultic functionality achieved by asking the deity to divide herself and making a conducive environment for her to do so by pursuing purity and divine pleasure. Perhaps then the officiants set the stage and create the mood, while the deity does the necessary work.[132] Whereas in Mesopotamia the deity seems to be present in or as the statue from the beginning, in Hittite Anatolia the primary concern is to make the deity present through multiple evocations and a plea to the

---

130. Incantations are commonly attested in ritual texts elsewhere in the Hittite corpus (see, e.g., Taracha, *Religions of Second Millennium Anatolia*, 152). In fact, although such texts often omit details that could be easily remembered, they generally include the precise wording of incantations (Beckman, "Temple Building," 72).

131. See, e.g., Taracha, *Religions of Second Millennium Anatolia*, 155.

132. The actors perform various actions to coax the deity to be present, and, once that presence is assumed, they merely ask the deity to divide herself in order to inhabit the new temple.

goddess to divide herself. Unlike in Mesopotamia, the deity also does not seem to be treated like a newborn who must be matured and empowered. Instead, once her presence is evoked and connected to the new statue, the goddess seems to possess her full faculties. Thus, rather than addressing the divine role and empowering the deity to perform it, the human actors focus their attention on luring the divine presence and ensuring her pleasure, leaving the deity herself to empower her statue and ensure the temple's efficacy.

Although the text nowhere disavows or disguises the human craftsmanship or attributes its crafting to the gods,[133] the complex ritual is required to transcend the initial crafting, to transform the newly crafted statue into a fully functioning locus of divine presence. Thus, although the divine role in crafting the statue remains unknown, the crafting of the deity is clearly insufficient alone, requiring an elaborate ritual involving significant divine action.[134]

### Ideology of Individual Elements

*The Old Temple.* Since the text is laconic in its description and interpretation of ritual actions, we tentatively reconstruct both from other texts that preserve similar rites. First, before the beginning of the primary ritual activity, it seems clear from the text that the new temple and its statue were intended to be copies of the originals, thereby establishing continuity between temples and the divine presence within them. On day two, the ritual proper begins with drawing the waters of purification. Although the expansion ritual includes only a list of necessary elements,[135] we may reconstruct the waters of purification rite especially from a ritual for Pirinkir.[136] The ritual actor[137] breaks the thin bread and throws it into a

---

133. Instead, it clearly affirms the statue human origins, as the explicit first step of the ritual is to appoint various artisans to form the statue. For a similar affirmation of the statue's human origins, see *KUB* 13.33 iv 1–6.

134. Divine participation simply may be assumed (and perhaps may be discerned, as the form of the cult image seems to be at least sometimes the prerogative of the deity [Collins, "A Statue for the Deity," 24 n. 41, 42; *KUB* 7.5 iv 11–16]). In the building of temples and royal statues, divine approval and participation must be scrupulously affirmed.

135. One *tarpala*(-fabric) of red wool, one *tarpala*(-fabric) of blue wool, one woolen *kisri*(-fabric), one shekel of silver, one *gazzarnul*-cloth, a little fine oil, three flat-bread loaves, and one pitcher of wine.

136. *KUB* 39.71 i 22–32; Beal, "Dividing a God," 203; see further David H. Engelhard, "Hittite Magical Practices: An Analysis" (Ph.D. dissertation, Brandeis University, 1970), 140–47; Haas, *Materia Magica I*, 141–60, esp. 146–53; Strauß, *Reinigungsrituale*, 34–38; cf. 98–101.

137. In the Pirinkir ritual, the *katra*-woman is the ritual actor. In the expansion ritual, the priest or ritual patron would be the most likely candidates.

well,[138] libates wine and drips fine oil into the well before drawing the water and tying the fabrics, the *gazzarnul*-cloth, and the silver shekel to the water vessel.[139] The various foodstuffs seem to be offerings presented to the gods in exchange for the waters of purification.[140] As its name indicates, the waters of purification are especially associated with purification, yet not simply in the instrumental sense of removing visible physical impurities like dirt and blood.[141] The waters are also associated with the removal of more intangible imperfections and their effects like bloodshed, perjury, sin, injury, oaths, curses, and tears.[142] Although not preserved in the expansion ritual, the cathartic potency of the water, like that of the Mesopotamian holy water basin, may be enhanced by the addition of various cathartic substances.[143]

Rather than serving to attract the deity (see the rites of the following day), placing the freshly drawn waters on the roof of the original temple for the night serves to heighten their purificatory potencies.[144] As in the Mesopotamian mouth-washing ritual,[145] the nocturnal encounter with deities in their celestial forms seems to be a means by which these deities lend their support and potency to the

---

138. The waters of purification may also have been drawn from a river (Strauß, *Reinigungsrituale*, 34; cf. Haas, *Materia Magica I*, 143–44).

139. Regarding the significance, use, and association of various colors, see Haas, *Materia Magica II*, 639–49.

140. Beal, "Dividing," 203; Haas, *Materia Magica I*, 146–47; Strauß, *Reinigungsrituale*, 34. In the Babylonian recension of the mouth-washing ritual, the libation of beer into the river also seems to be compensation for drawing water for the holy water basin (ll. 14–15).

141. Water in general and especially the waters of purification are some of the most potent cathartic ritual materials (Haas, *Materia Magica I*, 141; Strauß, *Reinigungsrituale*, 34).

142. E.g., *KBo* 10.45 obv. ii 30–35; *KUB* 43.58 obv. i 40–49 (Haas, *Materia Magica I*, 141; Strauß, *Reinigungsrituale*, 34).

143. Aromatic substances in particular add an olfactory component to the physical purification of water (cf. Haas, *Materia Magica I*, 142). Pebbles (ibid., 192–200), tamarisk (ibid., 283–84) and cedar wood (ibid., 277–81) are also especially prominent (see, e.g., *KUB* 41.13; Strauß, *Reinigungsrituale*, 38).

144. *Pace* Beal, "Dividing a God," 204; Feder, *Blood Expiation*, 31. In my understanding, there is no indication here or in any other ancient Near Easter ritual that a deity is drawn into water (though in some contexts a deity may be drawn from the water). Rather, water is typically used to provide a conducive environment for divine presence through its purificatory powers. Nonetheless, it remains possible that, if the *uliḫi* has been attached to the water vessel with or as the various wool strands (see further below), the deity in her aspect as morning star may be attracted into the *uliḫi*.

145. In the mouth-washing ritual, mouth washings—i.e., purification rites—are associated with each encounter with seven sets of stars and constellations, suggesting that in each encounter the deities are implored to lend their potencies to the purification process. In addition, each additional element placed in the holy water basin is accompanied by an incantation proclaiming the purity of the element and urging the gods to make the statue

purificatory process, in this case by enhancing the purificatory powers of the waters of purification.[146] In addition, if as in *CTH* 471 various additional purificatory elements are added to the water, the night under the stars gives them time to be absorbed into the water, thereby adding their powers to it.[147]

Instead of assuming that the deity is already present in the statue, the following evocation covers all the bases, summoning the deity from wherever she may be located, if by chance she is not in the temple.[148] The red wool and fine oil used for the evocation seem to function like a "red carpet,"[149] explicitly serving as the path along which the deity is invoked.[150] To make the path especially attractive, the oil lends its radiance and fragrance to the wool,[151] which in addition to functioning as a path also likely serves to absorb the deity and lead her along its length to the

---

perfectly pure. Thus, divine activity in and around the holy water basin seems to be aimed at heightening the already potent purificatory powers of the water.

146. Strauß, *Reinigungsrituale*, 43–44; cf. Haas, *Materia Magica I*, 152–53. The waters may also serve as an invitation to the goddess in her celestial form, getting her attention and inviting her in advance of the following days' evocations.

147. Strauß, *Reinigungsrituale*, 43. As in *CTH* 471, the waters may also be heated so that the substances can better dissolve (Haas, *Materia Magica I*, 152; cf. Strauß, *Reinigungsrituale*, 38). Practicaly, the pebbles also serve to delay the boiling point, enabling a longer extraction of the purificatory substances (*CTH* 409; Strauß, *Reinigungsrituale*, 38).

148. Though less likely, it is also conceivable that the deity in all her different manifestations is being drawn to the temple. In other words, rather than drawing the deity from wherever she may be, the ritual could be drawing the deity from everywhere she is present, so that the deity is made present in all of her fullness in the original temple. In other evocation texts, however, a vanished deity is summoned from wherever it has taken refuge, and thus from all of its normal stomping grounds. In this case, it seems that the ritual actors seek to ensure that if the deity has left the statue for any reason, she returns to ensure the efficacy of the ritual. Regarding evocation rites, see Haas, *Die hurritischen Ritualtermini in hethitischem Kontext* (ChS I/9; Rome: CNR, 1998), 37–51; idem, *Materia Magica I*, 94–99; Strauß, *Reinigungsrituale*, 44–56. For the texts, see Volkert Haas and Gernot Wilhelm, *Hurritische und luwische Riten aus Kizzuwatna* (AOAT Sonderreihe 3; Kevelaer: Butzon & Bercker, 1974), 7–33.

149. Jared Miller, personal communication. Although evocation is generally connected to the Telipinu myth (Strauß, *Reinigungsrituale*, 47), the expansion ritual gives no indication of such a connection.

150. *KBo* 24.45+ §16; Strauß, *Reinigungsrituale*, 48.

151. *KUB* 15.34 (*CTH* 483) obv. ii 26–31; Strauß, *Reinigungsrituale*, 48. See further Haas, *Materia Magica I*, 263–66.

desired location.[152] Although not listed here, food and drink are another typical evocation element,[153] which explicitly serve to satisfy the deity's appetite.[154]

The *uliḫi*, bound to the deity presumably in the form of its statue, seems to provide the means for the transfer of deity from the wool to the statue. What is this enigmatic *uliḫi*, which "is attested without exception in connection with the moving and/or evoking of a deity"?[155] The *uliḫi*, like the statue, serves as a locus of divine presence throughout the course of the ritual.[156] Although it is difficult to be more precise, certain clues within the ritual allow for a more specific, albeit tentative, reconstruction. The *uliḫi* is marked with the wool determinative (síg)[157] and appears following an evocation, except when it is attached to the deity or placed in the *tallai*-vessel. Thus, it would seem that the *uliḫi*, as a receptacle for divine presence, serves to bind the deity in the wool to the deity in or as the statue, thereby completing the divine evocation from elsewhere to the chosen vessel in the temple. Indeed, it is even possible that the *uliḫi* is the red wool itself.[158] Perhaps more likely, the *uliḫi* is some sort of woolen object that can easily be attached to both the wool used for the evocation and the divine statue, especially its clothing. Once attached to the statue, all other woolen strands used to summon the deity subsequently may be bound to the statue, thus completing the transfer.[159]

The waters of purification reenter the scene at the start of the third day. However, their role is unspecified. The text merely states that they are brought down from the roof. Presumably, as in Mesopotamia, the waters of purification are used to wash the divine image to ensure perfect purity and ward off any potential pollutants.[160] In fact, the initial inventory list of the divine accouterments mentions

---

152. Whereas elsewhere often employed to absorb and remove various pathogens, here it seems to absorb some of the divine essence. Regarding wool's specific qualities and its use, see Haas, *Materia Magica II*, 649–62. Regarding red wool in particular, see ibid., 653–57.

153. Haas and Wilhelm, *Riten*, 14–22; Strauß, *Reinigungsrituale*, 49, 51.

154. *KUB* 15.31 (*CTH* 483) obv. i 48–50; Haas, *Materia Magica I*, 95; Strauß, *Reinigungsrituale*, 52. Given the divine appetite for food and drink, spreading food along the way is a good way to elicit the deity's presence, not altogether dissimilar from luring birds with breadcrumbs.

155. Miller, *Kizzuwatna Rituals*, 410.

156. Hittite deities, like Hittite people, are also identified as having an immaterial aspect (*ištanza(n)-*, ZI), roughly translated as "soul" (Taracha, *Religions of Second Millennium Anatolia*, 158; see further below). The *uliḫi*, like the statue, seems to be a material receptacle for this "soul."

157. A iii 62; Miller, *Kizzuwatna Rituals*, 410.

158. Miller, *Kizzuwatna Rituals*, 409–10, followed tentatively by Feder, *Blood Expiation*, 27.

159. Beal, "Dividing a God," 204.

160. Cf. Strauß, *Reinigungsrituale*, 68–70.

a water basin in which the divine image is washed.¹⁶¹ In addition, the ritual later refers to "the water with which they wash the temple wall," which together with fine oil purifies the wall (§31). Since no other water is in view, this probably refers to the waters of purification, which may also be applied to the walls and other parts of the original temple to effect a purity befitting the divine presence. Finally, since both the deity and the ritual patron are treated with the purifying silver and *gangati*-plant (§15) and the priest and *katra*-women wash themselves (§8), it is conceivable that the waters of purification are also applied to them.¹⁶² However, it is perhaps more likely that the priest and *katra*-women bathe with regular water prior to their drawing of the waters of purification,¹⁶³ while the ritual patron may receive the purifying effects of the waters of purification as a perk for his benevolence.¹⁶⁴

Pulling the deity up from a ritual pit complements the evocation ritual of the preceding night.¹⁶⁵ Since it is daytime, the Deity of the Night, like many other celestial deities,¹⁶⁶ is located in the underworld.¹⁶⁷ Thus, rather than evoking her from various celestial and terrestrial locales, she is simply evoked upwards through the pit. However, in accord with the comprehensive approach,¹⁶⁸ the priest and the ritual patron each pull her up seven times to ensure ritual efficacy. Presumably, the foodstuffs are used as offerings to the emerging deity,¹⁶⁹ who once again seems to be absorbed into the oil-soaked wool, which is presumably affixed to the statue via the *uliḫi*.¹⁷⁰

There is unfortunately little evidence to explain the subsequent move to the storehouse and the *dupšaḫi*-ritual.¹⁷¹ After some free time, the ritual patron returns

161. *KUB* 29.4+ obv. i 43.

162. Cf. Strauß, *Reinigungsrituale*, 71–72.

163. I.e., before their contact with the divine realm. It is highly unlikely that they wash themselves with the waters of purification after having drawn them and before depositing them on the roof for the night, for such contact would render the waters impure.

164. Cf. Strauß, *Reinigungsrituale*, 71–72.

165. On the use of pits in Hittite ritual, see, e.g., Collins, "Necromancy, Fertility and the Dark Earth: The Use of Ritual Pits in Hittite Cult," in Mirecki and Meyer, eds., *Magic and Ritual*, 224–41; Strauß, *Reinigungsrituale*, 49–56; cf. Feder, *Blood Expiation*, 209–15.

166. Conversely, as in Egypt, celestial deities that manifest themselves during the daytime like the Sun Goddess of the Earth spend the night in the underworld.

167. Beal, "Dividing a God," 204.

168. And perhaps so that the ritual patron does not feel left out.

169. Cf. Strauß, *Reinigungsrituale*, 49. The offerings may also serve as gifts to the underworld gods for invading their terrain. The silver too may serve as payment for the use of the pit (Beal, "Dividing a God," 204).

170. Cf. Beal, "Dividing a God," 204.

171. Regarding the *dupšaḫi*, see Trémouille, *ᵈḪebat: une divinité syro-anatolienne* (Eothen

at night to present the offering of blood.[172] Whereas elsewhere blood is especially associated with ritual pits and evoking deities from the underworld,[173] here the ritual is postponed until the evening.[174] As such, and since during the evening the Goddess of the Night is no longer in the underworld, the blood is likely not used for evocatory purposes.[175] Instead, it may be a gift to the deity, who in her chthonic aspect enjoys blood.[176]

After the ritual actors finish summoning the goddess into the original temple through nightly and daily divine evocations, they welcome her with gifts and further purifications, of which the blood ritual is likely the first. As its name indicates, the praise ritual[177] seems designed to extol the deity and present her with various gifts. The subsequent treatment of the deity and ritual patron with silver and the *gangati*-plant serve as further purificatory procedures.[178] The burnt offering con-

---

7; Florence: Logisma, 1997), 179–83; *HEG* T/D: 453–54; Haas, *Materia Magica I*, 166; Miller, *Kizzuwatna Rituals*, 423. It is possible that, in accord with *CTH* 480, the *dupšaḫi* serves to burn away any maledictions (cf. Haas, *Materia Magica I*, 166). As a removal rite that handles potentially dangerous pollutants, the storehouse would be a more suitable locale than the temple sanctuary.

172. It is unclear why, at this point, the ritual patron explicitly does not bow until the end of the night and the completion of the night's ritual sequence.

173. See Feder, *Blood Expiation*, esp. 209–10; regarding the blood rite, see also Haas, "Ein hurritischer Blutritus und die Deponierung der Ritualrückstände nach hethitischen Quellen," in Janowski, Koch, and Wilhelm, eds., *Religionsgeschichtliche Beziehungen*, 67–85; idem, *Materia Magica I*, 511–16; Strauß, *Reinigungsrituale*, 92–98; Beckman, "Blood in Hittite Ritual," *JCS* 63 (2011): 95–102.

174. There is here no indication that a ritual pit is used. The animal chosen for the blood rite, in this case the fish, may be idiosyncratic to the deity being worshipped (Feder, *Blood Expiation*, 33).

175. *Pace* Feder, *Blood Expiation*, 29.

176. A possibility also mentioned by Feder, *Blood Expiation*, 29. Alternatively, it could be yet another means of purification (ibid., 227–28), serving as a ritual detergent that removes all pollution. Feder (*Blood Expiation*, 28) assumes that the blood was smeared on the statue itself, in accord with its later application to statue, wall, and paraphernalia. However, although applied to objects, blood is never applied to persons (Haas, *Materia Magica I*, 511).

177. Laroche, "L'adjectif *sarli-* 'supérior' dans les langues asianiques," in *Festschrift Johannes Friedrich zum 65. Geburtstag* (Heidelberg: Winter, 1959), 293–24; *CLL* 191.

178. Silver, one of the few materials with its own mythology (*CTH* 364: Hoffner, *Hittite Myths*, 45–48), seems to effect purification by transferring the purity evident in its radiant metal to the object to be purified (The rapid oxidation of silver serves as a visible sign that the pathogens have been absorbed; Haas, *Materia Magica I*, 214–17). It is even referred to as "the white" (*ḫargi*), the color of purity and perfection (Haas, *Materia Magica II*, 639). The *gangati*-plant is an especially important purificatory material (Strauß, *Reinigungsrituale*, 102), which likely spawned the verb *gangadai* ("to atone"). Cf. ibid.; Haas, *Materia Magica*

cludes the evening's welcome reception,[179] continued with the well-being offering for both Pirinkir and the Goddess of the Night.[180] The well-being offering often functions as a complement to the burnt offering, serving as a gift intended to evoke the well-being of the goddess.[181]

During the evening between the burnt offering and the well-being offering the following morning, the waters of purification reappear. The text lists the same ingredients used for their initial drawing before mentioning their placement once again on the roof, perhaps indicating that the waters must be drawn again. They may have been somehow contaminated by the pathogens they served to remove or perhaps fresh water and a fresh irradiation before the stars is necessary to ensure their potency.[182]

On the dawn of the fifth day, the presentation of the *tuḫalzi*-offering serves some as yet unidentified function.[183] After the ritual, fine oil is poured into a *tallai*-vessel and the text's only preserved utterance features, highlighting the centrality of its message: "preserve your being, but divide your divine manifestation (*šiuniyatar*)! Come to that new house, too, and take yourself the honored place! And when you make your way, then take yourself only that place!" The primary concern seems to be that the deity divide or duplicate herself so that she may inhabit both temples, rather than transfer her presence fully from the old temple to the new, thereby rendering the old temple defunct. Two important caveats appear alongside this primary plea. First, she is implored to preserve her being, to ensure that she retains all of her attributes, potencies, and faculties.[184] In other words, the speaker implores the deity to maintain her full and functional presence in both temples. Second, with all of her possible destinations in view, including enemy

---

*I*, 328. It presumably serves as a ritual sponge that absorbs impurities and transfers them from the bearer (cf. Strauß, *Reinigungsrituale*, 102). See *KBo* 35.139 1–12 for its use in purifying the gods (Haas, *Materia Magica I*, 334–35). See further *HED* K, 51–54; Haas, *Materia Magica I*, 328–35; Strauß, *Reinigungsrituale*, 101–8.

179. Haas and Wilhelm, *Riten*, 85–87; Schwemer, "Das alttestamentliche Doppelritual *'lwt wšlmym* im Horizont der hurritischen Opfertermini *ambašši* und *keldi*," *SCCNH* 7 (1995): 81–101; Haas, *Die hurritischen Ritualtermini*, 227–28.

180. See esp. Schwemer, "Das alttestamentliche Doppelritual," 81–101. The appearance of Pirinkir at this stage remains unexplained. Perhaps as an associated deity, her presence and well-being contribute to the presence and well-being of the Goddess of the Night.

181. Unlike its biblical counterpart (the *šlmym*), the offerings are entirely presented to the deity rather than forming a shared human-divine meal.

182. Cf. Haas, *Materia Magica I*, 157–58.

183. *HEG* T/D 408; Beckman, *Hittite Birth Rituals* (StBoT 29; Harrasowitz: Wiesbaden, 1983), 220; Miller, *Kizzuwatna Rituals*, 423.

184. Cf. Miller, *Kizzuwatna Rituals*, 260.

terrain, the speaker urges her to come only to the new temple so that the entire elaborate ritual process is not in vain.[185]

After imploring the goddess to divide herself safely, the ritual actors (continue to) enact this division, by pulling her from the wall with the red wool, completing the evocations in the old temple. Having drawn the deity from her various night and day locales outside of the temple, they now seem to draw her from the temple itself,[186] thus covering all conceivable locales. The *uliḫi* links the various evocations. With all of the various deity-absorbing wool strands attached to the *uliḫi* and the *uliḫi* attached to the statue, the divine presence is consolidated in the statue, the primary locus of terrestrial divine presence. With the evocations now complete, the *uliḫi* may be detached from the statue and placed in the *tallai*-container so that she may extend her presence from the old to the new temple without ever leaving the old temple. Together, the elaborate activities in the old temple are designed to ensure the full presence of the deity in the old statue, so that she can extend her full presence to the new statue via the *uliḫi*.

*The New Temple.* As the rites in the old temple conclude, those in the new begin in earnest with a purificatory waving of a kid and a lamb, which presumably absorb all potential pollutants, before installing the new deity and her accoutrements.[187] While not necessary in the fully functioning original temple, the waving rite seems to serve a dedicatory function, ensuring the temple's purity before the installation of its deity.

While the new statue is being deposited in the new temple, the ritual actors proceed to the riverbank[188] to draw the deity with various elements[189] "from Akkade, from Babylon, from Susa, from Elam, from ḪUR.SAG.KALAM.MA (=Kish) in

---

185. Cf. ibid.

186. The walls, perhaps standing *pars pro toto* for the entire temple, seem to represent any location within the temple. Miller (*Kizzuwatna Rituals*, 308) notes that this evocation finds no parallel in other Hittite texts.

187. For waving rites, see Haas, *Materia Magica I*, 75–76; Strauß, *Reinigungsrituale*, 108–11.

188. The riverbank with its life-giving, life-preserving and purifying powers seems to be a favorite place of ritual actors to appeal to the gods for support, especially the fate and mother goddesses responsible for human creation (see, e.g., Bo 3617 [*CTH* 409] obv. i 3'–17'). On the riverbank and its associations, see, e.g., Haas, *Der Kult on Nerik: Ein Beitrag zur hethitischen Religionsgeschichte* (Studia Pohl 4; Rome: Päpstliches Bibelinstitut, 1970): 102–5; idem, *Materia Magica I*, 144–45; Wilhelm, "Reinheit und Heiligkeit: Zur Vorstellungswelt altanatolischer Ritualistik," in *Levitikus als Buch* (ed. H.-J. Fabry & H.-W. Jüngling; BBB 19; Berlin: Philo, 1999), 208; Strauß, *Reinigungsrituale*, 30–33.

189. 1 *tarpala*-(fabric) of red wool, 1 red *kureššar* garment, a little refined oil, a *tallai*-vessel, 20 flat-bread loaves, 2 *mūlati* bread loaves of ½ an *upnu*-measure, 1 small cheese, and 1 pitcher of wine (§24). As with drawing the waters of purification, the foodstuffs likely serve as a gift to the river and its gods (cf. Strauß, *Reinigungsrituale*, 34–35).

the city that you love, from the mountain, from the river, from the sea, from the valley, from the steppe, from the spring, from the sky, from the earth, from the seven roads and from the seven footpaths." The list of cities is best understood as the most important Mesopotamian cities for the cults of the goddess' associated deities Ishtar and Pirinkir,[190] thereby extending the comprehensive parameters of their search. Once again characteristic of the additive approach, rather than simply transfer the goddess by means of the *uliḫi*, the ritualists evoke the deity from everywhere she might be located and perform these comprehensive evocations multiple times in multiple locations.

The deity drawn into this wool is then presumably attached to a new *uliḫi* for the new temple. The new *uliḫi* represents her presence in the tent erected by the river, where she is served by the welcoming party with the blood, praise, and burnt offerings as well as a meal. The deity, in the form of her *uliḫi*, is then transported to the ritual patron's house. To ensure her presence, pleasure, and purity along the way, percussion instruments are played, presumably for the divine enjoyment and to scare off evil spirits, food is spread beneath her to ensure she is sated and follows the trail, and a *ḫusti*-mineral substance is waved over her to preserve her purity.[191] The deity, in or as the new *uliḫi*, makes her journey progressively from the periphery to the center, from the river to the sanctuary via the house of the ritual patron and the storehouse. Eager not to neglect any stop along the way, they present the deity with a burnt offering in the storehouse.

After this final evocation and the entry into the temple, the new *uliḫi* may then be attached to the new statue. The day ends with the placement of the (new) waters of purification on the roof of the new temple, where their potency may be enhanced for the next day's purifications. The second day in the new temple begins with rites of purification, whereby the oil in the *tallai*-container is mixed with the waters of purification and applied to the walls to effect purity. Through the *tallai*-vessel and the oil it contains, the purity associated with the first temple may be joined with the waters of purification to suitably purify the new temple. The absorbed original deity present in the *uliḫi* enclosed in the *tallai*-vessel may even lend its support to the proceedings.

Only now, after all evocations have been completed and the new *uliḫi* is attached to the statue, may the old *uliḫi* containing the divine presence from the old temple be removed from the *tallai*-vessel and attached to the new statue, thereby completing her expansion and reduplication. The ritual actors then dig an offering pit and offer a sheep to the deity for reconciliation as a means of ensuring harmony with her so that she will remain present and benevolent.[192] The mechanism by

---

190. Miller, *Kizzuwatna Rituals*, 366.

191. Regarding the *ḫusti*, see Haas, *Materia Magica I*, 237–40. Here, it presumably absorbs all pollutants before they make contact with the travelling deity.

192. The text explicitly mentions that no evocation from the wall takes place, nor does

which reconciliation is effected remains unclear. Most simply, the sheep may be a gift intended to appease the deity and ensure her well-being and well-wishes toward her new subjects.[193] However, this does not explain the need for digging a pit.[194] Perhaps, slaughtering the blood into the pit elicits the presence and support of the Goddess of the Night in her chthonic aspect and the other chthonic deities, who are drawn by the blood for the following purification rite. In some contexts, blood itself seems to function as a ritual detergent that removes pollution.[195] In other contexts, the blood is a gift or bribe to the chthonic deities, who in return are expected to remove any lingering imperfections to their underground lair.[196] Either or perhaps both elements, in accord with the comprehensive approach, may be in view in the present rite. Either way, the blood is a (final) purificatory act that inaugurates the temple.[197]

## Purification

Given the multiple purifications in the expansion ritual (like its Mesopotamian counterpart), one wonders what pollutants are being removed and why so many purifications are necessary. It is unlikely that the ritualists had any concrete

---

it mention any pulling up from the pit. It would seem that evocations from the wall are unnecessary since the deity has just arrived in her new temple and is not lurking somewhere else in its precincts. Perhaps evoking the deity from the pit is also unnecessary since she has already been evoked from the underworld in the old temple and that aspect of her has been attached to the new statue via the *uliḫi*. Although plausible, this solution is not entirely convincing since the Hittite ritualists are by no means averse to "redundancy."

193. The blood of the sheep may also be a gift to the deity in her chthonic aspect. Alternatively, the sheep, and particularly its blood, could be an instrument of compensation. "Just as transgressions were conceived as debts for which the gods could exact payment in the form of the perpetrator's blood, so too, ... offering blood could serve as a payment to remove guilt" (Feder, *Blood Expiation*, 227; on blood as a means of compensation, see ibid., 215–27). In other words, the sheep and its blood could serve as payment for any perceived wrongs, thereby enacting reconciliation.

194. Although not its primary purpose, the pit reveals the dual presence of the deity both in the statue and in the underworld (Feder, *Blood Expiation*, 32). Alternatively, it is possible that the sheep itself is for the deity in her statue, while the blood spilled into the pit is intended for the underworld gods (and the goddess' chthonic aspect).

195. Feder, *Blood Expiation*, 227–28.

196. On blood as a bribe, see ibid., 209–15. The application of the blood to the objects to be purified—in this case the walls, the statue, and its equipment—serve as clear ritual instructions, attracting the chthonic beings to the very elements that need their attention. On the application of blood to the elements to be purified, see *KBo* 13.101 obv. 26'–31' and *CTH* 446 iii 1–12 and the interpretations in Feder, *Blood Expiation*, 210–11, 213.

197. "Final" appears in parentheses because we do not know what rites the second tablet contains.

pollutants in mind. Rather, here as elsewhere, the goal seems to be the general and comprehensive removal of all potential pollutants that may detract from perfect purity throughout the course of ritual activity.[198] In accord with the Hittite comprehensive approach, multiple purifications are necessary to achieve that end. In addition, it seems that, especially when no concrete pollutants are in view, purification, that is, the removal of pollutants, also serves to imbue the elements being purified with positive qualities.[199] Purification makes the statue, its accouterments, and its temple perfectly pure and thus suitable for the divine presence, which in effect "consecrates" them by preparing them for divine use.[200] Thus, according to Hittite thought, consecration, the addition of positive qualities, seems to be primarily achieved by subtraction, the removal of negative qualities.

## 2. DAILY CULT RITUAL

Before addressing the relationship of statue to deity and statue to statue in the expansion ritual and generally, we turn to the evidence for the daily cult. Among the Hittites, there is ample evidence for cult meals, indeed far more than in either Egypt or Mesopotamia.[201] However, despite the abundant evidence that the gods

---

198. Cf. regarding the biblical Priestly texts, Hundley, *Keeping Heaven*, 84.

199. Feder (*Blood Expiation*, 228) carefully and logically differentiates between purification as the removal of unwanted elements and consecration as the endowment of "sancta with a positive quality or force"; see also Haas, "Ein hurritischer Blutritus," 68 and Beckman, "Blood in Hittite Ritual," 101, who in particular identify the blood with life and associate its application with the impartation of vivifying qualities. However, the Hittites (as well as the other ancient Near Eastern peoples) seem to blur the distinction between purification and consecration (see briefly Hundley, *Keeping Heaven*, 76 and the references cited therein and with regard to the biblical material ibid., 75, 77–78).

200. Cf. Mesopotamian *ellu*, which "stands for perfection and integrity—moral, physical, spiritual, and social" (van der Toorn, "Sin, Pollution, and Purity: Mesopotamia," in Johnston, ed., *Religions of the Ancient World*, 500) and involves a visual brilliance that demonstrates a person or object's freedom from imperfection, much like a glistening floor shows that it has been freshly cleaned (see further E. Jan Wilson, *"Holiness" and "Purity" in Mesopotamia* (AOAT 237; Neukirchen-Vluyn: Neukirchener Verlag, 1995). Although blood does not impart a visual brilliance, the mixture of oil and water lends a brilliant quality to the walls that demonstrates their perfection. Cf. also Egypt, where purity (*wab*) is the absence of *bwt*, i.e., the pure individual or object is free from any of the various manifestations of evil, "whether this-worldly or other worldly, social or cosmological" (Paul J. Frandsen, "Sin, Pollution, and Purity: Egypt," in Johnston, ed., *Religions of the Ancient World*, 498); the related Hittite adjective is *parkui* (*CHD* P, 163–66).

201. Collins, "Ritual Meals in the Hittite Cult," in *Ancient Magic and Ritual Power* (ed. M. Meyer and P. Mirecki; Leiden: Brill, 1995), 78. Regarding cult meals, see Cord Kühne, "Hethitisch *auli-* und einige Aspekte altanatolischer Opferpraxis," *ZA* 76 (1986): 85–117; idem, "Zum Vor-Opfer im alten Anatolien," in Janowski, Koch, and Wilhelm, eds.,

were fed and cared for, texts say very little about their daily ritual.[202] The Instructions to the Priests and Temple Officials (*CTH* 264) refers to the gods' daily bread (§2) and a morning divine meal (§14).[203] In lamenting the plundering of temples, King Arnuwanda I and Queen Asmunikal also note that no one performs the daily, monthly, and yearly divine rituals.[204] At Nerik, there is even a brief text listing prescriptions for the daily ritual of the temple, which include daily water and bread.[205] Although it is impossible to know for certain, it is reasonable to assume that the deities' daily care and feeding took place along the same lines as their Mesopotamian counterparts.[206] More particularly, it seems that the daily staples consisted of bread and libations. For example, the so-called plague prayers of Mursili II repeatedly mention the deaths of those responsible for bread and libations in the hopes of persuading the gods to remove the plague so that regular offerings may be presented to them.[207]

While their daily regimen remains a mystery, it is clear that they were "clothed, fed, bathed (usually prior to a ritual service), entertained and their festivals were celebrated according to a regular calendar."[208] In other words, as in Egypt and Mesopotamia, the care of the deity in the anthropomorphic cult resembled that of the monarch. Such care, whether daily or not, was a natural outflow of the installation ritual, without which continued care would be meaningless. As in Egypt and Mesopotamia, its point was to keep the resident deity, so carefully installed, happy and healthy and well-disposed to offer its people protection and prosperity.

## Conceptions of Divine Presence in the Temple(s)

### Evocations

In order to determine the relationship between deity and statue and between a deity's multiple statues, we turn first to the issue of divine evocations, that is, the

---

*Religionsgeschichtliche Beziehungen*, 225–86; Collins, "Ritual Meals," 77–92. See now also Susanne Görke, "Hethitische Rituale im Tempel," in Kaniuth et al., eds. *Tempel im Alten Orient*, 123–45. Although no two descriptions are identical, such meals generally consist of the finest quality foodstuffs, especially sheep (Collins, "Ritual Meals," 89–90).

202. Goetze, *Kleinasien*, 162–63; Collins, "A Statue for the Deity," 13; cf. Taracha, *Religions of Second Millennium Anatolia*, 59.

203. For a convenient translation, see *COS* 1:83.217, 220.

204. *KUB* 17.21 iii 12–16; Collins, "Ritual Meals," 77.

205. *KUB* 31.113; see Haas, *Kult von Nerik*, 131–33 for text and translation.

206. Collins, "A Statue for the Deity," 13.

207. While it is clear that meat was presented to the deities on regular/festival occasions, it remains uncertain if it played any role in the daily cult meals.

208. Collins, "A Statue for the Deity," 13, 24.

common Hittite practice of evoking the divine presence. Why were so many evocations necessary and what did they achieve? What do they tell us about the Hittite understanding of the divine presence in the statue?

The multiple evocation rites in the larger expansion ritual and in other Hittite rituals indicate that the deity need not always be present in its statue. In order to ensure presence, such rituals summoned the deity comprehensively from all of its favorite places in case it was not in its image at that time, so that following communication and/or ritual activity could prove effective.[209] In addition, if the temple or cult image was defiled, the god could permanently leave its image. In response, various evocation rituals were performed to coax the angered deity to return.[210] Thus, it is clear that a deity was not considered coterminous with its image.

In the expansion ritual, the various evocations in the old temple likewise demonstrate that the deity was not always or necessarily present in its image. Since there was no way of concretely verifying presence, evocations were necessary to cover all of the bases before proceeding with ritual words and actions. Nonetheless, while it is clear that the deity had to be systematically summoned to ensure presence, it remains unclear if the multiple evocations were thought to have a cumulative effect. Although the Hittites themselves would likely not have articulated it in this way,[211] it is possible that comprehensive evocations were necessary to ensure full presence, whereby the goddess in all of her various manifestations and attributes—her celestial and chthonic aspects and various terrestrial manifestations[212]—was assembled so that she could be fully reproduced in her new setting.[213]

---

209. See, e.g., prayers 8 and 9 in Singer, *Hittite Prayers*, 50, 54, where the deity was summoned so that it could hear and respond to the suppliant's prayers.

210. Regarding the divine abandonment of its image, see Strauß, *Reinigungsrituale*, 44. For evocation rituals, see *CTH* 472, 483, 484; Strauß, *Reinigungsrituale*, 44; see further Haas and Wilhelm, *Hurritische und luwische Riten*, 7–33.

211. From analogous evocation texts, the Hittites likely would not have talked about gathering all of her parts, but rather making sure she was really and fully present by neglecting no single aspect or manifestation, such that her adlocation could be successful.

212. Hittite thoroughness even extended to evocation of the deity from cultic locales of the associated goddesses Ishtar and Pirinkir.

213. Although there is no way to verify this possibility, the continual evocations even after the summoned goddess had been attached to her statue speak in its favor. This differs from other evocations in that in other contexts the deity had already been fully installed in its various cult locales and need only be invoked to return, whereas the expansion required the divine totality, i.e., the divine constellation itself consisting of various manifestations and aspects.

## Relationship between Statue and Deity

In light of the fact that the deity was not necessarily considered to be always present in its cult image, how should we understand the relationship between a deity and its statue? An examination of the various terms used for statue is a good place to start.[214] *Ešri*, used to refer to anthropomorphic statues in both religious and secular contexts, denotes both "statue" and more generally "form, shape, stature, physical appearance."[215] Indeed, rather than distinguishing between the two uses, it seems better to understand *ešri* more broadly as "form" or "physical appearance," whether it refers to a statue or a living biological entity.[216] *Šiuniyatar*, used especially in cult inventories for cult images, is an abstraction of the word deity (*šiuni*) and is most often translated as "divine image" in the Empire period, whereas in the Old Hittite period it refers to a "divine manifestation," that is, the deity's (self-)presentation in a manner that could be perceived by the human senses.[217] Thus, it would seem that *šiuniyatar* as a manifestation of deity in the Empire period was used for a specific concrete manifestation, the cult image, understood to be a perceptible manifestation of deity on earth.[218]

Rather than completely replacing the older, more abstract meaning of "divine manifestation," *šiuniyatar* in the Empire period may be interpreted either as concrete or abstract manifestation.[219] For example, in the only utterance preserved in the expansion ritual—"Honored deity, preserve your body, but divide your divine manifestation (*šiuniyatar*)"—*šiuniyatar* may be understood abstractly as divinity or concretely as cult statue.[220] In effect, the text seems to be imploring the deity to

---

214. See the surveys in Collins, "A Statue for the Deity," 20–21; Petra Goedegebuure, "Hittite Iconoclasm: Disconnecting the Icon, Disempowering the Referent," in *Iconoclasm and Text Destruction in the Ancient Near East and Beyond* (ed. Natalie May; OIS 8; Chicago: University of Chicago, 2012), 407–52.

215. *HED* E 313–14; *HW²* E 124–25.

216. Taracha, *Religions of Second Millennium Anatolia*, 2; Goedegebuure, "Hittite Iconoclasm," 419.

217. Ibid., 420. *Šiuniyatar* may also be translated as "spirit holder," i.e., a receptacle for the immaterial aspect of a being (Haas, *Geschichte der hethitischen Religion*, 298; Goedegebuure, "Hittite Iconoclasm," 419).

218. Cf. Collins ("A Statue for the Deity," 21): "Where describing cult statues, as in the inventories, the reference is clearly to the statue as a receptacle for the deity's essence, its godhead. The application of the word *šiuniyatar* to a representation implies that, anthropomorphic or otherwise, the representation was imbued with the divine essence, i.e., that the deity was present. *Šiuniyatar*, then, is not simply the 'divine image,' but applies to the fully fused statue plus godhead. In other words, it is the cult image—the extraphysical reference to whatever object hosted the divine presence."

219. Goedegebuure, "Hittite Iconoclasm," 420.

220. Ibid., 421. Translating *šiuniyatar* as cult image does not suggest that the Hittites broke

divide her divine person so that she may make herself manifest in both cult images. Thus, it would seem that a cult image represented the physical, perceptible form of a deity that when occupied was understood as a manifestation of deity, in effect as the deity itself on earth in the form of a statue.[221]

How should we understand the division of a deity? By inhabiting an additional cult image, did the goddess halve her presence in each? In Hittite literature, there is no evidence that deities were imagined to possess a fixed amount of power. Instead, it would seem that they were divisible without diminishment, such that each manifestation could potentially possess all of the deity's powers in equal measure.[222] Although not always as well differentiated or articulated as in Egypt, the Hittite deity also appears to have possessed both material and immaterial aspects, *tuekka* and *ištanza*, roughly and somewhat anachronistically translated as "body" and "soul."[223] The cult image as a *tuekka*, *ešri*, or *šiuniyatar* then served as a form in which the immaterial aspect of the deity (its *ištanza*) could manifest itself. As an immaterial substance, it would seem that, as in Egypt, the deity's *ištanza* or other immaterial elements could be divided or multiplied infinitely without losing any potency. Thus, rather than producing two halves of the Goddess of the Night, the expansion ritual in effect produced two copies of the Goddess of Night, or the original manifestation of the deity in her statue and its clone in the new temple.[224] Nonetheless, while fully present in the statue, it is also clear that neither statue was

---

the statue in half. Rather, *šiuniyatar* refers to dividing the locus of manifestation between two sites, in each concretized as a discrete cult statue.

221. Although it approximates the Hittite usage, Goedegebuure's identification of a cult image as "an indexical nexus, medium, or portal" ("Hittite Iconoclasm," 243) seems to be alien to the Hittite way of thinking and suggests too strong a divide between deity and image. Rather, as we will see, it seems better to understand a statue as one of a deity's many forms or bodies that served as a potential locus for the divine presence without exhausting its plenitude.

222. However, this need not mean that every manifestation or aspect represented the deity in its fullness. Some divine elements, like deified "abstract" qualities, personified and thus possessed only a single divine attribute.

223. Annelies Kammenhuber, "Die hethitischen Vorstellungen von Seele und Leib, Herz und Leibesinnerem, Kopf und Person, 1. Teil," *ZA* 56 (1964): 150–212; Steiner, "Gott," 565; Haas, *Geschichte der hethitischen Religion*, 301; Theo P. J. van den Hout, "Death as a Privilege: The Hittite Royal Funerary Ritual," in *Hidden Futures: Death and Immortality in Ancient Egypt, Anatolia, the Classical, Biblical and Arabic-Islamic World* (ed. J. M. Bremmer, T. P. H. van den Hout and R. Peters; Amsterdan: Amsterdam University, 1994), 44; Miller, *Kizzuwatna Rituals*, 299; Taracha, *Religions of Second Millennium Anatolia*, 158. Thus, the Hittite deity was neither material nor immaterial, but a combination of both elements.

224. Cf. Beal, "Dividing a God"; Popko, "Der hethitische Gott und seine Kultbilder," *JANER* 5 (2005): 79–87; Wilhelm, "'Gleichsetzungstheologie,'" 68; Miller, *Kizzuwatna Rituals*, 260; Collins, "A Statue for the Deity,"; Taracha, *Religions of Second Millennium Anatolia*, 62. Rather than appearing in one manifestation at a time, it seems that a deity

the fullness of the deity, since the deity consisted of many of other manifestations, attributes, and aspects.

## Relationship between Statues

Were different statues of the "same" deity copies of the original deity or independent deities? More particularly, in the expansion ritual, was the deity as or in the new statue identical with, an extension of, or different from its prototype? As in Egypt and Mesopotamia, the answer is context specific. In some contexts, especially myths and hymns, deities and their various aspects were often treated as a unity, such that each statue could be considered a manifestation of the same god or as part of its constellation. Nonetheless, as noted, although treated as a unity, the divine person was by no means coterminous with its image. In accord with aspective theory, in other contexts (especially in ritual and oracle texts) each individual element was treated as a (semi-)independent self-propelled agent. Thus, in some contexts, each statue–deity symbiosis could be treated as a distinct yet related deity. For example, in the expansion ritual, although both were the Goddess of the Night, the deity in the old temple was referred to as the old deity, while the deity in the new temple was the new deity.[225] In effect, the incorporeal aspect of the same deity present in different "bodies" created two different deities. As in Mesopotamia, each statue–deity symbiosis could be treated like a clone, which, although it bore the same "DNA," was born in a different place and time and under different circumstances and developed traits peculiar to its cultic setting. For example, although often equated in scholarly circles, Ishtar of Nineveh and Ishtar of Samuha had different characteristic features. For example, the Anatolian Ishtar of Nineveh did not display either the pronounced astral or martial aspects characteristic of Ishtar of Samuha. Nor did she seem to share the latter's close relationship to the Hittite royal house.[226]

There is also evidence of multiple statues of a "single" deity in the same temple. For example, a festival text from Tahurpa refers to eight Sun Goddesses of Arinna

---

could theoretically be present in multiple locales at once (e.g., in the sun and in a cult statue or in two statues simultaneously [e.g., to receive its daily care and feeding]).

225. Cf. Beal, "Dividing a God"; Wilhelm, "'Gleichsetzungstheologie'"; Miller, *Kizzuwatna Rituals*, 260; Popko, "Der hethitische Gott"; Taracha, *Religions of Second Millennium Anatolia*, 62.

226. Beckman, "Ištar of Nineveh," 7; René Lebrun, *Samuha: Foyer religieux de l'empire hittite* (Louvain-la-Neuve: Institut Orientaliste, 1976), 17, 20–24. The Anatolian Ishtar of Nineveh even seems to have differed from her Assyrian archetype in that she had a chthonic aspect and could be summoned from the netherworld through a pit (Miller, *Kizzuwatna Rituals*, 374–75). These differences were likely products of different local conceptions of a deity that could incorporate elements of a pre-existing deity or add (or subtract) elements based upon the experiences and conceptions of its new environment.

in the form of three statues and five sun disks (*KUB* 25.14 i 10–31).[227] What was the relationship between these statues? Most simply, multiple statues of a single deity in a single temple established the prestige of the deity. Since deities distinguished themselves from other deities through the accumulation of manifestations, names, and attributes, multiple manifestations of a single deity in a single temple illustrated the importance of that deity, namely, that it was worthy of such reverence and its divinity was potent enough to be divided multiple times in the same setting.[228] Likewise, the possibility of multiple images pragmatically gave multiple monarchs the honor of presenting the deity with an image.[229]

Although theoretically all were copies of the same deity, each cult image also could be treated as a distinct entity capable of independent action.[230] In *KBo* 2.2, an oracle text designed to determine the cause of the king's fever, it becomes clear that a divine image is the responsible party (ll. 21–22). However, a further oracle is required to determine which image–deity symbiosis is responsible. In lines 50 and following, they narrow down the search to three possible manifestations of the Sun Goddess of Arinna. Although these images did not bear different names (as in Mesopotamia), they were treated as distinct and capable of individual action.[231] Thus, as Popko contends, in oracle practice, each cult image was understood to be a separate, independent deity.[232]

Although seemingly bizarre, this divine "fragmentation" was a natural product of the Hittite approach to the divine.[233] In order to be an effective and accessible locus of divine presence, each statue–deity symbiosis was capable of acting and thus was an actor. Thus, various images of the "same" deity localized in a single temple meant multiple actors. Rather than theorizing on the relationship between

---

227. Bin-Nun, *Tawannanna*, 197–202; Collins, "A Statue for the Deity," 28.

228. Again, although predicated on the human model, deities also established their otherness and superiority to both the other gods and humans by transcending that model. Having eight cult images in a single sanctuary seems to have established the greater importance of the Sun Goddess of Arinna than a deity with a single image.

229. The eight Sun Goddesses of Arinna were donated by six of the officiating queen's predecessors (Collins, "A Statue for the Deity," 28).

230. Popko, "Der hethitische Gott," 79–87.

231. *KBo* 16.97 rev. 12ff. is another oracle text that seeks to discover which Shaushka/Ishtar was angry, which Popko suggests refers to one of her cult images (Popko, "Der hethitische Gott," 81).

232. Ibid. 82. This comprehensiveness is akin to the Assyrian *tākultu* ritual texts, in which the ritual tradents took care to present offerings to each cultic manifestation in the temple, i.e., image, many of which were of the "same" deity, so as not to neglect any and thereby invite ritual failure. In both contexts, it remains unclear if each image was to be understood as a separate deity or if each simply had to be treated like a separate deity so as to avoid offending the deity to whom they were dedicated or for and by whom they were animated.

233. Regarding the term "fragmentation," see Sommer, *Bodies of God*, 13.

activated images, the Hittites pragmatically treated each as distinct in a cultic context. In accord with the aspective approach, rather than attempt to fit a deity's various elements into an organic unity in a cultic context, they simply juxtaposed them and treated them as independent. Since each was capable of (independent) action, any one could be responsible for a certain affliction. Thus, in order to find and remedy the cause of affliction, each had to be addressed as distinct, even if each was perceived to be effectively the same deity. Likewise, when presenting regular offerings in a temple, each image was afforded individual attention so as not to offend the deity (as manifest in that image). Thus, whatever the Hittites may have thought about the relationship between cult images, they treated them differently for practical purposes.

Although tangible evidence is lacking, it is also possible that, as in Mesopotamia, multiple images in a single temple could serve different functions. Just as there was a division of labor among temple personnel, so too could there have been a division of labor among divine manifestations. For example, one image could have been used for processions, while another remained in the temple to receive the daily care and feeding.

### The Role of the Uliḫi and the ḫuwaši-Stones

It would seem that the *uliḫi*, like the cult image, served as a potential receptacle for the divine presence, as a *šiuniyatar* or "spirit holder."[234] As the expansion ritual indicates, it too could be treated and addressed as the deity and receive various offerings including a ritual meal. However, unlike the cult image, rather than serving as a permanent locus of divine presence, the *uliḫi* seems to have served a more immediate and transitory function, either in enabling the installation of the deity in a statue or its transportation.

*ḫuwaši*-stones, like a cult statue in a temple, seem to have been another (potential) receptacle for divine presence or perhaps more distantly as an access point. Since the deity could theoretically take any form, the *ḫuwaši* and cult statue seem particularly suited to their different contexts. The cult image suited the intimate, restricted anthropomorphic cult, wherein the statue was dressed, fed, and entertained, and its size allowed for portability, elements for which the *ḫuwaši*-s were ill-suited.[235] As immovable objects located primarily outside of the city, *ḫuwaši*-s extended the sphere of the deity and provided another access point to it outside of normal temple channels. Likewise, a stone monument, even one thought to be imbued with divinity, was more suitable for open spaces and less restricted access, as it suggested some distance between object and referent, while a statue

---

234. Regarding *šiuniyatar* as "spirit holder," see Haas, *Geschichte der hethitischen Religion*, 298; Goedegebuure, "Hittite Iconoclasm," 419.

235. Cf. Collins, "A Statue for the Deity," 28–29.

was more suited to the guarded, enclosed, restricted, and regulated space of the temple, especially since, like the king, the anthropomorphic divine form required a home, servants, service, and protection from the mundane world. A *ḫuwaši* was also more suited to occasional rituals, requiring no full-time personnel or cultic care.[236] In effect, the *ḫuwaši* functioned like a poor man's sanctuary, a more accessible access point with less overhead.

How then should we understand the divine presence in the *ḫuwaši*? Given its open location and nonanthropomorphic and often nondescript form, the connection between deity and *ḫuwaši* may have been perceived to be more distant. The *ḫuwaši* may have been understood as a place to which the deity could be summoned, such that it could either be a temporary locus or more distantly a portal. Although distinct to the modern mind, the effect was practically the same—the deity could be approached, communicated with, and presented with offerings.[237] Thus, it is unlikely that the Hittites would have made any distinction.[238] In addition to a cult image and a *ḫuwaši*, various other physical forms also could serve as temporary vessels for divine presence. For example, a plant too could be a receptacle for a divine "soul" (*ištanza*).[239]

## DESTRUCTION AND DEPORTATION OF DIVINE IMAGES

In contrast to Egypt and Mesopotamia, in Hittite Anatolia there is little evidence of iconoclasm, inscriptoclasm, or the curses designed to protect against both.[240] Deportation or godnapping was instead a much more common phenom-

---

236. However, *ḫuwaši*-stones in temples, like their anthromorphic counterparts, probably enjoyed regular cultic care.

237. The conception of the *ḫuwaši* as a potential receptacle for divine presence (as a potential "spirit holder") seems to accord more with the general ancient Near Eastern mindset than the *ḫuwaši* as portal and finds distant support in the Aramaic stele found in what was formerly Hittite territory, which referred to a mortuary stele as containing the soul (*nbš*) of the deceased (Dennis Pardee, "A New Aramaic Inscription from Zincirli," *BASOR* 356 [2009]: 51–71).

238. Cf. Güterbock, "Hethitische Götterbilder," 215; Collins, "A Statue for the Deity," 26–27. Other elements also served as access points, yet the connection was considered somehow more diffuse, i.e., there was greater distance between the deity and these elements. For example, divine weapons served as extensions of divine potency, while other elements like the temple hearth functioned as self-propelled subordinate agents with access to the deity (see ch. 9).

239. Haas, *Geschichte der hethitischen Religion*, 304–7.

240. Goedegebuure, "Hittite Iconoclasm." The only apparent exception comes from the non-Hittite Gasgaeans (*CTH* 375; trans. Singer, *Hittite Prayers*, 42; Goedegebuure, "Hittite Iconoclasm," 411).

enon in the Old Hittite period,[241] while in the Empire period, by contrast, there is very little evidence of divine deportation.[242] Rather than destroy the cult images of conquered foes, Old Kingdom Hittites tended to take them, humiliating their enemies and appropriating the access point for themselves. In the Empire period, it seems that this godnapping gave way to divine adlocation or reduplication.[243] Instead of taking the divine image, they seem to have reduplicated it, as in the expansion ritual, such that the foreign deity (or statue as divine locus) could both remain in its original cultic environs and also be transferred into the heart of the Hittite empire. Rather than simply treating the cult images as plunder, they were incorporated into the Hittite pantheon and occasionally achieved prominent positions. The Hittite empire likewise benefitted, since, as an accumulation of aspects made a god greater, so too did the accumulation and care of deities render the Hittite Empire greater.

The general lack of destruction of images may indicate that the Hittites did not believe that damage to a divine image meant damage to its divine referent.[244] As the various evocation rituals attest, it seems that the Hittite deities were not bound to their statues, and, in potential contrast to Egypt and Mesopotamia, the divine–statue symbiosis was only in effect when the immaterial aspect of the deity chose to manifest itself. The cult image instead seems to have been one of the many places the deity manifested itself, though no doubt a favorite and regular place because of the cultic care offered to it. As an access point to the deity—i.e., a locus for divine manifestation—destruction of the cult image meant destruction of the access point.[245] The deity itself was not harmed, but inconvenienced, while the divine absence had a devastating effect on the people. The deity would no longer have access to that particular temple and its cult until a suitable replacement image was created, while the people no longer had access to the deity in the temple and, as such, no assurance of its protection and blessing.

---

241. Schwemer, "Fremde Götter in Hatti: Die hethitische Religion im Spannungsfeld von Synkretismus und Abgrenzung" in *Ḫattuša – Boğazköy - Das Hethiterreich im Spannungsfeld des alten Orients. 6. Internationales Colloquium der Deutschen Orient-Gesellschaft 22.–24. März 2006, Würzburg* (ed. G. Wilhelm; Wiesbaden: Harrasowitz, 2008), 137–58. In contrast to Mesopotamia and Syria-Palestine, here I primarily address the Hittite treatment of foreign statues.

242. Ibid.; Goedegebuure, "Hittite Iconoclasm," 412.

243. Gilan, "A Cultural Sponge? On the Hittite Fascination with Things Foreign," presented at the ANE Colloquium, University of Munich (LMU), 2012; cf. Singer, "Thousand Gods"; *pace* Schwemer, "Fremde Götter in Hatti"; Goedegebuure, "Hittite Iconoclasm."

244. Such reticence also demonstrates their general reverence for the gods, both domestic and foreign, and their reticence to do anything to them that would displease them. See Collins, "A Statue for the Deity," 34–35; Goedegebuure, "Hittite Iconoclasm."

245. Cf. ibid., 421–23, who refers to the cult image more distantly as a portal. It is perhaps better to understand the cult image as one of many potential loci for the divine presence.

With this data at hand, we may now assess the applicability of Bahrani's thesis to the Hittites, in which a cult image is presumed inherently to possess some of the divine essence. Unlike in Mesopotamia, the divine image did not seem to partake of the divine essence in itself. It only did so when the deity's immaterial presence chose to symbiotically join with the statue for the purpose of manifestation. When (or if) the deity left the image, the divine essence left with it. Thus, in the expansion ritual, elaborate crafting, care, and purifications made the statue as potential locus of presence as inviting as possible, so that through the evocations the deity could choose to inhabit it.

## Divine Nourishment

Human service, especially in the form of food, was clearly something the deities treasured and required of their human servants.[246] In the plague prayers of Mursili II,[247] the king repeatedly used offerings as leverage to persuade the gods to remove the plague.[248] In other words, if the gods continued killing the people who fed them, they would no longer receive the food they so clearly cherished.[249]

Nonetheless, it remains unclear if the Hittite deities needed such food to survive. As in Mesopotamia, cultic care was a means of receiving food without having to work for it. If the cultic care ceased, the Hittite deities, like their Mesopotamian counterparts, could have to work for a living. From the human side, whatever the Hittites may have thought about the matter, it behooved them regularly and lavishly to provide for the gods so that the deities would remain present and predisposed to offer protection and extend blessing. In effect, the cultic care of the deity in the temple determined the fate of the nation and its people.

---

246. In the expansion ritual, as elsewhere, these offerings are explicitly referred to as a divine meal.

247. See the translations in Singer, *Hittite Prayers*, 47–69 and more briefly COS 1:60.156–60.

248. See Singer, *Hittite Prayers*, nn. 8 §6; 10 §3; 11 §3; 12 §§8–9; 13 §3, pp. 52, 57, 58, 63, 65.

249. The Song of Hedammu (*CTH* 348; Hoffner, *Hittite Myths*, 49) uses the same argument from the divine side as Ea questions the divine destruction of humanity, noting that it will mean the cessation of human offerings.

# CHAPTER 11

# DIVINE PRESENCE IN
# SYRO-PALESTINIAN TEMPLES

OUR UNDERSTANDING OF DIVINE PRESENCE in the Syro-Palestinian cult is the murkiest of all.[1] Few relevant texts remain,[2] leaving interpreters to reconstruct their portraits primarily from the archaeological record and by analogy with surrounding cultures.[3] In addition, it is often difficult to determine if preserved images depict a deity or a human. Even if a deity may be conclusively identified, it is also difficult to assess whether the image represents the deity itself or its cult statue.[4] While some have especially lauded the merits of iconographical analysis, going so far as to equate its reconstructive value to the texts of Ugarit, such a claim is overstated.[5] While archaeology is by no means mute,[6] without accompanying texts and with few accompanying inscriptions,[7] the evidence is largely contextless. A statue, for example, may connote power, yet often does not indicate what kind

---

1. The following chapter will focus on evidence from the second half of the second millennium to the first half of the first millennium and leave aside any discussion of the laden biblical and Israelite material.

   Regarding the interpretive perils, see esp. Theodore J. Lewis, "Syro-Palestinian Iconography and Divine Images," in Walls, ed., *Cult Image and Divine Representation*, 71–82.

2. The primary textual information comes from Ugarit and Emar and provides limited access to the thought-world of the Syro-Palestinian cult.

3. As elsewhere in the ancient Near East, there is no guarantee that archaeological evidence and the conclusions drawn from it apply across Syria-Palestine or across time.

4. Berlejung, *Theologie der Bilder*, 293.

5. E.g. Izak Cornelius (*The Iconography of the Canaanite Gods Reshef and Ba'al: Late Bronze and Iron Age I Periods (c. 1500–1000 BCE)* [OBO 140; Fribourg: University Press, 1994], 264), who argues that the iconographic depictions "can fulfill a role comparable to the texts of Ugarit."

6. See esp. the communicative power of the temple of 'Ain Dara (e.g., Lewis, "Divine Images and Aniconism in Ancient Israel," *JAOS* 118 [1998]: 40; John Monson, "The New 'Ain Dara Temple: Closest Solomonic Parallel," *BAR* 26 [2000]: 20–35, 67; idem, "The 'Ain Dara Temple and the Jerusalem Temple," in Beckman and Lewis, eds., *Text, Artifact, and Image*, 273–99) and analogously of those in Egypt.

7. Lewis, "Syro-Palestinian Iconography," 77.

of power the deity bears and to what end. That is, whereas iconographic analysis can demonstrate that a raised hand is a symbol of power, "only texts describing Reshef as a god who listens to prayers and who heals informs us that Reshef's power [manifest in his raised hand] is an apotropaic power—an ability to ward of disease."[8]

When native interpretative statements are lacking, the interpreter must turn elsewhere to find meaning. Since primary data are insufficient for constructing a full picture, interpreters borrow from another context, most commonly either their own, the biblical texts, or the larger ancient Near Eastern world. The latter seems to be the best way forward,[9] and for good reason, yet this method is beset by various problems. First, although fuller, the data from the surrounding cultures is also poorly preserved and even more poorly understood. Second, and perhaps more tellingly, the data are merely analogous. Although there are many cross-cultural commonalities, there is no guarantee that features in one area apply to another and there is practically a guarantee that they apply in different ways.

Although our proposed reconstruction seems doomed from the start, there is reason for cautious hope. Iconographic remains are extensive and, while minimal in comparison with their more illustrious neighbors, various texts especially from Ugarit and Emar are also illustrative (e.g., myths, rituals, treaties, and royal correspondence). In addition, evidence exists from outside Syria-Palestine, particularly Assyria, pertaining to Syro-Palestinian cult statues (see figs. 11.1 and 11.2). Thus, we may begin to sketch the Syro-Palestinian portrait, proceeding cautiously and concluding tentatively in light of the various dangers, all the while hoping that our rendition captures some of the original and that better data and better interpretations will emerge to add depth and breadth to our portrait.

## PERCEPTIONS OF DEITY

As elsewhere in the ancient Near East,[10] Syro-Palestinian deities seem to have been predicated on the human model.[11] In mythological and epic literature,

---

8. Victor A. Hurowitz, "Picturing Imageless Deities: Iconography in the Ancient Near East," *BAR* 23 (1997): 69.

9. For example, Christoph Uehlinger's reassessment of anthropomorphic cult statuary in Iron Age Canaan proceeds "by way of analogy and on the basis of circumstantial evidence from neighbouring areas" ("Anthropomorphic Cult Statuary," 152).

10. Our understanding of Syro-Palestinian conceptions of deity comes primarily from Ugarit and, although we should expect significant overlap, we should also expect the configurations of deity to take different shape in different regions and different times.

11. Or, perhaps more in accord with the ancient Near Eastern mindset, humans were predicated on the divine model, i.e., theomorphic. Van der Toorn refers to the gods as "by and large ... anthropomorphic, both internally and externally" ("Theology, Priests, and

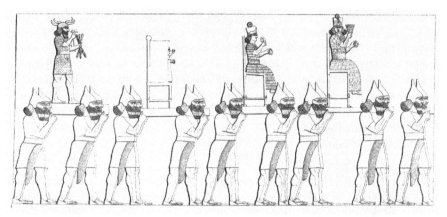

Fig. 11.1. Cult statues, presumably Syrian, carried away by Assyrian soldiers (wall relief, palace of Tiglath-pileser III, Nimrud, eighth century). From Layard, *Monuments of Nineveh*, pl. 65.

Fig. 11.2. The capture of cult statues, presumably from Ashkelon (Sennacherib's Southwest Palace, Room X, slab 11). From Layard, *Monuments of Nineveh II*, pl. 50.

they took human-like form, had human-like emotions, appetites, senses, and intellectual capabilities, engaged in human-like activities, and had human-like social relations.[12] Although human-like, the deities nonetheless were understood

---

Worship in Canaan and Ancient Israel," *CANE* 3:2044). While this is generally true, as we will see, the gods transcended the human model in various ways, such that they were far more than humans writ large.

12. At times, the anthropomorphism could be carried to an extreme. Like the statue of Nabu in Mesopotamia, the statue of Ashtart is said to have gone on a hunt at Emar (Emar 446 90; Fleming, *Time at Emar*, 274, 275; *COS* 1:125.440). Regarding the divine profile

to be grander in scale, exceeding their human counterparts in practically every respect.[13] For example, their visual and auditory capacities were simultaneously described in human terms and magnified.[14] In contrast to humans, they could see objects many miles away.[15] Likewise, while descriptions of the divine body were generally "literal,"[16] i.e., texts "realistically" described the divine body parts, the gods were nonetheless superhuman in size, such that gods could traverse "a thousand fields, ten thousand acres."[17] In addition, Kothar was so large that he could be seen approaching from the same distance.[18] Nonetheless, although they possessed great powers of perception and massive size, they were neither omniscient nor omnipresent.[19] Moral perfection was also not ascribed to them, as they were subject to the both the better and baser human emotions and wills.[20] They could act heroically and compassionately, yet also succumbed to flights of fancy, jealousy, sibling rivalry, and avarice. Thus, as in most polytheistic contexts, although they far exceeded human capabilities, the gods remained limited and interdependent. For example, Baal's absence in the Baal cycle seems to indicate that the gods could not produce rain without him and had to toil in vain to artificially irrigate the land.[21] El's subsequent dream of the heavens raining (*mṭr*) oil (*šmn*) and the wadis flowing with honey (*nbt*) indicated to him that Baal was still alive and that his return would mean that the gods could desist from their futile efforts.[22]

In addition to being bigger and better, the gods were also different in that they transcended the human form and function in various capacities. Divine powers extended to control over the very cosmic elements that humanity could not

---

in myths, see esp. the Korpel, *A Rift in the Clouds*, 88–552; see also Smith, *The Origins of Biblical Monotheism: Israel's Polytheistic Background and the Ugaritic Texts* (Oxford: Oxford University Press, 2001), 83–102.

13. For example, deities surpassed "humans in longevity, knowledge, authority and range of effective influence" (van der Toorn, "Theology, Priests, and Worship").

14. See Korpel, *A Rift in the Clouds*, 134–37, 140, 145–46.

15. *KTU* 1.1 ii 13–16; iii 2; 1.3 vi 18–19; Korpel, *A Rift in the Clouds*, 135. As noted in the preface, I use lower case roman numerals to refer to the column rather than the standard practice of upper case roman numerals for the sake of consistency across ancient Near Eastern cultures.

16. Korpel, *A Rift in the Clouds*, 127.

17. *KTU* 1.3 vi 17–19; 1.4 v 24; viii 24–26; Mark S. Smith, "Divine Form and Size in Ugaritic and Israelite Religion," *ZAW* 100 (1988): 424–27; idem, *Origins of Biblical Monotheism*, 84.

18. *KTU* 1.17 v 9–11.

19. Regarding their massive size, see the giant footprints at 'Ain Dara (see fig. 5.3).

20. See briefly van der Toorn, "Theology, Priests, and Worship."

21. *KTU* 1.6 i 67; ii 3. Unfortunately, the meaning of the text is not entirely clear in both places (Korpel, *A Rift in the Clouds*, 595).

22. *KTU* 1.6 iii 4–21; Korpel, *A Rift in the Clouds*, 595.

control. For example, Baal controlled the weather and Shapshu controlled the sun. Like the Egyptian, Hittite, and (to some extent) the Mesopotamian deities, Syro-Palestinian deities could adopt multiple forms. For example, in addition to their anthropomorphic forms, both El and Baal could transform themselves into bulls and oxen, while various deities, including Baal,[23] seem to have been able to change into avian form, especially for the purpose of travel.[24] The gods' power of and penchant for transformation is particularly evident in *KTU* 1.10, where it seems Anat appears as a winged bird, as anthropomorphic, as a cow, and again as a human.[25]

As in Egypt, Mesopotamia, and Hittite Anatolia, some deities had expansive and fluid enough profiles to be considered a constellation of aspects, anchored by the anthropomorphically conceived figure who controlled them. Each aspect could be treated as a distinct entity or as part of the divine person depending on the context.[26] The weather god Baal[27] in particular was identified by various locally and functionally determined epithets, such as Baal of Mt. Sapan, Baal of Ugarit, Baal-Shamem (heavenly Baal), and Baal-KNP (winged Baal), which were treated as distinct entities in cultic texts and treaties.[28] For example, in various offering lists from Ugarit, various Baals received distinct offerings. Likewise, the many elements of the weather that Baal controlled,[29] such as clouds, winds, thunderbolts,

---

23. Cf. Baal *knp*, "winged Baal" (*KTU* 1.46 6).

24. Korpel, *A Rift in the Clouds*, 524–32, 544–49.

25. Ibid., 526.

26. For example, Baal was treated as a single unified actor in the Baal cycle.

27. Baal itself was originally a title, "lord," applied primarily to the various West Semitic weather gods, which later seems to have become a personal name. On the expansive profile of Baal and the various similar names and entities that stood behind the label, see Korpel, *A Rift in the Clouds*; Schwemer, *Wettergottgestalten*; idem, "Storm-Gods I," esp. 152–68; idem, "Storm-Gods II," esp. 9–16; Allen, "Splintered Divine," 239–73. For iconography, see Cornelius, *Iconography of Reshef and Ba'al*.

28. See briefly the summary in Sommer, *Bodies of God*, 25 with references; see more fully, Pardee, *Ritual and Cult*, 11–72. For example, *KTU* 1.109 refers to a feast of Baal of Sapan (l. 5) in which offerings are presented to Baal, Baal of Sapan, Baal of Ugarit, and Baal of Aleppo (Pardee, *Ritual and Cult*, 29–33). The seventh-century treaty between Esarhaddon and Baal, king of Tyre, also mentions "Baal-Šamêm, Baal-Malagê and Baal-of-Ṣapān" (SAA 2.5 iv). Sommer (*Bodies of God*, 24 and 189 n. 82) contends that the three Baal-names refer to the same deity since the verb *lušatbâ* is singular and "no explicit copula" appears between Baal-Malage and Baal-of-Sapan. However, no other paired Phoenician deities in these curses are separated by an explicit copula, there is no other instance in which a divine name and its two epithets each bear a divine determinative, and the singular verb is better interpreted as referring to the unified actions of three distinct deities (esp. in light of the use of the singular verb *liškun* to refer to the shared activity of the seven Sebittu deities in the same text [l. 5']) (Allen, "Splintered Divine," 262–64).

29. For exceptions, see Korpel, *A Rift in the Clouds*, 598–99.

and rains, were presented alternatively as extensions of the divine person (such as the thunder as Baal's voice)[30] or as semi-independent self-propelled agents who did their divine master's bidding.[31] In addition, "the arms of the victorious warrior Addu were worshipped as movable cult symbols and could be taken into battle as a kind of field-standard."[32] Various qualities of the high god El— the Mercy (ḥnn) of El, the Constancy (nṣbt) of El and the Well-being (šlm) of El—also seem to have functioned as (semi-)independent divine beings.[33] Nevertheless, while significant and varied powers could be ascribed to the individual deities, none possessed all necessary powers, such that the gods had to work together to ensure the cosmos functions appropriately. For example, despite his potency, Baal was never responsible for the rising sun. In turn, the people also appealed to different gods with different competencies according to their different needs.

In addition to referring to a single deity consisting of a constellation of aspects, it seems Baal also referred to a category of similar yet distinct individual gods with their own constellations.[34] As in Hittite Anatolia, the dependence on rainfall meant that many cities had their own weather god upon whom they relied

---

30. In addition, Baal as the warrior god alone could hold lightning and thunder in his hand (cf. *KTU* 1.3 iii 26–28; 1.4 v 9; 1.5 v 7–8; Korpel, *A Rift in the Clouds*, 498). His lightning spears (ʿṣ brq) were presented elsewhere as wooden shafts (*KTU* 1.4 vii 40–41; Korpel, *A Rift in the Clouds*, 498).

31. Korpel, *A Rift in the Clouds*, 596–97; cf. 560–62. The different forms of dew were even presented as the animate daughters of Baal (ibid., 597–98). In other contexts, these elements were neither part of the divine person nor personified agents. Rather, they were simply presented as inanimate elements (ibid.).

32. Schwemer, "Storm-Gods I," 164; see further idem, *Wettergottgestalten*, 215–6, 217; A. 1858, edited as text 5 in Jean-Marie Durand, *Florilegium marianum VII: Le culte d'Addu d'Alep et l'affaire d'Alahtum* (Paris: SEPOA, 2002). This is not to say that the statue had detachable arms. Rather, in addition to the statue with arms intact, an additional cult object representing the divine arms was created.

33. Although there is no determinative to mark their divine status, these divine qualities appear in a list after other deities and thus seem to have been deified divine qualities (*KTU* 1.65; Smith, *Origins*, 76; Sommer, *Bodies of God*, 27). See also the list of (deified) divine qualities in *KTU* 1.123, Light and Firmness, Eternity and Rule, Right and Justice, Compassion of the sons of El and Glory and Light, which appear after a standard list of deities (Smith, *Origins*, 76; Sommer, *Bodies of God*, 27).

34. Since the evidence for differentiation comes largely from non-narrative and non-poetic texts (e.g., rituals and treaties), the various Baals, like all other gods mentioned in these genres, "show no individuation of personality, character, or function" (Sommer, *Bodies of God*, 25). In other words, these texts consist primarily of divine names and, in the case of ritual texts, a list of offerings received and thus have little interest in presenting a character profile. However, Baal (of Sapan) in Ugaritic mythology had a fully developed profile, and there is every reason to suspect that the other Baals likewise would have borne similar yet distinct full profiles had other mythologies (and texts of the like) been preserved.

for rain and protection.[35] It is likely that in some instances some of the locally distinct weather gods were assimilated by the more transregional manifestations of Baal (e.g., Baal of Mt. Sapan).[36] However, despite some merging, there is evidence that many of the weather gods were treated as distinct deities in some contexts.[37] For example, Baal of Mt. Sapan was the Baal of Ugaritic mythology.[38] In the myths, since there was no other Baal in view, he was simply Baal. However, in ritual and treaty contexts, he took the epithet Baal of Mt. Sapan to distinguish him from other Baals. Baal of Ugarit seems to have been an extension of Baal of Mt. Sapan, the Baal of mythology as manifest in that city.[39] Baal of Aleppo,[40] like the Hittite Goddess of the Night, had various other extensions in the Syrian sphere as far as Mari on the Middle Euphrates and the Hittite capital of Hattusa,[41] and likely had his own (as yet undiscovered) mythology.[42] Baal Shamem, especially prominent in the 1st millennium and probably originating in Phoenicia, likely had his own manifestations in the Phoenician city-states and mythological identity as the Lord

---

35. Any firm conclusions are elusive given the spotty nature of the evidence; so much comes from Ugarit and so little from everywhere else.

36. See, e.g., Schwemer, "Storm-Gods I," 158.

37. The turbulence in the region and the presence of multiple (semi-)independent states likely hindered the development of a single, unified Baal. In addition, different localized versions were preferred during different time periods. For example, the textual record indicates that Baal-Shamem rose to prominence in the 1st millennium. However, the lack of earlier texts from the region in which he emerged could mean that he was present earlier but as yet unattested textually.

38. Thanks are due to Mark Smith for pointing this out to me. Thus, there is no reason to suspect that an originally singular Baal of mythology "fragmented into a great number of Baal gods who could be worshipped and addressed separately" (Sommer, *Bodies of God*, 25). Instead, it would seem that from the beginning the Baal of mythology was Baal of Sapan, with Baal of Ugarit as his urban manifestation, while other Baal traditions, and thus Baal gods, were likely present as distinct deities elsewhere in Syria-Palestine.

39. See further below for a more detailed analysis of the relationship between the city Baals and the mountain, celestial, and mythological Baals.

40. Also prominent in the Hittite sphere. See, e.g., *Florilegium marianum VII.*

41. Schwemer, "Storm-Gods I," 155, 163, 165; idem, *Wettergottgestalten*, 464–5, 490, 494–502, 515, 521–2, 548.

42. Since the only Syro-Palestinian mythology discovered came from Ugarit, we often mistakenly assume that Ugaritic mythology was the only mythology of ancient Syria-Palestine, such that the mythology of Baal from Ugarit was shared by all other Syro-Palestinian peoples. While the various mythologies were likely mutually influential, they probably also carried their own distinctive elements.

of Heaven,[43] while Baal of Lebanon,[44] associated with a different mountain range, may also have had local manifestations and an associated mythology. Thus, the name Baal may be used to refer to a group of various deities of the weather god type (e.g., the Baals) and the various individual deities within the type (e.g, Baal of Ugarit) and their individual constellations of particular detachable aspects.

As the powers in charge of the cosmos and particularly those elements that humans could not control (like the weather), humans needed divine support to gain security in an otherwise insecure world. Since divine-human contact was otherwise sporadic, limited to myths, epics, dreams, and various other indirect media, temples regularized divine presence and afforded humans a consistent means of positively influencing the deities who now dwelt in their midst. In addition, unlike theophanies, encounters with the divine in the temple offered some level of predictability and less danger.

## The Statue and Its Craftsmanship

Although the data is fragmentary, the anthropomorphic cult statues generally seem to have been rather small. The extant metal statuary, none of which can be conclusively identified as a primary cult statue, ranges from approximately 5–40 cm (2–15 inches) in height, with far more clustering around 5 than 40 (see fig. 11.1).[45] Neo-Assyrian reliefs depict soldiers carrying off as booty cult statues, three of which appear to be almost ¾ life-sized.[46] Thus, although the evidence is limited and varied, statues were likely at most ¾ human size and often much smaller.

---

43. See, e.g., Herbert Niehr, *Baʿalšamem: Studien zu Herkunft, Geschichte und Rezeptionsgeschichte eines* phönizischen *Gottes* (OLA 123; Leuven: Peeters, 2003). Schwemer suggests that his association with the celestial realm led to his increased prominence especially in treaty contexts, since as the god of heaven he was able to bind people of different regions ("Storm-Gods II," 15).

44. Attested in a Phoenician inscription from Cyprus dated to the third quarter of the eighth century (KAI 31). See the discussion of Albert I. Baumgarten, *The Phoenician History of Philo of Byblos: A Commentary* (Leiden: Brill, 1981), 154. For convenient translations, see KAI 2:49–50; and John C. L. Gibson, *Textbook of Syrian Semitic Inscriptions: Volume III. Phoenician Inscriptions* (Oxford: Clarendon Press, 1982; reprinted, Oxford: Oxford University Press, 2002), 67–68. Regarding Baal of Hamon, see Paolo Xella, *Baal Hammon: Recherches sur l'identité et l'histoire d'un dieu phénico-punique* (Contributi alla storia della religione fenicio-punica 1; Rome: Consiglio Nazionale Delle Ricerche, 1991).

45. Ora Negbi, *Canaanite Gods in Metal* (Tel Aviv: Tel Aviv University, 1976). For questions of methodology, see esp. Peter R. S. Moorey and Stuart Fleming, "Problems in the Study of the Anthropomorphic Metal Statuary from Syro-Palestine before 330 B.C.," *Levant* 16 (1984): 67–90.

46. See briefly Uehlinger, "Anthropomorphic Cult Statuary," 124, 127–28. Although the

While data remains limited, there is every reason to suspect that they were crafted of the most precious materials, though perhaps less ostentatious and well-crafted than those of the surrounding empires (cf. the comparatively poorly crafted statue of King Idrimi of Alalakh with those of the wealthier Mesopotamian and Egyptian kings; fig. 11.3 vs. 2.5). Written sources are sparse but by no means absent. For example, in the Amarna archives (EA 55), the mayor of Qatna writes that he needs a sack of gold to refashion the Hurrian sun god. Other written evidence comes from the biblical text, referring to elements of gold, silver, bronze, iron, stone, wood, and fine jewelry.[47] Artifactual remains indicate the use of gold, bronze overlaid with gold, silver, stone, ivory, and terracotta in Syria and gold, bronze, silver, stone, ivory, and terracotta in Palestine.[48] It also seems that the gods wore lavish garments atop their valuable bodies.[49] Two texts from Ugarit (*KTU* 4.168, 4.182) mention a large amount of clothing.[50] Pardee concludes that this great quantity suggests either that the gods were well clothed and were often changed or that the "clothing of their priestly representatives was provided by this divine fiction."[51] The presence of garments in one of the so-called "entry" rituals suggests the former (*KTU* 1.43 4, 22), although the identification of the garments with the statue is unclear.[52] The biblical tradition also speaks of dressing the gods (e.g., a woven hanging for the asherah [2 Kgs 23:7] and crown of Milcom [2 Sam 12:30]).[53] As elsewhere, the images were likely made by specialized craftsmen. For example, among others, Ugaritic documents list metal workers (*nsk*), gold- and silversmiths (*nsk ksp*), and engravers (*mly*).[54] Ironically, the biblical image-ban texts

size of the images may be exaggerated, they nonetheless show an awareness of size variation since one image is significantly smaller than the others (ibid., 128 n. 154).

47. Lewis, "Syro-Palestinian Iconography," 84–87 and the references cited therein; cf. the reference to the Nergal stone at Emar (Daniel Arnaud, *Textes syriens de l'Âge du Bronze récent* [AuOrS 1; Barcelona: AUSA, 1991], 143–4).

48. Lewis, "Syro-Palestinian Iconography," 84–85.

49. Various Ugaritic texts mention the clothing of the gods (Korpel, *A Rift in the Clouds*, 364–67), from which one may infer that the statues also wore clothes, or at least that they were sculpted clothed and not nude.

50. See Charles Virolleaud, *Le Palais royal d'Ugarit, publié sous la direction de Claude F.-A. Schaeffer* (Mission de Ras Shamra 7; Paris: Imprimerie nationale, 1957), xxxi–xxxii, 137–42.

51. Pardee, *Ritual and Cult*, 226.

52. Gregorio del Olmo Lete argues that such passages refer to the "ritual attire of the gods" (*Canaanite Religion*, 260, 286 n. 96, 308–9). See also the reference to the red wool garment of NINKUR in the installation ritual of Baal's high priestess at Emar (Emar 369 23, 60; Fleming, *Installation of Baal's High Priestess*, 15, 23, 51, 56; *COS* 1:122.428–30).

53. Lewis, "Syro-Palestinian Iconography," 92.

54. Ibid.; cf. Joaquín Sanmartín, "Das Handwerk in Ugarit: Eine lexikalische Studie," *SEL* 12 (1995): 169–90; Juan-Pablo Vita, "The Society of Ugarit," in *Handbook of Ugaritic Studies* (ed. W. G. E. Watson and N. Wyatt; HO 1/39; Leiden: Brill, 1999), 486–90.

Fig. 11.3. A statue of Idrimi king of Alalakh from the fifteenth century BCE. Courtesy of the British Museum.

provide the best evidence for the artisans (e.g., metalworkers and carpenters) and their technique and skill by describing the craftsman and crafting of images they are polemicizing against.[55]

## Types of Statues

Syro-Palestinian gods were depicted in several (well-attested) forms, which can be subdivided into four broad categories: anthropomorphic, theriomorphic,

---

55. Lewis, "Syro-Palestinian Iconography," 89.

Fig. 11.4. A bronze statue with gold foil depicting the god El. Drill holes above the ears suggest that the statue originally had horns. Courtesy Mission to Ras Shamra-Ougarit and Ebla to Damascus Exhibit, Smithsonian Institute. Photo by Ingrid Strüben.

mixed, and as inanimate objects,[56] including cult symbols like a moon crescent and standing stones.[57] In most periods and places, anthropomorphic depictions

---

56. "Inanimate object" is an imperfect category, since to the ancient mind, celestial bodies, like the moon, probably would have been considered animate. It is used here merely as a modern label to help the reader differentiate human and animal forms from all others. Cf. Cornelius, "Many Faces of God," 41–42.

57. In addition to *GGIG*, see briefly Berlejung, *Theologie der Bilder*, 293–96, and more fully Silvia Schroer, *In Israel gab es Bilder: Nachrichten von darstellender Kunst im Alten Testament* (OBO 74; Fribourg: University Press, 1987), regarding Palestine. As elsewhere in

Fig. 11.5. A limestone stela of the anthropomorphic Baal with horned crown wielding a mace and carrying a staff sprouting vegetation (fifteenth–thirteenth centuries BCE; Ugarit). Courtesy of the Louvre. Photo by the author.

were especially prominent (fig. 11.4).[58] Like the Mesopotamian gods, they seem to have been adorned with the universal signs on the head and the specific attributes in the hand.[59] For example, in the famous stele from Ugarit (AO 15775) Baal wears

the ancient Near East, forms of cult images are generally conservative (Berlejung, *Theologie der Bilder*, 294).

58. As in Egypt and Mesopotamia, the anthropomorphic representation of deity was not necessarily intended to be a faithful and literal depiction of the true divine form, but rather a representation of the divine potencies and spheres of influence (cf. Berlejung, *Theologie der Bilder*, 294).

59. As in Mesopotamia, the horned crown was the primary marker of divinity (Berlejung, *Theologie der Bilder*, 294, 296).

a crown typical of divinity with horns and carries a mace in an upraised hand and a staff sprouting vegetation, both characteristic of the Weather God (fig. 11.5).[60]

The bull, associated with both Baal and El, was a particularly common theriomorphic form (fig. 11.6). However, given the lack of accompanying inscriptions and the uncertainty whether some such forms came from cultic contexts, there is some debate as to how to interpret them. Did they represent: 1) the deity itself in its animal form; 2) more distantly the deity in symbolic form; 3) the divine pedestal, mount, or accessory; or 4) votive offerings to the deity?[61] Various texts from Ugarit describe deities taking theriomorphic form,[62] suggesting that at least in some cases theriomorphic cult images may have been depictions of the deity in its theriomorphic form. However, there are also various instances that distinguished the deity from its associated animal, such as the common portrait of a deity astride its representative animal,[63] such that animal forms may have associated the image with a particular deity without actually visually depicting that deity (fig. 11.7).[64] Thus, an animal image could serve as a symbol for a deity, representing that deity by association rather than by physical resemblance. When the animal form appears alone, especially when the animal has post holes in its back, it is also possible that the originally attached deity has been lost.[65] Thus, we are left with a variety of options and, without further information, cannot easily decide between them.

---

60. See briefly Cornelius, *Iconography of Reshef and Ba'al*, 135–38.

61. Cf. Lewis, "Divine Images," 47–48. Here again, it must be stressed that we are talking about the ways in which the image visually represented the deity, not how and to what extent the deity was present in the image.

62. Korpel, *A Rift in the Clouds*, 524–28, 532–34; Lewis, "Divine Images," 47 and the references cited therein. See further below on the ability of the gods to change forms.

63. See, e.g., Negbi, *Canaanite Gods in Metal*, n. 1308, which depicts a warrior in smiting pose astride a crouching lion. See also the statue found at Hazor of a male deity, presumably Baal, as well as his animal pedestal, the bull (Cornelius, *Iconography of Reshef and Ba'al*, 226–29, BS 1, pl. 52) (see fig. 11.7); see also BM 16, 85 and cf. BM 4, 6, where he appears holding a bull. In addition, similar depictions in 1st millennium Mesopotamian may have been inspired by Syrian antecedents (J. E. Reade, "Shikaft-i Gulgul: Its Date and Symbolism," *Iranica Antiqua* 12 (1977): 42; Irene Winter, "Art as Evidence for Interaction: Relations Between the Assyrian Empire and North Syria," in *Mesopotamien und seine Nachbarn: Politische und kulturelle Wechselbeziehungen im alten Vorderasien vom 4. bis 1. Jahrtausend v. Chr* (ed. H. J. Nissen and J. Renger; BBVO 1; Berlin: Reimer, 1982), 367; Ornan, "Idols and Symbols—Divine Representation in First Millennium Mesopotamian Art and its Bearing on the Second Commandment," *TA* 31 (2004): 97–98; idem, "In the Likeness of Man," 137).

64. Or, as in the lion figures used to guard the temples, the animals depicted may not have represented the deity at all, but rather served to protect it and/or its precincts.

65. Attached in the sense of placed atop or alternatively next to the animal. Although there is little evidence for it, it is theoretically possible that the deity was imagined to be invisibly present upon the animal (Mettinger, *No Graven Image*, 137; Lewis, "Divine Images," 48).

Fig. 11.6. A bull statue found near Samaria (ca. 1200 BCE; 13 x 18 cm [5" x 7"]). Courtesy of the Israel Museum, Jerusalem.

As in Mesopotamia, the hybrid forms did not often seem to represent major deities, [66] instead commonly serving as monsters, protective figures, or elements of the divine throne (figs. 11.8, 11.9).[67] Symbolic representations appeared early but were especially prevalent in the Iron Age. For example, likely under Mesopotamian influence, the crescent of Sin, the spade of Marduk, and the stylus of Nabu appeared as early as the early eighth century.[68]

---

66. The winged female deities at Ugarit (Cornelius, "Many Faces of God," 39) may have been an exception (Lewis, "Syro-Palestinian Iconography," 99, fig. 32).

67. See, e.g., the Bes figurine in Lewis, "Syro-Palestinian Iconography," 74 fig. 4.6; the ivory panel from Megiddo with a sphinx throne (see fig. 11.8). See also the description of the monstrous sons of El (Smith, *Origins of Monotheism*, 32–35).

68. *GGIG* §§ 90, 168–88; B. Hrouda, "Göttersymbole und –attribute. A. Archäologisch. I. Syrien/Palästina," *RlA* 3 (1969): 490–95; Keel, *Studien zu den Stempelsiegeln aus Palästina/Israel IV* (OBO 135; Fribourg: Universitätsverlag, 1994), 135–202; Uehlinger, "Anthropomorphic Cult Statuary," 134.

Fig. 11.7. An anthropomorphic deity astride a bull (with legs reconstructed to connect figure to bull; Hazor, 14th century BCE; figure 26 cm [10.4"], pedestal 17 cm [6.8"]. Courtesy of the Israel Museum, Jerusalem.

Standing stones also featured prominently in Syria-Palestine,[69] occurring either as free-standing monuments or as focal points of sanctuaries (see fig. 11.10).[70]

---

69. See particularly the study of Mettinger, *No Graven Image*; note also the more cautious reviews (Oswald Loretz, "Semitischer Aniconismus und biblisches Bilderverbot: Review Article on T. Mettinger, *No Graven Image* [1995]," *UF* 26 [1996]: 209–23; Uehlinger, "Israelite Aniconism in Context," *Bib* 77 [1996]: 540–49; Hurowitz, "Picturing Imageless Deities"; Lewis, "Divine Images"). The use of standing stones was also rather static across the millennia as "the practice of setting up standings stones thirteen thousand years ago was nearly the same as it was two or three thousand years ago; stone aniconism was about as inert as the stones themselves (eleven millennia is a long time by anyone's standards)" (Hurowitz, "Picturing Imageless Deities," 68).

70. It would seem that standing stones originally were free-standing and only later

Fig. 11.8. An ivory of a hybrid being from Samaria (ca. 900–850 BCE). Courtesy of the Israel Museum, Jersualem.

Unfortunately, their interpretation is beset by archaeological and textual difficulties on all sides.[71] One could interpret a stone slab either as a cultic object, a house pillar, a table, or an altar.[72] In the biblical texts, standing stones also functioned as tombstones, boundary markers, markers for the twelve tribes, and even surrogates for a male heir.[73] When the slabs appear in a clear cultic context, they may be

enshrined in temples (cf. Mettinger, *No Graven Image*, 31–32, 181–82; idem, "Israelite Aniconism: Developments and Origins," in van der Toorn, *The Image and the Book*, 186), or perhaps the standing stones in the temples were smaller replicas of the open air standing stones, bringing the numinous power of the stones into the urban centers (cf. Fleming, *Time at Emar*, 85).

71. Hurowitz, "Picturing Imageless Deities"; Lewis, "Divine Images," 41; idem, "Syro-Palestinian Iconography," 76.

72. Lewis, "Divine Images," 41.

73. Ibid.; on the latter, see Johannes C. de Moor, "Standing Stones and Ancestor Worship," *UF* 27 (1995): 1–20.

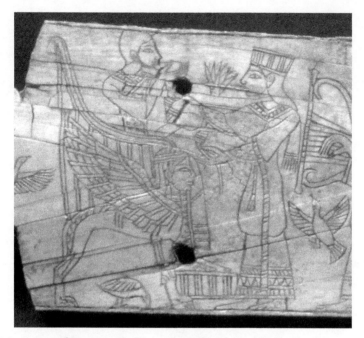

Fig. 11.9. An ivory from Meggido depicting a hybrid being beside or as the support for a throne (13th–12th centuries BCE). Courtesy of the Israel Museum, Jersualem.

regarded as a representation of divinity or, more minimally, as markers of sacred space where one could contact the deity.[74] The Emar texts in particular provide further cultic information. The texts about the *zukru* festival and the installation of Baal's high priestess refer to the presentation of offerings to the standing stone (*sikkānu*) of Hebat,[75] reflecting its close association with the deity, while within the same ritual oil and blood were applied to the stones,[76] indicating their association with ritual activity.

Before moving on to the rituals, it is worth discussing the posited general recession of anthropomorphic divine representations, especially the male deity, throughout the Iron Age II Palestine.[77] In its place, the glyptic evidence (i.e., small

74. Lewis, "Divine Images," 50–51.

75. Emar 369, 373; Fleming, *Installation of Baal's High Priestess*, 75–79; see conveniently *COS* 1:122.429, 123.435.

76. Emar 373 34, 60; *COS* 1:122.433.

77. Uehlinger, "Anthropomorphic Cult Statuary," 101 referring in particular to *GGIG* §§ 79–80, 82, 109, 111, 235 followed by Mettinger, *No Graven Image*, 16, 137. It must be noted that the following discussion says nothing about the presence or absence of a cult image

Fig. 11.10. Standing stones from Gezer. Photo by the author.

carved stones) in particular "displays a fairly clear tendency to gradually substitute straightforward anthropomorphic representations of deities with icons of blessing (such as suckling animals or scenes of tree worship), protection and/or solar symbolism (sphinxes, winged scarabs and uraei)."[78] Cultic symbols, like the moon crescent of Sin, also became especially prominent and in seals were depicted as the objects of worship instead of anthropomorphic statues, while anthropomorphic metal statuary appears to have been relatively rare compared to earlier periods.[79]

However, while it is clear that other visual media gained prominence, it is unlikely that anthropomorphic representations ever disappeared.[80] First, although modest compared to other periods, there is nonetheless considerable evidence for

in the Jerusalem temple (cf., e.g., Niehr, "In Search of YHWH's Cult Statue in the First Temple," in van der Toorn, ed., *Image and the Book*, 73–95 and Lewis, "Syro-Palestinian Iconography," 103–5).

78. Uehlinger, "Anthropomorphic Cult Statuary," 100; see further *GGIG* §§ 76–80, 87–95, 116–18 and *passim*. This is especially pronounced for male deities.

79. See generally James D. Muhly, "Bronze Figurines and Near Eastern Metalwork," *IEJ* 39 (1980): 148–61; for a list of the anthropomorphic metal statuary for Iron Age I–II A, II B and II C, see Uehlinger, "Anthropomorphic Cult Statuary," 103–4; 112–14, 129. As elsewhere in the ancient Near East, it is unsurprising that primary cult images have not been found, as they were subject to looting and reuse.

80. Uehlinger, "Anthropomorphic Cult Statuary."

anthropomorphic depictions of deity.[81] Second, as in Mesopotamia, the glyptic material is "far less marked by the relative conservatism of cultic practice and as a medium rather sensitive to transformations. . .does not share the relative conservatism of the terracotta production,"[82] and thus should not be given undo weight in assessing statuary. Third, metal production receded in general during the period, not just of anthropomorphic statues, probably as a result of the limited availability of the luxury materials and lack of technical expertise.[83]

It would seem that, in accord with the data from Mesopotamia roughly over the same time period (the second half of the second millennium BCE to the first half of the first), there was a general move away from anthropomorphic divine representation outside of the sanctuaries.[84] At the same time, it appears that within the (especially state-sponsored) temples cult images remained resolutely anthropomorphic.[85] Indeed, the only clear evidence we have of primary cult statues comes from the Neo-Assyrian reliefs and related inscriptions, which depicted these images anthropomorphically (figs. 11.1, 11.2).[86] These reliefs depict Assyrian soldiers carrying away the anthropomorphic cult statues of Syro-Palestinian temples in the late eighth century (Iron Age IIC), and suggest a continuity with earlier anthropomorphic forms that was likely not interrupted and then reinstituted. It is difficult to assess whether this shift was intentional—i.e., ideologically motivated—or a simple adoption of Neo-Assyrian ideas without careful reflection.[87] In either case, the shift effectively privileged the image in the sanctuary and put more distance between the deity and the people.[88]

---

81. See ibid., esp. 102–10, 113–22, 124–27, 129–33.

82. Ibid., 111.

83. Ibid.

84. Cf. Hendel, "Aniconism and Anthropomorphism," 210; Ornan, "Mesopotamian Influence on West Semitic Inscribed Seals: A Preference for the Depiction of Mortals," in *Studies in the Iconography of Northwest Semitic Inscribed Seals: Proceedings of a Symposium Held in Fribourg on April 17–20, 1991* (ed. B. Sass and Ch. Uehlinger; OBO 125; Fribourg: University Press, 1993), 71. However, the recession was likely less drastic than in Mesopotamia.

85. Nonetheless, nonanthropomorphic presentations of deity seem to have also found a foothold in the temples.

86. See Uehlinger, "Anthropomorphic Cult Statuary," 123–28 and the references cited therein.

87. For possible ideological motivations, see ch. 9 under "Anthropomorphic vs. Symbolic Representation." However, it is unlikely that the king benefitted much in the competition for iconic face-time since neither temples nor palaces carried much iconography.

88. See further ch. 9 under "Anthropomorphic vs. Symbolic Representation." The anthropomorphic element that represented the core of the divine constellation was effectively kept from the general public (or more likely simply not as prominent), who were presented with various more distant and short-hand forms (i.e., images related to

## RITUAL

There is no extant Syro-Palestinian ritual text that resembles the Opening of the Mouth, mouth-washing, or expansion rituals in the rest of the ancient Near East, which describe the activation and/or installation of the statue and deity in the temple. Nor is there any text that defines the relationship between statue and deity or how that relationship may change under different circumstances. Biblical texts potentially offer three brief consecration rituals involving anointing with oils and pouring out a libation,[89] yet these remain a far cry from the elaborate rituals in Egypt, Mesopotamia, and Anatolia.[90] However, a ritual text describing the installation and cultic activation of a high priestess is preserved from Emar, from which one may assume that if a priestess must be installed and activated, so too must a divine image.[91] One would expect some kind of ceremony that minimally ritualized the installation of the deity, as a sort of rite of passage to indicate the deity–statue symbiosis was ready to take up residence and rule. However, given the vicissitudes and relative poverty of the region, which may have inhibited the development or at least the preservation of such a ritual,[92] the ritual was probably relatively modest.[93] If an installation ritual occurred, it is unknown whether it was meant to install the deity in the statue, merely make the environment as pleasant as possible thereby prompting the deity to install itself, or simply mark the occasion.

On a smaller scale, there is some evidence that divine images received ritual attention in order to participate in rituals. For example, during the high priestess' installation ritual at Emar, the officiants twice "consecrate" (*qaddušu*) the gods of

---

and associated with the deity but not depicting his form, such as the spade of Marduk). In addition, the symbolic representation of the Mesopotamian gods served as a general extension of Mesopotamian iconographic policy, which restricted anthropomorphic forms to Mesopotamian sanctuaries, leaving symbols for the general public and the western portion of their empire (cf. Uehlinger, "Anthropomorphic Cult Statuary," 134).

89. Judg 17:3, Dan 3:1–7 (in Babylon), and Gen 28:18 (Lewis, "Syro-Palestinian Iconography," 90–91).

90. Cf. ibid. In addition, we do not even know for certain if divine statues were installed in the sanctuary. "Common sense tells us that those who fashioned divine statues then erected them in their temples and sanctuaries, yet we have no explicit ritual in our extant texts" (ibid.; on the Azatiwada inscription, see K. Lawson Younger, "The Phoenician Inscription of Azatiwada: An Integrated Reading," *JSS* 43 [1998]: 19, 36, 40; *COS* 2:31.150] *pace* Yitshaq Avishur, *Phoenician Inscriptions and the Bible* [Tel Aviv: Archaeological Center Publication, 2000], 193).

91. Emar 369; see esp. Fleming, *Installation of Baal's High Priestess*.

92. In other words, the kingdoms may neither have been stable enough nor wealthy enough to establish an installation ritual meaningful enough to be preserved.

93. Cf., e.g., the elaborate cultic rituals in Mesopotamia and Egypt and the more modest ones in Ugarit and especially the Hebrew Bible.

Emar, presumably in the form of their statues, with bread and beer.[94] In the *zukru* festival as well, blood and oil are applied to standing stones in preparation for the ritual proper.[95] In both cases, since the the statue or stone has already been installed, ritual attention serves instead to prepare it for ritual activity, in essence cultically (re)vitalizing them. The consecration with bread and beer serves to make the deities favorably disposed and to ensure their presence for and active participation in the following ritual activity. The application of blood and oil also seems to prepare the standing stones, perhaps by making them pure and/or charged with the necessary potency. If cult items were ritually (re)activated for participation in an important ritual, it follows that they were likely initially activated when cultically inaugurated.[96]

Likewise, there is little evidence for daily cultic care and feeding. Various ritual texts from Emar and Ugarit list the presentation of foodstuffs to divine images.[97] At Emar following the installation of the high priestess, offerings are even presented daily for seven days[98] and Emar 446 refers to offerings presented over six months,[99] while at Ugarit various offerings are presented during a portion or the entirety of a month.[100] However, none of them refers to daily care, and one would expect that the lavish offerings were not repeated on a daily basis. The biblical texts offer further evidence, referring to the weekly presentation of bread to YHWH.[101] Although one cannot say with any certainty, other evidence may enhance the possibility that Syro-Palestinian gods received regular meals akin to their ancient

---

94. Emar 369 6, 22; Fleming, *Installation of Baal's High Priestess*, 10–11, 49, 158–62. See conveniently COS 1:122.427, 428. Fleming defines *qaddušu* as "'to treat as sacred' by means of concrete offerings" (*Installation of Baal's High Priestess*, 162).

95. Emar 373 34, 60; Fleming, *Time at Emar*, 82–87, 238–41; see conveniently COS 1:123.433; cf. the analogous anointing and washing of *ḫuwaši*-s and statues in Anatolia (Goetze, *Kleinasien*, 168; Haas, *Geschichte der Hethitischen Religion*, 507–8; Collins, "A Statue, for the Deity" 33), which presumably follows their inauguration. Once rendered a "*bona fide* cult image" (Collins, "A Statue for the Deity," 33), the statue begins to function as such. Subsequent consecrations likely served to prepare the image for the ritual and invite the deity's active participation (cf. ibid., 33–34). It also marked the forthcoming ritual as important.

96. Or more minimally, cultic activation of divine images in some times and some places preceded their use in ritual activity.

97. See respectively Pardee, *Ritual and Cult*, 25–145; COS 1:122–126.427–43.

98. Emar 369 49–51; Fleming, *Installation of Baal's High Priestess*, 20–21, 54–55; COS 1:122.430.

99. Fleming, *Time at Emar*, 152–73, 268–80; COS 1:124.436–39.

100. RS 1.009; 24.248; 24.253; 24.256; 24.276; 24.284; 24.298; Pardee, *Ritual and Cult*, 26–40; cf. rituals for two months (ibid., 40–65).

101. Regarding the divine care, see more fully Hundley, *Keeping Heaven*, 95–117.

Near Eastern neighbors.[102] Syro-Palestinian temples were referred to as houses and the resident deities were often presented with food offerings, suggesting that the deity dwelled there and "ate" food. In addition, as offerings were the primary way for humans to influence the deities, it would follow that they would be done regularly. The Ugaritic literature also indicates the divine desire for food and that they could become hungry (*rġb*) and thirsty (*ġmʾ*) if not sated.[103] Divine meals in mythological literature are even occasionally referred to as offerings (*dbḥm*).[104] Thus, we may infer that regular, if not daily, offerings were presented to keep the resident deities resident and inclined to extend their protection and prosperity to the community around them. One may also imagine that regular offerings were more modest, perhaps bread and a beverage, while lavish offerings, like expensive meats, were reserved for festivals and times of explicit need.

## RELATIONSHIP BETWEEN STATUE AND DEITY

While the data is too sparse to allow for any firm conclusions, various clues in the texts and iconography allow for a tentative reconstruction. Since, although meager by ANE standards, Ugarit provides the best evidence, analysis will start there. At Ugarit, Baal of Mt. Sapan seems to have been the Baal described in Ugaritic mythology and thus the regional Baal prototype with his own distinct and expansive profile.[105] Baal of Ugarit seems to have been an extension of Baal of Sapan, bringing the deity inaccessibly and mythologically resident on the divinized mountain visible from the city into the city itself and its temple,[106] thereby extending his protection over the city and providing its citizens with the opportunity to positively influence him.[107] In effect then, Baal of Ugarit was Baal of Sapan as

---

102. Evidence is even more minimal for regular care, such as washing and clothing.

103. Korpel, *A Rift in the Clouds*, 171, 399–408, 414–18.

104. Ibid., 414.

105. In the Baal Cycle, Mt. Sapan is explicitly the site of action seventeen times (*KTU* 1.1 v 5, 18, 1.2 iii 19; 1.3 i 22, 1.3 iii 29, 1.3 iv 1, 19, 38; 1.4 iv 19; 1.4 v 23, 55, 1.4 vii 6, 1.5 i 11; 1.6 i 16, 57, 62; 1.6 vi 13), serving as the site of divine conflict and manifestation (Mark Smith, personal communication).

106. Regarding Baal's residence on the mountain, see, e.g., RS 1.009 ii 7; RS 24.284 i 8 (Pardee, *Ritual and Cult*, 27–28, 32–33). It is also possible that there was a temple of Baal of Sapan on the mountain itself.

107. The textual record clearly indicates the primacy of Baal of Sapan over Baal of Ugarit (Schwemer, "Storm-Gods II," 10–11; Smith, "The Problem of the God and His Manifestations: The Case of the Baals at Ugarit," presentation at the international SBL conference, London, 2011). See now idem, "The Problem of the God and His Manifestations: The Case of the Baals at Ugarit, with Implications for Yahweh of Various Locales," in *Die Stadt im Zwölfprophetenbuch* (ed. A. Schart and J. Krispenz; BZAW 428; Berlin: de Gruyter, 2012), 205–50. Indeed, Baal of Sapan and not Baal of Ugarit seems to have been the national

manifest in Ugarit (i.e., Baal of Sapan of Ugarit). More particularly, Baal of Ugarit was the deity-statue symbiosis of Baal of Sapan in the temple of Ugarit, which could be conceptualized differently depending on the context.

On the one hand, Baal of Ugarit could be presented as an extension of Baal of Sapan and thus part of his divine person or constellation. By adding a temple as a site of presence and worship, Baal of Ugarit served to expand Baal of Sapan's profile and sphere of influence. Nonetheless, although Baal of Ugarit was in a functional and cultic way Baal of Sapan, Baal of Ugarit was not the fullness of Baal of Sapan, since his fullness lay in the accumulation of his names, manifestations, and attributes.[108]

On the other hand, Baal of Ugarit could also be treated as distinct. He was localized in a different place, received his own offerings, and presumably could act as his own self-propelled agent. In other words, as the deity–statue symbiosis in Ugarit, Baal of Ugarit was distinct from all other Baals. In the end, rather than attempt to spell out the precise relationship between manifestations, cultic texts in particular simply juxtaposed the Baals and treat each as distinct so as to cover all the bases and not omit any aspect of the deity from cultic attention.[109]

Various other local Baals likely were also assimilated into or expanded from Baal of Sapan, thereby extending his profile and range of influence. In other contexts (e.g., the cult), the statue–deity symbioses too could be treated as distinct self-propelled agents. By extension, the other independent Baal constellations, like Baal of Aleppo and Baal-Shamem, probably developed their own manifestations either by assimilation or expansion, and these manifestations were likely considered functionally identical with the deity-statue symbiosis in the local temple.

Thus, it would seem that, although the precise relationship is nowhere articulated, the statue was an essential component of the locally manifested deity, without which it could not exist. For example, with the fall of Ugarit, Baal of Ugarit disappeared from the record.[110] Without a temple and statue, Baal of Sapan could no longer manifest in Ugarit and, without worshipers, would not want to do so. Thus, with the fall of Ugarit, Baal of Sapan lost part of his profile and Baal of Ugarit lost any independent existence.

---

god of Ugarit (ibid.). See, e.g., *KTU* 2.44, a letter from the king of Byblos to the king of Ugarit (ll. 1–3), which mentions Baal of Byblos and Baal of Sapan (ll. 8, 10), presumably as the national gods of the two parties, indicating that not only was Baal of Sapan the national god of Ugarit, but that the king of Byblos also recognized him as such.

108. In this way, Sommer's claim that each manifestation is a "diminution of the deity" (*Bodies of God*, 15) is somewhat justified, since while each manifestation is fully and functionally the deity, each is also not the fullness of the deity.

109. Treaties also juxtapose a deity's various manifestations so as to invoke the deity in its fullness to validate the treaty and enforce its fulfillment.

110. Allen, "Splintered Divine," 262.

The *zukru* festival from Emar offers additional information that suggests that at least in some contexts each statue bore its own name and played a distinct role in the local cult. The ritual lists the various deities of Emar that received cultic attention,[111] which in the context of the ritual seems to refer to the various cult images from the various shrines and likely several from the same shrine,[112] such that in some sense each was understood as a distinct entity.[113] The names of the various Dagan statues are particularly instructive. In addition to the unspecified Dagan, we find Dagan Lord of the Firstborn, Dagan Lord of the Offspring, Dagan of the Palace, Dagan Lord of Habitations, Dagan Lord of the Valley, Dagan Lord of Sumi, Dagan Lord of Buzqa, Dagan Lord of Yabur, Dagan Lord of Shade and Protection, Dagan Lord of the Fortress, and Dagan Lord of the Quiver. Several of these names referred to locally manifested Dagans (e.g., Dagan of the Palace, Dagan Lord of the Valley, Dagan Lord of Sumi), while others referred to a specific attribute or function of Dagan (e.g., Dagan Lord of the Firstborn, Dagan Lord of Shade and Protection, and Dagan Lord of the Quiver). Thus, Dagan cult images were resident in and protected various important places in and around Emar, while other images served specific functions, thereby dividing the labor of the larger Dagan into his various smaller manifestations. On the one hand, each image served as an extension of Dagan patron of the city, extending his sphere of influence to all important areas and aspects, not just those traditionally attributed to the deity. On the other hand, each was also treated as cultically distinct, such that depending on one's perspective, Emar had many Dagans or one Dagan with many detachable parts. Rather than appeal to a single Dagan, the people also could appeal to the particular manifestation that best suited their needs, such as the home, children, or hunting.

Standing stones or stele seem to have performed an analogous function. Clearly associated with particular deities, standing stones fundamentally served as access points to the otherwise distant deities.[114] More particularly, they seem to have comprised a space or form in which the deity could be incited to manifest itself, a proposition which finds support in the prominent West Semitic terms

---

111. Emar 373 75–162; Fleming, *Time at Emar*, 242–47.

112. Cf. ibid., 88.

113. See also from Ugarit RS 24.246 rev. 15–28 (Pardee, *Ritual and Cult*, 19–21); cf. RS 24.252 6–9 (ibid., 192–5), in which the various different names for Anat (e.g., Anat-of-Might and Anat-of-the-Wing) seem to be different epithets for a single deity; cf. also the Tell Fekheriye inscription, which seems to refer to a statue set up before the primary deity as Hadad-Yith'i ("Hadad is my salvation"; *COS* 2:34.153).

114. In addition to Hebat's standing stone, we also find the standing stone of Ninurta (Emar 375 16) and at Mari stones associated with particular gods (Durand, "Le culte des bétyles en Syrie," in *Miscellenea Babylonica: Mélanges offert à Maurice Birot* [ed. Dunand and J.-R. Kupper; Paris: Éditions Recherche sur les Civilizations, 1985], 79–84; Fleming, *Time at Emar*, 84).

for standing stones. Betyl[115] means "house or place of god," and thus seemingly indicates a place in which a deity may dwell or choose to manifest itself.[116] This finds corroboration in the first-century CE assertion of Philo of Byblos, who refers to the betyls as "animated stones" (λίθους ἐμψύχους).[117] The Ugaritic *skn* and the related Akkadian *sikkānum* appear to connote dwelling,[118] from which one may surmise that the *skn* served as a (temporary) residence of a god.[119] A recently discovered Aramaic mortuary stele from Zincirli offers tantalizing evidence, indicating that the stele itself was thought to contain the soul (*nbš*) of the deceased,[120] such that the stela was understood in some way to embody the immaterial essence of a person. Thus, it would seem that a standing stone may be understood as a vessel of potential manifestation or more generally as an accessible element in the divine constellation.[121]

At the same time, there is other evidence that may suggest that a stele was treated as a deity in its own right and in some cases may have broken off from its divine constellation completely and become fully autonomous. In addition to referring to a stone in which a deity could make itself manifest, Bethel (betyl) and *skn* likely functioned as divine names.[122] Although purely hypothetical, Bethel and

---

115. Greeks used βαίτυλος to refer West Semitic standing stones, which is a transliteration of the Aramaic בתי אלהיא and Hebrew בית אל, while English often uses betyl (alternatively bethel).

116. On betyl as a standing stone instead of a temple, see Joseph A. Fitzmeyer, *The Aramaic Inscriptions of Sefire* (Rome: Pontificium Institutum Biblicum, 1995), 131–32; KAI 2:262; Jacob Hoftijzer and K. Jongeling, *Dictionary of the Northwest Semitic Inscriptions* (HO 1/21; Leiden: Brill, 1995), 1:159.

117. Philo of Byblos in Eusebius's *Praeparatio Evangelica*. English translation in Harold Attridge and Ronald Oden, *Philo of Byblos: The Phoenician History: Introduction, Critical Text, Translation, Notes* (Washington: Catholic Biblical Association, 1981), 52–53; Sommer, *Bodies of God*, 28 and 192 n. 120.

118. The root *skn* in Mari seems to mean "to inhabit, to dwell" (Manfried Dietrich, Oswald Loretz and Walter Mayer, "Sikkanum 'Betyle,'" UF 21 [1989]: 134; Durand, "Le nom betyles a ebla en anatolia," NABU 8 [1988]: 6; Mettinger, *No Graven Image*, 130; Sommer, *Bodies of God*, 29 and 193 n. 130).

119. Van der Toorn, "Worshipping Stones," 7–10; Mettinger, *No Graven Image*, 116, 123–25, 130; Sommer, *Bodies of God*, 29. On the connection with betyls, see further Durand, "Le culte des bétyles"; Dietrich, Loretz, and Mayer, "Sikkanum 'Betyle.'" On the Northwest Semitic context of the term in Akkadian texts, see Fleming, *Installation of Baal's High Priestess*, 76 n. 2.

120. Pardee, "A New Aramaic Inscription," 51–71.

121. While it remains unclear whether the stone was understood to be the deity itself (i.e., its manifestation), a permanent body for the deity, or a potential and temporary vessel, the latter seems most likely.

122. Various texts refer to god named Bethel; see van der Toorn, "Worshipping Stones,"

Sikkun could have been originally the animated stones of certain deities, which later came to be independent divinized stones worshipped in their own rights. In other words, Bethel, the divine stone, could be worshipped on its own without any reference to the deity who was earlier thought to indwell it, such that people worshipped the immediate aspect while losing sight of the affiliated deity.

What was the relationship between a standing stone and an anthropomorphic cult image? Both means of divine representation seem to have served different and often complementary functions. The standing stone was more suited to the open air atmosphere or to a rural shrine. It is relatively immobile and aniconic and thus more impervious to the elements and to theft than its anthropomorphic counterpart. As a non-anthropomorphic (and indeed inanimate) representation, the standing stone also likely did not require the regular and expensive anthropomorphic care lavished on the anthropomorphic cult statues. As a relatively low maintenance access point to deity, it could be accessed and attended to ritually as the need arose. In addition, because of the potential transience and inanimate medium of divine manifestation, there was also a greater distance between deity and cult image, allowing greater lay access and lessening the likelihood of associating the stone with the deity in all its fullness.[123] By contrast, the anthropomorphic statue was more suited to the closed and intimate confines of the temple, modeled on or at least analogous to the care of the king in his palace, requiring more cultic personnel and a far greater expenditure. Here, in the protective enclave of the temple, the functional identity of deity and statue could be assumed, unless extreme circumstances prompted a theoretical distinction. The relatively small size and relative opulence of the statue was also more suited to processions.

## DEPORTATION AND DESTRUCTION OF DIVINE IMAGES

Evidence for deportation of Syro-Palestinian divine images comes primarily from Neo-Assyrian inscriptions and reliefs.[124] For example, Tiglath-pileser III's eighth-century inscriptions and a palace relief depict the exile of cult images from

---

3–7; Alexander Rofé, *The Belief in Angels in the Bible and Early Israel* (Jerusalem: Makor, 1979 [Hebrew]), 219–24; Röllig, "Bethel," in *DDD*, 173–75; Mettinger, *No Graven Image*, 35, 131–22; Smith, *Origins of Monotheism*, 137–38; Sommer, *Bodies of God*, 28. While not as strong as for Bethel, evidence for a divinized *skn* is also present, primarily in personal names such as Abdi-Sikkunni ("servant of Sikkun") and also in a Phoenician inscription where the divine name is written with a prosthetic aleph (KAI 58; see KAI 2:72; van der Toorn, "Worshipping Stones," 8; Sommer, *Bodies of God*, 29). Van der Toorn also notes the deities Abnu ("stone") and Ṣalmu ("image") ("Worshipping Stones").

123. Cf., however, the potential deification of standing stones noted above.

124. See Cogan, *Imperialism and Religion*, 22–41; with references Uehlinger, "Anthropomorphic Cult Statuary," 123–28; *COS* 2:118B.294. See more generally Amnon Ben-Tor, "The Sad Fate of Statues and the Mutilated Statues of Hazor," in *Confronting the*

Syria (see figs. 11.1 and 11.2).[125] The Amarna archives mention the capture of "the gods" from Gubla and record Lab'aya's complaint that "the city, along with my god, was seized."[126] The textual evidence for the destruction of divine statues also comes from primarily Neo-Assyrian sources,[127] while the archaeological evidence is more regionally dispersed.[128] For example, at Hazor "the heads and hands of the statues were the primary targets" of desecration.[129]

How then should we explain the evidence? In each of the sources, the exile of the statue was equated with the exile of the god. The statue-divine symbiosis was understood as the city deity, such that the statue's departure meant the deity's departure. In addition to the humiliation inherent in such an action, the statue's deportation meant that the city no longer had (regular) access to the deity and the deity's protection was no longer to be expected.[130] Destruction carried the humiliation and divine alienation one step further. Rather than being in exile, the destroyed statue meant that the deity as deity-statue symbiosis was no longer present in the human sphere. With regard to Baal, with the destruction of Ugarit and the

---

*Past: Archaeological and Historical Essays on Ancient Israel in Honor of William G. Dever* (ed. S. Gitin, J. E. Wright and J. P. Dessel; Winona Lake, IN: Eisenbrauns, 2006), 3–16.

125. Regarding the texts, see, e.g., Tadmor, *The Inscriptions of Tiglath-Pileser III*, 222–25. Regarding the relief, see A. H. Layard, *The Monuments of Nineveh: From Drawings Made on the Spot* (London: Murray, 1849), pl. 65; Barnett and Falkner, *Sculptures of Aššur-nasir-apli II*, 29, pl. 88, 92–93. The identity of the city depicted in the wall reliefs of Tiglath-pileser III remains disputed. For Gaza, see Hermann Thiersch, *Ependytes und Ephod: Gottesbild und Priesterkleid im Alten Vorderasien* (Geisteswissenschaftlichen Forschungen 8; Stuttgart: Kohlhammer, 1936), 210–11; Uehlinger, "Hanun von Gaza und seine Gottheiten auf Orthostatenreliefs Tiglatpilesers III," in *Kein Land für sich allein: Studien zum Kulturkontakt in Kanaan, Israel/Palästina und Ebirnâri für Manfred Weippert zum 65. Geburtstag* (ed. U. Hübner and E. A. Knauf; OBO 186; Freiburg: University Press, 2002), 94–127. For the more likely identification with Syria, see Barnett and Falkner, *Sculptures of Aššur-nasir-apli II*, xxiv–xxv, 29, 42; Tadmor, *The Inscriptions of Tiglath-Pileser III*, 240; Berlejung, "Shared Fates: Gaza and Ekron as Examples for the Assyrian Religious Policy in the West," in May, ed., *Iconoclasm and Text Destruction*, 156–58. There is also textual and/or pictorial evidence of the Neo-Assyrian deportation of statues from Samaria, Ashdod, Gath, Ashdod-Yam, Ashkelon, and Usû (see references in the previous note).

126. EA 134, 252; Lewis, "Syro-Palestinian Iconography," 100. See also the biblical evidence from Judg 18:24, Jer 48:7, and 2 Chr 25:14–16 (ibid.).

127. See Cogan, *Imperialism and Religion*, 22–41; Lewis, "Syro-Palestinian Iconography," 101–2. Regarding references to the burying of statues, see esp. Lewis, "Syro-Palestinian Iconography," 102; Ben-Tor, "Sad Fate of Statues."

128. Ben-Tor, "Sad Fate of Statues," 11–12.

129. Ibid., 14; cf. the description of Dagon (Dagan) in 1 Sam 5:4.

130. Interpretations of godnapping varied according to one's perspective. Conquerors often interpreted it as a demonstration of the superior might of their deity, while the conquered often saw it as a sign of divine disfavor.

disappearance of the cult image, Baal of Ugarit was no more, effectively dead, and the source deity Baal of Sapan lost part of himself (i.e., his manifestation at Ugarit). However, with the hypothetical repopulation of Ugarit and the reinstallation of an acceptable divine image in the temple, Baal of Ugarit could be reborn if the people could prompt Baal of Sapan to symbiotically join with the new cult image. In sum, it would seem that a statue is usually treated as a deity, whether as a deity in its own right or part of the larger divine constellation. Deportation did not dissolve the connection, and the deportation of one cult statue did not prohibit the installation of a new cult statue, enabling the otherwise absent deity to receive service and offer its protection in return. Since the (permanent) death of a god was unpalatable, the destruction of its statue prompted a theoretical distinction.[131] The statue as vessel of manifestation could be destroyed, yet the deity itself remained immaterially present somewhere in the cosmos or even materially and inaccessibly present beyond the bounds of the human sphere until a suitable replacement was found.[132]

## DIVINE NOURISHMENT

Realistically depicted divine meals played a central role in Ugaritic literature.[133] In these texts, it is apparent that the gods, like humans, enjoyed food and could become hungry (*rġb*) and thirsty (*ġm'*) when not properly sated.[134] Thus, it seems that the gods, as human-like beings, required food just like their human servants. However, not just any food would do. Like their most elite human counterparts, they demanded only the best nourishment.[135]

Although Baal as the provider of rain was responsible for the sustenance of the gods and humanity,[136] humanity also had an important role to play in nour-

---

131. Regarding divine death, see, e.g., Smith, "The Death of Dying and Rising Gods in the Biblical World," *SJOT* 12 (1998): 257–313; John Day, *Yahweh and the Gods and Goddesses of Canaan* (JSOTSupp 265; Sheffield: Sheffield Academic, 2000), 116–27; Mettinger, *The Riddle of the Resurrection: "Dying and Rising Gods" in the Ancient Near East* (CBOT 50; Stockholm: Almqvist & Wiksell, 2001); Machinist, "How Gods Die."

132. As in the case of Baal of Ugarit, the absent deity could re-merge with its parent deity. The status of a damaged statue remains an open question. Although evidence is minimal, it is perhaps best to assume that, as in Mesopotamia, there was some distance between statue and deity, but the connection was not fully abandoned.

133. Korpel, *A Rift in the Clouds*, 400.

134. Ibid., 171, 399–408, 414–18.

135. For example, the gods complain to Baal that he gives them sludge (*rṯn*) to drink (*KTU* 1.1 iv 9), while Baal laments the foul meat (*pgl*) placed on his table and the filth (*qlt*) he has to drink. In effect, he hates the inferior sacrifices presented to him (*KTU* 1.4 iii 14–22) (Korpel, *A Rift in the Clouds*, 408).

136. *KTU* 1.4 vii 49–51; 1.19 i 40–46; Korpel, *A Rift in the Clouds*, 407. With Baal's absence, the gods must toil in vain to irrigate the land in order to produce food (*KTU* 1.6 i 67; ii 3).

ishing the deities.[137] In fact, cultic offerings appeared to be transposed onto the mythic sphere, such that divine meals could be referred to as offerings (*dbḥm*).[138] Thus, as in Mesopotamia and Hittite Anatolia, it would seem that the cult was the primary way for deities to acquire food. It is unlikely that Syro-Palestinians would have pondered the potential starvation of the gods or considered the gods beholden to the same physical requirements as humanity. More simply, it was clear to them that the gods wanted food. Seizing on the opportunity, humans provided cultic care and feeding to influence divine activity and secure divine protection and national prosperity.

137. Ibid., 414.
138. Ibid.

# CHAPTER 12
## DIVINE PRESENCE: SYNTHESIS

ALTHOUGH THERE ARE OBVIOUS DIFFERENCES in the particulars, there is nonetheless a remarkable general commonality across ancient Near Eastern cultures regarding conceptions of deity and divine presence. The major gods were conceived of anthropomorphically, with human-like bodies, minds, emotions, and social structures. As befit their exalted status, they exceeded their human counterparts in practically every respect, for example, with larger bodies and greater mental capacities and sensory abilities. Rather than simply being humans writ large, they also transcended the anthropomorphic mold in several important capacities. First, the gods were thought to control the very elements in nature that humanity could not control, such as rain.[1] Second, in addition to a primary human-like form, deities could adopt multiple other forms, like animals, natural and celestial phenomena, and in some contexts switch between them at will.[2] In addition, it would seem that the gods could theoretically occupy multiple forms at once. Third, the gods were distinguished by the company they kept. In addition to their primary interactions with the other major gods and their divine subordinates, major ancient Near Eastern gods were often depicted as surrounded by and victors over "supernatural freaks," an amalgam of the most potent natural forces, thereby demonstrating a potency that belied their anthropomorphic presentations. By showing mastery over supernatural creatures and the forces of chaos, the gods demonstrated that they were superhumans who deserved their place atop the hierarchy of the created world. Nonetheless, within their polytheistic contexts, no ancient Near Eastern gods were supreme in power, presence, or perception. Although hierarchically ar-

---

1. While immeasurably important in Hittite Anatolia and Syria Palestine, rainfall was not as necessary in Egypt and southern Mesopotamia. Thus, various other non-weather gods occupied more prominent positions, e.g., the sun (Re) in Egypt. Without the obvious need for rainfall, some of the major deities could be more abstract, not as clearly or closely connected to natural phenomena, such as Amun in Egypt and Enlil, Assur, and Marduk in Mesopotamia.

2. As noted, Mesopotamian deities did not display the same shape-shifting tendencies as their ancient Near Eastern neighbors, especially in the first millennium and their connection to animals was more tenuous, while their relation to celestial phenomena was ambivalently expressed (see esp. Rochberg, "The Stars Their Likenesses"). Nonetheless, the range of elements in their divine networks, as or in which they could theoretically manifest, was vaster than those of the other ancient Near Eastern deities.

ranged, the gods were interdependent, together connected to creation, charged with its upkeep, and threatened by its dissolution.

In each culture, conceptions of the divine world seem to have been influenced by, if not the product of, the peoples' attempts to make sense of and gain some measure of control over their world. Since the gods were the supreme powers in the universe, understood to control the uncontrollable, humans naturally sought to secure divine favor so as to find some security in an otherwise insecure world. More than simply being unavoidable, primarily anthropomorphic conceptions of deity were also profitable. They made the otherwise incomprehensible deities more comprehensible and provided the assurance that gods could be communicated with and respond in ways analogous to humans.

Nonetheless, communication was not always easy since the gods rarely directly manifested themselves to humanity in the human sphere except through mediated forms. The temple, and more particularly its cult image, served as the ancient Near Eastern solution to the need for contact and commerce with the otherwise distant deities. Regardless of how one envisaged the exact relationship between deity and statue, the divine cult image functioned as the terrestrial locus of divine presence.[3] In the cult, the statue was treated like a god, constructed of materials befitting a god, addressed as such, and lavished with bounteous gifts and attention.

In addition to general conceptions of deity, this study has primarily been concerned with the practical elements of this all-important cult, namely, securing and maintaining divine presence and favor. Realizing the unnaturalness of divine presence in, as, or through human-made objects, the people of the ancient Near East employed various means to overcome this difficulty. First, appropriate cult images were necessary. Generally small, befitting the sheltered confines of the temple and the processions outside of it, deities were depicted as anthropomorphic, theriomorphic, mixed, and/or inanimate.[4] Each of these forms represented the deity either through visual likeness or association,[5] and in many contexts was considered to accord with the divine blueprint, in Mesopotamia drawn at the beginning of time. Each form was a suitable locus of divine presence, although, as we have seen, they served different purposes in different contexts.

Second, realizing that craftsmanship was not enough, Egyptians, Mesopotamians, Hittites, and perhaps Syro-Palestinians conducted elaborate rituals to

---

3. In a sense, the divine cult statue was a truer home of deity than the temple. The two were intimately joined in a way that defied adequate explanation.

4. As noted, inanimate is a problematic designator, as some of the elements that fall into this category were conceived of as animate in the ancient Near Eastern world. For example, a lunar crescent was likely conceived as a representation of the animate moon. Nonetheless, I have chosen to retain the category to help the modern reader.

5. Chapters 8–11 demonstrated the different configurations of representation prominent in each of the regions.

ensure cultic presence. In particular, the ritualists created and maintained a conducive environment for the deity to manifest itself. Although the divine role was primary, humans were by no means uninvolved. With the help of the gods and through the medium of ritual, the priests ensured the perfect purity of the statue and its environs to make a suitable environment for divine manifestation and empowered or ritually activated the new statue–deity symbiosis with the divine faculties and potencies necessary to function as god on earth.[6] Indeed, although conducted by humans, ritual activity was a primary means of bringing divine potencies to bear to ensure purity and cultic activation. Just as cult images must be regularly repurified and on special occasions reactivated for ritual participation (and to ensure continued presence),[7] so too must they be initially purified and activated for their installation.

In order to accomplish this lofty goal, ritual employed a multiplicity of often repeated means that functioned simultaneously on multiple levels to achieve the desired end. Although ritual complexity may make the modern interpreter uncomfortable and prone to search for different and incompatible ritual layers, ancient Near Eastern ritualists seem to have been perfectly content to juxtapose multiple and at times inconsistent means of achieving a single end. In accord with the aspective approach[8] and because the result was empirically unverifiable, they accumulated various complex and not always consistent parts without trying to incorporate them into a unified whole. Rather than choosing a single solution as the best option, they combined various solutions, adopting a comprehensive approach that sought to ensure efficacy by covering all bases.

Although in this respect ancient Near Eastern rituals are difficult for the modern mind to grasp, they nonetheless accord with modern ritual practice in various ways. Most fundamentally, the doing of ritual is generally considered much more important than understanding why one does it. In other words, the ritual actions themselves enact transformation, not their interpretations. Most rituals are deemed effective if the ritual participants agree that they are effective. Thus, although each ritual element is added for a reason, that is, to contribute to the ef-

---

6. In Hittite Anatolia, human actions focused on purification, while the deity herself was implored to activate her statue by dividing herself and taking up residence in the new temple. It is not improbable that the missing incantations associated human activity with divine activation.

7. In the Egyptian daily cult, for which we have by far the most information, cultic attention also involved ritual enlivening.

8. According to this approach, various individual elements were amassed and juxtaposed in order to present the whole, most often without systematically attempting to fit those elements into a consistently articulated, all-encompassing organic unity. In fact, focus centered on the individual aspects or elements to such an extent they could be treated (semi-)independently and in different ways in different contexts. See more fully ch. 8 under "Relationship of the Deity to Its Statue(s)."

ficacy of the larger ritual, that reason is often forgotten during the course of ritual practice. For example, in the modern West, people often agree that shaking hands is a necessary component of greeting. Nonetheless, although the result, greeting, is clear to all, no one remembers precisely why shaking hands accomplishes this goal. Likewise, in a graduation ceremony, there are specific reasons for the specific configuration of the robes and hats, yet few, if any, know what they are because the reason is not necessary for ritual efficacy. Based on tradition and the assent of the participants, the actions alone effectively ceremonialize the graduates' elevation in status, finalized with the receipt of a diploma, sometimes composed in Latin and thus unintelligible to most recipients. Similarly, in the ancient Near East, ritual activities in an installation ritual (in addition to being thought of as actually effecting divine presence) mark the transition from the crafting of the divine statue to its taking up its role as god on earth, without which the transition would be considered either incomplete or uncertain. Thus, since ritual practice is considered more important than ritual theory and the original functions of the individual rites are often forgotten or altered,[9] these original functions need not cohere to ensure ritual efficacy.

Third, installation alone was insufficient to ensure continued divine presence and blessing. The priests had to care for the resident deity continually so that it was persuaded to remain and to remain favorably disposed to its human servants. Since petition for the removal of individual and corporate ills did not serve this end, it often occurred outside of temple circles.[10] Regular service, instead, often took the form of anthropomorphic care, considered suitable for and desired by the anthropomorphized gods. By conceptualizing the deities according to these anthropomorphic categories, the ancient Near Eastern peoples brilliantly deduced that what they could offer the gods was in fact what the gods wanted or needed. Like human rulers, the gods liked to be pampered and, especially in Mesopotamia, it would seem that humans were created for this very purpose. While it is not always clear to what extent the gods or their statues needed food, it is abundantly clear that the gods desired it and would go to great lengths to get it. By providing it, humans gained some leverage over the gods, offering them something freely, easily, and opulently that they might otherwise have to work to get. Thus, they had something the gods desired and in return could reasonably expect divine presence and protection.[11]

---

9. At least for the practice of ritual, if not in its written form and as the object of academic inquiry.

10. For corporate and individual removal rites and their primary locus outside of the temple, see briefly Hundley, *Keeping Heaven on Earth*, 120–34.

11. Naturally, the gods would choose to presence themselves and protect the place where they were cared for and fed.

With this general framework in place, it remains to examine the little-articulated relationships between deity and statue and between different statues in various circumstances. As noted, the statue was considered the effective locus of cultic presence on earth, while its more precise identification depended on the context. Practically, the statue was understood to be the god. More precisely, through the medium of ritual and the participation of the gods, the statue and the deity symbiotically joined such that the statue and all it contained became the deity. Although people (and scholars) could theoretically distinguish between the statue and the deity, there was little practical impetus to do so. As the effective presence of the deity on earth and often as the only god within reach, people tended to identify the statue–deity symbiosis as their god and treat it accordingly with care and petitions even if they theoretically envisioned the god as far more than its image.[12]

The theoretical distinction likely touched down in reality only when the situation rendered maintaining the connection unpalatable. In most cases the deportation of a statue was not considered dire enough for the people to disassociate their deity from its statue. Rather than envisioning their deity as a helpless prisoner in a foreign land, they opted to believe that their deity had chosen to exile itself, often because of its dissatisfaction with cultic care, and could willingly return at any point. With the statue's deportation, the people had no further access to their god, which logically entailed the removal of divine protection and invited disaster. However, although their deity remained in exile, they could summon it back—this time from heaven—by creating and ritually activating a new and approved cult image. Thus, although the deity remained connected to the statue in exile, the people were nonetheless prompted by the circumstances to distinguish between deity and statue. They posited that the deity had an existence apart from its statue, which could be joined to a new statue when necessary. However, destruction of the divine image necessitated a different solution. Since (permanent) divine death or absence were unpalatable, the deity was disassociated from its statue, such that the statue was merely identified as the physical form in which the deity could chose to manifest itself. Although the particular statue was "dead," the deity-statue could be reborn when the same deity chose to reanimate a different statue.

Thus, on the theoretical level, active in academic circles and articulated most clearly and consistently in Egypt, the statue served as a form or locus in which the otherwise absent deity could manifest itself. In essence, each statue, like each sacred animal in Egypt, served as one among many potential receptacles of divine presence or, more loosely, potential divine bodies. However, rather than simply being a place where the deity showed up from time to time, the statue was consid-

---

12. There was also likely little opportunity to compare their local manifestation to other local manifestations and, when such comparisons were made, the people likely would have treated them as distinct (cf. the Hindu and Christian practices mentioned in ch. 7).

ered its (semi)permanent host or home.[13] In other words, each statue was considered to be an extension of the divine person that made her or him visible in the human sphere.

The geographic or descriptive surname (e.g., Baal of Ugarit or Ishtar Lady of Battle) accordingly served to distinguish one manifestation from another. In some cases, as with Baal of Ugarit, the so-designated manifestation referred specifically to the deity-statue symbiosis localized in a particular temple, while in others the designator distinguished a mythic prototype (e.g., Baal of Sapan) from other mythically and locally realized deities with the same forename. Thus, Baal of Ugarit was effectively the mythic Baal of Mt. Sapan as manifest in Ugarit. Likewise, Ishtar of Nineveh and Ishtar of Arbela seem to refer to the statue–deity symbioses of Ishtar of mythology localized in the respective cities' Ishtar temples. Deities with a descriptive epithet also could refer to a particular divine aspect or statue–deity symbiosis, which embodied a particular divine characteristic and to which one could direct one's appeal. For example, $^d$Aššur-$^d$Dayyāni (Assur-the-divine-judges) seems to refer to Assur in his role as judge.

In the Hittite realm, we find evidence for the extension of a locally realized deity to a new place. The expansion of the cult of the Goddess of the Night in particular demonstrates the ritual process by which a deity may take up residence in an additional temple. Through the medium of ritual, the mythic deity[14] and the statue–deity symbiosis, the "old" Goddess of the Night, were both summoned so that a "new" Goddess of the Night, a new statue–deity symbiosis, could be created from both its mythic and cultic prototypes. IŠKUR of Aleppo of Hattusa likewise seems to refer to the extension of IŠKUR of Aleppo, both as the statue–deity localized in the temple and as a mythological entity, to Hattusa in the form of a statue in the temple.

How one presented the individual extensions or manifestations depended on the context. On the one hand, each manifestation was part of a single divine entity, serving as an aspect of its larger divine constellation (e.g., Baal of Ugarit as an aspect or manifestation of Baal of Sapan). Many manifestations could be understood as fully god, that is, they could presence the deity and bring its powers to bear. However, they were not the fullness of the god, since that fullness—that is,

---

13. Among the Hittites, the connection between deity and statue seems to have been looser, evidenced by the repeated evocations, drawing the potentially absent deity back to its statue. In Mesopotamia as well, the lamentations recited with the daily cult suggest that the deity might not always be present or could choose to manifest itself (in Egypt, there is some uncertainty too). However, among the Hittites and Mesopotamians, there was likely an expectation of near-continual presence. Since this presence was unverifiable, the evocations and lamentations were designed to cover all bases, to ensure divine presence for the ensuing ritual activity.

14. I.e., the deity as theoretically present outside of the human sphere, encountered primarily in mythology.

the full constellation—lay in the accumulation of the deity's multiple names, attributes, and manifestations. For example, Ishtar was more than Ishtar of Nineveh or Ishtar of Arbela; she was also among other things Ishtar the anthropomorphically conceived divine person, the planet Venus, and the embodiment of love. Nonetheless, by being part of the larger divine constellation, the local Ishtar could partake of the other elements in the constellation and bring them to bear on behalf of the local populace.

On the other hand, in accord with the aspective approach, individual manifestations could be given their own names, presented with offerings and petitions, and expected to act as a distinct self-propelled agent. Thus, as in the case of the Goddess of the Night, although they were in some way connected, each manifestation could be treated as a (semi-)independent entity. Indeed, in the cult such treatment was often pragmatic. Rather than trying to sort out the relationship between a deity's many manifestations, rituals simply juxtaposed them and treated each as distinct to cover all the bases.[15] Thus, from a theoretical standpoint, a major ancient Near Eastern deity functioned like a constellation of divine aspects that, like LEGOs, could be taken apart and put back together depending on the context.[16]

This varied and flexible treatment of deities and their divine elements is especially apparent in the case of the destruction of a statue. Destruction of a cult statue signaled the destruction of a particular manifestation and simultaneously diminished the larger divine constellation. Without an image, the deity could not concretely and effectively presence itself in a particular locale. Thus, the deity's sphere of influence and worship decreased, thereby diminishing the divine constellation. At the same time, without a statue, there could be no deity-statue symbiosis, such that Shamash of Sippar effectively ceased to exist. However, his "death" was only temporary as the mythic Shamash could always reunite with an approved image and be "reborn."[17] Thus, the occasionally independent deity merged with the constellation upon the destruction of its host, yet could reemerge and regain its independence when joined with a new host. In turn, rather than being fixed and unyielding, such a fluid presentation of deity could adapt itself to fit the situation.

---

15. Treaties too juxtapose manifestations in order to ensure that all aspects of the deity are brought to bear to witness and enforce the contract.

16. In still other contexts, although deities might share a forename (e.g., Baal or IŠKUR), they could be understood as different deities altogether, who happened to belong to a larger god group of similar yet independent gods.

17. See the Sippar Stele. Such fluidity is also apparent when a statue was deported. While the statue–deity symbiosis could retain its divine identity even in exile, a new statue–deity symbiosis could be created to take its place in the temple. Thus, the exiled statue–deity symbiosis could remain distinct, while the deity was extracted from the larger constellation to form a new statue–deity symbiosis to take its place.

With these conclusions in mind, we may qualify Bahrani's claim[18] that an image inherently partook of but did not encapsulate the divine essence, such that the fate of the one affected that of the other. While at least in Mesopotamia the principle may have held true for humans, it seems that the gods played by different rules.[19] In Mesopotamia, in particular, certain cult images were understood to partake of the divine essence from their creation and proleptically from the time the deity planted the natural elements used to construct them. However, not every divine image in Mesopotamia possessed some of the essence of its bearer.[20] Even when an image partook of the divine essence, the statue did not become the fully functioning divine-statue symbiosis until the deity chose to complete the connection through the activation ritual.[21] Elsewhere, it is unclear if an approved image contained some of the divine essence before activation. Regardless, each divine image served as a potential receptacle for the divine presence, one which the deity chose, rather than was compelled, to join with or indwell. Even when an image became the fully functioning deity on earth through ritual activation, the link between image and deity was not indissoluble. The deity could theoretically sever it at any time, thereby inciting priests and kings to go to great lengths to ensure continued divine satisfaction and presence.

Until an image was activated, there is no indication that either care or harm to the image had any discernible effect on the deity. Once activated, the treatment of the divine image did affect the deity. The deity could enjoy care and nourishment offered to its activated image and in some cases be empowered by them. Rather than threatening the divine existence or physically harming the deity, the destruction of an image removed one of a deity's manifestations and the influence it exerted through (and the veneration it received from) that manifestation.

However, as noted, such damage was not irreparable. A new image could be fashioned and a new statue-deity symbiosis forged. Even if no replacement image was proffered, the deity theoretically could continue to exist in its various other celestial and terrestrial manifestations.[22] Indeed, it would seem that divine

---

18. See ch. 7 n. 47.

19. Regarding humans, see Karen Radner, *Die Macht des Namens: Altorientalische Strategien zur Selbsterhaltung* (SANTAG 8; Wiesbaden: Harrasowitz, 2005).

20. For example, *tamšīlu* refers to an image that resembled its referent without partaking of its essence (see, e.g., Bonatz, "Was ist ein Bild," 11–16).

21. Ritual in particular helped to accomplish this goal, as it joined together multiple times and in multiple ways the various elements that together constituted a deity or, more distantly, were necessary for the statue to function as the deity on earth.

22. Although not entirely precise, such a situation may be likened to the destruction of a Ford car. While an accident may destroy a particular model and in some way harm the company (e.g., since the driver would no longer drive a Ford), many other models would still exist and the larger entity Ford would continue to exist and could continue to manifest itself concretely in its various remaining models.

iconoclasm was not generally directed against the gods, but against the people who served and relied on them. Conquerors primarily aimed to subjugate their enemies, not inconvenience, or even destroy, their enemies' gods. Even when divine images were destroyed for more malicious purposes (e.g., in the struggle for supremacy between competing gods and their competing followers),[23] the iconoclasts likely did not believe that they were harming the essence of the deity,[24] but rather removing the deity from the human sphere, such that it was no longer worshipped. If its cult was not reinstituted, it could be forgotten and thus effectively cease to exist.[25] In the end, it seems that each cult image was a potential receptacle for presence that, once activated, functioned as the deity itself. Therefore, since deities were believed to control the cosmos, proper service of the deity-statue symbioses was considered absolutely essential for human prosperity.

---

23. See, e.g., Akhenaten's thorough destruction of Amun images and inscriptions (Baines, "Presenting and Discussing Deities," 64).

24. Or, if they were somehow true monotheists, destroying the names and images meant erasing the record of a false god.

25. See, e.g., the Restoration Stele of Tutankhamun, which refers to the gods' temporary withdrawal from the human sphere after the dereliction of their cults (for translations, see *ANET* 251–52; Murnane, *Texts from the Amarna Period*, 212–14). See also the various Mesopotamian god lists, which, among other things, served to preserve deities whose cults had gone out of favor, thereby remembering them.

# AFTERWORD

As its title indicates, this book has examined terrestrial divine abodes and the gods who dwelled in them in Egypt, Mesopotamia, Hittite Anatolia, and Syria-Palestine. More specifically, it analyzed the efforts taken to secure and safeguard the divine presence in the midst of human community. Rather than attempting an exhaustive survey of all relevant data, it focused on understanding the normative systems of thought and practice designed to keep heaven on earth, through an examination of their essential components. Part I analyzed the temple as the divine abode, exploring temple construction, use, and ideology. Part II investigated the divine presence in the temple, examining the conceptualization and concretization of divine presence as well as its installation and maintenance.

Rather than look back to the conclusions posited (see especially chs. 6 and 12), here I look forward to future avenues of exploration. Since this book represents an initial foray that no doubt will require revision in general and especially in the specifics, I invite specialists to assess my assertions. Although the study took note of different ways of formulating norms and divergences from those norms, its primary interest was synthetic. As such, it left a great deal of room to explore how norms were configured, altered, abandoned, and/or recreated in various specific times and places. In other words, I invite specialists to assess my macroanalysis and continue producing time- and place-specific microanalyses. Likewise, it would be a worthwhile endeavor to see how remarkable the commonality really is by performing a similar analysis of temples and divine presence in other cultures in other places and other times.

Although the book appears in a biblical studies series, I have explicitly refrained from making comparisons to biblical texts, instead letting each ANE system emerge in its own right and own context rather than simply using them as comparative fodder. Thus, as a reference tool, it invites biblical scholars (and scholars of other religions) to engage with its methodology and apply its data and interpretations.

Finally, this book promotes the examination of systems of thought and practice. Rather than simply comparing isolated rites, it invites the reader to compare the systems in which the rites are embedded.[1] Since each ANE region had various systems of thought and practice and many biblical scholars have limited access

---

1. In saying this, I recognize that not enough data remain to reconstruct these systems fully. Nonetheless, I believe that a partially reconstructed system is more illustrative than no system at all.

to those systems, much work remains in formulating those systems and making them accessible to a wider audience. In short, rather than serving as the last word, it is hoped that Gods In Dwellings will serve as the impetus for further discussion.

# REFERENCES

Abu Assaf, Ali. *Der Tempel von 'Ain Dara*. Mainz: Zabern, 1990.

Akurgal, Ekrem. *The Art of the Hittites*. Translated by C. McNab. London: Thames & Hudson, 1962.

Alexander, Robert L. "The Storm-God at Yazılıkaya: Sources and Influences." Pages 1–13 in *Aspects of Art and Iconography: Anatolia and Its Neighbors, Studies in Honor of Nemet Özgüç*. Edited by M. J. Mellink, E. Porada and T. Özgüç. Ankara: Türk Tarih Kurumu Basımevi, 1993.

Allen, James P. "Ba." Pages 161–62 in *The Oxford Encyclopedia of Ancient Egypt*. Vol. 1. Edited by D. Redford. Oxford: Oxford University Press, 2001.

———. *Genesis in Egypt: The Philosophy of Ancient Egyptian Creation Accounts*. Yale Egyptological Studies 2. New Haven: Yale Egyptological Seminar, 1988.

Allen, Spencer L. "The Splintered Divine: A Study of Ištar, Baal, and Yahweh Divine Names and Divine Multiplicity in the Ancient Near East." Ph.D. diss., University of Pennsylvania, 2011.

———. *The Splintered Divine: A Study of Ištar, Baal, and Yahweh Divine Names and Divine Multiplicity in the Ancient Near East*. SANER 5. Berlin: de Gruyter, forthcoming.

Allinger-Csollich, Wilfrid, "Birs Nimrud II: 'Tieftempel' – 'Hochtempel': Vergleichende Studien Borsippa – Babylon." *BaM* 29 (1998): 95–330.

———. "Gedanken über das Aussehen und die Funktion einer Ziqqurrat." Pages 1–18 in *Tempel im alten Orient: 7. Internationales Colloquium der Deutschen Orient-Gesellschaft 11.–13. Oktober 2009, München*. Edited by Kai Kaniuth, Anne Löhnert, Jared L. Miller, Adelheid Otto, Michael Roaf and Walther Sallaberger. CDOG 7. Wiesbaden: Harrassowitz, 2013.

Alp, Sedat. "Eine hethitische Bronzestatuette und andere Funde aus Zara bei Amasya." *Anatolia* 6 (1961/62): 217–43.

Alster, Bendt. "On the Interpretation of the Sumerian Myth 'Inanna and Enki.'" *ZA* 64 (1974): 20–34

Altenmüller-Kesting, Brigitte. "Reinigungsriten im ägyptischen Kult: Dissertation zur Erlangung der Doktorwürde der Philosophischen Fakultät der Universität Hamburg." Hamburg: Lüdke bei der Uni, 1968.

Ambos, Claus. "Building Rituals from the First Millennium BC: The Evidence from the Ritual Texts." Pages 221–37 in *From the Foundations to the Crenellations: Essays on Temple Building in the Ancient Near East and Hebrew Bible*. Edited by M. J. Boda and J. Novotny. AOAT 366. Münster: Ugarit-Verlag, 2010.

———. *Mesopotamische Baurituale aus dem 1. Jahrtausend v. Chr*. Dresden: Islet, 2004.

Amerlinck, Mari-Jose, ed. *Architectural Anthropology*. Westport, CT: Bergin and Garvey, 2001.

Andrae, Walter. *Coloured Ceramics From Ashur*. London: K. Paul, Trench, Truebner, 1925.

———. *Der Anu-Adad-Tempel in Assur*. WVDOG 10. Leipzig: Deutsche Orient-Gesellschaft, 1909.

Andrae, Walter, and Walter Bachmann. "Aus den Berichten über die Grabungen in Tulul Akir (Kar Tukulti-Ninib)." *MDOG* 53 (1914), 41–57.

Archi, Alfonso. "Formation of the West Hurrian Pantheon: The Case of Išḫara." Pages 21–33 in *Recent Developments in Hittite Archaeology and History: Papers in Memory of Hans G. Güterbock*. Edited by K. A. Yener and H. A. Hoffner, Jr. Winona Lake, IN: Eisenbrauns, 2002.

———. "The Former History of Some Hurrian Gods." Pages 39–44 in *Acts of the IIIrd International Congress of Hittitology, Çorum, September 16-22, 1996*. Edited by S. Alp and A. Süel. Ankara: Anit Matbaa, 1998.

———. "Trono regale e trono divinizzato nell'Anatolia ittita." *SMEA 1* (1966): 76–120.

Arnaud, Daniel. *Corpus des textes de bibliothèque de Ras Shamra-Ougarit (1936–2000) en sumérien, babylonien et assyrien*. AuOrS 23. Barcelona: AUSA, 2007.

———. *Textes syriens de l'Âge du Bronze recent*. AuOrS 1. Barcelona: AUSA, 1991.

Arnold, Dieter. "Egyptian Temples." Pages 174–79 in *The Oxford Encyclopedia of Archaeology in the Near East*, Vol. 4. Edited by E. Meyers. Oxford: Oxford University Press, 1997.

———. *Die Tempel Ägyptens: Götterwohnungen, Kultstätten, Baudenkmäler*. Zurich: Artemis & Winkler, 1992.

———. *Temples of the Last Pharaohs*. New York: Oxford University Press, 1999.

———. *Wandrelief und Raumfunktion in ägyptischen Tempeln des Neuen Reiches*. MÄS 2. Berlin: Hessling, 1962.

Aro, Jussi. *Mittelbabylonische Kleidertexte der Hilprecht-Sammlung Jena*. Sitzungsberichte der Sächsischen Akademie der Wissenschaften zu Leipzig 115/2. Berlin: Akademie-Verlag, 1970.

Asher-Greve, Julia M. "Reading the Horned Crown (A Review Article)." *AfO* 42 (1995–1996): 181–89.

Assmann, Jan. *Ägypten: Theologie und Frömmigkeit einer frühen Hochkultur*. Stuttgart: Kohlhammer, 1984.

———. *Ma'at: Gerechtigkeit und Unsterblichkeit im Alten Ägypten*. Munich: Beck, 1990.

———. *The Mind of Egypt: History and Meaning in the Time of the Pharaohs*. Trans. A. Jenkins. Cambridge, Mass.: Harvard University Press, 2003.

———. "Prayers, Hymns, Incantations, and Curses: Egypt." Pages 350–53 in *Religions of the Ancient World: A Guide*. Edited by S. I. Johnston. Cambridge, MA: Belknap Press of Harvard University Press, 2004.

———. *The Search for God in Ancient Egypt*. Translated by D. Lorton. New York: Cornell University Press, 2001.

———. *Tod und Jenseits im Alten Ägypten*. Munich: Beck, 2001. English Translation, *Death and Salvation in Ancient Egypt*. Translated by D. Lorton. Ithaca, NY: Cornell University Press, 2005.

———. "Die Verborgenheit des Mythos in Ägypten." *Göttinger Miszellen* 25 (1977): 7–43.

Aster, Shawn Zelig. "The Phenomenon of Divine and Human Radiance in the Hebrew Bible and in Northwest Semitic and Mesopotamian Literature: A Philological and Comparative Study." Ph.D. diss., University of Pennsylvania, 2006.

———. *The Unbeatable Light: Melammu and Its Biblical Parallels*. AOAT 384. Münster: Ugarit Verlag, 2012.

Attridge, Harold, and Ronald Oden. *Philo of Byblos: The Phoenician History: Introduction, Critical Text, Translation, Notes*. Washington: Catholic Biblical Association, 1981.

Avishur, Yitshaq. *Phoenician Inscriptions and the Bible*. Tel Aviv: Archaeological Center Publications, 2000.

Badawy, Alexander. *A History of Egyptian Architecture: Empire (the New Kingdom)*. Berkeley: University of California Press, 1968.

Bahrani, Zainab. *The Graven Image: Representation in Babylonia and Assyria*. Philadelphia: University of Pennsylvania Press, 2003.

———. *Women of Babylon: Gender and Representation in Mesopotamia*. London: Routledge, 2001.

Baines, John. "Egyptian Deities in Context: Multiplicity, Unity, and the Problem of Change." Pages 9–78 in *One God or Many? Concepts of Divinity in the Ancient World*. Edited by B. N. Porter. Transactions of the Casco Bay Assyriological Institute 1. Winona Lake, IN: Eisenbrauns, 2000.

———. "Palaces and Temples of Ancient Egypt." Pages 303–17 in *Civilizations of the Ancient Near East*. Vol. 1. Edited by J. M. Sasson. Peabody, MA: Hendrickson, 2000.

———. "Presenting and Discussing Deities in New Kingdom and Third Intermediate Period Egypt." Pages 41–89 in *Reconsidering the Concept of Revolutionary Monotheism*. Edited by B. Pongratz-Leisten. Winona Lake, IN: Eisenbrauns, 2011.

Barguet, Paul. *Le temple de Amon-Re à Karnak: essai d'exégèse*. Recherches d'archéologie, de philologie et d'histoire 21. Le Caire: Impr. de l'Institut français d'archéologie orientale, 1962.

Barnett, Richard D., Erica Bleibtreu, and Geoffrey E. Turner. *Sculptures from the Southwest Palace of Sennacherib at Nineveh*. London: British Museum, 1998.

Barnett, Richard D., and Margarete Falkner. *The Sculptures of Aššur-nasir-apli II, 883–859 B.C. Tiglath-Pileser III, 745–727 B.C. [and] Esarhaddon, 681–669 B.C., From the Central and South-West Palaces at Nimrud*. London: Trustees of the British Museum, 1962.

Barrie, Thomas. *The Sacred In-Between: The Mediating Roles of Architecture*. New York: Routledge, 2010.

———. *Spiritual Path, Sacred Place: Myth, Ritual, and Meaning in Architecture*. Boston: Shambhala, 1996.

Barta, Winfried. "Göttersymbole," *LÄ* 2 (1977): 714–16.

Barthelmess, Petra. *Der Übergang ins Jenseits in den thebanischen Beamtengräbern der Ramessidenzeit*. Studien zur Archäologie und Geschichte Altägyptens 2. Heidelberg: Heidelberger Orientverlag, 1992.

Baumgarten, Albert I. *The Phoenician History of Philo of Byblos: A Commentary*. Leiden: Brill, 1981.

Beal, Richard H. "Dividing a God." Pages 197–208 in *Magic and Ritual in the Ancient World*. Edited by P. Mirecki and M. Meyer. Leiden: Brill, 2002.

Beaulieu, Paul-Alain. "Antiquarianism and the Concern for the Past in the Neo-Babylonian Period." *BCSMS* 28 (1994): 37–42.

———. *The Pantheon of Uruk During the Neo-Babylonian Period*. Cuneiform Monographs 23. Leiden: Brill, 2003.

Becker, Katrin, Melanie Becker, and John H. Schwarz, eds. *String Theory and M-Theory: A Modern Introduction*. Cambridge: Cambridge University Press, 2007.

von Beckerath, Jürgen. *Chronologie des pharaonischen Ägypten*. MÄS 46. Mainz: Zabern, 1997.

———. *Handbuch der ägyptischen Königsnamen*. 2nd ed. MÄS 49. Mainz: von Zabern, 1999.

Beckman, Gary M. "Blood in Hittite Ritual." *JCS* 63 (2011): 95–102.

———. "The Goddess Pirinkir and Her Ritual from Ḫattuša (CTH 644)." *Ktema* 24 (1999): 25–39.

———. *Hittite Birth Rituals*. StBoT 29. Harrassowitz: Wiesbaden, 1983.

———. *Hittite Diplomatic Texts*. 2nd ed. WAW 7. Atlanta: Scholars, 1999.

———. "Ištar of Nineveh Reconsidered." *JCS* 50 (1998): 1–10.

———. "Mythologie A. II. Bei den Hethitern." *RlA* 8 (1993-7): 564–72.

———. "Pantheon. A. II. Bei den Hethitern." *RlA* 10 (2004): 308–16.

———. "Religion. B. Bei den Hethitern." *RlA* 11 (2007): 333–38.

———. "Royal Ideology and State Administration in Hittite Anatolia." Pages 529–44 in *CANE*.

———. "Sacred Times, Sacred Places: Anatolia," Pages in *Religions of the Ancient World: A Guide*. Edited by S. I. Johnston. Cambridge, MA: Belknap Press of Harvard University Press, 2004.

———. "Temple Building among the Hittites," Pages 71–89 in *From the Foundations to the Crenellations: Essays on Temple Building in the Ancient Near East and Hebrew Bible*. Edited by M. J. Boda and J. Novotny. AOAT 366. Münster: Ugarit-Verlag, 2010.

———. "The Tongue is a Bridge: Communication Between Humans and Gods in Hittite Anatolia." *ArOr* 67 (1999): 519–34.

Bell, Catherine. *Ritual Theory, Ritual Practice*. Oxford: Oxford University Press, 1992.

Bell, Lanny. "Luxor Temple and the Cult of the Royal *Ka*." *JNES* 44 (1985): 251–94.

———. "The New Kingdom Divine Temple: The Example of Luxor." Pages 127–84 in *Temples of Ancient Egypt*. Edited by B. E. Shafer. London: Taurus, 1997.

Bell, Paul A., Thomas C. Greene, Jeffery D. Fisher, and Andrew Baum. *Environmental Psychology*. 5th ed. Andover, UK: Thomson, 2001.

Ben-Tor, Amnon, ed. *Hazor III–IV: An Account of the Third and Fourth Seasons of Excavations, 1957–1958, Text*. Jerusalem: Israel Exploration Society, 1989.

———. "The Sad Fate of Statues and the Mutilated Statues of Hazor." Pages 3–16 in *Confronting the Past: Archaeological and Historical Essays on Ancient Israel in Honor of William G. Dever*. Edited by S. Gitin, J. E. Wright and J. P. Dessel. Winona Lake, IN: Eisenbrauns, 2006.

Berlejung, Angelika. "Geheimnis und Ereignis: Zur Funktion und Aufgabe der Kultbilder in Mesopotamien." Pages 109–43 in *Die Macht der Bilder*. Edited by I. Baldermann. *JBTh* 13. Neukirchen: Neukirchen Verlag, 1999.

———. "Notlösungen – Altorientalische Nachrichten über den Tempelkult in Nachkriegszeiten." Pages 196–230 in *Kein Land für sich allein. Studien zum Kulturkontakt in Kanaan, Israel/Palästina und Ebirnâri für Manfred Weippert zum 65. Geburtstag*. Edited by U. Hübner, E.A. Knauf. OBO 186. Fribourg: Academic Press, 2002.

———. "Die Reduktion von Komplexität: Das theologische Profil einer Gottheit und seine Umsetzung in der Ikonographie am Bespiel des Gottes Aššur im Assyrien des 1. Jt. v. Chr." Pages 9–56 in *Die Welt der Götterbilder*. Edited by B. Groneberg and H. Spieckermann. BZAW 376. Berlin: de Gruyter, 2007.

———. "Shared Fates: Gaza and Ekron as Examples for the Assyrian Religious Policy in the West." Pages 151–74 in *Iconoclasm and Text Destruction in the Ancient Near East and Beyond.* Edited by N. May. IOS 8. Chicago: University of Chicago, 2012.

———. *Die Theologie der Bilder: Herstellung und Einweihung von Kultbildern in Mesopotamien und die alttestamentliche Bilderpolemik.* OBO 162. Fribourg: University Press, 1998.

———. "Washing the Mouth: The Consecration of Divine Images in Mesopotamia." Pages 45–72 in *The Image and the Book: Iconic Cults, Aniconism, and the Rise of Book Religion in Israel and the Ancient Near East.* Edited by K. van der Toorn. CBET 21. Leuven: Peeters, 1997.

Bernstein, Jeremy. *Quantam Leaps.* Cambridge, MA: Belknap Press of Harvard University Press, 2009.

Bietak, Manfred. "Avaris and Piramesse: Archaeological Exploration in the Eastern Nile Delta." *Proceedings of the British Academy* 65 (1979): 225–96.

———. *Avaris, the Capital of the Hyksos: Recent Excavations at Tell el-Dab'a.* London: British Museum, 1996.

Bin-Nun, Shoshana R. *The Tawannanna in the Hittite Kingdom.* Texte der Hethiter 5. Heidelberg: Winter, 1975.

Bittel, Kurt. "Einige Kapitel zur hethitischen Archäologie." Pages 123–30 in *Neuere Hethiterforschung.* Edited by G. Walser. Historia, Einzelschriften 7. Wiesbaden: Steiner, 1964.

———. *Die Hethiter: Der Kunst Anatoliens vom Ende des 3. bis zum Anfang des 1. Jahrtausends v. Chr.* Munich: Beck, 1976.

———. "Hittite Temples and High Places in Anatolia and North Syria." Pages 63–73 in *Temples and High Places in Biblical Times.* Edited by A. Biran. Jerusalem: The Nelson Glueck School of Biblical Archaeology of Hebrew Union College-Jewish Institute of Religion, 1981.

Bjerke, Svein. "Remarks on the Egyptian Ritual of 'Opening the Mouth' and Its Interpretation." *Numen* 12 (1965): 201–16.

Black, Jeremy A., and Anthony Green. *Gods, Demons and Symbols of Ancient Mesopotamia: An Illustrated Dictionary.* Austin: University of Texas, 1992.

Blackman, Aylward M. "The House of the Morning." *JEA* 5 (1918): 148–65.

Blanton, Richard E. *House and Households: A Comparative Study.* New York: Plenum, 1994.

Block, Daniel I. *The Gods of the Nations: Studies in Ancient Near Eastern National Theology.* Grand Rapids, MI: Baker, 2001.

Blome, Friedrich. *Die Opfermaterie in Babylonien und Israel, Teil I.* Rome: Apud Pont. Institutum Biblicum, 1934.

Blyth, Elizabeth. *Karnak: Evolution of a Temple.* London: Routledge, 2006.

Boda, Mark J., and Jamie Novotny, eds. *From the Foundations to the Crenellations: Essays on Temple Building in the Ancient Near East and Hebrew Bible.* AOAT 366. Münster: Ugarit-Verlag, 2010.

Boden, Peggy Jean. "The Mesopotamian Washing of the Mouth (*Mīs Pî*) Ritual: An Examination of the Social and Communication Strategies Which Guided the Development and Performance of the Ritual Which Transferred the Essence of the Deity Into Its Temple Statue." Ph.D. diss., Johns Hopkins University, 1998.

Boehmer, R.M. "Hörnerkrone." *RlA* 4 (1975): 431–34.

Bolshakov, Andrey O. *Man and His Double in Egyptian Ideology of the Old Kingdom.* ÄAT 37. Wiesbaden: Harrassowitz, 1997.

———. "The Moment of the Establishment of the Tomb-Cult in Ancient Egypt." *AoF* 18 (1991): 204–18.

Bommas, Martin. "Schrein unter: Gebel es-Silsilah im Neuen Reich." Pages 88–103 in *Grab und Totenkult im Alten Ägypten.* Edited by H. Guksch, E. Hofmann, and M. Bommas. Munich: Beck, 2003.

Bonatz, Dominic. "Was ist ein Bild im Alten Orient?: Aspekte bildlicher Darstellung aus altorientalischer Sicht." Pages 9–20 in *Bild—Macht—Geschichte: Visuelle Kommunikation im Alten Orient.* Edited by M. Heinz and D. Bonatz. Berlin: Reimer, 2002.

Bonfil, Ruhama. "Area A: Analysis of the Temple." Pages 85–101 in *Hazor V: An Account of the Fifth Season of Excavation, 1968.* Edited by A. Ben-Tor and Bonfil. Jerusalem: Israel Exploration Society, 1997.

Bongenaar, A. C. V. M. *The Neo-Babylonian Ebabbar Temple at Sippar: Its Administration and Prosopography.* Leiden: Nederlands Historisch-Archeologisch Instituut te İstanbul, 1997.

Bonnet, Hans. "On Understanding Syncretism." *Orientalia* 68 [1999]: 181–98.

Borger, Rykle. "Gott Marduk und Gott-König Šulgi als Propheten: Zwei prophetische Texte." *BiOr* 28 (1971): 3–24.

———. *Die Inschriften Asarhaddons, Königs von Assyrien.* AfO Beiheft 9. Graz: E. Weidner, 1956.

———. "Review of *Brief des Bischofs von Esagila an König Asarhaddon*." *BiOr* 29 (1972): 33–37.

Börker-Klähn, Jutta. *Altvorderasiatische Bildstelen und vergleichbare Felsreliefs.* BaF 4. Mainz: von Zabern, 1982.

Bottéro, Jean. "Magie. A. In Mesopotamien." *RlA* 7 (1990): 225–28.

———. *Mesopotamia: Writing, Reasoning and the Gods.* Translated by Z. Bahrani and M. van de Mieroop. Chicago: University of Chicago, 1992.

———."Les noms de Marduk." Pages 5–28 in *Essays on the Ancient Near East in Memory of Jacob Joel Finkelstein.* Edited by M. de Jong Ellis. Memoirs of the CT Academy of Arts & Sciences 19. Hamden, Connecticut: Archon, 1977.

———. *Religion in Ancient Mesopotamia.* Translated by T. L. Fagan. Chicago: The University of Chicago Press, 2001.

Bourke, Stephen. "The New Pella Bronze Age Temple: The Largest 'Migdol' Ever Found." *Occident & Orient* 192 (1999): 57–58.

———. "The Six Canaanite Temples of Ṭabaqāt Faḥil: Excavating Pella's 'Fortress' Temple (1994–2009)." Pages 159–202 in *Temple Building and Temple Cult: The Architecture and Cultic Paraphernalia of Temples in the Levant (2nd–1st Millennium BCE).* Edited by J. Kamlah. Tübingen: Institute of Biblical Archaeology, 2012.

Boysan-Dietrich, Nilüfer. *Das hethitische Lehmhaus aus der Sicht der Keilschriftquellen.* Heidelberg: Winter, 1987.

Brand, Peter J. "Veils, Votives and Marginalia: The Use of Sacred Space at Karnak and Luxor." Pages 51–83 in *Sacred Space and Sacred Function in Ancient Thebes.* Edited by P. F. Dorman and B. N. Bryan. SAOC 61. Chicago: University of Chicago, 2007.

von Brandenstein, Carl-Georg. *Hethitische Götter nach Bildbeschreibungen in Keilschrift-texten*. MVAeG 46/2. Leipzig: Hinrichs, 1943.

Brinkman, John A. *Prelude to Empire: Babylonian Society and Politics, 747–626 B.C.* Occasional Publications of the Babylonian Fund 7. Philadelphia: University Museum, 1992.

Bryce, Trevor. *Life and Society in the Hittite World*. Oxford: Oxford University Press, 2002.

Brunner, Hellmut. "Herz." *LÄ* 2: 1158–68.

———. "Name, Namen und Namelosigkeit Gottes im Alten Ägypten." Pages 33–49 in *Der Name Gottes*. Edited by H. v. Stietencron. Dusseldorf: Patmos, 1975.

———. "Die Sonnenbahn in ägyptischen Tempeln." Pages 27–34 in *Archäologie und Altes Testament: Festschrift für Kurt Galling zum 8. Januar 1970*. Edited by A. and C. Kuschke. Tübingen: Mohr, 1970.

Brunner-Traut, Emma. *Frühformen des Erkennens: Am Beispeil Altägyptens*. Darmstadt: Wissenschaftliche Buchgesellschaft, 1990.

Bryan, Betsy N. "Designing the Cosmos: Temples and Temple Decoration." Pages 73–115 in *Egypt's Dazzling Sun: Amenhotep III and His World*. Edited by A. P. Kozloff, Bryan, L. M. Berman, and E. Delange. Cleveland: Cleveland Museum of Art, 1992.

Buchler, Justus. *The Philosophical Writings of Peirce*. New York: Dover, 1955.

de Buck, Adriaan. *The Egyptian Coffin Texts*, Vol. 6: *Texts of Spells 472–787*. OIP 81. Chicago: University of Chicago, 1956.

Budge, E. A. Wallis. *The Book of Opening the Mouth: The Egyptian Texts with English Translations*. Books on Egypt and Chaldaea 26–27. London: Kegan Paul, 1909.

Bull, Robert J. "A Re-examination of the Shechem Temple." *BA* 23 (1960): 110–19.

Burney, Charles A. *Historical Dictionary of the Hittites*. Oxford: Scarecrow Press, 2004.

Buzov, Emil. "The Role of the Heart in the Purification." Pages 273–81 in *Proceedings of the First International Conference for Young Egyptologists, Italy, Chainciano Terme, October 15–18, 2003*. Edited by A. Amenta. Egitto antico 3. Rome: L'Erma di Bretschneider, 2005.

Calmeyer, Peter. "Wandernde Berggötter." Pages 1–32 in *Languages and Cultures in Contact: Proceedings of the 42nd RAI*. Edited by K. van Lerberghe and G. Voet. OLA 96. Leuven: Peeters, 1999.

Campbell, Edward F. "Shechem: Tel Balâtah." Pages 1345–54 in *The New Encyclopedia of Archaeological Excavation in the Holy Land*. Edited by E. Stern. Jerusalem: Israel Exploration Society, 1993.

Cancik-Kirschbaum, Eva. *Die Assyrer: Geschichte, Gesellschaft, Kultur*. Munich: C. H. Beck, 2003.

Carlotti, Jean-François. "Considérations architecturales sur l'orientation, la composition et les proportions des structures du temple d'Amon-Rê à karnak." Pages 169–207 in *Structure and Significance: Thoughts on Ancient Egyptian Architecture*. Edited by P. Jánosi. Untersuchungen der Zweigstelle Kairo des österreichischen Archäologischen Institutes 25. Vienna: Verlag der Österreichischen Akademie der Wissenschaften, 2005.

Carter, Charles W. "Hittite Cult Inventories." Ph.D. diss., University of Chicago, 1962.

Cassin, Elena. "Forme et identité des hommes et des dieux chez les Babyloniens." Pages 63–76 in *Le temps de la reflexion* 7: *Corps des dieux*. Edited by C. Malamoud and J.-P. Vernant. Paris: Gallimard, 1986.

——. *La splendeur divine: introduction à l'étude de la mentalité mésopotamienne*. Civilisations et sociétés 8. Paris: Mouton, 1968.

Cauville, Sylvie. "Les statues cultuelles de Dendera d'après les inscriptions pariétales." *BIFAO* 87 (1987): 73–117.

Charpin, Dominique. *Archives familiales et propriété privée en Babylonie ancienne: Étude des documents de "Tell Sifr."* Hautes études orientales 12. Geneva: Droz, 1980.

Chassinat, Émile. *Le Temple de Dendara: Volume 5 (Plates)*. Cairo: Institut Français d'Archéologie Orientale, 1947.

Chavalas, Mark, ed. *Historical Sources in Translation: The Ancient Near East*. Malden, MA: Blackwell, 2006.

Civil, Miguel. "Remarks on 'Sumerian Bilingual Texts.'" *JNES* 26 (1967): 200–211.

Clemens, David M. *Sources for Ugaritic Ritual and Sacrifice: Ugaritic and Ugaritic Akkadian Texts*. AOAT 284. Münster: Ugarit-Verlag, 2001.

Clifford, Richard J. *The Cosmic Mountain in Canaan and the Old Testament*. Cambridge, MA: Harvard University Press, 1972.

Cogan, Mordecai. *Imperialism and Religion: Assyria, Judah and Israel in the Eighth and Seventh Centuries B.C.E.* Missoula: Scholars Press, 1974.

Cohen, Mark E. *The Canonical Lamentations of Ancient Mesopotamia*. 2 vols. Bethesda, MD: CDL, 1988.

——. *Sumerian Hymnology: The Eršemma*. HUCASup 2. Cincinnati: Ktav, 1981.

Collins, Billie Jean. *The Hittites and Their World*. SBL Archaeology and Biblical Studies 7. Atlanta: SBL, 2007.

——. "Necromancy, Fertility and the Dark Earth: The Use of Ritual Pits in Hittite Cult." Pages 224–41 in *Magic and Ritual in the Ancient World*. Edited by P. Mirecki and M. Meyer. Leiden: Brill, 2002.

——. "Ritual Meals in the Hittite Cult." Pages 77–92 in *Ancient Magic and Ritual Power*. Edited by M. Meyer and P. Mirecki. Leiden: Brill, 1995.

——. "A Statue for the Deity: Cult Images in Hittite Anatolia." Pages 13–42 in *Cult Image and Divine Representation in the Ancient Near East*. Edited by N. H. Walls. ASOR Book Series 10. Boston: ASOR, 2005.

Collon, Dominique. *First Impressions: Cylinder Seals in the Ancient Near East*. London: British Museum, 1987.

——. "Iconographic Evidence for Some Mesopotamian Cult Statues." Pages 57–84 in *Die Welt der Götterbilder*. Edited by B. Groneberg and H. Spieckermann. *BZAW* 376. Berlin: de Gruyter, 2007.

Conti, Giovanni. "Incantation de l'eau bénite et de l'encensoir et textes connexes." *MARI* 8 (1997): 253–76.

Cooney, Kathlyn M., and J. Brett McClain. "The Daily Offering Meal in the Ritual of Amenhotep I: An Instance of the Local Adaption of Cult Liturgy." *JANER* 5 (2006): 41–78.

Cornelius, Izak. *The Iconography of the Canaanite Gods Reshef and Ba'al: Late Bronze and Iron Age I Periods (c. 1500–1000 BCE*. OBO 140. Fribourg: University Press, 1994.

——. "The Many Faces of God: Divine Images and Symbols in Ancient Near Eastern Religions." Pages 21–43 in *The Image and the Book: Iconic Cults, Aniconism, and the Rise of Book Religion in Israel and the Ancient Near East*. Edited by K. van der Toorn. CBET 21. Leuven: Peeters, 1997.

Corti, Carlo. "The So-called 'Theogony' or 'Kingship in Heaven': The Name of the Story." Pages 109–21 in *Acts of the VIth International Congress of Hittitology*. Edited by A. Archi and R. Francia. Studi Micenci ed Egeo-Anatolici 49. Rome: CNR, 2007.

Crawford, Harriet. *Sumer and the Sumerians*. New York: Cambridge University Press, 1993.

Cunningham, Graham. *"Deliver Me from Evil": Mesopotamian Incantations, 2500–1500 BC*. Studia Pohl 17. Rome: Pontifcio Istituto Biblico, 1997.

Curtis, Edward M. "Images in Mesopotamia and the Bible: A Comparative Study." Pages 31–56 in *The Bible in the Light of Cuneiform Literature: Scripture in Context III*. Edited by W. W. Hallo, B. W. Jones, and G. L. Mattingly. Lewiston, NY: Edwin Mellen, 1990.

Dalley, Stephanie. "Statues of Marduk and the Date of *Enūma eliš*." *AoF* 24 [1997]: 163–71.

Damerji, Muayad Said Basim. *The Development of the Architecture of Doors and Gates in Ancient Mesopotamia*. Translated by T. Takase and Y. Okada. Tokyo: Institute of Cultural Studies of Ancient Iraq, 1987.

Daniélou, Alain. *The Myths and Gods of India: The Classic Work on Hindu Polytheism from the Princeton Bollingen Series*. Rochester, VT: Inner Traditions, 1991.

David, A. Rosalie. *Religious Ritual at Abydos (c. 1300)*. Warminster: Aris & Phillips, 1973.

Davies, Graham I. *Cities of the Biblical World: Megiddo*. Cambridge: Lutterworth, 1986.

Davies, Norman de Garis. *The Tomb of Rekh-Mi-Rē' at Thebes*. New York: Plantin, 1943.

Davis, Richard. *Lives of Indian Images*. Princeton: Princeton University Press, 1999.

Day, John. *Yahweh and the Gods and Goddesses of Canaan*. JSOTSupp 265. Sheffield: Sheffield Academic, 2000.

Delaporte, Louis. *Musée du Louvre, Catalogue des cylindres, cachets et pierres gravées de style oriental*. Paris: Hachette, 1920.

Deller, Karlheinz. "Götterstreitwagen und Götterstandarten: Götter auf dem Feldzug und ihr Kult im Feldlager." *BaM* (1992): 291–98.

Demisch, Heinz. *Die Sphinx: Geschichte ihrer Darstellung von den Anfängen bis zur Gegenwart*. Stuttgart: Urachhaus, 1977.

Derchain, Philippe. *Hathor quadrifons: Recherches sur la syntaxe d'un mythe égyptien*. Uitgauen van het Nederlandsch Historisch Archaeologisch Instituut te Istanbul 28. Istanbul: Nederlands Instituut voor het Nabije Oosten, 1972.

Dever, William G. "The Contribution of Archaeology to the Study of Canaanite and Early Israelite Religion." Pages 209–47 in *Ancient Israelite Religion: Essays in Honor of Frank Moore Cross*. Edited by P. D. Miller Jr., P. D. Hanson, and S. D. McBride. Philadelphia: Fortress, 1987.

Dick, Michael B. "The Mesopotamian Cult Statue: A Sacramental Encounter with Divinity." Pages 43–67 in *Cult Image and Divine Representation in the Ancient Near East*. Edited by N. H. Walls. ASOR Books 10. Boston: ASOR, 2005.

Dietrich, Manfried. "Der Werkstoff wird Gott: Zum mesopotamischen Ritual der Umwandlung eines leblosen Bildwerks in einem lebendigen Gott." *MARG* 7 (1992): 105–26.

Dietrich, Manfried, and Oswald Loretz. *'Jahwe und seine Aschera': Anthropomorphes Kultbild in Mesopotamien, Ugarit und Israel: Das biblische Bilderverbot*. UBL 9. Münster: Ugarit-Verlag, 1992.

Dietrich, Manfried, Oswald Loretz, and Walter Mayer. "Sikkanum 'Betyle.'" *UF* 21 (1989): 133–39.

van Dijk, Jacobus. "Inanna raubt den 'grossen Himmel': Ein Mythos." Pages 9–38 in *Eine Festschrift für Rykle Borger zu seinem 65. Geburtstag am 24. Mai 1994: Tikip Santakki Mala Bašmu*. Edited by S. M. Maul. Cuneiform Monographs 10. Groningen: Styx, 1998.

———. "Myth and Mythmaking in Ancient Egypt." Pages 1697–1709 in *CANE*.

Djikstra, Meindert. "The Weather God on Two Mountains." *UF* 23 (1991): 127–40.

Dombradi, Eva. *Die Darstellung des Rechtsaustrags in den altbabylonischen Prozessurkunden*. FAOS 20/1. Stuttgart: Steiner, 1996.

Donner, H., and W. Röllig. *Kanaanäische und aramäische Inschriften*. 3 vols. Wiesbaden: Harrassowitz, 1962–1964.

van Driel, G. *The Cult of Aššur*. Studia Semitica Neerlandica 13. Assen: van Gorcum, 1969.

Dunand, Françoise, and Christiane Zivie-Coche. *Gods and Men in Egypt: 3000 BCE to 395 CE*. Translated by D. Lorton. Ithaca, NY: Cornell University Press, 2004.

Durand, Jean-Marie. "Le culte des bétyles en Syrie." Pages 79–84 in *Miscellenea Babylonica: Mélanges offert à Maurice Birot*. Edited by Dunand and J.-R. Kupper. Paris: Éditions Recherche sur les Civilizations, 1985.

———. *Florilegium marianum VII: Le culte d'Addu d'Alep et l'affaire d'Alahtum*. Paris: SEPOA, 2002.

———. "Le nom betyles a ebla en anatolia." *NABU* 1988/8.

Ebeling, Erich. "Enki." *RlA* 2 [1938]: 374–79.

———. *Tod und Leben nach den Vorstellungen der Babylonier*. Berlin: de Gruyter, 1931.

Edzard, Dietz Otto. "Deep-Rooted Skyscrapers and Bricks: Ancient Mesopotamian Architecture and Its Imagery." Pages 13–24 in *Figurative Language in the Ancient Near East*. Edited by M. Mindlin, M. J. Geller, and J. E. Wansbrough. London: School of Oriental and African Studies, 1987.

———. "La vision du passé et de l'avenir en Mésopotamie: Période paléobabylonienne." Pages 157–66 in *Histoire et Conscience dans les Civilizations du Proche-Orient ancien: Actes du Colloque de Cartigny 1986*. Edited by A. de Pury. Les Cahiers du CEPOA 5. Leuven: Peeters, 1989.

Ellis, Richard S. *Foundation Deposits in Ancient Mesopotamia*. Yale Near Eastern Researches 2. New Haven: Yale University Press, 1968.

Emery, Walter, Henry Smith, and Anne Millard. *Excavations at Buhen 1, The Fortress of Buhen: The Archaeological Report*. London: Egypt Exploration Society, 1979.

Engel, Burkhard J. *Darstellungen vom Dämonen und Tieren in assyrischen Palästen und Tempeln nach den schriftlichen Quellen*. Mönchengladbach: Hackbarth, 1987.

Engelhard, David H. "Hittite Magical Practices: An Analysis." Ph.D. diss., Brandeis University, 1970.

Englund, Gertie. "Offerings." Pages 279–86 in *The Ancient Gods Speak: A Guide to Egyptian Religion*. Edited by D. Redford. Oxford: Oxford University Press, 2002.

van Ess, Margarete. "Babylonische Tempel zwischen Ur III- und neubabylonischer Zeit: Zu einigen Aspekten ihrer planerischen Gestaltung und religiösen Konzeption." Pages 59–84 in *Tempel im Alten Orient: 7. Internationales Colloquium der Deutschen Orient-Gesellschaft 11.–13. Oktober 2009, München*. Edited by Kai Kaniuth, Anne Löhnert, Jared L. Miller, Adelheid Otto, Michael Roaf and Walther Sallaberger. CDOG 7; Wiesbaden: Harrassowitz, 2013.

Falkenstein, Adam. *Topographie von Uruk, I. Teil: Uruk zur Seleukidenzeit*. Ausgrabungen der Deutschen Forschungsgemeinschaft in Uruk-Warka 3. Leipzig: Harrassowitz, 1941.

Farber, W. "Lamaštu." *RlA* 6 (1980–1983): 439–46.

Farber-Flügge, G. "Me." *RlA* 7 (1987–1990): 610–13.

Faulkner, Raymond O. *An Ancient Egyptian Book of Hours (Pap. BM 10569).* Oxford: Griffith Institute, 1958.

———. *The Ancient Egyptian Coffin Texts.* 3 volumes. Warminster: Aris & Phillips, 1973–1978.

Feder, Yitzhaq. *Blood Expiation in Hittite and Biblical Ritual: Origins, Context, and Meaning.* SBLWAWSup 2. Atlanta: Society of Biblical Literature, 2011.

Feldman, Marian. "Review of Zainab Bahrani, *The Graven Image: Representation in Babylonia and Assyria.*" *JAOS* 124 (2004): 599–601.

Finkbeiner, Uwe. "Emar 2001 – Bericht über die 4. Kampagne der syrisch-deutschen Ausgrabungen." *BaM* 33 (2002): 111–46.

———. "Emar 2002 – Bericht über die 5. Kampagne der syrisch-deutschen Ausgrabungen." *BaM* 34 (2003): 9–100.

———. "Neue Ausgrabungen in Emar, Syrien: Kampagnen 1996–2002." Pages 43–65 in *Colloquium Anatolicum IV.* Istanbul: Türk Eskiçağ Bilimleri Enstitüsü, 2005.

Finnestad, Ragnhild Bjerre. *Image of the World and Symbol of the Creator: On the Cosmological and Iconographical Values of the Temple of Edfu.* Wiesbaden: Harrassowitz, 1985.

———. "The Meaning and Purpose of *Opening the Mouth* in Mortuary Contexts." *Numen* 25 (1978): 118–34.

Fischer-Elfert, Hans-Werner. *Die Vision von der Statue im Stein.* Schriften der Philosophisch-historischen Klasse der Heidelberger Akademie der Wissenschaften 5. Heidelberg: Winter, 1998.

Fitzmeyer, Joseph A. *The Aramaic Inscriptions of Sefire.* Rome: Pontificium Institutum Biblicum, 1995.

Fleming, Daniel E. *The Installation of Baal's High Priestess at Emar: A Window on Ancient Syrian Religion.* HSS 42. Altanta: Scholars Press, 1992.

———. "The Israelite Festival Calendar and Emar's Ritual Archive," *RB* 106 (1999): 8–34.

———. "A Limited Kingship." *UF* 24 (1992): 59–71.

———. *Time at Emar: The Cultic Calendar and the Rituals from the Diviner's House.* Mesopotamian Civilizations 11. Winona Lake, IN: Eisenbrauns, 2000.

Folger, Tim. "If an Electron Can Be in Two Places at Once, Why Can't You?" *Discover Magazine,* June 2005. Online: http://discovermagazine.com/2005/jun/cover.

Foster, Benjamin R. *Before the Muses: An Anthology of Akkadian Literature.* 3rd ed. Bethesda: CDL, 2005.

———. *From Distant Days: Myths, Tales, and Poetry of Ancient Mesopotamia.* Bethesda: CDL, 1995.

Foxvog, D., W. Heimpel, and D. Kilmer, "Lamma/Lamassu. A. I. Mesopotamien. Philologisch." *RlA* 6 (1980-1983): 446–53.

Frame, Grant. *Babylonia 689–627 B. C.: A Political History.* Istanbul: Nederlands Historisch-Archaeologisch Instituut te Isstanbul, 1992.

Frandsen, Paul J., "Sin, Pollution, and Purity: Egypt." Pages 497–99 in *Religions of the An-*

*cient World: A Guide.* Edited by S. I. Johnston. Cambridge, MA: Belknap Press of Harvard University Press, 2004.

Franken, H. J. *Excavations at Tell Deir ʿAllā.* Leiden: Brill, 1969.

Frankena, Rintje. *Tākultu: De Sacrale Maaltijd in het Assyrische Ritueel met een Overzicht de in Assur Vereerde Goden.* Leiden: Brill, 1954.

Frankfort, Henri. *Ancient Egyptian Religion: An Interpretation.* New York: Columbia University, 1949.

———. *The Art and Architecture of the Ancient Orient.* Middlesex, UK: Penguin Books, 1977.

———. *Progress of the Work of the Oriental Institute in Iraq, 1934/35: Fifth Preliminary Report of the Iraq Expedition.* OIC 20. Chicago: Oriental Institute, 1936.

Frankfort, Henri, Seton Lloyd, and Thorkild Jacobsen. *The Gimilsin Temple and the Palace of the Rulers at Tell Asmar.* OIP 43. Chicago: The University of Chicago Press, 1940.

Frankl, Paul T. *Principles of Architectural Study.* Cambridge, MA: MIT Press, 1968.

Friedman, Richard E. *Who Wrote the Bible?* Englewood Cliffs, NJ: Prentice Hall, 1987.

Fuller, C. J. *The Camphor Flame: Popular Hinduism and Society in India.* Princeton, NJ: Princeton University Press, 1992.

Furlani, Giuseppe. *Riti babilonesi e assiri.* Udine: Istituto delle Edizioni Accademiche, 1940.

———. *Il sacrificio nella religione dei Semiti di Babilonia e Assiria.* Rome: Giovanni Bardi, 1932.

Gabbay, Uri. "The Performance of Emesal Prayers within the Regular Temple Cult: Content and Ritual Setting." Pages 103–22 in *Tempel im Alten Orient: 7. Internationales Colloquium der Deutschen Orient-Gesellschaft 11.–13. Oktober 2009, München.* Edited by Kai Kaniuth, Anne Löhnert, Jared L. Miller, Adelheid Otto, Michael Roaf and Walther Sallaberger. CDOG 7; Wiesbaden: Harrassowitz, 2013.

Gallagher, Winifred. *The Power of Place: How Our Surroundings Shape Our Thoughts, Emotions and Actions.* New York: Harper, 1994.

Gane, Roy E. *Cult and Character: Purification Offerings, Day of Atonement and Theodicy.* Winona Lake, IN: Eisenbrauns, 2005.

———. *Ritual Dynamic Structure.* Gorgias Dissertations 14. Piscataway, NJ: Gorgias Press, 2004.

Gee, John L. "The Requirements of Ritual Purity in Ancient Egypt." Ph.D. Diss., Yale University, 1998.

George, Andrew R. *Babylonian Topographical Texts.* OLA 40. Leuven: Peeters, 1992.

———. "The Bricks of E-Sagil." *Iraq* 57 (1995): 173–97.

———, ed. *Cuneiform Royal Inscriptions and Related Texts in the Schøyen Collection.* Cornell University Studies in Assyriology and Sumerology 17. Manuscripts in the Schøyen Collection, Cuneiform texts VI. Bethesda, MD: CDL Press, 2011.

———. *House Most High: The Temples of Ancient Mesopotamia.* Winona Lake, IN: Eisenbrauns, 1993.

———. "Marduk and the Cult of the Gods of Nippur at Babylon." *OrNS* 66 (1997): 65–70.

George, Mark K. *Israel's Tabernacle as Social Space.* SBL Ancient Israel and Its Literature 2. Atlanta: SBL, 2009.

Gevaryahu, H. M. Y. "Ghee and Honey He Will Eat (Isaiah 7)." Pages 169–74 in *Sepher Eliyahu Auerbach.* Edited by A. Birarn. Jerusalem: Kiryat Sepher, 5715 (Hebrew).

Gessler-Löhr, Beatrix. *Die heiligen Seen ägyptischer Tempel.* Hildesheimer Ägyptologische Beiträge 21. Hildesheim: Hildesheim Gerstenberg, 1983.

Gibson, John C. L. *Textbook of Syrian Semitic Inscriptions,* Vol. 3: *Phoenician Inscriptions.* Oxford: Clarendon, 1982. Repr., Oxford: Oxford University Press, 2002.

Gilan, Amir. "A Cultural Sponge? On the Hittite Fascination with Things Foreign." Paper presented at the ANE Colloquium, University of Munich (LMU), 2012.

———. "Epic and History in Hittite Anatolia: In Search of a Local Hero." Pages 51–65 in *Epic and History.* Edited by D. Konstan and K. A. Raaflaub. Oxford: Wiley-Blackwell, 2010.

Gitin, Seymour, Trude Dothan, and Joseph Naveh. "A Royal Dedicatory Inscription from Ekron." *IEJ* 47 (1997): 1–16.

Gladigow, Burkhard. "Gottesvorstellungen." Pages 32–49 in *Handbuch religionswissenschaftlicher Grundbegriffe,* Vol. 3: *Gesetz-Kult.* Edited by Hubert Cancik, Burkhard Gladigow and Matthias Laubscher. Stuttgart: Kohlhammer, 1993.

Glassner, J. J. "Mahlzeit." *RlA* 7 (1987–90): 259–67.

Goebs, Katja. "A Functional Approach to Egyptian Myth and Mythemes." *JANER* 2 (2002): 27–59.

Goedegebuure, Petra. "Hittite Iconoclasm: Disconnecting the Icon, Disempowering the Referent." Pages 407–52 in *Iconoclasm and Text Destruction in the Ancient Near East and Beyond.* Edited by N. May. IOS 8. Chicago: University of Chicago, 2012.

Goedicke, Hans. "727 vor Christus." *WZKM* 69 (1977): 1–19.

Goetze, Albrecht. *Kleinasien.* Munich: Beck, 1957.

Golvin, Jean-Claude, and Jean-Claude Goyon. *Karnak, Ägypten: Anatomie eines Tempels.* Tübingen: Wasmuth, 1987.

Gonnella, J., W. Khayyata, and K. Kohlmeyer, eds. *Die Zitadelle von Aleppo und der Tempel des Wettergottes: Neue Forschungen und Entdeckungen.* Münster: Rhema, 2005.

Görke, Susanne. "Hethitische Rituale im Tempel." Pages 123–45 in *Tempel im Alten Orient: 7. Internationales Colloquium der Deutschen Orient-Gesellschaft 11.–13. Oktober 2009, München.* Edited by Kai Kaniuth, Anne Löhnert, Jared L. Miller, Adelheid Otto, Michael Roaf and Walther Sallaberger. CDOG 7; Wiesbaden: Harrassowitz, 2013.

Goyon, Jean-Claude. *Le rituel du sḥtp Sḥmt au changement de cycle annuel: d'après les architraves du temple d'Edfou et textes parallèles, du Nouvel Empire à l'époque ptolémaïque et romaine.* Le Caire: Inst. Français d'Archéologie Orientale, 2011.

———. *Rituels funéraires de l'ancienne Égypte: Le Rituel de l'ouverture de la bouche, les Livres des respirations.* Paris: du Cerf, 1972.

Grallert, Silke. *Bauen, Stiften, Weihen: Ägyptische Bau- und Restaurierungsinschriften von den Anfängen bis zur 30. Dynastie.* Abhandlungen des Deutschen Archäologischen Instituts Kairo 18. Berlin, Achet, 2001.

———. "Pharaonic Building Inscriptions and Temple Decoration." Pages 35–49 in *Sacred Space and Sacred Function in Ancient Thebes.* Edited by P. F. Dorman and B. N. Bryan. SAOC 61. Chicago: University of Chicago, 2007.

Grandet, Pierre. *Le papyrus Harris I (BM 9999),* Vol. 1. Bibliothèque d'Étude 109. Cairo: Imprimerie de l'Institut français d'archéologie orientale du Caire, 1994.

Grayson, A. Kirk. *Assyrian Rulers of the Early First Millennia BC.* RIMA 2. Toronto: Toronto University, 1991.

————. *Assyrian Rulers of the Third and Second Millennia BC to 1115 BC*. RIMA 1. Toronto: University of Toronto, 1987.

Greene, Brian. *The Fabric of the Cosmos: Space, Time, and the Texture of Reality*. New York: Knopf, 2004.

J. Gwyn Griffiths, *The Conflict of Horus and Seth from Egyptian and Classical Sources: A Study in Ancient Mythology*. Liverpool: Liverpool University Press, 1960

————. "Myths: Creation Myths," Pages 249–55 in *The Ancient Gods Speak: A Guide to Egyptian Religion*. Edited by D. Redford. Oxford: Oxford University Press, 2002.

Gröndahl, Frauke. *Die Personennamen der Texte aus Ugarit*. Studia Pohl 1. Rome: Päpstliches Bibelinstitut, 1967.

Groneberg, Birgitte. "Aspekte der 'Göttlichkeit' in Mesopotamien: Zur Klassifizierung von Göttern und Zwischenwesen." Pages 131–65 in *Götterbilder, Gottesbilder, Weltbilder, I: Ägypten, Mesopotamien, Persien, Kleinasien, Syrien, Palästina*. Edited by R. G. Kratz and H. Spieckermann. FAT II/17. Tübingen: Mohr Siebeck, 2006.

————. "Review of Zainab Bahrani, *The Graven Image*." *Bryn Mawr Classical Review*, 2004. Online: http://bmcr.brynmawr.edu/2004/2004-02-06.html.

————. "Die sumerisch/akkadische Inanna/Ištar: Hermaphroditos?" *WdO* 17 (1986): 25–46.

Gubel, Eric. *Phoenician Furniture: A Typology Based on Iron Age Representations with Reference to the Iconographical Context*. Studia Phoenicia 7. Leuven: Peeters, 1987.

Guermeur, Ivan. *Les cultes d'Amon hors de Thèbes: Recherches de géographie religieuse*. Bibliothèque de l'école des hautes etudes sciences religieuses 123. Turnhout, Belgium: Brepolis, 2005.

Guglielmi, Waltraud. "Bemerkungen zum Maatopfer im Amunsritual." *Göttinger Miszellen* 40 (1980): 23–28.

————. "Die Funktion von Tempeleingang und Gegentempel als Gebetsort: Zur Deutung einer Widder- und Gansstelen des Amun." Pages 55–68 in *Ägyptische Tempel – Struktur, Funktion und Programm: Akten der Ägyptologischen Tempeltagungen in Gosen 1990 und in Mainz 1992*. Edited by R. Gundlach and M. Rochholz. HÄB 37. Hildesheim: Gerstenberger, 1994.

————. "Wortspiel." *LÄ* 6 (1986): 1287–91.

Gundlach, Rolf. "Tempelrelief." *LÄ* 6 (1986): 407–11.

————. "Temples." Pages 363–79 in *The Oxford Encyclopedia of Ancient Egypt*, Vol. 3. Edited by D. Redford. Oxford: Oxford University Press, 2001.

Gurney, Oliver R. "A Hittite Divination Text." Pages 116–18 in *The Alalakh Tablets*. Edited by D. J. Wiseman. Occasional Publications of the British Institute of Archaeology at Ankara 2. London: The British Institute of Archaeology at Ankara, 1953.

————. "Hittite Kingship." Pages 105–21 in *Myth, Ritual, and Kingship: Essays on the Theory and Practice of Kingship in the Ancient Near East and in Israel*. Edited by S. H. Hooke. Oxford: Clarendon, 1958.

————. *Some Aspects of Hittite Religion*. The Schweich Lecture 1976. Oxford: Oxford University Press, 1977.

Güterbock, Hans G. "The Composition of Hittite Prayers to the Sun." *JAOS* 78 (1958): 237–45.

————. "Hethitische Götterbilder und Kultobjekte." Pages 203–17 in *Beiträge zur Altertumskunde Kleinasiens: Festschrift für Kurt Bittel*. Edited by R. M. Boehmer and H. Hauptmann. Mainz: von Zabern, 1983.

——. "The Hittite Temple according to Written Sources." Pages 81–85 in *Perspectives on Hittite Civilization: Select Writings of Hans G. Güterbock*. Edited by H. A. Hoffner, Jr. Anatolian Studies 26. Chicago: The Oriental Institute of the University of Chicago, 1997.

——. "Some Aspects of Hittite Prayers." *Acta Universitatus Upsaliensis* 38 (1978): 125–39.

——. "Yazılıkaya: À propos a New Interpretation." *JNES* 34 (1975): 273–77.

Haas, Volkert. *Geschichte der hethitischen Religion*. HdO 1/15. Leiden: Brill, 1994.

——. *Die hurritischen Ritualtermini in hethitischem Kontext*. ChS I/9. Rome: CNR, 1998.

——. "Ein hurritischer Blutritus und die Deponierung der Ritualrückstände nach hethitischen Quellen," Pages 67–86 in *Religionsgeschichtliche Beziehungen zwischen Kleinasien, Nordsyrien und dem Alten Testament: Internationales Symposion Hamburg, 17.-21. März 1990*. Edited by B. Janowski, K. Koch, and G. Wilhelm. OBO 129. Fribourg: University Press, 1993.

——. *Der Kult on Nerik: Ein Beitrag zur hethitischen Religionsgeschichte*. Studia Pohl 4. Rome: Päpstliches Bibelinstitut, 1970.

——. *Materia Magica et Medica Hethitica: Ein Beitrag zur Heilkunde im Alten Orient*. 2 volumes. Berlin: de Gruyter, 2003.

——. "Substratgottheiten des westhurritischen Pantheons." *RHA* 36 (1978): 59–69.

Haas, Volkert, and Gernot Wilhelm. *Hurritische und luwische Riten aus Kizzuwatna*. AOAT Sonderreihe 3. Kevelaer: Butzon & Bercker, 1974.

Haeny, Gerhard. "New Kingdom 'Mortuary Temples' and 'Mansions of Millions of Years.'" Pages 86–126 in *Temples of Ancient Egypt*. Edited by B. E. Shafer. London: Taurus, 1997.

Haines, Richard C. *Excavations in the Plain of Antioch*, Vol. 2: *The Structural Remains of the Later Phases: Chatal Hüyük, Tell Al-Judaidah, and Tell Tayinat*. OIP 95. Chicago: Oriental Institute Publications, 1970.

Hall, Emma Swan. *The Pharaoh Smites His Enemies: A Comparative Study*. MÄS 44. Munich: Deutscher Kunstverlag, 1986.

Hallo, William W. "Cult Statue and Divine Image: A Preliminary Study." Pages 1–17 in *Scripture in Context* II. Edited by Hallo, J. C. Moyer and L. G. Perdue. Winona Lake, IN: Eisenbrauns, 1983.

——. "Texts, Statues and the Cult of the Divine King," Pages 54–66 in *Congress Volume, Jerusalem 1986*. VTSup 40. Edited by J. Emerton. Leiden: Brill, 1988.

Hamori, Esther J. *"When Gods Were Men": The Embodied God in Biblical and Near Eastern Literature*. BZAW 384. Berlin: de Gruyter, 2008.

Hannig, Rainer. *Großes Handwörterbuch Ägyptisch-Deutsch: Die Sprache der Pharaonen (2800-950 v. Chr.)*. 2d ed. Mainz: Zabern, 2003.

Haring, Ben J. J. *Divine Households: Administrative and Economic Aspects of the New Kingdom Royal Memorial Temples in Western Thebes*. Egyptologische Uitgaven 12. Leiden: Nederlands Instituut voor het Nabije Oosten, 1997.

Harrison, Timothy P. "West Syrian Megaron or Neo-Assyrian Langraum? The Shifting Form and Function of the Tayinat Temples." Pages 3–22 in *Temple Building and Temple Cult: The Architecture and Cultic Paraphernalia of Temples in the Levant (2nd-1st Millennia BCE)*. Edited by J. Kamlah. Tübingen: Institute of Biblical Archaeology, 2012.

Harrison, Timothy P., and James F. Osborne. "Building XVI and the Neo-Assyrian Sacred Precinct at Tell Tayinat." *JCS* 64 (2012): 125–43.

Hartenstein, Friedhelm. *Das Angesicht JHWHs: Studien zu seinem höfischen und kultischen Bedeutungshintergrund in den Psalmen und in Exodus 32–34.* FAT 55. Tübingen: Mohr Siebeck, 2008.

Hartmann, Benedikt. "Monotheismus in Mesoopotamien?" Pages 49–81 in *Monotheismus in Alten Testament und seiner Umwelt.* Edited by O. Keel. BibB 14. Fribourg: University Press, 1980.

Hays, Harold. "The Ritual Scenes in the Chapel of Amun." Pages 1–14 in *The Epigraphic Survey, Medinet Habu IX: The Eighteenth Dynasty Temple Part I: The Sanctuary.* OIP 136. Chicago: The Oriental Institute of the University of Chicago, 2009.

———. "The Worshiper and the Worshipped in the Pyramid Texts." *Studien zur altägyptischen Kultur* 30 (2002): 153–67.

Hazenbos, Joost. *The Organization of the Anatolian Local Cults During the Thirteenth Century B.C.: An Appraisal of the Hittite Cult Inventories.* Cuneiform Monographs 21. Leiden: Brill, 2003.

Heeßel, Nils P. "Evil against Evil: The Demon Pazuzu." *SMSR* 77 (2011): 357–68.

———. *Pazuzu: Archäologische und Philologische Studien zu einem altorientalischen Dämon.* Ancient Magic and Divination 4. Leiden: Brill, 2002.

Heinrich, Ernst. *Die Tempel und Heiligtümer im alten Mesopotamien: Typologie, Morphologie und Geschichte.* 2 volumes. Denkmäler antiker Architektur 14. Berlin: de Gruyter, 1982.

Heinz, Constance S. *Die Feldzugsdarstellungen des Neuen Reiches: eine Bildanalyse.* Vienna: Verlag der Österreichischen Akademie der Wissenschaften, 2001.

Helck, Wolfgang. "Einige Bemerkungen zum Mundöffnungsritual," *Mitteilungen des Deutschen Archäologischen Instituts Abteilungs Kairo* 22 (1967): 27–41.

———. "Kultstatue." *LÄ* 3 (1980): 859–63.

———. *Die Prophezeiung des Nfr.tj.* Kleine Ägyptische Texte 2. Wiesbaden: Harrassowitz, 1970.

———. "Torgötter." *LÄ* 6 (1986): 637–39.

———. *Untersuchungen zur Thinitenzeit.* ÄA 45. Wiesbaden: Harrassowitz, 1987.

———. *Urkunden der 18. Dynastie: Übersetzung zu den Heften 17.–22.* Urk. IV. Berlin: Akademie, 1961.

———. *Urkunden der 18. Dynastie, Heft 22.* Urk. IV. Berlin: Academie, 1961.

Hendel, Ronald S. "Aniconism and Anthropomorphism in Ancient Israel." Pages 205–28 in *The Image and the Book: Iconic Cults, Aniconism, and the Rise of Book Religion in Israel and the Ancient Near East.* Edited by K. van der Toorn. CBET 21. Leuven: Peeters, 1997.

———. "The Social Origins of the Aniconic Tradition in Early Israel." *CBQ* 50 (1988): 365–82.

Hilprecht, Hermann Vollrat. *Die Ausgrabungen der Universität von Pennsylvania am Bêl-Tempel zu Nippur.* Leipzig: Hinrichs, 1903.

Hoffmann, Friedhelm. "Zum Körperkonzept in Ägypten (P. Berlin P. 10472 A + 14400)." Pages 481–500 in *Menschenbilder und Körperkonzepte im Alten Israel, in Ägypten und im Alten Orient.* Edited by A. Berlejung, J. Dietrich, and J. F. Quack. ORA 9. Tübingen: Mohr Siebeck, 2012.

———. "Measuring Egyptian Statues." Pages 109–19 in *Under One Sky: Astronomy and Mathematics in the Ancient Near East*. Edited by J. Steele and A. Imhausen. AOAT 297. Münster: Ugarit-Verlag, 2002.

Hoffner, Harry A., Jr. "Bayit." *TDOT* II (1975): 107–11.

———. *Hittite Myths*. SBLWAW 2. Atlanta: Scholars, 1990.

———. "Paskuwatti's Ritual against Sexual Impotence (*CTH* 406)." *AuOr* 5 (1987): 271–87.

———. "The Royal Cult in Ḫatti." Pages 132–51 in *Text, Artifact, and Image: Revealing Ancient Israelite Religion*. Edited by G. M. Beckman and T. J. Lewis. BJS 346. Providence, RI: Brown Judaic Studies, 2006.

Hoftijzer Jacob, and K. Jongeling. *Dictionary of the Northwest Semitic Inscriptions*. HdO 1/21. Leiden: Brill, 1995.

Holloway, Steven W. *Aššur Is King! Aššur Is King! Religion in the Exercise of Power in the Neo-Assyrian Empire*. Leiden: Brill, 2002.

———. "The *ᵍⁱˢKakki Aššur* and Neo-Assyrian Loyalty Oaths." Pages 449–70 in *Proceedings of the XLV Rencontre Assyriologique Internationale: Part 1: Historiography in the Cuneiform World*. Edited by T. Abusch, P.-A. Beaulieu, J. Huehnegard, P. Machinist, and P. Steinkeller. Bethesda, MD: CDL, 2001.

Holly, Michael Ann. "Past Looking." *Critical Inquiry* 16 (1990): 371–96.

Hölscher, Uvo. *The Mortuary Temple of Ramses III, Part 1: The Excavation of Medinet Habu, Volume 3*. OIP 53. Chicago: University of Chicago Press, 1941.

Hornung, Erik. "Ancient Egyptian Religious Iconography." Pages 1711–30 in *CANE*.

———. *Das Buch der Anbetung des Re im Westen*. 2 volumes. Aegyptiaca Helvetica 2/3. Geneva: Faculté des Lettres de l'Université de Genève, 1975/1976.

———. *Conceptions of God in Ancient Egypt: The One and the Many*. Translated by J. Baines. London: Routledge, 1983.

Horowitz, Wayne. "The Babylonian Map of the World." *Iraq* 50 (1988): 147–65.

———. *Mesopotamian Cosmic Geography*. Mesopotamian Civilizations 8. Winona Lake, IN: Eisenbrauns, 1998.

van den Hout, Theo P. J. "Death as a Privilege: The Hittite Royal Funerary Ritual." Pages 37–75 in *Hidden Futures: Death and Immortality in Ancient Egypt, Anatolia, the Classical, Biblical and Arabic-Islamic World*. Edited by J. M. Bremmer, T. P. H. van den Hout, and R. Peters. Amsterdman: Amsterdam University, 1994.

Hrouda, Blahoslav. "Göttersymbole und –attribute. A. Archäologisch. I. Syrien/Paästina." *RlA* 3 (1969): 490–95.

———. "Zum 'Heiligen Hügel' in der altmesopotamischen Religion." *WZKM* 86 (1996): 161–75.

———. "Das Verhältnis zur Vergangenheit im alten Mesopotamien." *ArOr* 47 (1979): 4–14.

Hundley, Michael B. "Before Yahweh at the Entrance of the Tent of Meeting: A Study of Spatial and Conceptual Geography in the Priestly Texts." *ZAW* 123 (2011): 15–26.

———. "Divine Fluidity? The Priestly Texts in their Ancient Near Eastern Contexts." In *Reading Leviticus in Its Contexts*. Edited by F. Landy and L. M. Travaskis. Sheffield: Sheffield Phoenix Press, forthcoming.

———. "Here a God, There a God: Conceptions of Deity in Ancient Mesopotamia." *AoF*, forthcoming.

———. *Keeping Heaven on Earth: Safeguarding the Divine Presence in the Priestly Tabernacle*. FAT II/50. Tübingen: Mohr Siebeck, 2011.

———. "The Way Forward is Back to the Beginning: Reflections on the Priestly Texts." Pages 209–24 in *Remembering and Forgetting in Early Second Judah*. Edited by E. Ben-Zvi and C. Levin. FAT 85. Tübingen: Mohr Siebeck, 2012.

Hurowitz, Victor A. "Isaiah's Impure Lips and Their Purification in Light of Akkadian Sources." *HUCA* 60 (1989): 39–89.

———. "The Mesopotamian God Image, from Womb to Tomb." *JAOS* 123 (2003): 147–57.

———. "Picturing Imageless Deities: Iconography in the Ancient Near East." *BAR* 23 (1997): 46–51, 68–69.

———. "What Goes in Is What Comes Out: Materials for Creating Cult Statues." Pages 3–23 in *Text, Artifact, and Image: Revealing Ancient Israelite Religion*. Edited by G. M. Beckman and T. J. Lewis. BJS 346. Providence, RI: Brown Judaic Studies, 2006.

Hussy, Holger. *Die Epiphanie und Erneuerung der Macht Gottes: Szenen des täglichen Kultbildrituals in den ägyptischen Tempeln der griechisch-römischen Epoche*. Studien zu den Ritualszenen altägyptischer Tempel 5. Dettelbach: Röll, 2007.

Hutter, Manfred. "Aspects of Luwian Religion." Pages 211–80 in *The Luwians*. Edited by H. C. Melchert. HdO I/68. Leiden: Brill, 2003.

———. "Kultstellen und Baityloi: Die Ausstrahlung eines syrischen religiösen Phänomens nach Kleinasien und Israel." Pages 87–108 in *Religionsgeschichtliche Beziehungen zwischen Kleinasien, Nordsyrien und dem Alten Testament: Internationales Symposion Hamburg, 17.–21. März 1990*. Edited by B. Janowski, K. Koch, and G. Wilhelm. OBO 129. Fribourg: University Press, 1993.

———. "Religion in Hittite Anatolia: Some Comments on 'Volkert Haas: Geschichte der hethitischen Religion.'" *Numen* 44 (1997): 74–90.

İlaslı, A. "A Hittite Statue Found in the Area of Ahurhisar." Pages 301–8 in *Aspects of Art and Iconography: Anatolia and its Neighbors: Studies in Honor of Nimet Özgüç*. Edited by M. Mellink, E. Porada, and T. Özgüç. Ankara: Türk Tarih Kurumu Basımevi, 1993.

Jakob-Rust, Liane. "Zu den hethitischen Bildbeschreibungen. I. Teil." *MIO* 8 (1961): 161–217.

———. "Zu den hethitischen Bildbeschreibungen. II. Teil." *MIO* 9 (1963): 175–239.

Jacobsen, Thorkild. *The Gimilsin Temple and the Palace of the Rulers at Tell Asmar*. OIP 43; Chicago: University of Chicago Press, 1940.

———. "The Graven Image." Pages 15–32 in *Ancient Israelite Religion: Essays in Honor of F. M. Cross*. Edited by P. D. Miller, P.D. Hanson, and S. D. McBride. Philadelphia: Fortress, 1987.

———. *The Treasures of Darkness: A History of Mesopotamian Religion*. New Haven, CT: Yale University Press, 1976.

Janowski, Bernd. *Sühne als Heilsgeschehen: Studien zur Sühnetheologie der Priesterschrift und zur Wurzel KPR im Alten Orient und im Alten Testament*. WMANT 55. Neukirchenen-Vluyn: Neukircherner Verlag, 1982.

Jay, Nancy B. *Throughout Your Generations Forever: Sacrifice, Religion and Paternity*. Chicago: Chicago University Press, 1992.

Jean, Charles-Francis. *Tell Sifr: Textes cuneiformes conserves au British Museum*. Paris: Geuthner, 1931.

Junge, Friedrich. "Zur Felddatierung des sog. Denkmals memphitischer Theologie oder der

Beitrag der ägyptische Theologie zur Geistesgeschichte der Spätzeit." *Mitteilungen des Deutschen Archäologischen Instituts Abteilung Kairo* 29 (1973): 195–204.

Kammenhuber, Annelies. "Die hethitischen Vorstellungen von Seele und Leib, Herz und Leibesinnerem, Kopf und Person, 1. Teil." *ZA* 56 (1964): 150–212.

Karasu, Cem. "Why Did the Hittites Have a Thousand Deities?" Pages 221–35 in *Hittite Studies in Honor of Harry A. Hoffner Jr. on the Occasion of His 65th Birthday*. Edited by G. Beckman, R. Beal, and G. McMahon. Winona Lake: Eisenbrauns, 2003.

Karlshausen, Christina. "L'évolution de la barque processionelle d'Amon à 18ᵉ dynastie." *RDE* 46 (1995): 119–37.

———. "L'iconographie de la barque processionelle divine en Égypte au Nouvel Empire." Ph.D. diss., Université Catholique du Louvaine, 1997.

Kataja, L., and R. Whiting. *Grants, Decrees, and Gifts of the Neo-Assyrian Period*. SAA 12. Helsinki: Helsinki University Press, 1995.

Keel, Othmar. *Studien zu den Stempelsiegeln aus Palästina/Israel IV*. OBO 135. Fribourg: Universitätsverlag, 1994.

———. *The Symbolism of the Biblical World: Ancient Near Eastern Iconography and the Book of Psalms*. Translated by T. J. Hallett. London: SPCK, 1978.

Kempinski, Aharon. *Megiddo: A City-State and Royal Centre in North Israel*. Materialien zur Allgemeinen und Vergleichenden Archäologie 40. Munich: Beck, 1989.

Kertzer, David I. *Ritual, Politics, and Power*. New Haven, CT: Yale University Press, 1988.

Kilde, Jeanne Halgren. *Sacred Power, Sacred Space: An Introduction to Christian Architecture and Worship*. Oxford: Oxford University Press, 2008.

Kilmer, Anne D. "The Brick of Birth." *JNES* 46 (1987): 211–13.

King, L. W. *Babylonian Boundary Stones and Memorial Tablets in the British Museum*. London: Trustees of the British Museum, 1912.

Kingsbury, Edwin C. "A Seven Day Ritual in the Old Babylonian Cult at Larsa." *HUCA* 34 (1963): 1–34.

Kinsley, David. "Avatāra." Pages 14–15 in *Encyclopedia of Religion*. Edited by Mircea Eliade. Volume 2. New York: MacMillan, 1987.

Kitchen, Kenneth A. *Ramesside Inscriptions: Historical and Biographical: Ramesses II, Royal Inscriptions*. Volume 2. Oxford: Blackwell, 1979.

———. *Ramesside Inscriptions: Historical and Biographical: Translated & Annotated: Ramesses II, Royal Inscriptions*. Volume 2. Oxford: Blackwell, 1996.

Klingbeil, Martin. *Yahweh Fighting from Heaven: God as Warrior and as God of Heaven in the Hebrew Psalter and Ancient Near Eastern Iconography*. OBO 169. Fribourg: University Press, 1999.

Klinger, Jörg. "Reinigungsriten und Abwehrzauber: Funktion und Rolle magischer Rituale be den Hethitern." Pages 146–49 in *Die Hethiter und ihr Reich: Das Volk der 1000 Götter – Begleitband zur Ausstellung der Kunsthalle der Bundesrepublik Deutschland*. Edited by T. Özgüç. Bonn: Kunst- Und Ausstellungshalle Der Bundesrepublik Deutschland, 2002.

———. *Untersuchungen zur Rekonstruktion der hattischen Kultschicht*. StBot 37. Wiesbaden: Harassowitz, 1996.

Koch, Klaus. *Geschichte der ägyptische Religion: Von den Pyramiden bis zu den Mysterien der Isis*. Stuttgart: Kohlhammer, 1993.

Köcher, F. "Der babylonischen Göttertypentext." *MIO* 1 (1953): 57–107.

Kohlmeyer, Kay. *Der Tempel des Wettergottes von Aleppo.* Münster: Rhema, 2000.

———. "Der Tempel des Wettergottes von Aleppo." Pages 179–218 in *Tempel im Alten Orient: 7. Internationales Colloquium der Deutschen Orient-Gesellschaft 11.–13. Oktober 2009, München.* Edited by Kai Kaniuth, Anne Löhnert, Jared L. Miller, Adelheid Otto, Michael Roaf and Walther Sallaberger. CDOG 7; Wiesbaden: Harrassowitz, 2013.

———. "The Temple of the Storm God in Aleppo during the Late Bronze and Early Iron Ages." *NEA* 72 (2009): 190–202.

van der Kooij, Gerrit. "Deir 'Alla, Tell." Pages 338–42 in *The New Encyclopedia of Archaeological Excavation in the Holy Land.* Edited by E. Stern. Jerusalem: Israel Exploration Society, 1993.

Koldewey, Robert. *Das Ištar-Tor in Babylon. WVDOG 15.* Leipzig: Deutsche Orient-Gesellschaft, 1911.

Korpel, Marjo A. *A Rift in the Clouds: Ugaritic and Hebrew Descriptions of the Divine.* UBL 8. Münster: Ugarit-Verlag, 1990.

Kronasser, Heinz. *Die Umsiedlung der schwarzen Gottheit: Das hethitische Ritual KUB XXIX 4(des Ulippis).* Graz: Verlag der Österreichische Akademie der Wissenschaften, 1963.

Kruchten, Jean-Marie. "Oracles." Pages 609–12 in *The Oxford Encyclopedia of Ancient Egypt.* Volume 2. Edited by D. Redford. Oxford: Oxford University Press, 2001.

Kühne, Cord. "Hethitisch auli- und einige Aspekte altanatolischer Opferpraxis." *ZA* 76 (1986): 85–117.

———. "Zum Vor-Opfer im alten Anatolien." Pages 225–86 in *Religionsgeschichtliche Beziehungen zwischen Kleinasien, Nordsyrien und dem Alten Testament: Internationales Symposion Hamburg, 17.–21. März 1990.* Edited by B. Janowski, K. Koch, and G. Wilhelm. OBO 129. Fribourg: University Press, 1993.

Kurth, Dieter. *Edfu: Ein ägyptischer Tempel, gesehen mit den Augen der alten Ägypter.* Darmstadt: Wiss. Buch., 1994.

———, ed. *Systeme und Programme der ägyptischen Tempeldekoration: 3. Ägyptologische Tempeltagung Hamburg 1.–5. Juni 1994.* ÄAT 33. Wiesbaden: Harrassowitz, 1995.

Kuschke, A. "Tempel." Pages 333–42 in *Biblisches Reallexikon.* Edited by K. Galling. HAT 1. Tübingen: Mohr Siebeck, 1977.

Lambert, Wilfred G. "Ancient Mesopotamian Gods: Superstition, Philosophy, Theology." *Revue de l'Histoire des Religions* 207 (1990): 115–30.

———. "Donations of Food and Drink to the Gods in Ancient Mesopotamia." Pages 191–201 in *Ritual and Sacrifice in the Ancient Near East: Proceedings of the International Conference Organized by the Katholieke Universiteit Leuven from the 17th to the 20th of April 1991.* Edited by J. Quaegebeur. OLA 55. Leuven: Peeters, 1993.

———. "Gott. B. Nach akkadischen Texten," *RlA* 3 (1957): 543–46.

———. "Himmel." *RlA* 4 (1972–1975): 411–42.

Lambert, Wilfred G., and Alan R. Millard. *Atra-ḫasīs: The Babylonian Story of the Flood.* Oxford: Clarendon, 1969.

Landsberger, Benno. *Brief des Bischofs von Esagila an König Asarhaddon.* MKNAW Nieuwe Reeks 28/VI. Amsterdam: Noord-Hollandsche Uitg. Mij., 1965.

———. *Der kultische Kalender der Babylonier und Assyrer.* Leipzig: Hinrichs, 1915.

Langdon, Stephen. *Babylonian Penitential Psalms.* Oxford Editions of Cuneiform Texts 6. Paris: Geuthner, 1927.

———. *Neubabylonischen Königsinschriften.* Vorderasiatische Bibliothek 4. Leipzig: Hinrichs, 1912.

Lanier, Jaron. "Jaron's World: Shapes in Other Dimensions." *Discover Magazine*, April 2007. Online: http://discovermagazine.com/2007/apr/jarons-world-shapes-in-other-dimensions.

Laroche, Emmanuel. "L'adjectif *sarli*- 'supérior' dans les langues asianiques." Pages 291–98 in *Festschrift Johannes Friedrich zum 65. Geburtstag.* Edited by R. von Kienle. Heidelberg: Winter, 1959.

———. "La réforme religieuse du roi Tudḫaliya IV et sa signification politique." Pages 87–95 in *Les syncrétismes dans les religions de l'Antiquité.* Edited by F. Dunand and P. Lévêque. Leiden: Brill, 1975.

Layard, A. H. *Monuments of Nineveh: From Drawings Made on the Spot I.* London: John Murray, 1849.

———. *The Monuments of Nineveh II.* London: John Murray, 1853.

Lebrun, René. *Samuha: Foyer religieux de l'empire Hittite.* Louvain-la-Neuve: Institut Orientaliste, 1976.

Lefebvre, Henri. *The Production of Space.* Translated by D. Nicholson-Smith. Oxford: Blackwell, 1991.

Leicht, Michael. "Die erste Pflicht der Bildwissenchaft besteht darin, den eigenen Augen zu misstrauen." Pages 21-36 in *Bild—Macht—Geschichte: Visuelle Kommunikation im Alten Orient.* Edited by M. Heinz and D. Bonatz. Berlin: Reimer, 2002.

Leitz, Christian, ed. *Lexikon der ägyptischen Götter und Götterbezeichnungen.* 8 volumes. OLA 110-116, 129. Leuven: Peeters, 2002-2003.

Lesko, Barbara S. "Private Cults." Pages 76–81 in *The Ancient Gods Speak: A Guide to Egyptian Religion.* Edited by D. Redford. Oxford: Oxford University Press, 2002.

Levine, Aaron D. *Cloning: A Beginner's Guide.* London: Oneworld, 2007.

Levine, Baruch A., and William W. Hallo. "Offerings to the Temple Gates at Ur." *HUCA* 38 (1967): 17–58.

Lewis, Theodore J. "Divine Images and Aniconism in Ancient Israel." *JAOS* 118 (1998): 212–24.

———. "Syro-Palestinian Iconography and Divine Images." Pages 69–107 in *Cult Image and Divine Representation in the Ancient Near East.* Edited by N. H. Walls. ASOR Book Series 10. Boston: ASOR, 2005.

Jones, Lindsay. *The Hermeneutics of Sacred Space: Experience, Interpretation, Comparison.* 2 volumes. Cambridge, MA: Harvard University Press, 2000.

Liboff, Richard L. *Introductory Quantum Mechanics.* Reading, MA: Addison-Wesley, 2002.

Lichtheim, Miriam. *Ancient Egyptian Literature,* Vol. 1: *The Old and Middle Kingdoms.* Berkeley: University of California Press, 1973.

———. *Ancient Egyptian Literature,* Vol. 2: *The New Kingdom.* Berkeley: University of California Press, 1976.

———. *Ancient Egyptian Literature,* Vol. 3: *The Late Period.* Berkeley: University of California Press, 1980.

Linssen, Marc J. H. *The Cults of Uruk and Babylon: The Temple Ritual Texts as Evidence for Hellenistic Cult Practice.* Cuneiform Monographs 25. Leiden: Brill, 2004.

Livingstone, Alasdair. *Court Poetry and Literary Miscellanea.* SAA 3. Helsinki: Helsinki University, 1989.

———. *Mystical and Mythological Explanatory Works of Assyrian and Babylonian Scholars.* Oxford: Oxford University Press, 1986.

Lloyd, Seton. *The Archaeology of Mesopotamia: From the Old Stone Age to the Persian Conquest.* 2nd ed. London: Thames & Hudson, 1984.

Löhnert, Anne. "The Installation of Priests according to Neo-Assyrian Documents." *SAAB* 16 (2007): 273–86.

———. "Reconsidering the Consecration of Priests in Ancient Mesopotamia." Pages 183–91 in *Your Praise Is Sweet. A Memorial Volume Presented to Jeremy Allen Black by Colleagues, Students, and Friends.* Edited by H. D. Baker, E. Robson, and G. Zólyomi. London: British Institute for the Study of Iraq, 2010.

———. *"Wie die Sonne tritt heraus!" Eine Klage zum Auszug Enlils mit einer Untersuchung zu Komposition und Tradition sumerischer Klagelieder in altbabylonischer Zeit.* AOAT 365. Münster: Ugarit-Verlag, 2009.

Lohwasser, Angelika. *Die Formel "Öffnen des Gesichts."* BzÄ 11. Vienna: Afro-Pub, 1991.

Long, Bernard. "Le *ib* et le *ḥЗty* dans les textes médicaux de l'Égypte ancienne." Pages 483–94 in *Hommages à François Daumas,* Vol. 2. Edited by A. Guillaumont. Montpellier: University of Montpelier, 1986.

Loretz, Oswald. "Semitischer Aniconismus und biblisches Bilderverbot: Review Article on T. Mettinger, *No Graven Image* (1995)." *UF* 26 (1996): 209–23.

Lorton, David. "The Theology of Cult Statues in Ancient Egypt," Pages 123–210 in *Born in Heaven, Made on Earth: The Making of the Cult Image in the Ancient Near East.* Edited by M. B. Dick. Winona Lake, IN: Eisenbrauns, 1999.

———. "The Treatment of Criminals in Ancient Egypt through the New Kingdom." *JESHO* 20 (1977): 53–54.

Loud, Gordon. *Khorsabad I: Excavations in the Palace and at the City Gate.* OIP 38. Chicago: University of Chicago Press, 1936.

———. *Megiddo II, Seasons of 1935–1939, Text.* OIP 62. Chicago: University of Chicago, 1948.

Loud, Gordon, and Charles B. Altman. *Khorsabad, Part II: The Citadel and the Town.* OIP 40; Chicago: The University of Chicago Press, 1938.

Lubar, Steven, and W. David Kingery, eds. *History from Things: Essays.* New York: Smithsonian Books, 1993.

Luckenbill, Daniel D. *The Annals of Sennacherib.* OIP 2. Chicago: University of Chicago, 1924.

Lumsden, Stephen. "The Production of Space at Nineveh." *Iraq* 66 (2004): 187–97.

Machinist, Peter. "How Gods Die, Biblically and Otherwise: A Problem of Cosmic Restructuring." Pages 189–240 in *Reconsidering the Concept of Revolutionary Monotheism.* Edited by Pongratz-Leisten. Winona Lake, IN: Eisenbrauns, 2011.

———. "Kingship and Divinity in Imperial Assyria." Pages 152–88 in *Text, Artifact, and Image: Revealing Ancient Israelite Religion.* BJS 346; Providence: Brown Judaic Studies, 2006. ed. Lewis and Beckman

Mallowan, M. E. L. *Nimrud and Its Remains I.* London: Collins, 1966.

Margueron, Jean-Claude. "Meskene (Imar/Emar)." *RlA* 8 (1993–1997): 84–93.

———. "Sanctuaires semitiques." *Supplement au dictionnaire de la bible* 11 (1991): 1104–1257.

———. "Temples: The Mesopotamian Temple." Pages 165–69 in *The Oxford Encyclopedia of Archaeology in the Near East*, Vol. 4. Edited by E. Meyers. Oxford: Oxford University Press, 1997.

Margueron, Jean-Claude, and Veronica Boutte. "Emar, Capital of Aštata in the Fourteenth Century BCE." *BA* 58 (1995): 126–38.

Markus, Thomas A. *Buildings and Power: Freedom and Control in the Origins of Modern Building Types.* London: Routledge, 1993.

Matsushima, Eiko. "Divine Statues in Ancient Mesopotamia: Their Fashioning and Clothing and Their Interaction with the Society." Pages 209–19 in *Official Cult and Popular Religion in the Ancient Near East: Papers of the First Colloquium on the Ancient Near East: The City and its Life held at the Middle Eastern Culture Center in Japan (Mitaka, Tokyo) March 20–22, 1992.* Edited by E. Matsushima. Heidelberg: Winter 1993.

———. "Eleven Neo-Babylonian Texts Relating to the *lubuštu* (Clothing Ceremony)." Pages 235–43 in *Essays on Ancient Anatolia and Its Surrounding Civilizations.* Edited by H. I. H. P. T. Mikasa. BMECCJ 8. Wiesbaden: Harrosowitz, 1995.

———. "On the Material Related to the Clothing Ceremnoy." *ASJ* 16 (1994): 177–200.

Matthiae, Paolo. *Ebla: An Empire Rediscovered.* London: Hodder & Stoughton, 1980.

Maul, Stefan M. "Die altorientalische Hauptstadt - Abbild und Nabel der Welt." Pages 109–24 in *Die Orientalische Stadt: Kontinuität, Wandel, Bruch. 1. Internationales Colloquium der Deutschen Orient-Gesellschaft, 9.-10. Mai 1996 in Halle/Saale.* Edited by G. Wilhelm. CDOG 1. Saarbrücken: SDV Saarbrücker, 1997.

———. "Altorientalische Schöpfungsmythen." Pages 43–53 in *Mythos und Mythologie.* Edited by R. Brandt and S. Schmidt. Berlin: Akademie, 2004.

———. "Gottesdienst im Sonnenheiligtum zu Sippar." Pages 285–316 in *Minuscula Mesopotamica: Festschrift für Johannes Renger.* Edited by B. Böck, E. Cancik-Kirschbaum, and T. Richter. AOAT 267. Münster: Ugarit-Verlag, 1999.

———. "Das Haus des Götterkönigs: Gedanken zur Konzeption überregionaler Heiligtümer im Alten Orient." Pages 311–24 in *Tempel im Alten Orient: 7. Internationales Colloquium der Deutschen Orient-Gesellschaft 11.-13. Oktober 2009, München.* Edited by Kai Kaniuth, Anne Löhnert, Jared L. Miller, Adelheid Otto, Michael Roaf and Walther Sallaberger. CDOG 7; Wiesbaden: Harrassowitz, 2013.

———. *"Herzberuhigungsklagen": Die Sumerisch-akkadischen Eršahunga-Gebete.* Wiesbaden: Harrassowitz, 1988.

———. "Omina und Orakel. A. Mesopotamien." *RlA* 10 (2005): 45–88.

———. "Walking Backwards into the Future: The Conception of Time in the Acient Near East." Pages 15–24 in *Given World and Time. Temporalities in Context.* Edited by T. Miller. Budapest: CEU, 2008.

———. *Zukunftsbewältigung: Eine Untersuchung altorientalischen Denkens anhand der babylonisch-assyrischen Löserituale (Namburbi).* BaF 18. Mainz: von Zabern, 1994.

Mayer-Opificus, Ruth. "Die geflügelte Sonne: Himmels- und Regensdarstellungen im alten Vorderasien." *UF* 16 (1984): 189–236.

Mazar, Amihai. "Temples of the Middle and Late Bronze Ages and the Iron Age." Pages 161–87 in *The Architecture of Ancient Israel: From the Prehistoric to the Persian*

*Periods*. Edited by A. Kempinski and R. Reich. Jerusalem: Israel Exploration Society, 1992.

McCormick, Clifford Mark. *Palace and Temple: A Study of Architectural and Verbal Icons*. BZAW 313. Berlin: de Gruyter, 2002.

McEwan, Gilbert J. P. *Priest and Temple in Hellenistic Babylonia*. Freiburger Altorientalische Studien 4. Wiesbaden: Steiner, 1981.

McMahon, Gregory. "Theology, Priests, and Worship in Hittite Anatolia." Pages 1981–1995 in *CANE*.

Meeks, Dimitri. *The Daily Life of the Egyptian Gods*. Translated by G. M. Goshgarian. London: Pimlico, 1999.

Meijer, Diederik J. W. "Ground Plans and Archaeologists: On Similarities and Comparisons." Pages 221–36 in *To the Euphrates and Beyond: Archaeological Studies in Honor of Maurits N. Van Loon*. Edited by O. Haex, H. Curvers, and P. Akkermans. Rotterdam: A. A. Blakema, 1989.

Melchert, H. Craig. *Cuneiform Luvian Lexicon*. Lexica Anatolica 2. Chapel Hill, NC, 1993.

Menzel, Brigitte. *Assyrische Tempel*. 2 volumes. Rome: Biblical Institute Press, 1981.

Mettinger, Tryggve N. D. "Israelite Aniconism: Developments and Origins." Pages 173–204 in *The Image and the Book: Iconic Cults, Aniconism, and the Rise of Book Religion in Israel and the Ancient Near East*. Edited by K. van der Toorn. CBET 21. Leuven: Peeters, 1997.

———. *No Graven Image? Israelite Aniconism in Its Ancient Near Eastern Context*. CBOT 42. Stockholm: Almqvist & Wiksell, 1995.

———. *The Riddle of the Resurrection: "Dying and Rising Gods" in the Ancient Near East*. CBOT 50. Stockholm: Almqvist & Wiksell, 2001.

Meyers, Eric M., ed. *The Oxford Encyclopedia of Archaeology in the Near East*. 5 volumes. Oxford: Oxford University Press, 1997.

Michalowski, Piotr. "The Torch and the Censer." Pages 152–62 in *The Tablet and the Scroll: Near Eastern Studies Honor of William W. Hallo*. Edited by M. Cohen, D. Snell, and D. Weisberg. Bethesda, MD: CDL, 1993.

Milgrom, Jacob. *Leviticus 1-16*. AB 3. New York: Doubleday, 1991.

Miller, Jared L. "The *katra/i*-women in the Kizzuwatnean Rituals from Hattuša." Pages 423–31 in *Sex and Gender in the Ancient Near East: Compte Rendu de la XLVIIe Rencontre Assyriologique Internationale, Helsinki 2001*. Edited by S. Parpola and R. M. Whiting. Winona Lake, IN: Eisenbrauns, 2002.

———. *Studies in the Origins, Development and Interpretation of the Kizzuwatna Rituals*. StBoT 46. Wiesbaden: Harrassowitz, 2004.

Modéus, Martin. *Sacrifice and Symbol: Biblical Šĕlāmîm in a Ritual Perspective*. CBOT 52. Stockholm: Almqvist & Wiksell, 2005.

Monson, John. "The ʿAin Dara Temple and the Jerusalem Temple." Pages 273–99 in *Text, Artifact, and Image: Revealing Ancient Israelite Religion*. Edited by G. M. Beckman and T. J. Lewis. BJS 346. Providence: Brown Judaic Studies, 2006.

———. "The New ʿAin Dara Temple: Closest Solomonic Parallel." *BAR* 26 (2000): 20–35, 67.

de Moor, Johannes C. "Standing Stones and Ancestor Worship." *UF* 27 (1995): 1–20.

Moorey, Peter R. S., and Stuart Fleming. "Problems in the Study of the Anthropomorphic Metal Statuary from Syro-Palestine before 330 B.C." *Levant* 16 (1984): 67–90.

Morenz, Sigfried. *Egyptian Religion*. Translated by A. Keep. Ithaca, NY: Cornell University Press, 1973.

Moret, Alexandre. *Le Rituel du culte divin journalier en Égypte, d'après les papyrus de Berlin et les textes du temple de Séti Ier, à Abydos*. Paris: Leroux, 1902.

Muhly, James D. "Bronze Figurines and Near Eastern Metalwork." *IEJ* 39 (1980): 148–61.

Müller-Karpe, Andreas. "Ein Großbau in der hethitischen Stadtruine Kuşaklı: Tempel des Wettergottes von Sarissa?" *Alter Orient aktuell 1* (2000): 19–22

———. "Zu einigen archäologischen sowie archäoastronomischen Aspekten hethitischer Sakralbauten." Pages 335–54 in *Tempel im Alten Orient: 7. Internationales Colloquium der Deutschen Orient-Gesellschaft 11.–13. Oktober 2009, München*. Edited by Kai Kaniuth, Anne Löhnert, Jared L. Miller, Adelheid Otto, Michael Roaf and Walther Sallaberger. CDOG 7; Wiesbaden: Harrassowitz, 2013.

———. "Kuşaklı-Sarissa: A Hittite Town in the 'Upper Land.'" Pages 145–55 in *Recent Developments in Hittite Archaeology and History: Papers in Memory of Hans G. Güterbock*. Edited by K. A. Yener and H. A. Hoffner Jr. Winona Lake, IN: Eisenbrauns, 2002

———. "Kuşaklı-Sarissa. Kultort im oberen Land." Pages 176–89 in *Die Hethiter und ihr Reich: Das Volk der 1000 Götter – Begleitband zur Ausstellung der Kunsthalle der Bundesrepublik Deutschland*. Edited by T. Özgüç. Bonn: Kunst- Und Ausstellungshalle Der Bundesrepublik Deutschland, 2002.

———. "Untersuchungen in Kuşaklı 1992–1994." *MDOG* 127 (1995): 5–36.

———. "Untersuchungen in Kuşaklı 1995." *MDOG* 128 (1996): 69–94.

———. "Untersuchungen in Kuşaklı 1992–1996." *MDOG* 129 (1997): 103–42.

———. "Untersuchungen in Kuşaklı 1997." *MDOG* 130 (1998): 93–172.

———. "Untersuchungen in Kuşaklı 1998." *MDOG* 131 (1999): 57–113.

———. "Untersuchungen in Kuşaklı 1999." *MDOG* 132 (2000): 311–53.

———. "Untersuchungen in Kuşaklı 2000." *MDOG* 133 (2001): 225–50.

———. "Untersuchungen in Kuşaklı 2001." *MDOG* 134 (2002): 331–51.

———. "Untersuchungen in Kuşaklı 2002." *MDOG* 136 (2004): 103–35.

———. "Untersuchungen in Kuşaklı 2004." *MDOG* 137 (2005): 137–72.

———. "Untersuchungen in Kuşaklı 2004 and 2005." *MDOG* 138 (2006): 15–42.

Munn, Nancy D. "Symbolism in Ritual Context: Aspects of Symbolic Action." Pages 579–612 in *Handbook of Social and Cultural Anthropology*. Edited by J. Honigmann. Chicago: Rand McNally, 1973.

Munro, Peter. "Die Nacht vor der Thronbesteigung—zum ältesten Teil des Mundöffnungsrituals." Pages 907–28 in *Studien zu Sprache und Religion Ägyptens zu Ehren von Wolfhart Westendorf*, vol. 2. Edited by F. Junge. Göttingen: Hubert, 1984.

Murnane, William J. *Texts from the Amarna Period in Egypt*. SBLWAW 5. Atlanta: Scholars Press, 1995.

Nakhai, Beth Alpert. *Archaeology and the Religions of Canaan and Israel*. ASOR Books 7. Boston: ASOR, 2001.

———. "Temples: Syro-Palestinian Temples." Pages 169–74 in *The Oxford Encyclopedia of Archaeology in the Near East*, vol. 4. Edited by E. Meyers. Oxford: Oxford University Press, 1997.

Negbi, Ora. *Canaanite Gods in Metal*. Tel Aviv: Tel Aviv University, 1976.

Nelson, Harold Hayden. "Certain Reliefs at Karnak and Medinet Habu and the Ritual of Amenophis I," *JNES* 8 (1949): 201–32.

———. *The Great Hypostyle Hall at Karnak 1*, Part 1: *The Wall Reliefs*. OIP 106. Chicago: Oriental Institute, 1981.

———. "The Rite of 'Bringing the Foot' as Portrayed in Temple Reliefs." *JEA* 35 (1949): 82–86.

Nelson, Harold H., and Uvo Hölscher. *Work in Western Thebes, 1931–33*. OIC 18. Chicago: University of Chicago Press, 1934.

Neve, Peter J. "Boğazköy-Ḫattuša: New Results of the Excavations in the Upper City." *Anatolica* 16 (1989): 7–20.

———. "The Great Temple in Boğazköy-Ḫattuša." Pages 77–97 in *Across the Anatolian Plateau: Readings in the Archaeology of Ancient Turkey*. Edited by D. Hopkins. Annual of ASOR 57. Boston: American Schools of Oriental Research, 2002.

———. "Der Große Tempel (Tempel 1) in Boğazköy-Ḫattuša." *Nürnberger Blätter zur Archäologie* 12 (1996): 41–62.

———. "Hattusha, City of Gods and Temples: Results of the Excavations in the Upper City." *Proceedings of the British Academy* (1991 Lectures and Memoirs) 80 (1993): 105–132.

———. *Ḫattuša-Stadt der Götter und Tempel: Neue Ausgrabungen in der Hauptstadt der Hethiter*. 2nd ed. Mainz: von Zabern, 1996.

———. *Die Oberstadt von Ḫattuša: Die Bauwerke II: Die Bastion des Sphinxtores und die Tempelviertel am Königs- und Löwentor*. Boğazköy-Hattusa: Ergebnisse der Ausgrabungen 23. Mainz: Zabern, 2001.

Niehr, Herbert. *Ba'alšamem: Studien zu Herkunft, Geschichte und Rezeptionsgeschichte eines phönizischen Gottes*. OLA 123; Leuven: Peeters, 2003.

———. "In Search of YHWH's Cult Statue in the First Temple." Pages 73–95 in *The Image and the Book: Iconic Cults, Aniconism, and the Rise of Book Religion in Israel and the Ancient Near East*. Edited by K. van der Toorn. CBET 21. Leuven: Peeters, 1997.

Nielsen, Kjeld. *Incense in Ancient Israel*. VTSup 38. Leiden: Brill, 1986.

Novotny, Jamie. "Temple Building in Assyria: Evidence from Royal Inscriptions." Pages 109–40 in *From the Foundations to the Crenellations: Essays on Temple Building in the Ancient Near East and Hebrew Bible*. Edited by M. J. Boda and J. Novotny. AOAT 366. Münster: Ugarit-Verlag, 2010.

Oates, David. "The Excavations at Tell al Rimah, 1964." *Iraq* 27 (1965): 62–80.

———. "The Excavations at Tell al Rimah, 1965." *Iraq* 28 (1966): 122–39.

———. "The Excavations at Tell al Rimah, 1967." *Iraq* 29 (1967): 70–96.

———. "The Excavations at Tell al Rimah, 1967." *Iraq* 29 (1967): 115–38.

del Olmo Lete, Gregorio. *Canaanite Religion: According to the Liturgical Texts of Ugarit*. Winona Lake, IN: Eisenbrauns, 2004.

Omnès, Roland. *Understanding Quantum Mechanics*. Princeton: Princeton University Press, 1999.

Oppenheim, A. Leo. *Ancient Mesopotamia: Portrait of a Dead Civilization*. 2nd ed. Chicago: University of Chicago, 1977.

———. "The Golden Garments of the Gods." *JNES* 8 (1949): 172–93.

Ornan, Tallay. "Idols and Symbols—Divine Representation in First Millennium Mesopotamian Art and Its Bearing on the Second Commandment." *Tel Aviv* 31 (2004): 90–121.

———. "In the Likeness of Man: Reflections on the Anthropocentric Perception of the Divine in Mesopotamian Art." Pages 93–151 in *What is a God? Anthropomorphic and Non-Anthropomorphic Aspects of Deity in Ancient Mesopotamia*. Edited by B. N. Porter. Transactions of the Casco Bay Assyriological Institute 2. Winona Lake, IN: Eisenbrauns, 2009.

———. "Mesopotamian Influence on West Semitic Inscribed Seals: A Preference for the Depiction of Mortals." Pages 52–73 in *Studies in the Iconography of Northwest Semitic Inscribed Seals: Proceedings of a Symposium Held in Fribourg on April 17–20, 1991*. Edited by B. Sass and Ch. Uehlinger. OBO 125. Fribourg: University Press, 1993.

———. *The Triumph of the Symbol: Pictoral Representation of Deities in Mesopotamia and the Biblical Image Ban*. OBO 213. Fribourg: Academic Press, 2005.

Osing, Jürgen, and Gloria Rosati. *Papiri geroglifici e ieratici da Tebtynis*. Florence: Istituto Papirologico, 1998.

Otto, Adelheid. "'Gotteshaus und Allerheiligstes in Syrien und Nordmesopotamien während des 2. Jts. v. Chr." Pages 355–84 in *Tempel im alten Orient: 7. Internationales Colloquium der Deutschen Orient-Gesellschaft 11.–13. Oktober 2009, München*. Edited by Kai Kaniuth, Anne Löhnert, Jared L. Miller, Adelheid Otto, Michael Roaf and Walther Sallaberger. CDOG 7; Wiesbaden: Harrassowitz, 2013.

Otto, Eberhard. *Das Ägyptische Mundöffnungsritual*. 2 volumes. Ägyptologische Abhandlungen 3. Wiesbaden: Harrassowitz, 1960.

Otto, Rudolf. *The Idea of The Holy*. Translated by J. Harvey. Oxford: Oxford University Press, 1958.

Ottosson, Magnus. *Temples and Cult Places in Palestine*. BOREAS 12. Uppsala: Acta Universitatis Upsaliensis, 1980.

Özgüç, Tahsin, and Nimet Özgüç. *Karahöyük Hafriyati Raporu 1947: Ausgrabungen in Karahöyük*. Ankara: Türk Tarih Kurumu Basımevi, 1949.

Pardee, Dennis. "A New Aramaic Inscription from Zincirli." *BASOR* 356 (2009): 51–71.

———. *Ritual and Cult at Ugarit*. SBLWAW 10. Atlanta: SBL, 2002.

———. *Les textes rituels*. Ras Shamra-Ougarit 12. Paris: Editions recherche sur les civilisations, 2000.

Parpola, Simo. *Assyrian Prophecies*. SAA 9. Helsinki: Helsinki University, 1997.

Parpola, Simo, and Kazuko Watanabe. *Neo-Assyrian Treaties and Loyalty Oaths*. Helsinki: Helsinki University Press, 1988.

Perroudon, Marie-Claire. "An Angry Goddess." *SAAB* 6 (1992): 41–43.

von Pfeil-Autenrieth, Christiane Gräfin. *Der Gotteslohn für die Pharaonen: Untersuchungen zu den Gegengaben in ägyptischen Tempeln der griechisch-römischen Epoche*. SRaT 6. Dettelbach: J. H. Röll, 2009.

Piankoff, Alexandre. *Le "Coeur" dans les textes égyptiens depuis l'Ancien jusqu'à la fin du Nouvel Empire*. Paris: Geuthner, 1930.

———. *The Litany of Re: Texts Translated with Commentary*. Egyptian Religious Texts and Representations 4. New York: Bollingen Foundation, 1964.

Pitard, Wayne T. "Temple Building in Northwest Semitic Literature of the Late Bronze and Iron Ages." Pages 91–108 in *From the Foundations to the Crenellations: Essays on*

*Temple Building in the Ancient Near East and Hebrew Bible.* Edited by M. J. Boda and J. Novotny. AOAT 366. Münster: Ugarit-Verlag, 2010.

Podella, Thomas. *Das Lichtkleid JHWHs: Untersuchungen zur Gestalthaftigkeit Gottes im Alten Testament und seiner altorientalischen Umwelt.* FAT 16. Tübingen: Mohr, 1996.

Pongratz-Leisten, Beate. "Divine Agency and Astralization of the Gods in Ancient Mesopotamia." Pages 137–87 in *Reconsidering the Concept of Revolutionary Monotheism.* Edited by Pongratz-Leisten. Winona Lake, IN: Eisenbrauns, 2011.

———. *Ina šulmi īrub: Die kulttopographische und ideologische Programmatik der* akītu-*Prozession in Babylonien und Assyrien im I. Jahrtausend v. Chr.* BaF 16. Mainz: von Zabern, 1994.

———. "Mental Map und Weltbild." Pages 261–80 in *Das biblische Weltbild und seine altorientalischen Kontexte.* Edited by B. Janowski and B. Ego. FAT 32. Tübingen: Mohr Siebeck, 2001.

———, ed. *Reconsidering the Concept of Revolutionary Monotheism.* Winona Lake, IN: Eisenbrauns, 2011.

———. "Sacred Places: Mesopotamia." Pages 253–55 in *Religions of the Ancient World: A Guide.* Edited by S. I. Johnston. Cambridge, MA: Harvard University Press, 2004.

Popko, Maciej. "Aniconische Götterdarstellungen in der altanatolischen Religion." Pages 319–27 in *Ritual and Sacrifice in the Ancient Near East: Proceedings of the International Conference Organized by the Katholieke Universiteit Leuven from the 17th to the 20th of April 1991.* Edited by J. Quaegebeur. OLA 55. Leuven: Peeters, 1993.

———. "Der hethitische Gott und seine Kultbilder." *JANER* 5 (2005): 79–87.

———. *Kultobjekte in der hethitischen Religion.* Warsaw: Wydawnictwa Uniwersytetu Warszawskiego, 1978.

———. *Religions of Asia Minor.* Warsaw: Academic Publications Dialog, 1995.

Porter, Barbara Nevling. "The Anxiety of Multiplicity: Concepts of the Divine in Ancient Assyria." Pages 211–72 in *One God or Many? Concepts of Divinity in the Ancient World.* Edited by Porter. Transactions of the Casco Bay Assyriological Institute 1. Casco Bay, ME: Casco Bay Assyriological Institute, 2000.

———. "Blessings from a Crown, Offerings to a Drum: Were there Non-Anthropomorphic Gods in Ancient Mesopotamia?" Pages 153–94 in *What Is a God? Anthropomorphic and Non-Anthropomorphic Aspects of Deity in Ancient Mesopotamia.* Edited by B. N. Porter. Transactions of the Casco Bay Assyriological Institute 2. Winona Lake, IN: Eisenbrauns, 2009.

———. *Images, Power, and Politics: Figurative Aspects of Esarhaddon's Babylonian Policy.* Philadelphia: American Philosophical Society, 1993.

———. "Introduction." Pages 1–13 in *What is a God? Anthropomorphic and Non-Anthropomorphic Aspects of Deity in Ancient Mesopotamia.* Edited by B. N. Porter. Transactions of the Casco Bay Assyriological Institute 2. Winona Lake, IN: Eisenbrauns, 2009.

———. "Ishtar of Nineveh and Her Collaborator, Ishtar of Arbela, in the Reign of Assurbanipal." *Iraq* 66 (2004): 41–44.

———, ed. *One God or Many? Concepts of Divinity in the Ancient World.* Transactions of the Casco Bay Assyriological Institute 1. Casco Bay, ME: Casco Bay Assyriological Institute, 2000.

———, ed. *What is a God? Anthropomorphic and Non-Anthropomorphic Aspects of Deity in Ancient Mesopotamia.* Transactions of the Casco Bay Assyriological Institute 2. Winona Lake, IN: Eisenbrauns, 2009.

Postgate, Carolyn, David Oates and Joan Oates. *The Excavations at Tell al Rimah: The Pottery.* Iraq Archaeological Reports 4. Warminster, England: Aris & Phillips, 1997.

Postgate, J. Nicholas. *Early Mesopotamia: Society and Economy at the Dawn of History.* London: Routledge, 1992.

Propp, William H. C. *Exodus 19–40.* AB 2A. New York: Doubleday, 2006.

Proshansky, Harold M. et al., eds. *Environmental Psychology: People and Their Physical Settings.* 2nd ed. New York: Holt, Rinehart and Winston, 1976.

Quack, Joachim Friedrich. "Bilder vom Mundöffnungsritual – Mundöffnung an Bildern." Pages 18–28 in *Bild und Ritual: Visuelle Kulturen in historischer Perspektive.* Edited by C. Ambos, P. Rösch, and S. Weinfurter. Darmstadt: Wissenschaftliche Buchgesellschaft, 2010.

———. "Fragmente des Mundöffnungsrituals aus Tebtynis." Pages 69–150 in *The Carlsberg Papyri 7: Hieratic Texts from the Collection.* Edited by K. Ryholt. Copenhagen: Museum Tusculanum Press, 2006."

———. "Opfermahl und Feindvernichtung im Altägyptischen Ritual." *Mitteilungen der Berliner Gesellschaft für Anthropologie, Ethnologie und Urgeschichte* 27 (2006): 67–80.

———. "Ein Prätext und seine Realisierungen: Facetten des ägyptischen Mundöffnungsrituals." Pages 165–85 in *Text und Ritual: Kulturwissenschaftliche Essays und Analysen von Sesostris bis Dada.* Edited by B. Dücker and H. Roeder. Hermeia 8. Heidelberg: Synchron, 2005.

———. "To clothe or to wipe? On the semantics of the verb *nms.*" Pages 379–86 in *Lexical Semantics in Ancient Egyptian.* Edited by E. Grosman, S. Polis, and J. Winand. Lingua Aegyptia Studia Monographica 9. Hamburg: Lingua Aegyptia, 2012.

Quirke, Stephen. *Ancient Egyptian Religion.* New York: Dover, 1992.

———. *Egyptian Literature 1800 BC: Questions and Readings.* London: Golden House, 2004.

Rapoport, Amos. *The Meaning of the Built Environment: A Nonverbal Communication Approach.* London: Sage Publications, 1982.

Reade, J. E. "Shikaft-i Gulgul: Its Date and Symbolism." *Iranica Antiqua* 12 (1977): 33–44.

Refai, Hosam. "Notes on the Function of the Great Hypostyle Hall in the Egyptian Temple: A Theban Approach." Pages 393–99 in *Egyptology at the Dawn of the Twenty-First Century: Proceedings of the Eighth International Congress of Egyptology, Cairo 2000,* Vol. 1: *Architecture.* Edited by Z. Hawass. Cairo: American University in Cairo Press, 2003.

———. *Untersuchungen zum Bildprogramm der großen Säulen in den thebanischen Tempeln des Neuen Reiches.* BzÄ 18. Vienna: Afro-Pub, 2000.

Reiner, Erica. *Astral Magic in Babylonia.* Transactions of the American Philosophical Society 85. Philadelphia: American Philosophical Society, 1995.

———. *Šurpu: A Collection of Sumerian and Akkadian Incantations.* AfO Beiheft 11. Graz: E. Weidner, 1958.

Renger, J. "Kultbild A. Philologisch (in Mesopotamien)." *RlA* 6 (1980–1983): 307–14.

Ritner, Robert K. "Magic." Pages 191–8 in *The Ancient Gods Speak: A Guide to Egyptian Religion.* Edited by D. Redford. Oxford: Oxford University Press, 2002.

———. *The Mechanics of Ancient Egyptian Magical Practice.* SAOC 54. Chicago: University of Chicago, 1993.

Roaf, Michael. "Palaces and Temples in Ancient Mesopotamia." Pages 423–41 in *CANE*.

Robins, Gay. "Cult Statues in Ancient Egypt." Pages 1–12 in *Cult Image and Divine Representation in the Ancient Near East.* Edited by N. H. Walls. ASOR Books Series 10. Boston: ASOR, 2005.

Rochberg, Francesca. *The Heavenly Writing: Divination: Divination, Horoscopy, and Astronomy in Mesopotamian Culture.* Cambridge: Cambridge University Press, 2004.

———. "'The Stars Their Likenesses': Perspectives on the Relation Between Celestial Bodies and Gods in Ancient Mesopotamia." Pages 41–91 *What Is a God? Anthropomorphic and Non-Anthropomorphic Aspects of Deity in Ancient Mesopotamia.* Edited by B. N. Porter. Transactions of the Casco Bay Assyriological Institute 2. Winona Lake, IN: Eisenbrauns, 2009.

Roeder, Günther. *Naos: Catalogue Général du Musée du Caire.* Catalogue général des antiquités égyptiennes du Musée du Caire 75. Wiesbaden: Breitkopf & Härtel, 1914.

Roeder, H. "'Mit dem Auge sehen': Ägyptisches und Ägyptologisches zum 'Auge des Horus.'" *Göttinger Miszellen* 138 (1994): 37–69.

Rofé, Alexander. *The Belief in Angels in the Bible and Early Israel.* Jerusalem: Makor, 1979 (Hebrew).

Röllig, W. "Bethel." Pages 173–75 in *DDD*.

de Roos, Johan. "Hittite Prayers." Pages 1997–2005 in *CANE*.

Roth, Ann Macy. "Buried Pyramids and Layered Thoughts: The Organisation of Multiple Approaches in Egyptian Religion." Pages 991–1003 in *Proceedings of the Seventh International Congress of Egyptologists.* Edited by C. J. Eyre. OLA 82. Leuven: Peeters, 1998.

———. "Fingers, Stars, and the 'Opening of the Mouth': The Nature and Function of the *nrwj*-Blades." *JEA* 79 (1993): 57–79.

———. "Opening of the Mouth." Pages 605–9 in *The Oxford Encyclopedia of Ancient Egypt*, vol. 2. Edited by D. Redford. Oxford: Oxford University Press, 2001.

———. "The *pss-kf* and the 'Opening of the Mouth' Ceremony: A Ritual of Birth and Rebirth," *JEA* 78 (1992), 113–47.

———. "The Representation of the Divine in Ancient Egypt." Pages 24–37 in *Text, Artifact, and Image: Revealing Ancient Israelite Religion.* BJS 346; Providence: Brown Judaic Studies, 2006.

Rothöhler, Benedikt, "Die vierzehn Kas des Re." Pages 183–206 in *Mythos & Ritual: Festschrift für Jan Assmann zum 70. Geburtstag.* Edited by B. Rothöler and A. Manisali. *Religionswissenschaft: Forschung und Wissenschaft* 5. Münster: LIT, 2008.

Routledge, Carolyn. "Parallelism in Popular and Official Religion in Ancient Egypt." Pages 223–38 in *Text, Artifact, and Image: Revealing Ancient Israelite Religion.* Edited by G. M. Beckman and T. J. Lewis. BJS 346. Providence: Brown Judaic Studies, 2006.

Roux, Georges. *Ancient Iraq.* Middlesex, UK: Penguin, 1964.

Rudnitzky, Günter. *Die Aussage über "Das Auge des Horus": Eine Altägyptische Art Geistiger Äusserung nach dem Zeugnis des alten Reiches.* Analecta Aegyptiaca 5. Copenhagen: Ejnar Munksgaard, 1956.

Russell, John Malcolm. *Sennacherib's Palace without Rival at Nineveh.* Chicago: University of Chicago Press, 1991.

Sallaberger, Walther. "Pantheon A. I. In Mesopotamien." *RlA* 10 (2004): 294–308.

Salonen, Armas. *Die Möbel des alten Mesopotamien nach sumerisch-akkadischen Quellen: Eine lexikalische und kulturgeschichtliche Untersuchung.* Helsinki: Suomalainen Tiedeakatemia, 1963.

Sanmartín, Joaquín. "Das Handwerk in Ugarit: Eine lexikalische Studie." *SEL* 12 (1995): 169–90.

Sasson, Jack M., ed. *Civilizations of the Ancient Near East.* 2 volumes. Peabody, MA: Hendrickson, 2000.

Schachner, Andreas. *Hattuscha: Auf der Suche nach dem sagenhaften Großreich der Hethiter.* Munich: Beck, 2011.

Schäfer, Heinrich. *Von ägyptischer Kunst: Eine Grundlage.* 4th ed. Wiesbaden: Harrassowitz, 1963.

Schaudig, Hanspeter. *Die Inschriften Nabonids von Babylon und Kyros des Grossen samt den in ihrem Umfeld enstandenen Tendenzschriften: Textausgabe und Grammatik.* AOAT 256. Münster: Ugarit-Verlag, 2001.

———. "The Restoration of Temples in the Neo- and Late-Babylonian Periods: A Royal Prerogative as the Setting for Political Argument." Pages 141–64 in *From the Foundations to the Crenellations: Essays on Temple Building in the Ancient Near East and Hebrew Bible.* Edited by M. J. Boda and J. Novotny. AOAT 366. Münster: Ugarit-Verlag, 2010.

Scheer, Tanja S. *Die Gottheit und ihr Bild: Untersuchungen zur Funktion griechischer Kultbilder in Religion und Politik.* Zetemata 105. München: Beck, 2000.

Schirmer, Wulf. "Stadt, Palast, Tempel: Charakteristika hethitischer Architektur im 2. und 1. Jahrtausend v. Chr." Pages 204–17 in *Die Hethiter und ihr Reich: Das Volk der tausend Götter: Kunst- und Ausstellungshalle der Bundesrepublik Deutschland (Bonn 2002).* Edited by T. Özgüç. Darmstadt: Wiss. Buchges., 2002.

Schlereth, Thomas J., ed. *Material Culture: A Research Guide.* Lawrence, KS: University Press of Kansas, 1985.

Schlüter, Arnulf. *Sakrale Architektur im Flachbild: Zum Realitätsbezug von Tempeldarstellungen.* ÄAT 78. Wiesbaden: Harrassowitz, 2009.

Schmid, Hansjörg. *Der Tempelturm Etemenanki in Babylon.* BaF 17. Mainz: von Zabern, 1995.

Schoske, Sylvia. "Das Erschlagen der Feinde: Ikonographie und Stilistik der Feindvernichtung im alten Ägypten." 2 volumes. Ph.D. diss., Heidelberg University, 1982.

Schröder, Stefanie. *Millionenjahrhaus: Zur Konzeption des Raumes der Ewigkeit im konstellativen Königtum in Sprache, Architektur und Theologie.* Wiesbaden: Harrassowitz, 2010.

Schroer, Silvia. *In Israel gab es Bilder: Nachrichten von darstellender Kunst im Alten Testament.* OBO 74. Fribourg: University Press, 1987.

Schwabe, Calvin W. "Bull Semen and Muscle ATP: Some Evidence of the Dawn of Medical Science in Ancient Egypt." *Canadian Journal of Veterinary Research* 50 (1986): 145–53.

Schwabe, Calvin W., and Andrew Gordon. *"Live Flesh": Rudiments of Muscle Physiology in Ancient Egypt.* Working Paper Series 54. Davis: Agricultural History Center, University of California, 1989.

Schwaller de Lubicz, R. A. *The Temples of Karnak: A Contribution to the Study of Pharaonic Thought.* London: Thames & Hudson, 1999.

Schweitzer, Ursula. *Das Wesen des Ka im Diesseits und Jenseits der alten Ägypter.* Glückstadt: Augustin, 1965.

Schwemer, Daniel. "Das alttestamentliche Doppelritual 'lwt wšlmym im Horizont der hurritischen Opfertermini *ambašši* und *keldi*." *SCCNH* 7 (1995): 81–116.

———. "Fremde Götter in Hatti: Die hethitische Religion im Spannungsfeld von Synkretismus und Abgrenzung." Pages 137–58 in *Ḫattuša – Boğazköy - Das Hethiterreich im Spannungsfeld des Alten Orients. 6. Internationales Colloquium der Deutschen Orient-Gesellschaft 22.–24. März 2006, Würzburg.* Edited by G. Wilhelm. Wiesbaden: Harrassowitz, 2008.

———. "The Storm-Gods of the Ancient Near East: Summary, Synthesis, Recent Studies: Part I." *JANER* 7 (2007): 121–68.

———. "The Storm-Gods of the Ancient Near East: Summary, Synthesis, Recent Studies: Part II." *JANER* 8 (2008): 1–44.

———. *Die Wettergottgestalten Mesopotamiens und Nordsyriens im Zeitalter der Keilschriftkulturen.* Wiesbaden: Harrassowitz, 2001.

Seeber, Christine. *Untersuchungen zur Darstellung des Totengerichts im Alten Ägypten.* MÄS 35. Munich: Deutscher Kunstverlag, 1976.

Seeher, Jürgen. "Chronology in Hattusa: New Approaches to an Old Problem." Pages 197–214 in *Strukturierung & Datierung in der hethitischen Archäologie:Voraussetzungen – Probleme – Neue Ansätze: Internationaler Workshop Istanbul, 16.–27. November 2004.* Edited by D.P. Mielke, U.-D. Schoop and J. Seeher. BYZAS 4. Istanbul: Ege Yayınları, 2006.

———. "Hattusa - Tuthalija-Stadt? Argumente für eine Revision der Chronologie der hethitischen Hauptstadt." Pages 131–46 in *The Life and Times of Hattusili III and Tuthaliya IV: Proceedings of a Symposium Held in Honour of J. de Roos, 12–13 December 2003, Leiden.* Edited by Th. P. J. van den Hout. Leiden: NINO, 2006.

———. *Hattuscha-Führer: Ein Tag in der hethitischen Hauptstadt.* 3rd ed. Istanbul: Ege Yayınları, 2006.

———. *Die Lehmziegel-Stadtmauer von Hattusa: Bericht über eine Rekonstruktion.* Istanbul: Ege Yayınları, 2007.

———. "Die Techniken der Steinbearbeitung in der hethitischen Architektur des 2. Jahrtausends v. Chr." Pages 119–156 in *Bautechnik im antiken und vorantiken Kleinasien. Internationale Konferenz vom 13.–16. Juni 2007, DAI Istanbul.* Edited by M. Bachmann. BYZAS 9. Istanbul: Ege Yayınları, 2009.

Seidel, Matthias. "Götterstäbe." *LÄ* 2 (1977): 711–13.

Seidl, Ursula. "Babylonische und assyrische Kultbilder in den Massenmedien des 1. Jahrtausends v. Chr." Pages 89–114 in *Images as Media: Sources for the Cultural History of the Near East and the Eastern Mediterranean (1ˢᵗ millennium BCE).* Edited by Ch. Uehlinger. Fribourg: University Press, 2000.

———. *Die Babylonischen Kudurru-Reliefs: Symbole Mesopotamischer Gottheiten.* OBO 87. Fribourg: University Press, 1989.

———. "Bildschmuck an mesopotamischen Tempeln des 2. Jahrtausends v. Chr.," in *Tempel im alten Orient: 7. Internationales Colloquium der Deutschen Orient-Gesellschaft 11.–13. Oktober 2009, München.* Edited by Kai Kaniuth, Anne Löhnert, Jared L.

Miller, Adelheid Otto, Michael Roaf and Walther Sallaberger. CDOG 7. Wiesbaden: Harrassowitz, 2013.

———. "Göttersymbole und –attribute. A. Archäologisch. I. Mesopotamian." *RlA* 3 (1969): 484–90.

Selz, Gebhard J. "'The Holy Drum, the Spear, and the Harp': Toward an Understanding of the Problems of Deification in Third Millennium Mesopotamia." Pages 167–209 in *Sumerian Gods and Their Representations*. Edited by I. J. Finkel and M. J. Geller. Groningen: Styx, 1997.

Shafer, Byron E., ed. *Temples of Ancient Egypt*. London: Taurus, 1997.

———. "Temples, Priests, and Rituals: An Overview." Pages 1–30 in *Temples of Ancient Egypt*. Edited by B. E. Shafer. London: Taurus, 1997.

Shaw, Ian, ed. *The Oxford History of Ancient Egypt*. Oxford: Oxford University Press, 2000.

Silverman, David P. "Divinity and Deities in Ancient Egypt." Pages 7–87 in *Religion in Ancient Egypt: Gods, Myths, and Personal Practice*. Edited by B. E. Shafer. Ithaca: Cornell University Press, 1991.

Simpson, William Kelly. "Egyptian Sculpture and Two-Dimensional Representation as Propaganda." *JEA* 68 (1982): 266–71.

Singer, Itamar. "A City of Many Temples: Ḫattuša, Capital of the Hittites." Pages 32–44 in *Sacred Space: Shrine, City, Land: Proceedings of the International Conference in Memory of Joshua Prawer*. Edited by B. Z. Kedar and R. J. Z. Werblowsky. Basingstoke: Macmillan, 1998.

———. *Hittite Prayers*. SBLWAW 11. Atlanta: Scholars Press, 2002.

———. "'The Thousand Gods of Hatti': The Limits of an Expanding Pantheon." Pages 81–102 in *Concepts of the Other in Near Eastern Religions*. Edited by I. Alon, I. Gruenwald and I. Singer. Israel Oriental Studies 14. Leiden: Brill, 1994.

Slanski, Kathryn A. *The Babylonian Entitlement narûs (kudurrus): A Study in their Form and Function* (ASOR Books 9. Boston: ASOR, 2003.

———. "Representation of the Divine on the Babylonian Entitlement Monuments (*kudurrus*): Part I: Divine Symbols." *AfO* 50 (2003): 308–23.

Smith, Mark S. "The Death of Dying and Rising Gods in the Biblical World," *SJOT* 12 (1998): 257–313.

———. "Divine Form and Size in Ugaritic and Israelite Religion." *ZAW* 100 (1988): 424–7.

———. *The Origins of Biblical Monotheism: Israel's Polytheistic Background and the Ugaritic Texts*. Oxford: Oxford University Press, 2001.

———. "The Problem of the God and His Manifestations: The Case of the Baals at Ugarit." Paper presented at the international SBL conference, London, 2011.

———. "The Problem of the God and His Manifestations: The Case of the Baals at Ugarit, with Implications for Yahweh of Various Locales." Pages 205–50 in *Die Stadt im Zwölfprophetenbuch*. Edited by A. Schart and J. Krispenz. BZAW 428. Berlin: de Gruyter, 2012.

———. "The Structure of Divinity at Ugarit and Israel: The Case of Anthropomorphic Deities versus Monstrous Divinities." Pages 38–63 in *Text, Artifact, and Image: Revealing Ancient Israelite Religion*. Edited by G. M. Beckman and T. J. Lewis. BJS 346. Providence, RI: Brown Judaic Studies, 2006.

———. *The Ugaritic Baal Cycle*, Vol. 1: *Introduction with Text, Translation & Commentary of KTU I.I–I.2*. VTSupp 53. Leiden: Brill, 1994.

Smith, Mark S., and Wayne T. Pitard. *The Ugaritic Baal Cycle,* Vol. 2: *Introduction with Text, Translation and Commentary of KTU/CAT 1.3–1.4.* VTSupp 114; Leiden: Brill, 2009.

Snape, Steven. *Egyptian Temples.* Buckinghamshire, UK: Shire, 1996.

von Soden, Wolfram. *The Ancient Orient: An Introduction to the Study of the Ancient Near East.* Translated by D. Schley. Grand Rapids, MI: Eerdmans, 1994.

Sommer, Benjamin D. *The Bodies of God and the World of Ancient Israel.* Cambridge: Cambridge University Press, 2009.

Sonik, Karen. "Daimon-Haunted Universe: Conceptions of the Supernatural in Mesopotamia." Ph.D. diss., University of Pennsylvania, 2010.

Sørensen, Jørgen Podemann. "Redundans og abstraktion i det ægyptiske daglige tempelritual." *Chaos* 1 (1982): 49–60.

Soskice, Janet. *Metaphor and Religious Language.* Oxford: Clarendon, 1985.

Spencer, Patricia. *The Egyptian Temple: A Lexicographical Study.* London: Kegan Paul, 1984.

Spycket, A. "Lamma/Lamassu. B. Archäologisch." *RlA* 6 (1980–1983): 453–55.

Staal, Frits. "The Meaninglessness of Ritual." *Numen* 26 (1979): 2–22

———. *Rules Without Meaning: Ritual, Mantras and the Human Sciences.* New York: Peter Lang, 1989.

Staehelin, Elisabeth. *Von der Farbigkeit Ägyptens.* Leipzig: University of Leipzig, 2000.

Steiner, Gerd. "Gott. D. Nach hethitischen Texten." *RlA* 3 (1957): 547–75.

Steinkeller, Piotr. "Studies in Third Millennium Paleography, 2: Sign Šen and Alal: Addendum." *OrAnt* 23 (1984): 39–41.

Stockfisch, Dagmar. "Bemerkungen zur sog. 'libyschen Familie.'" Pages 315–25 in *Wege öffnen: Festschrift für Rolf Gundlach.* Edited by M. Schade-Busch. ÄAT 35. Wiesbaden: Harrassowitz, 1996.

Stone, Elizabeth. "Ziggurat." Pages 390–91 in *The Oxford Encyclopedia of Archaeology in the Near East,* vol. 5. Edited by E. Meyers. Oxford: Oxford University Press, 1997.

Strauß, Rita. *Reinigungsrituale aus Kizzuwatna: Ein Beitrag zur Erforschung hethitischer Ritualtradition und Kulturgeschichte.* Berlin: de Gruyter, 2005.

Sullivan, Elaine A. "Visualizing the size and movement of the portable festival barks at Karnak Temple." *BMSAES* 19 (2012): 1–37.

Tacke, Nikolaus. "Das Opferritual des ägyptischen Neuen Reiches." Pages 27–36 in *Rituale in der Vorgeschichte, Antike und Gegenwart; Studien zur vorderasiatichen, prähistorischen und klassischen Archäologie, Ägyptologie, alten Geschichte, Theologie und Religionswissenschaft; interdisziplinäre Tagung vom 1. – 2. Februar 2002 an der Freien Universität Berlin; Internationale Archäologie; Arbeitsgemeinschaft, Symposium, Tagung, Kongress 4.* Edited by C. Metzner-Nebelsick. Rahden: Leidorf, 2003.

Tadmor, Hayim. *The Inscriptions of Tiglath-Pileser III, King of Assyria: Critical Edition, with Introductions, Translationss and Commentary.* Jerusalem: The Israel Academy of Sciences and Humanities, 1994.

Taracha, Piotr. "Bull-Leaping on a Hittite Vase: New Light on Anatolian and Minoan Religion." *Archeologia* 53 (2002): 7–20.

———. *Religions of Second Millennium Anatolia.* DBH 27. Wiesbaden: Harrassowitz, 2009.

de Tarragon, Jean-Michel. *Le Culte a Ugarit: D'apres les textes de la pratique en cuneiformes alphabetiques.* CRB 19. Paris: Gabalda, 1980.

Teeter, Emily. *The Presentation of Maat: Ritual and Legitimacy in Ancient Egypt*. SAOC 57. Chicago: The Oriental Institute of the University of Chicago, 1997.

———. *Religion and Ritual in Ancient Egypt*. Cambridge: Cambridge University Press, 2011.

———. "Temple Cults." Pages 310–24 in *The Egyptian World*. Edited by T. A. H. Wilkinson. London: Routledge, 2007.

*The Temple of Khonsu*, Vol. 1: *Scenes of King Herihor in the Court*. OIP 100. Chicago: University of Chicago, 1979.

Thiersch, Hermann. *Ependytes und Ephod: Gottesbild und Priesterkleid im alten Vorderasien*. Geisteswissenschaftlichen Forschungen 8. Stuttgart: Kohlhammer, 1936.

Thompson, Stephen E. "Cults." Pages 61–71 in *The Ancient Gods Speak: A Guide to Egyptian Religion*. Edited by D. Redford. Oxford: Oxford University Press, 2002.

Thureau-Dangin, F. *Rituels Accadiens*. Paris: Leroux, 1921.

Tobin, Vincent Arieh. "Myths." Pages 239–46 in *The Ancient Gods Speak: A Guide to Egyptian Religion*. Edited by D. Redford. Oxford: Oxford University Press, 2002.

———. *Theological Principles of Egyptian Religion*. New York: Lang, 1989.

Toombs, Lawrence E. "The Stratification of Tel Balâtah (Shechem)." *BASOR* 223 (1976): 57–59.

van der Toorn, Karel. "The Iconic Book: Analogies between the Babylonian Cult of Images and the Veneration of the Torah." Pages 229–48 in *The Image and the Book: Iconic Cults, Aniconism, and the Rise of Book Religion in Israel and the Ancient Near East*. Edited by van der Toorn. Leuven: Peeters, 1997.

———. "Sin, Pollution, and Purity: Mesopotamia," in *Religions of the Ancient World: A Guide*. Edited by S. I. Johnston. Cambridge, MA: Belknap Press of Harvard University Press, 2004.

———. "Theology, Priests, and Worship in Canaan and Ancient Israel." Pages 2043–58 in *CANE*.

———. "Worshipping Stones: On the Deification of Cult Symbols," *JNSL* 23 (1997): 1–14.

Traunecker, Claude. *La chapelle d'Achôris a Karnak II: Texte*. Paris: ADPF, 1981.

———. *Les Dieux de l'Égypte*. Paris: University of France Press, 1992.

———. *The Gods of Egypt*. Translated by D. Lorton. Ithaca, NY: Cornell University Press, 2001.

Trémouille, Marie-Claude. *ᵈHebat: une divinité syro-anatolienne*. Eothen 7. Florence: Logisma, 1997.

———. "La religion des Hourrites: état actuel de nos connaissances." *SCCNH* 10 (1999): 277–91.

Turner, Victor W. *Dramas, Fields and Metaphors: Symbolic Action in Human Society*. Ithaca, NY: Cornell University Press, 1974.

———. *Forest of Symbols*. Ithaca, NY: Cornell University Press, 1967.

Uehlinger, Christoph. "Anthropomorphic Cult Statuary in Iron Age Palestine and the Search for Yahweh's Cult Statue." Pages 97–155 in *The Image and the Book: Iconic Cults, Aniconism, and the Rise of Book Religion in Israel and the Ancient Near East*. Edited by K. van der Toorn. CBET 21. Leuven: Peeters, 1997.

———. "Hanun von Gaza und seine Gottheiten auf Orthostatenreliefs Tiglatpilesers III." Pages 94–127 in *Kein Land für sich allein: Studien zum Kulturkontakt in Kanaan, Israel/Palästina und Ebirnâri für Manfred Weippert zum 65. Geburtstag*. Edited by U. Hübner and E.A. Knauf. OBO 186. Freiburg: University Press, 2002.

———. "Israelite Aniconism in Context." *Bib* 77 (1996): 540–49.

Ullmann, Martina. *König für die Ewigkeit – Die Häuser der Millionen von Jahren: Eine Untersuchung zu Königskult und Tempeltypologie in Ägypten.* ÄAT 51. Wiesbaden: Harrassowitz, 2002.

Van den Mieroop, Marc. *A History of the Ancient Near East, ca. 3000–323 BC.* Malden, MA: Blackwell, 2004.

Vandier, Jacques. "Un don des amis du Louvre au départment des antiquités égytiennes." *La revue du Louvre et des musées de France* 19 (1969): 49–54.

Vanstiphout, Herman. "Die Geschöpfe des Prometheus: Or How and Why Did the Sumerians Create their Gods?" Pages 15–40 in *What Is a God? Anthropomorphic and Non-Anthropomorphic Aspects of Deity in Ancient Mesopotamia.* Edited by B. N. Porter. Transactions of the Casco Bay Assyriological Institute 2. Winona Lake, IN: Eisenbrauns, 2009.

te Velde, Herman. "Relations and Conflicts Between Egyptian Gods, particularly in the Divine Ennead of Heliopolis." Pages 239–57 in *Struggles of Gods: Papers of the Groningen Work Group for the Study of the History of Religions.* Edited by H. G. Kippenberg. Berlin: de Gruyter, 1984.

———. "Theology, Priests and Worship in Ancient Egypt." Pages 1731–49 in *CANE.*

Verbovsek, Alexandra. *"Als Gunsterweis des Königs in den Tempel gegeben...": Private Tempelstatuen des Alten und Mittleren Reiches.* ÄAT 63. Wiesbaden: Harrassowitz, 2004.

Vernant, Jean-Pierre. *Mortals and Immortals: Collected Essays.* Edited by Froma I. Zeitlin. Princeton: Princeton University Press, 1991.

Versnel, Henk S. "Thrice One: Three Greek Experiments in Oneness." Pages 79–164 in *One God or Many? Concepts of Divinity in the Ancient World.* Edited by B. N. Porter. Transactions of the Casco Bay Assyriological Institute 2. Maine: Casco Bay Assyriological Institute, 2000.

Virolleaud, Charles. *Le Palais royal d'Ugarit, publié sous la direction de Claude F.-A. Schaeffer.* Mission de Ras Shamra 7. Paris: Imprimerie nationale, 1957.

Vita, Juan-Pablo. "The Society of Ugarit." Pages 455–98 in *Handbook of Ugaritic Studies.* Edited by W.G.E. Watson and N. Wyatt. HdO 1/39; Leiden: Brill, 1999.

Waerzeggers, Caroline. "The Babylonian Priesthood in the Long Sixth Century BC." *Bulletin of the Institute of Classical Studies* 54 (2011): 59–70.

———. "On the Initiation of Babylonian Priests." *Zeitschrift für altorientalische und biblische Rechtsgeschichte* 14 (2008): 1–38

Waghorne, Joanna Punzo. "The Divine Image in Contemporary South India: The Renaissance of a Once Maligned Tradition." Pages 211–43 in *Born in Heaven, Made on Earth: The Making of the Cult Image in the Ancient Near East.* Edited by M. B. Dick. Winona Lake, IN: Eisenbrauns, 1999.

Waghorne, Joanna Punzo, and Norman Cutler, eds. *Gods of Flesh/Gods of Stone: The Embodiment of Divinity in India.* New York: Columbia University Press, 1985.

Wagner, Andreas. *Gottes Körper: Zur alttestamentlichen Vorstellung der Menschengestaltigkeit Gottes.* Gütersloh: Gütersloher Verlaghaus, 2010.

Walker, Christopher, and Michael B. Dick. "The Induction of the Cult Image in Ancient Mesopotamia: The Mesopotamian *mīs pî* Ritual." Pages 55–121 in *Born in Heav-*

*en, Made on Earth: The Making of the Cult Image in the Ancient Near East.* Edited by M. B. Dick. Winona Lake, IN: Eisenbrauns, 1999.

——. *The Induction of the Cult Image in Ancient Mesopotamia: The Mesopotamian* mīs pî *Ritual.* SAALT 1. Helsinki: University of Helsinki, 2001.

Walls, Neal H., ed. *Cult Image and Divine Representation in the Ancient Near East.* ASOR Book Series 10. Boston: ASOR, 2005.

Wasilewska, Ewa. "Sacred Space in the Ancient Near East." *Religion Compass* 3 (2009): 263–70.

Watanabe, Chikako E. *Animal Symbolism in Mesopotamia: A Contextual Approach.* Wiener Offene Orientalistik 1. Vienna: University of Vienna, 2002.

Watanabe, Kazuko. "Seals of Neo-Assyrian Officials." Pages 313–66 in *Priests and Officials in the Ancient Near East: Papers of the Second Colloquium on the Ancient Near East—The City and Its Life, Held at the Middle Eastern Culture Center in Japan (Mitaka, Tokyo), March 22–24, 1996.* Edited by Watanabe. Heidelberg: Winter, 1999.

Watkins, Calvert. *How to Kill a Dragon: Aspects of Indo-European Poetics.* Oxford: Oxford University Press, 1995.

Wegner, Ilse. *Gestalt und Kult der Ištar-Šawuška in Kleinasien.* AOAT 36. Neukirchen-Vluyn: Neukirchener Verlag, 1981.

von Weiher, Egbert. *Spätbabylonische Texte aus Uruk* II. ADFU 10. Berlin: Mann, 1983.

Werner, Peter. *Die Entwicklung der Sakralarchitektur in Nordsyrien und Südostkleinasien vom Neolithikum bis in das 1. Jt. v. Chr.* Munich: Profil, 1994.

Westenholz, Joan Goodnick. *Cuneiform Inscriptions in the Collection of the Bible Lands Museum Jerusalem: The Emar Tablets.* Cuneiform Monographs 13. Groningen: Styx, 2000.

Wiggermann, F. A. M. "Lamaštu Daugher of Anu: A Profile." Pages 217–52 in *Birth in Babylonia and the Bible: Its Mediterranean Setting.* Edited by M. Stol. Cuneiform Monographs 14. Groningen: Styx, 2000.

——. *Mesopotamian Protective Spirits: The Ritual Texts.* Cuneiform Monographs 1. Leiden: Brill, 1992.

——. "Mischwesen A. Philologisch. Mesopotamien." *RlA* 8 (1994): 222–46.

——. "Pazuzu." *RlA* 10 (2004): 372–81.

——. "Scenes from the Shadow Side." Pages 207–30 in *Mesopotamian Poetic Language: Sumerian and Akkadian.* Edited by M. E. Vogelzang and H. L. J. Vanstiphout. Cuneiform Monographs. Groningen: Styx, 1996.

——. "The Staff of Ninšubura: Studies in Babylonian Demonology, II." *JEOL* 29 (1985–1986): 3–34.

——. "Theologies, Priests and Worship in Ancient Mesopotamia." Pages 1857–70 in *CANE.*

Wightman, Gregory J. *Sacred Spaces: Religious Architecture in the Ancient World.* Leuven: Peeters, 2007.

Wilcke, Claus. "Zum Geschichtsbewusstsein im Alten Mesopotamien." Pages 31–52 in *Archäologie und Geschichtsbewusstsein.* Edited by H. Müller-Karpe. Munich: Beck, 1982.

Wildung, Dietrich. "Götterstandarte." *LÄ* 2 (1977): 713–14.

——. "Naos." *LÄ* 4 (1982): 341–42.

Wilhelm, Gernot. "'Gleichsetzungstheologie', 'Synkretismus' und 'Gottesspaltungen' in Polytheismus Anatoliens." Pages 53–70 in *Polytheismus und Monotheismus in der Religionen der Vorderen Orients*. Edited by M. Krebernik and J. van Ooorschot. AOAT 298. Münster: Ugarit-Verlag, 2002.

———. *Grundzüge der Geschichte und Kultur der Hurriter*. Darmstadt: Wissenschaftliche Buchgesellschaft, 1982.

———. "Reinheit und Heiligkeit: Zur Vorstellungswelt altanatolischer Ritualistik." Pages 197–217 in *Levitikus als Buch*. Edited by H.-J. Fabry & H.-W. Jüngling. BBB 119. Berlin: Philo, 1999.

Wilkinson, Richard H. *The Complete Temples of Ancient Egypt*. Cairo: The American University in Cairo Press, 2005.

———. *Symbol and Magic in Egyptian Art*. London: Thames & Hudson, 1999.

———. "Symbolism." Pages 239–47 in *The Ancient Gods Speak: A Guide to Egyptian Religion*. Edited by D. Redford. Oxford: Oxford University Press, 2002.

Wilmut, Ian, and Roger Highfield. *After Dolly: The Promise and Perils of Cloning*. New York: W. W. Norton, 2007.

Wilson, Brian. *Systems: Concepts, Methodologies, and Applications*. Chichester: Wiley, 1984.

Wilson, E. Jan. *"Holiness" and "Purity" in Mesopotamia*. AOAT 237. Neukirchen-Vluyn: Neukirchener Verlag, 1995.

Wilson, John A. "The Nature of the Universe." Pages 39–70 in *The Intellectual Adventure of Ancient Man: An Essay of Speculative Thought in the Ancient Near East*. Edited by H. A. Frankfort, J. A. Wilson, T. Jacobsen, and W. A. Irvin. Chicago: Chicago University Press, 1946.

Winer, Jerome A., James William Anderson, and Elizabeth A. Danze, eds. *The Annual of Psychoanalysis, Vol. 33: Psychoanalysis and Architecture*. Catskill, NY: Mental Health Resources, 2005.

Winter, Irene J. "Art as Evidence for Interaction: Relations Between the Assyrian Empire and North Syria." Pages 355–82 in *Mesopotamien und seine Nachbarn: Politische und kulturelle Wechselbeziehungen im alten Vorderasien vom 4. bis 1. Jahrtausend v. Chr.* Edited by H. J. Nissen and J. Renger. BBVO 1. Berlin: Reimer, 1982.

———. "Art in Empire: The Royal Image and the Visual Dimensions of Assyrian Ideology." Pages 359–81 in *Assyria 1995: Proceedings of the 10th Anniversary Symposium of the Neo-Assyrian Text Corpus Project, Helsinki, September 7–11, 1995*. Edited by S. Parpola and R. M. Whiting. Helsinki: The Neo-Assyrian Text Corpus Project, 1997.

———. "Le Palais imaginaire: Scale and Meaning in the Iconography of Neo-Assyrian Cylinder Seals." Pages 68–74 in *Images as Media: Sources for the Cultural History of the Near East and the Eastern Mediterranean (1st millennium BCE)*. Edited by Ch. Uehlinger. Fribourg: University Press, 2000.

Wiseman, D. J. "The Vassal-Treaties of Esarhaddon." *Iraq* 20 (1958): i–ii, 1–99.

Woodward, Ian. *Understanding Material Culture*. London: Sage, 2007.

Woolley, Leonard. *Alalakh: An Account of the Excatvations at Tell Atchana in Hatay, 1937–1939*. Oxford: Oxford University Press, 1955.

———. *Ur Excavations, V: The Ziggurat and it Surroundings*. London: Oxford University Press, 1939.

Wright, David P. *The Disposal of Impurity: Elimination Rites in the Bible and in Hittite and Mesopotamian Literature*. SBLDS 101. Atlanta: Scholars, 1987.

———. "Histories: Syria and Canaan." Pages 173–80 in *Religions of the Ancient World: A Guide*. Edited by S. I. Johnston. Cambridge, MA: Belknap Press of Harvard University Press, 2004.

Wright, George Ernst. "Shechem." Pages 1083–94 in *Encyclopedia of Archaeological Excavations in the Holy Land*, vol. 4. Edited by M. Avi-Yonah and E. Stern. Englewood Cliffs, NJ: Prentice-Hall, 1978.

Wright, George R. H. *Ancient Building in South Syria and Palestine*. 2 volumes. Leiden: Brill, 1985.

Xella, Paolo. *Baal Hammon: Recherches sur l'identité et l'histoire d'un dieu phénico-punique*. Contributi alla storia della religione fenicio-punica 1. Rome: Consiglio Nazionale Delle Ricerche, 1991.

Yadin, Yigal. *Hazor: The Head of All Those Kingdoms*. London: Oxford University Press, 1972.

———. *Hazor: The Rediscovery of a Great Citadel of the Bible*. London: Weidenfeld and Nicolson, 1975.

Yamamoto, Kei. "The Materials of Iykhernofret's Portable Shrine: An Alternative Translation of Berlin 1204, lines 11–12." *Göttinger Miszellen* 191 (2002): 101–6.

Younger, K. Lawson. "The Phoenician Inscription of Azatiwada: An Integrated Reading." *JSS* 43 (1998): 11–47.

Žabkar, Louis V. *A Study of the Ba Concept in Ancient Egyptian Texts*. SAOC 34. Chicago: University of Chicago Press, 1968.

Zandee, Jan. *De Hymnen aan Amon van Papyrus Leiden I 350*. Leiden: Brill, 1948.

Zick, Michael. "Sarissa - die Heimat des Wettergottes." *Bild der Wissenschaft* 6 (2000): 34–38.

Ziedler, Jürgen. „Zur Frage der Spätentstehung des Mythos in Ägypten." *Göttinger Miszellen* 132 (1993): 85–109.

Zimansky, Paul. "The 'Hittites' at 'Ain Dara." Pages 177–91 in *Recent Developments in Hittite Archaeology and History: Papers in Memory of Hans G. Güterbock*. Edited by K. A. Yener and H. A. Hoffner Jr. Winona Lake, IN: Eisenbrauns, 2002.

Zuckerman, Sharon. "The Temples of Canaanite Hazor." Pages 99–126 in *Temple Building and Temple Cult: The Architecture and Cultic Paraphernalia of Temples in the Levant (2nd–1st Millennium BCE)*. Edited by J. Kamlah. Tübingen: Institute of Biblical Archaeology, 2012.

Zwickel, Wolfgang. *Der Tempelkult in Kanaan und Israel. Ein Beitrag zur Kultgeschichte Palästinas von der Mittelbronzezeit bis zum Untergang Judas*. FAT 10. Tübingen: Mohr Siebeck, 1994.

# INDEX OF NAMES

## PLACE NAMES

# Index of Ancient Sources